Rockwell College

1864-2014

Seán O'Donnell

ISBN No: 978-0-9926949-0-6

Typesetting and design by Artwerk Limited
Printed in Ireland by Brunswick Press Ltd

Typeset in 11.5 pt Goudy

First published 2013 by
Cashel Publications,
Rockwell College,
Cashel,
Co. Tipperary

CONTENTS

APPENDICES

ABBREVIATIONS

ISR	*Irish Spiritans Remembered* (Seán Farragher)
JCT	Junior Cup Team
JNL	Journals of the Rockwell College Community
RCA	Rockwell College Annuals
SCT	Senior Cup Team
SFFC	*The French College: Blackrock 1860-1896* (Seán Farragher)
SFLM	*Père Leman: Educator & Missionary 1826-1880* (Seán Farragher)

PREFACE

Writing the history of Rockwell College has been an exercise more in compilation than research. This is so because of the immense research already accomplished on the history of the Congregation of the Holy Spirit in Ireland. In this regard the work of Fr. Seán Farragher is especially impressive and any further study on Spiritan education in Ireland is deeply dependent on his publications.

The journals which were kept by the Spiritan Community in Rockwell recording daily happenings in the College are a rich source of information not only on life within the narrow confines of Rockwell but also on the reaction of the Community to the wider scenario of unfolding major developments in the course of Irish history. The *Rockwell Annual* provides an insight to student life since 1926 and is a useful pictorial resource.

The production of this work has been greatly helped by Spiritans, especially by Fr. Patrick J. Ryan in Kimmage Manor and by the Rockwell Community members Fr. James Hurley, Fr. Brendan Hally, Fr. William Kingston and Fr. Peter Queally. Assistance has also been provided by Mr. Pat O'Sullivan, Ms. Audrey O'Byrne, Mr. Michael Doyle, Ms. Eileen McCormack, Ms. Joan Kennedy, Ms. Caroline Kelly, Ms. Siobhán Nolan, Mr. Tony Smith, Mr. Domhnall Blair and Mr. Gay Mangan. The assistance of Ms. Mary Guinan-Darmody and Mr. John O'Gorman at Tipperary Local Studies in Thurles is also appreciated.

Where sources are not mentioned in the narrative for the years following 1926 it can be taken for granted that the source of any event is the *Rockwell Annual* of that year.

– 1 –

FROM FRANCE TO TIPPERARY

The story of Rockwell College begins in France. It begins with the accomplishment of two remarkable Frenchmen who were founders of religious congregations which later amalgamated to become The Congregation of the Holy Spirit under the protection of the Immaculate Heart of Mary. The members of this Congregation were known in Ireland for many years as the Holy Ghost Fathers.. Their mission is to spread the Christian message together with the advancement of education in general and of Catholic education in particular.

The story begins with Claude Francis Poullart des Places who was born in Rennes, Brittany in 1679, the son of a rich merchant, Francois Claude Poullart des Places. His mother, Jeanne, was a teacher and a woman of deep Christian faith. He studied law at the University of Nantes. Instead of entering the legal profession after graduation, however, he gave up a promising career as a lawyer and decided to become a priest.

In 1703 while studying for the priesthood, Claude founded in Paris a house for disadvantaged theological students and a community consecrated to the Holy Spirit under the invocation of the Blessed Virgin Conceived without Sin, which later

Claude Francis Poullart
des Places

became the Congregation of the Holy Spirit. He was ordained priest on 17th December 1707. He died on 2nd October 1709 at the age of thirty. After Claude's death the Congregation he had founded continued to flourish and to maintain his tradition of high academic standards, a simple lifestyle and a religious commitment to difficult ministries.[1]

The second remarkable personality in this story is Francis Libermann. He was born in 1802 in Severne, Alsace, the son of a Jewish rabbi. While studying in Paris he was baptised into the Catholic Church in 1826. Soon afterwards he experienced the call to become a priest and in 1827 he entered the seminary of St. Sulpice. Because of ill health, however, he was not ordained until 1841. That same year he opened the novitiate of a new society, the Society of the Holy Heart of Mary, for the pastoral care and education of freed slaves in the French colonies. In 1848 this society joined with the congregation founded by Des Places and under Libermann's leadership the Congregation continued to grow

1

Francis Libermann

and to develop its educational, missionary and pastoral work in many countries outside France and her colonies.

In February 1842 Fr. Libermann became aware of reports in French newspapers which suggested that all French priests were to be expelled from the island of Mauritius by the British Government, and that clergy from France would no longer be permitted to operate in the British colonies. This was at a time of tension between France and Britain over their respective interests in Canada following a rebellion by French colonists and some Irish there in 1837.[2]

Fr. Libermann now began to explore the possibilities of finding vocations for the missions in the British colonies. The Paris seminary of the Congregation was within sight of the Irish College and so a close contact between the two developed. Francis Libermann died on 2nd February 1852, but the contact was retained by his successor, Fr. Schwindenhammer, and after lengthy deliberations the Congregation decided on opening a new foundation in Ireland. The person chosen to undertake this challenging task was Fr. Jules Leman and it was he who became the founder and first president of Blackrock College in Dublin in 1859.

Blackrock College was still in its infancy in 1864 when Fr. Leman received a letter from Co. Tipperary, written in French, inviting him to give serious consideration to a rather unusual proposal. The writer of the letter, Charles Thiébault, was a native of Beaurains, near Aras in France, but had settled in Dundee, Scotland, where he had built up an extensive business in the flax trade and had become very rich in the process. A devout Catholic, he was concerned about the lack of a strong Catholic presence in Scotland; so with the blessing of the Scottish bishops, he set about encouraging religious communities from France to take charge of various works of charity in Scotland. In this way he helped set up communities of the Marist Brothers and of the Little Sisters of the Poor. He formed the idea of founding a seminary to provide priests for the Scottish mission and he chose to locate this seminary not in Scotland but in Co. Tipperary.[3]

His choice of Tipperary is explained by the fact that in 1856 he had acquired a large property between Cashel and Cahir known as Rockwell. The name Rockwell is derived from the Irish *Carraig an Tobair*, meaning the Rock of the Well or perhaps from *Ceathrú an Tobair*, meaning the quarter (land division) of the well. Rockwell is situated in an area of great beauty and rich history with views of the

Père Jules Leman

Galtee Mountains to the west, the Knockmealdowns to the south, the Comeraghs to the south-east and Slievenamon to the east and half way between the historic towns of Cashel and Cahir.

The land of Rockwell and of the surrounding parishes had been acquired by Richard Boyle, later Earl of Cork, who had purchased from Sir Walter Raleigh lands he had been granted following the Munster Plantation. Boyle then became the owner of vast tracks of land throughout Munster. Rockwell and the surrounding area came into the possession of the Roe family in 1756 when Andrew Roe owned "in fee simple" the mansion, demesne and lands of Rockwell containing then about two hundred and eighty one acres. Thomas Chidley Moore leased sixty acres of Rockwell to Andrew Roe, "for lives renewable forever" in 1765. This land was in the town land of Garranlea.[4] The Roes were descendants of Sir Thomas Roe, who was Lord Mayor of London in 1568. His great grand-son, James Roe, had settled in Co. Wexford in 1645 and James's son, Andrew, who died in 1714, had settled in Tipperary Town. One of Andrew's four sons, also Andrew, first acquired Rockwell.[5]

In 1806 William Roe, barrister, with a residence at Kingstown (now Dún Laoghaire) is named as lessee of Carrigeen, the property opposite the present College front gate, and now part of the Rockwell farm. He had obtained this land, consisting of just over five acres, from Robert Carew of Woodenstown, Co. Tipperary.[6] This land was owned in 1854 by John and Elizabeth Roe and on the land stood a row of cottages, seven in number, built as a segment of a circle, with the concave side, which was the back, towards the College gate. But having become unsightly the entire row was later removed by the Rockwell Community.[7]

In 1837 this William Roe is set down as landlord of the Rockwell estate where John Roe occupied the house later known as "The Old Mansion". He had founded a National School on the estate. In 1834 William Roe had commissioned the architect William Tinsley of Clonmel to carry out improvements on the mansion changing it into a Gothic-style residence. The flat Tudor arches of the present entrance hall and the branching staircase are the work of Tinsley. He had built chapels of the Established Church at Clogheen,

A painting of a "peasant" cottage in the Rockwell neighbourhood by James Roe *c. 1794.*

Lisronagh, Kilbehenny and the Wesleyan Methodist chapel at Gordon Street, Clonmel and had remodelled buildings such as Curraghmore House, Comeragh House, Turtulla House and Tullamain Castle, all within a short distance of Rockwell. He emigrated to the United States in 1851 where his first major work was the design of the North Western Christian University (Butler University) at Indianapolis. Its Gothic style was new to the American mid-west and it won him many other design contracts which included Wabash College, Indiana University, Oskaloosa College in Iowa and the University of Wisconsin.[8]

In 1841 Henry, third Marquis of Waterford, a member of the Beresford family, rented the Old Mansion from the Roes as a hunting lodge and maintained on the farm the Tipperary Foxhounds known as the Grove Pack from their place of origin near Fethard where they had been founded in 1816 by Thomas Barton. The field nearest the road on the Cahir side of the property was used by the Marquis for his horses and was for a long time known to Rockwell students as "The Exercise".

The Rockwell property had been for over sixty years in the possession of the Roe family, a family noted for their style of high living with little concern for their tenants. They were in fact absentee landlords and as such were detested by their tenants. They relied on an agent to collect the rent from their tenants in the surrounding farms. Merciless evictions followed in the wake of the Famine when tenants found themselves unable to pay the rent. William Roe, the Dublin barrister, was the owner of the Rockwell property in 1847 and his agent was his cousin, George Roe, who lived at Belview, Boytanrath, about a mile and a half from Rockwell.

William Roe, while visiting Rockwell, set out walking on Saturday 2 October 1847 to visit his cousin George. Mindful of the high level of agrarian crime in the area, he carried a loaded shotgun and was accompanied by a large dog. Despite these precautions, he was overpowered and brutally murdered. A local man, John Lonergan, whose family had been recently evicted by Roe, was accused of the murder.[9] Many of Roe's tenants were in serious arrears of rent at this time and it was reported that the tenants had conspired to kill William Roe, rather than his agent, because his children were very young and the estate would

A painting by James Roe of the old Mansion as seen across the lake.

therefore be placed under the Court of Chancery in which case rents were likely to be reduced.[10]

Following the murder, a large military force under the civil authority seized upon the produce of such farms in Boytonrath as owed rent and arrears to William Roe, the deceased landlord, to be transmitted to Dublin for sale there, if not redeemed within fourteen days. There were two hundred soldiers and their officers garrisoned at Rockwell during this operation.[11]

John Lonergan absconded after the murder, but with a large reward offered for his capture, he was arrested on the morning of 26th December in the neighbourhood of his farm. He was tried for murder in Clonmel Court House in January 1848, the same Court House in which the Young Ireland leaders were to be tried eight months later. The trial lasted for two days during which eighteen witnesses were called for the prosecution, but none for the prisoner. Lonergan was found guilty and sentenced to death by hanging.[12] As was the custom in Clonmel, hangings were held in public and took place outside the gate of the County Gaol. On the morning of the 1st March 1848 John Lonergan was due to be hanged at 11. a.m. with two brothers of the name Cody. Thousands had assembled since early morning and the place was surrounded by military and police. As the three were led to the scaffold the two Cody brothers attempted to overpower the executioner and almost succeeded. When order was restored the three fell to their deaths and their bodies were cut down and buried within the precincts of the gaol.[13]

William Roe was buried in the family vault in the churchyard of Boytonrath, but in the course of the same year his body was exhumed and interred in the vault of his wife's people in Mount Jerome Cemetery, Dublin.[14]

This incident left Rockwell very much under a cloud, so the Roe family decided to sell it.[15] Following the death of Roe the Rockwell Mansion was occupied for a short time by a Robert Bushe, a popular gentleman. Being placed under the jurisdiction of the Encumbered Estates Court, however, it was bought in 1856, along with properties in the neighbourhood, by Monsieur Charles Thiébault, a French merchant living in Dundee, for the sum of £5,850. It consisted of over 398 acres.[16]

As Thiébault's principal interests were still in Scotland, he did not come to live in Rockwell himself. Instead he got his brother Gustave, a naturalised British subject, to act as his agent. Gustave with his wife Eugénie and their two children Gustave and Marie came to reside in the Old Mansion. He soon resorted to evictions as a method of dealing with unprofitable tenants. In November 1861 he took the fatal step of evicting a Halloran family from their holding in Boytonrath for non-payment of rents. This eviction caused great tension in the area and five months later, perhaps sensing danger, he agreed with his wife to leave Rockwell on 27th April. For reasons unknown, however, he put back the date and on the following day as he walked through his estate, and like William Roe fifteen years earlier, accompanied by a big dog and carrying a loaded shotgun, he was overpowered and brutally murdered in the townland of Killeenasteena. Similar to the incident fifteen years earlier there were rumours of a conspiracy to kill Thiébault because his children were young with the hope of reduced rents through the Landed Estate Court.[17]

Thomas Halloran, a member of the evicted family, was known to have been walking with Thiébault at the time of the tragedy and at the inquest held in Rockwell on the following day the jury laid a charge of wilful murder against him. He was tried at Clonmel on 20th June 1862 in an atmosphere of high drama. Halloran, "fully six feet in height, an exceedingly mild, intelligent looking man, about twenty three years of age" proved a successful alibi and was acquitted. The number of witnesses for the defence was three. Among these was Fr. John Ryan, Parish priest of New Inn who stated that Halloran was a parishioner of his, that he had known him since his childhood, and that he was extremely well conducted and religious.[18] His two brothers and two sisters subsequently emigrated to Australia while Thomas afterwards went to the United States and died in Chicago.[19]

The remains of Gustave Thiébault were laid to rest in New Inn cemetery. Later they were transferred to the family burial ground in Bouvais. On 8th May Madame Thiébault left to rejoin her relations in France taking with her the four children, two of whom had been born in Rockwell. A special force of police was quartered at Rockwell for the next fifteen months, at the expense of the local townlands, to give a salutary lesson on what to expect for such attacks on landlords in future.

Meanwhile Charles Thiébault had decided to hand over the Rockwell estate to a religious body, which by the nature of its work would expiate the crime. He got approval for his plan from Bishop John Murdoch, Vicar Apostolic of the Western District of Scotland, and the Scottish bishops and from the Archbishop of Cashel and Emly, Dr. Leahy.[20] The plan was to establish a seminary in order to provide a sufficient number of priests to attend to the spiritual needs of Irish Catholics who were constantly going over to Scotland.

Accordingly by deed executed in 1864 M. Thiébault made over to Bishop Murdoch and others, in trust, the whole demesne of Rockwell and a portion of his estate of Dangan Dargan, in all about four hundred acres. The demesne included a beautiful artificial lake of about twenty four acres, dotted with miniature islands, wooded, and discharging its superfluous waters by a fine waterfall at the western verge, all situated at a short distance westwards from the Mansion. It had been formed by the Roe family from what would otherwise appear to be marshy land, and is fed by a stream from the eastward side. At one point on the eastern side, the lake approaches quite near to the eponymous well. A stone canopy erected over the well bears the inscription: A.S.R. 1799. This inscription stands for *Anno Salutis Redemptae* meaning the Year of World's Redemption. Adjacent to the same point there is also a well on the floor of the lake, and from it is derived, by mechanical power, a water supply for the College.[21] The beauty of this lake was described in her book *Retrospections* by the writer Dorothea Herbert who was familiar with the area because of her younger brother who was rector of nearby Knockraffon. It was a case also of Dorothea's unrequited love for John Roe, who owned Rockwell at the time.[22]

The old Mansion
with later
modifications

Mr. Thiébault invited over from Brittany a congregation of the Fathers of the Immaculate Conception of Rennes to whom he allocated the Rockwell mansion and part of the property for the purpose of educating students from Scotland for the priesthood. They did not establish a permanent foundation, however, and it was then that Thiébault approached Fr. Leman at Blackrock College. Fr. Leman was supportive of the idea. Following a visit to Rockwell he wrote to his superiors in Paris saying "we need a second leg in Ireland if we are to survive." He described Rockwell as "a real paradise" to become that second leg. But his superiors in Paris were less enthusiastic, feeling that Thiébault's conditions lacked clarity on matters such as the duration of the contract, the place of residence of Thiébault in the house, the right of the Holy Ghost Fathers to undertake other subsidiary works at Rockwell and the right of visitation on the part of the Scottish bishops. After voluminous correspondence between Fr. Leman and his superiors in Paris and other interested parties, the Superior General eventually put his signature to a civil contract with which he was fully satisfied. It was agreed to found a seminary for the education of priests for the Scottish diocese with freedom to develop at Rockwell any other work which might further the ends of their own Congregation.[23]

On 20th July 1864 Fr. Leman arrived in Rockwell to take over possession. He was accompanied by Fr. Huvétys, Br. Aloysius and five Scottish students. There to greet them were Fr. Orriere, Provincial of the Fathers of the Immaculate Conception, two "reliable" domestics, Michael and Martin Connors, Denis McLoughlin (a mechanic) and two women housekeepers.[24] Fr. Orriere departed within a few days. Fr. Huvétys was appointed Superior on 8th September 1864 the Community was officially established under the title of *The College of the Immaculate Conception*.

The Holy Ghost Fathers had come to Tipperary at a time when rural Ireland was undergoing great changes caused by the Famine and in its aftermath by estate clearances and by emigration. The parish priest of New Inn, Fr. John Ryan, who welcomed the Holy Ghost Fathers to his parish, remembered the Famine as "a visitation of God's providence" and held out hope of better times in the next world. As a curate in Cashel he had witnessed an unprecedented influx of over 4,000 starving paupers into the local workhouse and had been deeply affected by it for the rest of his life.[25] The area within the immediate vicinity of Rockwell suffered its share of population decline. In the parish of Knockgraffon, where most of the Rockwell land was situated, each of the townlands of Farranliney, Graigue Little and Loughkent West had lost more

The Old Parlour

than half of its population between 1841 and 1851. And as in all rural areas the people worst hit were the labourers who were faced with low wages, irregular employment and extremely poor housing conditions.[26] The Fathers in Rockwell were obviously sensitive to these conditions and to the actions of previous landlords of their estate when it is considered that nearly thirty years after they came to Rockwell it was revealed that their tenants had not been asked to pay rent for most of that period.[27]

Notes

[1] SFPL p. 29.
[2] ibid pp. 18-35
[3] ibid pp 196 ff.
[4] Lease of 30th March 1765.
[5] Marnane, D.G., *Land and Violence: A History of West Tipperary from 1660*, p. 15.
[6] Lease of 31st March 1806.
[7] RCA 1926.
[8] O'Donnell, S., *Clonmel 1840-1900: Anatomy of an Irish Town*, p. 291.
[9] *Tipperary Free Press* 6/10/1847.
[10] ibid 16/10/1847.
[11] RCA 1926.
[12] *Tipperary Free Press* 29/1/1848.
[13] ibid 4/3/1848.
[14] RCA 1926.
[15] ibid.
[16] Conveyance Certificate copy of Landed Estates Court to Charles Thiébault, 19th July 1856.
[17] *Clonmel Chronicle* 30/4/1862.
[18] ibid 24/6/1862.
[19] RCA 1926.
[20] Deed of Trust. Thiébault to Scottish Bishops 13th July 1864.
[21] RCA 1926
[22] RCA 1948.
[23] SFPL pp 198 ff.
[24] JNL 1864 p. 2
[25] O'Shea, J., *Priest, Politics and Society in Post- famine Ireland*, pp 58-59.
[26] D.G. Marnane, The Famine in South Tipperary, *Tipperary Historical Journal* 2000, pp 73-121.
[27] JNL 1892 p. 15.

– 2 –

THE SCOTCH COLLEGE
1864-1874

In the first decade of the history of Rockwell College the Holy Ghost Fathers provided a seminary for the Catholic Church in Scotland and a seminary for their own Congregation in Ireland. Both were modest achievements but with their own seminary they had laid the foundation of an institution which was later to blossom into a substantial contributor to the world-wide Irish missionary movement of the nineteenth and twentieth centuries. And unintentionally the Holy Ghost Fathers had laid the foundation of a lay secondary school with a national reputation which educated pupils who later contributed to various strands of Irish life. This was happening at a time of civil unrest in the aftermath of the Famine in Ireland with agitation for tenant right and the advent of fenianism.

EPISCOPAL AND LOCAL APPROVAL

Père Huvétys
President 1864-1880

Two days after his arrival in Rockwell Fr. Huvétys, accompanied by Fr. Leman, visited the Archbishop of Cashel and Emly Dr. Patrick Leahy at Thurles. Fr. Leman would have been aware of Leahy's reputation as a leading theologian and prelate who had been the first vice-rector of the Catholic University which had been established following one of the most important decrees at the Synod of Thurles in 1850.[1] Fr. Leman had regular dealings in Blackrock College with this university. The archbishop made it quite clear to his visitors that he was not allowing them to take in as boarders at Rockwell any students of Irish origin, nor any students for the priesthood from his diocese. Apart, then, from the Scottish students, they were allowed to have as boarders only aspirants for their own Congregation, and as day-boys, such students from the area as might present themselves. These limitations were intended to protect the status of St. Patrick's College, Thurles which had been the diocesan seminary since 1837.[2]

The archbishop advised Frs. Leman and Huvétys to cultivate good relations with the local clergy and to have "as far as possible" friendly relations with the parish priest of New Inn, Fr. John Ryan.[3] The archbishop probably had his tongue in cheek as he offered this advice because he knew Fr. Ryan to be so extremely outspoken on political issues that he had to suspend him for a time.[4] Fr. Huvétys may have had difficulty coming to terms with this aspect of Irish culture but the archbishop himself, together with other well-known Irish theologians saw political involvement as a civil right which did not interfere with purely spiritual matters. It was a hangover from the days of struggle for Catholic Emancipation when Daniel O'Connell had been so successful in encouraging priests to become politically active.[5]

Whatever about Fr. Ryan's political involvement he became a close friend of the Rockwell Community from then until his death in 1891, was present at all major feast days and occasions of celebration and mourning in the College while the Rockwell Fathers took part in all liturgical celebrations in New Inn.[6] He erected schools at Knockgraffon in 1871 and at Lagganstown in1889; he brought the Sisters of Mercy from Charleville to make a foundation in New Inn in 1879 and willed them his house and farm after his death. A wise, genial and zealous pastor, he lived for the people; a patriot priest, he strove for justice during his long life against an unsympathetic landed ascendancy and unsympathetic alien rulers.[7] The Rockwell Community was fortunate to have had such a friend for the most part of its first thirty years in Tipperary.

The French Fathers were just settling in to Rockwell when they had visits from two local influential celebrities to wish them well. The renowned transport pioneer, Charles Bianconi and the Member of Parliament for Tipperary, Charles Moore, together with their families visited in August 1864.[8] Bianconi, who had purchased the nearby Longfield estate at Boherlahan in 1846 had been a promoter of Catholic education in the area.[9] Moore had been a champion of all Catholic causes at Westminster.[10]

THE EARLY ROCKWELL COMMUNITY

During the ten year life of the Scotch College the Holy Ghost Community in Rockwell consisted for the most part of Fathers, Brothers and prefects who came from Blackrock College and who frequently interchanged between the two colleges. Fr. Pierre Huvétys was a young priest of only twenty nine years of age when he became the first and longest-serving Superior of the Rockwell Community. Born in the French colony of Martinique he was appointed to the Langonnet College in Brittany after his ordination in 1862. Fr. Leman requested his service as Dean of Studies in Blackrock College where he had made such an immediate impression that he seemed the ideal choice for the Rockwell position. He adapted quickly to his Irish surroundings

Notre Dame de Rockwell from the printed crest of old delft

and made rapid progress in mastering the English language. Fr. Leman, who was responsible for his appointment to Rockwell, thought very highly of Fr. Huvéyts, expressing himself as follows: "He is certainly one of the most valuable and most all-round members in the Congregation. He is devoted, faithful in all his duties; he is possessed of a sound judgement, is talented, gifted with prudence and firmness; and with all this richness of character he is endowed with tact and delicacy".[11]

Eight Fathers, apart from Fr. Huvétys, ministered in Rockwell in its first decade, they being Frs. Bartholmew Stoffel, Joseph Hofbaur, Prosper Goepfert, Jacques Richert, Denis O'Farrell, Bernard Graff, Anthony Clauss and Edward Mooney. (Appendix II) Of these, the longest serving was Fr. Goepfert who was in Rockwell from 1867 to 1889 and was to become a future Superior.

Fr. Leman brought with him to Rockwell as helpers for Fr. Huvétys two scholastics from Blackrock College, Michael Clarke and John O'Dwyer, who were to act as prefects, or junior masters. Another prefect who joined the Congregation in May 1865 was Edward Gallagher. Fr. Leman also brought with him a novice, Br. Alban Crean, who was to act as a general factotum until the arrival later in the year of four professed Brothers from France. Brother Crean, who was a native of Claremorris, Co. Mayo, remained in Rockwell for a year before departing for the missions in The Gambia and thus became only the second native Irish member of the Congregation to arrive in Africa. Like many of those early missionaries he soon developed an illness which made his return to Europe imperative and he died *en route* at Dakar.

The four Brothers who arrived in Rockwell from France in 1864 were Brothers Hippolyte Matasse, Vincent de Paul McNally, John Joseph O'Donoghue and John Aloysius McGrath. Brother Hippolyte was the only French Brother in the Community and he served in Rockwell until his death in 1916. Br. Vincent de Paul was the first Irishman to complete his postulancy and novitiate in Ireland. He remained in Rockwell until 1868 before departing for Langonnet in Brittany where he died in 1907. Br. John O'Donoghue was a Tipperaryman and spent four years in Rockwell while Br. John McGrath was from Waterford and was in Rockwell for three years. Br. Silas Laffan arrived in 1868 and remained in Rockwell until his death in 1922. Other Brothers to arrive in Rockwell during its first decade were Brs. James Elzear, Edward Flynn, Tobias Fitzpatrick and Roland Mahony. (Appendix II)

Among the prefects of 1868 was James Cotter who was President in 1893-4 and who died in Rockwell in 1921 having filled the office of Bursar for twenty years. Other prefects of those years who served before their ordination were Jules Botrel and Prosper Duval. The earliest lay masters of whom the records make mention were Messrs Reidy and Courtnay, and the first music professor was a Mr. Etterlen.[12]

THE FIRST STUDENTS
The five students who arrived with Frs. Leman and Huvéyts in July 1864 were joined on 13th September by a further eight students from Scotland.[13] It would

The first photo

seem that one of these may have returned to Scotland by 11th October when the first school year opened and the following students were mentioned in attendance: John Golden, Joseph Lynch, Laurence Finin, James Harris, Daniel Donnelly, H.G. McKenzie, William Golden, Laurence McGlinchy, Stephen McGlinchy, Harry Logan, George Middleton and Samuel Sutherland.

A student from New Inn, Patrick Ryan was enrolled on 31st October and in 1865 a new student, Thomas Tighe, arrived from Scotland. Irish students who enrolled in 1865 included Cornelius O'Sullivan, Thomas O'Connor, James Keating, John Ryan, John Keane, Michael Hickey, the Campbell brothers from Waterford who were sons of the Principal of Waterford High School, Edmund Connolly from Kilteely, the Cleary brothers, Michael and John who were from the Rockwell locality as was Mike Heffernan, the son of a local farmer. Five of the Irish students were day students.[14]

The number of students increased throughout 1866 and 1867 but it was in 1868 that there was a dramatic increase. By the end of March that year the number of boarders, not counting the scholastics, had risen to twenty nine and by June the total Rockwell student population had reached sixty four. In December of that year a further increase was reported.[15] By January 1869 it had reached eighty three.(Appendix XI) The increase in numbers was partly due to the fact that in May 1867 Archbishop Leahy had withdrawn his reservation on the admission of boarders to Rockwell.

The first three boarders were John and Thomas Cooney from Shanballard near Fethard and Thomas Halloran from near the College. The Mullins brothers, William and Richard of Cashel, came next. Richard was the first Rockwell boarder to be ordained to the priesthood, for the diocese of Girvan where he became a Canon; he was still coming back to Rockwell for his summer holidays in the 1920s. John Coman of Cashel entered the same day as the

Mullins brothers. The Scots seminarians included two notable brothers, Dan and Peter Donnelly of Grennock. Peter became parish priest of Hamilton, Lanark, and Dan worked as a curate at Strathaven. Both were men of considerable classical scholarship; they corresponded for years in Greek and to the end of his days Peter read his Scripture in Hebrew. They both had affectionate memories of the Scotch College and used to recall with amusement one of the French Fathers, their professor of Physics, who gave demonstrations of electricity and became known locally as "the priest who could make lightning."[16] This was a reference of course to Fr. Bernard Graff who was an expert on pyrotechnics and was responsible for the fireworks displays which were a feature of special occasions in the early days of Rockwell.

The number of students in Rockwell increased in 1870 following the outbreak of war between France and Prussia in July of that year. The repercussions of the war for the Holy Ghost Congregation were serious. Its houses in Paris had to be evacuated and were taken over as infirmaries. Fr. Leman, the Irish Superior, was concerned about the welfare of the German members of the Congregation in France. They had already suffered from Bismarck's *Kulturkampf* and were now open to ill-treatment at the hands of the French military. Leman offered to educate them in Blackrock together with the Irish senior scholastics in France who had returned to Ireland at the outbreak of war. Most of the students who came from France finished up in Rockwell where, as will be seen, there was already the nucleus of a senior seminary.[17]

St. Joseph's

It was in 1866 that the Rockwell Juniorate, known as St. Joseph's Scholasticate, was founded. Known from its inception as the Scholasticate of Our Lady of Rockwell, the Lake House was in the course of time confided to the special patronage of St. Joseph. It was a seminary for the education of future members

An early group

of the Holy Ghost Congregation. St. Joseph's had only three scholastics in its first year. The very first scholastic to enter was Thomas O'Flaherty of Sandymount who arrived on 29th November 1866 but who left two years later. The other two, John O'Keeffe and James Cotter were later ordained. Fr. O'Keeffe died at Blackrock in 1877 while Fr. Cotter, as has been seen, was for many years Bursar in Rockwell where he died in 1925. Among the notable members of St. Joseph's prior to 1874 were James Hickey who became parish priest of Clontarf, Innocent Ryan, Dean of Cashel and first president of the Rockwell College Union in 1925 and Eugene Phelan who was provincial of the American province of the Holy Ghost Congregation for seventeen years. There was a noticeable increase in numbers in 1870 when the students from France arrived; and coupled with Irish names on the register of that year are found such unfamiliar ones as Berkessel, Dujardin, Deisner, Muller, Koeber, Dickhopof, Schmidt and Wolf, most of whom later became priests in the Congregation. The scholastics of St. Joseph's took up permanent residence in the Lake House about 1874 where for the next hundred years many students were to be prepared for entry to the Congregation of the Holy Spirit.[18]

The experience of two of these early scholastics in St. Joseph's, John Hogan and Joseph Lynch may mirror the fate of others. John Hogan was born within sight of Rockwell. When he left his home at Carron to enter Rockwell, the College was then but three years old. It was a small school having only seventy three names on its rolls. Seventeen were in the Scots College, five were scholastic aspirants of the Holy Ghost Fathers, twenty eight were boarders and twenty three were day students. John spent six years at Rockwell, the final two being devoted principally to the duties of prefect. In 1873 he went to the Senior Scholasticate in Brittany and later to Chevilly near Paris where he completed his studies and was ordained in 1878.[19]

Joseph Lynch came from Dundee in 1869 to the Scots College with the intention of returning as a priest to Scotland. After the transfer of students to the Colonial Seminary in Paris, Joseph opted for the Holy Ghost Fathers. Nothing is known of his people except that his parents were Irish emigrants and that he never had the opportunity of visiting them after he had left home for Rockwell; not even before he was sent on his first appointment to Chandernagore in India. Some years later as he stopped over at Mauritius he received orders from Paris to join Fr. John Hogan in Angola.

Fr. Hogan had established a mission in Angola with the help of his contemporary from Rockwell, Br. Cooney. For six years they laboured in conditions which were totally foreign to them and for which they were poorly prepared. Far from all means of communication with Europe and even with the nearest supply depot, they felt at times abandoned and forgotten. They were not forgotten, however, and when Fr. Joseph Lynch arrived the common experience of life in Rockwell may have helped to counteract the uncongenial conditions which surrounded them. Such a common bond, however, was no shield against the dangers that were always lurking in a climate against which there was little medical protection. Disaster struck in the spring of 1885. Fr.

Hogan died from fever on 10th March and Fr. Lynch on 6th April. Br. Cooney survived until a relief party arrived, but he too was doomed to lay down his life in Angola within a few years.[20]

THE FIRST CHAPEL

On the feast of St. Andrew, patron saint of Scotland, 30th November 1867, the first Rockwell Chapel was built. It was needed to accommodate the growing numbers. It had stained glass windows of St. Andrew, St. Patrick and the Holy Spirit hovering over the Immaculate Heart of Mary. It has long since disappeared. It was on the first floor of a probably new building and replaced Mr. Thiébault' chapel, itself a conversion of a pre-existing building dating from the time of the Roes. The new chapel was probably on the same site.[21]

A FRENCH EDUCATION SYSTEM

With Rockwell and Blackrock College being so closely related, it seems likely that the same system of education operated in both colleges. The French Fathers operated the system in use in France with its strong emphasis on a liberal education. In the French system students were graded subject by subject, acknowledging that a student's ability differed from subject to subject. In the absence of public examinations other incentives were provided. These took the form of weekly "Notes" for application and conduct. Monthly examinations in each subject were held. Certificates and testimonial cards were given for each month and each year. A generous allocation of book prizes was presented on Prize Day. Physical punishment was forbidden. Scripture, Greek, Latin, English, French, History, Mathematics and Public Speaking were the subjects on the original curriculum. In November 1864 Fr Huvétys conducted the first note-reading ceremony in Rockwell.[22] The "note system", with a few modifications, has survived in Rockwell to the present day. Teaching of the Catechism was of course central to the curriculum and it is notable that the students of 1865 had not yet made their First Communion, it not being until the papacy of Pius X that frequent Communion was encouraged. Music was introduced to the curriculum in 1865 by Jules Botrel, a future Provincial Superior and then a prefect and teacher of Art and Music at Blackrock College. He spent the summer months in Rockwell that year and it was during his stay that a new piano for the College arrived by train at Cahir station.[23] He was a musician and artist of note and was recognised as a portrait painter of some merit. It was probably on one of his many visits to Rockwell that he painted a portrait of Fr. John Ryan, Parish Priest of New Inn.

The daily routine under the French regime may have seemed strange to the Irish students. In October 1864 the daily time-table was recorded. Students rose at 6 a.m., with morning prayer and meditation at 6.20. Morning Mass at 6.30 was followed by study at 7 a.m. Breakfast was at 8.30 and was followed by manual labour before a short recreation at 9.15. Class continued from 9.30 until noon with a break for lunch and resumed at 12.30 until 3.30 when dinner was served. Recreation followed until 5.00 when study commenced. A spiritual conference commenced at 7.35 and continued until supper was served at 8.00. Night prayer was at 8.30 followed by bed. Silence was observed at all meals throughout the day as one of the Fathers read aloud on a spiritual topic. On Sundays High Mass at 9.00 was followed by recreation till 10.45 when there was a three quarter hour study to prepare for Catechism. At noon the students took lunch and went for a walk. Vespers took place at 2.45. Dinner at 3.30 was followed by study until 7.30. Then supper and recreation were followed by night prayer and bed.[24]

The first Rockwell Prize Day was held in July 1868. This was the beginning of a custom whereby the Fathers used the occasion to invite not only the parents, but also the clergy from parishes throughout the archdiocese and dignitaries from the neighbourhood, and entertained them afterwards to a three course

Fr. Bernard Graff
Dean of Studies 1869-1878

meal. The distribution of prizes was accompanied by instrumental music, a few piano duets, a short dialogue in French and a simulated debate between O'Connell and Grattan.[25] In June 1869 Rockwell students gave their first public entertainment which demonstrated the standards achieved in English literature, history and music. The *Tipperary Free Press* described it as a dramatic entertainment at which clergy and "notable people" from the surrounding area attended. The large room usually occupied as a refectory was fitted up tastefully for the occasion "with banners, emblems and other devices covering the walls and giving a festive appearance." When the performance had concluded the students and guests adjourned to one of the lawns overlooking the lake where they witnessed a brilliant display of fireworks. This pyrotechnic spectacle excited loud applause and admiration and lasted until a late hour.[26]

Reporting on Prize Day of 1871 *The Cashel Gazette* commented that "the College hall was beautifully decorated; purple hangings and garlands of evergreen, in all devices, lent freshness and gaiety to the happy occasion." The College band under the direction of Mr. Etterlen, it reported, opened proceedings. It noted that in the published results of the Catholic University examinations Rockwell candidates had received five honourable mentions in Latin and Greek while in the same examinations of 1868 and 1869 Rockwell students had taken first and second place in English essay writing. At Prize Day 1872 it mentioned all the dignitaries from the surrounding areas in attendance and stated that the highlight of the proceedings was a lecture by one of the students relating to experiments on electricity.[27]

Newspaper accounts of proceedings in Rockwell prior to 1874 had all been submitted by the College. For Prize Day of that year, however, a reporter from the *Tipperary Free Press* was invited to attend, so a more detached account of proceedings followed. He described the "spacious study hall" in which the event was held, as tastily decorated with flowers and banners bearing the national colours of France and Ireland. He was especially struck by the standard of the orchestra which consisted of members of the Community and students and which he found "above average of instrumentalists at a collegiate seminary". It was led by Fr. Graf on first violin who he described as a thorough musician possessing brilliant execution and artistic taste. He was less impressed by the standard of choral singing but enjoyed the one-act French comedy. Prizes were distributed for Religious Instruction, English literature, prose composition and grammar, Latin, Greek, French, Mathematics, Commerce, Piano, Singing and Art.[28]

RECREATION AND OUTINGS

A system of education was never complete, however, without a time for recreation. And so it was in the early days in Rockwell. The first mention of sport in the College was in August 1864 when the students took part in the ancient sport of archery. No mention was made of their targets but it seems likely they confined themselves to the nearby woods. Cricket is first mentioned in May 1869 when the crease was located on the lower side of the lake on the left of the back avenue on the approach to the back gate. In June of that year Rockwell beat a visiting team from Cashel by 176 runs to 14.[29] From then

Fr. Jules Botrel
visited Rockwell in 1865

and for many years later cricket was a popular sport for students from the months of April to June. Each year matches were played against teams from Thurles, Cashel, Dundrum, Cahir and Clonmel. In June 1874 when Dundrum was the visiting team the Rockwell players were: R. McCluskey, J. Lynch, E. Phelan, J. Harris, J. Conaghan, J. Foley, T. Heaney, J. Bergin, J. Mealy, C. O'Donnell and A. McLaughlin.[30]

Swimming and boating on the lake were popular in the summer months and when the students went fishing in the nearby River Suir Fr Huvétys usually accompanied them. On one occasion in September 1864 students followed the hounds and raised seven hares. By the end of that month they had travelled in horse-drawn coaches to Tipperary Town, Cahir, Cashel and twice to Clonmel. Walking, however, was the principal form of physical exercise and walks to the Rock of Cashel, to New Inn, around the lake and up and down the back avenue were regular. Fr Huvétys often set out on foot for Cashel. Students usually brought their musical instruments with them when they went walking and were often a source of amusement to the resident population.[31]

In those days, when traffic was mostly confined to horse-drawn vehicles and individuals on horseback, walking on the public roads was quite safe with the only irritant being the dust from the gravel-surfaced roads in the vicinity of Rockwell which were un-tarred until the mid 1920s. Nor did the walkers of those days have to cope with Cork-Dublin bound traffic which was then routed from Fermoy to Ardfinnan, Clonmel and Kilkenny. It was not until the mid-1920s that the Free State Government designated the main Dublin-Cork road as that from Port Laoise through Cashel and past the front gates of Rockwell.[32] The nearest railway station to Rockwell on the Cork-Dublin line was at Gould's Cross and it was from there that Rockwell students departed for and arrived from Dublin. The most common mode of transport for the individual on short journeys was on horseback and for this reason it seemed a very sensible decision by the Rockwell Fathers to have introduced for students in August 1865 lessons in horseback riding.[33]

Outings to places of interest appealed to the French Fathers and Scotch students who were keen to acquaint themselves with their new habitat, and an outline of their schedule for 1865 provides a further insight to early life in Rockwell. On Easter Monday, 17th April, they set out at 7.00 a.m. for the Galtee Mountains, returning at 6.p.m. Two weeks later they travelled to Mitchelstown Caves and Lismore Castle. Rising at 4.30 a.m., a breakfast of bread and milk followed morning prayer and at 6.00 a.m. the journey began with the singing of *Ave Maria*. Arriving at the Caves at 10.a.m. they had a meal of bread and eggs before journeying to Lismore. At 4.00 p.m. in the Castle they enjoyed a meal of ham, bread and wine and began the return journey singing hymns to Our Lady. They were back in Rockwell by 8 p.m. for a supper of soup and meat before night prayer and bed.

In early June they paid their first of many later visits to Mount Mellery. Rising at 3.30 a.m., a light breakfast of bread and milk followed morning prayer and they were on the road at 4.00 a.m. They attended Mass in Cahir at 5.00 a.m before resuming their journey to Mount Mellery. They enjoyed their breakfast on the roadside at that popular scenic spot, the Vee, and on reaching Mellery they were brought on a tour of the monastery by the Lord Abbot followed by dinner. They were back in Rockwell by 9.pm.

A trip to Waterford was undertaken in early August. Leaving Rockwell at 6.30 they arrived in Clonmel where they took the train which arrived in Waterford at 10.30. A visit to the cathedral and junior seminary and a tour of the port followed. Later that month they visited the Agricultural Show in Clonmel. In early September they visited the estates of the Bagwell family at Marlfield, of the Roe family at Roesgreen, of Lord Kingston at Mitchelstown and of the Maude family at Dundrum. Later they travelled by train from Gould's Cross to Dublin and had an overnight stay in Blackrock College. The last outing of the year for some of the students was to the races in Cashel. The Fathers and the scholastics did not go, however, on account of a law forbidding such pastime for clerics.

Indoor recreation was also catered for. A billiard table was part of the furniture from the beginning. On certain occasions, such as St. Patrick's Day, the vigil of All Saints and St. Andrew's Day a soirée was held at which students and staff entertained each other with stories and musical items. Until the arrival of the silent films in the early 1900s, these events usually included a magic lantern show. The lantern had a concave mirror in front of a light that projected it through a slide with an image scanned into it and on to a large screen. Not all lantern shows had an equal appeal as is evident from a comment following a show in 1871 "The scenes were excellent and the lighting very good, but without interesting and amusing commentary, the presentation was somewhat dead."[34]

HEALTH AND WELFARE

Memories of famine and fever were very much alive in the public mind in Ireland when Rockwell College was established. People feared the return of the dreaded fever which had been the principal cause of death in Ireland for centuries and which could break out upon the slightest provocation. There was a tendency to use the terms *fever* and *consumption* for various ailments such as typhoid, diphtheria, scarlet fever, tuberculosis and influenza, all of which were common in those days and all of which could be fatal. In a boarding school precautions against such ailments were essential.

The Fathers had no sooner arrived in Rockwell than they employed Dr. McCormack from Cashel as physician to the College at the rate of £10 a visit. A special part of the building was designated as an infirmary with Bro. Aloysius in charge. A dentist was employed to examine all the students and floors were thoroughly scrubbed regularly.

The first death recorded in Rockwell was that of Edward Gallagher who died suddenly in June 1865. He had only come to Rockwell the previous month with the intention of joining the Congregation and since then had been on the teaching staff. Fr. Huvéyts presided at his funeral Mass and the Fathers accompanied his coffin down the front avenue for burial in New Inn singing the *Benedictus*.

There were outbreaks of fever in the College in September 1865 and again in March 1868 but on both occasions the outbreak was successfully contained although they did cause great worry and the suspension of many activities. In December 1870 the fever took its first victim with the death of Thomas Tighe. He had come to Rockwell as a student from Scotland in April 1865 and his talent had been noted at the first Prize Day in 1867 and at the first public entertainment in 1869. When he died Fr. Goepfert went to Thurles to ask the archbishop for permission to have a cemetery for the Community on the grounds of the College. Permission was given. Thomas Tighe was buried near the Rock and his body was exhumed and re-buried soon afterwards when the new cemetery was ready.[35] This was the first interment in that cemetery in a secluded area near the Rock which became the final resting place of members of the Community from then until the present day.

THE FRENCH FLAIR

The Scots College was typical of any French seminary with the Fathers lending their own style and élan to incidents and events, a style that was often very different to what the Irish were accustomed. One event which caught the imagination of many people in Tipperary was the celebration in Rockwell of the feast of Corpus Christi. It took the form of a procession of the Blessed Sacrament through the College grounds with more than twenty priests from the surrounding parishes taking part. It is said that twelve thousand people attended the celebration in 1868. A large crowd was also present in 1869 when triumphal arches were erected at intervals with an array of flags of the Pope, of France and of Ireland along the route and hanging from windows. There were two altars of repose, one in front of the main entrance and one at the Lake House and both were lavishly decorated with drapes and garlands. The procession proceeded around the lake accompanied by the College band and choir with hymn singing along the way.[36] Irish people had been unaccustomed to public profession of faith because of the penal laws and the splendour of the Rockwell celebration was a new experience.

The reception for Archbishop Leahy in May 1868 afforded the French Fathers another opportunity to demonstrate their style of celebration. Earlier that day the archbishop had administered Confirmation in Knockfaffon and New Inn. At 2.30 p.m. the procession to Rockwell set out from New Inn with triumphal arches erected along the route. The chapel was beautifully decorated with drapes and garlands and the ceremony raised much excitement in the locality and was described in detail by the *Freeman's Journal*.[37]

Another new experience for the natives was the sight of the Scots and junior scholastics in their soutanes and broad French hats walking to the Rock of Cashel with their prefects. Such a sight had not been witnessed in Tipperary since before penal times and it was now welcomed with excitement by the locals. The French Fathers were bringing an air of freshness to Tipperary and this was evident in the requests to Fathers to give retreats and to officiate at ceremonies in the local parishes. Fr. Huvéyts celebrated Mass on feast days in Cashel and New Inn while Fr. Graf officiated at ceremonies in Clonmel and Fr. Riebert was a regular preacher at missions in the West of Ireland. This freshness was also evident in the visits of Fathers and students to the estates of the local gentry, especially to the Maude family in Dundrum and the Bagwells in Marlfield, both families prominent members of the Established Church and both having close associations with the execution of Fr Nicholas Sheehy a hundred years previously.[38] The memory of Fr. Sheehy still lingered in Tipperary but the new Rockwell was devoid of local prejudice and was injecting an air of freshness and ecumenism.

There was an air of freshness too in the way that Rockwell students endeared themselves to the local community. Whenever they went walking or on their day trips with their musical instruments they broke into song. When, for example, they visited Mitchelstown in June 1869 as their carriages moved through the town the band struck up some lilting airs. The townspeople expressed their appreciation by breaking into applause with shouts of enthusiasm and admiration. On the way home the same cheers of goodwill greeted them in Cahir.[39]

THE POLITICAL CLIMATE

When the French Fathers arrived in Rockwell in July 1864 Ireland was preoccupied by the growing influence of the Fenians and by the attempts of the more cautious majority to counteract them. And both of these courses had a strong Tipperary input. Two of the leading Fenian proponents, John O'Leary and Charles J. Kickham were from within a short distance of Rockwell, O'Leary from Tipperary Town and Kickham from Mullinahone. And one of the most prominent leaders at national level attempting to deflect attention from the Fenians was none other than Archbishop Leahy, close confidant of the Rockwell Fathers. Rockwell, therefore, cannot have felt remote from the course of events.

Less than a fortnight after Fr. Huvéyts met Archbishop Leahy in Thurles, the archbishop called to Rockwell on 1st August on his way from Confirmation in New Inn.[40] A week later Leahy was the centre of attention in Dublin at the laying of the foundation stone of the O'Connell monument, attended by an estimated half-a-million people, at which he made a speech calling for moderation. The following December he was one of the supporters of The National Association of Ireland, a movement founded to promote   reform of the land laws, the disestablishment of the Church of Ireland, and the solution of the education question.[41] And in February 1865 Leahy had a hand in having one of the founders of that movement, the Young Irelander John Blake Dillon, elected to parliament for one of the two Tipperary seats.[42] Charles Thiébault, being a wealthy land owner, was entitled to vote in that election. He actually voted twice. He travelled to Clonmel to vote in the county election and then to Cashel which had a parliamentary seat until 1868 when it was abolished because of charges of corruption.[43]

Fr. Leman in Blackrock College was always in close contact with the Fathers in Rockwell and it can be assumed that he reflected their views on current events. Writing to his superiors in Paris on 1st August 1866 it is clear that he had a good grasp of the Irish situation. He was unsympathetic to landlordism and he understood the emotional attraction of Fenianism. Continuing he wrote "This poor country is very unfortunate, and recently the case has been made worse by American Fenianism. It is said there is danger of an uprising, but I do not think it likely. In any event there is not the slightest chance of its success. It is only the poorest classes who are plotting at the moment, and all they can succeed in doing is to add to the misery of the country". In a later letter while referring to Fr. Huvétys and fears for their safety in Rockwell, he remarked that they were in no danger at all and that the only ill-will was directed towards Thiébault, who was cordially detested by his tenants, but who was then out of the country and would remain so until the troubles were over. He felt that the agitation had left the Holy Ghost Fathers in Ireland untouched. There might be a loss of some students, he felt, because of the troubled state of trade.[44]

Following the abortive rising in 1867 the political focus changed to the issue of political prisoners, and Tipperary was at the centre of attention again with the election of the veteran Fenian, Jeremiah O'Donovan Rossa as M.P. for

Tipperary in 1869 and the candidature of Charles J. Kickham for the same seat when O'Donovan Rossa's seat was annulled. Of a more immediate concern for the Fathers in Rockwell, however, was the outbreak of the Franco-Prussian War which, as has been seen, led to an influx of students from France.

CHARLES THIÉBAULT IN RESIDENCE

After the arrival of the Holy Ghost Fathers to Rockwell Charles Thiébault spent most of four years in the College during which time he attended to the welfare of the Scotch students and enhanced the property of the College. One of his first projects was the building of a house for himself by the lake which appropriately became known as Lake House. The architect for this house was a Mr. Butler and the building was complete in March 1865. Residing with him in Lake House was his valet Martin who looked after all his personal needs and who drove his two-horse carriage on Thiébault's many journeys around South Tipperary.[45] His first farm manager, Michael Connors, also lived in Lake House with his wife Mary who became the housekeeper and who had previously been Thiébault's housekeeper in Dundee.[46]

Thiébault spared no expense in the development of Rockwell's natural beauty and while in residence he personally supervised a task-force of masons, carpenters and gardeners. A third storey was added to the Mansion. Roads and walls were built or repaired. The orchard was stocked with hundreds of fruit trees brought from France. Thousands of ornamental and forest trees were planted. "The Rock" was laid out with its charming rustic pathways and artificial monastic ruins in the manner of the time, rockeries and fancy gates, and crowned with statues of Our Lady and St. Joseph. In this respect Thiébault was in keeping with other Tipperary landlords of that time who were inveterate travellers and collectors of demesne plants. Charles Bianconi, on purchasing the nearby Longfield House had experts brought from Italy to lay out an Italian garden with a yew hedge. He also planted a rose garden with white and yellow roses to represent the "Joyful and Glorious Mysteries, and red roses to represent the "Sorrowful Mysteries".[47]

A reporter from the *Tipperary Free Press* who visited Rockwell in July 1874 described the College "which is most picturesquely situated, and, at first sight looks like a lordly mansion in the midst of grounds on which timber, hundreds of years old, diversifies the landscape and reminds one of a noble demesne." He walked around the lake "and then through a winding shrubbery on to the pleasure ground above where are erected two magnificent statues of Our Lord and the Holy Virgin under whose patronage the establishment is placed and beheld a view of undulating hills profuse in many foliaged trees, and luxuriant vales that would gladden the heart of the most apathetic beholder of the beauty."[48]

Thiébault laid on gas-light to the College from a plant which he set up near the site of the present pavilion. The piping which conveyed the gas from the gasometer to the House was purchased in Clonmel and the fittings were installed in September 1864.[49] How the gas was generated is unknown.

During these years Charles Thiébault acquired a quantity of furniture for the College. Much of this he acquired at auctions in big houses in Holycross, Cashel and Fethard. He attended no less than six auctions in 1865 alone. He also had furniture made by the Graham Brothers who were high class furniture makers in Clonmel whose furniture had adorned many big houses in South-East Ireland.[50] He purchased two large book cases from a Protestant minister in Cahir and a fine horse-drawn carriage at an auction in Fethard. He attended a cattle sale in Dundrum in April 1866 and the following month he purchased thirty eight acres of land at Dangan Dargan which he donated to the Congregation.[51] He made frequent trips to Clonmel to purchase goods, including books, and on most of these occasions he was accompanied by Fr. Huvéyts.

Mr. Thiébault was very attentive to the welfare of the students from Scotland, accompanying them on outings and relaying messages from their parents and relatives following his twice yearly trips to Dundee. That his kindness was appreciated by the students was evident in November 1864 when they invited him to a party in the parlour for which they had composed a song for him. One of the students read a short complimentary address to which Mr. Thiébault responded with much emotion. He was then presented with a small gold cross.[52]

While Mr. Thiébault was in Dundee in 1866 the Fathers converted two twin buildings at the eastern end of the complex into classrooms and dormitories. A glass roof was placed between the two buildings thus providing a covered space which was used as a refectory. This refectory doubled as a theatre with a temporary stage erected. A kitchen block and scullery were built around the same time.[53]

DARK CLOUDS GATHERING

It was in November 1868 that the first sign of Mr. Thiébault's tetchiness with the course of events became apparent. It took the form of a very public disagreement with the parish priest of New Inn, Fr. John Ryan whom he accused of making a derogatory statement about him. He took the issue so seriously that he resorted to writing letters to the *Cashel Gazette*. He reported the matter to Archbishop Leahy and following a meeting in Thurles between the Archbishop, Fr. Ryan and himself, he attended Mass in New Inn at which Fr. Ryan made a public retraction of his statement.[54]

Whatever was the source of this disagreement it came at a time when a disagreement of a very serious nature was developing between Thiébault and the Holy Ghost Fathers. When a contract was signed in 1864 by the Holy Ghost Congregation with Mr. Thiébault and Bishop Murdoch of Glasgow acting on behalf of the Scottish bishops who were appointed trustees, it was agreed that complete responsibility for the running of the project should be shouldered by the Holy Ghost Fathers rather than having a dual control, while Mr. Thiébault retained a life interest in the property. All went well until the death of Bishop Murdoch when Mr. Thiébault demanded a new contract.[55]

The Front Gates until 1943

Much time and legal expertise was spent throughout the year 1868 in the drawing up of various reports, and the modification of the agreement. Fr. Leman and Fr. Huvétys went over to Scotland to discuss matters in person with Thiébault and the representatives of the Scottish bishops. Agreement was finalised and all seemed to be going satisfactorily until late in 1870 when Thiébault returned to Rockwell after a long absence. He objected to the buildings erected during his absence. Tension mounted almost immediately once he began to take an active part in the direction of the establishment, interfering with the day-to-day life and management. Matters were aggravated by the arrival of a number of senior scholastics from France as a result of the Franco-Prussian war. Courses in philosophy and theology were conducted for these students as well as for the Scots and this new situation added to misunderstandings. The Scottish bishops, against the advice of Fr. Leman, decided to submit the matter to the Landed Estates Court to seek a legally binding decision as to their respective claims. This attempt failed and both parties then decided to submit the matter to Rome for arbitration.[56]

Rome appointed Cardinal Cullen as arbitrator. Negotiations dragged on until 1874 when a final settlement was reached. Ownership of Rockwell was legally decided in favour of the Holy Ghost Congregation on condition that they indemnify the Scottish bishops to the tune of £7,000. The Scotch College closed and the Scots seminarians, ten theologians, three philosophers and one secondary student, worked industriously until the day of their departure and left full of respect and affection for the Fathers to whom they expressed their profound gratitude. Two of their number joined the Holy Ghost Congregation. Henceforth the institution adopted the name of the French College under the titular designation of Notre Dame de Rockwell. This was modified in later years by the omission of the French reference in the name.

Meanwhile Charles Thiébault died in the hospital of St. John of God in Paris on 5 June 1873. He left his entire fortune to the poor of his native parish of Beaurains, to the Little Sisters of the Poor, to the building fund of a church in Dundee and to the establishment of Catholic schools for the poor in England. In Rockwell he was given a Solemn Requiem Office and High Mass and a Month's Mind. Father Huvétys wrote "These charitable bequests of Thiébault show the generous and truly Christian sentiments which animated him to the end of his life. We hope that he has already received his eternal reward."[57]

Notes

[1] O'Dwyer, C., "The Beleagurered Fortress", St. Patrick's College, Thurles, 1937-1988. p. 240 in *Thurles: The Cathedral Town*. Eds W. Corbett, W. Nolan.

[2] SFLM p. 201.

[3] JNL 1864 p. 2.

[4] W.G. Skehan, *Cashel and Emly Heritage* pp 157-8.

[5] O'Shea, J., *Priests, Politics and Society in Post-famine Ireland*, p. 43.

[6] JNL 1964-1891 passim.

[7] W. G. Skehan, op. cit. pp 157-8.

[8] JNL 9/8/1864.

[9] W. Hayes & A. Kavanagh, *The Tipperry Gentry* p. 52.

[10] R. V. Comerford, Tipperary Representation at Westminster, 1801-1918 in W. Nolan & T. G. McGrath, *Tipperary: History and Society* pp 331-2.

[11] SFLM p. 201, ISR 163.

[12] JNL 1864-5 passim

[13] JNL 1864 p. 7.

[14] JNL 1864-5 passim

[15] JNL 29/3, 1/6, 30/12/1868.

[16] RCA 1957.

[17] SFFC pp 113-4.

[18] RCA 1964.

[19] RCA 1932.

[20] ibid

[21] RCA 1977.

[22] JNL 6/11/1864.

[23] JNL 29/7/1865.

[24] JNL 16/10/1864.

[25] JNL 21/7/1868.

[26] *Tipperary Free Press* 29/6/1869

[27] *The Cashel Gazette* 22/7/1871, 20/7/1872.

[28] *Tipperary Free Press* 17/7/1874.

[29] JNL 7/6/1869.

[30] *The Cashel Gazette* 4/7/1874.

[31] JNL 1864-1869 passim

[32] O'Donnell, S., op.cit. pp 36-8, 102-3.

[33] JNL 24/8/1865.

[34] JNL 2/11/1871.

[35] JNL 1864-1870 passim

36 JNL 27/5/1869
37 JNL 12/5/1868
38 W. Hayes & A. Kavanagh, *The Tipperary Gentry* pp 148-159.
39 JNL 29/6/1869.
40 JNL 1/8/1864.
41 R. V. Comerford, *The Fenians in Context,* pp 105-7.
42 J. O'Shea, *Priest, Politics and Society in Post-famine Ireland,* pp 156-160.
43 JNL 24/2/1865, 27/2/1865.
44 SFLM pp 298 ff.
45 JNL 20/3/1865.
46 JNL 16/7/1865.
47 W. Nolan, Patterns of Living in Tipperary 1750-1850, in W. Nolan & T.G. McGrath, op. Cit. pp 256-287.
48 *Tipperary Free Press* 17/7/1874.
49 JNL 6/91864, 17/9/1864.
50 O'Donnell, S., *Clonmel 1840-1900: Anatomy of an Irish Town.* P. 262.
51 JNL 16/4, 5/5/1867.
52 JNL 3/11/1864.
53 RCA 1977
54 JNL 15/11, 19/11/1868.
55 SFPL pp 336 ff.
56 ibid
57 RCA 1964.

– 3 –

THE FRENCH COLLEGE
1875-1889

Following the closure of the Scotch College, Rockwell College for a time became known as the French College. Its sister College, Blackrock College, was also known by the same name. These two Colleges were called the French Colleges, not merely because they were founded by Frenchmen but because the system of education followed in them was based on the system operated in France, modified to suit the Irish situation.[1] Even after the Irish system of education was introduced in 1879 the name persisted for a time.

THE COMMUNITY

Between 1875 and 1889 five French Fathers had at times been members of the Rockwell Community together with one German and ten Irish. In the same years twenty two Irish Brothers and one French Brother had also been members. In 1875 the only members still in residence since the 1860s were Frs Huvéyts and Goepfert and Br. Hippolyte. All of the Fathers were teachers in the College. Of the five French Fathers, three were from Alsace, a province together with Lorraine which had been taken over by Prussia by the Treaty of Frankfurt in 1871 following the Franco-Prussian War. These Fathers from Alsace were Fr. Goepfert who had been in Rockwell since 1867, Fr. John George Ott, who was Bursar from 1883 to 1889 and Fr. Louis Leiniger who taught Music, French and Latin from 1888 to 1891. With Fr. Huvétys the other French Father was Fr. Achilles Lemire who was appointed Director of St. Joseph's in 1887. The only German Father was Fr. Dominique Schleweck who was from Würtemburg.[2]

An interesting feature of these Fathers was that they were all relatively young. When Fr. Huvétys was appointed President of Blackrock College in 1880, having served as President of Rockwell for sixteen years, he was still only forty five and when Fr. Achilles Lemire was appointed Director of St. Joseph's he was only twenty seven. Fr. Goepfert was thirty eight when he became President of Rockwell and Fr. Dominique Schleweck was only thirty three when he came to Rockwell. The age profile of these Fathers can explain why they all had a relatively short tenure in Rockwell, they being young enough to be involved in new foundations and other developments of the growing Congregation.

Of the Irish Fathers who served for a time in Rockwell between 1875 and 1889 three had completed their novitiate in St. Joseph's, they being Fr. Patrick

McDermott who became Director of St. Joseph's in 1881, Fr. John O' Keeffe who was the first student of Rockwell to be ordained for the Congregation and Fr. James Cotter who was to become a future President of the College. With the exception of Fr. Edward Conyngham, who completed his novitiate in Lagonnet, all the other Irish Fathers completed their novitiate in Blackrock College.

Like their French confreres, these Irish Fathers were very young. Frs. McDermott, O'Keeffe. Fogarty and Healy were in their twenties when appointed, Frs Murphy and Kenneally were in their thirties and Fr. Conyngham, aged forty, was the oldest among them. And like their French confreres most of these Irish Fathers had a short tenure in Rockwell and were destined to play important roles in the work of the Congregation in other foundations.[3]

Together with Br. Hippolyte, twenty two Brothers were members of the Rockwell Community at times between 1875 and 1889. Six of these did not continue in the Congregation after their time in Rockwell but of the eighteen who did, twelve had completed their novitiate at St. Joseph's and the remaining four at Blackrock College. They all had developed skills which qualified them to carry out various important tasks which an institution such as Rockwell demanded. Br. Aidan Ryan, a native of Killenaule, Co. Tipperary and a former student at St. Joseph's, was in charge of the College infirmary and acted as College receptionist. He was a source of guidance to students. Br. Celsus McCabe from Co. Cavan had been a primary school teacher before joining the Congregation and was therefore ideally suited to take charge of the junior students. Br. Congal Gleeson from Moycarkey, Co. Tipperary attended to housekeeping and bookkeeping.

The College farm was looked after by a few Brothers. Br. Killian Cunningham from nearby Aherlow, Co. Tipperary took charge in 1880 and he was so successful that Fr. Leman asked him to take charge of the Blackrock College farm at Leixlip, Co. Kildare. He was succeeded as farm manager by Br. Kieran Egan from Ferbane, Co. Offaly who was in charge for the rest of his life until his death in 1905. Helping on the farm and in the kitchen garden developed by Mr. Thiébault were Br. John O'Donoghue from Hospital, Co. Limerick, Br. Raol Condon from nearby Ballylooby, Co. Tipperary and Br. Senan Mulligan from Corflugh, Co. Fermanagh.

The kitchen and catering areas of the College were looked after by five Brothers. Br. Paulinus Colgan from Clonbrin, Co. Kildare and Br. Dunstan Dunne from Monastereven were in charge of the refectory and Br. Dalmas Colgan, also from Monasterevan was in charge of the bakery where he was assisted by Br Colmkille Heffernan from Moycarkey, Co. Tipperary. Br. David Doran from Aherlow, Co. Tipperary was cook.

The dormitories in a boys' boarding school demanded special attention and this was supplied between 1873 and 1897 by Br. Mary Ignatius O'Dea from nearby Ballydoyle, Rosegreen, Co. Tipperary who was engaged all the remainder of his life in the minor but essential functions of looking after the tidiness of rooms and dormitories, replenishing the supply of water for wash basins and baths. He also served as sacristan for many years.

The Fathers wore their soutanes and birettas at all times in public and which often needed repairs or replacement; and for boys who were prone to horseplay torn clothes was not unusual. A tailoring service was therefore necessary. And this was supplied from 1880 by Br.Nicephorus Barrett from Ballylooby, Cahir. He is said to have learned the art of tailoring from a Mr. Duggan, a Carlow man operating in Cahir. It is also possible that he was sent to France to learn how to make soutanes to CSSp specifications. In later years when his eyesight failed, he supervised the work of those he had trained, in particular Joe Moloney his relative.

Br. Silas Laffan, a native of Kildare Town, left a mark on Rockwell which is visible to this day. He supervised the building of the main north wing, often referred to as the Silas wing. He was a talented man who also learned the art of shoemaking which he plied almost to the end of his days.

DEVELOPMENT

There had been a gradual increase in the student population in the early 1870s and by September 1876 there were ninety boarders and fifteen day boys. To cope with these numbers, development of the infrastructure was a necessity. Since the foundation of the College, water had been carried from a well by the lake to the main building. This chore came to an end in 1876 when a hydraulic pump was installed in the well which was cut off from the rest of the lake by the erection of a circular protecting wall. The water was pumped to the yard of St. Joseph's and from there to the main building. It was also at this time that a cricket pitch, a handball alley and a bakery were built.[4]

It was between August 1877 and November 1879 that the main north wing of the College, known as the Silas wing, came into existence. No professional architect seems to have been employed.[5] (See Chronological Floor Plan) On the plan it covers the stairs at the eastern end and what until recently were the science rooms. The ground floor became the second Rockwell Chapel. The Chapel was greatly enhanced in April 1886 with the arrival from France of new Stations of the Cross. They were shipped from France packed in crates.[6] The second floor for many years contained "The Pink" and St. Joseph's dormitories. Two of the three rooms on the first floor, and next to the stairs, were occupied by the Deans of Discipline and Studies. The rest of this floor was a smaller dormitory.[7]

There was an important development with regard to communications in 1886. Previously mail arrived at the College at irregular intervals. But in April of that year Fr. Goepfert arranged with the Post Master General whereby incoming mail arrived each morning at 7.20 a.m. and outgoing mail was collected each evening at 6.40. A significant reduction in the cost of telegrams was also achieved. They now cost only one shilling and sixpence whereas formerly they cost four shillings.[8]

TRANSITION

The Archbishop of Cashel, Patrick Leahy, died on 26th January 1875. He had been a friend and mentor of Fr. Huvéyts and the Rockwell Community since

The new building

1864. His successor, Dr. Thomas Croke, who held the position until 1902, became a lifelong friend of Rockwell and a frequent guest of the Community. One of his early appointments was a visit to Rockwell in February 1876 when Fr. Huvéyts greeted him with a presentation of addresses in English and French.[9]

On his appointment Archbishop Croke selected five senior clergy of the diocese to advise him on diocesan matters and one of the five was Fr. John Ryan of New Inn, Rockwell's friend.[10] The archbishop's link with Rockwell was therefore further strengthened because of Fr. Ryan's affinity with the College. Dr. Croke spent the months of May, June and July 1876 visiting thirty parishes in his archdiocese and he reported to Archbishop Cullen that he had been received everywhere and by everyone with the most extraordinary enthusiasm.[11] His popularity was enhanced by his support for the rights of tenant farmers.

Archbishop Croke

This extraordinary enthusiasm for him was evident when he visited Rockwell in June 1881 on the feast of *Corpus Christi*. On his way from Thurles he passed through Cashel unnoticed. However, at the racecourse, half way between Cashel and Rockwell, he was met by a most enthusiastic and warm-hearted gathering of tenant farmers and labourers of the Ryan, Hogan, Davett and Coughlan families. The Boytonrath fife and drum band was present with a green flag fluttering in the breeze and bearing in gold letters *Ireland for the Irish, The Land for the People* and *Tis grand to see brave Parnell free*. A splendid triumphal arch bore the inscription *We hail thee with delight*. At that point the archbishop alighted from his carriage and walked to Rockwell with the crowd.

The entrance gate to the College was decorated with banners supporting in the centre an Irish cross from which branched off on either side a graceful wreath which bore the motto *Benedictus qui venit in nomine Domini* with an Irish harp beautifully festooned. Along the magnificent avenue at short intervals were the Pontifical French and Irish flags. Approaching the College, the President Fr. Goepfert, the President of Blackrock College, Fr. Huvétys, Fr. FX Liberman (nephew of the founder of the Congregation who was on official visitation) and Fr. Murphy met the archbishop and falling on bended knees kissed his ring and obtained his blessing. Dr. Croke later visited the village of New Inn which was decorated with flags and flowers with music from the Cashel Temperance Band, the Rockwell College Brass Band, the Drangan Brass Band and the Boytonrath Fife and Drum Band.[12]

Archbishop Croke's appointment was followed five years later in 1880 by a major change in the history of Rockwell caused by the death of Fr. Leman, founder and President of Blackrock College. Fr. Huvéyts was appointed his successor and Rockwell's loss was Blackrock's gain. The achievements of Fr. Huvéyts during his sixteen years in Rockwell were remarkable. He had established Rockwell College as a national institution. He had, with Fr. Leman, steered the College through very difficult negotiations following the death of Mr. Thiébault and it was not until 1st November 1876 that the Fathers were fully recognised as the legal owners of the Rockwell property. He had overseen structural developments since 1864 culminating in the erection of the Silas wing between 1877 and 1879. He had also prepared Rockwell for the transition from the French education system to the Irish Intermediate system. His post-Rockwell career was also impressive. While at Blackrock he was much involved in the struggle for fair play for Irish Catholics in the area of higher education. On his return to France in 1889 he was appointed secretary for all matters to do with the English-speaking areas of the Congregation. He died at Chevilly on 15th March 1898 aged 63.[13]

Fr. Huvétys was succeeded as President of Rockwell in 1880 by Fr. Prosper Mary Goepfert who like Fr. Huvétys was a relatively young man when he took this responsible position. Fr. Goepfert was born in Alsace, then part of France, in 1842. He entered the senior scholasticate in 1862 at rue Lhomond, Paris, going to Chevilly when the scholasticate was located there as from 1864. He was ordained by the Papal Nuncio to France in 1866 and was appointed the following year to Rockwell where he was to serve for twenty two years, at first teaching Latin, Greek and French while trying to master English. He served as director of St. Joseph's from 1870 to 1880 and as President from 1880 to 1890. Fr. Goepfert is remembered for his life of Fr. Libermann, the

Fr. Prosper Goepfert
President 1880-1889

first to appear in English and for the first religious magazine of the Congregation in English, *The Messenger of St. Joseph*. Both of these publications relied heavily on earlier French editions.[14]

THE INTERMEDIATE

Secondary education in Ireland in the post-reformation era had been very much affected by the political and religious policies of Britain. As a result of legislation or state patronage a number of secondary schools were established with a view to fostering English language and culture and Protestant belief. Such grammar schools had been established in Clonmel and in Tipperary Town. Catholic education was forbidden and restrictions were intensified during the penal period. When the penal laws were relaxed in the 1780s Catholic religious orders began founding secondary schools without public endowment. For three quarters of the nineteenth century a dual system of secondary schools existed, Protestant schools, many of them benefiting from older public endowment, and Catholic schools operating with no support from public funds.[15]

When Rockwell College was founded, second-level education was officially referred to as intermediate education, a term which was to remain for many years. The problem of financing intermediate education in Ireland was a matter of concern to interested parties in the 1860s and a number of proposals were made for a system of payment by results. Patrick Keenan, as a special commissioner, introduced such a system in Trinidad in 1869. One of the colleges which benefited from the system there was St. Mary's College which was owned and run by the Holy Ghost Fathers. In 1871 Edward Howley, a barrister who had taught at Blackrock College, was encouraged by Fr. Leman, President of the College, to write a pamphlet urging the introduction of a results system for Irish schools. The suggestion was welcomed in Irish political circles and it was incorporated into the Intermediate Education (Ireland) Bill which was introduced into the House of Commons in June 1878. There was little opposition to the bill and it received the royal assent in August of that year. The Intermediate Board was established to operate the system.[16]

The first examinations under the Intermediate Board took place in June 1879. At first there were three grades of examination, junior, middle and senior. The subjects were arranged in seven divisions as follows: Greek, Latin, English, Modern languages, Mathematics, Natural Sciences, Music and Drawing. The subjects were not treated equally, however, because subjects such as the classics and English received more favourable mark weighting and higher results fees. The Education Act had many limitations. It took no cognisance of the need to support, equip or fund schools. It made no mention of teachers and laid down no conditions for teacher competence or remuneration, nor did it support any schemes for teacher training.[17] The result was that the quality of much of the teaching was highly suspect and by the turn of the century only 11.5 % of male teachers in Catholic secondary schools were university graduates. The assumption that to pass certain stereotyped written tests was the main goal of a child's career had a stultifying effect upon good, if individualistic teaching.[18] It was this system, with later minor modifications, that Patrick Pearse referred to as "the murder machine".

With all its limitations, the Act was welcomed in Rockwell by Fr. Huvétys. He realised how important it was for Rockwell's academic reputation and funding that good performances in the public examinations be recorded. With this in mind, he was aware that there was in the Congregation a young man with an outstanding reputation as a teacher and administrator and he persuaded the authorities that he be appointed to Rockwell. That man was Fr. John T. Murphy. He was appointed to Rockwell in 1879 as Dean of Studies and Dean of Discipline and over the next seven and a half years he was to have a major influence over events in the College.

Fr. John T. Murphy
Dean of Studies 1879- 1887

Fr. John T. Murphy was born in Meenhanivan, Castleisland, Co. Kerry, in 1854 and educated at Blackrock College where he proved to be a student of great ability. He served as a prefect in Trinidad where he excelled as a teacher and became familiar with the new system of payments by results. He was ordained in 1878 and on his arrival at Rockwell his vision for the College was soon apparent. In the first Intermediate examination in June 1879, Rockwell entered fifty three candidates. Of these, forty four were successful and included two "of the highest exhibitions." In 1880, 43 passed and four of them were within the first hundred in Ireland.[19] In the six years between 1879 and 1884 Rockwell gained no fewer than eighty five distinctions, leading all the schools of Ireland in 1884 with a total of ten exhibitions and the unprecedented number of nine medals. The prize winners in 1884 were Matthew H. Auer, Michael A. Hughes, Charles Kempel, Michael Delaney, Thomas P. O'Connor, Michael J. McLoughlin, John Hussey, Edward A. Cahill, Edward P. McLoughin, Timothy O'Sullivan, William J. O'Connor, Michael O'Brien, John Ahern, William Collins and Patrick Coffey. The editor of the *Cashel Gazette*, John Davis White, was so impressed by the performance of Rockwell students that year that he commented that the "education given at Rockwell must be of a first class character.[20] Dr. Croke pointed out in a lengthy letter to the *Freeman's Journal* that this achievement was more striking as Rockwell presented only forty two candidates. "Rockwell stands just now absolutely at the head of all the Intermediate Colleges in Ireland", he wrote.[21] The academic successes continued to be so remarkable that Fr Goepfert proposed Fr. John T. Murphy's name for a Fellowship in the Royal University and he was seconded in this by Archbishop Croke.[22]

Fr. Goepfert proceeded to promote the College by placing advertisements in the local and national press. The first of these appeared in August 1880 and interestingly the address given was *Rocwkell College, Cahir*. This was also the address used initially by the Intermediate Board. By 1884, however, the address had become *Rockwell College, Cashel*. The advertisement described the College as situated "in a beautiful and picturesque locality within three miles of Cashel and five of Cahir. With its well-wooded demesne, four hundred acres in extent, and its beautiful lake, Rockwell affords advantages altogether unparalleled for the outdoor exercise and recreation of the students. The large and commodious buildings which have been erected recently, enable the Fathers to give superior accommodation to the students entrusted to their care."[23] While one could question Fr. Goepfert's description of the extent of the demesne and its distance from Cahir and Cashel it has to be remembered that in 1880 acreage and distance were determined sometimes in statue and sometimes in Irish measurements.

The advertisement continued that the course of instructions embraced English language and literature, Greek, Latin and most modern languages "of which French and German are taught by natives." Also included were Mathematical, Physical and Natural Sciences, Composition, Elocution, History and Geography (ancient and modern), Music, Drawing "and the various other branches of a sound liberal education." The classical studies included Rhetoric and comprised the entrance and undergraduate courses required for any of the universities. There was also a commercial course in Economics and Bookkeeping catering for students interested in applying to the civil service or banks. The advertisement stressed that junior students formed quite "a distinct department" from senior students. The annual fee for students was twenty eight guineas with a reduction for brothers and ecclesiastical students.[24]

Fr. Laurence Healy
Dean of Studies 1887-1890

ST. JOSEPH'S

During Fr. Prosper Goepfert's tenure as Director of St. Joseph's ninety two postulants had entered. The largest number in any year was fourteen in 1870, 1875 and 1877. In other years there were at times only a few entrants. Among these who later had notable associations with Rockwell were Innocent Ryan and Edward Schmidt in 1869 and Daniel Murphy ten years later.[25]

Fr. Patrick McDermott was Director from 1881 to 1883. A native of Mullinahone, Co. Tipperary, he had entered St. Joseph's himself at the age of twelve in 1871. Twenty three postulants entered while he was in charge, among them Thomas Pembroke in 1882, a future President of Rockwell. Fr. McDermott was appointed to the senior scholasticate at Chevilly where he taught Philosophy and later to Pittsburgh, USA where he spent most of his life. He was succeeded as Director of St. Joseph's by Fr. Thomas Fogarty who spent three years in Rockwell before departing for the missions in South Africa. Fr. Achilles Lemire was director of St. Joseph's for a year before it closed temporarily in 1888. The students in St. Joseph's at the time of its closure transferred to the scholasticate in Blackrock College. There were four senior scholastics and sixteen junior scholastics in St. Joseph's in August 1887.[26]

By 1888 one hundred and sixty one students had entered St. Joseph's. Those of them who continued their studies for the priesthood went to France and studied either at Langonett or Chevilly. Following ordination they departed for the early Holy Ghost mission fields as far apart as South Africa, Angola, Mauritius, Zanzibar and USA.[27]

THE POLITICAL CLIMATE

During the final years of the presidency of Fr. Huvétys and that of Fr. Goepfert the two issues which dominated the Irish political scene were the movements for home rule and land reform. It would have been difficult for anyone in Rockwell, even the French Fathers, to escape the animation engendered by these issues. The general election of 1874 had raised particular excitement in Tipperary when the Young Irelander, John Mitchel, was elected for the county, although unseated by the government on the grounds that he was a convicted criminal. The obstruction tactics of Charles Stewart Parnell and his colleagues at Westminster during 1877 raised further excitement.

Unprecedented bad weather in the late1870s had caused a sharp fall in potato and grain production, while at the same time greatly increased competition from America caused Irish grain prices to plummet. Hardest hit were the subsistence farmers in the West of Ireland and as thoughtless landlords continued to demand the payment of rents, evictions became commonplace. An agrarian protest followed which led to the setting up of the Irish National Land League in 1879. Its chief architect was Michael Davitt and the decision of Charles Stewart Parnell to accept its presidency greatly widened its scope.[28]

The feelings of local people in the vicinity of Rockwell on these issues were highlighted in June 1881 on the occasion of the visit of Archbishop Croke to the College. At the opening of a concert in the College following the annual sports of 1882 Fr. James Cantwell of Thurles read a telegram he had just received announcing the release of Parnell under the terms of the Kilmainham Treaty and the crowd erupted into loud cheering.[29]

Rockwell students were given a clear insight into the problem of evictions when they visited Mitchelstown in July 1888 when the Plan of Campaign was at its height. Each summer it was customary for them to travel on an outing to the Kingston estate there where they enjoyed a picnic. In September the previous year a crowd gathered outside the courthouse in Mitchelstown in which William O'Brien, the Nationalist politician, and John Mandeville, a local farmer, were summoned on a charge of incitement to resist eviction of tenants on the Kingston estate. The police retreated to their barracks under assault, and opened fire, killing two and injuring dozens of their assailants, one of whom subsequently died.[30] O'Brien and Mandeville were imprisoned in Tullamore jail where they refused to wear prison uniform. Mandeville was kept naked in his cell and he died in July 1888, a few months after his release and only a few days before the visit of the Rocwkell students. Feelings were running high in the town and the students were invited to a pageant depicting the Mandeville experience. They were deeply affected by the experience.[31]

VISITORS

There were some important visitors to the College in the 1880s. Archbishop Croke had made it a rule to "drop in" on the Fathers whenever a Confirmation tour or other business took him to South Tipperary. In June 1881 he stayed for a whole three days rest following his formal visit which has already been noted. On the occasion of one of his visits he said "There are good colleges in Ireland and in England, but unfortunately there are others too. I am convinced that at Rockwell you are in a house which, in religion and education, yields to no other institution in Ireland. It is a school which I am proud to have in my diocese." [32]

Another important visitor in June 1881 was Fr. Francis Xavier Libermann, nephew of the founder, who was sent from Paris to make an official report on the works of the Congregation in Ireland. Another reason for his visit was to make a decision on the acceptance of an offer being made to the Congregation by Bishop George Buckley of Limerick and Lord Emly, namely the taking on of the direction of Mungret College. Fr. Libermann turned down the offer and Mungret was later taken over by the Jesuits.[33]

In June 1883 the College was visited by the Superior General of the Holy Ghost Congregation, Fr. Ambrose Emonet. This was, in fact, the first ever visit to Ireland by a Superior General of the Congregation. He had been ordained together with Fr. Leman the founder of Blackrock College and it was while in charge of St. Pierre College, Martinique, that he had singled out one of the students, Peter Huvétys, first President of Rockwell, as an ideal candidate for the Holy Ghost Congregation.[34] He would have been familiar, therefore, with the fortunes of Rockwell under the guidance of Fr. Huvétys. He must have been impressed by the warm and joyous reception accorded to him all the way from the railway station in Thurles to the hall-door at Rockwell. The school band was at the front gate as were workers and neighbours and later in the evening a fireworks display on the lake heralded his arrival.[35]

Michael Davitt may have seemed an unlikely visitor to Rockwell in 1884. He was an ex-Fenian, a revolutionary and a land agitator. That was but a side in the character of a man whose achievements by 1884 in the cause of land reform had been heroic. Davitt was also an orthodox practising Catholic who appreciated the immense social and moral importance of the Catholic Church in Irish society. He had close and friendly relations with individual Catholic clerics, most notably Archbishop Croke of Cashel and Bishop Duggan of Clonfert. In 1884 he was campaigning on behalf of the Irish National League in Tipperary, a county he considered "national and reliable" because of the controlling influence of Archbishop Croke whose long association with the cause of tenant farmers he appreciated.[36]

Michael Davitt

The Fathers in Rockwell may have viewed with some apprehension the visit of this great man because of the stormy past of the Rockwell property. Their fears were soon dispelled, however, as is clear from the reference to his visit in the Journal. "He is a man ardently devoted to his country and above all to the poor tenants whom he wants to see independent owners of their property as in France; but he seeks to achieve his purpose by fair means. He is far from being the fierce and blood-thirsty revolutionary so frequently depicted in the Protestant press of England.

'Ah!' he said to us 'how I should love to spend my last days in a charming retreat like Rockwell! I would never oppose properties such as it is, destined to educate our youth and to spread the faith. Believe me …you will never hear it said that Michael Davitt defended unjust principles.'

And seeing the statue of Mary Immaculate he said with great emotion ' And I too am a Child of Mary. My mother often repeated that I was born on the 25th of March, 1845.'

We gave him a hospitable and religious reception without demonstration and he left us grateful and edified. This man has almost suffered martyrdom for his political faith; but in spite of the years spent in English prisons he pursues his aim with the same confidence and ardour."[37]

An interesting visitor to Rockwell in August 1887 was the Archbishop of Damietta, Ignazio Persico, accompanied by Monsignor Enrico Gualdi.[38] Archbishop Persico was an Italian Capuchin who served in the Vatican Diplomatic Service on whose behalf he came to Ireland with the Under Secretary of Propaganda, Monsignor Gualdi, to investigate the Plan of Campaign, that stratagem employed by tenants against landlords between 1886 and 1891, prompted by the depression in the prices of dairy produce which left many tenants in arrears with rent. The Vatican was concerned about the attitude of Catholic clergy to the Plan. In the course of their visit, the papal envoys visited Archbishop Croke in Thurles where they spent a few days. The visit to Rockwell could be seen as part of Croke's attempt to impress them.[39]

SPORTING ACTIVITIES

The annual Rockwell Sports was first held in June 1877 and it gained in popularity each year, one reason being that originally it was not confined to the College but was open to the public and the grounds of Rockwell were a public attraction. Its popularity was further enhanced by Fr. John T. Murphy because of his passion for boating. His model for most matters in Rockwell was Oxford and he envisaged regattas on the lake in imitation of Henley.[40] He founded a boat club in Rockwell but the expense of building a boat house and the purchase of a fleet of boats may not have been a priority with the President Fr. Goepfert who was then also in charge of the purse strings as Bursar. Fr. Murphy overcame this problem, however, by using the annual sports of 1882 as a fund-raiser for the boat club. He advertised the entry to the sports and "fancy fair" as free of charge, but a charge of half a crown was levied for entry to a concert which was to follow the sports in the College.[41]

The Sports of 1882 was a gala affair with "the elite" of the county in attendance. Prominent business and professional people from the towns of Thurles, Cashel, Cahir and Clonmel were in attendance as were many of the local farming community and clergy from local parishes. The Rockwell band under the direction of Thomas Griffin together with the Holy Family band from Thurles entertained the crowd. Stalls were managed by the ladies and the refreshment marquee at the sports was managed by the Misses Hayes of The Commercial Hotel, Thurles, in which hotel the Gaelic Athletic Association was to be founded two years later.[42] Sprint and hurdle races were keenly contested as were the long jump, high jump, pole vault and the throwing of a cricket ball. The sports ended with a pony race. The concert attracted a large crowd and finished with a performance of the play *Rory O'More* which had been written by Samuel Lover in 1836.[43]

Fr. John T. Murphy's success in organising the boat club reached fruition in 1883 with the holding of Rockwell's first regatta. It was held on Whit Monday and it was an event separate from the annual sports which had been held earlier. It consisted of races for juniors and seniors in rigged gigs, in four-oared outriggers and in canoes. The Cashel Temperance Band entertained the visitors who were also entertained to a meal in the College. The athletic sports which had been held in March included the usual competitions together with a sack race and throwing of a cricket ball for seniors and juniors.[44]

The regatta was incorporated as part of the annual sports from 1885. That year the regatta was held in the morning and the athletics in the afternoon.[45] The sports of 1886 followed a similar time-table but tragedy struck in the afternoon following the final of the 100 yards sprint. That race had finished in a dead heat between Edward McLoughlin and James Holland who felt unwell at the end of the race. He collapsed into the arms of another student, Patrick O'Neill. Fr. Fogarty, who was nearby, administered the Sacrament of Extreme Unction and Dr. Moloney pronounced him dead. James was from Dungarvan.[46] Two years later tragedy struck again when a student drowned while swimming in the lake. His body was pulled out of the water by Fr. Healy. The coroner concluded that he had died as a result of cardiac arrest.[47]

Cricket continued as a popular sport with Rockwell students. Other Tipperary schools with cricket teams included Tipperary Grammar School, St. John's College, Newport and Clonmel Grammar School. Over the years the cricket teams of these schools could comfortably compete with any cricket club in the county. Cricket was also played in the seminaries of St. Patrick's College,

Thurles and Mount Mellary.[48] Among its matches in 1882 the Rockwell eleven travelled in May to Tipperary to play Clanwilliam and then to the Cahir Cricket Ground at the military barracks on Whit Monday where they beat the local team by 78 runs to 17.[49] Rockwell returned to the Cahir Cricket Ground in June 1883 to play the Twentieth Hussars while the regimental band entertained those in attendance. Three days earlier Rockwell played host to a visiting team from Carrick-on-Suir.[50] A team of Rockwell past students returned to the College in 1883 to play the present students.[51] Cricket was to remain a popular sport in Rockwell for many years.

Rugby football was introduced to Tipperary by the military. The 50th (Queen's Own) Regiment, based in Nenagh, took on a local club in December 1875. The Abbey Grammar School in Tipperary had its own rugby team a few years later and by 1882 rugby was well established in the county with teams in Clonmel and Clanwilliam.[52] The first reference to rugby at Rockwell's sister College, Blackrock, was in 1881.[53] Rockwell was to become a noted rugby centre a decade later, but in the meantime it is likely that football of some nature was enjoyed by the students.

Rockwell College was affiliated to the Gaelic Athletic Association on 20th October 1887, just three years after the association was founded in Thurles. For the first few years of its life the new association was much more concerned with athletics than with games. To Michael Cusack, the association's founder, the need for nationalists to control Irish athletics was at this stage more important than the revival of hurling and football.[54] As a promoter of athletics and as a friend of Archbishop Croke, the association's patron, Rockwell's affiliation therefore seemed natural. There was a Holy Ghost connection with Michael Cusack, of course, he having been a teacher at Blackrock College.

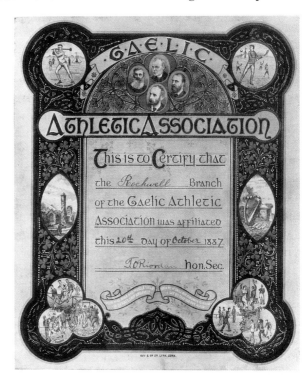

G.A.A. Certificate

PROMINENT STUDENTS

A number of students during the presidency of Fr. Goepfert later became distinguished members of the clergy, of academia and of the public service. John Paul Dowling from Freshford, Co. Kilkenny entered the Dominican Order and was appointed Archbishop of Port of Spain, Trinidad, Thomas Shine from New Inn became the Bishop of Middlesboro. Students who joined the Holy Ghost Congregation included John Stafford from Ballinacroone, Co. Waterford who became the first Superior of Kimmage Manor, Michael J. Downey from Cork who became President of Blackrock College from 1916 to 1925 and James Nolan from Fadden near Birr who spent many years on the missions before returning to Rockwell. Students who joined the secular clergy included William Lockhart who was a priest of the Archdioce of Dublin and John Rogers of the diocese of San Francisco. Students who were priests of the diocese of Waterford and Lismore were Henry Gavin from Burncourt who became parish priest of Ardmore and William P. Burke from Clonmel, the noted historian.

Denis Kennedy became an eminent surgeon while P. J. Lennox was later head of the Department of English in the Catholic University of Washington and E.P. McLoughlin became professor of anatomy at University College Dublin. He was holder of the College record for the high jump which up to 1926 had not been broken. T.P. O'Connor became chief inspector of national schools. James John O'Shee from Carrick-on-Suir entered the legal profession and built up a big practice. In 1895, following the retirement of Alfred Webb, he was elected a Nationalist M.P. for West Waterford. He died in 1946. Daniel Heffernan from Drangan Mór, Cahir became prominent in the Land League and James McCarthy Roche from Castleisland was prominent in the early days of

Professor Lennox

the Rockwell Union. Charles Whitaker became a marine engineer but lost his life in the Great War when his ship was torpedoed by a German submarine.

DEPARTURES

Fr. John T. Murphy had been a leading light in Rockwell since his appointment in 1879 as Dean of Discipline and Dean of Studies. He had steered the College through the early years of the Intermediate with great distinction. His great talents were in demand elsewhere, however, and in 1886 his departure from Rockwell marked the continuation of an even more impressive career in the promotion of the Congregation. His future roles included that of director of the Holy Ghost College in Pittsburgh which paved the way for it to acquire university status as Duquesne University, President of Blackrock College, founder of the first Irish novitiate at Kimmage Manor in 1911 and his appointment as Bishop of the diocese of Port Louis, Mauritius. He died in Port Louis in 1926.[55]

Three years after Fr. Murphy's departure Fr. Goepfert's presidency came to an end. He transferred to the U.S.A. where he took on pastoral work and occasionally wrote to the press in defence of the Catholic Church. He died in Pittsburgh in 1914. During the last years of his presidency Rockwell was in recession. Numbers had dropped in the school and finances were in a precarious state, due it would seem, in part at least, to Fr. Goepfert's lack of taste for administration and his penchant for socialising in the local community.[56] In June 1888 Rockwell was again visited by the Superior General of the Congregation, Fr. Ambrose Emonet, accompanied by Fr. Huvétys, now Provincial Superior. The visitors spent nine days studying matters on the spot and one of their decisions was the temporary closure of the Junior Scholasticate.

The year 1888 could be termed an *annus horribilis* for Rockwell. It was the year of the closure of St. Joseph's, the year of the drowning of a student in the lake and the year when the Intermediate results were disappointing. Rockwell had previously been among the top schools in Ireland but this year it had dropped to twenty fifth place.[57] The following year was not much better with a serious outbreak of scarlet fever. Panic gripped the students and Community as quarantine regulations were enforced. One student from Bansha became so ill that Fr. Fogarty and Br. Aidan travelled by carriage to inform his parents.[58] The Intermediate results of 1889 were also poor and for the first time the results in Rockwell were poorer than those achieved by schools in Clonmel and Tipperary Town.[59] The student population had dropped to fifty.

Rockwell College was in crisis in 1889. Its possible closure was even being discussed.

Notes

1   SFFC p. 234.
2   ISR passim
3   ibid
4   RCA 1977 pp 7-40.
5   See Chronological Floor Plan
6   JNL 16/4/1886.
7   RCA 1977 pp 7-40
8   JNL 9/4/1886.
9   RCA 1964 p. 20.
10 M. Tierney, *Croke of Cashel: The Life of Archbishop Thomas William Crok, 1823-1902*, p. 78.
11 ibid p. 83.
12 *Tipperary Free Press* 14/6/1881.
13 ISR p. 77.
14 ISR pp 259-260.
15 J. Coolahan, *Irish Education: History and Structure*, p. 52.
16 ibid pp 62 ff.
17 ibid.
18 F.S.L. Lyons, *Ireland Since the Famine*, pp 92, 93.

19   *Tipperary Free Press*27/8/1880.

20   *Cashel Gazette* 27/9/1884.

21   *Freeman's Journal* 18/12/1884.

22   ISR p. 104.

23   *Tipperary Free Press* 27/8/1880.

24   ibid.

25   Register of Junior Scholasticate

26   JNL 31/8/1887.

27   ibid.

28   J. Lee, *The Modernisation of Irish Society 1848-1918*, pp 65 ff.

29   *Clonmel Chronicle* 15/4/1882.

30   D.G. Boyce, *Nineteenth Century Ireland: The Search for Stability*, p. 271.

31   JNL 26/7/1888

32   RCA 1964, p. 22.

33   SFFC pp 270, 297, 349.

34   ibid p. 291-2.

35   RCA 1964 p. 23.

36   T.W. Moody, *Davitt and Irish Revolution 1846-82*, pp 338, 513.

37   RCA 1964 p. 23.

38   JNL 31/8/1887.

39   M. Tierney, *op. cit.*, pp 216 ff.

40   ISR p. 104.

41   *Clonmel Chronicle* 1/4/1882.

42   M. de Búrca, *The GAA: A History* p. 20.

43   *Clonmel Chronicle 15/4/1882*.

44   *Cashel Gazette* 31/3/1883, 19/5/1883.

45   *Cashel Gazette* 30/5/1885.

46   JNL 15/5/1886.

47   JNL 25/5/1888.

48   P. Bracken, *Foreign and Fantastic Field Sports: Cricket in County Tipperary*, pp 49,50.

49   *Clonmel Chronicle*, 20/5/1882, 31/5/1882.

50   *Clonmel Chronicle*, 13/6/1883.

51   *Cashel Gazette*, 19/5/1883.

52   P. Bracken, op. cit. pp 50,72, 89.

53   SFFC pp 117-8, 279.

54   M. de Búrca, op. cit. p. 23.

55   ISR pp 103-5.

56   ISR pp 259, 260.

57   JNL 31/9/1888.

58   JNL 19/11/1889, 20/11/1899, 23/11/1899, 11/12/1899.

59   *Nationalist* 11/9/1889.

– 4 –

AN EMINENT ASSEMBLY
1890-1905

Few Irish schools can claim to have had so many persons of distinction within their walls as Rockwell College had in the years between 1890 and 1905. These were the years in Rockwell of Joseph Shanahan, Edward Crehan, David Browne, Pádraig de Brún Thomas MacDonagh, Eamon de Valera and Pádraig Ó Conaire. These were the years when Rockwell quickly recovered from its temporary depression and rose to new heights in the chronicle of post-primary Irish education.

The depression which Rockwell had reached by 1889 was quickly reversed due for the most part to the ability of Fr. Amet Limbour and Dr. Edward Crehan. The reverse was notable in the increase in student numbers, the improvement in Intermediate examination results, in developments of the College infrastructure and in the extension and improved production on the farm.

Fr. Limbour from Port-Aven, Brittany, succeeded Fr. Goepfert as President. He had served in Réunion and St. Louis before taking charge of the newly founded apostolic school at Beauvais. He was a man of dynamic character. He set about reviving the fortunes of Rockwell at all levels. Much of what he saw in the Irish way of life displeased him as a waste of money and lacking in style. Even the style of life lived by the Community met with his disapproval. He viewed it as a deviation from the French Spiritan standards with too much socialising and going to political meetings and too much time wasted organising sport and games.[1] His management skills, however, were a great help to Rockwell's recovery but his time in Ireland was short and in 1893 he was called on to supervise an ambitious project in Haiti. He later served in Canada and Senegal where he died in 1916.[2]

Edward Crehan was born in Clonmel, Co. Tipperary, in 1862, the son of John Crehan and Margaret Dwyer. He went to Blackrock College as a junior scholastic and obtained his Senior Grade in 1879, winning an exhibition. He was an excellent sportsman, excelling in gymnastics in particular, but a footballer too,

Fr. Amet Limbour
President 1889-1893

43

Dr. Edward Crehan
Dean of Studies 1890-1900

winning his place on an Irish Youths XV. He was a prefect in the Castle, Blackrock from 1880 to1884, while continuing his studies. He graduated in 1884 from the Royal University and went to France to pursue his philosophical studies. The following year he was transferred to Rome where he obtained his Ph.D. and D.D., winning the gold medal for Scripture. He was ordained in 1889 and following his novitiate year, was professed as a Holy Ghost Father in 1890 and sent to Rockwell as Dean of Studies. From 1898 he combined the posts of Dean of Studies and Discipline, while at the same time teaching full-time classes in Mathematics and Italian. He was short in stature but strongly built and had a most dynamic personality.[3]

A student and teacher at Rockwell from 1897 to 1907, D.J. O'Connor, described Dr. Crehan as "the source of energy that moved mountains, who inspired students to cultural greatness in the class-room and physical greatness in the fields of sport. He was the greatest man I ever knew, and with all his greatness, he was at heart a very humble priest. He was an inspiring orator who roused his students to carry the flag of the class-room and the ball-field to leadership in Ireland." Mr. O'Connor, who later became principal of a private school in Pittsbourgh continued "When Dr. Crehan took over the double deanship in 1898 Rockwell was a strictly Tipperary college dominated by a large number of local students. By 1900 Rockwell was a national institution with students from all over Ireland.[4]

FOUR PRESIDENTS

Rockwell had four Presidents between 1890 and 1905. Fr. Limbour was succeeded in 1892 by Fr. James Cotter, a native of Bruree, Co. Limerick. He came to Rockwell in 1867 and was the second student to enter St. Joseph's. Following his ordination in 1874 he was appointed to Rockwell where he was to serve for the rest of his life. He reluctantly accepted the position of President and at the end of his first year in office he asked to be relieved of his post because of his inability to cope.[5] He was succeeded by another reluctant candidate in Fr. John Stephens.

Fr. Stephens was a native of Gurtapuntane, Co. Mayo where he was born in 1839. Following his ordination in 1871 he sought permission to serve as a curate in his native diocese of Tuam. He was a close friend of Archbishop John McHale and was an ardent supporter of the Land League. A spectacular achievement of his was the construction in 1882 of

Fr. James Cotter
President 1893-1894

the first oratory erected in modern times on the top of Croagh Patrick. On rejoining the Congregation he served as Bursar in St. Mary's before his appointment to Rockwell as Director of St. Joseph's. He agreed to succeed Fr. Cotter as President on condition that it was only for one year. He was then called on to serve as Bursar under Fr. Nicholas Brennan.[6]

Fr. John Stephens
President 1894-1895

Fr. Brennan was born in Sart, Co. Kilkenny in 1854. He studied at Blackrock College and is reputed to have been the best Latin scholar the school ever produced. He won several scholarships at the Catholic University examinations. In later life he had a great reputation for his knowledge of classical authors and for his talent at Latin composition, particularly in hexameters.[7] He taught Latin and Greek and one of his pupils, Pádraig de Brún, later considered him one of the greatest classical scholars in Europe. His custom of giving a Latin translation for even the most mundane events of the day were legendary and he even reported the complicated moves of a rugby match in lines of Virgilian style. Here is the first stanza of his exquisite Latin rendering in hexameter verse of the spirited Irish ballad "O'Donnell Abu"[8]

Pro Patria Mori
Consonat omne solum litui clangori superbo
Martis atrox caelo tollit se turbine clamor;
Carpit iter sonipes agilis Vadimonis ad undam,
Tibris ut in viridi jungat se valle catervis.
De patriis montana jugis rue cuncta juventus
Nescia corda fugae, nullo torrenda periclo!
Signa sub intrepidi properent ducis agmina Turni!
Militibus variis densae prodite phalanges
Omnibus effusae saltus montisque latebris,
Pro patria veteri sanctum pugnate duellum!

O'Donnell Abú
Proudly the note of the trumpet is sounding
Loudly the war-cries arise on the gale;
Fleetly the steed by Lough Swilly is bounding
To join the thick squadron in Saimer's green vale.
On every mountaineer
Strangers to flight and fear!
Rush to the standard of dauntless Red Hugh!
Bonnaught and Gallowglass
Throng from each mountain pass,
On for old Erin, O'Donnell Abú.

Fr. Brennan was one of the most vociferous local personalities in a campaign championing the building of a railway line from Goold's Cross to Cashel. Such a line would have shortened the journey to and from Rockwell for students. The campaign was successful and Dean Kinane ceremoniously dug the first sod at Goold's Cross on 4th March 1903. The line was complete and Fr. Brennan was a passenger on the first train which arrived in Cashel on 12th October 1904. The line remained open for the next fifty years and was used regularly by Rockwell students.[9]

Fr. Nicholas Brennan
President 1895-1905

A REMARKABLE RECOVERY

Rockwell emerged from the crisis it had reached in 1899 with remarkable speed. The first mark of recovery was the re-opening of the scholasticate on 18th October 1890. The Community rejoiced with a Mass of thanksgiving and a meal to celebrate. Fr Demaison had been sent by the Mother House as the new Director of this important part of the College. The first four students who went to reside there were William Evans from Kilmallock, Thomas Coman from Clonoulty, Dan Maher from Dundrum and Pat Meade from Dungarvan.[10]

There was a steady increase in the student population of the secondary school and a vast improvement in examination results. The system of education that persisted under the Intermediate Board was so competitive that schools had to perform well in examinations if they were to survive. Cash prizes were awarded to schools by the Government based on examination results. The Grand Prizes, or Exhibitions, were worth £25 to £30; other results, called Distinctions, were worth £1. 10s. to £2. Rockwell gained eight Exhibitions and fifteen Distinctions in 1892 with similar gains in 1893 and there was a notable increase in student numbers in those years, with a large number coming from Clonmel.[11]

By 1894 the President, Fr. Stephens, was unable to accept all the applications for student places. The student population for the first time ever had reached one hundred and eighty. Of these, one hundred and thirty were boarders, thirty were scholastics and twenty were day students.[12] The examination results improved each year and when twenty four exhibitions were obtained in 1896 the *Freeman's Journal* reported that this was the second highest for any Irish school. From 1895 to 1899 Rockwell remained among the top schools in Ireland obtaining one hundred and nine exhibitions and four gold medals.[13] These medals were awarded to a student who obtained the highest mark in Ireland in a particular subject. What was regarded as the most spectacular individual result was achieved in 1904 when the young Patrick Browne (Pádraig de Brún) from Grangemockler gained first place in Ireland in Mathematics while still two years underage.[14]

Rockwell introduced a scholarship system in 1900. Eighteen scholarships to the value of £15 each were awarded to students following a competitive examination in the College. This was an attractive offer at a time when the full annual boarding fee was £30. It was introduced when Fr. John Byrne succeeded Dr. Edward Crehan as Dean of Studies. The scheme continued for the following number of years.

Rockwell could not afford any modesty about its academic success. Its very future depended on good examination results because of the competitive nature of the education system at the time. Like all second level schools it published its examination results each year. It also published advertisements portraying the wonderful facilities that the College offered, its vast playing areas, its cycle track and its location in an area of great beauty. It was regularly featured in the *Freeman's Journal* at the time of publication of examination results and in 1902 it received very favourable treatment in an article in the *Evening Herald*.

THE COLLEGE CHAPEL

The Community was considering building a little chapel as an annex to the Sacred Heart chapel and in May 1890 Br. Silas and his team were about to start work on it when there was a change of plan.[15] The Mother House in Paris had been pressing for the erection of a new separate chapel, sacristy and annex since 1892 and it was during the presidency of Fr. Amet Limbour that it was decided to proceed with this project following an interview with Mr. Patrick Ryan, the principal benefactor. He had taken a room in the Lake House and had promised to cover a great part of the cost. Brother Aidan Ryan was sent off to America to collect for the remainder.[16]

An architect, George Ashlin, was employed. He presented his plan in February 1895 in the presidency for Fr. John Stephens.[17] George Ashlin (1837-1921), was one of Ireland's most distinguished architects. He trained with the great English architect, Welby Pugin (1812-1852) who with Charles Barry designed the Houses of Parliament in London and who did much for the revival of Gothic architecture. Pugin, who was associated with Cardinal Newman and the Oxford Movement, designed a number of churches in Ireland including the chapel of St. Patrick's College, Maynooth, Cobh Cathedral, St. Aidan's Cathedral Enniscorthy and St. Mary's Cathedral, Killarney. Ashlin worked with Pugin on these Irish designs and married Pugin's sister. Following Pugin's death, Ashlin designed a number of churches and other buildings in Ireland including the McCabe Memorial (1887) in Glasnevin Cemetery.[18]

Building on the College Chapel commenced during the presidency of Fr. Nicholas Brennan in February 1896.[19] The work was done by direct labour

The College Chapel

Interior of College Chapel

under the supervision of the Fathers and Brothers. The first barrow of concrete was thrown into the foundation in March and the foundation stone was laid in April.[20] The foundation stone was blessed by Archbishop Croke in June at a ceremony attended by the clergy and notable people of the district. In his address on this occasion the archbishop made a strong appeal for funds for this worthy project. He initiated the fundraising by contributing a handsome cheque. At the conclusion of the ceremony Dr. Croke was presented with a silver trowel suitably inscribed. It was richly carved, had an ornamental handle and was enclosed in a silk-lined Moroccan case. The cost of building the Chapel was estimated at £4,000.[21] Stain glass windows were installed in August 1897 and work on the Chapel was completed in early 1898 when heating was installed. The previous chapel in the Silas building was converted into a dormitory. In July 1898 the high altar in the Chapel was donated by the Ryan/O'Connor family and in March 1900 the Chapel was dedicated to St. Patrick by Monsignor Allgeyer who was visiting Ireland and deputising for the ailing Archbishop Croke.[22] He was from Alsace and had been educated at Blackrock College and when he was ordained bishop in 1897 he was the first former student of a Holy Ghost Irish college to be raised to the episcopate.

The College Chapel is one hundred and ten feet long, thirty two feet wide and fifty feet in height and can accommodate four hundred people. The façade in rusticated cut-stone with its elegant belfry gives a joyous appearance. The interior is plain with excellent acoustics. The absence of aisles and pillars gives an uninterrupted view of the high-altar from all parts of the interior. The arrangement of the roof trusses gives the impression of true Romanesque barrel vaulting from either end of the building. This impression is intensified from the eastern end by the Romanesque architrave over the high altar. The roof trusses and panelling are of pitch-pine and the craftsmanship in them is very fine.[23]

The stain glass windows were installed in August 1897. Above the door on both sides are two windows representing in various colours Our Saviour giving the keys to St. Peter, and sending out the Apostles to preach. Above this is a rose window, representing the Patron Saint of Ireland. Over the main altar are three large windows in various colours, where one can view the scene of Calvary. The side chapels are lit by two rose windows, representing the Sacred Heart and the Holy Virgin. The sacristy is in perfect harmony with the architecture of the whole edifice.

The organ in the College Chapel was built by the English firm of William Hill. It was purchased for Rockwell following discussions between the Provincial, Fr. Jules Botrel, himself a noted musician, and the President Fr. Nicholas Brennan. It was regarded at the time as an excellent instrument with seventeen stops, two keyboards and separate pedals. Before the introduction of an electric blower, it was hand-pumped. It was valued at £400 but was purchased by Rockwell for £180. It is not clear why there was such a reduction in price but it seems possible it was built originally for another customer who was anxious to sell it. Fr. Muller was to exploit the sonorous potential of this instrument for the next thirty years.[24]

The College Chapel and New Wing

A NEW WING

The building of the College Chapel was only at the early stages when the plans for a new building block were presented by the architect, George Ashlin, to the newly appointed President, Fr. Nicholas Brennan.[25] An alternative plan supplied by the Mother House was turned down.[26] On this occasion it was decided to employ a contractor and in March 1901 the tender of Mr. Holloway of Cahir at a cost of £4,000 was accepted.[27] Work commenced immediately.[28] The ground floor contained the corridor joining the Silas Building with the Chapel and for years what was known as the Big Study. The middle floor contained the Fathers' rooms and the top floor became the Sacred Heart Dormitory.(See Chronological Floor Plan) Central heating was installed in the ground and top floors, serviced from the Chapel furnace and a new furnace erected beyond the western end of the Silas Building. Fireplaces were installed in the Fathers' rooms.[29] This new wing became known as the Study Block.

A new kitchen was built at this time and a room was set aside for a Fathers' refectory to permit reading at meals. Classrooms, known as the New Tipperary classrooms were also built. They were only temporary structures but remained in place until 1939. They probably received their title from the temporary structure built outside the town of Tipperary during the Plan of Campaign and known as New Tipperary. From the students' point of view, however, probably the greatest novelty of the time was the building of a splendid *vélodrome* around the Big Field which provided an outlet for enthusiastic cyclists for a number of years, and the banking of which was still visible up to the 1960s.[30]

A further measure of the confidence which prevailed in Rockwell in these years was the extension of the farm. In December 1892 Frs Limbour and Cotter went to Fethard to request the Grand Jury, which was in session, to grant Rockwell a right of way running beside the College property and adjoining the

Dr. Crehan with group of students

property of Mr. Rice. It facilitated communication for Rockwell with New Inn, being roughly 300 perches. The request was granted.[31] On 26th June 1897 Fr. Brennan purchased the interest in Tom Ryan's farm in Carrigeen, consisting of approximately fifty acres for £90. In May 1900 Fr. Brennan purchased the interest in Lonergan's farm, also in Carrigeen and consisting of about one hundred and sixty acres, for £700.[32]

THE COMMUNITY

A notable feature of the Rockwell Community between 1890 and 1905 was the continuing high degree of interchanging of Fathers within the growing new missionary projects of the Congregation including the opening of St. Mary's College, Rathmines in 1890. The result was that many spent only a short while in Rockwell before moving to another missionary centre. Also notable was the dominance of Irish Fathers in the Community.

Thirty one Fathers served in Rockwell in these years. (Appendix II). Ten of them were either French or German but only two of these, both German, Frs Christian Schmidt and John Muller, remained in Rockwell for a long term. Fr. Schmidt spent most of his life in Rockwell having first come to St. Joseph's as a young aspirant because of Bismarck's Kulturkampf. He served as a prefect and following his senior studies and ordination in France, he returned to Rockwell in 1892 where he remained for the rest of his life. He taught German, French and Latin and took a keen interest in sport, especially in cricket and handball and was one of Rockwell's most colourful characters for many years.[33] Fr. Muller also came as an aspirant to St. Joseph's and later served as a prefect. He did his senior studies in France and was ordained in 1888. He returned to Rockwell in 1898 as teacher of German and Music where he remained until 1930. He was a very talented musician and his presence marked a new era for music in Rockwell.[34]

Of the twenty one Irish Fathers, ten of them, including Fr. Joseph Shanahan, spent less than five years in Rockwell. Of the eleven others, five served as Presidents and two as Deans of Study. Fr. Michael Colgan had been a student in Rockwell from 1882 to 1888 and following his ordination in 1896 he was assigned to Rockwell. He was a brother of Br. Dalmas who also served in Rockwell.[35] Fr. Michael Walsh spent two terms in Rockwell teaching classics.[36] Fr. Daniel Egan was Director of St. Joseph's from 1904 to 1907 and later a popular member of the teaching staff while Fr. John McGrath was a teacher of Irish and French for many years.[37] Fr. Bernard Carey from Rathkeale, Co. Limerick was on the teaching staff from 1903 to 1906.

Br. Kieran Egan from Ferbane continued in charge of the Rockwell farm in these years with the assistance of Br. Nicholas Quinlan from Athassel and Br. Raoul Condon from Ballylooby. Br. David Doran from Aherlow was cook from 1877 until 1893 when he set out for Nigeria and became the first Irish member of the Congregation to serve there. He was later joined by two more Rockwell men, Fr. Joseph Shanahan and Fr. Patrick McDermott. Br. Elimien Gaschy from the diocese of Strasbourg became chef in Rockwell in 1898 and in 1933 he moved to Kilshane where he remained for the rest of his life. Br. Dalmas Colgan from Co. Kildare was in charge of the bakery; and looking after the refectory were Br. Brendan Coffey from Clonmel and Br. Albert Cody from Dublin, both of whom spent a number of years in the Gambia. Brother Aidan Ryan from Killenaule continued to look after the infirmary as did Br. Edgar Stafford from Ballymore, Co. Wexford until he was transferred to Kimmage. In charge of dormitories were Br. Mary Ignatius O'Dea from nearby Ballydoyle and Br. Gregory Power from Cappoquin and the linen room was looked after by Br. Patrick McCarthy from Co. Kerry.

Br. Hippolyte Matasse continued in charge of the College shop while Br. Agricola Kennedy from Co. Clare was in charge of the book shop. Br. Virgilius Ryan from nearby Annacarty was librarian and Br. Silas Laffan continued to attend to all building and maintenance matters while Br. Nicephorus Barrett continued as tailor. Br. Adelm Walsh, from Silvermines, Co. Tipperary, was an uncle of Joseph Shanahan and had spent most of his religious life in France. After three years in Sierra Leone he was posted to Rockwell in 1896 where he taught French until 1909 when he replaced Br. David Doran in Nigeria.

Br. Adelm Walsh

Br. John Baptist Hourigan from Lattin, Co. Tipperary, also spent most of his life in France and in 1903 his last appointment was to Rockwell where he acted as sacristan.

JOSEPH SHANAHAN AND ROCKWELL

Born 6th June 1871 in Glankeen, Borrisoleigh, Co. Tipperary, Joseph Shanahan had spent eleven years in France before coming to Rockwell. When finished in the primary school, he went in 1886 to the Apostolic School in Beauvais, France, where his uncle, Br. Adelm Walsh, was a member of the Holy Ghost Community conducting that school. When that school closed in 1889 Joseph was transferred to the French juniorate in Cellule, where he completed his secondary studies and did part of the university course. In 1894 he went to the senior scholasticate in Langonnet to do Philosophy. The following year he transferred to Chevilly with all the senior students and started Theology. In Christmas 1895 he was appointed as a

Bishop Joseph Shanahan

prefect for a short time at a college conducted by the Congregation at Merville in the north of France. In August 1897, after eleven years away from Ireland, he was unexpectedly appointed as a prefect in Rockwell. He made his profession on Easter Sunday 1898, the first such ceremony to be held in the new College Chapel.[38]

Joseph Shanahan was one of ten prefects in Rockwell in 1897. One of his fellow prefects, Thomas Mac Donagh, may well have been a close friend seeing that they were both from more or less the same part of Tipperary and students later recalled that they were the prefects in charge of the large study. As part of his duties as prefect Joseph Shanahan taught French, Latin, Greek and Mathematics. One of his students in the French class was the young James Mellett on his first year in Rockwell. Mellett recorded that Shanahan spoke French perfectly, he "had the gracious manners of an aristocrat and discoursed so freely and feelingly of French Catholicism and of France that we felt sure he was a Frenchman."[39]

Surprisingly the most vivid recollections people retained of Shanahan at this period were not of his classroom performances but his athletic appearance and prowess on the rugby field. This was one aspect of his formation which he did not owe to his French training which regarded such physical field games as unsuited for students destined for the priesthood. This view was strongly held by the President of Rockwell Fr. Amet Limbour. But following Fr. Limbour's departure, Dr. Crehan took over as Dean of Discipline and he was strongly in favour of prefects playing with the College team. Dr. Crehan had himself been a fine rugby player during his days in Blackrock and had been considered worthy of a place in a representative Irish side in matches against an English youths' team. It was at this time too that the Ryan brothers from the neighbouring farm became involved, relishing the distraction from farming.[40]

It was arranged through contacts in St. Mary's College that the Ryan brothers could play occasionally for the Dublin club, Bective Rangers, and so catch the selectors' eye for a place on the Irish team. Rockwell basked in the publicity given to the performances of Jack and Mike Ryan on the Triple Crown winning Irish side between 1897 and 1904. Rockwell beat the leading clubs in Limerick, Cork and Dublin and Joseph Shanahan played a major part alongside the Ryans in those victories. He won for himself a reputation that still lives in the annals of Munster rugby as one of the finest players in the southern province for strength, unremitting drive and splendid sportsmanship.[41]

When a senior scholasticate was launched at the Lake House in 1898, Joseph Shanahan was among the eleven students selected to do Theology there. Some of them were also drafted in as part-time prefects in the College, among them Joseph Shanahan. During his two years study at the Lake House, Joseph Shanahan's directors were Fr. Paul Meistermann who lectured in Dogma, Canon Law and Church History and Fr. Jean Michel Desnier who taught Moral Theology, Sacred Scripture and Liturgy. Fr. Meistermann, a native of Alsace, was previously known to Joseph Shanahan. He had taught at Cellule while Joseph Shanahan was on his final year there and Fr. Desnier, born in Riom, Puy de Dome, France, had been posted to Blackrock the year before his Rockwell appointment.

The senior scholasticate at the Lake House only lasted for the two years of Joseph's Shanahan studies there. Fr. Meistermann was very critical of the situation at St. Joseph's. He felt that it suffered especially from its proximity to the College which continually impinged on the quiet routine of the scholasticate where past and current prefects among the scholastics were in continual contact with the College staff and events. Despite the distractions, two of the students, John McGrath and Alphonsus Murphy, who had already missed out for health reasons, were ordained on 20th November 1898 by Archbishop Croke in his private oratory in Thurles. St. Joseph's resumed as a juniorate in 1891.

Joseph Shanahan was ordained to the priesthood at Blackrock College on 22nd April 1900. The music on that occasion was conducted by Fr. John Kearney with the assistance of the recently ordained Fr. Alphonsus Murphy and in the congregation was the young Eamon de Valera, then a student at Blackrock College. Following his ordination Joseph Shanahan returned to Rockwell where until 1902 he served as Dean of Discipline.

As Dean of Discipline Fr. Shanahan had responsibility for the welfare of two hundred and fifteen students in all matters outside classroom hours. This covered not merely the care and supervision of dormitories, dining room and recreation areas inside the house, but also games, recreation and sorties outside the College grounds. He had of course the help of the Brothers and prefects but the ultimate responsibility rested with him. The Dean of Studies, Fr. Johnny Byrne, worked closely with him. Apart from his duties as Dean of Discipline, Fr. Shanahan also had a pretty full day's class. His influence on his students was immense, as was recalled by many. Fr. Edward Leen, a student in those days, who thought that Fr. Shanahan felt cramped by the narrow horizons of school life. He laboured to enkindle in the souls of the students something of the lofty idealism and deep religious spirit which he had brought with him from France, according to Fr. Leen.

Many stories are told about Fr. Shanahan as Dean of Discipline but a particular one seems to have lingered in Rockwell longer than others. It concerns a rugby match between Rockwell and Dolphin to be played at the Mardyke in Cork on St. Patrick's Day 1902. Fr. Shanahan set out with the Rockwell team on a horse-drawn carriage on the fourteen mile journey to Limerick Junction to catch the train to Cork. When they arrived at the station, however, they discovered to their dismay that the train for Cork had left. With no further trains scheduled for that day and no other means of transport available the situation seemed desperate. An important match had to be played for which there was great anticipation, with a large crowd expected at the Mardyke. The station master was consulted and he said the only possibility open was to charter a special train from Dublin. This would be enormously expensive of course. With characteristic generosity of spirit Fr. Shanahan said that honour was at stake in fulfilling an important engagement and expense could not be allowed to weigh against that. The decision was taken. The wires were sent to Dublin and Cork and the line was cleared. The train from Dublin reached the Junction in record time and the Rockwell team took to the field at the Mardyke amidst roars of applause, for news of this splendid sportsmanship had reached the ground. Rockwell won the match and Fr. Shanahan's deeds became legendary.[42]

Fr. Shanahan's appointment to Nigeria followed soon after but there is no evidence that the two incidents were related. The unremitting drive, the idealism and generosity of spirit which he displayed in Rockwell were to feature in his amazing missionary career. In Nigeria, having helped Fr. Léon Lejeune build the first mission house, he opened the first permanent mission in the interior of the country at Ozubula and the first Teacher Training centre and a network of schools. The Southern Nigeria mission was given the status of a Vicariate in 1920 and he was ordained bishop at Maynooth College. He founded the Missionary Sisters of the Holy Rosary and was an inspiration for missionaries who followed, many of them from Rockwell College. He died and was buried in Nairobi in 1943 but in 1956 his remains were transferred for burial in Onitsha Cathedral in Nigeria. Always revered as a saint by those in close contact with him his cause for Beatification was introduced officially in 1997.[43]

THOMAS MACDONAGH AND ROCKWELL

A man who spent nine years of his young life in Rockwell and who is remembered with enduring affection in his *alma mater* is Thomas Mac Donagh, the 1916 leader and patriot.

Thomas MacDonagh was born on 1st February 1878 in Cloughjordan, Co. Tipperary where his parents, Joseph and Mary, were teachers. He was baptised in Grawn church, then the parish church about a mile from the town. His elder sister, Mary, became a nun, entering the Sisters of Charity, taking the name sister Francesca, and spending her life helping the poor and ill of Dublin. He had three younger brothers, John, who became an actor and after the foundation of Radio Éireann in 1926 frequently contributed to plays and poetry readings, James, who became principal oboist with the London Symphony Orchestra and Joseph, who was elected to Dáil Éireann in 1918.[44]

Thomas MacDonagh

Thomas entered the juniorate in Rockwell with the intention of studying for the priesthood on 29th August 1892 when Fr. Louis Leiniger was Director. He sat for the junior grade examination of the Intermediate Board in 1893 and the middle grade the following year. The subjects he took, with average results, were Latin, French, English, Arithmetic, Euclid, Algebra and Drawing.[45] After two years in St. Joseph's he applied to enter the Holy Ghost Congregation.

He was appointed a prefect in the College in 1896 and as such he was a member of the teaching staff. Among the subjects he taught was Mathematics and among his students in October 1898 was the young James Mellett who said of him "He was a fine Maths professor and a kindly one. But at heart he was a visionary and poet and he gave his life for Ireland in 1916.[46] Another student, J.P. Brennan, remembered Thomas MacDonagh , then senior prefect of studies "of low stature, refined disposition, with eyes glittering like diamonds reflecting the spiritual enthusiasm that illuminated his soul, this young man who was to die for his country's freedom in 1916, contributed to generations of Rockwellians an example of patriotism which inevitably must lead to the liberation of the land he loved."[47]

Among the friends Thomas MacDonagh made in Rockwell was Michael Smithwick from nearby Carron, later a Commissioner of Income Tax. Both worked together in helping Pádraig Pearse in founding St. Enda's School, of which he was made a director and where he served as a teacher in the early years. His years of preparing students for the Intermediate Board examinations in Rockwell would have made him aware of the highly competitive nature of the system which Pearse referred to as "the murder machine".

He continued in Rockwell until 1901 when eventually he abandoned the idea of becoming a priest. His years in Rockwell were years of study, poetry, music and teaching and he left the peace and security of the College with regret:

I found that when my childhood's
Home I left
And grew to love thee fondly through the years
Of blissful quiet in the half-lost past.[48]

One of his books of poetry was written while a prefect in Rockwell. His second book of poems *April and May* was dedicated to Dr. Crehan and the autographed copy bears the inscription "To my best friend Very Reverend Dr. Crehan C.S.Sp from Thomas MacDonagh.[49]

There was a dark irony to the surrender of Thomas MacDonagh in 1916 in that there was a distant Rockwell connection. Arthur Dickens, a student in Rockwell from 1912 to 1915, revealed in later life that Thomas MacDonagh had surrendered to his father. While Arthur was in Rockwell his father was a British Army officer based in Cahir and was in command of the Artillery in Dublin during the Easter Rising.[50]

THE LAY TEACHERS

There were a few instances of very bright students later returning to Rockwell for a time as teachers such as Thomas J. Morrissey from Clonmel and Michael Smithwick. Morrissey had been a student from 1890 to 1892. He returned to Rockwell as a teacher in 1897 having graduated from the Royal University at an early age and remained for a few years until his appointment as assistant keeper in the Public Records Office. He later became secretary of the Department of Education. Michael Smithwick had been one of the most successful students of the decade in Rockwell. He was a pillar of cricket and rugby and as has been seen he was a close friend of Thomas MacDonagh at Rockwell and later at Scoil Éanna. After several years teaching at Rockwell, while studying for his BA under the Royal University system, he transferred to Blackrock College where he continued his studies. Another past student who taught for a few years was D.J. O'Connor from Castleisland.

Joseph Shanahan's brother, Daniel, was appointed to the lay staff in 1897. Thomas Griffin from Cashel had been a part-time teacher of music for many

Some members of teaching staff 1898
Seated:
Frs: Nicholas Brennan,
Edward Crehan,
Patrick Dooley
Standing:
Michael Smithwick,
Thomas Morrissey,
Thomas MacDonagh

years. Michael Ryan, a native of Solohead, Co. Tipperary was also on the teaching staff. He was a former student of Blackrock College and in later years he was a lecturer at St. Patrick's Teacher Training College, Drumcondra, Dublin.

The most widely known of all Rockwell lay teachers was of course Eamon de Valera.

EAMON DE VALERA AND ROCKWELL

Having been educated by the Holy Ghost Fathers at Blackrock College, Eamon de Valera's appointment as a teacher at Rockwell College in 1903 was an occasion for him to meet up with some of his former acquaintances from Blackrock and to forge new friendships, some of which remained life-long. The fact that he boarded in Rockwell meant that very soon he was part and parcel of the life of what was a very closed community.[51]

Lay teachers and prefects 1903:
Back: Tom O'Donnell, James Cremer,
Eamon de Valera, Daniel Leen.
Front: Thady O'Connor, Timothy Cunningham.

There were three other laymen on the teaching staff of Rockwell in 1903, Jack Barrett, Tom O'Donnell and James Cremer. Tom O'Donnell is on record as being the first adult who addressed the future Chief as "Dev". O'Donnell was later a T.D. for Sligo and a life-long friend of Dev, even though he had voted in favour of the 1921 Anglo-Irish Treaty. The lay professors dined with the prefects, many of whom Dev would have known from Blackrock as they were about the same age. He became friendly with the Dean of Studies, Fr "Johnny" Byrne with whom he shared a life-long interest in the Irish language.

A photograph of Dev in the College orchestra in 1904 has raised some eyebrows because even his closest friends were unaware of his musical talents. Dev himself had a special regard for that picture and had it displayed in his private study. The orchestra was conducted by the German priest Fr. Muller and he trained Dev in the use of one of the percussion instruments for which Dev did not need the guidance of any musical notation. All he needed was a simple mathematical formula to guide him.

In Rockwell Dev taught Mathematics and Physics and among his students were Henry Gogarty, later bishop in East Africa, Paddy Browne, later president of University College, Galway, Michael O'Malley, later professor of surgery at University College, Galway, Henry Barniville, later professor of surgery at

University College, Dublin, Michael Hillery, father of future President of Ireland, Fionán Lynch, future government minister and the Leen brothers from Abbeyfeale. Among his students too was James Mellett, then the captain of the senior Rugby team. He remembered Dev's arrival from Blackrock. "He scintillated with academic distinctions; exhibitions in the "Grades" and a scholarship in Mathematics from the Royal University. That was all very well, but where did he stand in football? Would he be an addition to the team? The first day he togged out we appraised him critically.[52]

In his book *If Any Man Dares* Mellett describes Dev as a useful rugby player who was noted for the lengthy clearances he made when playing at full back and that he was very unlucky in a Munster trial when instead of scoring a spectacular try, his opposite number left him flat-footed and scored in the opposite direction, cheating Dev out of his chance of a final trial. On one occasion when Rockwell played Clonmel in Magner's Field the reporter from The *Nationalist* who covered the match listed fourteen Rockwell players "and another player", thus highlighting the difficulty people had in those early days with Dev's unusual surname.

The Ryan brothers, Jack and Mike, were at that time the pillars of the Rockwell team. Little did Dev imagine in 1899, as he watched them in wonder at Lansdowne Road in the Triple Crown match, that he would one day, not only be on the same team with the Ryans, but that he would become a close friend of the Ryan family. He became a regular visitor to the Ryan homestead where he enjoyed with the brothers the country pursuits of shooting, fishing

The College orchestra in 1904:
Back: Eamon de Valera at centre. Fr. John Muller in second row centre.

and card-playing. Dev's friendship with Mike Ryan did not wane over the years and significantly in 1916 as he awaited execution, Dev wrote one of his farewell letters to Mike.

While in Rockwell, Dev had other interests apart from rugby. The lay professors were regular visitors to Stewart's Hotel in Cashel where Mary Stewart, daughter of the proprietor, had taken a special fancy for Dev and it was felt there was a real romance in the making. It was said that Dev had taught her a simple cipher whereby they communicated with each other by card.

It is no wonder that Dev, looking back over his varied and troubled career, could so often refer to those Rockwell days as among the most carefree and personally satisfying in his life. The problem was that it was a distraction from the further study which he hoped to pursue to obtain an honours degree. And it was for this reason that at the end of the school year of 1904 Dev headed back to Blackrock College where he was to spend the next fourteen weeks in intensive study. For the remainder of his life, however, he remained in contact with Rockwell.

De Valera used the Rockwell connection to his advantage in 1922 when he attended a meeting of the Irish Race Congress in Paris. He was one of the eight delegates from Ireland and he decided to travel from London to Paris in the guise of Fr. Patrick Walsh with whom he had been friendly in Rockwell. He devoted proper care to his new identity, and jotted down vital pieces of information regarding Fr. Walsh in his diary. In a studio near Charing Cross he was photographed in clerical garb. The picture was attached to a passport which was forged or, at least, had been tampered with.[53]

THE STUDENTS

The student population in Rockwell between 1890 and 1905 was remarkable for the number who later played significant roles in the Church and State. Among those students was a future cardinal, six future bishops and a number of missionaries, academics and public servants.

Joseph Byrne from Clonmel, was a future Provincial of the Congregation and Bishop of Kilimanjaro and brother of John, a future President of Rockwell. John Heffernan from Brosna, Co. Kerry became Bishop of Zanzibar, and Henry Gogarty, originally from Cavan town and later from Cahir, Co. Tipperary, became Bishop of Kilimanjaro. Michael McGrath, who was a student from 1896 to 1900 became Bishop of Menevia and Bartholomew Wilson from Cobh, Co. Cork became Bishop of Bagomoyo.[54] (He was an uncle of Fr. Robert Madigan who served in Rockwell and Sierra Leone)

The four Leen brothers from Abbeyfeale, Co. Limerick made a major contribution to the Congregation. John, born in 1881, came to Rockwell in 1893 and having served as a prefect from 1900 to1902 he died suddenly. Daniel, born in1882, entered Rockwell in 1894 and served as a prefect. Ordained in 1910 he was a member of the Community of St. Mary's, Rathmines from 1911 to 1916 and Rockwell from 1917 to 1926. He later served in St. Mary's, U.S.A., Rockwell and Blackrock. Edward, born in 1885, was a student at Rockwell from

1896 to 1904. He excelled as a student and later studied in Rome where he was awarded a D.D. He served in Nigeria and later was appointed Dean of Studies at Blackrock. He became widely known for his spiritual writings on theological themes which were considered highly academic and sometimes controversial. James Leen was the youngest of the brothers. Born in 1888, he entered Rockwell in 1905 and excelled as a student. He later studied in Rome where he obtained doctorates in philosophy and theology. He was appointed Coadjutor Bishop of Port Louis, Mauritius, to John T. Murphy, another ex-Rockwell man. He succeeded Bishop Murphy and was later appointed archbishop. [55]

The Browne brothers of Grangemockler were Rockwell students in those years. David was the future Cardinal, Paddy (better known as Pádraig de Brún), became a distinguished academic and President of University College Galway, while Maurice became a parish priest in Co. Kildare and popular novelist in the Canon Sheehan tradition, his best known works being *The Big Sycamore* and *In Monavalla*. The niece of the three Browne brothers, the distinguished poet and diplomat Máire Mhac an tSaoí, describes in her autobiography the first contact of the brothers with Rockwell.

PAST STUDENTS

Bishop John O'Gorman

Bishop John Pius Dowling

Bishop John G. Neville

Bishop Bartholomew Wilson

Bishop Henry Gogarty   **Bishop James Leen**

David was the eldest and he later took the name Michael when he entered the Dominican Order. He was as tall as his father, Maurice, and terrifyingly strong. It was time for him to go to boarding school. Rockwell College was the obvious choice as it was within easy range by pony and trap. Mac Donagh and De Valera were teaching there at the time but that was not a factor in the family's decision. David was accepted and invited to sit the scholarship examination on the first day of term. They set off by pony and trap in the morning, David in his new suit and Eton collar with his bags packed and little Paddy who came for the jaunt. Kate, his mother, decided to wait till the exam was over, to have an idea how David fared. She had friends among the staff and they persuaded her to let Paddy sit the exam as well as his brother, which he did. In due course Kate was asked to come and meet the Dean of Studies, Dr. Crehan. "Madam", he said, "your boy David will certainly qualify for a scholarship". This was undoubtedly good news, for money was indeed a consideration. Then the Dean continued, "but the little fellow is a genius, you must leave him with us right away." Paddy had come first on every paper. Kate was overwhelmed. "But he has no suit" she said. "The tailor will fix him up" And his boots "We have a shoemaker also." Kate asked Paddy would he like to stay. His eyes shone; he would love to. She drove home alone and very uneasy as to what would be her reception, for she knew how much this particular pupil meant to his father and how he would be missed. She did not dare tell her husband what she had done, and when Maurice, in puzzlement, kept asking where Paddy was, she told him brusquely to stop annoying her; she had to see to the cows. Eventually of course, the truth came out, and a sad Maurice accepted the *fait accompli*.[56]

James Mellett referring to David who was a friendly rival of his on the rugby field said "One day in the last term he challenged me to a wrestling match on the cricket field. I won, but in the fall David broke a collar bone". Referring to his younger brother, Paddy, Mellett says "In appraising his scholarship and genius one can only speak in superlatives. Two years younger than his classmates, he was still under sixteen when he sat for the Senior Grade examinations in which he came first, not only in his own special Mathematics group but in Classics too. It was taken for granted that in every examination that Paddy would come first."[57]

Among the students in those days too were future missionaries and secular clergy. Daniel Murphy, future Dean of Studies and later Provincial, came to Rockwell from Knocknagoshel, Co. Kerry, in 1903. Richard A. Harnett from Abbeyfeale, future Provincial, came in 1895. James Mellett, legendary missionary in Nigeria, came from Crosboyne, Co. Mayo, in 1898, Thady O'Connor, future missionary came from Millstreet, Co. Cork, also in 1898. Charles Mulcahy, who later became a Jesuit and Michael F Kivlehan who became a priest of the Dublin Archdioce came to Rockwell in 1902. John A. Fahey became Dean of the Archdiocese of Adelaide and when remembering his days in Rockwell said "I have never forgotten my Rockwell days; the "gangs", the Big Study with its oil lamps, the Chapel, so lovely always, the lake and all the surroundings where we laid the foundations of our lives."[58]

Among the students who later became prominent in public life were Fionán Lynch, future Minister for Education and Fisheries, Pierce McCan who was elected M.P. for East Tipperary while serving a prison sentence in England, Senator Henry Barnville, Professor of Surgery at U.C.D. and senior surgeon at the Mater Hospital, Michael O'Malley, Professor of Surgery at University College, Galway, Thomas Morrissey from Clonmel, later Secretary of the Department of Education, Tim Cleary from Birr, later Assistant Secretary of the Revenue Commissioners, James Lynch of Marlhill, New Inn, later a journalist with the *Drogheda Independent* and founder of the *Dungarvan Observer*. Henry S. Moylan became Secretary of the Department of Local Government and Martin Connolly became a Circuit Court judge. William Martin became an investment manager at the banking House of Baring Brothers in London and Cormac Ó Cadhla became Professor of Irish at U.C.D. John Burke of Cahir and Michael J. Bowman of Kanturk, Co. Cork were among the founding members of the Rockwell Union. Two young people of that vintage died while still in Rockwell. Frederick Rausch, who was a prefect, died in April 1897 and is buried in Rockwell. His parents had emigrated from Germany to the U.S.A. Frederick entered the juniorate in Pittshurgh in 1886. He was a good musician but weak in health. He came to Rockwell as a prefect in 1894.[59] Thomas Bennet, a young student died of pneumonia in January 1900.[60]

Of all those students of those years, perhaps the one who evokes the fondest memories was the Galway writer Pádraig Ó Conaire. He was born in Galway in 1882 and orphaned at a young age. He was reared for a time by his grandparents in Conamara and with relatives in Co. Clare. He arrived in Rockwell early in 1898 with his younger brother intending to study for the priesthood at St. Joseph's. His arrival in Rockwell was due to the influence of Fr. John Kingston, who was then a prefect at the College, and his uncle who was the Parish Priest of Miltown-Malbay, Co. Clare. Pádraig's stay in Rockwell was short because later that year the junior seminary was closed to make way for the senior seminary and most of the scholastics, including Pádraig, were transferred to the juniorate at Blackrock College.

All students retained memories of their days in Rockwell. James Mellet later wrote "There was the Big Study looking out on the lake and the blue of the Galtees. There were the long halls, the glass-roofed refectory, the Chapel where at least one could slip in and have a small cry unnoticed. There was the dormitory, so vast for a small boy, and yet with so little room for his goods and chattels; and the soutaned prefect's handclap to waken us in what seemed the small hours, and the booming Angelus bell."[61]

Few students escaped home-sickness. Cormac Ó Cadhla, writing in Irish in the Annual of 1927 remembered "When he is in the study hall in the evening peering over his books he becomes lonely. The sight of his native place appears before his eyes and between the tears he sees his mother and father sitting by the fire and discussing the business of the day. He imagines himself at home again learning his lessons under the caring eyes of his mother. He imagines that he hears her kind voice but suddenly he is awakened from his dream by the sound of the bell announcing the end of study and a call to the Chapel for night prayer. And when he goes to bed he dreams again about the wonderful life he had at home listening to the neighbours tell their stories by the fireside. Life in College is not what he thought it would be like and he longs to be at home again".

Cormac Ó Cadhla

The pressure to perform well in examinations in those days was intense. Cormac Ó Cadhla remembered: "Examinations were held at Christmas and Easter and books were given as prizes to those who did best. The prizes were distributed on the day before the Easter holidays. We all gathered in the study hall in the presence of all the teachers. The President sat on the rostrum and the Dean of Studies stood beside him. The President spoke first about our preparations for life and gave us advice but we took little heed of what he was saying because we were waiting for the results. Then the Dean stood up with a long paper in his hand. Some of us were white with fear in dread of the results. And then he read out the marks. Sighs of delight and disappointment were heard throughout the room. Then there was the prospect of the stick, or worse still, to be kept back during the Easter holidays. There was little excitement after Easter because we were in preparation for the end of year exams so our heads were always in the books." [62]

James Mellett also felt the examination fever as he wrote: "The burning topic of conversation on all sides was the results sheets of the Intermediate examinations. In those days the race for distinctions was in full cry. The newspapers featured the leading schools in banner headlines and the tide of inter-college rivalry ran strongly. The year before I arrived, Rockwell had led, a clear first in Ireland and in September 1898 I found that the hero of the hour was Willie Martin who had won the Gold Medal in Senior Grade Mathematics, the most coveted distinction of all. He was the son of my old school teacher."

MUSIC AND DRAMA

The tension of examinations found relief in musical and dramatic proceedings. By 1894 the Rockwell Brass Band, which had featured in earlier years numbered twenty five, seven of whom were German. The band had previously been under the direction of Thomas Griffin from Cashel, but was now under the direction of William Griffin, perhaps his son. A new addition to the staff that year was Mr. Walsh who was a skilled piano instructor.[63] Concerts and lantern shows provided regular entertainment for students. It had become a custom to have such an entertainment on the evening prior to the students' departure for the Christmas holidays. At such an occasion in December 1896 the Magic Lantern showed scenes from London, Rome, Paris and New York with a performance by the College String Band and comic items from local artists from Cashel. It was at this concert that Fr. John McGrath unveiled his new gramophone.[64] This was a contraption unlikely to have been seen by students before.

A new era for music and drama in Rockwell began in 1898 with the appointment of Fr. Joseph Muller and Fr. Hugh Evans. Fr. Muller had been previously in Rockwell as a student and prefect and Fr. Evans as a prefect. Within weeks Fr. Evans had organised a concert of music and sketches with Fr. Muller on the piano. On the Feast of the Immaculate Conception their new choir, The Cecilian Society, performed in the new Chapel, conducted by Fr. Evans with Fr. Muller on the new organ. A week later Rockwell had its first experience of a Gilbert and Sullivan operetta. It was *The Gondoliers*, produced by Fr. Evans with music by Fr. Muller and with more than fifty students participating.[65] This was a remarkable achievement considering that it was only nine years since that popular operetta had been first produced in London and that information in those days travelled so slowly. It was the first of many Gilbert and Sullivan productions in Rockwell over the next seventy years.

Over the next few years Fr. Evans produced *Macbeth*, *The Merchant of Venice* and a play about the life of Robert Emmet while at the same time the choir and orchestra were thriving under the direction of Fr. Muller.[66]

A POLITICAL AWARENESS

The politics of Ireland from 1870 to the end of the century were dominated by agitation for home rule and land reform. The Community and students in Rockwell were kept abreast of political events in the country. The *Freeman's Journal* was freely available and with extracts publicly read at mealtimes. On an outing to the Devil's Bit in May 1890 the students were accompanied on their carriages by the College band with loud entertainment, but on entering Cashel the military was in force on account of a Land League meeting. The band was ordered to stop playing and the carriages were directed on another route. On entering Thurles the students recognised the two politicians, John Dillon and

William O'Brien, who were electioneering. They descended from their carriages, shook hands with the celebrities and raised three cheers for Ireland.[67]

The turmoil which accompanied the Parnell divorce case in 1890 did not pass unnoticed in Rockwell. The case had come up for trial in November of that year and was not contested by Parnell. Calls for Parnell's resignation were immediate, the most influential being that from Michael Davitt. The reaction of clergy, notably that of Archbishop Croke, was awaited. Croke was slow to publicly react to the crisis.[68] Meanwhile a meeting was held in Cashel in support of Parnell. It was attended by the Fathers from Rockwell. Their attendance was justified in the Journal by the fact that the meeting had been convened by the clergy.[69] The reaction of individual Fathers in Rockwell is a matter for speculation.

Later pronouncements by Archbishop Croke and the Irish Catholic Hierarchy were influential in their anti-Parnell stance. An indication that Rockwell may have followed the archbishop's line was evident in the general election of 1892. Rockwell was in the constituency of East Tipperary and the candidates were the outgoing member of the Irish Party, Thomas J. Condon from Clonmel and the Parnellite Dr. P.R. Dennehy who was considered by the Rockwell Journal to be somewhat anti-clerical. Rockwell had forty votes between Fathers, Brothers, prefects, boarders and domestic staff. Even Fr. Limbour and Br. Hippolyte, who were of French nationality, had a vote. The Journal was confident that all forty votes went to Condon, who had an easy win.[70] The secret ballot was then twenty years old, of course, and it can be assumed that Rockwell was not without men of independent mind.

In the immediate aftermath of the Parnell split the division and bitterness which gripped Irish politics were intense as was the internecine feud within the Irish Parliamentary Party between the Parnellites who believed that home rule could only be achieved by an independent Irish Party and the anti-Parnellites who believed that home rule depended on the good will of the Liberal Party and that an alliance with them was therefore essential. The leading characters in this feud were John Dillon who believed in the Liberal alliance, Tim Healy who did not, John Redmond who led a Parnellite rump but distanced himself from the squabbles, and William O'Brien who wanted the party to lead a revival of land agitation. The speeches of these men were frequently read aloud at meals in Rockwell.[71] It is likely that each of these characters had their fans in Rockwell and were the subject of heated debates.

SPORT AND RECREATION

Cormac Ó Cadhla remembered that despite the loneliness there was also great fun in Rockwell. On a free day a long walk in the countryside with a visit to an old castle or an old ruin, probably Athassel Abbey or the Rock of Cashel was enjoyable and hearing about the people who dwelt in them long ago. Listening to the old boys telling about the great things that happened in previous years was fun as was the excitement at the end of the journey seeing the carts full of food and drink; "and how the stories shortened the journey and we were suddenly back at the College again. And the next day we were back at study but fully refreshed after our walk in the country side" He remembered the excitement on the sideline at football matches as they encouraged their side when teams from Limerick, Cork or Dublin visited. And when the team was playing away he remembered that as the carriage left the College there was great cheering.[72]

Cricket continued in popularity during the summer term in Cormac Ó Cadhla's time and whenever the weather was unsuitable practice took place in the handball alleys. Matches were played against local clubs and against teams from the army barracks in Cahir and Thurles. In 1893 a new cricket club was formed in Clonmel and in early May it visited Rockwell and recorded a comfortable win by forty six runs in the first innings. On the Rockwell team on that occasion were two prefects, John Kingston, a future Rockwell Bursar, and John Stafford, a future Provincial Bursar. Rockwell's return match was played a week later with Clonmel on the Marlfield estate outside the town with permission from Richard Bagwell, then lord of the manor.[73]

John Kingston figured on Rockwell cricket teams every year during the eight years he spent as prefect. He was the outstanding player in June 1898 when Rockwell defeated a visiting team of railway officials from Thurles. Also prominent on the Rockwell team that day was another prefect and future Dean of Discipline in Rockwell, Joseph Baldwin, who is better remembered for his prowess on the rugby field than on the cricket crease. Also prominent on the Rockwell team in those years were the Shephard brothers. On some occasions visiting cricket teams were entertained after the match by an aquatic display on the lake.[74]

Cricket had an assured future in Rockwell because of the continued enthusiasm of Fr. Christian Schmidt who had joined the staff in 1892 and who was one of Rockwell's great characters. He was an outstanding batsman and handball player and the stories of his exploits are legendary.[75]

The annual Rockwell Sports, which was first held in 1877, continued as a significant sporting and social occasion not only in Rockwell but also in South Tipperary. During Dr. Crehan's term, the sports received great publicity in the area because of a guest list which was published in the local papers and included all the Tipperary celebrities from Archbishop Croke to the prominent members of the business, farming, professional and political communities.[76] The guest list also included the editors and proprietors of all Tipperary local newspapers, thus assuring a favourable account of the proceedings.

The Sports day of June 1890 was described in the Journal in great detail. It was open to the public. The field was well prepared, surrounded by a railing, making it a very appropriate setting for the various events. Benches from the Chapel were put in place for the guests to watch the contestants. Two tents loaned by the Barracks in Cahir were set up, one for the athletes and one for cool drinks. The second one was kept very busy. Bordeaux wine, seemingly without official authorisation, was available. The weather was good and the attendance numbered about eight hundred. A checkpoint was set up in the refectory. There the guests produced their passes. Two students, appointed by the committee, did not allow anyone to pass through without showing their ticket. Many priests from the neighbourhood were present.

The refectory was lavishly decorated for the occasion. Students were in charge of cutting the meat: beef, mutton and ham. For dessert there was jelly, blancmange, biscuits and dry raisins. For drinks there was Bordeaux wine and sherry, porter, lemonade and more than anything else, urns of tea. Everyone was drinking tea, especially the ladies. No whisky was available. Drinks were given only to those who had come a long distance. Carriage drivers took bread and butter and some a piece of meat and a mug of porter. Newspaper reporters were served lunch. For the first serving about 150 entered the refectory and about 50 for the second. A second refectory was in use.

After lunch, which took place at 3.00 p.m. there was a walk through the grounds and then the Sports began and lasted until 6.00pm. One accident occurred during the regatta with one of the boats but no one was injured. At 6.30 the prizes were distributed by the President. By 7 pm all had departed. The newspapers represented at that Sports were The *Freemans' Journal*, the *Cashel Sentinel*, the *Cashel Gazette*, the *Clonmel Chronicle*, the *Clonmel Nationalist* and the Waterford and Cork papers. The cost of entertaining the guests was estimated at £40 and was regarded as good value for the money because of the great impression which it created.[77] About two hundred and forty were served meals at the Sports of 1891.[78]

All newspaper accounts of the Sports referred to the beautiful site that is Rockwell. A report of the 1894 sports described the new bicycle track which had become a recent valuable acquisition and voiced its only criticism of the proceedings being that the programme was so long that it had to be completed on the following day.[79] At the 1896 sports the newly formed Cashel Brass Band added to the attraction.[80] And at the 1898 sports the courtesy extended to the visitors was noted whereby they were met by the staff and students and escorted to their seats. One of the most popular events that year was the throwing of the cricket ball. That sports, as every other year ended with a sumptuous meal for the visitors in the College dining rooms.[81]

In the early 1890s rugby in Rockwell was in its infancy. There were two Rockwell rugby teams, the students' team and the senior team which consisted of students, prefects and outside players. In October 1892 the students team played the Abbey School, Tipperary. Two weeks later the Limerick Rugby Club came to Rockwell for a match against the students. They easily beat the Rockwell youngsters. They were hardened experienced players, trained for rough bouts. They also spent far too much time in the refectory after the meal, even when the hint was given that it was time to break up, according to the Rockwell Journal which opined that moderation and regularity needed to be a part of the sport.[82]

James Mellett opined that for most boys the happiest memories of schooldays are bound up with games. For him there was football, Gaelic and rugby, hurling, cricket, and in the idyllic days of the summer term, boating and swimming. With hurling he was unable to match himself against the boys of the famous hurling counties of Tipperary, Kilkenny, Cork and Limerick. He had never seen rugby before but he seemed to fit into it more naturally and rugby became his game. Before he was seventeen he found himself on the senior team in the company of the Ryan brothers. David Browne was also on that team. The following year he was captain of the team.[83]

J.P. Brennan, a student in those years, later spoke of the influence of the Ryan brothers. The names of Mike and Jack Ryan, he said, will live forever as long as the game of rugby is played. "In every respect they were giants. The accounts of their deeds in international matches were accepted by young Rockwellians with reverential admiration. Their rivalry with the towering McEwan of Scotland, Bancroft of Wales and others has been immortalised." J.P. Brennan also felt that Fr. Baldwin and Fr. McGuirk were perhaps the finest pair of three-quarters in Ireland.[84]

D.J. O'Connor remembered that in those days rugby football was practically his only sport in Rockwell. He dreamed it, he talked it, and he played it. Dr. Crehan, he felt, believed that every student should play it and play it to the limit. Dr. Crehan personally took over the coaching and training of the senior team. He was a great football strategist and he had at his disposal the greatest bunch of rugby footballers to wear the blue and white. He took Mike and Jack Ryan from the backs and threw them into the scrum where their weight and strength belonged. With them in the forwards were Mike Cleary and Dan Egan. In the backs were prefects Joseph Baldwin and James J. McGurk, with little fleet-footed Johnnie Ryan on the wing.[85]

Rockwell had a number of new players on the team when the 1898 season opened with a draw against St. Kieran's College, Kilkenny, and a win over Cork Constitution. The match against Constitution was played in Rockwell and the referee was Dr. Crehan. The star players that day were the Ryan brothers and Joseph Baldwin.[86] A week later Rockwell travelled to Turners' Cross for a return match and for another victory, this time by two tries to nil. The Rockwell captain was Joseph Baldwin, then a prefect and later Dean of Discipline at Rockwell. The full-back was Mortimer Vaughan from Mullinahone, then a student at St. Joseph's and the forwards included Joseph Shanahan alongside the Ryan brothers. When Rockwell later played Garryown in Cahir the match ended in a draw, both sides having scored a try.[87]

A newcomer to the Rockwell team which was at home to Cork County in February 1900 was lay teacher and former student Michael Smithwick.[88] In March of that year Rockwell faced the great Garryown in the Munster Cup. The game was played in Magner's Field in Clonmel and Rockwell were the surprising winners by a try and drop goal to a drop goal. The match had to be stopped for a while as Joseph Shanahan was attended to following a collision with another player.[89] Later that year Joseph Shanahan had recovered sufficiently to take his place on the team which drew with Cork Constitution.[90]

A new full-back on the Rockwell team in 1902 was the recently ordained Fr. James J. McGurk who was a member of the Rockwell Community for only one year before his appointment to another ministry. He played a prominent part in Rockwell's game against Clanwilliam and later in the season when Rockwell defeated Queen's College, Cork.[91] This was Joseph Shanahan's last season with the team before his departure for Nigeria.

Eamon de Valera was a prominent member of the Rockwell rugby team in 1903 and 1904 and in those years he played alongside a number of prefects who were also fine rugby players. They included Thaddeus O' Connor, better known as Thady, a future missionary and teacher of chemistry in Rockwell, Edward Leen, one of the Leen brothers who later became a distinguished writer on religious topics, Prosper Bisch from Alsace who had studied at Blackrock, and was afterwards a pioneering missionary in Sierra Leone, Leonard Graf from the Rhineland who later did most of his missionary work in Trinidad, Frank Howell, later a missionary in Nigeria, John Heelan, later Dean of Discipline at Blackrock, Richard Harnett, later Irish Provincial, and two future members of the Rockwell Community Tim Cunningham and Martin O'Mahony. Other players in Dev's time included the legendary Ryan brothers, lay teacher Tom O'Donnell and James Mellettt, the colourful and legendary future missionary in Nigeria., still a student in St. Joseph's who often mentioned a flying tackle he made on Dev which could have changed the course of Irish history.

Rockwell reached the Munster senior cup final in 1904. The campaign started in early March with a victory over Clonmel. This was followed later in the month with a win over Cork County. This match was played in Cork and it was the first appearance on the Rockwell team of the new full-back Prosper Bisch. Early in the first half Thady O'Connor passed to De Valera who dived over the line near the posts for a try which was converted by Tim Cunningham. Thady O'Connor added another try in the second half. The opposition had been held scoreless and Rockwell had now qualified for the final.[92]

Senior XV 1904
Back: Dick Power, Michael Kennedy, Edward Leen, Con Liddane, Tom Cusack, John O'Dwyer,
Jack Ryan, Dick Conway, Mike Ryan, J.J. O'Sullivan.
Seated: Michael Flannery, Prosper Bisch, Thady O'Sullivan, Eamon de Valera, Jack Barrett.
In front: John O'Dwyer, Denis Joy.

The final was played in the Market Field in Limerick against Garryowen. D.J. O'Connor recalled that these were also the golden days of Garryowen, the pride and joy and the toast of the citizens of Limerick By the thousands they crowded the historic old Market Field to cheer on their heroes when they engaged in football contests. He remembered the excitement in Rockwell on the morning of the match. "After breakfast we gathered in the College square to wish our boys God speed. With our cheers and our prayers the two-horse wagonette whirled ahead." When the team reached Cahir they took the train to Limerick. A record crowd had assembled in the Market Field. The first half was fought with great ferocity but both sides failed to score. The struggle continued in the second half and it was near full-time when Garryowen went over for the only score of the game. It was a great disappointment for the Rockwell team, the members of which were: Prosper Bisch, Johnny Ryan, Eamon de Valera, Tim Cunningham, John Rice, Thady O'Connor (captain), Denis O'Connor, Mike Ryan, Jack Ryan, Tom O'Donnell, John Franklin, Michael Dwyer, Leonard Graf, James Mellett and John Kennedy.[93]

* * *

No period in the history of Rockwell has given the College a national profile to surpass that of the years 1890-1905. This profile was earned by the unusually high number of individuals gracing its halls who later in life distinguished themselves in Church and State.

Chapter 4 Notes

[1]   S. Farragher, *Bishop Joseph Shanahan CSSp.Seleccted Studies*, p.89.
[2]   ISR p. 201.
[3]   ISR pp 13-15.
[4]   RCA 1955, pp 74-77.
[5]   ISR pp 223-4.
[6]   ISR pp 253-4.
[7]   ISR pp 252-3.
[8]   RCA 1926 p. 14.
[9]   *Cashel Sentinal* 27/1/1900, *Nationalist* 11/8/2011
[10] JNL 19/10/1890
[11] *Nationalist* 3/9/1892, 30/8/1893, 23/9/1893.
[12] *Cashel Sentinal* 18/5/1894
[13] *Cashel Sentinal* 29/8/1896, 20/8/1898, 25/8/1900.
[14] *Cashel Sentinal* 7/9/1904.
[15] JNL 31/5/1890.
[16] RCA 1964 p. 26.
[17] JNL 22/2/1895
[18] B. De Breffny, *Ireland: A Cultural Encyclodaedia*, pp 37-8.
[19] cf Chronological Floor Plan, section 3.
[20] JNL 2/2/1896, 12/3/1896, 13/4/1896.
[21] *Cashel Sentinal* 20/6/1896, 12/9/1896.
[22] JNL 18/7/1898, 17/3/1900.

[23] RCA 1977 p. 12. Description of Fr. Michael Comerford.
[24] RCA 1996, pp 147-149.
[25] JNL 15/8/1896.
[26] RCA 1977 p. 13.
[27] JNL 25/3/1901.
[28] cf Chronological Floor Plan, section 4.
[29] RCA 1977 p. 13.
[30] RCA 1964 p. 25.
[31] JNL 18/12/1892.
[32] Deeds of Rockwell Property June 1897 and May 1900.
[33] ISR 169-70.
[34] ISR p. 18.
[35] ISR p. 54.
[36] ISR p. 83
[37] ISR pp 168, 217.
[38] ISR p. 336.
[39] RCA 1961, pp 24-26, 49.
[40] *Shanahan in the Making,* (Record in Rockwell Archives)
[41] RCA 1942 p. 42.
[42] *Shanahan in the Making*
[43] ISR pp 336-7.
[44] T.R. Mac Uilliam, The MacDonaghs of Cloughjordan, *Tipperary Association Year Book 1981/82* pp 15-17.
[45] *Nationalist 23/9/1893, Cashel Sentinal 22/9/1894.*
[46] RCA 1961, pp 24-5.
[47] RCA 1953 pp 19-22.
[48] ibid
[49] S.F.F.C. pp 252-3.
[50] RCA 1970 p. 37-8.
[51] This section on Eamon de Valera is summarised from S.P. Farragher, *Dev and his Alma Mater* pp 73-79.
[52] RCA 1961, p 25.
[53] The Earl of Longford and Thomas P. O'Neill, *Eamon De Valera,* pp 182-3.
[54] ISR passim
[55] idem.
[56] M. Cruise O'Brien, *The Same Age as the State,* pp 22-3.
[57] RCA 1961 pp 24-27,
[58] RCA 1958 p. 39.
[59] ISR p 113.
[60] JNL 19/1/1900.
[61] RCA 1961 pp 24-49.
[62] RCA 1927 pp 42-45.
[63] *Cashel Sentinal 18/5/1894.*
[64] *Cashel Sentinal 26/12/1896.*
[65] *Cashel Sentinal 5/11/1898, 10/12/1898, 21/12/1898.*
[66] *Cashel Sentinal 28/6/1902, Nationalist 19/3/1904.*
[67] JNL 20/5/1890
[68] F.S.L. Lyons, *Charles Stewart Parnell* pp 478-487.
[69] JNL 21/12/1890.
[70] JNL 9/7/1892.
[71] JNL 1890-1900 passim.
[72] RCA 1927 pp 42-45.
[73] *Nationalist 3/5/1893*

74   *Nationalist* 11/6/1898.
75   ISR pp 169-70.
76   *Nationalist* 27/5/1893
77   JNL 9/6/1890
78   JNL 18/5/1891
79   *Cashel Sentinel* 18/5/1894.
80   Cashel Sentinel 30/5/1896.
81   Cashel Sentinal 28/5/1898.
82   JNL 31/10/1892, 11/11/1892.
83   RCA 1961 pp 24-26.
84   RCA 1953 pp 19-22.
85   RCA 1955 pp 74-77.
86   *Cashel Sentinal* 12/11/1898.
87   *Cashel Sentinal* 12/2/1898, 17/2/1898, 19/3/1898.
88   *Cashel Sentinal* 10/2/1900.
89   *Cashel Sentinal* 24/3/1900
90   *Cashel Sentinal* 24/11/1900.
91   Cashel Sentinal 18/1/1902 and 25/1/1902.
92   *Nationalist* 9/3/1904, 30/3/1804, 2/4/1904.
93   *Nationalist* 6/4/1904.

– 5 –

CONTINUED SUCCESS
1906-1915

The presidencies of Fr. Pembroke and Fr. Evans between 1906 and 1915 were marked by continued academic success, an increase in the number of students and the erection of a new building and extension. It was a time in Ireland of political impasse and growing nationalism when the horrors of World War I began to unfold.

Fr. Thomas A. Pembroke
President 1905-1912

Fr. Thomas A. Pembroke was President from 1905 to 1912. He was born in Castleisland, Co. Kerry in 1864. He came to Rockwell as a boarder in 1878 and in 1882 he joined St. Joseph's. After prefecting in Rockwell from 1884 to 1887 he went to France to do his senior studies and was ordained in 1891. He was appointed to St. Mary's College, Rathmines and later to Blackrock College where he served as Dean of Studies and later as Director of the juniorate there.

He was succeeded in Rockwell by Fr. Hugh Evans who served as President from 1912 to 1916. Fr. Evans was born in Newcastlewest, Co. Limerick in 1860. He studied at Blackrock College and in France and served as prefect in Blackrock and in Rockwell from 1884 to 1887. Following his ordination in 1889 he was appointed to St. Mary's College, Rathmines, where he taught music and art. He served as Bursar in Rockwell from 1898 to 1900 and as Director of St. Joseph's from 1900 to 1903. He was Bursar in Blackrock from 1904 before serving as President of Rockwell.

THE COMMUNITY

When Fr. Pembroke became President there were thirteen Fathers in the Community. Fr. John Byrne had been Dean of Studies from 1900 to 1907 when he was succeeded by Fr. Thomas Naughton who held the position until 1911. Dr. James O' Neill from Downpatrick, Co. Down became Dean of Studies in 1911. Fr. James Cotter was Bursar all those years. Fr. Michael Walsh from Tullaroan was Dean of Discipline for just the one

Fr. Hugh Evans
President 1912-1916

year 1908-1910, having previously served in that position in Blackrock and St. Mary's. He was succeeded by Fr. Patrick Brennan from Freshford, Co. Kilkenny, who held the position until 1917. A student in those days, W.E. Fogarty, later remembered Fr. Brennan as a wonderful rugby referee who showed no favours. "In his capacity as Dean of Discipline I have often cowered before him for some unusually flagrant breach of etiquette, and sitting down was a painful procedure for a long time after his ministrations. A hard man but a just one." [1]

Fr. Daniel Egan from Ferbane, Co. Offaly came to Rockwell as Director of St. Joseph's from 1904 to 1907 and remained on the teaching staff until his untimely death in 1922. He was succeeded as Director of St. Joseph's by Fr. Edmund Cleary from nearby Rosegreen who, like Fr. Egan, had been a student in St. Joseph's and a prefect for many years. Fr. Philip O'Shea from Ballyragget, Co. Kilkenny, served in Rockwell from 1910 to 1912 and Fr. Martin O'Mahony from Castleisland, Co. Kerry taught Irish from 1909 to 1913. Members of the Community from the previous presidency were Fr. Michael Colgan, Fr. John Muller, Fr. John McGrath and Fr. Christian Schmidt.

There were fifteen Brothers in Rockwell when Fr. Pembroke became President, five of whom were new to the Community since Fr. Brennan's presidency. Br. Ephanius O'Leary, who had earlier helped Br. Kieran in running the farm, returned to Rockwell in 1913, having in the meantime served in Blackrock and St. Mary's. Brother Brendan Coffey also returned having previously helped in the refectories and in the meantime having worked on the missions in Africa. Br. Edmond McSweeney had previously served in France, Trinidad and Africa before retiring to Rockwell. Three Brothers arrived in Rockwell in 1906 to help with the new wing which was then being built. They were Br. Materne Comte and Br. Gomes Proptasio, who were French and Br. Alphonsus Biggemann from Germany. Still attending to their duties were Br. Kieran, Br. Elimien, Br. Dalmas, Br. Albert, Br. Edgar, Br. Ignatius, Br. Silas, Br. Nicephorus, Br. John Baptist and Br. Hippolyte who was the longest serving of all.

ACADEMIC DISTINCTIONS

The high achievement of Rockwell students in the Intermediate examinations while Dr. Crehan was Dean of Studies continued under his successors Fr. John Byrne, Fr. Thomas Naughton and Dr. James O'Neill. In 1911 Rockwell came first of the colleges in Ireland in the number of exhibitions and prizes achieved.[2] The following year it was first again, but this time in a tie with Clongowes Wood when it had ten exhibitions, nine book prizes, two medals, eight composition prizes, totalling twenty nine, one less than achieved the previous year.[3] It had twenty nine again in 1913, sixteen in 1914 and twenty two in 1915.[4]

Among the exhibition winners in 1909 were Maurice Browne from Grangemockler, future author of *The Big Sycamore*, Thomas Collins, future editor of *Dublin Opinion*, William Cahill of Clonmel and Joseph Walsh of Cahir.[5] A prize winner in the middle grade in 1910 was Francis Griffin, future Superior General of the Holy Ghost Congregation. And in the preparatory grade of that

Group of junior students 1906

year Liam O'Flaherty, future writer, obtained honours in English, Greek, Latin, French, Irish, Mathematics and Physics.[6]

The failure rate in the Intermediate examination at national level was very high. In 1908, when Rockwell considered its result was good, it had ninety passes and sixty failures.[7] The following year the pass rate in Rockwell was 86 out of 131 at senior grade, 33 out of 55 at junior and 22 out of 26 at preparatory level. These pass rates were far in excess of the national average which was 55%.[8] Because the income from the government to schools was based on examination results it was important for Rockwell to have good results. In these years the highest grant it received for examination results was £1.046.[9] Changes were made to the system at this time, the most notable being the introduction of an inspectorate in 1909, the dropping of the preparatory grade in 1913 and the greater emphasis on commercial subjects in 1914.[10]

Group of senior students 1906

DEVELOPMENT

It was during the presidency of Fr. Pembroke that a new building and an extension were erected. They were the Chapel Hall, which was an extension to the Study block and the Library block which was a new building. (See Chronological Floor Plan). Three Brothers who were skilled in special trades, were transferred to Rockwell to oversee the work. Br Materne Comte was an expert mason and plasterer, Br Gomes Protasio was a carpenter and Br Alphonsus Biggemann was a painter and decorator.[11]

Work on the Chapel Hall, which joined the Silas Building with the Chapel, commenced in 1907. The masonry work on this extension was done by Br Materne and the work was complete in September 1907. Br. Alphonsus was responsible for the painting and decorating of the Study Hall which was completed in 1909.[12]

Work on the Library block commenced on Monday 17th May 1909.[13] Some of the outer walls had been completed by January 1910 when the workmen were involved in uprooting three fine beech trees to make way for the building.[14] Progress was slow because of only a skeleton staff and poor weather conditions, but the building was complete by the end of 1911. The block completely joined the western wing to the northern wing. The top floor contained the Sacred Heart Dormitory and a washroom annex to St. Joseph's Dormitory. In the first floor there were five toilets. The corridor leading to these had two rooms on the western side and a washroom annex to the Pink Dormitory on the other side.[15] The cost of this new wing was £5,000.[16]

Prior to the commencement of work on the Library block a road was built from the Cashel Road to the farmyard for the purpose of diverting farmyard traffic from the main avenue.[17]

Rockwell in 1910

GOLDEN JUBILEE CELEBRATIONS

In December 1913 a number of past students met in Cashel to make arrangements for the celebration of Rockwell's golden jubilee in 1914. The majority of these past students were priests of the archdiocese of Cashel and Emly and of the diocese of Waterford and Lismore, the most prominent among them being Archdeacon Ryan of Fethard and the historian Fr. William Burke who was then a curate in Cahir. It was felt that the best way to honour their *alma mater* was to launch a fund-raising campaign for the erection of three classrooms.[18]

The golden jubilee was an occasion for the media to highlight Rockwell's record over the previous fifty years. In an editorial the *Nationalist* commented that "Rockwell's wonderful development is another marked evidence of the constructive forces of the Catholic Church, and the marvellous growth of educational houses under its fostering care.[19] Commenting on the jubilee the *Freeman's Journal* said that "Rockwell takes front-rank place in classical teaching and in modern languages and science. It has sent out pupils who are distinguished in every rank of life, Church, State, commerce and industry; and its reputation has become international, students coming from all parts of Ireland and foreign lands to receive instruction in its halls."[20]

The actual celebration of the jubilee took place in September 1914 when the guest of honour was the newly ordained Archbishop of Cashel and Emly, Dr. Harty. Prominent among the guests was the Dean of Cashel, Monsignor Innocent Ryan who was one of the earliest students in Rockwell. High Mass was followed by a lunch at which many laudatory speeches were made. Rockwell's missionary spirit was praised by the archbishop who referred to the large number of past students who were priests in Africa and throughout the world. Monsignor Ryan remarked that in the previous seven years Rockwell had presented 346 candidates for the Intermediate exam and that 294 of them had passed. This was followed in the evening by a concert at which the College orchestra under the baton of Fr. Muller performed.[21]

Archbishop Harty

ST. JOSEPH'S

Under directors Fr. Egan and Fr. Cleary the average number of scholastics in St. Joseph's each year between 1906 and 1915 was about thirty. On his visit to Rockwell in 1909 the Provincial expressed disappointment that the numbers were not higher.[22] By 1912, however, the number had reached thirty four.[23] It was usual that a few boarders transferred to the scholasticate each year.

As usual the scholastics joined the boarders for class and sporting activities and during these years they joined the boarders in Fr. Muller's choir and orchestra.[24] They studied on their own in St. Joseph's, however. Some of the scholastics were among the leading performers academically and the "Galaxy" which awarded the top performers annually with a surprise trip away from the College usually included scholastics. The "Galaxy" of 1913 included three, and one of them was Liam O'Flaherty who was destined to become an acclaimed writer.[25]

In November 1909, the Sodality of the Children of Mary, which had formerly been so flourishing in Rockwell and which had been considered responsible for giving many vocations to the priesthood, was revived.[26] In March 1910 the scholastics became involved with the Brothers in Sacristy duties.[27] They were also involved in the annual Corpus Christi procession, especially in decorating the route around the grounds. St. Joseph's was visited regularly by returned missionaries who talked of their experience and among the visitors in 1913 were Bishop Neville and Bishop O'Gorman.[28]

EDUCATIONAL ISSUES

Fr. Pembroke was concerned about developments in education at a national level and like Fr. Leman and Fr. Huvéyts in previous years, the university question was a concern to him. The British government made a final attempt to resolve this issue in 1908. The Irish Universities Act (1908) dissolved the Royal University and established the Queen's University of Belfast and the

Community and visitors with Archbishop Harty 1915.
Seated: Fr. Kelly, Canon Byrnes, Fr. E vans C.S.Sp, Archbishop Harty, Mgr Nolan, Dr. Crehan C.S.Sp, Fr. Schmidt C.S.Sp.
Back: Fr. M. Meagher C.S.Sp., Fr. J. Murphy C.S.Sp., Fr. J. Nolan C.S.Sp., Fr. T. O'Connor, Fr. McElligott, Dr. Kennedy C.S.Sp., Fr. F. Griffin C.S.Sp., Fr. J. Hayes, Dr. D. Murphy C.S.Sp, Fr. E. O'Donnell, Fr. J. McGrath, Fr. Coady, Fr. J.J. McCarthy C.S.Sp.

National University of Ireland, the latter a federal body comprising University College Cork, University College Galway and a reconstituted University College Dublin. Maynooth became a recognised college in 1913.

During his presidency Fr. Pembroke was a very active member of the Catholic Headmasters' Association and was in regular attendance at its meetings in Dublin. A matter of concern to this body was the issue of school inspection. The government wanted an inspectorate to replace examinations, while many schools were suspicious of the powers of the inspectorate, acting as an agent of the state, to inquire into private institutions. Eventually in 1909 permanent inspectors were appointed. When the preparatory grade examination was dropped in 1913 payments were made on a capitation basis for pupils at this level on the reports of the inspectors.[29]

In the immediate aftermath of the appointment of inspectors, inspections of Rockwell were frequent and unannounced. The first inspection took place in October 1909 when the Dean of Studies, Fr. Naughton was asked to submit time-tables of house examinations. There were two more inspections by the end of that year, one for drawing and one for science. In February 1910 inspectors spent three days in the College and the following November there were two further inspections. On all occasions satisfaction with procedures was expressed but the frequency of these inspections initially caused concern to the Community. And on one occasion when inspectors arrived on the morning of an important Cup match there were sighs of exasperation.[30]

The question of Irish as an Intermediate subject was an issue for the Headmasters' Association on two occasions. An attack on Irish as being culturally unsound had been mounted by Professor Robert Atkinson of Trinity College and was met by opposition from the Association and the Gaelic League.[31] There was great controversy in 1909 when it was alleged that Irish was marked much harder than any other language in the Intermediate examination. In Rockwell, for example, students performed much poorer in the subject than in any other language. This had financial implications for the College.[32]

General Sir William Butler, who was guest of honour at Prize Day in 1909, expressed a rather sober opinion when he spoke to the students on the Irish language question. He felt that the study of Irish could in the near future become an influence of intense importance. He would not favour compulsion in the study of the language, however, and he warned that "English, the language we now speak, the language of the mart and commerce and of the professions, will remain what it is. I don't see how the tide can now be changed when the enormous masses of the people around us only know that language."[33]

Another issue which confronted Fr. Pembroke and the Catholic Headmasters Association was the question of the qualification and payment of teachers. The Education Act of 1878 had made no provision for it. Members of religious communities could view their educational work as part of their religious commitment but for the average lay teacher the remuneration and conditions of employment were unsatisfactory. Dr. Starkie, chairman of the Intermediate

Board commented in 1911 "Any man or woman, no matter how incompetent, may be appointed to a position in a secondary school. Although many teach for a year or two while they are preparing for other work, no layman wilfully takes up teaching as a permanent occupation." The Association of Secondary Teachers of Ireland (ASTI) had been formed in 1909 and the matter was then addressed.[34] In Rockwell since 1864 there had been a number of lay teachers, but none of them for long. In October 1909 there were seven lay teachers in Rockwell, which was a record number.[35] Of these, Michael Cremin was the only one long term. He was indeed to teach in Rockwell for a record forty five years.

Fr. Pembroke was known for his outspokenness and his vigorous defence of Catholic educational interests. He had plans for opening an agricultural school at Rockwell in 1912 but by then his health was deteriorating. He resigned and returned to Blackrock as an invalid.[36]

ROCKWELL AND THE RISE OF NATIONALISM

Irish Nationalist politics in 1900 was beginning to recover from the Parnellite split of a decade earlier. The Irish Party was eventually united under John Redmond in 1900 but its attendance at Westminster was seen by some as irrelevant while others looked instead to the emerging cultural nationalism as a more satisfying alternative. The idea that Ireland had a distinctive cultural identity took hold. This idea was promoted originally in Tipperary by the Gaelic League and later by political and separatist movements.

Two early champions of the Gaelic League in Tipperary were Fr. Matt Ryan, parish priest of Knockavilla-Donaskeigh since 1897 and Canon Arthur Ryan, parish priest of Tipperary Town since 1903. These two men typified the two strands of thinking within the League, Fr. Matt being a committed separatist and an early member of *Sinn Féin,* and Canon Arthur content to promote the language and Irish industry.[37] Both men organised annual *feiseanna* in the area and both were regular visitors to the Rockwell Community.

There was a certain rivalry between the Ryan clergymen as they organised their *feiseanna* which at times clashed. In 1909, however, Fr. Matt pulled a stroke which he felt would put his *feis* on a splendidly beautiful site with a wide catchment area. He would have it on the grounds of Rockwell College. Permission was granted and the *feis* commenced in Rockwell on Sunday 20th June. But the fates were against Fr. Matt for as soon as proceedings began the rain came down in torrents and the *feis* had to be abandoned.[38]

Fr. Matt had better luck in 1910. Rockwell was again the venue for his *feis* and it was held in glorious sunshine and with huge crowds. Reporters from the *Nationalist* and *Cork Examiner* were in attendance and the seats reserved for special guests were occupied by local clergy and by a few lay persons including the future M.P. for Tipperary, Pierce McCan.[39] This *feis* provided an opportunity to observe the thinking within the Rockwell Community on current affairs when Fr. Pembroke addressed the crowd at length. He was full of praise for the great strides made by the Gaelic League in promoting the language. . Some good people asked occasionally, he said "What is the good in studying Irish? Would it not be better to teach the boys French, German, Italian and mathematics?" His answer was that French, German, Italian and mathematics were all excellent; but there was only one thing that would tend to make us national; there was only one thing that would tend to develop in us the manhood of nationality and to give us self respect; and that was the language and history of our country.

Thinking men, he said, had begun to see that Ireland was slipping fast away from her noble traditions and that we were fast becoming merely a second-rate colony tacked on to the great England across the Channel. The Gaelic League, he said, had been trying to instil some practical patriotism into our people who had been too taken up with the land laws and the landlords. "Now, thank God," he said, "the landlords are passing away and we have time for the study of our history and time to develop in our people that strength of character, that manhood and backbone that went to make up a people and that would go to make us an Ireland independent of our neighbours across the Channel."

There was no movement in modern times, he said, that had helped Irish industries more than the Irish language movement. "We saw that we had a language and a history of our own; then why should we not ourselves manufacture the things that we wore and the things that we ate" he asked. If everyone in Ireland wore Irish-made clothes and boots, thousands would not be emigrating, he felt. And then he told his listeners what practical work Rockwell was doing "Every cap worn by the boys was Irish made; every candle burned on the altar, every piece of soap that came into the house, all the materials for the soutanes of the priests and brothers, all were made in Ireland."[40]

This speech of Fr. Pembroke suggests that there was sympathy for Fr. Matt's way of thinking in Rockwell. Further evidence of this is that three days earlier at the annual Rockwell Prize Day the guest of honour who presented their prizes to the students was Fr. Matt. And among the guests at that Prize Day were two close and influential friends of Fr. Matt, Pádraig Ó Cadhla, headmaster of Coláiste na Rinne and Pierce McCan.[41] It cannot be assumed, however that sympathy for the views of Fr. Matt was universal in Rockwell. A balancing act prevailed when the guest of honour at Prize Day in 1911 was Canon Arthur Ryan who made a strong plea that Irish should never be a compulsory subject.[42] The Speeches of John Redmond, John Dillon and William O'Brien, which heralded a sometimes alternative course, were read at meals in the College. And when John Redmond addressed a public meeting in Tipperary Town in April 1910 a number of the Fathers went to hear him.[43]

There were signs, however, that the spirit of the Gaelic League was having an influence on events in Rockwell. An official school holiday to mourn the death of King Edward in May 1910 was ignored and class continued as usual.[44] On St. Patrick's Day 1911, for the first time ever in Rockwell, the prayers after Mass were recited in Irish.[45] In May 1911 it was reported that the Irish revival movement in Rockwell was making great headway and that the students were preparing a play in Irish to be performed at Fr. Matt Ryan's *feis* the following month.[46] In December 1911 Fr. O'Mahony produced a play in Irish by the students which was well received.[47] In February 1912 an Irish dancing class for the students was introduced and in March of that year Fr. O'Mahony was the founder of The Gaelic Literary Society for students and on St. Patrick's Day he preached the sermon at Mass in Irish.[48]

The association of Pierce McCan, with Rockwell is interesting. He had been a student in Rockwell until 1899 when he and his brother were transferred to Clongowes Wood, possibly because one of the Jesuits there was an uncle of his mother. He dined with the Rockwell Community in November 1909 and again in June 1910;[49] and he was one of only a few lay people who were guests at Prize Day and at the *Feis* that year. At that time he was greatly

An tAthair Ó Mathúna

involved in the Gaelic League.[50] It may be that his visits to Rockwell had nothing to do with the Gaelic League and that he may have been a friend of a member of the Community. He was interested in craftwork, and succeeded in making a boat for the small lake on the McCan estate which was similar to the Rockwell lake. He had gone to France in 1900 where in Pau he studied French under Abbé Pedoupe and had visited Denmark to study Danish farming methods. Both of these interests may have struck a chord for someone in Rockwell.

Of more interest in an era of developing nationalism was the arrival in Rockwell in May 1914 of Seamus O'Neill. He was employed as an Irish teacher in Rockwell to substitute for another teacher who had got ill.[51] He was at that time a more advanced nationalist than either Fr. Matt Ryan or Pierce McCan but he was an acquaintance of both. He had been involved in the Gaelic League in Clonmel since 1904. He was leader of the Clonmel branch of Fianna Éireann, an organisation set up by Countess Markievicz and Bulmer Hobson in August 1909. It was a Republican youth movement modelled on the boy scout structure but with the object of establishing an independent Ireland. The Clonmel branch was set up by Seamus O'Neill following a meeting he attended in Dublin in the house of Countess Markievicz attended also by Bulmer Hobson and Con Colbert. He was sworn in as a member of the Irish Republican Brotherhood and was a member of the Irish Volunteers. Five months after his appointment to Rockwell he was involved with Pierce McCan and others in an organisation incorporating all branches of the Gaelic League in South Tipperary.[52] No one in Rockwell, of course, could have known that the teaching staff included a member of the I.R.B

THE STUDENTS

The Rockwell students between 1906 and 1915 varied in number between one hundred and eighty and two hundred.[53] Many distinguished themselves in later life. Francis Griffin from Kilmurry, Ibricken, Co. Clare arrived in Rockwell in 1907 and was later the first non-Frenchman to become Superior General of the

Congregation of the Holy Spirit. Maurice Browne, the youngest of the brothers from Grangemockler, and the winner of a distinction at the Intermediate of 1908, was author of *The Big Sycamore*. Michael J. Fahy was on the senior rugby team of 1909 and he later became a canon of the diocese of Dunkeld, Scotland. Michael B. Langford, a native of Ballybunion, Co. Kerry, came to Rockwell in 1908 at the early age of twelve and obtained first place in Ireland in Irish in the Intermediate. He later was ordained a priest for the Archdiocese of Dublin and was chaplain to the Governor General Tim Healy and to his successor James MacNeill.

Rockwell students, too from this era, later featured in the War of Independence. Bill Quirke from Clonmel was in Rockwell at this time. He was prominent in the War of Independence in South Tipperary and was elected Senator in 1929. He shared the secretaryship of Fianna Fáil with another old Rockwellian, Seamus Davin. John C. O'Sullivan was from Kenmare and was active in the Volunteers in Kerry. He later joined the National Army and was A.D.C. to Tim Healy and James McNeill. Daniel J. Browne was from Listowel and later qualified as a solicitor and practised in Tralee. In 1920 in the thick of the troubles he went to Dublin at the request of Austin Stack, then Minister for Home Affairs in Dáil Éireann to act as secretary of that Department. Its tasks were mainly to set up, organise and maintain Republican Courts throughout the country and to establish a police force. Ned Shanahan from Farranfore, Co. Kerry was medical officer to the Kerry No. 2 Brigade during the War of Independence. While in Rockwell he played centre-threequarter with Fr. David Heelan on the Schools Cup team and scrum-half to Vincent Vaughan on the Senior Fifteen. In contrast to the activists in the War of Independence, Gerard Grey, who finished in Rockwell in 1911 was awarded the O.B.E. in the 1955 Birthday Honours List. He joined the English Civil Service in 1913 and filled many important posts in the Department of Customs and Excise. Edward C. Powell captained the S.C.T. in 1913-14.[54]

The writer, Liam O'Flaherty, was a student in Rockwell from 1909 to 1913. Fr. Thomas Naughton, Dean of Studies, while on holidays in the Aran Islands met the young O'Flaherty and suggested to him that if he had a vocation for the priesthood he should come to Rockwell. O'Flaherty arrived in St. Joseph's but after four years discovered that his vocation was elsewhere. In one of his works, *Benedicamus Domino*, Rockwell is mentioned.[55]

Seán Ó Suilleabháin, Professor of Irish at University College, Cork, spent five years in Rockwell. P.J. Roche left Rockwell in 1909 and qualified as an engineer. He went into partnership with J. A. McConnell as Roche & McConell Ltd which was associated with the electrical and engineering requirements for the extension of Rockwell during Fr. Dinan's presidency. Denis Bowman was in Rockwell from 1904 to 1908. He later became an extensive farmer at Pallasgreen, Co. Limerick. J.J. Griffin was in Rockwell from 1908 to 1911. He was later a member of the company Davis, Griffin & Co. the well-known firm of auditors, accountants and taxation consultants. He was a great mathematician while at Rockwell. His vivid memories of Rockwell were of Fr. Colgan and his rabbits at the Rock, Fr. Naughton and his pointed mnemonics and Fr. Dan Murphy, who as a prefect lectured a class for Senior Grade Trigonometry of which J.J. Griffin was the sole member. James A. Nugent was in Rockwell from 1912 to 1916 and was a founder member of the Rockwell Union. Paddy Stokes from Fethard who was capped many times for Ireland was in Rockwell from 1907 to 1910, as was his brother Tom. Jack Sewell from Killarney, a future founder member of the Union was in Rockwell from 1912 to 1916. He played senior and junior football for Kerry and was an Irish delegate to the Olympic Games Congress in Berlin in 1930. Willie and Louis Quinlan form Tralee were in Rockwell from 1911 to 1915. Willie became the first County Manager for Kerry. Both were great sportsmen in Rockwell.Tom O'Carroll from Carrick-on-Suir was in Rockwell from 1912 to 1916. He became a broadcasting engineer with 2RN when it was first founded.[56]

Thomas J. Collins (1894-1972) co-founder and co-editor of *Dublin Opinion* was born in Dublin and educated at Rockwell and U.C.D. He was co-author with Fr. Andrew Egan (President of Rockwell 1949-1955) of two operettas *Trágadh na Taoide* and *Nocturne sa Chearnóg* performed at the Gaiety Theatre, Dublin, in the 1940s.[57] An article of his, *The Old School Tie*, was first published in *The Bell* magazine, edited by Seán Ó Faoláin, in February 1946. The article was a depiction of his time as a student in Rockwell which commenced in September 1906. The following are edited extracts from that article:

> From the windows of the big Study you can see the Galtees. I still remember the unsubstantial fairy-blue look of Galteemore on early June evenings. From the Study windows, too, you could watch the shining level of the lake and the tree-tops of its rather magical islands.
>
> So there we were, 300 of us between the ages of twelve and eighteen, as nicely mixed up as any experimental educationist could desire. But our education wasn't experimental; its roots went a very long way back, and those in charge of us knew exactly where they were going and kept a well-charted course.
>
> The boys were placed in two divisions, the Juniors and the Seniors. Up to fifteen you were a Junior; thereafter you were Senior. It was a rigid division. Juniors didn't speak to Seniors. Seniors didn't speak to Juniors. Their games and most of their classes were separate. All the Seniors looked enormous when you were a Junior, six feet high and fourteen stone. All the boys, Senior and Junior, were in the immediate charge of prefects, but these were not the prefects of the English Public School system. They were students from the scholasticate at the other side of the lake who were studying for, or had obtained their university degrees, and were going to be priests in the Order. They wore soutanes, which gave them a dignified appearance, and they knew how to keep us in order. They also mixed with the Seniors in the football matches without any loss of dignity and some of those powerful young men must have toughened the fibre of the College's teams with whom they exchanged knocks.
>
> The routine of the school was similar to that of other boarding schools. We arose, or were aroused, at 6.30 in winter and 6.00 in summer. Then we went to Mass.

After Mass there was a half-hour's study before breakfast. Breakfast was a simple affair, tea and bread and butter, but plenty of both. Then off we went for a walk around the lake. Classes began about 9.00. There was a break at 11.30, during which you ate a bun, supplemented by jam, if you had any jam, or if any of your friends had any. Back to class then until 3.00, when the dinner bell rang. Dinner was our real meal, a good one, and simple. You got a good helping of meat, plenty of potatoes and one other vegetable, usually cabbage. There was always some kind of dessert which occasionally took curious forms. Sometimes it was a slice of ham, served by itself, sometimes stewed apples, sometimes pineapple, tinned of course.

That is the setting of the Rockwell to which I went down from Dublin at the age of twelve. It was a big school even then, about 300 boys from all parts of Ireland and from other places too. In my time we had two from Burma, two from Waterbury, Connecticut, one from Belgium, one from South Africa and one dark stranger from Siam.

On Sundays a slice of fruit cake was served in addition to the usual dinner and this cake, which was much esteemed, formed the currency in which all school bets were made. If you wanted to bet that Rockwell would beat Blackrock you bet "half-a-cake" and if you won you'd receive a half slice from your victim the following Sunday, and eat it before his suffering eyes. Nobody ever bet a whole cake; there are limits to human endurance. On feast days, luxuries were added. Lemonade appeared at dinner, cake and oranges. Barm-brack graced the tea. For supplementary rations the school shop was open, I think, twice a week, and in those days two pence would get you a penny packet of biscuits and twelve caramels.

After dinner, we had recreation till five o'clock when we were either training for matches or playing matches. In between times, we dashed for places in the big handball alley, and the little alley, and in case we weren't getting enough exercise we also played, on the side, Gaelic football, hurling, soccer and whatever else was going.

At five o'clock we went to the Study Hall, not so reluctantly. At seven o'clock we had tea and a break which we spent walking around the quadrangle. At eight we returned to study. At 9.15 there was "Library" during which you could read any book you could grab out of the huge bookcases at the ends of the hall. And at ten we went to bed.

Wednesday was our half-day. On Wednesday classes ceased at 11.30 and there were the rugby matches in which a couple of hundred boys took part, carefully graded as to size, age and ability. These games were refereed by the Fathers, or by prefects, and talent was unlikely to miss being spotted. Competition for places on the teams which played other colleges was fierce.

Sunday was another day on which we had plenty of free time. There was High Mass and Benediction and a special time set apart for writing letters home in the Study hall. Invariably these letters told our parents we were working hard and doing fine and to send along some pocket money, as soon as possible, or sooner.

In the summer term we played cricket and there was the Boat Club, which you paid something extra for the privilege of joining; something big like five shillings. In the boathouse were outriggers and ordinary rowing boats and lovely little one-man canoes in which you could paddle round the islands and up all kinds of lost little waterways to the annoyance of water hens. One of the practical jokes which was current in my time was to place a water hen's egg in a friend's pocket and push up against him accidentally.

I imagine it is unnecessary to say that religious instruction took its rightful place.

The very first class I went to in Rockwell, in the Babies' Division, was conducted by a hallmarked character who was an authority on rabbit-shooting and an authority on Moran's French Grammar. (Fr. Michael Colgan) He brought with him into class a short stick which he called the pen handle and a short black dog called Rex. His homely kindness put us at our ease in our first days in the strange world of school. He taught us the elements of French with great speed and thoroughness. When we were guilty of forgetting points like ne before the verb and pas after it, he appealed to Rex to witness our shame.

My second class was quite different. (Fr. Johnny Byrne) It was an English class in charge of one whom we afterwards knew to be a fine scholar. He was a peculiarly neat and pungent satirist. He seemed to us then a severe and stern-looking priest, but his scathing remarks were looked forward to and respected. He was a vivid contrast to our French teacher.

I remember too, a Latin teacher (Fr. James O'Neill) who made Pliny's villa so real to us that I can still tell you about the central heating plant. There was a teacher of Mathematics (Fr. Patrick Brennan) whose name is a legend. There was a sturdy and lovable priest (Fr. Thomas Naughton) who spent all his spare time trying to get us to love the Irish language, even if we weren't concentrating on it as a subject. There were two German priests vastly different in every way except one. One was a biggish man with a beard (Fr. Christian Schmidt) who loved cricket and looked like W.G. Grace at the wicket and once hit one over the pavilion. He sang songs like Kramhambuli and Paddy Flynn at the school concerts, soirées we called them. The other (Fr. Joseph Muller) was a different type altogether. He was small-sized with a funny little smile that wasn't just on the surface but went the whole way down. All of him was kindness and usefulness. He taught us German by magic; you hardly knew you were working. He rounded us up into the school orchestra; he even got me to play the oboe; and he got the contribution made by this mixed bunch from the playing fields to sound like music. Whenever I talk about Germany these days I can't help thinking of Fr. Schmidt and Fr. Muller.

The person in Rockwell who most impressed Tom Collins was Fr. Johnny Byrne who was a highly effective Dean of Studies and later a rather controversial President. Describing him on another occasion, Collins wrote:

I met Fr Johnny Byrne for the first time in the year 1906 when I was twelve, and I had never met anyone like him. I have never met anyone like him since. Johnny was Dean of Studies at the time. He was also our teacher of English in the long vanished Preparatory Grade. In English, as in other things, Johnny was a purist. He took a lot of trouble with all of us, from the careful to the wild, and he taught us to know what was good, even if we didn't always put his precepts into practice

Fr. John Byrne, Dean of Studies 1900-1908 with a group of prize winners

in our essays. Any class Johnny conducted was well conducted. He had an eye and a presence. He would have been awesome had he not an occasional little Johnnyesque twinkle in his eyes as he made one of his dry little satiric remarks on a passage in an essay, or for that matter, in a text, which didn't do the writer credit…He was a man of great personal dignity, high principle, high courage and fine mind.[58]

A character very popular with students in those days was Fr.Christian Schmidt. When he chose Ireland as his adopted home he became more Irish than the Irish themselves. In his speech he developed the pleasant cadence which one associates with the Glen of Aherlow at the foot of the Galtees. His favourite songs were *O'Donnell Abú, The Donovans* and *Paddy Flynn*. He followed Irish affairs with the deepest interest and identified himself completely with the national view-point.

Fr. Schmidt taught French and German and his pupils appreciated his fatherly concern for their welfare; and that he himself had nothing but the happiest memories of them was always apparent when one asked him if he remembered so-and-so. Fr. Schmidt was a generous contributor to the lighter side of Rockwell. Whenever the lake froze he would give a spectacular display on the skates. In the handball alley he was a constant figure, and a challenge match featuring Fr. Schmidt never failed to draw an enthusiastic gallery. It was, however, as a cricketer that he was best remembered. He was a reliable fielder at any

Fr. Christian Schmidt

position, a fast, sure bowler, and a devastating batsman. He was always at his best at the soirées and after dinner sing-songs. He was a keen supporter of all things Rockwellian, in particular the Rugby Club XV. It is reported that when he noticed a Garryowen player treat a Rockwell player with a lack of respect which was not duly punished by the referee, Fr. Schmidt waited for the scrum to be sufficiently near the touch-line for him to bring his pointed umbrella to bear on the offender's rear end.[59]

Not every aspect of student life in those years was as golden as that portrayed by Tom Collins. (There were never three hundred students in his time.) The education system which then prevailed put pressure on students to perform well academically. The "notes" system kept a regular check on one's performance and the consequences for a student who was considered not to have reached the required standard could be severe. Detention in the study hall during recreation was common. A student with continuous "bad notes" or one who failed more than three subjects in the end-of-term examinations could be detained on the day of the holidays and not allowed home for a day or two after the others.[60] Notes were also given for discipline and at times the most common misdemeanour was smoking.[61] More serious offences, however, merited expulsion.[62]

The fear of sickness was always present. Any illness which was contagious was dreaded in a boarding school and could cause panic. Two outbreaks of scarlet fever caused the deaths of two students. The first was in January 1910 when Patrick Murphy from Ennis, Co. Clare died and the second was in November 1911 when Patrick Keane, who was a scholastic, died.[63] Great precautions were taken when an outbreak of measles occurred in March 1909 and an outbreak of mumps in February 1911.[64] Similar action was taken with outbreaks of influenza in 1913 and 1914.[65]

On Sunday evening, 24th September 1911 when study was due to commence, forty seven senior students and twenty one juniors walked down the back avenue and claimed they were on strike. They were quickly rounded up and marched to the Dean's office. Four were expelled. The strike had been crushed. The boys' retreat began two days later during which some of the strikers went to the President to apologise, while thirty sent him written apologies.[66] It is doubtful if this strike was due to any serious grievance and would appear to have been a prank that misfired.

WORLD WAR I

Few Irish institutions were untouched by the horror which befell Europe from 1914 to 1918. It is not possible to know exactly how many former Rockwell students were involved but it is known there were some. There had been a tradition since the foundation of the College for some past students to follow a military career in the British army. Some may also have answered the call of John Redmond. The following were killed in action at the front: Martin Moroney of Miltown Malbay, William Mallen of Grange, Joe Walsh of Cahir, Patrick Guerin from Kerry and George Mariano of Rangoon. Tom McClure of

Athlone was killed in an air accident in Scotland and Paddy Keohane of
Waterford sank with *The Hawk* on which he was a wireless operator. Among
those who came home alive from the Great War were Tom Dowling of
Balbriggan, Jack and Willie Power of Cashel, Louis Jones of Athlone, Michael
Hunt of Thurles, Jim Duffy from Galway and E.K. Powel who served in the
Royal Navy.[67] Another past student who survived, Arthur Dickens, served in
Egypt and Palestine and when he moved to India he was joined by another
officer, A.P. Kennedy, who had been with him in Rockwell.[68]

At least seven Rockwell past students who were members of the Holy Ghost
Congregation served as army chaplains during World War I. Fr. Bartholomew
Wilson, later Bishop, volunteered as a military chaplain shortly after the
outbreak of war. He served in the 15th Division of the British army. One of his
daring deeds was to bring in from "No Man's Land" five wounded men. He was
awarded the Military Cross and recommended for the V.C. "for conspicuous
gallantry and devotion to duty in action" and was featured for this in the *London
Gazette*. Eventually he was wounded by a shell fragment and had to be invalided
home where he was to serve as Dean of Discipline in Rockwell.

Another future Bishop, Fr. Henry Gogarty, served as chaplain to the troops
in Nairobi and Fr. Patrick Frawley was a chaplain in Sierra Leone. Fr. Bernard
Carey served in the Middle East and Fr. Denis Fahey in Switzerland. The two
O'Brien brothers from Mullinahone were also chaplains, Fr. Thomas in Salonica
and Fr. David in Belgium.

Those war years cannot have been easy for the two German Fathers in
Rockwell at the time, Fr, Joseph Muller and Fr. Christian Schmidt. Fr. Schmidt
maintained that the terms imposed on Germany by the Treaty of Versailles were
a mistake. He was proved to be correct.[69] During the war years the movements
of Fr. Muller and Fr. Schmidt were confined by the government to specified area
within a certain distance of Rockwell. Even after the war the restrictions were
still in force in July 1919. Finally in September 1919 Fr. Schmidt was officially
informed that he was "no longer an alien enemy, but simply an alien" and that
he was free to go wherever he wished for any period not exceeding three
months.[70] It can be assumed that Fr. Muller was given the same latitude. As Fr.
Schmidt cycled his bicycle around South Tipperary he would have enjoyed
telling his many friends about his restrictions.

Summer Sport
The summer term in Rockwell each year was marked by the opening of the
cricket season, swimming and boating on the lake and preparation for the
annual sports. The first swim of the year in April attracted only the brave-
hearted but as the weather improved the swimmers increased. On occasions
when there were relaxations in the study schedule, a swim before bed-time was
enjoyed.[71] The Boat Club usually marked its first outing with the first swim. The
boats on the lake had been in use for the previous thirty years and were
beginning to show the worst of the wear, so in May 1910 Fr. Brennan and Fr.
Colgan set out for Waterford where they purchased a new set. Another purchase

was made the following year. Swimming and boating races on the lake were an attraction for many students.[72]

It was during the summer term that the handball tournaments were completed. Athletic competitions culminated in the annual sports. In previous years the sports had been open to the public with invitations to local dignitaries. But in recent years the sports had been private. It was private in 1912 and lasted for two days when the Ryan brothers of Racecourse were the referees.[73] Tennis was introduced to Rockwell in 1910 when a tennis court for the Fathers was laid out and after a slow start the sport became popular.[74] Its popularity in the Tipperary area may have been due to the success of Lena Rice who won the Wimbledon singles title in 1900. The Rice family lived next to Rockwell on the Cahir side.

While the Fathers were involved in tennis they were also very much involved in cricket. When the Rockwell XI played the Clonmel Asylum in May 1910 in a return match, the team consisted of five Fathers, two prefects and four students. The Fathers on the team were Fr. Schmidt, Fr. Colgan, Fr. O'Neill, Fr. Brennan and Fr. Meagher. The same Fathers were part of the Rockwell team each year up to 1915. Games were played against teams from Cahir and Cashel each year, but no season was complete without a home and away match with Clonmel Asylum. This was due to the fact that the founder and leading player on the Asylum team was Dr. Patrick Heffernan, a past student and friend of Rockwell.[75] (He later wrote a memoir in which he referred to these cricket matches and his days in Rockwell.)[76] In 1914 Rockwell played a home and away match with Clonmel Grammar School.[77] This demonstrated the ecumenical nature of Rockwell, the Clonmel school being under Church of Ireland patronage. Cricket in the South Tipperary area had always been promoted by the military, but the withdrawal of troops from neighbouring towns on the outbreak of World War I in 1914 halted the progress of the sport.

RUGBY
Rugby continued as a popular sport among Rockwell students. Competitive rugby for Rockwell in the Munster championship continued in the senior grade with teams consisting of prefects, outside players and students. In 1908, however, there was debate in the Rockwell Community as to whether students should continue in senior rugby contests. The welfare of students at this level of competition was obviously a matter of concern. It was agreed, however, to leave matters as they were.[78]

Despite the indecision it would seem that in 1909 the focus in Rockwell was more on the schoolboys' team than on the senior. The schoolboys beat Christians College, Cork by a try to nil and beat a Blackrock under18 team by two tries to nil and a Blackrock under 16 team by a try to nil. Both Blackrock matches were played in Rockwell. An under 18 match against Roscrea College followed.[79]

The under 18 players against Blackrock were: Cleary, Power, Murphy, Kelly, O'Connor, Sammon, McGurk, Blackburn, Browne, Cahill, Egan, Fahy,

Heffernan, Hogan and Mc. Mahon. The under 16 players were: M.B. Kennedy, L.Power, P. Leen, Ml. O'Shaughnessy, Moran, Dee, Walsh, Dowling, Foley, J.J. Griffin, Horan, Kelly, Kennedy, McDonnell, J. Ryan.[80]

It was proposed to hold a competition for the first time in 1909 confined to Munster schools with an upper age limit of 19. The Rockwell Community discussed the feasibility of Rockwell entering this competition but felt it was not suitable because most Rockwell students left the College at 18. Because of the age difficulty, most Munster schools either withdrew from the competition or did not enter. Despite its reservations, Rockwell entered and was one of only three schools in the competition, the other two being the Cork schools, Presentation College and Christians College.[81]

On Shrove Tuesday, 1909 Rockwell travelled to Cork to play its very first match in the Munster Colleges Senior Cup and beat Presentation College by three tries to nil. The final against Christians was not played until the end of March and Rockwell travelled again to Cork but with great hope, having already beaten Christians in a challenge in January. The team was accompanied by Fr. Walsh and Fr. Schmidt. Rockwell lost narrowly in its first ever final by one try to nil. The team had to wait for a late train home and did not arrive back in the College until early next morning.[82]

Rockwell won the senior Cup for the first time in 1910. Fr. Walsh, Dean of Discipline, was in charge of the team. There were four teams in the competition, Rockwell together with the two Cork teams of the previous year and North Monastery of Cork, the latter being more famous as a hurling centre. Rockwell had a home venue for the semi-final against North Mon and the game was attended by the College staff and students and a small number of outsiders. On a bitterly cold day Rockwell won by two tries to nil in a good contest.[83] The final against Christians was played in the Mardyke, Cork and the referee was the President of the Irish Rugby Football Union C.W.L. Alexander. Frs Pembroke, Walsh and Colgan and two senior prefects accompanied the team.

Rockwell won by 2 goals (one penalty and a try) to nil. The team which brought the first Munster Schools Cup to Rockwell was: Fullback: Merlehan, three quarters: Kennedy, Kenny, Walsh and Power, halves: Salmon (captain) and Mulcahy, forwards: Blackburn, Stokes, Horgan, Dowling, Egan, Fitzgerlad, Cahill and Casey. The scores came from Stokes and Casey.[84]

Expectations of winning the Cup for the first time had been very high. D.J. O'Connor, a former student, later described the scene on such an occasion:

For us left behind it was a long day of waiting, an endless day. When three o'clock came we realised that our heroes had started their battle for us and Rockwell. As the shadows crept across the campus we tried to picture the play and the result. Six o'clock came and we were in the Big Study trying to focus our minds on cube roots and irregular Latin verbs. It was no go. As the minutes ticked on, our hopes and spirits dropped to deeper depths of despondency. Surely if Rockwell had won we would have had a telegram by now. The clock rang out six thirty. Then there was confusion and uproar. The big glass and wooden doors of the study hall blew open as if impelled by an atomic blast. Fr. Schmidt came through the doors holding aloft a pink telegram. He was exhausted and breathless. Sweat poured down from his brow. He had run all the way from the post office in New Inn with the news. In a body we rushed forward to find what it was all about.[85]

Fr. Pembroke had sent the telegram on this occasion. There was much cheering and schoolboy enthusiasm. The workers lit a bonfire in one of the adjoining fields. The team arrived home in the small hours of the morning and the whole house awoke. The next morning at breakfast the team carried the Cup into the refectory and Fr. Pembroke announced a free day. Five Rockwell players were later picked to play for Munster in the first schools' inter provincial.[86]

Rockwell won the Cup again in 1911. There were only three teams in the competition, Pres, Christians and Rockwell. The two Cork teams played each other in the semi-final with a win for Christians. For the third year in a row Rockwell travelled to the Mardyke, Cork to meet Christians in the final. The Rockwell team consisting of twelve boarders and three scholastics won by twelve points to nil and arrived back in the College at three o'clock the following morning.[87] The team which brought the Cup for the second time to Rockwell was: Fullback: Leen, three-quarters: Kenny, Walsh, Ronan, Power, halves: Duffy and Coyle, forwards: Horgan, Fitzgerald, Dowling, O'Grady, O'Sullivan, Quinlan, Neenan and Kinsella.[88]

For the third year in succession, Rockwell won the Cup in 1912. Again there were only three teams in the competition and the two Cork teams having played in the semi-final Rockwell played Christians in the final for the fourth year in a row and won by eleven points to nil. This win was a surprise to all as the Cork team was regarded very highly.[89] The winning streak came to an end in 1913, however. The final of 1913 between Rockwell and Christians was played in the Markets Field, Limerick and ended in a scoreless draw. The replay was in Cork and Christians won by seven points to five.[90] The team which played in the drawn game was: Fullback: O'Shea, three-quarters: Heslan, Kenny, Hurley, Murphy, halves: Fitzgerald and McDonagh, forwards: Tierney, O'Sullivan, Heffernan, Ryan, Stokes, Fitzgerald, Scully and Hynes. The team in the final was: Full: W.J. Hennebry, three quarters: D. O'Shea, W. Hurley, D.J. Heslan, T. Kenny, halves: M. Dwyer and W. Murphy, forwards: F. Tierney, H. Heffernan, P. O'Sullivan, J.B. Ryan, P. Stokes, R. McDonagh, T. Fitzgerald and P. Jones.[91]

The same three teams took part in the Cup in 1914 and 1915 and Rockwell won in both years. In the semi-final of 1914 Rockwell beat Pres by six points to nil and beat Christians in the final in Limerick by a try to nil.[92] In 1915 it was a repeat of the previous year, Rockwell beating Pres in the semi-final and Christians in the final.[93] Rockwell had established a remarkable record in this competition, winning it five times in its first seven years. Each season it also enjoyed challenge matches against Blackrock College and Cistercian College Roscrea.

Meanwhile the Rockwell senior team continued to take part in Munster competitions. The team which played Landsdowne, a Limerick club, in 1908 included four prefects.[94] The senior team played matches annually against Landsdowne, Garryowen, Clanwilliam, Cork County, Cork University and Blackrock College. A senior Cup match against Garryowen in 1910 generated particular interest. Rockwell College, having played a drawn game with Garryowen at the Markets Field Limerick decided that the replay should be in Clonmel, much to the disapproval of the Limerick side. Garryowen had no alternative but to undertake the journey to Clonmel and accordingly they chartered a special train by which they travelled to Clonmel accompanied by over 470 supporters. The match was played on Magner's field, the scene of many a Cup fight. The playing pitch was well enclosed by a stout wire paling, and the turf was in sound condition, though a trifle uneven. Garryown were very confident because they had dominated play for most of the drawn game. In this replay they dominated the first half but failed to get over the line.

The second half opened sensationally. The Garryowen full-back had his kick blocked down and Rockwell forwards swarmed over the line for a try. The tempo increased immediately and one of the Garryowen players received his marching orders. Garryown frequently attacked with vigour but failed to get over the line. Towards the close of the game, when Garryowen were unable to equalise and the match was lost, their supporters became aggressive and started shouting abuse at the referee. When the final whistle sounded the referee, Mr. O'Regan of University College Cork, was surrounded by the Limerick crowd with a very menacing attitude and would have received rough treatment were it not for the intervention of the police, the Garryowen captain and the father of the Rockwell player, Paddy Stokes, who escorted Mr. O'Regan to the exit and to his hotel. Garryowen unsuccessfully lodged an objection to Rockwell being awarded the match on the grounds that the pitch was not properly enclosed and that spectators encroached on the playing area. The Rockwell team that day was: M. O'Connor, P.J. Kennedy, D.J. Murphy, P. Salmon, J. Power, D. Joy, James Leen, James Mellett, J. English, Bill. Blackburn, W. Heffernan, D.J. Casey, Joseph Horgan, Paddy Stokes, T. Griffiths.[95] Notable members of that team were the prefects, future Archbishop James Leen and future missionaries James Mellett and Joseph Horgan and future international Paddy Stokes. The Rockwell senior team of 1914 included two prefects who were future archbishops. They were Archbishop Charles Heery of Onitsha and Archbishop John McCarthy of Zanzibar.[96]

Irish International Paddy Stokes

Cup winning XV 1914
Front: K. Temple, M. McDonnell.
Seated: P. Kelly, L. Hennessy, J. Barry, D. Heelan, P. Scully, J. McCormack, E. Shanahan.
Back: V. Vaughan, D. Egan, D. Brown, P. Stokes, W. Henebry, J. McCarthy, T. Rowan, E.C. Powell.

* * *

The presidencies of Fr. Pembroke and Fr. Evans had marked a continuation in the formation of future missionaries and high academic standards together with further development of the College infrastructure. They also marked the birth of Rockwell's reputation as a bastion of Munster schools' rugby.

Notes

[1] RCA 1941 p. 52
[2] JNL 12/9/1911.
[3] *Freeman's Journal* 10/9/1912.
[4] *Freeman's Journal* 9/9/1913, 12/9/1914, 11/9/1915.
[5] *Nationalist* 15/9/1909.
[6] *Nationalist* 18/9/1910.
[7] JNL 6/9/1908.
[8] JNL 4/9/1909.
[9] JNL 18/12/1909.
[10] J. Coolahan, *Irish Education: History and Structure*, pp 68-9.
[11] ISR p. 134.

12   RCA 1977, p. 15.
13   JNL 18/5/1909.
14   JNL 25/1/1910, 31/1/1910.
15   RCA 1977, p. 15
16   *Nationalist* 22/6/1910.
17   JNL 10/1/1909.
18   JNL 18/12/1913.
19   *Nationalist* 15/4/1914.
20   *Freeman's Journal* 18/4/1914.
21   *Freeman's Journal* 22/9/1914.
22   JNL 26/11/1909.
23   Journal of the Scholasticaate 1911-1913., 15/1/1912.
24   JNL 23/10/1910.
25   Journal of the Scholasticate 1911-1913, 7/6/1913.
26   JNL 14/11/1909.
27   JNL   1/3/1910.
28   JNL 10/10/1913.
29   J. Coolahan, *Irish Education: History and Structure*, pp 66-7.
30   JNL 23/10/1909, 14/11/1909, 2/12/1909, 14/2/1910, 17/11/1910, 24/11/1910.
31   F. X. Martin and F.J. Byrne (eds), *The Scholar Revolutionary: Eoin MacNeill, 1867-1945, and the Making of the New Ireland*, p. 294.
32   JNL 15/9/1909.
33   *Nationalist* 21/5/1909.
34   J. Coolahan, *Irish Education: History and Structure*, pp 69, 70.
35   JNL 10/10/1909.
36   ISR p. 176.
37   D.G. Marnane, The Road to Soloheadbeg, *Tipperary Historical Journal* 2011, pp 84-126.
38   JNL 20/6/1909.
39   JNL 19/6/1910.
40   *Nationalist* 22/6/1910.
41   ibid
42   *Freeman's Journal* 20/6/1911.
43   JNL 11/2/1910, 25/2/1910, 3/4/1910, 11/4/1910
44   JNL 7/5/1910, 20/5/1910.
45   JNL 17/3/1911.
46   JNL 8/5/1911.
47   JNL 8/12/1911.
48   JNL 21/2/1912, 2/3/1912, 17/3/1912.
49   JNL 31/11/1909, 5/6/1910.
50   Pierce McCan M.P. *Tipperary Historical Journal* 1988 pp 121-132.
51   JNL 5/5/1914.
52   S. O'Donnell, *Clonmel 1900-1932: A History*, pp 253, 256, 259, 267.
53   JNL 14/9/1909, 6/9/1910, 14/9/1910, 16/1/1912, 12/1/1914.
54   RCA passim
55   RCA 1985 p. 151.
56   RCA passim
57   H.Boylan (ed.) *A Dictionary of Irish Biography* p. 73.
58   RCA 1953, pp 71-73.
59   ISR pp 169, 170.
60   JNL 21/12/1909, 23/3/1910.
61   JNL 24/1/1909, 28/2/1909.
62   JNL 21/3/1910, 1/3/1913.
63   JNL 30/1/1910, 2/11/1911.

64 JNL 1/3/1909, 18/2/1911.
65 JNL 19/1/1913, 9/2/1914.
66 JNL 24/9/1911.
67 JNL 25/10/1921.
68 RCA 1970 pp 37-8.
69 ISR passim
70 JNL 1/7/1919, 24/9/1919.
71 JNL 24/5/1910.
72 JNL 5/5/1910, 12/6/1910, 4/5/1911
73 JNL 12/6/1912.
74 JNL 27/4/1910, 4/5/1911.
75 S. O'Donnell, *Clonmel 1900-1932: a History*, p. 164.
76 Heffernan, P., *An Irish Doctor's Memoirs*, (Dublin 1958)
77 JNL 27/5/1912, 10/6/1912.
78 JNL 24/9/1908.
79 JNL 28/1/1909, 2/2/1909, 10/2/1909.
80 *Freeman's Journal* 6/2/1909.
81 JNL 11/2/1909, 13/2/1909.
82 JNL 23/2/1909, 31/3/1909.
83 JNL 11/2/1910, 15/10/1910.
84 *Nationalist* 26/2/1910
85 RCA 1955, pp 74-77.
86 JNL 22/2/1910, 23/2/1910.
87 JNL 21/3/1911.
88 *Nationalist* 25/3/1911.
89 JNL 17/4/1912.
90 JNL 13/3/1913, 9/4/1913
91 *Nationalist* 15/3/1913, 16/4/1913.
92 JNL 14/2/1914, 7/4/1914
93 JNL 11/2/1915, 9/3/1915.
94 JNL 11/11/1908.
95 RCA 1931 pp 21-2.
96 RCA 1946 p. 58.

– 6 –

TROUBLED TIMES
1916-1924

This was a difficult chapter in the history of Rockwell College. Falling farm prices in the aftermath of World War I and circumstances relating to the War of Independence and Civil War led to a fall in student numbers as did the serious disruption to everyday life in South Tipperary during these times. For the second time in its history, the closure of Rockwell was up for discussion.

THE COMMUNITY
Fr. John Byrne succeeded Fr. Hugh Evans as President in 1916 and remained in that position until 1925. Known to his confreres and students as Fr. Johnny, he was born in Clonmel in 1872. He entered Rockwell in 1886 and was a prefect during Dr. Crehan's term as Dean of Studies. Following his studies in France and his ordination in Cobh in 1900, he succeeded Dr. Crehan as Dean of Studies and held that position until 1907. He spent the following nine years as a very popular teacher.[1]

During Fr. Byrne's presidency Fr. James Cotter stepped down as Bursar, having held the position for sixteen years and was succeeded by Fr. John Kingston. The position of Dean of Discipline was held in turn by Fr. Patrick Brennan, Fr. Bartholomew Wilson, Fr. Daniel Leen and the future Superior General of the Congregation Fr. Francis Griffin, while the Deans of Studies were Dr. James O'Neill, Fr. John Kingston, Fr. John McGrath and Fr. Daniel Murphy

Fr. John Byrne	**Fr. Daniel Leen**	**Fr. Francis Griffin,**
President 1916-1925	*Dean of Discipline 1919-1923*	*Dean of Discipline 1923-1925*

who took up the position in 1924. The Directors of St. Joseph's were Fr. John English, Fr. Patrick Walsh and Fr. John McCarthy.

Apart from the Fathers who held special positions there were usually six or seven other Fathers in the Community who were engaged in teaching. The two German Fathers, Fr. Muller and Fr. Schmidt were still there and in 1913 they were joined by their countryman Fr. Charles Meyer who had returned from the missions and was to teach in Rockwell until 1922 when he departed for Trinidad. Fr. Michael Colgan had been in Rockwell since 1897 and was still a popular member of the teaching staff. Fr. John English taught English and Maths from 1914 to 1916 and was Director of St.Joseph's from 1917

Fr. Michael Colgan
French teacher.

to 1918. Fr. Daniel Egan continued in Rockwell from 1903 until his untimely death in 1922. Fr. Michael Meagher from Ballingarry, Co. Limerick on his return from the missions taught in Rockwell from 1913 to 1916. Fr. Patrick McAllister from Glenravel, Co Antrim served in Rockwell from 1917 to 1924 and attended many of the wounded during the War of Independence and Civil War. Fr. Louis Ward from Donegal served for a year in Rockwell on his return from Nigeria in 1921. Dr. David Heelan joined the Rockwell Community in 1924.

In Fr. Byrne's presidency there were thirteen Brothers in Rockwell, some of whom had been there for a long time. Br. Patrick looked after the shop and Br. John Baptist was sacristan. Br. Nicophorus continued as tailor and Br.Silas as cobbler. Br. Elimien was cook while Br. Finbar was in charge of the Fathers' refectory and Br. Albert looked after the boarders' refectory. Br. Brandon was in charge of the linen room and Br. Malachy of the bookshop. Br. Dalmas was plumber while Br Canice was in charge of the dairy and poultry and Br. Kieran looked after the garden,

Three long serving members of the Community died in these years. Fr. James Cotter had come to Rockwell as a student in 1867 and following his ordination returned to Rockwell where he spent the rest of his life. He served as Dean of Studies and Bursar and in many other capacities before his death in 1922. Br. Hippolyte Matasse who had been in Rockwell since its foundation in 1864, fulfilling many duties, died in 1916. Br. Silas Laffan died in 1922. He had spent all his religious life in Rockwell since his appointment in 1868. He was in charge of building the new wing which bears his name. He served in several other capacities and in later life he was the cobbler. Fr. John Stephens, who had been President for a short while, died in 1916. Four Brothers who had spent most of their lives on the missions before retiring to Rockwell, died in those years; Br Edmond McSweeney and Br Tobias Tobin in 1918, Br Virgillius Ryan in 1920 and Br John Baptist Hourigan in 1924. Br Edmond McSweeney, who had spent much of his life in Trinidad and Zanzibar before retiring to Rockwell in 1904, died in 1918. Br. Tobias Tobin, who had retired to Rockwell from the missions, also died in 1918. Br. John Baptist Hourigan, who retired to Rockwell from the missions, died in 1924.

THE TROUBLES

Rockwell did not escape the disruption and emotion which followed the Easter Rising in Dublin. The execution of former teacher Thomas MacDonagh had a particular resonance. So too did the execution of the young Con Colbert whose five first cousins from West Limerick had been in Rockwell between 1913 and 1922. The personal body-guard to the executed leader, Seán Mac Diarmada, was Eamonn Dore, a native of Glin, Co. Limerick who had been in Rockwell from 1912 to 1914. The roundup of suspects in the immediate aftermath of the Rising was also sensed in Rockwell with the arrest of the Irish teacher, Seamus O'Neill early one morning.[2] He was one of a number of suspects from South Tipperary lodged initially in Cork Prison. The majority of these were later interned in Frongoch but O'Neill was sent to Lewes Prison.[3] Despite these events, 1916 was a normal school year in Rockwell. So too was the following year 1917, although the change in public opinion, which followed the Rising and executions, was in evidence when the Rockwell students were given a free day to celebrate the victory of Count Plunkett in the Roscommon election. And when O'Neill was released and returned to the class room he was given a rousing reception by the students.[4] An influential voice which did not share these sentiments or enthusiasm, however, was that of Archbishop Harty who had consistently urged support for John Redmond's party.[5]

Public opinion remained unchanged throughout 1918 and was reflected in Rockwell with the *Rockwell Journal*, which was a diary of the daily life of the College, now recorded in the Irish Language and showing enthusiasm for the growth of Sinn Féin and especially for the election of the imprisoned Pierce McCan in the December General Election.[6] The mood was more sombre in March 1919, however, with the death from flu in Gloucester Prison of Pierce McCan. The President, Fr.Byrne, and two more Fathers met his funeral cortege in Thurles and more Rockwell Fathers were in Dualla to receive his remains and to officiate at his High Mass the following day. They were also in attendance at Requiem Masses for Pierce McCan in New Inn and Fethard.[7]

Over the next few years Rockwell was unlucky to be located in an area where there was intense activity by the IRA and Crown forces. It was located in an area only a few miles distant from three RIC. barracks in New Inn, Clerihan and Rosegreen which were the target of the IRA. In the final three months of 1920 thirty two members of the Crown forces and sixteen IRA members were killed or wounded in Tipperary, mainly in the South Riding.[8] When three soldiers were killed and five wounded in an ambush in the Rockwell locality near Thomastown it was feared that reprisals could take place close to the College.[9]

In September 1920 Rockwell was raided by a party of Lancers, numbering about eighty, who completely surrounded the College. Soldiers held up everyone and having searched them let them go. A party of soldiers entered the main building and searched many rooms, especially the room of Seamus O'Neill who had been arrested again at Rosegreen a few days earlier. The farmyard, outhouses and wooded areas on the grounds were all searched. The entire operation took about three hours.[10] A few days later the Rockwell houses in Carrigeen, where some of the Brothers and farmyard staff lived, were raided by the military.[11] And a few months later when a lorry of soldiers came up part of the back avenue it was evident that Rockwell was under constant surveillance.[12]

The introduction of martial law in Tipperary in December 1920 severely restricted movement around Rockwell and the strike of railway workers regularly interrupted the arrival of newspapers and post with a consequent feeling of isolation. Further isolation followed the trenching of what was known locally as the Rockwell Bridge located on the road to Cashel a few hundred yards from the College front gates. Indeed the state of the country was so disturbed in December 1920 that some parents requested that their sons be allowed home a week before the scheduled Christmas holidays; and midnight Mass on Christmas Eve which was usually attended by people from the district had to be cancelled for visitors.[13]

Disturbances continued into 1921. Movement was greatly curtailed and newspapers and post went undelivered because of the continuous trenching of roads and bridges. The road from Cashel to Golden was trenched in January and the Rockwell Bridge was trenched again in February and again in April and on both occasions Rockwell workmen, at the request of the County Council, helped to fill in the trenches. The Boytonrath Bridge was blown up in May and when the Rockwell Bridge was trenched yet again in June a convoy of military lorries halted there and the soldiers commandeered some of the Rockwell goalposts from the nearby playing fields to help them cross over.[14]

There was intense military activity in the Rockwell neighbourhood at the end of May and early June 1921. When six students who had been convalescing in the Infirmary decided to take a walk in the nearby field they were rounded up by a passing military convoy and ordered to disperse. In the afternoon of 8th June a party of Crown forces numbering about fifty and consisting of Black and Tans and RIC searched the College. Most of the troops remained outside while the students' dining hall and the Fathers' corridor were searched. The raid lasted about half an hour and when the troops had departed it was discovered that the statues of the Blessed Virgin and St. John at the Rock had been shattered.[15]

The Truce was declared in July 1921 and some work was carried out in filling in trenches and making bridges passable. The Truce period was also used in many places to disinter the remains of IRA men who had been given a secret burial. These were now re-interred with great solemnity. One such ceremony was the re-interment of the former O/C of the 5th Battalion, Commandant Denis Sadleir, who had been killed accidentally by a comrade's rifle shortly before the Truce. His remains were removed from a temporary resting place in Grangemockler and re-interred in the family plot in Drangan on 11th August 1921.[16] Denis Sadleir was a past-student of Rockwell and his funeral was attended by a number of the Fathers.[17]

The situation in the Rockwell area was relatively calm following the Truce. In September, however, a section of the IRA took up their quarters on the Rockwell property in Carrigeen and acted as police of the district. One of the Rockwell farm hands was arrested by the IRA and detained at Carrigeen for some misdemeanour. After a short detention he had his locks shorn off and was released. Seamus Robinson, who was in command of the 2nd Southern Division of the IRA and James Flynn, a recent past-student, called to meet the President, probably to assure him that order would be maintained. There was a feeling of relief in Rockwell when the Anglo-Irish Treaty was signed and the students were given a half day in celebration.[18]

Not everyone was celebrating the Treaty, however, as it had soon become an extremely divisive issue. It was important for Rockwell therefore that it not be seen to be taking sides. That was not easy when two of the most vociferous Anti-Treaty members of Dáil Éireann had Rockwell connections. Eamon de Valera was known to have been a teacher in Rockwell and Cathal Brugha was brother in-law of Rockwell's Bursar, Fr. John Kingston. Adding to the difficulty were two members of the farmyard staff, Patsy Carey and John O'Brien who were loud in their denunciation of the Treaty. O'Brien was even known in the locality by his nickname "de Valera".

The situation in the Rockwell area in early 1922 became so lawless that the O/C 2nd Battalion, 3nd Tipperary Brigade, IRA, ordered that "owing to the numerous acts of lawlessness, destruction and commandeering of property" the area come under martial law. The area affected included the parishes of Kilfeacle, Golden, New Inn, Cashel, Dualla and Ballyfowloo.[19] A tense situation in Rockwell under martial law cannot have been relieved when at 9. p.m. on the night of St. Patrick's Day a motor approached up the front avenue and out of it stepped Eamon de Valera, Seán MacBride, Cathal Brugha and Joe MacDonagh T.D, a past student and younger brother of the executed 1916 leader Thomas MacDonagh. The four stayed the night and on the following morning, before setting out for an anti-Treaty rally in Kilkenny, they signed autographs for the students who were given a free day on their behalf.[20]

South Tipperary continued in a state of lawlessness throughout 1922 with very poor communications because of trenched bridges and broken railway lines. Conditions were so bad that most of the Rockwell Fathers spent the month of July in the safety of Blackrock College. This was at a time when two columns of Republicans, of some thirty men each, made their way into the College and commandeered one of the dormitories for a night. In early November a party of Free State soldiers surrounded the house of William Heffernan of Marlhill near the back gate of the College. In the house was Commandant Michael Sadleir, the O/C. of the 2nd Battalion, a past student and a brother of Denis whose funeral the previous year had been attended by Rockwell Fathers. Michael was shot and as he lay dying Fr. McAllister and the Rockwell nurse were sent for to attend to him. He died the next day and Rockwell Fathers attended his funeral in Drangan.[21]

Events during 1922 revealed that Rockwell past-students were involved on both sides of the Civil War. In November when six Republican prisoners were captured at nearby Ballydoyle, two of them, Gus McCarthy of Fethard and Andy Moloney of New Inn, were past students, while at the same time the Quinlan brothers of Golden were in command of the Free State troops in Cashel. Other past students on the Free State side included William Keane of Galway, Denis O'Donovan and John O'Leary of Bantry and John McGroarty of Killorgan. Fionán Lynch and Bill Quirke were in senior positions on either side, the former on the Free State side. And the first past student on the Free State side who was a casualty was Michael Hogan of Golden who was shot while driving a Free State ambulance in Dublin. Another past student General Liam Deasy on the Republican side had called in vain for an end to hostilities in February 1923.[22]

Fionán Lynch

The leader of the Third Tipperary Brigade, Dinny Lacey, was killed in the Glen of Aherlow on 18th February 1923 and earlier that morning Rockwell was raided. A student at that time remembered troops barging into the Chapel during Mass.[23] Following the death of Dinny Lacey Free State troops were in the ascendant and for the remainder of that year they proceeded to round up Republicans in the South Tipperary area. By the end of the year they had made eight raids on Rockwell College, the overriding motive of their searches being their

Bill Quirk

belief that Eamon de Valera was in hiding there. In early March they searched the grounds and the servants' quarters. Two weeks later they searched the farmyard and the area around St. Joseph's and arrested John O'Brien (aka de Valera) In mid April a detachment from Clonmel arrived at 10 o'clock on a Saturday night and searched the house for two hours. They arrived back at 5 o'clock in the morning and remained on the grounds until after the People's Sunday Mass. They made three further searches during the month of May, one at 4 o'clock in the morning, and as in all cases except when John O'Brien was arrested, no prisoners were taken. The final search took place at the beginning of October and when they were assured by Fr. McGrath that no "wanted men" were in residence, they departed.[24]

The ending of the Civil War was a relief to Rockwell.

STUDENT HEALTH

There were occasional outbreaks of influenza in Rockwell in previous times but none to compare with the epidemic that ravaged the western world between the spring of 1918 and early 1919. Before that outbreak, however, there were outbreaks of flu and scarlet fever in Rockwell in February 1917. In the middle of the month fourteen students were initially sent to the infirmary suffering from flu, but the numbers rapidly grew and classes were reduced to half their size. The outbreak was contained however. Later in the month four cases of scarlet fever were diagnosed and all four victims were removed to Cashel hospital. The authorities were advised that if the situation got worse, all students would have to be sent home. Fortunately this was not necessary.[25]

In mid-October 1918 when a long spell of very bad weather was being reported and when the flu was rampant throughout the country, the first cases were reported in nearby Bansha and Golden. It was decided therefore that all day students should stay at home for two weeks or until further notice. The first victim in the College was one of the lay teachers. It was decided as a precaution to close all entrances to the College and that no visitors be allowed enter, not even parents. The People's Mass on Sundays was discontinued and when a neighbour died it was decided that none of the Fathers should attend the funeral in New Inn for fear of getting the flu. By the end of October no student had so far contracted the flu but a sister of Fr. Meagher and a sister of Fr. McAllister had died from it. One student had become seriously ill, suffering from meningitis and his parents were asked to take him home.[26] Further outbreaks of flu were reported in the immediate neighbourhood of the College in early November but

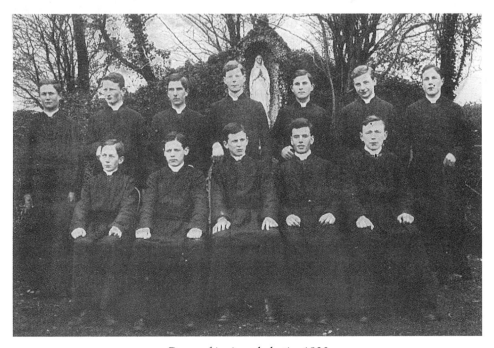

Group of junior scholastics 1920

The Fathers 1921/22
Seated: *Frs. James O'Neill, John Kingston, John McGrath, Joseph Byrne (visiting). Laurence Healy,
Christian Schmidt, Patrick McAllister*
Standing: *Frs. Patrick Brennan, Michaael Colgan, Daniel Leen, Peter Meagher, Louis Ward, John McCarthy.*

the precautions taken in the College had been successful and no case of flu had been reported by the time the students went home for the Christmas holidays.[27]

The College re-opened on 13th January 1919 and within a few days a number of Fathers and teachers and up to forty students were in bed with flu but none of them was in danger. When Nurse Armstrong died and her replacement fell seriously ill, Br. Malachy and Portuguese Br. Protasio stepped into the breach.[28] It was decided however to close the College exactly a week after it had re-opened. Students who were well were sent home immediately and those in the infirmary went home as soon as they recovered. Rockwell remained closed for more than six weeks as a second bout of flu raged throughout the country. The College re-opened on 25th February and parents were informed that to make up for lost time there would be no Easter holidays in 1919. [29]

On re-opening, precautions against flu continued to be taken. In April when the Rockwell hurlers were due to play Boherlahan the match was cancelled when it was discovered that there had been an outbreak of flu in the Boherlahan area. It was at that time too that one of the scholastics, Paddy O'Connor, suffered seriously from an illness which does not seem to have been the flu. He was attended to by Dr. Dowling from Tipperary Town and Dr. Cusack from Cashel. He died on Easter Monday and following his funeral Mass the following day the students lined the back avenue as the hearse carrying his remains set out for his home in Tarbert, Co. Kerry.[30]

The flu had disappeared from most parts of Ireland by the end of 1919 but in May 1920 there was an outbreak of mumps in Rockwell. There were seven cases in all and the patients were sent into quarantine in what was popularly known as the "Home Rule" dormitory and the problem was contained. In December there was an outbreak of a mild flu with nearly forty students confined to the infirmary.[31]

A case of scarlet fever was reported in April 1921 and another outbreak of mumps the following month. The following three years were free of any serious illness. In May 1924 a prefect who was a native of Cahir, William Law, died from tuberculosis. His funeral Mass was celebrated in Rockwell.[32]

DEVELOPMENT
Following World War I coal became very expensive and scarce. It had been the source of heating in Rockwell. Carbide, which was a requisite for the gas lighting system in the College, also became difficult to obtain. On two occasions when the gas lighting failed due to a shortage of carbide, the students, much to their delight, were sent to bed early.[33] A more secure system of lighting was therefore called for and electricity seemed the answer.

A dynamo and an oil engine were purchased and installed in the sawmill shed in June 1922 and in mid September Rockwell had its first electric light.[34] The light was initially very faint and blackouts, which were a great source of joy to students, were common in the early months. Electricity was installed in St. Joseph's in January 1923.[35] To compensate for the shortage of coal it was decided to use more timber in the furnace. A programme of tree felling in the area of the Rock and opposite the front house was carried out throughout 1920 and early 1921.[36] This was accompanied by a programme of tree planting along the back avenue and adjacent to the lake.[37]

A new development on the Rockwell farm in 1917 was the appointment of Mr. Enright as farm steward and an assistant steward who took charge of the poultry and pigs.[38] Flower beds and shrubs were planted on the front avenue in 1919 and tarmac was laid on the front and back avenues for the first time in 1923.[39] Rockwell entered into a new era in 1924 with the purchase of a motor car and the training of Mr Luke Lyons as chauffeur.[40]

IN THE FREE STATE
Rockwell College, like all educational establishments, had to adjust to the new circumstances when the administration of the educational services was taken over by the Provisional Government of the Irish Free State on 1 February 1922. On 8th June 1923 the Board of Commissioners of Intermediate Education was dissolved and was replaced by the Department of Education. A fundamental change was the new system of funding schools. Grants were no longer to be payable on examination results but were to be paid on a capitation basis for pupils who followed an approved course of study. In June 1924 the Intermediate Education (Amendment) Act was passed and this allowed changes in the examination system and the programme of instruction. Under the new system the three grades of examination were abolished and were replaced by two certificate examinations, the Intermediate and Leaving Certificates. A number of scholarships, tenable for two years, were awarded by the state on the results of the Intermediate Certificate.[41]

In these years of transition between 1916 and 1924 there were many students in Rockwell who were later prominent. Three future members of the Congregation were students then; Phil Judge, who spent eight years in Nigeria before his untimely death in 1942, came to Rockwell as a student in 1922; Tom Maher from nearby Lagganstown where his father was school principal, also came in 1922 and Seán Nealon, who was to spend much of his life in Rockwell had come from his native Toomevara in 1921.

Two future leading surgeons were students then; Andy Butler was a student from 1916 to 1918 and James J. Maher from Ardmayle in the parish of Boherlahan was on the 1918 Harty Cup team. There were future academics among the students then; Tomás Ó Laoi did his Senior Grade at Rockwell in 1922 and is best remembered as the fair-haired stalwart of the Harty Cup fifteen and the athletic team which cleaned up at the Schools contest at Croke Park. He won five gold medals on that occasion and later became Professor of History and Geography at St. Patrick's Training College, Drumcondra. He broadcast the first running commentary in Irish of the Munster versus Leinster hurling final at Croke Park on St. Patrick's Day 1939. Michael V. Duignan from Catlebar did his Leaving Certificate in 1924 and later became Professor of Celtic Archaeology at University College Galway. Donal McCarthy, future president of University College Cork sat his Leaving Cert in June 1925. He obtained first place in Ireland in several subjects and first place in the Cork county scholarship. Donal was an outstanding hurler when in Rockwell as was his brother Terry.[42]

Niall Harrington came to Rockwell in 1916. He was son of Tim Harrington, former Lord Mayor of Dublin and one of the faithful followers of Parnell. Niall later became a prominent member of the Free State army. Thomas Gerard Clarke from Ballybunion came to Rockwell in 1917. He was nephew of Philip Clarke, a member of the citizen Army killed in action during Easter Week 1916. He was later State solicitor for Kerry. Denis Jones, who represented Clare in Dáil Éireann for many years was a student from 1919 to 1924 and future Senator John J. Nash took Senior Grade in 1923.[43]

Sport

Sporting facilities for Rockwell students were good and afforded them plenty of activity with house leagues throughout the year. Handball continued to be very popular and in the Summer term croquet was played. Rockwell continued to produce some fine athletes. At the All Ireland Schools and Colleges Sports in Croke Park in May 1922 the two most successful schools were St. Finian's College Mullingar and Rockwell College. In the final of the senior relay the Rockwell team of W.F Byrnes, J. Scanlon and Tomás Ó Laoi, beat Drogheda C.B.S. Tomás Ó Laoi came first in the senior 200 and 400 metres and in the long jump, and T.J. Moloney was first in the 110 hurdles. J. Scanlon won the hop step and jump.[44]

Billiards was a popular indoor sport when the weather was unfavourable and the large room on the bottom floor of the newly built Library Wing was reserved for billiards. In February 1922 Rockwell purchased a billiard table complete with balls and cues for the bargain price of £35. It was on offer at an auction in the military barracks in Cahir when the British Army was vacating the town.[45]

Since the Munster Schools rugby competition commenced in 1909 there had only been three schools taking part, (except for North Monastery in 1910), they being Presentation Brothers Cork, Christian Brothers Cork and Rockwell and each year Presentation had been beaten in the semi-final by one of the other two and each year the final was played between Rockwell and Christians. The same trend continued in 1916 and 1917.

In 1916 Rockwell beat Presentation but lost in the final to Christians in a replay, the first match finishing with three points each. The replay was won controversially by Christians by a try to nil, Rockwell claiming that the referee had ended the match ten minutes before the due time. Despite the defeat, seven Rockwell players were picked to represent Munster.[46]

Rockwell won the Cup for the sixth time in 1917, having had a bye to the final against Christians. Rockwell won by two tries to nil and some of the players were: P. Breen (capt) E. O'Reilly, B. McGlade, J. Walsh, P. Burke, J. Breen, J. Lyons, H. Harrington, J. O'Donnell, M. Davin, J Arrigan, M. Ryan The tries were scored by Davin and Ryan. Eight of that team were chosen to play for Munster. Fr. Meagher was in charge of the team. There was great rejoicing over that victory. The following morning the team carried the Cup around the lake before presenting it to the President at the front door. For the first time ever the Rockwell team had travelled to the Mardyke in Cork for that match by charabanc, which was an early form of bus.[47] Rockwell had to wait another eleven years before its next victory in the Cup.

It was in October 1917 that a notable decision was taken about sport in Rockwell. Cricket and Rugby were to be replaced by hurling and Gaelic football. This was obviously a reaction to the British Army personnel who had been promoters of cricket and rugby in the region. From September to Christmas Gaelic football was to be played and from January to June hurling was the game.[48] The Munster Council of the Gaelic Athletic Association presented a Cup in 1917 for competition among colleges playing Gaelic football. Rockwell travelled to Kilmallock to play St. Brendan's College Killarney in the semi-final of that competition and won by 2-5 to 0-3. The final against St. Colman's College Fermoy was again played in Kilmallock and Rockwell were the surprise winners by 2-5 to 0-3. The team which brought the first ever Munster Schools Gaelic Football Cup to Rockwell Was: J. O'Reilly, J. Lyons (captain), J. Moran, N. Moroney, T. Ryan, C.M. Vaughan, J. Quinn, W. McCarthy, P. O'Dwyer, T. O'Callaghan, M. Costigan, M. Fox, A. Hughes, M. Quinn, J. Healy.[49] Fr. Meagher and Fr. Leen were in charge of the team. So two football trophies won by Rockwell in 1917 sat beside each other the front parlour, the Munster Schools Rugby Cup and the Munster Schools Gaelic Football Cup. Rockwell won the Munster Colleges Gaelic Football Cup for the second time in May 1919 by defeating St.Colman's College Fermoy the only other team in the competition.[50] In the next few years there is no record of any Munster Schools

Cup games and Rockwell Gaelic footballers in the first term each year confined themselves to games against local clubs Cahir, Cashel and Fethard.

In January 1918 it was the turn of hurling. Archbishop Harty had presented a Cup for hurling to be competed for by Munster schools. Like the rugby and Gaelic football competitions in those years, very few schools competed but Rockwell never shied from competition. In the 1918 semi-final in Thurles Rockwell defeated Cistercian College Roscrea by 3-3 to 3-1. A month later Rockwell were back in Thurles for the first final of the Harty Cup which was played in the presence of the archbishop himself who threw in the ball at the start of play. The opponents were Christian College, Cork, the old rugby rivals. It was a fine game which Rockwell won by 5-5 to 3-1. The Cup and medals were presented by the archbishop to the winners after the game. The team which brought the first ever Harty Cup to Rockwell was: J. Daly, M. Collins, E. O'Donnell, M. Fox, K. Egan, J. Quinn (captain), M. Quinn, P. Power, W. Heron, W. McCarthy, T. Ryan, T. Lynch, T. O'Connor, J. Maher, W. Ryan. On the way home the team paraded through Cashel and on the following morning paraded around the lake. Fr. Leen was in charge of the team.[51] In September 1918 Rockwell took part in a sports in Croke Park organised by the GAA and took home a Cup and seven medals.[52]

Rockwell lost to Thurles C.B.S. in the semi-final of the Harty Cup of 1919 by 6-1 to 4-0, blaming the defeat to the flu which had been rampant in the College. The Rockwell team was the bigger of the two, but the Thurles boys were more active.[53] Rockwell got revenge over Thurles in 1920 by beating them by 5-7 to 4-0 but lost in the semi-final to Limerick C.B.S. by 4-1 to 2-4.[54] The Rockwell team which beat Thurles C.B.S. in 1920 was: P. Power (captain), J. Crowe, P. Gillmore, W. Croke, J. O'Leary, J. Donovan, J. Daly, M. O' Rourke, T. Gillmore, J. Geoghan, G. O'Connell, J. Brett, P. O'Dwyer, J. Slattery, E. Hickey. And the referee was Mr. John Leahy of the famed Toberadora hurling family.[55]

There is no record of any Harty Cup matches in 1921 but the following year Fr. Leen hired a bus in Clonmel to take the team to Knocklong for the final of the Harty Cup against St. Munchins which Rockwell lost by one point.[56] In preparation for Harty Cup matches Rockwell had regular challenge matches in those years against the Boherlahan junior hurlers.

Rockwell won the Harty Cup for the second time in 1923. When Rockwell defeated Thurles C.B.S. in the semi-final in March that year at Thurles, the archbishop himself was among the spectators. The final was also played in Thurles and Rockwell easily defeated Limerick C.B.S. by 5-3 to 2-1. That match attracted a big crowd in Thurles and before the match the teams were paraded round the field by the Workmen's Band from Limerick. The winning team was: Brosnihan, Chawke, Coll, Duffy, Fleming, Foley, Hackett, Hickey, McCall, McCarthy, Poole, O'Connell, Ryan, Sheehan.[57]

Fr. Leen had managed the Rockwell team to three Harty Cup titles and he was surprised in May 1923 when he was invited to take the team to Croke Park to play the Leinster champions, Cistercian College Roscrea, in the All Ireland

Schools' Hurling Championship final. Roscrea had beaten St. Kieran's College Kilkenny in the Leinster final but put up a poor show against Rockwell who won easily by 6-1 to 1-0. The Rockwell scores came from Sweeney, Brosnihan, Foley, Tobin, Sheehan and Hickey while the Rockwell goalkeeper, Fleming, was reliable. The Rockwell team stayed overnight in Blackrock College and on the following morning lost in a match to their sister College.[58]

For the third time Rockwell won the Harty Cup in 1924. Rockwell beat North Mon in the semi-final in Thurles. And for the second year in succession Rockwell beat Limerick C.B.S. in the final by 7-3 to 3-4. The leading Rockwell players on that occasion were Powell, Dunphy, Kennedy and Gahan.[59] A special train from Cashel was hired to take the students to Thurles and a number of Fathers, including the Provincial who was in Rockwell at the time, motored there. The team, headed by the College band, paraded through Cashel on the way home.[60] Roscrea refused to return to Croke Park in June 1924 for the All Ireland final against Rockwell, so the match was awarded to Rockwell and the medals arrived in the College the following October.[61] For the second year in a row, therefore, Rockwell were declared All Ireland Colleges Hurling Champions.

A Crisis

The Rockwell Journal on 20th January 1924 recorded "We are working under depressing conditions. Our numbers have dwindled. The sword of Damocles hangs over us for the question of closing the College has been revisited." This reference to the "revisit" was to a similar crisis in 1899 when there had been a dramatic drop in student numbers and when it was proposed that the secondary school be closed and that Rockwell become a senior seminary.

That Rockwell had reached a crisis in January 1924 is evident from the dramatic drop in student numbers over the previous years. (Table 6.1). The fall in numbers of course led to a fall in revenue and so it was necessary to increase the annual fee. For many years this fee had been £30 but by 1919 it had been raised to £40.[62] Many questions were raised as to the reason for the fall in numbers. The Rockwell Journal attributed it to the slump in farmers' profits which followed World War I, to the unsettled state of the country in recent years and to "our reputation for die-hard republicanism.[63]

TABLE 6.1. STUDENT POPULATION 1920-1925

Year	Boarders	Scholastics
1916-17	224	12
1918-19*	182	27
1920-21	150	44
1921-22	125	36
1922-23	100	25
1923-24	101	24
1924-25	85	36

* There were 15 day pupils in 1918-19.
Source: JNL 28/9/1918, 3/12/1923, 19/9/1924.

The slump in farmers' profits was a valid reason. By 1920 the boom years of the First World War, when agricultural prices had been high, had given way to an economic recession made the more severe by the turbulent years of revolution.[64] Indeed it was accepted in Rockwell that the drop in wool and bacon prices spelt a loss to the College farm.[65] When it is considered that a large number of Rockwell students down through the years came from the farming areas of Munster, the drop in student numbers is understandable. The unsettled state of the country was also a factor since much of the fighting, especially during the Civil War was located in South Tipperary. The political reputation of Rockwell was no more than an inevitable perception as it seems likely that the Community and staff reflected the divided shades of public opinion on the Treaty.

The future of Rockwell would obviously be influenced by the Provincial of the Congregation. The Provincial at the time was Dr. Joseph Byrne, younger brother of the President of Rockwell, Fr. Johnny. He was very familiar with the Rockwell scene, having been a student there with Thomas MacDonagh. He had been a student of great ability and later studied in Rome where he obtained doctorates in philosophy and theology and where he was ordained in 1903. Having worked on the missions in Sierra Leone and the United States, he was appointed Provincial in 1922. During the Civil War, Dr. Byrne was in close contact with Eamon de Valera in an effort to work out a cessation of hostilities and it was he who

Dr. Joseph Byrne

arranged the meeting between de Valera and the Papal Envoy, Monsignor Luzio in the hope of reaching a settlement.[66]

Dr. Byrne was greatly concerned about the financial state of the Congregation and would have been kept in touch about the finances of Rockwell by the Provincial Bursar Fr. John Stafford who since 1920 had been arriving in Rockwell on his motorcycle on frequent occasions to check the books. Dr. Byrne concluded that Rockwell should be closed as a college and that it become the central house of formation for the Congregation. To that end he produced a booklet which reviewed the future development of the Congregation.[67]

Dr. Byrne's booklet was received by the Rockwell Community with an accompanying letter which stated that the matter would be discussed at a Provincial Chapter in Blackrock College on 22nd April.1924.[68] Meanwhile a committee of five was set up to interview the Fathers individually and to seek their views on the matter. One person who had expressed a determined opposition to the closure of Rockwell was the Archbishop of Cashel and Emly,

Dr. Harty.[69] The matter was finally resolved at the Chapter when Dr. Byrne's proposal was resoundingly defeated by twenty nine votes to nine.[70] Rockwell College had been saved for the second time in its history and it was in Rockwell that Dr. Byrne, who later became Bishop of Kilimanjaro, enjoyed the last years of his life until his death in 1961.

Notes

[1] ISR p. 101.
[2] JNL 4/5/1916.
[3] S. O'Donnell, *Clonmel 1900-1932: a History*, p 275.
[4] JNL 6/2/1917, 16/11/1917, 26/11/1917.
[5] J. Aan de Wiel, *The Catholic Church in Ireland 1914-1918: War and Politics*, p. 98.
[6] JNL 1918 passim
[7] JNL 9/3/1919, 11/3/1919, 26/3/1919, 3/4/1919.
[8] J. Augusteijn, The Operations of South Tipperary IRA 1916-1921, *Tipperary Historical Journal* 1996 pp 145-163.
[9] JNL 28/10/1920
[10] *Freeman's Journal* 21/9/1920, *Nationalist* 23/9/1920.
[11] JNL 28/9/1920
[12] JNL 19/12/1920.
[13] JNL 13/12/1920, 25/12/1920, 30/12/1920.
[14] JNL 24/1/1921, 18/2/1921, 25/4/1921. 19/5/1921, 15/6/1921.
[15] JNL 18/5/1921, 30/5/1921, 8/6/1921.
[16] An tAthair Colmcille, The third Tipperary Brigade: From Truce to Civil War, *Tipperary Historical Journal* 1990, pp 9-26.
[17] JNL 11/8/1921.
[18] JNL 29/9/1921, 9/11/1921, 25/11/1921, 9/12/1921.
[19] An tAthair Colmcille, op. cit.
[20] JNL 17/3 and 18/3/1922.
[21] An tAthair Colmcille, op. cot. JNL 3 and 7/11/1922.
[22] JNL 9/11/1922, 10/2/1923.
[23] Submission of Frank Madden whose uncle was the student mentioned. 14/2/2013
[24] JNL 3/3, 16/3, 14/4, 15/4, 7/5, 13/5, 17/5, 1/10/1923.
[25] JNL 13/2, 14/2, 15/2, 19/2, 20/2, 27/2/1917.
[26] JNL 13/10, 22/10, 27/10/1918.
[27] JNL 3/11, 8/11, 11/11/1918.
[28] ISR p. 34.
[29] JNL 13/1, 18/1, 19/1/20/1, 25/2/1919.
[30] JNL 7/4, 13/4, 21/4, 22/4/1919.
[31] JNL 20/5, 21/5, 7/12, 11/12/ 1920.
[32] JNL 27/4, 6/5, 17/5, 23/5/1921, 18/3, 25/5, 26/5/1924.
[33] JNL 17/11/1916, 9/10/1917.
[34] JNL 22/6, 19/9/1922.
[35] JNL 12/10, 17/10, 27/11/1922, 11/1/1923.
[36] JNL 27/1, 19/2, 4/3/1920, 14/2/1921.
[37] JNL 22/3/1919.
[38] JNL 21/2/1917, 15/11/1917.
[39] JNL 17/11/1919, 23/1, 3/2/1923.
[40] JNL 11/9/1924.
[41] J. Coolahan, *Irish Education: History and Structure*, pp 73-78.

42 S.J. King, RCA 1998-2001
43 ibid
44 *Irish Independent* 29/5/1922.
45 JNL 9/2/1922.
46 JNL 12/2/1916, 23/2/1916, 7/3/1916, 1/4/1916, 8/4/1916.
47 *Nationalist* 10/3/1917, JNL 10/3/1917, 11/3/1917, 12/3/1917.
48 JNL 24/10/1917.
49 *Nationalist* 22/12/1917.
50 JNL 28/11/1917, 15/12/1917, 29/5/1919.
51 *Nationalist* 29/4/1918. JNL 25/3/1918, 25/4/1918.
52 JNL 22/9/1918.
53 *Nationalist* 22/3/1919.
54 JNL 19/3/1919, 27/3/1920, 25/4/1920.
55 *Nationalist* 27/3/1920.
56 JNL 30/3/1922.
57 *Nationalist* 25/4/1923.
58 *Nationalist* 6/6/1923.
59 *Nationalist* 21/5/1924.
60 JNL 10/5/1924, 18/5/1924.
61 *Freeman's Journal* 4/6/1923. JNL 28/5/1923, 2/6/1923, 13/6/1924, 7/10/1924.
62 JNL 3/1/1919.
63 JNL 19/1/1924.
64 T. Brown, *Ireland: A Social and Cultural History 1922-2002*. p. 4.
65 JNL 28/1/1921.
66 ISR p. 267.
67 ibid.
68 JNL 28/2/1924.
69 JNL 18/3, 2/4/1924.
70 JNL 22/4/1924.

− 7 −

RECOVERY
1925-1934

The crisis which had faced Rockwell College in 1924 was reminiscent of a similar crisis in 1899 when there was talk of closure and when the person credited with having played a major part in its recovery was Dr. Edward Crehan, then Dean of Studies. Now in 1925 Dr. Crehan was back in Rockwell as President and he is credited with having for the second time played a major role in leading Rockwell to recovery.

Dr. Edward Crehan
President 1925-1934

Since leaving Rockwell in 1900 Dr. Edward Crehan had served as President of St. Mary's Rathmines from 1900 to 1904 and President of Blackrock College from 1904 to 1910 overseeing the laying out of new grounds and the reconstruction of the Castle. He had been President of St. Mary's, Trinidad from 1910 to 1920 and General Prefect of Studies for the Congregation in Paris from 1920 to 1925, leaving his mark on all the positions of responsibility which he held.[1] Now at the age of 65 he was about to restore Rockwell to its former position as a leading second level institution in Irish education.

Dr. Crehan was fortunate to have as his Dean of Studies in Rockwell Dr. Daniel Murphy another formidable member of the Congregation who was destined to high offices in the future. Following his student days in Rockwell and the completion of his novitiate in Kimmage in 1913, Daniel Murphy had a brilliant academic career at University College Dublin obtaining an M.A. in classics followed by his studies at Fribourg where

Dr. Daniel Murphy
Dean of Studies 1924-1934

he qualified *maxima cum laude* in the double doctorates in philosophy and theology. His first appointment in 1923 was to the teaching staff at Blackrock College and the following year as Dean of Studies in Rockwell.[2] Dr. Crehan and Dr. Murphy were to leave an indelible print on Rockwell.

During Dr. Crehan's presidency there were two Deans of Discipline. Dr. David Heelan occupied the position from 1925 to 1928. A native of Hospital, Co. Limerick, he was a past student and had captained the Cup winning team of 1914. Following his studies in Rome he was awarded a doctorate in theology and Rockwell was his first appointment following his ordination. He was succeeded as Dean of Discipline in 1928 by a future President, Fr. Andrew Egan. Fr. Kingston continued as Bursar throughout those years and the only new member of the Community in 1925 was Fr. David O'Brien who retired to Rockwell in poor health following a lifetime on the missions in Trinidad, Belgium and the USA. All of the eleven Brothers in Rockwell in 1925 had served during the previous presidency.

THE PROSPECTUS

Students entering Rockwell in 1925 were required to provide a birth certificate together with a reference from their parish priest and from the headmaster of the last school attended. The fee for the academic year was £50. In the case of brothers attending the College together, a reduction of £2 for the second and £4 for any other was made. Each student was required to provide at least two suits of clothes, an overcoat, six day-shirts, three night-shirts, six pairs of stockings, six pocket-handkerchiefs, twelve collars, four towels, three pairs of boots, one pair of slippers, two pairs of sheets (8feet by 5), three pillow cases (24 inches by 18), four napkins, a napkin ring, a knife, fork, dessert-spoon, tea-spoon, a dressing case, a College cap (which could be procured at the College), one pair of football boots and a rug. Every article of outfit coming to the College was required to be marked with the owner's name and number.

The College Band with Fr. Schmidt 1926

Intending students were advised that the general course of studies was based on the Intermediate Programme. It embraced the Irish Language and Literature, History and Geography, Greek and Latin, English, French and German, Mathematics and Science, Drawing, Commercial subjects, Typewriting, Shorthand and Singing. There were special courses for commercial life, the banks, the Civil Service, the learned professions, University Matriculation and the County Council Scholarships. There was a special Elementary Department for boys from 10-12 years of age, and such young students as were not sufficiently advanced to enter the general or special courses. There was Religious Instruction in all classes for one half-hour each day. Piano and violin lessons were available at one guinea per term. Students had at their disposal playing fields of thirty acres in extent for football and hurling and the lake of twenty four acres which was suitable for boating and bathing.[3]

TABLE 7.1. ROCKWELL COLLEGE STUDENT POPULATION 1925-1929

Date	Boarders	Scholastics
5/12/1925	115	44
1/9/1926	92	54
6/9/1927	174	57
5/9/1928	240	61
5/9/1929	237	75

Source: JNL on dates specified.

ACHIEVEMENTS

A notable achievement of the presidency of Dr. Crehan was the increase in student numbers, both among boarders and scholastics. (Table 7.1) By 1934 the total number of students had reached 500. This was a record for Rockwell. During these years the number of day students never exceeded a dozen.

Speaking at the Rockwell Prize Day in June 1925 Archbishop Harty congratulated the College on its academic achievements. "There was a class of college attended by boys, and convent attended by girls" he said "seemingly with only one object in view—that of passing examinations. Rockwell was not one of those. It was a college where boys got a general training, and where the examinations held a secondary place; where boys were trained to be good Irishmen and good Catholics." He was glad to be able to congratulate the Fathers on their success in this direction. "Rockwell has trained many of the young men of the archdiocese to go into the priesthood. Many of the finest priests in the archdiocese were trained in Rockwell. Nearly all the members of the teaching staff of Thurles College began their life in Rockwell as did also several distinguished ecclesiastics at Maynooth".

Nevertheless, the academic distinctions of Rockwell students during Dr. Murphy's term as Dean of Studies were notable. In 1925, for example first place in Ireland in Mathematics and History were obtained and eight other students obtained county council scholarships. In 1926 fourteen students were presented

Group of senior students 1930

for the Leaving Certificate. Of these, twelve passed, eleven with honours, this being the highest number to obtain honours in any school in Ireland that year. First place in Ireland was obtained in Chemistry, third in Commerce, fourth in French, fifth in Irish and sixth in Latin. Seven County Council (University) Scholarships were won by Rockwell students in Tipperary (South Riding) and Limerick.

In the Intermediate Certificate Examination of 1926 thirty four Rockwell students were presented. Twenty eight of these passed giving a pass rate of 82% while the rate for all Ireland was only 61%. Of these twenty eight, thirteen passed with honours, securing first place in Ireland (full marks) in Latin, second in Commerce, sixth in French. Two of these junior students secured Intermediate scholarships. The Intermediate scholarships were worth £80.

In June 1930 Rockwell presented forty one candidates for the Leaving Certificate Examination. Of these thirty five were successful, twenty six securing the certificate with honours. These included first and third places in Ireland in Physics, second and fourth in Greek, second in Chemistry and third in History. Of the local council scholarships that year Rockwell students obtained first place in Dublin Corporation, Dublin County Council and Tipperary (S.R.) County Council.

Rockwell presented ninety two candidates for the Intermediate Certificate of 1930, seventy nine of whom were successful. These included first, second and fourth places in Ireland in Greek, first, second, fourth, fifth, seventh and eighth in Latin, first in Mathematics and third in French. Of the seventy Intermediate scholarships offered for competition among the schools and colleges of Ireland by the Department of Education, Rockwell students secured fourteen. Rockwell students also featured prominently in the Civil Service examinations of that year. Archbishop Harty, writing to congratulate Dr. Crehan on these results said "Rockwell has more than maintained the foremost place among the educational institutions of this country."[4]

Community group 1925
Seated: *Fr. Daniel Leen, Bishop James Leen, Fr. John Byrne, Bishop Henry Gogarty, Fr. John McGrath.*
Standing: *Fr. John Kingston, Fr. John McCarthy, Fr. James O'Neill, Fr. Michael Colgan,*
Fr. Christian Schmidt, Fr. Michael Walsh, Fr. Patrick Brennan, Fr. David Heelan.

STUDENT LIFE

Examination statistics, however spectacular, were far from the thoughts of the student who described his feelings in the Annual of 1925: "After a week spent in Rockwell a fellow is fit to bunk; after two weeks, he is either gone or in the blues, and after three, assuming that he remains, he begins to say to himself that after all, the temperature is quite bearable and that there are only one hundred days, four hours and three minutes to the Christmas vacation. This thought cheers him up wonderfully."

Among the students who attended Rockwell during Dr. Crehan's presidency were Ruairi Brugha, son of Civil War veteran, Cathal Brugha, Thomas Cummins, future Irish Ambassador to the Holy See, and Patrick Lennon, the future Bishop of Kildare and Leighlin and the first former Rockwell student to become a member of the Irish Hierarchy. The O'Brien brothers, Patrick, Tim and Willie arrived in Rockwell from the Capuchin College, Rochestown in 1928. Patrick excelled in hurling, Gaelic football and rugby and later rose to the rank of Surgeon-Lieutenant in the British Navy. Martin Byrne from Knockgraffon later became Professor of Surgery at the Veterinary College, Dublin. Students who were later ordained to the priesthood included John English of Knockgraffon, John Casey of Quilty, Co. Clare, David O'Donnell of Ardfinnan, John J. Barry of Golden, Phil Noonan of Oola, James Noonan of Galbally and Willie O'Brien, the youngest of the three brothers.

The schedule of events of the school year differed little from year to year. Class was held everyday except Sunday, with half days on Wednesday and Saturday. The annual walk to Cashel took place in early September. Students set out at 11.30 and after an hour or so of leisurely walking they arrived in Cashel. Every nook and cranny of the town was invaded. Dinner was served at the Rock and then they adjourned to the local cinema. A two day Retreat was held in mid- September and at the end of that month the annual walk to Athassel Abbey took place. Lunch was served at the College at 11 a.m. and at 11.40 the juniors led the way and the seniors fell into line at 11.55. Dinner was eaten beneath the shadows of the ruin and students returned to Rockwell tired. After tea soirées were held for both seniors and juniors until 9 p.m.

Occasional incidents cling to the memory of students such as the visit of the dentist in November 1925, recorded in the *Annual* when "the poor victims were trotted out to the chamber of horrors. When the ordeal was past the victims retired to the Infirmary where the nurse restored their equilibrium". And on a cold December morning "the Drill Master appeared in the quadrangle and put us through a round of callisthenics that well-nigh rendered us incapable of active locomotion for a week afterwards."

Free days were a welcome respite. The Feast of All Saints on 1st November 1925 was a free day. High Mass was celebrated in the morning and was followed by a rugby match in the afternoon between the Second Seniors and Juniors. A concert was held in the evening in which the College orchestra, under the direction of Fr. Muller, took part. The Feast of the Immaculate Conception on 8th December was also a free day with High Mass in the morning and rugby match in the afternoon. After Benediction in the evening the students went down to the Rock where they gathered around the statue of Our Lady which was fittingly decorated and illuminated by Fr. Brennan and Br. Canice for the occasion. Here they sang several hymns. They had a concert and play in the evening at which the College orchestra gave a splendid recital.

Examinations began in mid-December and Christmas holidays commenced on 23rd December. The new term commenced in the middle of January and students looked forward to a free day on 2nd February in memory of the

Group of junior students 1930

anniversary of the death of Venerable Libermann. St. Patrick's Day was the next occasion of freedom and by mid-April there was a feeling that summer was not far away when the lake was swarming with boats, the playing fields were dotted with footballers, hurlers and athletes with the tennis courts and handball alleys fully occupied.

Rockwell missionary priests
Bishop Shanahan, Bishop Wilson and Fr. Thady O'Connor

The annual May Procession was held on an evening in the middle of the month and commenced with Rosary in the Chapel after which the whole Community, preceded by the students, moved towards the Rock where an altar had been erected adjoining the statue of Our Lady. The band played hymns en route, alternating with the singing of the choir. The Litany of Loreto was then chanted, a hymn to Our Lady sung and the procession passed on and returned by the back avenue to the Chapel. Solemn Benediction followed. On the Feast of Corpus Christi each year a procession formed after High Mass. The route through which it passed was decorated with banners, pictures and flowers. Two altars were erected the previous night, one near the boat-house and the other further on, near the gate leading to the back avenue. Benediction was given at each of these. The procession then proceeded to the Chapel where the *Magnificat* was sung and the final Benediction given.

The annual Prize Day at the end of May was attended each year by the Archbishop of Cashel and by a number of priests from the area. The year came to a colourful close with the annual Sports Day which during Dr. Crehan's presidency featured a gymnastic display, under the direction of Mr. Frazer, in which drills were performed to the accompaniment of the College orchestra.

St. Joseph's

Fr. John J. McCarthy became Director of St. Joseph's Missionary House (The Lake House) in 1921, a position he held until 1934. He transformed the Juniorate. He set out to instil in his future missionaries a spirit of sacrifice and hard work. He had them involved in serious manual labour as they laid down paths, and roadways, built shrines and erected a ball alley.[5]

St. Joseph's had forty four scholastics in 1925 and this number was to almost double by 1934. Among the scholastics during Fr. McCarthy's directorship were Patrick Nolan Christopher Meagher and James Hurley, later Directors of St. Joseph's, Peter Kelly, later Superior of the Kenya Mission, Patrick Burke, later Provincial Procurator, Joseph Nolan, later Dean of Studies and Michael Troy,

Sodality of Children of Mary 1930

founder and first Superior of the Neil McNeil High School in Toronto. Among the visitors to St. Joseph's in 1927 were Bishop Wilson of Bagamoyo, Bishop Gogarty of Kilimandjara and Bishop Leen of Mauritius, all former students of St. Joseph's. Another visitor in 1928 was Fr. Harnett, the newly appointed Provincial who was also a past student. The best known past student of St. Joseph's, Bishop Shanahan, visited in 1929 and again in 1934. Fr. McCarthy had an extra affinity to Bishop Shanahan in that he was present in St. Patrick's College, Maynooth at his ordination as bishop and in 1920 he had been among a favoured few who took part in a series of fireside chats on the missions with Monsignor Shanahan then recuperating from some severe surgical operations.[6]

Fr. James Mellett
On leave from the missions in 1930

SPORT

Rockwell had been a "Gaelic Games Only" since 1916 but on 28th October 1925 Dr. Keane, Bishop of Limerick observed "Rockwell will never be the place she was until she takes up rugby again". His view was that of many and the following year Rockwell returned to competing in the Munster Cup and won the Senior Cup in 1928, 1929 and 1930 and the Junior Cup for the first time in 1934. In the first term each year Rockwell played home and away matches with

Senior Cup winning Team 1930
Front: *M. Neligan, D. Madden.*
Seated: *P. Kennedy, V. Nunan, J. O'Connor, J. McCarthy, P. Kennedy.*
Standing: *E. D'Olier Moore, M. O'Sullivan, R. Kiely, E. Kennedy, J. Andrews, F. Walsh, T. Maher,*
J. Miller, T. O'Connor.

Fethard, Clonmel, Cashel, Clanwilliam and Cistercian College, Roscrea. The senior players of 1926 were: G. Casey, J. Cashman, D. Fitzgerald, D. Cummins, P. Noonan, F. Linnell, E. O'Connell, M. Dore, J. Deegan, J. Lonergan, R. Kiely, J. Breen, A. Kierce, V. Quirke, J. Condon. W. Clarke, F. Mangan, P. Noonan. The Junior pack of 1925 was led by Matt Aherne and Dermot O'Shea and the team was: P. Heffernan, M. O'Sullivan, O. O'Keeffe, J. Corcoran, J. O'Brien, C. McLaughlin, P. O'Shea, M. Kelleher, D. Commins, J. Leo, M. Blake, J. Blake, J. Cregan, Dermot O'Shea, H. O'Neill, and substitute J. Wall.

The Rockwell team which won the Cup in 1930 was: V. Nunan, J. O'Connor, E. D'Olier Moore, P. Kennedy, M. O'Sullivan, R. Kiely, E. Kennedy, J. Andrews, T. O'Connor, J. McCarthy, J. Miller, T. Maher, F. Walsh, M. Neligan, D. Madden.

No member of the 1930 team was eligible in 1931 when Rockwell travelled to the Markets' Field, Limerick and beat Christians in the first round. The second round against Mungret was played at the Mardyke Grounds, Cork. The game finished level but Rockwell lost the replay. The Rockwell team was: P. Ward, J. Griffin, G. Keeley, J. O'Flaherty, Michael O'Sullivan, E. Clancy, F. Hazel, W. Kennedy, J.J. Ryan, M. Neligan, B. Curtin, J. McAuliffe, C. Martin, J. K. Murphy and T. O'Donnell.

HURLING

Speaking at Prize Day in 1925 Archbishop Harty remarked "The Cup, which I had presented for hurling in Munster colleges, has been won nearly every year by Rockwell" This was a slight exaggeration but Rockwell's record in the Harty

Cup was impressive. In 1925 Rockwell was in hope of a three-in-a-row victory. On St. Patrick's Day students set out for Thurles where the hurlers beat Presentation College Cork in the Harty Cup semi-final by four goals to two points. The match was a splendid one and Victor Byrne, Tom Butler and Peadar Kelly in the forward line as well as Willie O'Connor, Gerard Casey and Dick Kiely in the backs gave a fine display. On the first Sunday in May students walked to Cashel to see the hurlers of Cork and Tipperary play a league match. As a curtain-raiser the Rockwell senior team played Boherlahan and won by a narrow margin.

The following Sunday Rockwell was beaten by Christians of Limerick in the final of the Harty Cup, played at Thurles. Students travelled to that match by train from Goold's Cross. In 1926 Rockwell lost to Christians in the first round. Players mentioned on that occasion include M. Foley, M. Barron, T. Kiely, E. Kierce, M. Waldron, J. O'Connell, G. Casey, W. Clarke, J. Casey, D. Grant and R. Kiely.

Rockwell won the Dean Ryan Cup for under 16 hurling in 1928 and 1929 and won the Harty Cup in 1930 and 1931. In 1931 Rockwell hurlers were flattered to be invited to play the Tipperary minor team who were All Ireland champions of the previous year. The game finished level. In the first round of the Harty Cup that year Rockwell met Mallow Training College and won by 6-2 to 3-1, the outstanding Rockwell players being P. Kennedy, M. Mc.Carthy, P. O'Sullivan and J. McMahon. A special word of praise was due to Michael Burke from Cashel, the youngest and probably the lightest player on the field, who at

Hurling inter-pros 1930

all times proved a stumbling block to his capable adversary. Walsh in the goal was a perpetual source of encouragement and reliance. Rockwell then had challenge games with Boherlahan and Cashel before meeting Doon C.B.S. in the final of the Harty Cup, played at Mitchelstown. The sides were level for most of the first half and at half-time Rockwell led by a point. The second half was disappointing with Rockwell completely dominating the play. The final score was Rockwell 6-2; Doon 1-1. The team which played in the final was: J. Brennan, M. Burke, D. Coughlan, D. Cronin, T. Cummins, T. Dillon, P. Kennedy, P. Maher, C. Meagher, J. McCarthy, P.McMahon, M. O'Dwyer, T. O'Dwyer, P. O'Sullivan, T. Walsh. The C. Meagher on that team was none other than Fr. Christy Meagher, later a household name in Rockwell.

Munster beat Leinster in the 1931 All-Ireland Colleges Hurling Final played at Nowlan Park, Kilkenny by 6-1 to 4-2. This was the fifth successive victory for Munster. The Leinster team was composed of ten from St. Kieran's, while Munster had a much wider selection picked from Midleton C.B.S., Rockwell, Mallow, Thurles, Doon, Mount Sion, Dungarvan C.B.S. Rockwell had the largest membership with five players and one sub. The Rockwell players were Kennedy, McCarthy, O'Donnell, Smith and Walsh.

In 1932 Rockwell was seeking three-in-a-row winnings of the Harty Cup. That target proved to be elusive. Having defeated Doon in the first round Rockwell lost to Limerick C.B.S. in the second round. The hurlers of 1932 were: Leo Harte (Waterford), James Brennan (Kilkenny), Edward Barry (Tipperary), James Donnelly (Wexford), Patrick Noonan (Limerick), Michael Creedon (Dublin), Michael Burke, captain (Cashel), Thomas Cummins (Littleton), Edmond O'Neill (Rosegreen), James O'Meara (Dungarvan), John O'Flaherty (Clonmel), Christy Ryan (Mitchelstown), James Purcell (Upperchurch), John Quill (Killarney), Nicholas Carey (Kilkenny).

Some of these Rockwell hurlers later won honours with their counties. These included Jerry McCarthy of Cork and Donal McCarthy (afterwards president of U.C.C), Michael Tubridy of Clare, Michael Burke of Cashel who hurled with Tipperary from 1936 to 1940, Bill O'Donnell of Golden who won an All Ireland with Tipperary in 1937 and who was later to delight readers of The *Nationalist* with his penetrating comments on Tipperary hurling under the name of *Divot*. Among these hurlers too were Tom Cummins of Littleton who afterwards became Irish Ambassador to the Holy See, Michael Creedon who later built the Rockwell extension from the Tower to the Senior Refectory, Toddy Walsh and Paddy Kennedy, noted Limerick hurlers. Noted hurlers too were Paddy and Con Bresnihan whose son Barry was capped many times for the Irish rugby team.

ATHLETICS

Whenever the state of Rockwell athletics in these years is discussed, the name of Michael "Sparky" O'Sullivan jumps out. At the All Ireland Colleges Championships in Croke Park in 1929 "Sparky" O'Sullivan accomplished a feat which has been likened to that of Jesse Owens at the Munich Olympics. He won the College of Science Cup for Rockwell on his own. He came first in most

Michael "Sparky" O'Sullivan

of the track and field events and brought this prestigious trophy to the Rockwell for the first time.

For many years afterwards the students of Rockwell have marvelled at the heroics of "Sparky" in 1929. Thirty years later the story was still fresh and the unusual nature of "Sparky"s deeds was relished. It was believed that at the time of the All Ireland Championships many of the Rockwell athletes were laid low with flu. "Sparky" was fit and well and rearing to go, but because of some disciplinary issue was forbidden to travel. Undaunted by this sanction, "Sparky" sauntered down to the back gate where he was picked up by his father who drove him to Dublin.[7]

"Sparky's problems with the Dean of Discipline, Fr. Andy Egan, were soon mended and on 10th June 1930 on a miserable day he was back in Croke Park with the full Rockwell team. On this occasion he won the 100, 200, 440 and long jump and his all-round athletic ability enabled Rockwell to retain the Cup and thus equal the record of the C.B.S. Synge Street team. Another notable Rockwell performance on that occasion was that of Paddy Bresnihan, in the intermediate high jump. In 1931 Rockwell created a record by winning the College of Science Trophy for the third year in succession. In that season the athletic team made their debut in the Munster Championship Sports held at Mallow where their efforts were rewarded with 19 medals. In the senior section Michael "Sparky" O'Sullivan was first in the 100 yards, 220 yards, 440 yards and long jump in which he jumped 20 feet and 10 inches. Rockwell was also first in the senior relay race. It was a wait of another twenty seven years before Rockwell won the College of Science Cup for the fourth time.

NEW STRUCTURES

Major development of the Rockwell infrastructure occurred during Dr. Crehan's presidency. Because of an increase in the number of scholastics St. Joseph's was completely restructured in 1928 and its capacity was extended to eighty. The ever increasing number of applicants for places in the secondary school made it imperative to extend the building. Every year numerous applications had to be turned down. Thanks to the generosity of past students and of kind benefactors it was decided to build a new wing to the College which later came to be known as the Crehan Wing. Work commenced on this building in 1932. Some grand old trees had unfortunately to be torn from their roots. The work was completed in 1934. Solidly built in a type of castellated perpendicular Gothic, it is attractive enough to look at when taken in isolation, but in conjunction with the buildings as a whole, there is a marked clash in style. It is a three-storey building and originally the top floor housed dormitories with a theatre in the middle floor and class rooms at the bottom.[8] The dormitory on the top floor was not entirely heated to the satisfaction of some students who duly named it *Siberia*, the exploits of a certain Mr. Joseph Stalin being then a topical issue in Ireland. The nickname eventually adhered to the entire building.

On the completion of the Crehan Wing in 1934 a new Pavillion was built adjacent to the playing fields and two new ball-alleys were erected near it. In the summer of 1934 the College changed from its own direct current generator to the Electricity Supply Board. Lines were brought overhead from the eastern side of the main road round the southern and western side of the farmyard to a transformer west of the Big Study. An overhead line from there connected St. Joseph's to the system.[9]

ROCKWELL COLLEGE UNION

The Rockwell Union was founded on Sunday 20th December 1925. It was founded on an occasion when a large number of past students had returned to the College with a two-fold intention, firstly to honour the former President, Fr. John Byrne on the occasion of the silver jubilee of his ordination and secondly to form the Union.

Proceedings commenced at 11.00 a.m. with High Mass at which the principal celebrant was Bishop O'Gorman of Sierra Leone, a past student, who had brought with him from Rome a papal blessing for Fr. Byrne and for the proposed Union. A football match between past and present students was played in the afternoon. Among those who donned the "blue and white" for the past students was the newly elected T.D. for Tipperary, Michael R. Heffernan, who had been capped for Ireland's rugby team four times in 1911. Interested spectators who envied Heffernan's youthful enthusiasm included Eamon de Valera and former rugby internationals Mike and Jack Ryan and Dr. Paddy Stokes.

The presentation to Fr. Byrne took place in the large study-hall at which the spokesman for the past students was Thomas J. Morrissey, former Assistant Commissioner of Intermediate Education and at that time Assistant Registrar General, and like Fr. Byrne and Dr. Crehan a native of Clonmel. A banquet

Members of Rockwell Union committee 1925 with Dr. Crehan

was served in the students' refectory which had been sumptuously decorated for the occasion. The launching of the Union followed. Monsignor Innocent Ryan, Dean of Cashel, was elected President and Eamon de Valera Vice-President. Elected secretaries were Dr. J.P. Brennan of Blackrock, Co. Dublin and Mr. Jack Sewell of Killarney. The treasurer was Mr. Frederick T. Byrne of Rathmines. The committee members were Fr. William Lockhart, Dublin, Mr. T.J. Morrissey, Assistant Registrar General, Mr. Robert V. Walker, Clones, Mr. James Dudley, Mallow, Dr. Paddy Stokes, Fethard, Mr. W.J. Moloney, Thurles and Mr. Mike Ryan, Cashel. A preamble to the constitution stated the objects of the Union "to strengthen the bonds of affection between us and our *Alma Mater*; to render more effective, through organisation, that feeling of loyalty to old comrades which should characterise the alumni of any great institution; to afford opportunities of renewing old friendships and of forming new ones; to render, as opportunities arise, the mutual aid so profitably exercised by similar Unions in every sphere of life."

The constitution had eighteen articles by which past and present students and professors of Rockwell were entitled to membership. An annual subscription of five shillings was payable in advance. The functions of officers were outlined as were the methods of election, funding and procedures.

A remarkable feature of the new Union was the election of the first president and vice-president. In the highly charged atmosphere of the immediate aftermath of the Civil War in Ireland, no two people could have been as politically opposed as Innocent Ryan and Eamon de Valera. The anti-Treaty campaign had been led by De Valera who had spent eleven months in Kilmainham jail following his arrest in Ennis in August 1923. On 10th December 1925, only ten days before the Rockwell meeting, de Valera, as President of Sinn Féin, had led an anti-partition protest in Dublin. Innocent Ryan, on the other hand, had vigorously campaigned against Sinn Féin in the 1918 General Election and was an ardent supporter of Cumann na nGaedheal, the party founded by William T. Cosgrave for supporters of the Treaty in April 1923. In November 1925, only a month before the Rockwell meeting, Innocent Ryan had addressed a public meeting of that party outside the Town Hall in Clonmel.[10] The election of Innocent Ryan and Eamon de Valera to their respective positions was an indication of the ability of Rockwell College and the Rockwell Union then and in the future to absorb people of opposing political persuasions.

In their choice of president and vice-president the Rockwell past students of 1925 cannot have been unaware of these differences. Indeed it seems likely that by their choice they were actually mending fences. The Rockwell Union was from its beginning always accommodating to members of varying political persuasions.

The first annual Union Day was held on Monday 24th May 1926. The day was marred by very unfavourable weather and the College Sports had to be cancelled. Some two hundred past-students attended, in many instances accompanied by lady friends, and a very pleasant day was spent, the visitors being hospitably entertained. The recitals by the school band under Fr. Muller made up for the bad weather. Solemn High Mass was celebrated in the College

Union Dinner 1926

Union meeting in the study hall 1926 with Bishop O'Gorman and Dr. Crehan

Chapel at 10 a.m. The members assembled in the spacious Study Hall. Dean Ryan was re-elected President. The secretary, Dr. J.P. Brennan said he expected that Mr. de Valera would be present later during the proceedings, as he had written stating nothing but an accident would prevent his presence. A prize for athletics was presented for competition among present students of the College. The membership of the Union was already one hundred and fifty. An application for permission to establish a branch of the Union in America had been received from some past students in that country and the committee had authorised its establishment. It was agreed that a medal for general excellence be donated annually by the Union to a student chosen by the teaching staff. Mr. de Valera was voted Vice-President on the proposal of Dean Ryan. In the evening members assembled in the spacious students' refectory for a banquet.

The annual dinner of the College Union in 1930 was held in the Gresham Hotel, Dublin. President William T. Cosgrave, in proposing a toast to the College, said it was one of the foremost of a number of similar institutions in this country which appealed to the interest and pride of every Irishman who had at heart the prestige of his country's educational progress. This great College, he said, which now houses over 500, had its beginnings 66 years ago in a Community of one priest, two prefects and four brothers. Rockwell also had a great athletic tradition as well as a distinguished educational record, he said. Dr. Crehan, he continued, had already held the presidency of every college of the Holy Ghost Order in Ireland, but it was no secret, and he himself made no secret of it that, no matter in what part of the world he had served, his heart had always been in Rockwell where he had spent the greater part of his religious

Union Dinner 1930 at the Gresham Hotel
Included in the group with President W. T. Cosgrave are Dr. Crehan, Alfie Byrne, Lord Mayor of Dublin, P.J. Duffy President of the Rockwell Union and Professor O'Sullivan, Minister for Education.

life. Dr. Crehan had also re-organised the farming operations of the college, with the result that it now boasted prize potatoes, and excellent Angus cattle. To-day the college was so popular that Dr. Crehan, he said, was compelled each year to refuse fifty applicants for admission as pupils. He had put the matter before the Council of the Order and before doing so he paid the Rockwell Union the compliment of being allowed to be associated with any building extension which might be authorised, he concluded. Present at the dinner were the Lord Mayor of Dublin, Alfie Byrne, and the Minister for Education Professor O'Sullivan

The first edition of the *Rockwell Annual* was published in June 1926. Its editor, Dr. Daniel Murphy, Dean of Studies, in its first editorial stated that it was because of the importance of such institutions as Rockwell in the life of a nation that the *Annual* was being published. It was meant, he said, for the present students and for the past. The present would recognise therein many a scene in which they were themselves the actors, or of which they were the interested spectators. The past would see their long-lost youth live again. "The college traditions they knew, they will see continued. The old haunts they can re-visit, the old associations, revive, and old familiar faces see once more. It is meant also to be a link between to-day and long ago." Dr. Murphy continued as editor until he was succeeded in 1933 by Fr. Andrew Egan.

* * *

Following his term in Rockwell Dr. Crehan went on a pilgrimage to the Holy Land, arranged for him by the Rockwell Union. He died in 1938. In 1934 Dr. Murphy was appointed Provincial of the Irish Holy Ghost Fathers. Under his guidance the Province prospered and expanded with an increase in the number of missionary priests. In 1948 he became Superior in Kenya and in 1950 he was called to Rome to become Procurator General of the Holy Ghost Fathers. In 1962 he became Director of the International Scholasticate at Fribourg where he had earlier studied.

Notes

[1] ISR 4.
[2] ISR 204.
[3] RCA 1926
[4] RCAs 1926-1930.
[5] ISR 484
[6] ibid
[7] Submission of Gay Mangan 23/3/2013
[8] RCA 1977
[9] ibid
[10] O'Donnell, S. *Clonmel 1900-1932: A History*, 285-6, 357.

— 8 —

MAINTAINED STANDARDS
1934-1939

The high academic standards which had been set during the presidency of Dr. Crehan were maintained by his successor Fr. John J. McCarthy who was President from 1934 to 1939. Born in 1889 in Baurleigh, Killbrittain, Co. Cork, he was a native Irish speaker and was educated at Blackrock College. He was ordained in 1920. He had come to Rockwell in 1920 and had been Director of St. Joseph's since 1921. He took over as President at a time of great changes of personnel, the departures of Dr. Crehan and Dr. Murphy being momentous and the deaths in 1938 of Fr Muller and Fr Schmidt divesting Rockwell of two long-standing colourful German characters. Fr. McCarthy succeeded in steering Rockwell along the same pathway that had been designed by his immediate predecessor with continued academic success and further major development to the infrastructure.

Fr. John J. McCarthy
President 1934-39

The Vice-President during these years was Fr. Timothy Cunningham who had been a member of the Community since 1922. Fr. Cornelius Daly succeeded Dr. Daniel Murphy as Dean of Studies in 1934 and Fr. James White became Dean of Discipline. Fr. John Cahill was Dean of Discipline in 1937 and was replaced in 1938 by Fr. James Barrett. Fr. John Kingston retired as Bursar in 1934, having served in that position for sixteen years, and was succeeded by Fr. Michael Sexton. In 1936 Fr. Edward Kinsella returned from Sierra Leone and replaced Fr. Sexton who for health reasons returned to St. Mary's Rathmines. Fr.

Fr. James White
Dean of Discipline

Michael Comerford became Director of St. Joseph's in succession to Fr. McCarthy. Other new members of the community during Fr. McCarthy's presidency were Fr. Thomas Gough and Fr. James Burke in 1935, Fr. Reginald

Walker in 1936 and Fr. Joseph Mullins in 1938. Br. Canice Butler, who had been a member of the Community from 1916 to 1929 returned to Rockwell in 1936, having spent the intervening years in Trinidad. New members of the lay teaching staff in 1934 were Mr. James A. White, Mr. Martin Farragher and Mr. Jerry Hayes. Dr. Arthur Foley was the house physician and Miss Galwey-Foley the resident nurse. Mr. John Frazer was the gymnastic instructor.

Fr. Timothy Cunningham
Vice-President

A notable development in 1936 was the introduction into the College of Sisters of St. John of God who for many years were to take charge of the infirmary, the laundry and the kitchen. The first Sisters in 1936 were Sr. Stanislaus, Sr. Rose and Sr. Emmanuel. Other Sisters who served up to 1939 were Sr. Lelia, Sr. Magdalen, Sr. Canisius and Sr. Bosco. A private oratory for the Sisters was located adjacent to the infirmary.

DEVELOPING THE INFRASTRUCTURE

Major development of the Rockwell infrastructure was carried out during the presidency of Fr. McCarthy. Two new ball alleys were built in 1935. A new kitchen was developed in 1936. The same year the College front avenue was re-designed and surfaced with tarmac as was the back avenue and all the walks throughout the grounds. At the same time all of the "old mansion" was stripped of its exterior lime-mortar pebble dash, which was no longer damp proof, and finished instead with a smooth cement plaster. The same year the sewerage system was up-dated. In the summer of 1937 some changes were made in St. Joseph's with the erection of new toilets and the insertion of dormer windows.[1]

Fr. Edward Kinsella
Bursar

The biggest improvement of these years in the College came in 1937 and 1938. The first connecting cross hall between the northern side of the College and the old mansion was made. The cross hall made it possible for the first time to go from anywhere to anywhere on the ground floor of the College without having to go into the open. At the same time a new refectory for the priests (now the Community refectory) was built on the site of the dayboys' hall with a narrow corridor leading to the parlours in the "old mansion" and the new refectory. (See chronological floor plan). A new dining room for the Sisters was built adjacent to the infirmary. In 1938 a more ambitious development plan was proposed which would re-produce the existing Northern Block (The Silas

Building) with another of the same size extending eastwards: and a new Eastern Block, almost similar to the Western Block of 1900-1911 (The Study and Library Block). The plan for this development was drawn up by Fr. Jim Burke, then a member of the Community. The proposal was agreed but it was felt it should only be done in stages.[2]

The laying out of a golf course had been under consideration for quite a long time and in 1939 it was then finally decided to develop it on the spacious pasture known in the College as Connor's Field. Some twenty acres in area, it was situated above the grove on the left, half-way down the back avenue. There were five holes which took about an hour to cover. The quarry, house and trees in the centre made an interesting hazard.[3]

STUDENT LIFE

Rockwell students continued to perform well in public examinations and in 1936 the Rockwell Union congratulated the College "for obtaining the premier place amongst the Colleges in the Free State in the Intermediate and Certificate examinations for the ninth year in succession." When Fr. Daly took over as Dean of Studies in 1934 an "A School" and a "C School" were introduced. This was an experiment with the intention of devoting more time to the intellectually "bright" student while at the same time giving more time to the needs of weaker students. This experiment may have been in response to the bonus marks on offer to students taking subjects through the medium of Irish in certificate examinations. In the first few years of the experiment the final year students were divided evenly between the two schools with the *Annual* giving the names of those in the "A School" in Irish and those in the "C School" in English. This experiment was controversial of course from an educational point of view and would not have been welcomed by all parents. Whatever the outcome of the experiment it is interesting that by 1939 the two "Schools" had petered out and all students were back in the same fold.

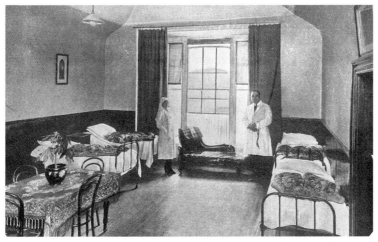

The College infirmary in 1934 with Dr. Foley and Nurse Foley

It was still the culture of the time to publish examination results in detail and in the month of September each year every local newspaper throughout Ireland was littered with results of the Leaving and Inter Cert from the local schools. Rockwell was not backward in this respect with its results in the *Tipperary Star* and the two Clonmel papers, the *Clonmel Chronicle* and the *Tipperary Nationalist*. The *Rockwell Annual* also continued to publish the results every year.

The spiritual welfare of students was always a concern of the College management and societies such as the Sodality of the Children of Mary were encouraged. This sodality had over eighty members each year. The Pioneers had a similar membership. Missionary exhibitions portraying the work of the Holy Ghost Fathers in Africa were organised and exhibited in the College theatre and were usually on display on Parents' Day. Bishop Shanahan visited Rockwell during May 1936 and gave a glowing account of his recent visit to Nigeria, the scene of his twenty-eight years' apostolate. In 1934 a movement called the *Students' Burse Circle* had been founded in Blackrock College by students and teachers in response to Pope Pius XI speaking in praise of the help given by the laity to the Catholic Missions. The movement was set up with the object of providing small contributions for the maintenance of students destined to become missionary priests. The movement spread to Rockwell in 1935 when Bishop Shanahan celebrated Mass for the students at the launch of the movement.

The Debating Society was directed by Fr. Walsh up to 1937 when Fr. Walker took charge of debating in English and Fr. Mullins directed debating in Irish. Motions for debate reflected issues that were topical in Ireland at the time. In 1936, for example, a motion that the entire population of the Gaeltacht should be transplanted into fertile farms in the midlands was debated. In 1937 one of the motions was "That Ireland should help the Spanish patriots" and another "That monarchies have outlived their usefulness." Among the motions debated in 1939 was "That the re-afforestation of Ireland is not at the present moment a practical possibility" and "That an Irish speaking state is necessary for our national welfare."

The English Dramatic Society usually performed a few sketches in the first term with a major production before Easter. St. Joseph's occasionally also had their own dramatic society and in 1939 it performed *Dermot O'Hurley* a dramatized version of the vocation, betrayal and subsequent martyrdom of the Archbishop of Cashel. It was produced by Fr. Comerford. *Órd San Mhicil* was the Cumann Gaelach founded in 1934. It had a debating team and it performed plays in the Irish language. Two plays in Irish were performed in 1938, *An Dochtúir* and *Breachadh an Lae* by the St. Joseph's House Dramatic Society

Music continued to occupy a prominent part of the student's experience. Students were presented each year for the examinations of the Royal Irish Academy of Music. Interestingly the majority of these students were entered for stringed instruments (mainly violin) rather than piano. It is not surprising therefore that the College orchestra was vibrant, especially when it was augmented by Mr. Cremin on violin and Fr. Walker on cello. The Operatic

The Band of the Garda Síochána in 1937
With Fr. McCarthy and Mr. White and members of the College Orchestra

Society in 1936 performed *H.M.S. Pinafore* conducted by Mr. White and with Mr. Cremin leading the College orchestra on piano. The Band of the Garda Síochána visited Rockwell in 1937, much to the delight of the students. The College choirs were directed by Fr. Daly and Mr. White and each year they were entered for the Plain Chant Festival held in Thurles. The main competition for senior choirs was the Ailbe Shield which Rockwell won in 1937 and 1938.

THE ROCKWELL UNION
During Fr. McCarthy's presidency the Rockwell Union presidents were Andrew Butler, James A. Nugent, Malachy Martin, Edward C. Powell and James Gleeson, all of them with high reputations in their own professions. In 1936 the question of holding an annual dance was considered by the committee but the idea was abandoned in favour of a Bridge and Whist Drive, which was held in the Dolphin Hotel in December. The annual dinner was held in the same venue in February. Union Day was observed each year on a Sunday in late May or early June with High Mass celebrated by the President of the College and the election of the new President of the Union. Union Day often coincided with Parents' Day. A number of Rockwell past students were ordained to the priesthood each year. One of the highest numbers was in 1939 when nineteen were ordained, six of whom were Holy Ghost Fathers. Each year a number of past students were commissioned as cadets in the Irish Army and among the six commissioned in1939 was Richard Bunworth, who was later to command United Nations forces in the Congo.

A STUDENT'S MEMORY
An insight into life in Rockwell during those years, as perceived by a student, is provided by Patrick Hillery, future President of Ireland who came to Rockwell as a twelve-year old in 1935. He was sent to Rockwell from his home in Miltown Malbay by his parents because his father, who had preceded him as a student in Rockwell, had a high regard for the Holy Ghost Fathers.[4]

Walk around the lake in 1936

It was a difficult transition for a twelve-year-old boy, who was separated from his family and friends for the first time. What he missed most was Spanish Point itself and its closeness to the sea. "If you're reared near the sea and you're sent off inland, you feel it. I did not realise it at the time, but other times when I was away form the sea I was uncomfortable."

His abiding memories of the first days at Rockwell were of "big rooms, the enormous corridors, huge dormitories and refectories and a young child's loss of the beloved seaside of Miltown Malbay." Yet his initial loneliness passed quickly as he settled into the rhythm of life at a boarding school. He remembered the prefects who were training for the priesthood and took day-to-day responsibility for discipline in the dormitories and common areas of the school such as the refectory. Hillery did well in his first-year exams, securing first place in his class in three subjects and second place in three more. This marked the high point of his academic career at Rockwell. He himself admitted "That was the last of my interest of study in school: I did not exhibit any interest in books again until I was in medical school learning my profession".

He did not take academic work too seriously, becoming immersed in various sports and enjoying the camaraderie of the boarding school environment. He played hurling and Gaelic football. He excelled in rugby and played for the College's Junior Cup team. Hillery became captain of the Junior Cup team in 1938 and was selected on the Senior Cup team the same year.

Hillery was by no means a model student, by his own admission. His academic record after his first year was mediocre and he clashed with the school authorities on a few occasions. He rebelled against some of the strict rules maintained by the school management. The students were divided into senior and junior groups; the groups were kept apart not only in their dormitories but also in the refectory and during their leisure time. Hillery broke this rule in his final year at Rockwell by speaking to his vice-captain of the Junior Cup team in the refectory. He fell foul of the Dean of Discipline, Fr. Barrett, for this and he was caned on the hands. The harsh punishment for such a minor breach of the rules did not bother him greatly; like most boys of his generation he accepted physical punishment as a normal part of the educational experience.

Fr. Cornelius Daly
Dean of Studies

He felt that by the standards of the time, Rockwell was mild in administering physical punishment, especially in comparison with schools run by other religious orders in the same period. He greatly enjoyed his time in Rockwell and valued the strong sense of community that he found in the school. He remembered Rockwell with great affection and paid a handsome tribute to the College in an interview some years later. "They were good. They didn't push you. At that time it was a bit like the old university: you just mixed with the others; you were there for the experience. I felt that Rockwell was my university."

RUGBY

In the five years between 1934 and 1939 Rockwell won the Munster Junior Rugby Cup on four occasions. Their four-in-a-row victories commenced in 1934 when the Junior Cup came to Rockwell for the first time ever. In 1935 Rockwell beat Crescent and Mungret before meeting Christians, Cork in the final and winning by 8-6. The team was: D.B. Kennedy, Terence Foley, Arthur Tracey, Thomas Kelly, Raymond Busby, Cecil O'Driscoll (captain), Joseph Holohan, Liam Mulcahy, Michael O'Gorman, Joseph Roantree, James Cummins, Michael O'Driscoll, Patrick Holohan, Thomas Jordan, Liam Madden.

In 1936 Rockwell beat Mungret and Christians to win the Junior Cup. In 1937 Rockwell beat Mungret and Limerick C.B.S. to reach the final. The final was against Presentation in Cork and finished with a nil all draw. The replay was in Clonmel and Rockwell won by 6 points to 3. The team was: William Crowley, Timothy O'Shea, John O'Brien, Thomas O'Sullivan, John Delaney, Michael Ryan, Michael O'Donoghue, Jeremiah O'Mahony (captain), Seán Fahy, Thomas O'Sullivan, Thomas O'Beirne, Patrick Mullane, William Lafford, Hugh O'Connell, John Martin.

The S.C.T was not so successful but did win the Cup in 1937 for the first time since 1930. In 1935 they drew with Christians, Cork in the semi-final. Rockwell won the replay but lost to Presentation in the final. In 1936 the S.C.T.

Junior Cup team 1935
Front: D. Kennedy, J. Holohan.
Seated: J. Cummins, A. Tracey, J. Roantree, C. O'Driscoll, J. Kelly, M. O'Driscoll, R. Busby.
Back: E. O'Sullivan, T. Jordan, L. Madden, M. O'Gorman, L. Mulcahy, T. Foley.

Munster Senior Cup winners 1937
Front: J. Cummins, J. Aherne, P. Murray, M. O'Keeffe
Middle: E. O'Sullivan, J. Holohan, L. Madden, P. Ryan, C. O'Driscoll, M. Murphy, R. Busby.
Back: P. Liddane, T. Kelly, P. O'Sullivan, E. O'Mahony, P. Fitzpatrick, P. Holohan.

24 Junior Cup winners 1937
Front: M. O'Donoghue, W. Crowley.
Middle: D. Delaney, L. Lafford, S. Fahy, J. O'Mahony, M. Ryan, M. O'Shea, T. O'Sullivan.
Back: P. Mullane, H. O'Connell, C. O'Beirne, D. O'Sullivan, J. Martin, J. O'Brien.

defeated Presentation in the semi-final but lost to Christians, Cork in the final and had five inter-provincials.

1937 was a memorable season for Rockwell rugby. For the first time in the history of Munster Schools rugby the Senior and Junior Cups came to the same school, to Rockwell. The S.C.T. beat Christians, Cork by two tries to one. In the semi-final at Thomond Park they drew with Mungret with a penalty goal each. In the replay in Tipperary Rockwell won by a try to nil. The final was played in Cork and Rockwell beat Presentation College by 3 points to nil. The winning team was: Patrick Liddane, Thomas Kelly, Thomas O'Sullivan, Eamon O'Mahony, Patrick Fitzpatrick, Patrick Holohan, Thomas O'Sullivan, John Holohan, Liam Madden, Patrick Ryan (captain), Cecil O'Driscoll, Michael Murphy, Raymond Busby, James Cummins, John Aherne, Patrick Murray, John O'Keeffe. The following year the Junior Cup team was captained by Paddy Hillery.

GAELIC GAMES
Rockwell Gaelic footballers competed in the Munster Schools' Cup each year between 1934 and 1939 but failed to win the big prize. Prior to Cup matches

each season they had home and away matches with local clubs such as Ardfinnan and Arravale Rovers. In 1935, under the management of Fr. White, the players felt confident because they were strengthened by a few versatile players from "The Kingdom". They lost, however in the Cup to North Mon. Two members of that team, Redmond Walsh and Joe Nolan, later became prominent members of the Rockwell Community. They suffered the same fate against the same opposition in 1936. They beat Kilrush C.B.S. in the first round in 1937 but lost to Ennis C.B.S. in the semi-final. They lost to North Mon in 1938 and again in 1939 and yet they had six players on the Tipperary minor team of 1939 and one on the Wicklow team.

The Rockwell hurlers took part in the Harty Cup each year between 1934 and 1939. They had pre-Cup challenges with Cashel, Golden and Roscrea College each season. Their most successful season was in 1936 when they reached the Harty Cup final. They had an easy win over Ennis C.B.S. in the first round which was played at St. Munchin's College Ground in Limerick. The semi-final was played in Clonmel Sportsfield against Thurles C.B.S. and finished in a draw. Rockwell easily won the replay and met North Mon in the final at Mitchelstown. Although narrowly losing that final, Rockwell had six players on the Munster Colleges team of that year including Tony Brennan who was later to win senior hurling medals with Tipperary. Rockwell lost to North Mon in the Harty Cup semi-finals of 1937 and 1938 and to Thurles C.B.S in 1939. There were two Rockwell hurlers on the Tipperary minor team of 1939 and one on the Limerick team. The Rockwell junior team competed each year for the Dean Ryan Cup.

Senior Gaelic Football team 1935
Front: J. Joy, F. O'Neill, W. Noonan, J. Daly.
Middle: *P. Corry, D. McAuliffe, A. McGuinness, R. Walsh (capt), C. Savage, J. Dennehy, T. O'Sullivan.*
Back: *K. Delaney, M. Troy, J. Magner, J. Cahalane, C. Holly, J. Nolan.*

The Rockwell hurlers of 1935
Front: P. Griffin, C. Gleeson, L. O'Connell.
Middle: *J. McCarthy, J. Daly, D. Ryan, T. McCarthy, M. O'Connor, T. Healy, W. Gavin.*
Back: *W. Leahy, J. McCarthy, J. Nolan, P. Hanly, A. Brennan, J.J. Meagher, J.P. McCarthy,*
D. McAauliffe.

That game against Thurles C.B.S. in 1939 seems to have marked a watershed for Rockwell hurling. The referee was from Thurles and so also were the umpires. Dissatisfaction with a decision led to a heated argument. Thurles was awarded the match and Rockwell withdrew from the Harty Cup. They were joined in this move by most of the boarding colleges of Munster. A principal factor seems to have been the difficulty in competing at under 19. The age limit for the Harty Cup had been raised to 19 in 1933. Few boarding schools had many players of that age. No doubt the G.A.A. ban on rugby players was also a consideration. Rockwell henceforth competed in the Munster Colleges Hurling Cup where the age limit was under 18 and there was no ban. The Harty Cup was henceforth a competition almost confined to the Munster schools of the Irish Christian Brothers.

Handball continued as a very popular sport. Junior and senior leagues generated great interest and excitement. Regular tournaments were held against Roscrea College. Leading players of 1935 were James McElligot and Patrick Hanly who represented Rockwell in the Dr. McRory Shield.

ROWING
The Rockwell Rowing Club received a much-needed impetus in 1934 following the purchase of two "fours" from Shannon Rowing Club. A team was entered for the Schools' Metropolitan Challenge Cup organised by the Dolphin Rowing Club in Dublin on 21st. July. The entrance for this regatta was only made possible by the splendid offer from Dolphin Rowing Club to place a boat at

The Boat Race. Sports Day 1934

Winning crew at 1937 Cork regatta:
F. Mulcahy, T. Healy, P. Morrissey, C. Crowley, C. Mangan

Winners of the Schools Metropolitan Rowing Cup 1934
Seated: J. McElligott, F. Mulcahy, M. Crowley.
Standing: C. Mangan, T. O'Sullivan

Rockwell's disposal and give the rowers a week's training before the regatta. Blackrock College also came to Rockwell's aid by welcoming the rowers as guests during their stay. They arrived in Dublin a week before the race and were on the water every morning at eight o'clock. Unfortunately there was no other entrant for the designated race so Rockwell had to row over the course alone. This was Rockwell's debut and they were greatly praised by the judge. The captain was Colman Mangan and the vice-captain James McElligott. The other rowers were Henry Hayes and Timothy Cronin. Rockwell was the first Munster college to compete in Dublin. Fr. Walsh did great work in the launching of the Rockwell College Rowing Club.

Rockwell competed in the Dublin regatta every year up to 1939 and during those years it also competed in regattas in Galway, Cork, Fermoy and Clonmel.

OTHER SPORT
A little flutter of excitement ran around the Study when the Dean announced in the farewell "spiff" before Easter 1939 that those who possessed bicycles were invited to bring them back after the holidays. "Seniors, only, that is." A day after coming back the first muster of about forty cyclists set out for Thurles for the Dean Ryan cup and on 30th April they cycled again to Thurles for the Dublin-Waterford hurling match. The next trip was to Tipperary for the Harty Cup match. Trips to The Glen of Aherlow, Sliabh na mBan and Horse and Jockey followed. Students began to realise that Rockwell was planted in the centre of a glorious cyclist's paradise.

Sport in Rockwell concluded each year with Parents' Day. The *Cork Examiner* describing Parents Day on Whit-Sunday 31st May 1936 reported that

Rockwell was *en fete* for the annual festival, known as Parents' Day. Relatives of students came from all parts of Ireland, it stated. The magnificent grounds never looked prettier in their beautiful setting, ornamented with bunting and flags. The drill display, in which the whole student body of more than three hundred boys participated was a striking and delightful affair, according to the report. Mr. Fraser had been for some years responsible for the development of this attractive branch of the College activities. The College orchestra gave a pleasing musical selection. Athletic competitions, tennis matches and boat races delighted the parents who were entertained to refreshments.

* * *

Old Entrance c. 1935

Fr. McCarthy retired from the presidency in 1938 because of illness. He retired to the Holy Ghost Fathers' rest house at Montana in the Canton of Valais in Switzerland. His health recovered after some time and on his return to Ireland in 1940 he was appointed Provincial Bursar. In the summer of 1946, however, a decline in his health forced a return to Switzerland and it was there that he died on 20th August 1948. During his presidency in Rockwell standards had been maintained and plans had been envisaged for major development of the infrastructure.

Notes
[1]   RCA 1977
[2]   ibid
[3]   ibid
[4]   Walsh, J., *Patrick Hillery: The Official Biography* (Dublin 2008) pp 8, 15-19.

– 9 –

A MAJOR DEVELOPMENT
1939-1949

A major reconstruction of Rockwell College was completed during the presidency of Fr. Dinan. It was a reconstruction which was to give Rockwell some of its most endearing features such as the long hall, the present senior refectory, the clock tower and front entrance.

When Fr. Vincent Dinan was appointed President of Rockwell in the summer of 1939 he was the youngest ever to hold the office in the history of the College. Born in Borrisokane, Co. Tipperary in 1907, he received his secondary education at Blackrock College. Ordained in 1929 he was appointed to the staff of Blackrock College the following year. He had been intimately associated with many aspects of the life of Blackrock College during the thirties under the presidency of Dr. John Charles McQuaid as Dean of the Day-school, Director of the Juniorate, Director of sodalities and trainer of teams, as well as being a very dynamic force in the classroom.[1]

Fr. Timothy Cunningham continued as Vice-President. Fr. Cornelius Daly was succeeded as Dean of Studies in 1940 by Fr. James Barrett who was succeeded in 1942 by Fr. Maurice Curtin. The positions of Bursar and Dean of Discipline changed hands on a number of occasions in the 1940s. Fr. Patrick J. Nolan succeeded Fr. Michael Comerford as Director of St. Joseph's in 1942. There were many changes in the Rockwell Community during these years because of the regular comings and goings to and from the missions and to and from Blackrock College and St. Mary's College Rathmines. Two new lay teachers, Xavier Gibson and Patrick J. O'Connor, joined the staff in 1942. In 1943 Rockwell

Fr. Vincent J. Dinan
President 1939-1949

Fr. James Barrett
Dean of Studies 1940-1942

Pre-secondary 1943-44
Front: *J. Duffy, M. Lavery, V. Forster, B. Kingston, G. Larkin*
Seated: *M. O'Donoghue, M. Moloney, D. Wall, Mr. F. McCabe C.S.Sp., F. Lawless, M. Moylan, J. Campbell.*
3rd row: *J. O'Leary, L. Lawlor, W. O'Brien, J. Howard, P. Martin, J. Ryan, M. Chadwick.*
Back row: *T. Farrell, R. Moloney, M. Campbell, G. Studdard, D. Lavery, W. Dargan.*

welcomed Br. Benedict from Blackrock College and he was soon radiating energy in pre-secondary classes and the bookshop. The Sisters of St. John of God in those years were Sr. Loreto, Sr. Fabian, Sr. Bosco, Sr. Monica, Sr. Aquinas and Sr Eucharia. The Rockwell Community and Teaching Staff were well supplemented as ever during Fr. Dinan's presidency by the prefects who assisted in many departments such as teaching classes, supervising dormitories, assisting with choirs, orchestras and supervising games. They numbered at least ten in those years and at most fourteen. The prefects of 1948, for instance, included two notable sportsmen, Bernie Murphy and Jim Aherne, the former a Cork senior hurler and the latter a Cork senior footballer. Both were greatly involved with the promotion and organisation of sport.

A RECONSTRUCTION

As has been seen, the reconstruction of Rockwell was planned during the presidency of Fr. McCarthy and it was to be carried out in stages. World War II had broken out only a month after Fr. Dinan became President and it did not seem an appropriate time for any major development. Fr. Dinan, however, had other ideas. From the beginning he was against any curtailment of the original outline plan proposed by Fr. Jim Burke. He succeeded in convincing the Provincial Council and the Mother House in Paris that going ahead with the entire project at once was the wiser course. By January 30th 1940 permission to proceed had been granted. Fr. Dinan also got permission to add the northern projecting gable (not in Fr. Burke's outline plan) to the new eastern wing to make it correspond exactly with the old western wing. (See Chronological Floor Plan)

Because of the War it was thought that building materials could easily become scarce and expensive so the builders were instructed to procure immediately all the materials on the bill of quantities. The necessary loans were procured through the banks and other sources. It was a Dublin building firm, Messrs Creedon & Co. which carried out the work, the owner of that company being a past student.

The project had its own growing pains. It was found that the original electrical contractor was not carrying out the work according to specifications and was therefore paid-off and replaced by the firm of Roche & McConnell who took over all electrical and engineering requirements. A partner in that firm, P.J. Roche, had been a student in Rockwell from 1904 to 1909. Disagreements with the original architect emerged and he was replaced by the consultants Messrs Jones & Kelly. The plan involved the complete demolition of the New Tipperary classrooms, of the existing students' refectory and of other classrooms and offices. The finding of an alternative temporary refectory was the greatest difficulty. The Theatre Hall was commandeered. The stage became a kitchen and a food storage space. The classrooms on the ground floor of the Crehan Wing were the only regular classrooms left in operation and were therefore not sufficient. Classes were held in the Big Study and in the smaller study (now the College Library) and sometimes more than one class at a time was held at each of these venues. It was a difficult time for staff and students.

However, by the end of 1942 the interior work was completed. The exterior of the College got a new dominating feature, the clock tower. This was built on the stairs well of the Silas House. It is neatly designed in Neo-Romanesque, but in the opinion of Fr. Comerford it is too tall for the long Northern wing of which it is the focal point, and a two storey tower would have been better in proportion. Fr. Dinan, however, wanted a belfry with chiming bells striking the hours and quarters. The belfry added another story to the tower but the bells were too costly. The result, according to Fr. Comerford was an empty belfry, a silent clock and a tower that was too tall.

In the interior the long hall is the outstanding feature of the reconstructed building. The Romanesque motif of the Chapel hall was continued right through the long hall. It measured ninety eight yards to the base of the terrazzo main stairs and with ample width and height, its mahogany dado height panelling, its rather unusual pattern ceramic tiled floor, broken regularly by three mosaic crests and its general architecture make this hall a treasured feature. On the first landing of the main staircase there is a beautiful stained-glass window of Our Lady of the Woods presented by the late Archbishop of Dublin, Dr. John Charles McQuaid. It is a very fine example of the later work of the Harry Clarke Studios and was designed by William Dowling. There were originally two Ivie Hone windows on the ground floor level, at either side of the main stairs. These were later removed because of impending structural changes.

The refectory with its entrance at the bottom of the main stairs is also beautifully designed with a fine ceiling, nice window sashes and a low mahogany dado panelling. It was enhanced by the addition of the three southern decorative stained-glass windows, also the work of William Dowling. Two of these were presented by the Rockwell Union and the central one by Canon O'Meara, uncle of Fr. John Byrne and Bishop Byrne. The space between the refectory and the kitchen was utilised to improve the kitchen annexes with the installation of a cold room, a new vegetable pantry and a dessert pantry.

The long hall

Walking down the long hall, starting at the western end, the first entrances on the left hand side were to the three Science laboratories. Next were the locker rooms, toilets and exit to the outdoor recreation facilities. Further down the rooms on the left hand side have changed in their use many times since from classrooms to reading rooms computer room and recreation rooms to the present-day secretary's office, Principal's office and surgery. At the end of the Long Hall opposite the refectory is another very fine large room, identical in proportion to the College Library. Its function has also changed many times over the years.

The senior choir in 1939 with Fr. Daly and Mr. White

With the new building complete, attention turned to the renovation of the Old Mansion and in the summer of 1942 a new and more imposing hall door and entrance was completed. In 1943 extensive improvements were carried out in St. Joseph's. The whole exterior was re-plastered and this together with the demolition of minor buildings completely transformed the picturesque house by the lake.

The front avenue to the College from the Dublin-Cork road was re-shaped and the impressive entrance portal and gates erected. The new avenue measured two hundred and fifty yards long. It was in 1949 that the final stage of this new front entrance and avenue was completed, namely the planting of the borders and shelter belts. The planning and arranging of the trees and shrubs for this work had been going on for almost two years. In the planting two distinct things had to be considered, the shelter belts on either side and the actual avenue border. Many varieties of deciduous trees and ornamental conifers were planted on either side of the avenue and in the existing belt of conifers directly in front of the College which was extended to meet the new avenue. Where the avenue opens out to meet the front of the College a striking bed of rhododendron containing twenty four choice hybrids was laid down, and all along the College frontage the terraced border on the conifer belt was edged with smaller annual plants. The maintenance of this magnificent entrance was overseen by Fr. Comerford for the rest of his life. It was a labour of love for a man who was such a talented gardener and who was regularly seen by visitors to the College pottering with his beloved plants and flowers.

Another major initiative undertaken in 1940 was a three-year programme providing for the clearance, drainage and afforestation or re-afforestation of thirty five statute acres of the College property. Of the fifty to sixty thousand trees to be planted the greater number belonged to the rather neglected hardwoods, oak, walnut and beech. The remainder consisted for the most part of softwoods such as Austrian pine, silver birch and Lombardian poplar. The beauty of the already well-wooded Rock was further enhanced by a plantation of special ornamental trees including cedar, Spanish chestnut, pseudo-acacia, the tulip tree, maple, the Chinese ghost tree, the Japanese cedar and cherry-trees. It was proposed to plant a demonstration avenue for educational and botanical purposes with one tree from every family, each tree being labelled with its name, together with a new orchard with modern lay-out. Timber from the existing plantations which was ready for harvesting was treated in the college saw-mills.

A journalist, Miss Gertrude Gaffney, who visited Rockwell in 1941 wrote in the *Irish Independent*:

"I have never seen anything more lovely than the setting of Rockwell, the great stretches of lusciously rich land with islands of spreading trees, cupped by three ranges of mountains, The Galtees, the Comeraghs and Knockmealdown; the land blindingly green, the mountains changing every few minutes from cobalt to misty grey-blue.

Since my return from Rockwell I have been thinking how much the country owes to institutions of this kind. Over a hundred men have been employed on the construction of the new school buildings, now completed. When farms of the size attached to the College were owned by individuals they employed at best fifteen or twenty people; The Holy Ghost Fathers employ eighty five at Rockwell. They have one hundred and sixty acres of tillage this year, probably the largest single tillage effort in the country. They have started to build houses for the workers, five-apartment houses with fine rooms and big windows that overlook a lovely stretch of country to the mountains."[2]

The great impression which the new development of Rockwell had on visitors was also shared by those within the College as is evident from the pen of Fr. Walker. *And as we look around on the long hall of the forty arches with its mosaic inlays, the great terrazzo staircase crowned with its exquisite window of Our Lady of the Wood from the Harry Clarke studios, the billiard rooms and reading rooms, the new dormitories, the sunlit classrooms and the soaring tower, we feel that we may breathe a fervent prayer of thanks to God. The kitchen has been re-adjusted and equipped with several new large-size electrical labour-saving devices, a long awaited refrigerator room and (cheers!) an ice-cream producer. The dairy has installed a new butter-making plant, a new poultry farm has been set up, new piggeries are under construction, the saw-mills are being extended to keep pace with the steady progress of the forestry scheme. And a sound film projector has been installed in the Theatre.[3]*

WARTIME ROCKWELL

Despite the feel-good factor about the development of the College, Rockwell did not escape the restrictions which the War had placed on society, with parents and College authorities trying to cope with the rationing of bread, tea and sugar. Management of the Rockwell Farm had to adjust its programme because of the compulsory tillage policy introduced by the Government in 1940 which, during the War years almost doubled the acreage under crops. It was the shortage of coal, gas and petrol which caused most disruption to parents and College authorities. Private motoring became almost impossible by 1942 and was replaced by many resurrected horse-drawn vehicles. Because of the location of Rockwell in the heart of the countryside this caused problems in the ferrying of students to and from Goold's Cross Railway Station at holiday time and at the opening of term. Even simple necessary daily trips to Cashel became a burden. Student travel to sporting fixtures was also curtailed.

Rockwell was conscious of the much more serious deprivation caused in countries in the war-front and it was for this reason that in 1944 twelve students from war-torn France spent the year in Rockwell. They returned home at the end of the school year in June and were replaced the following September by another twelve French students who spent the year in Rockwell. This arrangement was facilitated by the Holy Ghost Fathers in the Mother House of the Congregation in Paris. Another arrival in Rockwell in 1939 because of the war was Fr. James Kromer, an exile from the Third Reich. He came to carry on

Sixth Year 1944-45
Front row: J. Gleeson, M. Sheedy, P. Roche, P. Ryan, F. Heelan, B. Hoare, O'O'Riordan, J. O'Mahony.
2nd row: J. Kennedy, J. Keane, J. O'Carroll, B. Conlon, D. O'Sullivan, Rev. P. Liddane C.S.Sp.,
J. Keyes, T. O'Regan, R. Conway, P. Murray, J. Crean.
3rd row: F. Hudney, M. Moran, J. Moynihan, J. Dunne, B. Keating, C. Martin, T. Finucane,
M. Griffin, J. Kennedy, K. Mackey, J. McGrath, M. Power, W. Gaynor.
4th row: P. Devlin, J. Flavin, L. Cusack, S. O'Dea, F. O'Farrell, B. McInerney, J. Nunan, A. Doyle,
P. Conway, M. Delaney, P. Marron, M. McNeela, W. Ryan.
5th row: P. Blackwell, J. Harris, F. Cainan, W. Nolan, P. Corish, J. Heffernan, M. Fahey, J. Ryan,
G. O'Shea, D. Beddy, M. Maher.
6th row: D. Maher, A. Tobin, J. Whelan, J. Peters, J. Harrington, S. O'Byrne, J. Daly, T. O'Farrell,
T.K. Murphy, R. Shanahan, P. Shelley.

the German tradition maintained for many years in Rockwell by the late Frs Muller and Schmidt. For the next decade he was to engage in the teaching of arts and crafts to students.

Rockwell was also concerned for its past-pupils who were actively involved in the conflict. The first Allied prisoner of war was a Rockwell man. On 4th September 1939 when Britain and France had been at war for barely twenty four hours a squadron of R.A.F. planes was detailed to make a low-level attack on German shipping in the Kiel Canal. On one of the planes was Laurence Slattery of Littleton, a Rockwell student of the early thirties, as wireless operator and gunner. His plane was hit and as it plunged into the sea it rebounded into the air and Slattery was flung clear. He landed in the cold sea and regained sufficient consciousness to operate the inflator of his life-jacket before again passing out. The next thing he sensed was being lifted aboard a rescue vessel as a German voice in English informed him that he was now a prisoner. Of the plane's crew of three he was the only survivor and spent the entire remaining five years of the war in captivity.[4]

Among those to share the unenviable distinction of being the first to enter the Belsen horror camp was Dr. Paddy O'Donnell of Kildorrery who was a student in the 1920s. Having qualified as a doctor he joined the British Army

Legion of Mary
1949 with Fr.
Comerford

Medical Service and was with the Guards Armoured Brigade from the landing on D-Day and with them reached Belsen in April 1945. His work was to organise and supervise the transfer of camp internees to the decontamination centre. From Belsen he went to Norway to tend the German prisoners of war at Narvik. Major Kevin Mallen, was with the intelligence section of the American Air Force Commandos on a special mission to India. His brother Brendan also served in the American army and his brother Ciaran served in the British Army. All three Mallen brothers were past-students.[5]

On a cycling
tour in 1939

CLASS AS USUAL.

The Rockwell student population grew steadily during the presidency of Fr. Dinan increasing from 400 in 1944 to just 3 short of 500 in 1948. (Appendix XIII) It is evident from these figures that not all students followed the five year course. Approximately 12 of the 2nd Year students each year followed what was the Preparatory or Pre-School course. An increase in numbers each year came in 4th Year, the year of the Intermediate Certificate. There was a notable drop-

The College orchestra in 1940 with Fr. Walker and Mr. White

out rate between 4th and 6th Year as is evident from comparing the numbers in 4th Year with those two years later in 6th Year. It can be concluded from these figures that the majority of students aspired to doing the Leaving Certificate while a sizeable minority may have been content with enjoying a period in Rockwell without any academic ambition. It is evident that past students found Rockwell an attractive school for the education of their sons when it is considered that in 1946 there were twenty nine students who were sons of past students.[6]

Of the seventeen subjects on the Department of Education's programme for Boys' Secondary Schools in the 1940s, Rockwell offered fourteen. These included Latin Greek, the modern continental languages French, Spanish, Italian and German and Physics, Chemistry, Drawing, Music and Commerce. The winning of University and Intermediate Scholarships by Rockwell students throughout the 1940s was regular. Fr. Dinan reported that in the public examinations of 1945 Rockwell set a new record when it won eight scholarships and that in the Intermediate Examination of that year a Rockwell student obtained either first or second place in Ireland in Irish, English, Maths, Physics, French, Spanish, Italian, Latin and Greek. Fr. Dinan reported that in the public examinations of 1947 Rockwell obtained its highest number of successes ever secured: five University scholarships and four first places in Ireland obtained in the Leaving Certificate. First and second places were obtained in Mathematics, Spanish, Latin, English, Italian and Chemistry in the Leaving Certificate with first places in the Intermediate Certificate in Commerce, Spanish and Italian.

The promotion of the Irish Language was a major policy of the Department of Education in the 1940s and each year it presented the Department Shield to the school which it considered did most during the year to promote the language. This Shield was awarded to Rockwell in 1940 and 1941. In those years Eamon de Valera was acting as Taoiseach and Minister of Education and it was in the latter capacity that in 1941 he came to Rockwell to personally present the Shield. He availed of the visit to remain for a few days rest during which he renewed acquaintance with old faces and old places.[7]

The promotion of the Irish language was evident not only from examination results but also from the work of the Irish language groups in the College such as Na Réadóirí and Cumann Díospóirechta, both promoted fervently by Fr. Mullins, but also from the number of articles in Irish by students and invited contributors which Fr. Walker included each year in the *Rockwell Annual*. In 1945 a number of parents asked if it was possible that their boys could be taken for a spell in the Gaeltacht under the care of their Rockwell teachers. Fortunately The Holy Ghost Congregation owned a house in the Waterford Gaeltacht, An Rinn. This house in Helvick had originally been used to stage Irish courses for the prefects and staff of the three Holy Ghost colleges. The emergency had curtailed arrangements and so the house was available in July 1945 and a three week course was organised for eight students from Rockwell and one from Blackrock.

While some Rockwell students achieved great fluency in the Irish Language and obtained outstanding results in examinations, there were others who struggled and found the academic side of life difficult. One such student penned his feelings in a poem which Fr. Walker felt merited inclusion in the *Annual* of 1940. Despite its poetic limitations, its sentiments might strike a chord for some parents, teachers and students.

I don't mind slogging now and then   *He tells him that I've tons of brains*
And even I can stand it when   *And if I'd only tame the pains*
I'm put at penance each day   *To study hard and persevere*

English debating team 1940
M. White, F. O'Meara, P. Leahy, G. O'Carroll, H. McCay, W. Roycroft.

While all the rest are out at play.
The Dean may spiff me and may scold
Because I don't do what I'm told
But Gosh! It fairly makes me mad
When he writes a letter to my dad.
My dad is easy to annoy
He doesn't understand a boy
He says to me "Now listen James
You're spending too much time at games
I want to see you lead your class
And not be one of those who Pass"
You see now why it makes me mad
When the Dean of Studies writes to dad

I'd be a dab in every sphere.
Then dad expects me win a prize
As he did when he was my size.
Is it any wonder I get mad
Each time the Dean writes to my dad
It's very easy to complain
That "James is falling off again"
But I'd prefer my work could be
A question 'twixt the Dean and me.
I'd take the sloggin's by the score
And penances and spiffs galore
But honestly it makes me mad
Each time the Dean writes to my dad

The academic year came to a close with Prize Day at the end of May. For many years this function had been presided over by Archbishop Harty and from 1942 by his successor Archbishop Kinane. The occasion commenced with High Mass presided over by the Archbishop in the College Chapel and the singing of the *Te Deum* in thanksgiving for the year's work. Prize Day was an occasion when the President congratulated the prize-winners, highlighted the events of the year and reiterated the ethos of Rockwell. In 1941 Fr Dinan mentioned the visit of the new Archbishop of Dublin to Rockwell soon after his consecration. Both men were well known to each other of course from the days when Dr. McQuaid was President of Blackrock College. Dr. McQuaid visited again in 1943 as did President Seán T. O'Kelly and on another occasion that year when Mr. de Valera visited he was accompanied by Mr. McEntee, Minister for Local Government and Mr. Derrig, Minister for Education.

An Taoiseach Eamon de Valera presents the shield to Fr. Dinan.

Reflecting on war-time conditions in the Western World Fr. Dinan stated at Prize Day in 1943 "It is the lot of our boys now passing through our halls to step into a world ominously dominated by broken covenants and propagandist lying. In Rockwell we have laboured to ensure that the young men whom we are sending from our College will be schooled to live their lives with that single faced rectitude which is the honour and crown of a just living man and which alone can guarantee the survival of the noble traditions of our Catholic Irish nation." And at Prize Day in 1947 he said "Whatever emphasis one may wish to set on this or that element of Catholic training we here in Rockwell have desired to stress the essential need of supernatural standards in the guidance of youthful life together with that courage which is one of the fruits of the full living of the true Faith. It is in a spirit of crusader-like manliness that we wish our boys to go forth to challenge and give battle to the pagan arrogance of our times".

Archbishop Leen, an illustrious past student, was the guest at Prize Day in 1948 and he

An Taoiseach with Fr. John Byrne and Fr. Dinan

Prize Day 1948
Past student Archbishop Leen with Fr. Curtin and Fr. Dinan

paid a compliment to Rockwell when he said "But we of the old Rockwell take off our hats to the new Rockwell that we see before us, and if we did not do so we would be deviating from the truth. It is not without reason that the word "Rock" appears in the name of the College. It stands for a spirit of rock-like constancy to the Catholic Faith and a spirit of manly effort in Catholic living. I am delighted to see the Rockwell of to-day not only carrying on this tradition but even going forward to an even greater success....I find that there has been in recent years in Rockwell a great development of all the things that go together to make the thorough training of the complete Catholic boy."

MUSIC AND DRAMA

Rockwell music students continued to take the examinations of the Royal Irish Academy of Music. In the early forties the majority of these students took examinations in string instruments, especially the violin with the result that the College orchestra was quite strong and was supplemented by Fr. Walker on cello and Mr. Cremin on violin. There were twenty two students in the orchestra in 1940 and their repertoire included minuets by Beethoven and Mozart, a selection of jigs and hornpipes and the overture to *The Gondoliers*.

The departure of Fr. Daly to Blackrock in 1939 was a loss to choral singing in Rockwell but the baton was taken up by Fr. Walker and Mr. White until the appointment in 1943 of Mr. J.G. Croghan as Professor of Music and Mr. Xavier Gibson in 1945. Two choirs, a senior and junior, took part in the plain chant competition in Thurles in 1940. The following year there were forty students in the senior choir and their repertoire included Gounod's *Ave Verum*, a *Tantum Ergo* and *O Salutaris* by Mr.Stein, a former professor of Music at Blackrock College. For the visit of Archbishop McQuaid the choir sang Ett's *Ecce Sacerdos* then for Pentecost Stein's *Veni Sancte Spiritus*, for Corpus Christi Stoeklin's *Pie Pellicane*. For the Feast of the Ascension Gounod's chorus *Unfold! Unfold! Unfold Ye Portals Everlasting* from the *Redemption* oratorio. Fr. Botrel's *Requiem Mass* was rendered on a number of occasions. The singing of the Common of the *Missa de Angelis* and *Orbis Factor* by the entire student body was part of the Rockwell tradition. Elgar's *Ave Verum* was in the repertoire of 1943 and was performed by the choir at the Sligo Feis Cheoil which it had entered for the first time.

Brother Benedict produced *H.M.S. Ambassador*, an operetta, in May 1944, the first of his many productions. His annual productions from 1945 had Mr.

Combined orchestra and choir 1941

Gibson as musical director with the sets painted and designed by Fr. Comerford and the wardrobe provided by Burke's of Dublin. Brother Eugene was the stage electrician and Johnny Moore the stage carpenter. The orchestra for these productions was led by musicians from Clonmel, Tipperary and Cashel and included students, prefects, Fr. Walker and Mr. White. In the 1947 production of *The Pirates of Penzance* parts were played by Herbert Hanna, Patrick Baynton, Tim Murray, Michael Finlan, Frank Foster, Paddy Lynch and John Moloney. The

English Debating Society 1947
Seated: *B. Murphy, M. O'Regan, D. Foley, J. Hogan.*
Standing: *W. Corrigan, J. Berkery Inset K. Walsh*

1948 production of *The Gondoliers* had leading roles played by Herbert Hanna, Patrick Baynton, John Geary, Alan Hanna, Laurence Breen, Patrick Walsh, Patrick McInerney, Thomas Deehan and Brendan Thompson. In the 1949 production of *The Mikado*. Paddy Baynton, Herbert Hanna, Alan Hanna, Colm O'Regan, John Geary, Paddy McInerney, Tommy Deehan, Danny Hale and Paddy Walsh were the principals.

While greatly involved with the production of Gilbert and Sullivan operettas, Fr. Comerford and Br. Benedict were also involved with production of plays and short sketches, as was Fr. Mullins. At least two plays in Irish were produced each year by Fr. Mullins, usually at St. Patrick's Day and in December. Fr. Comerford regularly produced plays for the students of St. Joseph's with Br. Benedict looking after the make-up.

CLUBS AND SOCIETIES

The English Debating Society, under the patronage of St. Thomas Aquinas and directed by Fr. Walker, debated topics that were issues of the time, such as the quality of education, the Irish economy, the flight from the land and unemployment. The auditor of the English Debating Society in 1946 was Leo Nealon who afterwards became a journalist with *The Irish Independent* and a sports commentator with Radio Éireann. An Cumann Díospóireachta, which was directed by Fr. Mullins, tended to focus on issues such as partition and the status of the Irish language (issues which were close to his heart).

Fr. Kromer directed the Arts and Crafts Club which in 1942 had eighty members who were involved with book binding, lino cutting, wood carving, fret work, painting and carpentry. Building models of aeroplanes and boats was very popular. The club sent a number of exhibits to an exhibition which was held each year in Mungret College, Limerick.

The Camera Club concentrated on the unique scenic beauty surrounding Rockwell which had ample scope for developing photographic talent. Promising photographers in the early 1940s included Risteard Ó Colmáin, Lorcan Connaughton and Joe Walsh. Lectures were held regularly on matters photographic and exhibits were displayed in the Long Hall on Union Day each year. The Club affiliated to the National Film Institute of Ireland in 1946.

The Chess Club was directed by Fr. Meaney who presented medals in 1948 for the winners of senior and junior competitions which were won respectively by Denis Wall and Kenneth O'Riordan. Home and away competitions were regularly held with Blackrock College. In 1948 the first junior championship of Munster was held. It was won by Kenneth O'Riordan who was picked to represent Ireland in a schoolboy tournament with England. Rockwell was the only College to have two representatives at the All Ireland Schoolboy Championship held in Dublin in 1949, they being Charles Cantwell and Kenneth O'Riordan.

The Cycling Club which had been founded in 1939 had been confined to seniors. At Easter 1940, however, the invitation to "bring back your bike" was extended to juniors and there was a big response with bikes of all shapes and sizes appearing. Cycling on the roads of Tipperary during the War years was less hazardous because the shortage of petrol had greatly reduced vehicle traffic. On Whit Monday 1940 a cycle to Slievenamon was organised for seniors while the juniors cycled to the Glen of Aherlow.

The 18th Tipperary Troop of the Catholic Boy Scouts of Ireland was founded in Rockwell on May 18th 1949. Order and discipline, colour and pageantry, these would seem at first sight to have been the keynotes of the inaugural reception held in the College Theatre. First of all the Scouts candidates filed into the hall, attired in College blazer, Scout tunic, shorts and socks, and they had already taken up their positions before the dais, when the colour parties marched in, carrying the official Scout colours, (the flag of St. Patrick.). They were followed by the President of the College, the national chaplain, the Chief Scout and the diocesan commissioner and members of the College Community flanked by a guard of Scouts. The ceremony opened with the *Veni Sancte Spiritus* rendered by the Scout schola. The Troop Flag was then blessed and the investiture commenced. The Scout Master was Br Benedict. The Boy Scouts were to be part of official Rockwell functions for a number of years.

On a cycling tour in 1940

THE LAKE HOUSE

In an article in the *Annual* of 1940 about St. Joseph's, its Director Fr. Comerford, wrote that for a decade and more about one quarter of Rockwell's annual student population had been composed of missionary students. That year was no exception, he wrote, and the Junior Scholasticate was full to capacity. Throughout the 1940s there were about eighty students each year in St. Joseph's. While following the same academic programme as the other students, they also enjoyed the regular talks and film shows on the missions given by missionaries home on leave. The legendary missionary and past student of St. Joseph's, Fr. Mellet made a big impression when he visited in 1941.

Many St. Joseph's students were members of the Legion of Mary which was introduced into Rockwell on 8th December 1942. Twelve senior students were chosen to found the first praesidium. By Easter there were 34 active and 66 auxiliary members. It was therefore decided to form a second praesidium. The titles of the praesidia corresponded to the two College windows, *Our Lady of Rockwell* and *Our Lady of the Woods*. Every legionary was expected to do some definite good work every week. The scope for such action was necessarily limited in a boarding school but the legionaries were allotted a separate oratory from which they could prepare the altars and arrange chalices and vestments. They also sold pamphlets of the *Catholic Truth Society*. Manual work was also undertaken and legionaries were frequently seen hard at work with hoe and spade, rake and hedge-clippers, tending the paths in the graveyard and around the shrine of Our Lady in the Rock. During wet half days in the winter term they organised Whist Drives and concerts for the students. They helped in the College Theatre getting it ready for various functions and acting as stewards when called upon. Each year they got the grounds in order for the May and Corpus Christi processions and erected the temporary altars. They took charge of the annual Holy Childhood collection and sold leaflets of the League of

Junior scholastics 1939

Prayer for the canonisation of Blessed Oliver Plunkett. The work in which they had proved most successful was in providing a combined book-stall and Catholic Repository. Students from St. Joseph's were also involved with The Pioneers directed by Fr. Mullins and in Na Réideoirí, which was the Irish language version of the movement.

RUGBY

During Fr. Dinan's presidency Rockwell won the Senior Cup twice and the Junior Cup on five occasions. The seniors did not take part in the Bowen Shield until 1948 and pre-Cup matches were played against Clonmel, Clanwilliam, Mount St. Joseph's College Roscrea and the two sister colleges, Blackrock and St. Mary's. The first Cup match in 1940 was against Mungret and was played in Clonmel. It ended in a draw and the replay in Thomond Park also ended level. The second replay in Clonmel generated great excitement with a six point victory for Rockwell. An easy win over Crescent College by 24 points to nil followed. The final in Cork against Presentation College was fixed for Monday 19th March at the Mardyke. At the very last moment word came that the match was off because Pres had objected to the referee. Rockwell was awarded the match without fielding a team. The team which reached the final was: Vincent Keane, Frank O'Meara, Thomas O'Sullivan, Patrick Ryan, Michael Farrell, Michael O'Donoghue (captain), Michael Ryan, Colm .Danaher, Timothy Moriarty, Tom Sweeney, John Wall, William Burke, Billy Roycroft, James Maher. The five inter provincials in 1940 were Michael Ryan, Billy Roycroft, Arthur Lawlor, Tommy O'Sullivan and Frank O'Meara.

Frank O'Meara captained the team in 1941 which beat Pres Cork at the Mardyke but lost to Mungret in the semi-final at Clonmel. The four inter-provincials of 1941 were Frank O'Meara, Mick Dunne, Frank Kavanagh and Billy Hartnett. The Cup returned to Rockwell in 1942 with victories over Crescent and Mungret to reach the final against Pres. That final finished scoreless, even after extra time. In the replay in Thomond Park Paddy Ryan's try was the only score of the game but was enough to bring the Cup back to Rockwell. The winning team, captained by Mick Dunne was: Des Healy, C. Coghlan, B. Fitzgerald, J. Neenan, T. Enright, J. Mannion, J. Maher, E. McSweeney, N. Fitzgerald, Gerald Ahearne, Bertie O'Hanlon, Mick Dunne, Joe Dudley, Paddy Ryan. The best known player on that team was Bertie O'Hanlon, the future international. He was an all-round athlete. In the summer of 1943, having completed his Leaving Certificate, he won the 100 yards, 200 yards and long jump at the Munster Inter-County Athletic Championship held in Mitchelstown. At the Cork County Championship he repeated the same three victories and equalled the record for the 100 yards.

Bertie O'Hanlon

And in the same season he reached the final of the Irish Tennis Championship at Rushbrook and later in the year was on the Cork Constitution senior rugby team.

Des Healy captained the 1943 team with Norman Fitzgerald as vice captain. Both of them were inter-provincials as were Joe Dudley and Gerald Ahearne. In the first Cup match against Mungret an unconverted try by Charlie O'Reilly was the only score of the match. For the final Rockwell travelled to Cork to meet Christians. It ended in a scoreless draw but Rockwell lost the replay. Joe Dudley captained the 1944 team with Dermot O'Connor as vice-captain. In the first Cup match against Crescent Billie O'Brien got the only scores of the match, two unconverted tries. A victory over Mungret by 12 points to 3 followed. In the final at Thomond Park Rockwell lost to Christians for the second year in a row.

Paul Murtagh was captain in 1945 with Paddy Conway vice-captain. Victories over Glenstal and Mungret earned a place in the final against Presentation College, Cork which Rockwell lost by 10 points to 3. The first cup match in 1946 was against Crescent. Rockwell won that match but for the second year in a row was beaten in the final by Presentation College Cork. Reporting on that match the *Irish Independent* referred to boys waving banners and "chewing rhythmically on caramels which they pouched mysteriously to chant war-cries and school songs at the frenzied admonition of puce-faced cheerleaders. The team was: Jim Brosnan, A. Harris, Paul Murtagh (captain), Noel Keane, J. Dunne, J. Maguire, P. Ryan, G. Ryan, W, McSweeney, J. Spillane, L. Dineen, Paddy Houlihan, T. English, B. Hanley, P. Kissane.

A future President of Rockwell, Fr. Paddy Holohan, captained the 1947 team with Brendan O'Farrell as vice-captain. The Munster Branch changed the date of age limit from February to August, thus depriving three members of the previous year's team of eligibility. Rockwell entered the Bowen Shield competition for the first time and won it but was beaten in the Cup by Crescent. Jim Brosnan and Gerry Kenny were the most prominent members of the 1948 team which lost in the semi-final to C.B.C. while the 1949 team beat Mungret and Pres but lost in the final to Crescent. Jim Brosnan was later to distinguish himself as the great Kerry All Ireland winning footballer.

The record of the J.C.T, trained for a number of years by Fr. Meaney, was impressive in those years. The Cup-winning team of 1942 was captained by Joe

Senior Cup Winners 1942
Row 1: B. O'Hanlon, M. Dunne,
J. Dudlley, M.Ryan
Row 2: N. Fitzgerald, G. Ahearne,
M. Hassett.
Row 3: T. Enright, J. Mannion,
J. Maher, E. McSweeney.
Top Row: D. Healy, C. Coghlan,
B. Fitzgerald, J. Neenan

Junior Cup Winning Team 1949
Front: *M. English, R. Walsh.*
Seated: *J. McInerney, J. Buckley, P. McGrath, M. McEvoy, P. Casey, J. Cosgrove, E. Martin, J. Bernard.*
Back: *J. Farrell, A. Fitzpatrick, T. Redmond, T. McGrath, J. Bennett, C. Burke, S. Murray.*

Dudley and beat Mungret, Crescent and Presentation College, Cork The team was: Joe Dudley, Charlie O'Reilly, Denis Finnucane, Ted Crofton, Jack Sheerin, Tim Richardson, Mick Ryan, D. O'Connor, M. O'Sullivan, F. Cummins, D. Brosnan, M. Meagher, R. Burke, R. Murphy, Liam Lynch, J. Murphy, W. O'Brien. They beat Mungret in Tipperary by eleven points to nil. Rockwell was due to meet Crescent in semi-final but they withdrew at the last minute. The final was against Presentation College, Cork and Rockwell won by two converted tries to nil.

The Junior Cup returned to Rockwell in 1943 with victories over Mungret, Crescent and Pres. That team was captained by Ray Murphy with Paul Murtagh as vice-captain. Other players included Gerry Crean, Bertie Hanly, Phil Ryan, John Hindle, Jack Dee, Charlie O'Reilly, Peadar Devlin, Joe Keane, Brian Fitzgerald, Jack O'Regan, J. Maguire, M. Griffin, Rory O'Connor, A. Harris, T. English.

The J.C.T. of 1947 which won the Cup was trained by Fr. Crowley, with the assistance of the prefect, Mr. Holland. Jerry Kenny was captain and Mick Brosnan vice-captain. Other players included Jarlath Fahy, Seán Conway, Pat Casey, Jim Burke, Pat Burke, Frank Gallagher, Oliver O'Sullivan Paddy Horgan, Noel Keane, Seán D'Arcy, Brian King and David Duffy. Rockwell drew with Crescent in the semi-final at Thomond Park and secured victory in the replay in Clonmel with tries from Jim Burke and Jarlath Fahy. In the final against Pres in Thomond Park Jarlath Fahy kicked a penalty between the posts for the only score of the game in which Mick Brosnan and Jerry Kenny were influential.

Mr. Holland trained the Cup-winning J.C.T. of 1948 with Mick Brosnan as captain and Pat Casey as vice-captain. Other prominent players included Jack

Manning, Bobby Walsh, Jim Corry and Denis Bernard. The team beat Mungret and Crescent before beating Pres in the final played in the Mardyke in Cork. The J.C.T. of 1949 was in search of three-in-a-row and had a bye into the semi-final in which it drew with Pres but won the replay by 6 points to 3. The final was against Crescent and the fact that Crescent had already beaten the senior team added spice to the game which was played at Thomond Park on 7th April on a day of very high wind. Mick English, playing at out-half dropped a goal in each half and that was sufficient for Rockwell to win by 6 points to 3.

GAELIC GAMES

As has been seen in the previous chapter, Rockwell hurlers withdrew from the Harty Cup in 1939 and in 1940 the seniors competed for the first time in the Munster Colleges Hurling Cup and the juniors in the Munster Colleges Hurling Shield. Each year throughout the 1940s the hurling season opened with friendly matches against Mount St. Joseph's College, Roscrea, St. Kieran's College, Kilkenny, Thurles C.B.S. and the local clubs of Cashel and Golden. On a few occasions in the 1940s Rockwell had a challenge against the Tipperary minor team. Rockwell made hurling history in 1940 by capturing the two trophies. The seniors beat St. Colman's College Fermoy in the first round of the Cup following goals from Mick Ryan, Jerry Ryan and Tom Joye. They then had an easy win over Farrenferris and in the final, played in Mitchestown on 16th March they beat St. Munchin's by 5-5 to 3-3. Mick Ryan was captain and Jerry Ryan vice-captain. The juniors beat St. Colman's in the Shield and in the final they beat Ballinasloe by 6-4 to 4-1. The junior captain was Billy Roycroft with Paddy Ryan as vice-captain.

In 1941 the seniors won the Cup for the second year in a row. In the Gaelic Grounds in Limerick they drew with Farrenferris in the first round but won the replay. The final was against St. Flannan's College, Ennis and Rockwell won by 5-4 to 2-2, the leading players being Martin and Paddy Ryan, Mick Hassett and Tom Joye. The juniors lost to Farrenferris in the first round of the Shield. Fr. O'Driscoll was in charge of the senior team in 1942 with Eamonn McSweeney as captain. Other prominent players included Mick Hassett, Paddy Creamer, Seán Mannion, Paddy Ryan, Martin Ryan, Joe Heavey, Frank Cummins, Leo Leydon and Jerry Purcell. The seniors lost narrowly to Farrenferris in the first round as did the juniors.

The seniors won the Cup for the third time in 1943 by beating St. Colman's, Roscrea and St. Flannan's. The team was captained by goalkeeper Paddy Creamer with Frank Cummins as vice-captain. Other players on that team were Leo Leyden, Rory Leahy, Joe Whelan, Mick Delaney, Ernan Neville, Martin Ryan, John O'Mahony Jerry Harney, Nick O'Dea, Jim O'Shea, John Mannion, Paddy Meagher, Liam Lynch. Gerry Ahern and Christy Foley.

Rockwell failed to advance beyond the first round in either senior or junior championship matches in 1944 or 1945. In 1946, however, the seniors beat Roscrea and Farrenferris to qualify for the final against St. Flannan's. That final was postponed on a number of occasions for various reasons and when it was finally fixed, Flannan's refused to play on the grounds that it was too near to exam time. Rockwell was awarded the match but refused to accept the Cup because the final had not been played.

The seniors lost to Roscrea in the first round of the Cup in 1947 but in 1948 they drew with St. Colman's in the first round and won the replay. They then travelled to Thurles for the semi-final against St. Flannan's but were decisively beaten. The team captain that year was Jerry Kelly and the other players were Brendan Deegan, Mickey Buckley, Jarlath Fahy, Henry O'Brien, Pat Horgan, Joe Heenan, Denis Bernard, Seán O'Sullivan, Pat Moran, Seán Richardson, Patsy Halloran, Seán Conway, Tadhg Keane. Rockwell was fortunate to have among its prefects in 1949 the distinguished Cork senior hurler Bernie Murphy. The Munster Senior Cup had ended so Rockwell had no senior team that year. The under 17s, trained by Bernie Murphy, lost to Thrules C.B.S.

In the years 1940 to 1943 some notable names appear among the Rockwell hurlers. Paddy Creamer from Cappamore was later a captain of the Limerick senior team. Rory Leahy was a member of the famous Boherlahan hurling family and nephew of the former Tipperary hurler, Tommy Leahy, whose farm was adjacent to that of Rockwell. Tom Joye later played for Tipperary and Mick Hassett captained the Dublin hurlers. Frank Cummins also captained Dublin and was regarded as one of the leading players of his time. John O'Mahony of

Athletic team 1941
Front: *E. Noonan, J. Lynch, E. Ahearne.*
Middle: *G. Fitzgerald, M. Fitzgerald, M. Dunne, B. Fitzgerald, J. Sheerin.*
Back: *B. O'Hanlon, J. Mannion, T. Hunt, D. Healy.*

Kilcrohane played for Cork and Joe Whelan of Bodyke captained the Clare team. Mickey "Jinks" Ryan made the Tipperary minor team and Seán Nash was a forceful player for many years in Limerick hurling. In 1941 the Rockwell hurlers were trained by Fr. Joe Nolan, then a prefect and later Headmaster and in 1942 the hurlers were trained by Fr. Oliver Barrett, then a prefect and brother of Jack Barrett who hurled at centre field for Cork alongside Jack Lynch. Jim Aherne, the great Cork and inter-provincial Gaelic footballer was a prefect in Rockwell in 1948 but he was involved more with the hurlers that the footballers that year.

Rockwell Gaelic footballers won the Munster Senior Cup in 1941. They beat St. Colman's Fermoy in the semi-final and then travelled to Buttevant for the final against Rochestown Capuchin College which they won by 5-4 to 1-2. Teams were not entered in the Munster championship for the remainder of the 1940s because of a concentration on rugby and hurling. There was great interest, however, in the Gaelic football house leagues which commenced at the end of the rugby season each year. In 1948 a Rockwell Gaelic football team, consisting of students and three prefects, Jim Ahearne, Bernie Murphy and Pat Holland played University College Cork in a challenge match. Jim Aherne was centre-half forward and was closely marked by his fellow Cork player and U.C.C. captain, Paddy Tyers. Among the Rockwell students who were prominent in that match were Seán Lynch, Jarlath Fahy, Jim Brosnan (the future Kerry footballer) and Denis Bernard (the future Cork footballer) who was that year only in 4th Year. Rockwell won that match by 6-7 to 2-7.

Handball continued to be popular with students throughout the 1940s and the stampede from the refectory to acquire an alley was legendary. The handball leagues were also keenly contested and prominent players in the 1940s included Bernie Brady, Tom Casey, Mick Fahey, Paddy O'Connell, John Ryan and Frank Hudner.

ROWING

In the 1940s rowing was one of the most successful sports in Rockwell and brought to the College almost as much notoriety as rugby. Its success was due for the most part to Fr. Patrick Walsh who had been teaching French in Rockwell since 1916, having served as Director of St. Joseph's from 1918 to 1921. He had the traumatic experience of witnessing the drowning of his confrere despite his own valiant effort to save him. For the rest of his life he trained students in swimming, life-saving and rowing.[8]

The 1940 rowing crew was picked in April and consisted of Paddy Hoare, Terry Sweeney, Donal O'Sullivan, Denis Kelly and Tim O'Brien. As usual Fr. Walsh was in daily attendance from the very beginning of training. Mr. John Scully came in from Fethard in the cool of the evening and tore up and down the lake-side on a bicycle, shouting instructions. And so to Dublin where for a week before the race the crew enjoyed the hospitality of sister college, Blackrock and were chaperoned to Island Bridge every evening by past student Mr. Gerald O'Shaughnessy and coached to the last available minute by Mr. Colman

The crew that won the Metropolital regatta in 1941
T. O'Brien, B. Hoare, T. Sweeney, J. Ryan, M. Hassett.

Mangan, another past student. In the preliminary heat on Friday Rockwell beat Belvedere and on Saturday, after beating Methodist College, the Metropolitan Challenge Cup was Rockwell's for the fourth time. The disqualification of Presentation College, Cork, on a technical issue, was a disappointment to the Rockwell five who had looked forward to a keen race with the Lee-siders. Rockwell took part in the Fermoy regatta. The last fixture of the season was at Galway where Rockwell beat St. Joseph's College and Galway Technical College.

The crew for 1941 was on the lake before the end of January, with snow on the bank and consisted of Dick Godley, Billy Hartnett, Terry Sweeney, Brendan Hoare and Tim O'Brien. When they set out for the Dublin regatta Blackrock College was again host and Colman Mangan and Gerald O'Shaughnessy helped as usual. Rockwell won the Cup by a length and a half. Celebrations afterwards took place in the Dolphin Hotel, organised by the Rockwell Union and was attended by parents and many past students. In the following weeks Rockwell took part in regattas at Fermoy and Galway. Soon after the Metropolitan Regatta the following article appeared in an English newspaper *The People*:

Ireland's champion rowing college has no river. Rockwell College, County Tipperary has to train in unusual quarters. In the past few years Rockwell College has taken up rowing; and just as they excel in hurling and rugby, they are now excelling at rowing. There is no big river at Cashel, but the boys train on a lake, and not a very big lake. In fact, when the boys are doing their rowing they travel round and round the mulberry bush, which is the island in the centre. Any rowing man will tell you the difference between rowing on the still waters of a lake and on a river. There is a different zip in a river's flowing waters. Yet Rockwell go to the

Colman Mangan
Coach to Rockwell crews

Metropolitan Regatta at Dublin and beat the best rowing schools there. Rockwell would like a rowing eight, but have to be content with fours. The reason is that there would be no room for such a gig on their little lake. An eight there would be as manageable as the Queen Mary would be in the Manchester Ship Canal.[9]

The article was not entirely accurate. The 24 acre lake gave a straight run of over a quarter of a mile. There were six islands on it. Rockwell had two eights boats with crews to man them and eights races at the College Regatta. There were no eights race for schoolboys at the Metropolitan Regatta.

In 1942 Rockwell broke new ground by sending two crews to Islandbridge, a Schools Four and a Maiden Four. The Maiden Four beat Trinity but lost to U.C.D. by the narrow margin of two feet. The Schools four defeated the Royal Academical Institute (Belfast) and Belvedere to qualify for the final against Methodist College, Belfast which Rockwell won by a distance. So the Metropolitan Challenge Cup came to Rockwell for the third year in succession, the sixth in all since the inauguration of the contest in 1934.

Rockwell's greatest success in rowing came in 1943. Rockwell had competed at Islandbridge every year since 1934 except 1938 and 1939 and in eight attempts had won six times. Other competitors included Coleraine Academical Academy, St. Ignatius College, Galway and Portora School. In 1943 a Rockwell eight made its appearance in the Head of the River race on the Liffey and finished sixth of the eleven starters. Then came the splendid successes of the Metropolitan regatta when Rockwell won the Schools' Cup and the Visitors'

Maiden Eight 1944
Mr. C. Mangan (coach), B. Duffy, C. Ryan, S. McDonald, J. Cahill, F. Hoare (cox), P. Burke, J. Walsh, F. Blair, C. Martin, Mr G. O'Shaughnessy.

Cup and reached the final of the Civic Cup (Maiden Fours). Much of the success was due to Fr. Walsh, Mr. John Scully, Mr Colman Mangan and Mr. Gerald O'Shaughnessy. For years Mr. O'Shaughnessy had been the connecting link between the Dublin clubs and the College crews. Mr. Denis Kennedy was also helpful. When Colman Mangan was a student in Rockwell he was a schoolboy pioneer oarsman. By 1943 he had become sculls champion of Ireland, captain of Dolphin Rowing Club and Rockwell's coach. Every year, at the commencement of the rowing season a picturesque ceremony took place at the Rockwell lakeside. The entire fleet was assembled at the slip, outriggers and pleasure craft, and the blessing was given. In 1943 for the first time the entire school assisted at the function which was performed by the President.

Rockwell competed at the Trinity regatta in 1944 and 1945 and in the same years won the Schools Four at the Metropolitan regatta. Colm Lawless was one of Rockwell's finest oarsmen and stroked to victory in the Maiden Eight of 1944. His love of the water was his reason for joining Irish Shipping when he completed his Leaving Certificate. In September 1956 he was Chief Officer on the new 9,700 tons *Irish Larch* on her maiden voyage across the Atlantic and back.

The death of Fr. Walsh in 1946 had a huge impact on rowing in Rockwell which was never to reach the heights it did while he was in charge.

CRICKET

After a lapse of nearly thirty years cricket was revived in Rockwell in 1945. The revival was at the behest of some Dublin students who had family

Cricket XI: Winners of Munster Schools Senior Cup 1945
Front: *S. Williams, L. O'Reilly, W. Corrigan.*
Seated: *F. Foley, D. Sweeney, J. Maguire, P. Murray, J. McDonnell.*
Back: *J. O'Dowd, E. Hayes, H. Hanna (12th man), G. McConnell.*

Tennis team 1946
Michael Ryan, John O'Hara, Nicholas Walsh, Fr. Barrett, Emmet Smyth, Gerald Dodd. Gerald Deehan

connections with the city cricket clubs and who were not endeared by the physical contact sports of rugby and Gaelic games. They looked forward from Easter to June of the sound of willow smacking the leather. The crease of thirty years earlier was re-discovered and with infinite care it was doctored back to playability. Through the kindness and generosity of a good friend an adequate outfit of bats, pads and gloves was provided. Then on Ascension Thursday, 10th May twenty two players took to the field in immaculately laundered whites for a trial match. On Sunday 13th May Glenstal were guests and they beat Rockwell because of the superior fielding of a carefully trained team. The Rockwell team was greatly encouraged by the presence on the boundary line of Fr. Dinan and many Fathers. On Sunday May 20th Glenstal hosted a return match which ended in a draw. On Whit Monday Rockwell took on a team from Cahir and won by twenty two runs.

In the summer of 1946 the Rockwell XI won the Munster Schools Senior Cricket Cup in the first year of the competition. A practice was held against a team consisting of players from Cashel, Cahir and Clonmel. The first cup match was against Glenstal which Rockwell won easily. The semi-final was against Bishop Foy School, Waterford and again Rockwell were the winners. The final was against Midleton College. It was on the 6th June, second anniversary of D. Day. It was played at the Mardyke. The final score was Rockwell 81, Midleton 64. Supper at the Savoy followed. The next morning the presentation of the Cup took place and the President in his balcony address had words of encouragement for the cricket players. The Cup final of 1947 was a repeat of the previous year but on that occasion Midleton were the winners. Bad weather in the last term of 1948 greatly hampered play. In 1949 Alex Miller and Finbarr Gallagher were elected captain and vice-captian, respectively and with three of the previous year's team, John Geary, Bernard Flusk and Bobby Walsh, there was an air of confidence. The first Cup match was against Midleton College in the Mardyke. Tim Beary and Martin Dwyer played very well but Rockwell lost.

THE ROCKWELL UNION.

The presidents of the Union during Fr. Dinan's presidency were John Gleeson, William Chadwick, James J. Comerford, Robert V. Walker, Martin Gleeson, T.J. Horgan and Michael K. O'Connor. The annual subscription in 1941 was reduced to £1 probably because of wartime conditions; and because of the shortage of petrol members did not travel to Rockwell and instead held Mass for deceased members in St. Mary's Rathmines. A branch of the Union was established in Cork to accommodate members from the Munster area. The annual dinner at the Dolphin Hotel and the annual golf outing continued as usual.

A number of members were associated with a lay Catholic organisation for the help of young Dublin boys called Comhairle Le Leas Óige. Two past students, Martin Gleeson and Gerard O'Shaughnessy were members of this organisation and in July 1943 they organised a holiday in Rockwell for a number of boys from deprived Dublin areas. For one of the boys the highlight of the holiday was a trip around the farm led by Fr. O'Driscoll who answered in a courteous and amusing manner about the nature of crops, how fast cattle could run, the difference between spring wheat and winter wheat and between oats and barley.

Rockwell Union Cup Golf Outing 1943
W. O'Neill, P. J. Fogarty T. D., G. Ring, Fr. Dinan, Major J.J. Comerford, T. Cleary.

In November 1943 the Rockwell Union established a Boys' Club in the parish of City Quay, Dublin. Membership of the parochial sodality was an essential qualification for membership of the club. Initially fourteen boys were enrolled. The Club was open on Tuesdays and Thursdays from 8 to 9.30 and on Sunday mornings and supervised by members of the Union. Indoor games of billiards, table tennis, draughts and dominoes were available. The boys had football on Sunday afternoons. A canteen was established to provide refreshments. Within three months the membership had increased to forty three. After Easter the outdoor programme on Sundays was varied to include hikes. The Club was affiliated to Comhairle le leas Óige. By invitation of Fr. Dinan, thirty one boys from the Club spent an enjoyable holiday in Rockwell in the summer of 1945 as well as over sixty boys from Comhairle le leas Óige. The Boys Club continued to thrive in 1946 with senior boys having an average attendance of nineteen and junior boys with an average attendance of twenty four. A library was established in 1947 when one of the most successful activities was the instruction in boot repairing. The highlight of the year was the annual holiday in Rockwell. An adult club was inaugurated in 1948 and was confined to former members of the Boys Club.

Early in 1945 a number of Rockwell Union members living in Dublin decided to form a lawn tennis club in the city as a means of keeping past students in touch with each other. The club opened in May at Brighton Square Rathmines and at the end of the season it had one hundred and forty members. Among those involved in the formation of the club were Daniel Mullane, Niall Sheerin, Frank Lawless, Gerard O'Shaughnessy and Fionnán Blair. The club closed for the season in mid September with a Fancy Dress American Tournament. At the meeting at which it was proposed to form a tennis club it was also decided to form a rugby club but this did not come to pass.

After the War, Union Day in Rockwell resumed. On Union Day, 6 June 1948, the new Boat House with its white-railed enclosure and club colours fluttering bravely from the flagstaff caught the attention of nearly four hundred past students who returned. High Mass was presided over by Archbishop Kinane. The regatta proceeded to the lakeside accompaniment of the No. 2 Army Band under the direction of past student Lieut Kealy. The Dining Hall was decorated in fine colours for lunch with two of the lay teachers, Mr. Gibson, assisted by Mr. White and guest musicians providing the appropriate atmosphere. The presence of the Shannon Airport waiters and waitresses in their colourful uniforms gave added colour to the occasion as did the blazered schoolboy stewards who helped so splendidly. It was seven o'clock by the time the speeches were complete. Union Day on Whit Sunday 1949 followed a similar pattern. On both occasions the Boy Scouts performed their rituals.

Members of the Rockwell Union were always keen to point to those who had come to prominence in Irish society. In the Leaving Cert class of 1947 was Alphonsus O' Brien of Chruchtown, Mallow. Better known as "Fonsie", he rode Royal Tan in the Grand National of 1951. He was brother of Vincent, the renowned trainer. The number of former Rockwell students holding major

Union Dinner 1946
Mr. S. McKenzie (President Blackrock Union, Fr. Dinan, Mr. Martin Gleeson (President Rockwell Union) Dr. Daniel Murphy (Provincial)

positions in the National University reached ten in 1947 with the appointments of Michael O'Kelly and Kieran McGrath. They were Pádraig de Brún, President of U.C.G, Michael O'Malley, Professor of Surgery, U.C.G., Michael V Duignan, Professor of Archaeology, U.C.G., Donal McCarthy, Professor of Mathematical Physics and Warden of Honan Hostel, U. C.C., Michael O'Kelly, Professor of Archaeology, U.C.C., Monsignor Shine, Professor of Logic and Psychology, U.C.D., Senator Henry Barniville, Professor of Surgery, U.C.D., Cormac Ó Cadhla, Professor of Modern Irish, U.C.C., Kieran McGrath, Professor of Dental Mechanics U.C.D. Michael O'Kelly was in the Leaving Cert class of 1934 and was from West Limerick. In April 1948 John O'Meara, a past student, was appointed professor of Latin at U.C.D.

* * *

On completion of his term as President of Rockwell Fr. Dinan became President of Blackrock College from 1950 to 1956 and again from 1962 to 1965. In 1965 when the office of Provincial was to be filled, Fr. Dinan was a popular choice. His humanity and his vision were well known by then and there were great expectations. Poor health, however forced him to resign his position in 1970. He died in 1975, aged 69 years.

OBITUARIES
Rockwell lost many valuable members of its community and staff during the presidency of Fr. Dinan. In 1940 former Bursar, Fr. Kingston died as did Dr. Foley, former medical officer and Tom Meehan of the maintenance staff. Fr.

Michael Colgan, Fr. Daniel Leen and Br Austin Tobin all past students, died in 1941. Fr. Michael Colgan came to Rockwell from his native Kildare in the early 1880s. He spent almost forty years in Rockwell and was an exceptional teacher. Fr. Daniel Leen came to Rockwell in 1895 and was one of three brothers who were prominent in the Holy Ghost Congregation. Following his ordination in Paris he was appointed to Rockwell and became Dean of Discipline during the presidency of Fr. Byrne. For a time he was Bursar in St. Mary's but returned to Rockwell to the teaching staff. He returned to Blackrock in 1934 and before his death he asked to be buried in Rockwell. Brother Austin Tobin was a native of Clonmel and had been in Rockwell since 1927, having previously served on the missions in Africa.

Brother Albert Cody died in 1942. Born in Dundrum, Co. Dublin in the 1870s, he served in Blackrock College, The Gambia in West Africa and St. Mary's College before coming to Rockwell in 1900. He was in charge of the refectory in Rockwell for nearly forty years. Bishop Joseph Shanahan, the legendary missionary died in 1944 as did Fr. Evans, one time President, Bursar, Director of St. Joseph's, and Fr. Martin O'Mahony of the teaching staff. Fr. James Nolan, Rockwell's oldest past pupil, died in 1945 as did Patsy Heaney who was connected with the College for over sixty years as grounds man and gardener. He was part of Rockwell and had many a good story to tell of the past. Fr. Patrick Walsh, patron of the boat club, died in 1946. A native of Thurles, as a boy he served Mass for Archbishop Croke. He did his secondary studies in Rockwell and was one of the few members of the Congregation who had the distinction of having done his theology in St. Joseph's when the Lake House was the Senior Scholasticate of the Irish Province. Ordained in 1900 he taught in Blackrock, St. Mary's and Rockwell and returned to Rockwell in 1933. He was a powerful swimmer and expert at life-saving. His greatest service to Rockwell in the realm of sport was rendered as patron and trainer of the Boating Club. He made a close study of rowing in all its aspects, and although he had never been an oarsman himself, he coached a long line of crews.

Former President of Rockwell, Fr. John McCarthy, died in 1948 as did Fr. Pat McAllister and Brother Eusebius. Fr. Pat McAllister was born in Glenravel Co. Antrim in 1889. He studied at Blackrock College and entered the novitiate at Kimmage. He went to Chevilly for his senior studies but because of the War he finished his studies at Langonnet, Brittany where he was ordained in 1917. He came to Rockwell in 1918. He involved himself not only with the College but also the surrounding district. During the War of Independence and Civil War he frequently exposed himself to personal danger to administer the Last Sacraments to the dying. He went to America in 1925 and gave retreats up and down that country and after a time in Nigeria he returned to Rockwell in 1936.[10]

Brother Eusebius Ahearne was born in the Sliabh gCua area of Co. Waterford in 1873 and was a native Irish speaker. He spent many years in Calabar in Southern Nigeria but poor health forced him to return to Ireland.

He became sacristan in Rockwell in 1913 but poor health continued to afflict him. He died in January 1948.[11]

Prize Day 1947
Past student Monsignor O'Donnell, Archbishop Harty, Past student Bishop Heffernan and Fr. Dinan.

Notes

1	ISR 446.
2	RCA 1941
3	RCA 1943
4	RCA 1947
5	RCA 1946
6	ibid
7	RCA 1941, 1942.
8	ISR 494
9	RCA 1941
10	ISR 519
11	ISR 24

– 10 –

AN EMPHASIS ON AGRICULTURE
1949-1955.

Fr. Andrew Egan who was appointed President of Rockwell College in August 1949, placed a great emphasis on the importance of Agricultural Science in the school curriculum. He was born in Loughmore, Co. Tipperary in 1900. Fr. Egan had been a student, a prefect and Dean of Discipline in Rockwell. He was known nationally for his work for the Irish language with Oireachtas na Gaeilge, Comhdháil Náisiúnta na Gaeilge, Cumann na Sagart and other national bodies and was known locally for his great interest in agriculture. He was an elected member of the Governing Body of University College, Dublin.[1]

Fr. Michael Comerford continued as Vice-President during those years with Fr. Joe Nolan as Bursar. Fr. Maurice Curtin continued as Dean of Studies until 1954 when he transferred to the same position in St. Mary's College, Rathmines and was replaced by Fr. Patrick Murray who came from St. Mary's. Fr. Patrick Meaney continued as Dean of Discipline until 1954 when he was replaced by Fr. Denis O'Brien. The deans and teaching staff had the assistance of a generous number of prefects with as many as sixteen on occasions. (Appendix VI) They were of great assistance in

Fr. Andrew Egan
President 1949-1955

Fr. Francis Griffin
conferred with
LLD 1952
Mgr. O'Rahilly, Fr. Griffin, Eamon de Valera (chancellor), Prof E. P. McLoughlin (past student), Prof. Pádraog de Brún (past student)

the class room, in study and dormitory supervision and in the organisation of games and other student activities. The Sisters of St. John of God in the early 1950s were Sr. Fabian, Sr. Loreto, Sr. Aquinas and Sr. Rufina. The Sisters of Divine Providence took over the duties of the Sisters of St. John of God in 1954.

There was a drop in the student population in the early 1950s with a continuing trend of students not availing of the full five-year course.(Appendix XIII) This may be due in part to a casual approach to promotion. The remarkable increase in the number of 2nd Year students in 1955 may be due to a more active attempt at promotion. The fall in numbers cannot be attributed to a fall in academic standards because the high achievement by students in public examinations continued. In 1950 five university scholarships were obtained with first place in Ireland in the Leaving Certificate obtained in Spanish and Italian while in the Intermediate Certificate that year first place was obtained in Spanish, Italian and Commerce. In 1951 two students obtained full marks in Mathematics in the Leaving Certificate while in the Intermediate two students obtained full marks in Algebra while one was first in Ireland in Commerce.

AGRICULTURAL SCIENCE
A notable feature of Fr. Egan's presidency was the emphasis he placed on Agricultural Science. Speaking at Union Day in 1951 he stressed the duty of educators "to inculcate a true appraisal of the value, the dignity, the nobility of work and a contempt for seeking after the easy tasks of life. One type of work has, unfortunately, not been esteemed at its proper value, agriculture. We hope

Archbishop Kinane is welcomed by the President and Fr. Comerford and a guard of honour of boy scouts.

Community Group 1951
Seated: Fr. Nolan O.P., Fr. A. Egan, Fr. P. O'Carroll, Fr. F. Griffin, Cardinal Browne, Fr. J. Byrne.
Second row: Frs. J. Cronin, M. Neenan, T. O'Connor, T. Cunningham, E. O'Shea, J. Burke, F. Nolan, M. Comerford, J. Cahill, M. O'Quigley.
Behind: Frs. S. Nealon, E. Holmes, C. Meagher, J. Nolan, J. Mullins, D. O'Brien.

that every student of ours will in future have a true esteem for those who direct their energies to the cultivation of the soil." He announced the intention of the College authorities to incorporate in the curriculum a course in Agricultural Science for those students who aimed at managing their own farms in the future, or who may have wished to proceed to a University degree in Agriculture. The remarkable progress made on the College farm in recent years, he felt, gave solid ground for hope that Rockwell's latest contribution to education in the southern province would be blessed with success. Agricultural Science became a subject on the Rockwell curriculum in 1952.

Fr. Egan returned to the same theme on Union Day 1955. He said he hoped the boys studying the subject would help to stem that flight from the land which was such a disturbing symptom in the life of our country. We would be proud, he said, to be able to say that our system of education did not, while necessarily catering for students who would join professional classes, turn the minds of its pupils away from, or make them contemptuous of a life on the land. Rockwell was fortunate in its geographical position, he said, to be in a position to train future leaders in agriculture who would help in the development and organisation of agricultural unions, in promoting collective activity on the part of farmers, in seeing that the State would not forget the rural population in the matter of sound legislation. He hoped that the new ideas of Agricultural Science, would change completely that idea of the "uneconomic holding" and that by sewing new crops and the adoption of new methods, and the improvement of the soil, our Irish land would be able to provide a living, a comfortable living, for farmers and farm labourer alike. Continuing he said "You may think that it is strange that I chose Agricultural Science for special mention amongst our varied activities and that something less materialistic, something spiritual, something scholarly, something patriotic, would be a more suitable subject for a Union Day speech. I have no worries that a school from which came writers like Pádraig Ó Conaire, patriots like Thomas MacDonagh, missionaries like Dr. Shanahan, will prove to be what a nation's schools should be- an organ of its life whose special function it is to consolidate its spiritual strength, to maintain its historic continuity, to secure its past achievements, to generate its future."

DEVELOPMENT

As Bursar, Fr. Joe Nolan had responsibility for developments on the Rockwell Farm. In 1951 two hundred and seventy seven acres were under tillage and for the harvest of that year a combined harvester was in operation for the first time. In the autumn of 1954 at the Carrigeen side of the farm there were four combined harvesters involved in a race to save the harvest. Seventy five acres in the north-east area of the farm underwent a massive programme of reclamation and drainage in 1952. While Fr. Joe Nolan was dealing with increased acreage of tillage, Fr. O'Brien was developing an extensive apiary and a new orchard. In 1954 the old bull paddock was transformed into a large-scale vegetable, fruit and flower garden with two centrally heated glass houses and Mr. John Seery having responsibility for this operation.

A new entrance to the farm was completed in 1952 to avoid heavy traffic on the front avenue. An entrance gate was erected and the roadway to the farm was flanked on either side by a row of young beech trees. For reasons of safety it was necessary to level the great beech grove along the main road boundary wall. New saplings were planted in its place. This grove had been a route for "bunkers" to New Inn. While this work was in progress, the bridge to the St. Joseph's grounds was rebuilt and widened. Over two thousand trees were planted by Fr. Meagher and the junior scholastics in the grounds of the Lake House.

The lake had dried up in September 1949 and the poor condition of the bank on the southern end became visible. In 1951 work began on erecting a protective concrete wall. Johnnie Moore and his team built a wall three hundred and seventy yards in length to protect the west and south banks. The lake dried up again in 1954 because of a prolonged drought from April to October. It began to re-fill in November but two months later it was covered with ice. The Tower was flood-lit in 1951 and the Chapel was completely re-roofed in 1954.

SPIRITUAL AFFAIRS

Fr. Christopher Meagher was Director of The Lake House during the presidency of Fr. Egan when the scholastics numbered between seventy and eighty. The scholastics were prominent in the Legion of Mary and when the custom of having the Corpus Christi procession around the lake was revived in 1952 they were involved in decorating the altars. They took part in all of the College sporting activities and helped in a tree planting programme in the grounds of the Lake House. They had frequent talks from priests home from the missions and in 1954 they enjoyed an inspiring talk from the veteran missionary Fr. Mellett.

In 1955 Fr. Murray led a pilgrimage of students to Rome. They travelled by boat from Dublin to Liverpool and from there by train to London where they visited Westminster Cathedral. A train journey to Folkstone followed where they boarded the *Maid of Orleans* for Boulogne. From Boulogne they travelled to Paris and visited the Mother House of the Holy Ghost Congregation. In Rome they were greeted by Fr. Daniel Murphy, former Dean of Studies in Rockwell and then Procurator General of the Holy Ghost Fathers. They met the Irish Ambassador to the Holy See, Mr. Cremin, and visited the Vatican, the Sistine Chapel and the Church of the Spanish Franciscans where they paid their respects to the remains of the Earls of Tyrone and Tirconnell.

CLUBS AND SOCIETIES

Fr. Murray took charge of the English Debating Society with interesting topics debated such as: that patriotism in Ireland was dead; that the ban on foreign games should be abolished; that chivalry was on the decline; that life in the country was better than life in the city; and that the educational value of games was exaggerated. The annual debate between 6th and 5th Years continued as did the home and away debates with Glenstal. Fr. Mullins continued to direct Cumann Díospóireachta Na Gaeilge with regular topics on political matters and even on one occasion that the world would be a better place if Columbus had not discovered America.

Fr. Kromer, founder of the Arts and Crafts Club returned to Germany in 1950 and he was succeeded as director by Br. Ambrose. That year some excellent works in oil painting were accomplished by George V. Moloney, Michael Gilligan and Joe Gallagher. Among the juniors Vincent Mahon, Alan O'Regan and Manuel Janku impressed. Vincent Mahon carved a pleasant study of a child's head in red pine. There were also promising beginners in water colours. In the crafts, plastic work was introduced and became very popular. In this area Stefan Schmeltz and Brian Flanagan were prominent. Daniel King and Joe Gallagher were among the most enthusiastic leather workers. Paul and Eucharius McKiernan set high standards for wood-carvers. Fret work was the most popular of all the crafts. One of the most tireless members of the club in those years was George V. Maloney, doyen of the corps. In 1952 Joseph Gallagher was one of the most skilled members of the club. In the painting section between 1953 and 1955 oils predominated and some very fine work was done by Patrick Hurley, Seán and Patrick Smith and Michael Gilligan. Edward T. Liston and Cornel Metternich were also prominent in this medium. Brian Reidy proved himself very adapt in water-colours and produced, among other things, a very good seascape. Thomas O'Gorman was prominent among the leather workers.

Fr. Nealon directed the Rockwell troop of the Catholic Boy Scouts of Ireland (18th Tipperary Troop) who performed their duties on ceremonial occasions. Such an occasion occurred in February 1950 when the President of Ireland, Seán

A guard of honour for President Ó Ceallaigh on his 1950 Visit.

T. Ó Ceallaigh visited. As his car passed up the avenue he received a great ovation from the four hundred waiting students and on his arrival at the main entrance he was welcomed by Fr. Egan. The President inspected a guard of honour of the College Troop of Catholic Boy Scouts. President Ó Ceallaigh addressed the boys entirely in Irish in the College Theatre, much to the pleasure, no doubt of Fr. Egan. The Scouts paraded each Prize Day and Sports Day and in 1954 the whole troop turned out in full uniform for the Cashel Historical Pageant.

The Boy Scouts were taught all the skills associated with scouting but the camps arranged away from Rockwell were especially popular with boarders. In those years they camped at locations including Helvick, Mount Mellery and Crosshaven. In June 1954 the Scouts set out on a five-mile hike to Ballycarron where they set up camp in the convent grounds. The same year they took part for the first time in the annual camp held in the National Camping Grounds, Larch Hill, in the Dublin Mountains where they won awards   for compass work, first aid and personal hygiene.

MUSIC AND DRAMA

A Gilbert and Sullivan operetta was performed by the students each year during the presidency of Fr. Egan, produced as usual by Br. Benedict with the painting and set by Fr. Comerford. The musical director of these performances was Mr. Xavier Gibson until Fr. O'Quigley took over in 1954. By then Br. Benedict had been laicised and was now Mr. Tobin. Most members of the orchestra came from Clonmel, Tipperary and Thurles. Costumes were supplied by Gings of Dublin. Leading roles in the 1950 production *The Yeomen of the Guard* were played by Daniel Hale, Michael English, Patrick McInerney, Colm O'Regan, Michael Keane, Denis Allman, Alexander Miller and Patrick Lynch. Present at the first

Richard Mulcahy
(Minister for Education)
and Fr. O'Carroll
(Provincial) at the 1950
performance of Yeomen
of the Guard

night of that production were the Provincial of the Congregation, Fr. O'Carroll, and the Minister for Education, Richard Mulcahy. The 1951 production of *H.M.S Pinafore* had Alexander Millar, Brendan Thompson, Michael Burke, Francis Sheerin, Arthur Breen, David Ryan, Francis Smith, Louis Donnelly, Denis Corrigan and Seán Gardiner in the leading roles.

The Pirates of Penzance in 1952 had Cornelius O'Donovan, Francis Sheerin, Seán Gardiner, Patrick McInerney and Vincent Molony in the leading parts and when *The Gondoliers* was performed in 1953 Noel Kingston, Patrick Fenoughty, Michael Comerford, Martin O'Boyle, Danny, Hale, Noel O'Callaghan, Denis O'Carroll, Benedict Meade, Timothy Hurley, John Comerford, Patrick Sheehy and Michael O'Farrell all had parts. The 1954 production of *The Mikado* starred Michael Burke, Geoffrey Palmer, Fergus O'Brien, John Comerford, Noel Kingston, Joseph Sadlier, Ciarán O'Reilly, Luke Casey and Parick Fenoughty. Among the audience at that performance was Delia Murphy, the famous ballad singer, who with her husband, the Irish Ambassador to Australia, was on a visit to Rockwell. Earlier she had given an afternoon recital of her incomparable ballads.

Musical societies from the neighbouring towns performed in Rockwell for the students. St. Mary's Choral Society, Clonmel, directed and conducted by Rockwell teacher, James A. White, gave a three hour performance in January 1951 and the following month the Cashel Operatic Society gave a performance of *Bitter Sweet*. The Tipperary Operatic Society performed *The Gondoliers* and in 1954 St. Mary's Choral Society returned to Rockwell with a production of *Maritana*.

Students continued to take the examinations of the Royal Irish Academy of Music with an increase in those taking the piano. There was a notable decrease in those taking string instruments with the result that less students were playing in the orchestras for the Gilbert and Sullivan productions. In the 1954 production, for example, only one student took part. Fr. O'Quigley formed a junior flageolet band in 1952. For the first time, in 1954 a Music Appreciation society was formed. Fr. Murray was behind it. Regular meetings were held and at the beginning of each meeting a member was called upon to read a paper on the life and work of some composer. Music of that composer was then listened to. Thanks to the Arts Council, recitals by visiting artists were regular. In 1954 two of Ireland's best known artists, pianist Charles Lynch and singer Máire Ní Scolaí, performed in Rockwell.

Anew McMaster, who had last visited Rockwell in 1937 returned in 1952 with a production of *The Merchant of Venice*. And he returned with his company in 1954 to perform *Julius Caesar*. At least one play in the Irish language was produced by Fr. Mullins each year while Fr. Comerford produced a number of plays in English.

ATHLETICS

Rockwell teams competed in the North Munster Sports in Limerick and the Munster Sports in Cork each year between 1949 and 1955 with the winners at

Athletic team 1950
In front: G. Mullins.
Seated: P. Casey, J. Bennett, M. Manning, N. Keane, S. F. Gallagher, B. O'Connor, M. English, P. Buckley.
Standing row 1: J. McInerney, J. Manning, J. Cosgrove, J. Burke, F. Forster, D. Ryan, S. Givins.
Standing row 2: J. Lenihan, R. McGrath, P. O'Mara, J. Hynes, S. Quinn, K. Prendergast.

these competing in the All Ireland Sports in Dublin. Prior to these Rockwell competed against Mount St. Joseph's, Roscrea. The leading athlete between 1950 and 1952 was Michael Manning who won the 100yards and 220 yards at the All Ireland in 1952. The same year Jerry Tackaberry was first in the discus at the North Munster and Munster Sports. In 1954 at the All Ireland Schools Championship at the Iveagh Grounds Michael McSweeney was first in the senior high jump and second in the long jump. The annual Sports Day was revived in 1953 with Mr. Frazer Junior in charge of the drill display and the Clonmel Boys Pipe Band adding to the occasion. Nicholas Tierney and his team had the grounds in good shape.

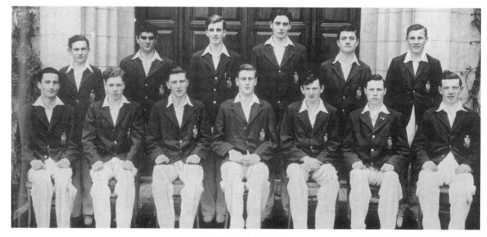

1950 Cricket XI
Seated: T. Beary, B. Flusk, S.F. Gallagher, A. Miller, J. Hogan, M. Dwyer, A. Fitzpatrick
Standing: T. Deehan, R. Abdo Zaidan, P. Nearman, J. Gallagher, M. English, B.Dwyer.

CRICKET

In the Spring of 1950 the Cricket Club had no fewer than seven of the previous year's first XI. April and May were so cold, wet and windy that practice had to be snatched at odd moments and in the ball alleys only. The first Cup match against Bishop Foy School was played away and Rockwell won by six wickets but with no particular distinction. The semi-final was played at home against Newtown who had recently beaten Presentation College, Cork. Rockwell had managed to produce a reasonably playable crease. Alec Miller was captain and other players featured included Tommy Deehan, Finbar Gallagher, Seán Hogan, Martin Dwyer, Brendan Dwyer, Michael English and Tony Fitzpatrick. Rockwell lost. The last fixture of the year was on Union Day when the Past played the Present. Rockwell did not field a team in the Cup in the following years.

HURLING

After a lapse of twelve years Rockwell entered a team for the Harty Cup in 1950. Fr. Joe Nolan with the help of prefect John Spriggs took on the task of training the team. Joe Heenan and Tim Holland were elected captain and vice-captain respectively. Friendly matches were played against Thurles C.B.S. Mount St. Joseph's, Roscrea, Mugret College and St. Kieran's College, Kilkenny. In the first round of the Harty Cup Rockwell played Christians College, Limerick in the Seán Treacy Park in Tipperary. The Limerick side was the better in this match despite good displays from Joe Heenan, Tim Holland, Dermot O'Sullivan, Paddy O'Hara and Dan Healy. The junior team of 1950 beat St. Flannan's College in the semi-final of the Canon Kennedy Shield. Denis Bernard, the future Cork footballer, was captain of the side. Tim McGrath and Michael English, two future rugby internationals, were prominent members of that team as were Eamon Martin and Dermot O'Sullivan. Rockwell lost in the final to St. Finbar's College, Farrenferris.

The seniors lost again in the first round of the Harty Cup in 1951 despite a stalwart display by Bernard Frawley who later played for Clare and who later still became a prominent member of the Rockwell Community. Fr. Christy Meagher trained the senior team for the next few years but lost to Mount Sion in the Harty Cup in 1952 and again in 1953 when Dan Delaney was goalkeeper and other prominent players were Noel O'Callaghan, Seán Hayes, Jim Foley, Stephen Maher, Ned Ryan and Seán Broderick, a future President of Rockwell. Dan Delaney was captain in 1954 but because of illness, he was absent for the Harty Cup match against St. Flannan's and Seán Broderick deputised for him. Rockwell lost that match. Despite the absence of trophies during the presidency of Fr. Egan, the house leagues, both senior and junior, were very competitive.

RUGBY

In 1950 the S.C.T, captained by Mick Brosnan with Jim Burke as vice-captain, won the Cup for the first time since 1942. The usual friendly matches opened the season. In early November the first Bowen Shield match was against the holders Crescent. Tries by Brendan O' Connor and Noel Keane and a drop goal by Mick English in the first half laid the foundation for a Rockwell victory. The second Shield tie was against Christians in the Mardyke in which Rockwell won by 16-0. The deciding Shield game was against Pres in Cork and it finished Rockwell 6, Pres nil. Rockwell had now won the Bowen Shield for the sixth time.

In the first Cup match Rockwell faced a Crescent XV that showed great improvement on the Bowen shield form. Despite this improvement the superiority of the Rockwell forwards especially was evident from the kick-off. Crescent had gone into a six point lead when just before half time Jack Manning spread-eagled the Crescent defence to score a try at the corner flag. Early in the second half Noel Keane dropped a goal from far out. Then Paddy Casey gathered a cross kick and beat two defenders for the touch down. Just before the final whistle Crescent kicked another penalty goal to leave the final score Rockwell 12 pts. Crescent 9 pts.

After two postponements due to bad weather Rockwell faced Presentation at the Mardyke on March 22nd. Heavy rain had rendered the pitch almost

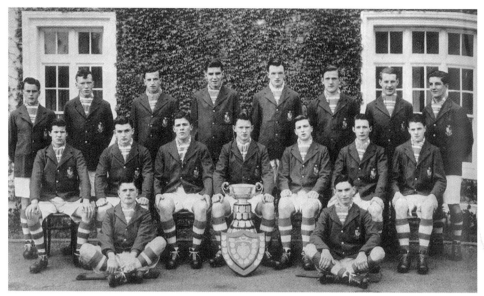

Senior Rugby Cup Winning Team 1950
Front: M. English, B. O'Connor.
Seated: *J. Manning, P. Casey, J. Burke, M. Brosnan, S.F. Gallagher, N. Keane, R. Walsh.*
Back: *K. Prendergast, K. Dodd, F. O'Keeffe, D. Bernard, J. Cosgrove, M. McEvoy, S. Darcy, G. Bernard.*

unplayable and after a short period it became increasingly difficult to recognise the teams. Half time yielded no score. After ten minutes of the second half Mick Brosnan kicked a delightful penalty which livened up proceedings. Kevin Prendergast rallied his forwards while John Cosgrave and Denis Bernard dominated the line-out allowing Mick Brosnan to increase the lead with a drop goal and leaving the final score Rockwell 6 pts. Pres nil.

Rockwell travelled to Limerick for the final against Mungret on Thursday 30th March. Denis Bernard crossed the line for the only score of the first half. Three scores followed in quick succession on resumption. Finbar Gallagher brought off a fine double which was capped with a third from Noel Keane. Rockwell were well ahead when Finbar Gallagher brought off his hat-trick and Paddy Casey put the finishing touch with a touch down which left the final score Rockwell 18 Mungret nil. The Cup was back in Tipperary. The seven inter-provincials that year were Malachy McEvoy, Michael Brosnan, Noel Keane, Seán D'Arcy, Jim Burke, Paddy Casey and Mick English the future Irish International.

Mick English had been in Rockwell from 1946 to 1950. His first sporting interest was hurling which he played at Limerick C.B.S. but the four English brothers, Des, John, Mick and Christy all later went to Rockwell and soon Mick easily took to rugby. He quickly settled down at out-half and hit the headlines in 1949 when as a fifteen year old he dropped two goals in the replay junior Cup final in which Rockwell defeated Crescent 6-3 at Thomond Park. Mick was on the senior side that year that lost the decider to Crescent. In 1950 at the age of sixteen he was out-half on that Rockwell team that beat Mungret. That was a

Senior Cup winning XV 1953
Front: G. Mullins, B. O'Hart
Seated: T. Coffey, J. Kiely, S. Maher, D. Hale, D. Allman, J. O'Neill, T. McGillicuddy.
Standing: D. Mullins, S. Burke, P. Molloy, F. Gallagher, S. Givens, D. Burke, E. Marren, P. O'Dea.

great side containing flying wingers like Noel Keane and Finbar Gallagher, a highly competent full-back and captain in Kerryman Mick Brosnan and a big, able pack in which some of the shining lights were Jim Burke of Cahir, Cork's Denis and Jerry Bernard and Kevin Prendergast the hooker and later well-known race horse trainer. Mick was capped sixteen times for Ireland between 1958 and 1964. Mick was on the Rockwell Athletic team of 1950 as a javelin thrower and as a member of the senior relay team and was a member of the Rockwell cricket XI. And Mick's talents were not confined to sport as was evident in 1950 when he played the leading role in the Rockwell production of *The Yeomen of the Guard*.

The 1952 S.C.T. was captained by another future international, Tim McGrath, with Michael Manning as vice-captain. Fr. Meaney trained that team which beat Christians and Crescent to retain the Bowen Shield but was beaten by Christians in the Cup. The 1953 S.C.T. was captained by Danny Hale with Seamus Maher as vice-captain.

In the Bowen Shield Rockwell had wins over CBC and Crescent followed by a draw against Pres in the final in the Mardyke. Rockwell lost the replay. On the morning of the final, the refectory as usual rang with the College songs, chants and yells:

> *Our support's behind the team chanting loud and clear*
> *Rockwell, Rockwell S.C.T. gallant, without fear*
> *In blue and white our brave men fight, we'er sure they'll never yield*
> *And back to Rockwell College we will bring the Bowen Shield*

In the first round of the Cup St. Munchins gave Rockwell a walk-over because of flu in their college. The semi-final was played in the Mardyke against Pres. That morning in the refectory the chants were loud:

Hurrah, Hurrah for the Munster Cup
Hurrah, Hurrah for the Munster Cup
Let the forwards do their duty and the backs will back them up
And back to Rockwell College we will bring the Munster Cup.

Seán Givens, Jack O'Neill and Seán Burke were the leading players in a game which ended after twenty minutes extra time in a scoreless draw. In the replay in Clonmel Rockwell dominated in all departments winning by 6 points to nil. Denis Allman and Paddy O'Dea were prominent on that occasion. And so to the final in Thomond Park against Crescent where vocal support was prominent:

Heel, heel, heel, the gallant forwards
Fearless backs await the ball,
Since to-day the Cup's at stake
Score and score for Rockwell's sake
And the blue and white shall triumph over all.

Paddy Prendergast was full-back. The *Cork Examiner* reported that in the forward tussle Rockwell came out well on top led by the Burke brothers, George Mullins and Pat Molloy. Rockwell had won the Cup for the fourteenth time. The Inter- provincial players of 1953 were Jack O'Neill, Seán Burke, Danny Hale, Denis Allman, Paddy O'Dea, Donal Burke and George Mullins.

The S.C.T. captain of 1954 was Donal Burke with Tom McGillycuddy as vice-captain. It was a season of mixed fortunes winning the Bowen Shield but relinquishing possession of the Munster Cup. The first match in the Bowen Shield tournament, which was originally intended to be a series of friendly matches but which in recent years had become very competitive, was against Christians. A future President of Rockwell, Fr. Seán Broderick was on that team. Players mentioned in the game against Christians which Rockwell won, were Donal Burke, Tom Coffey, Jim Foley and Denis Mullins. Rockwell then beat Crescent with a try by Paddy Kirwan. In the final against Pres, Bob Lynch scored the winning try. The S.C.T. had friendlies before Christmas with Bohemians and Blackrock and after Christmas with Rathdowney, Clonmel, Kilrush and Cashel. The first Cup match was against Crescent College in Limerick and even after twenty minutes of extra time there was no score. In the replay in Clonmel the only score was a try by Rockwell. An easy win over Munchins followed in semi-final. In the final against Pres in the Madryke, Pres dominated throughout and were deserving winners. A record was established that season for never before in the history of Rockwell were nine Munster caps gained in one season. Those honoured were Tom McGillycuddy, Tom Coffey, Donal Burke, who captained the Munster side in all matches, Denis Mullins, Giorgio Ghio, Tony Gleeson, Brendan O'Hart, Bobbie Cotter and Jim Foley.

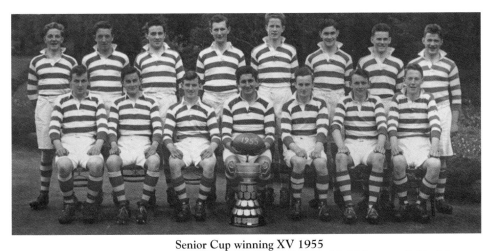

Senior Cup winning XV 1955
Seated: *P. Kirwan, D. Rice, J. Coakley, T. Coffey, B. O'Hart, M. McSweeney, J. Nesdale.*
Standing: *D. O'Connell, M. Mullins, E. Ryan, D. Hickey, A. McCabe, E. P. O'Dwyer, J. King, E. Doran.*

1955 was one of the most successful and one of the most enjoyable for many years of Rockwell rugby. The Seniors won the Bowen Shield and the Cup and the Juniors won the Cup. Tom Coffey was captain of the S.C.T. and Brendan O'Hart vice-captain. Christians visited Rockwell for the first Bowen Shield match which Rockwell won by eight points to nil. In the second match, also at home, Rockwell beat Crescent by six points to three. Rockwell then travelled to Cork to meet Presentation College in the third match of the competition in which the two Rockwell unconverted tries were the only scores. The final encounter was against Crescent in Limerick and again Rockwell was victorious becoming the proud possessor of the Bowen Shield.

The first Cup match of 1955 was against Crescent in Clonmel and resulted in a nil-all draw, even after extra time. Rockwell won the replay in Limerick by 15 points to nil, the scores coming from Donal Lynch, Paddy Kirwan and Tom Coffey. St. Munchin's College proved to be a weak opposition in the second round with Rockwell winning by 29 points to nil. Presentation College were the opponents in the final played in Thomond Park. Both sides failed to score and they met a week later to decide the destination of the Cup. The replay was hard fought. Tim O'Sullivan dropped a goal for the only score of the first half. Pres forwards staged some dangerous raids in the second half and would have scored but for the whole-hearted display by Tom Coffey. Tim O'Sullivan dropped another penalty mid-way through the half and in the last few minutes of the game the Pres full-back dropped a neat goal for their only score. Rockwell survived further pressure to win by 6 points to 3.

The Rockwell J.C.T. captained by Jerry Bernard, had hopes of winning the Cup for the fourth year in a row in 1950 but these hopes were dashed in the final by Crescent. The following year the J.C.T. lost to Christians. Tom Coffey was captain in 1953 when they lost to Pres as a number of the leading players

**Senior Rugby
Trophies 1955**
*Tom Coffey with the
Munster Schools Cup
and Brendan O'Hart
with the Bowen Shield.*

were in bed with flu. Fr. O'Brien trained the 1954 team which had Maurice Mullins as captain and Eamonn Doran as vice-captain but lost to Glenstal in the Cup.

Loman Conway captained the Cup-winning J.C.T. of 1955 which was trained by Fr. Walsh with Pat Murphy as vice-captain. The team showed promise in friendly matches against Shannon, Glenstal, Crescent, St. Mary's, Blackrock, Mungret and Presentation College. In the first Cup match in February Rockwell had an easy win over Crescent in Limerick. A week later Limerick was again the venue for the match against Glenstal. A very close encounter ended in a draw with both sides scoring an unconverted try. In Clonmel ten days later Rockwell crossed the Glenstal line twice but on both occasions failed to convert. Glenstal failed to score so the next outing was to Musgrave Park for the final against Presentation College. An early try by Pat Murphy was converted by Loman Conway and proved to be the only score of the game. Pres had the advantage of a strong breeze in the second half but the Rockwell defence held firm and the Cup returned to Rockwell.

ROCKWELL UNION

The Rockwell Union celebrated its silver jubilee in 1950. The presidents of the Union during Fr. Egan's tenure were Michael K. O'Connor, P.J. Roche, Thomas Collins, Martin Byrne and Stanislaus O'Brien. The Union celebrated its silver jubilee in 1950 and at the annual dinner in the Dolphin Hotel that year the President, Michael K. O'Connor, reflected on the fear of Communism, a fear which was widespread in Ireland at that time.

In his presidential address in 1951 P.J. Roche spoke of the contribution made by Rockwell past students to banking. In that year, he said, fifteen past students were in the National Bank, twelve in the Munster and Leinster Bank, nine in the Bank of Ireland three in the Hibernian Bank, three in the Provincial Bank of Ireland, one in the National City Bank, one in the Royal Bank of Ireland and one in Lloyd's Bank, London.

The Union continued to assist the College in various ways each year and this was acknowledged by Fr. Egan on Union Day 1955 when he said "We thank you for your generosity through the years in helping our building schemes, in the foundation of burses, in the donation of equipment of which we have an example in the beautiful 16 m.m. film projector which you presented to us this year."

Union Day in Rockwell was usually held on the last Sunday in May and the level of enjoyment was often determined by the weather. Union Day in 1955 was on Whit Sunday, 25th May and the weather was ideal. A large number of past students were in attendance with their wives and girl friends. The Clonmel Boys' Pipe Band enhanced the holiday atmosphere and in general the day was a very pleasant one with the family spirit very much in evidence. High Mass was followed by luncheon and in his address Fr. Egan welcomed all, including local T.D. Dan Breen and Mr. Thomas Walsh, former Minister for Agriculture who was of course a past student. Fr. Egan referred to the deaths that year of two prominent past students, Dr. Andrew Butler and Senator Bill Quirke

OBITUARY

The death took place in 1954 of Mr. Michael Cremin who had been professor of French and Music for many years and had lived in the College for fifty two years. A native of Kerry, he had received his secondary education at Rockwell and later became a graduate of the old Royal University. He was organist in the College Chapel for many years and assisted in the College orchestra as a violinist. He had the Latin name for every flower and weed on the back avenue. Also in 1954 the death took place of Martin Hewitt who had been herdsman on the Rockwell Farm for forty five years.

Following his retirement from Rockwell, Fr. Egan returned to the classroom in Blackrock College. He assisted the Carmelite Sisters, Blackrock, in their major building scheme and he assisted the Irish Sisters of Charity in connection with acquiring the site for St. Vincent's Hospital. He died in 1971, aged 70 years.[2]

Notes

[1]   ISR 74
[2]   ISR 74

– 11 –

A NEW ENDEAVOUR
1955-1961

The founding of the Rockwell Hotel and Catering School was the highlight of
the first presidency of Fr. James M. Finucane. It was a brave attempt by Rockwell
to contribute to Ireland's developing tourist industry while at the same time
enhancing the catering facility within the College.

Fr. Finucane became President of Rockwell in August 1954. Born at Tarmon,
Knock, Ennis, Co. Clare in 1904, he was a student at Rockwell from 1918 to
1922. Ordained in 1929 he was appointed to Blackrock College where he
became Dean of the Day School and later Dean of Discipline and Bursar.[1] He
was to serve two terms as President of Rockwell.

Former President, Fr. Egan, returned to Blackrock College and Fr. Michael
Comerford continued as Vice-President. Fr. Patrick McMahon and Fr. David
Heelan were Bursars. Fr. Denis O'Brien was Dean of Discipline until he was
succeeded by Fr. Aidan Lehane in 1957. Fr. Patrick Murray continued as Dean
of Studies until succeeded in 1958 by Fr. Joseph Nolan. Fr. Alfred Chamberlain
became Director of St. Joseph's in 1958. Among the new members of the
Community in 1959 was Fr. James Hurley, a future President of the College.
There were fifteen prefects each year until 1958 and by 1961 the number had
reduced to ten. The Sisters of St. John of God had been succeeded in 1954 by
the Sisters of Divine Providence and they in turn were succeeded in 1956 by
the Sisters of St. Joseph of Chambery with those serving up to 1961 being Sr.
Mary Emerita, Sr Mary Elizabeth, Sr. Mary Winnifred and Sr. Mary Bernadette.

STUDENTS AND STANDARDS
The Rockwell student population steadily increased during the first presidency
of Fr. Finucane and exceeded five hundred for the first time in the history of
the College in 1961.(Appendix XIII) As in previous years not all students
completed a full five year programme in Rockwell as is evident from the number
of 1st Years in 1956 compared to the number five years later in 6th Year. Some
students entered Rockwell at a very young age and were considered in need of
a preparatory year before embarking on the secondary syllabus. In 1956, of the
59 1st Years 32 were classified as Preparatory, 24 in 1958 and 11 in 1959. None
were classified as Preparatory in 1960 or 1961. Another feature of the student
population was an increase in the number of foreign students. In 1957 all
previous records in this regard were broken with students from United Kingdom,
France, Spain, United States, Cairo, Morocco, the Lebanon, Kenya, South

Prize Day 1957
Archbishop congratulates prize winners: M. O'Mahony, M. Foley, C. Kavanagh, D. O'Brien,
M. Casey and E. Tuffy.

Africa, Sierra Leone, Nigeria and Gambia.[2] There was a continuing tendency too for families whose father had been to Rockwell to send their son there. In 1957, for example, the student population included twenty one sons of past students.

The high academic standards which prevailed in previous years continued during Fr. Finucane's presidency. He reported at Prize Day in 1956 that in the public examinations of 1955 five scholarships were obtained and that a first or second in Ireland was obtained in Irish, Arithmetic, Algebra and Commerce. The most unique distinction, he said, was the gaining of three of the four possible medals presented by the Department of Education for excellence in Irish composition, the two for Leaving Certificate and one in the Intermediate. Fr. Finucane said that while they honoured and encouraged academic success for itself and as a stimulus to greater effort and to higher scholarship, they by no means worshipped brilliance or forgot the plodder, nor did they place mere intellectual achievement in the forefront of what went to constitute the curriculum of an academic year, especially in an Irish Catholic college. In the Leaving Certificate of 1956 five University scholarships were obtained with first and second places in Ireland obtained for Irish essay.

Speaking on the same occasion in 1956 Archbishop Kinane said "For well nigh a century Rockwell has been a leader among the educational institutes of our country, and the future will see that fine academic tradition fully maintained. But education was concerned with the heart and the emotions as well as with the intellect." Speaking at Prize Day in 1960 Dr. Patrick Hillery,

Prize Day 1959
Fr. Nolan (Dean of Studies), Fr. O'Driscoll (Provincial), Mr. Condon (President of Rockwell Union),
Mr. Lynch (Minister for Education), Bishop Byrne, Fr. Finucane (President), Fr. Comerford (Vice President)

Minister for Education and a past student, in the course of his address said "It may be said that the worth of a College is reflected in the achievements of its past pupils and of their loyalty to the College. There is scarcely any field of human endeavour in which past pupils of this College are not to be found, all adding lustre to the College which guided their early steps in building up that moral fibre of character which made it possible for them to give of their best in whatever occupation they may have chosen. But the greatest tribute of all to the College is the large number of its past students who, as priests, are doing such wonderful work in the various mission fields." Tributes to the high standards of Rockwell were also paid by the Minister for Education, Mr. Jack Lynch, at Prize Day in 1959 and by Dr. St. John Atkins, President of University Cork, at Prize Day in 1961.

For most of its history Rockwell retained the "notes system" whereby a weekly mark was given to students as a measure of their academic progress. This system had originally been introduced by the French Fathers and was retained by the three Holy Ghost colleges in Ireland. The system rewarded not only the bright student who attained high standards but also the academically weak student for the effort made. Students who obtained high marks were rewarded on Prize Day with certificates or medals. They were also rewarded by a day tour away from the College during the last term, known as the Galaxy. This was a prize especially relished in a school where the majority of students were boarders. After a lapse of some years the annual Galaxy had been revived in 1955, and in 1956 the excursion was to Ard na Crusha Power Station followed by a film and a meal in Limerick. In the following years the Galaxy visited places of interest throughout Munster.

Educational tours to Europe had become popular in the 1950s, always taking place in June when the College was closed for holidays and initially confined to 5th Year students. The third trip of the decade in 1956 was to the Rhineland. These trips were by land and sea with overnight stops in London and Paris. Fr. Joe Nolan led the 1957 tour to Rome and tours to the north of Italy and Spain followed in 1960 and 1961.

SOME STUDENT INDOOR ACTIVITIES

Fr. Mullins involved students in promoting the Irish language with organisations such as *An Fáinne, Ógraí na Croise Deirge and Cumann Lán-Staontha na Réadóirí* as well as debating through Irish. Br. Ambrose did much in the promotion of Arts and Crafts and each year on Union Day and Parents' Day the work of students was on display in leatherwork, woodcarving, marquetry and aero modelling which was especially popular. In the 1961 exhibition seventy five paintings were on view. In 1959 Br. Ambrose held fortnightly meetings on art appreciation. He also supervised the Stamp Club which fostered a great interest in geography. Fr. O'Brien encouraged the Chess Club which was especially active during the dark days of the second term with afternoon and evening sessions. Senior and junior tournaments were organised and Rockwell had a

Preparatory 1957
Seated: *A. Faulkner, C. Ransom, F. Madden, Mr. T. Barron, L. Stapleton, I. Harrison, D. Hill.*
2nd row: *P. Clancy, O. Hill, P. Conway, T. Stapleton, D. Hunt, D. O'Brien.*
3rd row: *P. English, P. Moynihan, M. Kerrigan, P. Hecksher, D. Kiely, V. Ryan, E. McManus.*
4th row: *H. Gaffney, P. Hardiman, R. Hecksher, J. Gaffney.*

home-and-away fixture with Tipperary Chess Club. *The Rock*, that occasionally published student magazine, appeared in 1960 with Al Conroy as editor and Maurice Manning as assistant.

ST. JOSEPH'S

There were eighty eight scholastics in St. Joseph's in 1956 when they were visited by the Provincial Fr. Patrick O'Carroll. They had a special welcome in 1957 for the new Provincial, Fr. Tim O'Driscoll, who was no stranger to Rockwell. Fr. Meagher had been Director of St. Joseph's for nine years in 1958 when he was succeeded by Fr. Chamberlain who had previously been a director of a Juniorate in Nigeria. For the first time in its history in 1959 St. Joseph's had a Deputy Director with the appointment of Fr. Patrick Leonard.

Visits to St. Joseph's by missioners home on leave continued as a regular feature of life for the scholastics who were given talks and slide shows depicting life on the missions. In 1958 a past student of St. Joseph's, Dr. Moloney, Bishop of Bathurst, Gambia, visited the scholastics. A special welcome was extended in 1961 to Bishop Anthony Nwedo of Eastern Nigeria who had been educated in a Holy Ghost mission school and seminary and had been one of the earliest African bishops.

Junior Scholastics 1958
In front: M. Higgins.
Seated: J. White, W. Crowe, V. McLoughlin, L. Ahern, T. O'Shea, P. McGovern, Fr. Chamberlain,
Mr. J. Flynn, P. Carroll, J. Wall, P. Peters, M. Herriott, P. Moran, P. Healy
1st row: A. Kelly, M. Brennan, P. Ranahan, L. Gillespie, D. O'Sullivan, C. McGrath, P. Queally,
S. Tobin, D. Moloney, B. Nolan, J. Power, M. O'Neill, P. Dalton.
2nd row: J. Fox, M. O'Connor, P. Wall, P. Walsh, J. Moriarty, J. Brogan, P. Doody, S. Hogan,
J. Meehan, M. Keane, A. McSweeney, J. Riordan.
3rd row: K. Lewis, T. Walsh, P. Daly, P. O'Brien, P. Keogh, P. Murphy, J. Reidy, N. Ferris, S. Tierney,
J. Roche, M. O'Grady.
4th row: E. Tierney, L. Grogan, M. Morgan, M. O'Donoghue, S. Cahill, T. Byrne, J. Costello,
D. Dennehy, P. Doherty, P. Taylor.
5th row: M. Halligan, M. Tierney, O. Lewis, J. Gough, D. O'Donnell, T. Kenny, S. O'Rourke.

The Legion of Mary was very much part of the religious formation of scholastics. The work of members included preparations for the liturgy in the College Chapel and preparing for events in the College Theatre. The Legion stalls stocked rosary beads, scapulars, miraculous medals, prayer books and religious literature. Legionaries enrolled members in the Confraternities of the Holy Ghost and of the Immaculate Heart of May and the White-Star League. The scholastics joined with the general body of students for the annual retreat given by the Redemptorists each October.

Legion of Mary 1960
Seated: M. Gallagher, Fr. Comerford, J. Finucane.
Standing: D. Kelly, W. Gardiner.

MUSIC AND DRAMA

In 1956 *The Yeomen of the Guard* was performed with production by Mr. Tobin, scenery by Fr. Comerford and music by Fr. O'Quigley. Leading roles were played by Thomas Kirby, Patrick Fenoughty, the veteran of the society, Declan Hickey, Fintan Fagan, Edward Flannery, Don Henihan, Donal Kelly, David Timlin, Michael Kirby and James Burke.

The Music Society was very active in those years with over a hundred members in 1956. Regular meetings were presided over by Fr. Murray at which recordings of classical and popular music were played. A vast collection of long playing records had been built up which included Decca's recording of Handel's *Messiah* and the H.M.V's recordings of the great Irish tenor John McCormack which were extremely popular. Three films were kindly loaned by the German Legation in 1956 and of the three the most popular was the film on the history of the famous Berlin Philharmonic Orchestra. Films on the lives of French composers and on the instruments of the orchestra were loaned by the French Embassy in 1958. Papers on the lives of the great composers were regularly read by students.

More than forty students sat for the examinations of the Royal Irish Academy each year. In 1958 thirty five students took piano while nine took violin and four took singing. In 1959 the junior choir took part in the Gregorian chant competition in the Clonmel festival. The College orchestra in 1960 was directed by Mr. O'Callaghan and in 1961 by Mr. Guckian.

On St. Patrick's Day 1956 the premier of *Pilate*, a sacred drama based on the Roman governor who sent Our Lord to His death was performed by the students. Written and produced by Fr. Brian Ward, the sets were designed by Br. Ambrose with Fr. Redmond Walsh in charge of the make-up. Fr. Campbell produced *The Merchant of Venice* in 1959 with parts played by Michael Gallagher, Eoin White, the Faulkener brothers, Michael and Anthony, Anthony Deevey, Ian Tamplin, David Bradley, Liam O'Gorman, John L. Murray, William Gardiner, Donal Kelly, Noel Connaughton, Liam Brophy, Paul Walsh, Michael Kirby, Martin Hanihan, John O'Dowd, Michael Neal, Joseph O'Loughlin and Henry Mangan. The same year Fr. Campbell produced a performance of Patrick Pearse's play *Íosagán* by first year students.

Fr. James Murray produced *Julius Caesar* in 1960 with parts played by Richard Nyholm, Albert Daniels, Howard Napier, Conor Anderson, Terence Murphy, David Langton, Barry Moynihan, Michael Gallagher, Eoin White, Hugh O'Connor, Domhnall Blair, Vincent Hannon, Alfred Berkeley, Aloysius Conroy and Donal O'Donnell. Fr. Campbell produced a number of short sketches for junior students in which parts were played by Tom Holmes, Harry Crosby, Christopher Baker, Pat O'Shaughnessy, David Bradley and Paul Moynihan. A musical drama, *Róisín*, written and produced by Fr. Campbell was performed in 1961.

DEBATING

Debating was popular with students and was encouraged by the Deans. 5th and 6th Years had their separate debates and the annual debate between the two years in May attracted great attention and was sometimes chaired by an invited celebrity. In 1960 the guest chairman was Mr. P.I. Maher, former president of Macra na Feirme and in 1961 the inter-year debate was presided over by distinguished past student Senator John Nash, President of the Incorporated Law Society of Ireland. An inter-schools debate was held each year with Glenstal. In 1960 it was held in Glenstal with the motion *That the present system of education in Ireland produces good citizens.* Mr. Justice Cearbhall Ó Dálaigh, Judge of the Supreme Court and future Uachtarán na hÉireann, graciously acted as chairman.

Cumann Díospóireachta na Gaeilge continued to promote debating in the Irish language under the direction of An tAthair Ó Maoláin with topics that were relevant to the time, such as: that Ireland should have its own television service, that the party system of government suits Ireland, that state censorship is necessary and that the G.A.A. Ban is an injustice.

Sixth Year Debating Committee 1957
Seated: H. Nash, Fr. Murray, M. Foley.
Standing: H. Behan, D. Bodley
Front: E. Tuffy.

Coiste na Gaeilge 1960
Seated: G. Crowley,
Fr. Mullins, M. Ryan
Standing: K. O'Connor,
M. Manning,
W. Gardiner, T. Walsh,
C. Comerford.

A student who played a prominent role in debating in those years was Maurice Manning, future senator and Chancellor of the National University of Ireland. Maurice remembers his time in Rockwell with great affection.

Rockwell in 1958 was for me a sort of liberation. Coming from a small school in a small town Rockwell offered such a variety of new experiences; a great choice of subjects, every sort of sporting activity, students not just from all over the country but many from exotic overseas countries.

Fifth Year English Debating Committee 1960
Seated: K. O'Connor,
Fr. Murray, O. White.
Standing: K. Lewis,
P. O'Hourihane, M. Ryan.

What I came to value most in Rockwell was the range of extra curricular activities. We all, even those like myself who were not athletically gifted, were proud of our rugby teams and I still cherish the memory of the three-in-a-row teams of 1958-1961and most especially the great Tadgh Houlihan, a raw, untamed talent which sadly never reached anything like its true potential.

But life was not all about rugby. There was so much else on offer. I remember to this day Fr. Tommy Nolan, without doubt the best teacher of English I ever had, Fr. Reggie, "Johnny" Walker as a fine, if somewhat precocious stylist and the infectious enthusiasm of Fr. Conor Kennedy as a young teacher of History. Their influences were, for me, lasting.

One of the great memories is that 6th Year Sunday "spiff" when Fr. Lehane (a truly great educator) arrived in with two of the greatest rugby players of the time, Tony O'Reilly and Andy Mulligan. To this day I still remember many of O'Reilly's stories.

I edited a College newspaper- crude but readable, and which actually made a small profit. It was there I think I began my writing career! We had vigorous debating and acting societies, but most of all we learned to get on with other people.

What I learned in Rockwell did stand to me in university and in later life. Many of the friendships made then endure after a half century and my memories are good ones.[3]

F.C.A.

The Tipperary 18th Troop of the Irish Catholic Boy Scouts, which had been part of student life in Rockwell since 1949 held their last annual camp at Castlegregory in the summer of 1956 and were disbanded later that year. They were replaced in September 1957 by the F.C.A. which offered a more adventurous and more adult activity to students. Captain Beary administered the oath to the one hundred and twenty members who initially signed on. They were to perform the ceremonial duties in the College life formerly performed by the Boy Scouts. Membership was originally confined to 5th Year students. A weekly rifle practice class was held on half-days in the Cahir barracks which proved attractive to boarders who relished any occasion that brought them legitimately beyond the front gates. A fortnight's training, with pay, during holiday time on Spike Island was an added attraction.

Eight of those who trained on Spike Island in the summer of 1958 were promoted to the rank of corporal and they, for the first time, helped in the training of the members in 1959 which numbered close on a hundred. At the 1959 summer camp on Spike Island eight of the corporals did a lieutenant's course and during the term they organised field days and a refresher course in Clonmel. A group formed a guard of honour at the funeral of Archbishop Kinane in Thurles. Several misty days were spent on the Kilcoran Range. The average turn-out for the year was about sixty-five. Much of the co-ordination between the group and the regular army was done by Fr. Leonard.

In 1960, the third year of the F.C.A. in Rockwell, a marked improvement in all spheres of training was noted by Captain O'Grady. Since its integration

Bishop Moloney (Past student) inspects a guard of honour on Confirmation Day 1958

during the year with the regular army, the troop had benefited in the training in new weapons including the Bren gun, the Vickers machine gun and the Energa grenade. The Rockwell F.C.A. was now part of the Cahir Company 1st Brigade, Southern Command and was closely attached to four other companies, Mallow, Fermoy, Kanturk and Dungarvan to form the 13th Battalion of which Lt. Col. Byrne was Commanding Officer. Three former members of the Rockwell F.C.A., Billy Egar, Jim Condon and Colm Mangan, had won cadetships in the army and were studying at the Military College. From the beginning, membership was confined to 6th and 5th Years but for the first time in 1960 4th Year students were enlisted. On Prize Day of 1960 the F.C.A. formed guards of honour for Dr. Hillery, the Minister for Education, and for Dr. Morris, the new Archbishop of Cashel. There were one hundred and twenty five on the roll in 1961 and parade attendances were moderately good. As in other years the summer camp was on Spike Island.

THE LEAGUES
The House leagues each term in all sports, as in every year, formed a major part in the outdoor recreation of Rockwell students. They offered the chance of participation to students of varying sporting ability at junior and senior level. They also provided an opportunity for the mentors of the J.C.T. and S.C.T. to spot form. The students picked their own captains and the prefects organised matches which they usually refereed. Each team in the league usually adopted

the name of some famous club in that sport and the four teams which reached the semi-finals of the junior rugby league in the first term of 1959, for example, were Garryown, Wanderers, Wolfhounds and Dolphin. Students from St. Joseph's liked to enter their teams as the Lakesiders and any team with a few students from Kerry was known as the Kerrymen. More bizarrely named teams in the leagues of 1960 and 1961 included the Bombers, the Otters, the Beatniks and the Crazy Men. Leagues in Basketball, at senior and junior level, were very popular at the end of the 1950s. Swimming in the lake was permitted only in the last term, and in 1957 thirty two candidates presented themselves for swimming tests under the auspices of the Red Cross, and a number were awarded Life-saving certificates.

Sports Day, often referred to as Parents' Day, on the last Sunday of the summer term continued as a platform for students to show their prowess to their parents and visiting dignitaries. In the late 1950s it included a gymnastic display. Qualifying heats were run off in the weeks prior to the event. The President of the Rockwell Union was usually in attendance to present prizes. A visiting band was always in attendance. In

William Egar throws the discus

1959 it was an Army Pipers' Band and in 1960 it was the Band of the Southern Command under the command of Captain Kiely, a past student.

ATHLETICS

Rockwell had some fine athletes during Fr Finucane's first presidency. Kevin Prendergast set a new record for the 7lb shot at the All Ireland schools' championship in 1956, held in Ballinasloe. He also came third in the 12lb shot and discus. At the same sports other athletes who were in receipt of medals were Seán Murphy, Ted O'Brien, Joe King, Declan Mulligan, Seamus Behan, Michael Ryan and William Lee who was Rockwell's leading pole-vaulter. In the 1957 Munster championship Kevin Prendergast was beaten in the discus by his fellow Clonmel townsman, Brian O'Callaghan, son of the legendary Olympic champion, Pat O'Callaghan. Yet, Kevin won the discus at the All Ireland championship at which he also set a new record for the 12 lb shot and came second in the javelin. Other prominent athletes in 1957 were Michael O'Leary,

William Egar, Dermot Moloughney, William
Lee, Kevin O'Connell, Donal Kelly, Matt
O'Mahony, John Broderick, Seamus Behan,
Michael Ryan and Louis Bermudez from Trinidad
who won the junior shot at the All Ireland,
setting a new Irish record.

At the All Ireland championships of 1958
Kevin Prendergast won the discus and 12 lb shot,
setting new records in both and later competed
for the Irish Universities in Louvain. At that
1958 event William Lee became senior all
Ireland pole vault champion and Pat McGrath
junior pole vault champion. The All Ireland
championships of 1959 were held in Ballinasloe
and Rockwell brought home the College of
Science Cup for the first time in twenty eight

Pat McGrath with College of
Science Cup 1959

years. Team captain was Pat McGrath who competed in the pole vault, long
jump and 120yds hurdles. Denis Murphy was vice-captain and came second in
the 100 yards at the All Ireland while Louis Bermudez won the intermediate
pole-vault. Fr. O'Brien, as Dean of Discipline, did much to promote athletics in
Rockwell but the sport got a new impetus with the arrival of Fr. Lavelle to the
Community in 1957. He took over the coaching of the pole-vault, shot and
discus and his influence was immense.

The leading senior athletes in 1960 were Michael Ryan and Seán Tierney at
the mile and 880 yards, Chris Liddy at 220 and 440 yards, Tony Egar at the
hurdles and Simon Onwu at the high jump. In the intermediate class Roger
Cumiskey was prominent in the long jump, Michael Cole in the 4-kilo shot and
Roger Kelly in the pole vault. Joe Cumiskey was the leading junior athlete in
1960 winning the 100 and 220 yards at the All Ireland and winning the junior
relay with Anthony Finn, Brendan Dempsey and David Hill. In the senior
category in1961 Tony Egar was prominent in the shot and discus, Michael Ryan
in the mile and 880 yards and Louis Bermudez who was the only Rockwell
winner at the All Ireland Sports. Joe Cumiskey was first in the Munster
intermediate 100 and 220 yards and won the relay with Des O'Brien, Stephen
Tam and Brendan Dempsey. Liam Stapleton won the junior shot at the Munster
Sports.

To cater mainly for those with no great inclination for football or hurling
and yet with some running ability, the Rockwell Cross-Country Club was formed
in October 1958. About twenty runners joined. The club affiliated with the Co.
Tipperary N.A.C.A. The first outing was to nearby Barne for a race organised
by the Clonmel Club. The club later took part in races at Thurles and Nenagh.
By the end of the season there was a solid core of seasoned runners in Seán
Cooney, Brendan Coleman, Paddy Ryan, Maurice Mullins, Chris Liddy, Michael
Ryan and Brian O'Keeffe.

GAELIC GAMES

Handball was a popular recreation especially during the final term when the handball leagues were in full swing. In 1957 more than twenty players took part in the leagues and the leading players were William Lee, Michael Heelan, Paddy Hickey, Matt McGrath, John Synnott, Liam Lewis, Billy Egar and Paddy Morris. In the handball leagues of 1958 the leading senior players were Paddy Hickey, Liam Ahearne, Mick Butler and Seamus Behan. Paddy Hickey and Liam Ahearne became senior doubles champions. In the junior league final Des Harris and Kieran Kelly beat Joe Kerrigan and Colm Corcoran.

The Rockwell hurlers, in preparation for the Harty Cup each year had challenge matches against Thurles C.B.S., St. Kieran's, Kilkenny, Roscrea and local clubs. Roger O'Donnell was senior captain in 1956. The first round of the Harty Cup was played against Dungarvan C.B.S. in Clonmel and Rockwell lost by 5-9 to 4-6. Leading players were John Malone, John McCarthy and Eamon Lonergan. The juniors of 1956 lost to St. Flannan's in the first round of the Canon Kennedy Shield, played at Patrickswell.

The seniors lost to Farrenferris in the first round of the Harty Cup in 1957 while the juniors failed to progress in the Dean Ryan Cup and the under 15s in the Dr. Croke Cup. Although no hurling trophies were won in 1957 a pointer to the standard of hurling in the College can be gauged by the number of players who were invited for trials for their county minor teams, they being Bernard O'Callaghan for Kerry, John. Heffernan, Eamonn Lonergan, Matthew McGrath and Edmond O'Donnell for Tipperary William Lee and Michael Heelan for Limerick and Michael Crowley for Waterford.

Senior Hurlers 1957
Front: M. O'Donoghue, M. McGrath, M. Ryan, G. Manning
Seated: E. O'Donnell, J. Malone, E. Lonergan, J. O'Mahony, C. Cooke, L. Crowe, J. Beere.
Standing: M.O'Donoghue, M. Heelan, B. Casserly, W. Lee, J. Moloney, J. O'Regan

Rockwell, captained by William Lee in 1958, beat Ennis C.B.S. in the first round of the Harty Cup by 4-6 to 4-3 but lost in the second round to Thurles C.B.S. The following year Rockwell travelled to Fermoy for the first round of the Harty Cup against Farrenferris and secured a draw. The following week Rockwell won the replay by 5-9 to 3-4 but in the semi-final suffered a heavy defeat to the Harty Cup holders and All Ireland champions, St. Flannan's College. The juniors that year beat Clonmel High School in the Dr. Rodgers Cup by twelve points but lost to Mount Sion in the second round.

The Harty Cup team of 1960 was captained by Noel Drew and lost to De La Salle, Waterford in the first round by 5-2 to 1-4, in a game played at Carrick-on-Suir. This was the last time that Rockwell played in the Harty Cup. It was a competition in which Rockwell had been dominant in the early days but had lost its prominence in the late 1950s due to a growth of the student population of schools in the hurling heartlands of Tipperary, Limerick, Cork, Clare and Waterford. Rockwell continued to participate in the Dr. Rodgers Cup and the Dr. Croke Cup and in 1961 reached the semi-final of the Dr. Rodgers Cup, narrowly losing to Ennis C.B.S. The leading players in that match were Tony Roche, Thomas Duggan, William Quaid, Thomas Hickey, Edward McManus, Keith Lancaster and John O'Brien.

After a lapse of a number of years Rockwell entered a senior Gaelic football team in the Munster Championship of 1960. This team was trained by Fr. Joe Nolan. A number of challenges with local teams were held before losing to St. Flannan's in the championship. In 1961 challenges were held with local clubs, Clonmel High School, Copswood College, Pallaskenry, Roscrea and Limerick C.B.S. St. Flannans were again the opponents in Corn na Mumhan. St. Flannans won by 3-6 to 1-8.

JUNIOR RUGBY

Rockwell won the Junior Cup for the second year in a row in 1956. The team was trained again by Fr. Redmond Walsh with Michael O'Leary as captain and David Sheahan as vice-captain. Among the early challenge matches was one against St. Joseph's College, Ballinasloe which was paying its first visit to Rockwell. In the Cup, Rockwell beat St. Munchins 9-0 and then drew 3-3 with Crescent but won the replay 6-0. A narrow win in the final over Presentation College Cork by 6-5 followed. In 1957 the team was captained by Seamus Behan with Seán Gillen as vice-captain but hopes of winning three in a row were dashed in the first round by Pres.

The Cup returned to Rockwell in 1958 with Pat Leyden as captain. A tight struggle against Pres in the first round resulted in a 6-3 win for Rockwell. The semi-final against Munchins was played at Clanwilliam Rugby Ground and Rockwell won by 11-3. The final against Crescent was postponed until after Easter which meant in a boarding school there was a complete break in the training schedule. The team returned a few days before the general body and in the delayed final scores from Tom Ryan, Matt O'Mahony, Pat Leyden and John Daly assured a Rockwell win. Other players who were prominent in

Junior Cup Winners 1959
Front: *P. Tierney, M. Hackett.*
Seated: *T. Synnott, P. O'Connell, A. Egar, M. O'Mahony, A. Butler, K. O'Connor, U. Conway.*
Standing: *M. Cole, G. O'Sullivan, D. O'Shea, J. Wallace, J. Molloy, S. O'Sullivan.*

the campaign were Jim Harrington, Andy Butler, Tadhg Houlihan and Donal Kelly.

Fr. Lavelle was in charge in 1959 when the Cup was won for the second year in a row. He was indeed to take charge of every J.C.T. from then until 1982. Matt O'Mahony was captain in 1959 and Tony Egar vice-captain. Other prominent members were Kevin O'Connor and Andy Butler whose older brother captained the senior team to victory in the Cup that year. Rockwell beat Glenstal in the first round by 9-0 and had a comfortable win over Christians, Cork, in the semi-final by 23-0. Rockwell beat Pres in the final by two penalty goals to one. In the 1960 final Pres got their revenge and won by two points. In 1961 Rockwell beat Munchins and drew with Crescent in the semi-final but lost the replay.

SENIOR RUGBY
Rockwell won the Senior Cup on two occasions during Fr. Finucane's first presidency, in 1959 and in 1961. In 1956 Rockwell won the Bowen Shield but lost to Pres in the first round of the Cup. Maurice Mullins was captain and Joe King vice-captain. The inter-provincial players that year were Loman Conway, Frank Byrne, Billy Egar, Maurice Mullins, Declan Hickey and Joe King. Pat Murphy and Billy Egar were captain and vice-captain respectively in 1957 and for the second year in succession lost to Pres in the Cup. The six inter-provincials of 1957 were Kevin Prendergast, Billy Egar, Michael Crowley, Cathal Kavanagh, Tom O'Brien and John Coakley. Kevin Prendergast captained the 1958 side with Matty McNamara as vice-captain. Rockwell drew with Pres in

Senior Cup Winners 1959
Front: *P. Leyden, H, Moody.*
Seated: *P. McGrath, M. Dennehy, S. Behan, M. Butler, J. Clancy, B. Nolan, T. Kerins.*
Standing: *J. Byrne, S. Cooney, D. Murphy, S. Gillen, J. Harrington, T. Houlihan, N. Elliot, D. Corry.*

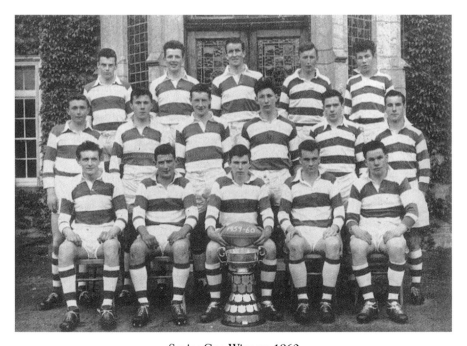

Senior Cup Winners 1960
Seated: *D. Timlin, T. Houlihan, P. Leyden, J. Harrington, C. Guiney.*
Middle: *D. Shanahan, M. Cole, A. Butler, J. Molloy, G. Davey, J. Daly.*
Back: *D. Harris, W. Gardiner, D. Kelly, M. O'Mahony, M. Cooke.*

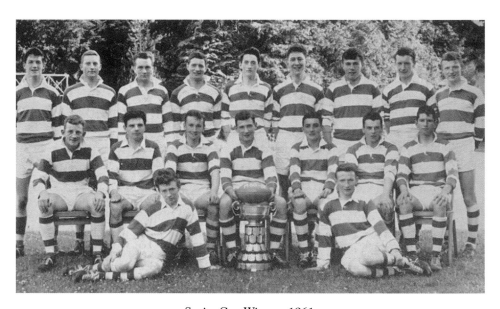

Senior Cup Winners 1961
Front: J. Cumiskey, R. Cumiskey
Seated: B. O'Keeffe, K. Lannen, M. O'Mahony, T. Houlihan, D. Houlihan, D. Harris, J. Hawkins.
Standing: F. Egan, J. O'Sullivan, J. Harrington, A. Egar, O. Breen, J. Molloy, M. Cole, A. Butler,
M. Hackett.

the first round of the Cup but lost the replay. The seven inter-provincials of 1958 were Brendan O'Dowd, Kevin Prendergast, Michael O'Leary, David Geaney, Matty McNamara, Mick Butler and Seamus Behan.

The Cup returned to Rockwell in 1959 for the first time since 1955. This was the first in a three-in-a-row sequence. As was the case in previous years, challenge matches were played against Blackrock, St. Mary's, Roscrea, Cashel and Carrick-on-Suir. The Cup campaign began with a 42-0 victory over a weak Mungret. The semi-final was against C.B.C. It finished level at 6-6 but after extra time Rockwell won 12-6. The final was against P.B.C. which Rockwell won for the seventeenth time. Seamus Behan had been elected captain but in his absence because of injury Michael Butler captained the team for the final. The inter-provincials of 1959 were Denis Murphy, Neil Elliott, Michael Butler, John Clancy, Tadhg Houlihan and Gerard O'Brien. Other players who featured on the Cup winning side were Jim Harrington, Joe Byrne, Paddy Leyden, Paddy McGrath, Seán Cooney, Bernard Nolan, Declan Corry, Seán Gillan, Tadhg Kerins, Seamus Behan, Hugh Moody and Michael Dennehy

Paddy Leyden was captain in 1960 when the Cup returned. Rockwell beat Munchins 17-3 in the first round and Mungret 22-3 in the semi-final. The final in Limerick was against Crescent who had already won the Bowen Shield. It finished in a draw but in the replay in Cork Rockwell won possession of the Cup. The inter-provincials of 1961 were Tadhg Houlihan, Jim Harrington, Andrew Butler and Paddy Leyden. Other players who featured in the Cup campaign were Derek Harris, Con Guiney, John Daly, Denis Shanahan, Roger Cumiskey, Matt O'Mahony, Donal Kelly, David Timlin and Billy Gardiner.

When Rockwell won the Cup for the third year in a row in 1961 the team was captained by Tadhg Houlihan with Matt O'Mahony as vice-captain. Rockwell beat Munchins 15-3 in the first round and beat Pres by 11-9 in the semi-final after a very close encounter in Cork. The final was against Christians and Rockwell won 9-0. The inter-provincials of 1961 were Jim Harrington, Tony Egar, Andy Butler, Tadhg Houlihan, Michael Cole and Matt O'Mahony.

ROCKWELL UNION

During the first presidency of Fr. Finucane the presidents of the Rockwell Union were Edward Morkan, James G. Maher, Jack Condon and William J. O'Neill. The annual Union dinner was held in those years in the Dolphin Hotel in Dublin. At the annual dinner in 1956 Edward Morkan announced that because of changing circumstances the Union reluctantly had to wind up the Boys' Club which it had been running in Dublin since 1943. With this Catholic social activity no longer functioning, he said it was decided to substitute for it some form of help for the missions "and accordingly we have inaugurated it with an initial contribution of two burses for the training of two students for the priesthood." The annual dinner also provided a platform for the President of the College to speak on current affairs and at the dinner of 1956 Fr. Finucane said "We are to-day grappling with a very grave problem in what a Vatican pronouncement referred to as the eruption in our society of modern communication techniques and their threat to personal living. The "mass media" as they are called of press, movies, radio and television with their unrelenting enticements and their tireless propaganda, tend more and more to atrophy the critical judgement, to induce the dumb acquiescence of the herd and to substitute for the Catholic ideal of life the bogus and highly dangerous alternative of a pleasure-loving paganism".

Union Day 1957
John Condon, Fr. Finucane, James G. Maher (Union President). Fr. Comerford, Seán McKenna.

Bishop Brosnahan
(past student) with
James G. Maher and
Fr. Finucane on Union
Day 1958

The custom of holding an annual retreat in Rockwell from Holy Thursday to Easter Saturday for Union members had been introduced in 1955 and had attracted a good attendance each year. Union Day in Rockwell continued as a popular occasion. On the 5th January 1958 a preliminary meeting was held in Rockwell by a group of seventeen past students from all parts of Munster with a view to establishing a branch of the Union in the South. Frank Mulcahy of Cork took the chair and Jim Burke of Cahir acted as secretary. A dinner was held in Mallow in February. In 1959 a target of £1,000 for mission burses was set. And at Union Day 1960 a centenary year committee was established and was already planning for the celebration. The following year a ladies' committee was established to help with the planning.

HOTEL AND CATERING SCHOOL
The Rockwell Hotel and Catering School had begun as a catering course in 1958 under the auspices of Bord Fáile Éireann. The course was planned and organised with the help of the catering officers of Bord Fáilte, Shannon Airport and Córas Iompar Éireann, and by the members of the Irish Hotel Federation and the Irish Hotel and Restaurant Managers' Association. On 15th June 1960 the Hotel and Catering School was formally opened by the Minister for Education, Dr. Patrick Hillery. In the same year the Vocational Education Committee of South Tipperary undertook to sponsor the catering course at Rockwell. In 1963 the Council for Education, Recruitment and Training for the hotel industry (C.E.R.T.) took over from Bord Fáilte Éireann the responsibility for hotel staff training in Ireland, and the Rockwell Hotel and Catering School came under the control of this new body.

The aim of the school was to provide a basic training in dining room service and cookery for boys who wished to take up a career in the hotel and catering industry as chefs and waiters. The contents of the course included the practice and theory of dining room service, restaurant operations, cookery, kitchen operations, menu planning, hygiene, food costing and care of equipment. As well as this specific training the students, who usually entered the school on the completion of the Group Certificate in Vocational Schools, were able to continue their academic training and take the Leaving Certificate Examination after two years if they wished.

There were practical advantages to the Hotel and Catering School being attached to Rockwell College. They included the facilities offered in the College kitchen and dining rooms. With a view to providing the proper training facilities, the College kitchen was built and equipped in accordance with plans approved by Bord Fáilte Éireann and leading Irish hoteliers. The kitchen area consisted of the kitchen proper, two still rooms, a larder with adjacent cold rooms, a patisserie, a vegetable preparation room, store rooms and two wash-up sections.

The duration of the course was two years for waiters and three years for chefs. During this time of training the students were released occasionally to gain experience in local hotels. With the same purpose in view they were placed in approved Irish hotels and restaurants during the summer holiday period. At the termination of the course the students went to work in Irish hotels to spend a further two years' practical training, during which time they remained under the supervision of the Rockwell school authorities.

OBITUARIES

The death took place in September 1955 of Fr. Timothy Cunningham, former Vice-President. Born in 1881 in the Glen of Aherlow, Co. Tipperary, he did his secondary studies at Blackrock College and it was at this time that he became a life-long friend of Eamon de Valera. He had been a prefect in Rockwell and apart from a few years in Blackrock and later in the English Province, he lived all his priestly life in Rockwell. He taught Latin and was especially popular with the "plodders". He had been a good rugby player in his youth and was a fine referee. He cultivated with great taste a little garden-retreat near the boat house.[4]

Fr. Anthony Meaney died in 1957. He was born in Limerick City in 1909 and studied at Blackrock College. Following his ordination in 1937 he taught science in Mauritius and Trinidad. He had come to Rockwell from Blackrock in 1946 and the following year departed for the missions again in both Mauritius and later in Trinidad, returning to Rockwell in 1953. One of his tasks in Rockwell was the organisation and conducting of classes in Agricultural Science.[5]

Fr. James J. Burke died in 1958. He had written the words of the missionary hymn of the Holy Ghost Fathers *Go Ye Afar*. And it was he, in collaboration with Fr. John Kearney, who composed the hymn *De Profundis* "Out of the Depths." Born at Attanagh, Co. Laois in 1877 his student and priestly life was centered in Blackrock College until he arrived in Rockwell in 1935 where he became a very popular French teacher. He celebrated the golden jubilee of his ordination in October 1958 when over four hundred students in the College Chapel sang his missionary hymn *Go Ye Afar*. Six weeks later, on 17th December, at his funeral the same student body sang his *De Profundis*.[6]

Brother Malacy Fleming died in 1959. He was born in Ballinspittal, Co. Cork in 1887. When Kimmage was opened in 1911 he joined the Community there. In 1917 he was appointed to Rockwell where he was to spend the next forty years. He was a very effective teacher and he also looked after the Book Shop. He later transferred to the Bursar's office where he acted as accountant and secretary to seven successive Bursars.[7]

Fr. Thady O'Connor died in 1960. Born in Millstreet Co. Cork in 1882 he came to Rockwell as a student in 1898 and later as a prefect he captained the Rockwell Senior Munster Cup team of 1904 which included the famous brothers Jack and Michael Ryan and Eamon de Valera. He was ordained in Chevilly, Paris, where he had done his studies, and he departed for the missions in Southern Nigeria in 1912. After twenty years of missionary work he returned to Ireland because of poor health and he became professor of Chemistry at Rockwell in 1932. He held this post until his death. He was a dynamic character and a very popular teacher.[8]

Bishop Joseph Byrne died on 20th October 1961. A native of Clonmel where he was born in 1880, he was a younger brother of Fr. John Byrne, President of Rockwell (1916-1925) and he was a Rockwell student in the late 1890s. He studied in Paris and Rome where he was ordained in 1903. He was a missionary in Sierra Leone from 1905 to 1910 and was Master of Novices, Director of Scholastics and Professor of Theology at Ferndale, Connecticut with the American Province of the Holy Ghost Fathers. He became Provincial of the Irish Province in 1922 and in 1926 was appointed to the General Council of the Order in Paris where he served for seven years. On the death of Bishop Henry Gogarty, a fellow Rockwellian and Tipperary man in 1933 Dr. Byrne was appointed Vicar Apostolic of Kilimanjaro in East Africa and was consecrated at Rockwell. His life-long friend, Eamon de Valera, was present at his consecration. When the Vicariate of Kilmanjaro was amalgamated into the diocese of Moshi in 1953, Dr. Byrne became its first bishop. He pioneered the training of African-born priests. Five years later, in his 79th year he retired to Rockwell. His funeral was attended by President de Valera and Dr. Patrick Hillery, Minister for Education and many members of the Irish Hierarchy.[9]

Two lay teachers died during Fr. Finucane's first presidency. Patrick J. O'Connor died suddenly in 1956. He had been teaching in Rockwell since 1943 and was very popular with students. Patrick Ryan died in 1958. He had been on the Rockwell staff since 1954 where he taught Irish and English and was an accomplished artist.

Notes

[1] ISR 778
[2] RCA 1957
[3] Submission of Dr. Maurice Manning 27/2/2013
[4] ISR 553
[5] ISR 647
[6] ISR 736
[7] ISR 53
[8] ISR 469
[9] ISR 620

– 12 –

THE CENTENARY CELEBRATIONS
1964

The most notable event of the 1960s in Rockwell was the celebration in 1964 of the centenary of the College. It was an occasion to honour all those who had served the College in the past and to take pride in their achievements. It was an occasion to assess the enormous contribution the College had made to the missionary Church and to the development of the early Irish State. And it was an occasion for its past students to acknowledge their gratitude and for its authorities to plot its future.

STRUCTURAL DEVELOPMENTS
The centenary provided an opportunity to focus on necessary developments of the College which would come to fruition in 1964. In the three years prior to the centenary major initiatives were achieved. Chief of these was the building of St. Joseph's Oratory adjacent to the Lake House. The decision to proceed with the oratory was taken in 1961 and by coincidence at the same time the Ancient Order of Hibernians offered a substantial endowment to honour the recently deceased James D. Nugent, a high ranking member of the Order and a loyal Rockwell past student and prominent member of the Rockwell Union since its inception in 1925.

The new oratory at the Lake House

213

Rockwell Union organisers of centenary celebration 1963
Thomas V. Cummins (Irish ambassador to the Holy See), Tim Cleary (founder member of Union), Lieut. Col. Liam Bergin (Organising secretary), Col. Eddie Morkan (former Union President)

Work on the oratory commenced under the direction of Fr. Michael Comerford who embraced the project with an endearing enthusiasm. Johnnie Moore, as foreman, assembled a team of skilled craftsmen and work commenced. On Fr. Comerford's suggestion a tabernacle donated by the Ancient Order of Hibernians was to be the centrepiece of the oratory. Messrs Jones and Kelly were appointed architects and in their restrained modern-style design, all features had a focus on the tabernacle with its decorative motifs repeated throughout the church.[1]

The skilful cut-stone work in the chancel interior and exterior was perfected by Br. Senan Smith who had come to Rockwell from Ardbracan in 1961 and whose manifold skills and great organising ability were evident in many Rockwell structural projects. The suspended ceiling and canopy over the altar were the work of Messrs Creedon Brothers, the plastering contractors, who presented the plaques of the Evangelists, the Holy Spirit image and the Eucharistic symbols. Tipperary Glass Ltd. (Templemore) supplied the coloured leaded lights and Mrs. Elizabeth Fleming, architect, was responsible for the décor. Fr. Comerford himself designed the modern pews in keeping with the rest of the Church

The altar was consecrated by past student Bishop Brosnahan of Sierra Leone on 9th October 1963 and on the following morning the oratory was blessed by Fr. Connors of the General Council.

Preparations for the centenary included major works under the direction of Denis Kelly a past student and architect. These works included an updating of toilets and locker rooms to the east of the Silas building and a rejuvenation of toilets and wash rooms adjacent to dormitories throughout the building. The provision of individual lockers was greatly welcomed by students. The then Dean of Discipline, Fr.Lehane, put much effort into the design of the lockers, especially with regard to drying, ventilation and storage space. There was a general scheme of painting and redecoration throughout the house. A new floor was installed in the Big Study and changes in the College Chapel included a new lighting system and a redecoration of the Stations of the Cross.

One of the exterior improvements for the centenary was probably unnoticed by many although it may have been the most expensive. It consisted of a new sewage and drainage system with pipes running westwards from the Crehan wing across the field at the back of the Study Block to a new and improved septic tank. Two more exterior improvements which were much more visible, however, were the tarmac area and the golf links. Prior to these developments Rockwell had no hard surface playing grounds and in damp weather the boys frequently came to class in sodden footwear, even after short morning recreations. Originally there had been a rapid slope (partly terraced) right down to the handball alleys and to the orchard behind the alleys. In the change now made the top level terrace near the house was retained and bulldozers got to work on the lower terraces. Levelling of the surface necessitated the demolition of the alleys (with aspirations to restore them in the future) but the outcome was more than three acres of a tarmac surface with floodlighting sited on the northern wing.

The development of the golf course was very much the aspiration of Fr. Aidan Lehane, himself a low-handicap golfer. Eddie Hackett, professional golfer and golf course designer, was responsible for the lay-out of the Rockwell course. Originally a three-hole course was developed in the two fields between the Chapel and the lake, the separating fence having been removed. During subsequent years three more holes were placed in the long rectangular field below the lake on the south side of the back avenue. Finally the paddock west of the farmyard provided three more holes, thus providing Rockwell with its nine-hole course.

THE CELEBRATIONS
Almost a hundred years to the day that Fr. Leman arrived in Rockwell to take over possession, celebrations to mark the centenary commenced on Sunday 19th July 1964. Dignitaries of church and state attended a Solemn Pontifical

The President's Guard of Honour
President De Valera inspects the Guard of Honour

The procession of prelates

Mass in the College Chapel. Prior to the Mass President Eamon de Valera inspected a guard of honour of a hundred troops of the Southern Command to the accompaniment of the Band of the Southern Command. Almost twenty bishops and other church dignitaries including the Superior General of the Holy Ghost Congregation, Archbishop Lefebvre, walked in procession from their robeing rooms to their places in the chapel. The Papal Nuncio and Cardinal Browne followed. Last to enter at 12 noon was the Archbishop of Cashel, Dr. Morris, who was celebrant. He was greeted by the *Ecce Sacerdos* sung by the choir of the senior scholasticate, Kimmage, conducted by Fr. Desmond Reid.

The congregation included An Taoiseach, Seán Lemass, An Tánaiste, Seán McEntee, The Minister for Education, Patrick Hillery, Seán T. O'Kelly, former President of Ireland, John A. Costello, former Taoiseach, William T. Cosgrave, first President of the Irish Free State, General Richard Mulcahy, first Minister for Defence in the Irish Free State, General Seán McKeon, veteran of the War of Independence, the Lord Mayors of Cork and Limerick, the Mayors of Clonmel and other towns and councils and several other public figures and past students. The presence of such leading public figures was testament to the status and esteem with which Rockwell was held throughout Ireland.

The sermon was preached by Dr. Peter Birch, Bishop of Ossory, himself a former Professor of Education at St. Patrick's College Maynooth. He spoke of the difficult times with which the founders of Rockwell had to cope in 1864. It was surely a time, he said, when educational advance seemed imperative, a time of economic and political as well as religious expansion. Not even the most sanguine, he continued, can have anticipated that the pitiable stream of junior clerics would swell so soon into the steady flow of missionaries, the eminent men of state, the Church dignitaries of today.

After the Pontifical Mass
Fr. Finucane, Archbishop Lefebre, Archbishop Morris, Cardinal Browne, President de Valera,
Archbishop Sensi, An Taoiseach Seán Lemass, Archbishop McCarthy.

Following the Mass the guests assembled for a reception in the Big Study, now denuded of the desks where so many of the past students had sat in former years. This re-union was a most pleasant introduction and "ice-breaker" to the luncheon which commenced at 2 p.m. At the end of the luncheon Archbishop Marcel Lefebre proposed a toast to the President of Ireland. He referred to Mr. de Valera as a senior statesman of Europe and thanked him for his lifelong loyalty to the Holy Ghost Fathers. In reply President de Valera spoke of his happy times in Rockwell and wished the Holy Ghost Fathers many more centuries of equal service to God and to our country. Toasts were proposed to Cardinal Browne, to the Papal Nuncio, Archbishop Morris, to Rockwell College and finally to the guests.

On 22nd July Rockwell continued her centenary celebrations by inviting to the College all the Irish Holy Ghost Fathers of the Irish Province and of the missions. These were joined by diocesan priest past students and by priests of the archdiocese of Cashel and Emly. The invited guests numbered 320 and came from all over the world. President de Valera was also in attendance.

The ceremonies on this occasion began with Pontifical High Mass celebrated by Archbishop Marcel Lefebre. The Kimmage choir was again conducted by Fr. Reid. In his sermon the Bishop of Owerri, Nigeria, Dr. Joseph Whelan, praised the work of all Rockwell past students who had served on the missions. He paid especial praise to Rockwell's past student, Bishop Joseph Shanahan, for his exceptional role in the development of the Nigerian Church and describing him as one of Rockwell's greatest sons. He also stressed the importance of the teachers in the building up of the Church. "Where they fail, the Church fails" he said.

Guard of honour of past student army officers
Comdt. M. O'Farrell, Lieut. J. O'Brien, Capt. M. Duggan, Lieut. A. Egar, Lieut. S. J. Stokes,
Lieut. C. Mangan, Capt. J. Finucane, Capt. G. Kenny, Lieut. W. Egar, Capt. T. O'Mahony,
Capt. M. Harrington, Capt. B. Cantwell, Lieut. Col. L. Bergin.

The High Mass was followed by a reception in the Big Study and later by lunch. After lunch the Superior General Emeritus Fr. Griffin, proposed a toast to President de Valera who in his reply raised a smile (from those who remembered the Treaty Debates of 1921-2) when he said that he always enjoyed an "external association" with the Holy Ghost Congregation. Fr. Joseph Nolan proposed the toast to Cardinal Browne who in his reply referred to his own days in Rockwell. He insisted that the training both intellectual and moral which he received in Rockwell were the foundation on which all his subsequent attainments were based. Canon Christopher Lee, parish priest of Fethard proposed the toast to the Superior General who in his reply expressed the wish that Rockwellians should be all good "Rock" men, meaning that they be loyal to the Rock which is Peter. The president of the Rockwell Union, Surgeon James Maher, proposed the toast to the College referring to the great work of past students on the missions. Rockwell, he said, was producing a stream of highly educated laymen whose impact on the recent history of our country was evident. "But let us not forget our unsung hero from Cloughjordan, Thomas MacDonagh" he said. "Scholar, poet, soldier, patriot, who to me exemplifies more than any other the spirit of the ideal Rockwell student. Only he could write" he continued:

> *But I found no enemy, no man in a world of wrong*
> *That Christ's word of charity did not render clear and strong.*
> *Who were I to grudge my kind—blindest groper of the blind*

Surgeon Maher concluded that an officer who witnessed the execution of the 1916 leaders said "They all died well, but MacDonagh died like a prince"

In part of his reply Fr. Finucane said "We are a missionary society and here in Rockwell it is our constant endeavour to foster both priestly and missionary vocations. "We do not try to indoctrinate. A vocation comes from God, not from man. Apart from the Junior Scholasticate we realise that we are a secular College. But I think that we may lay claim that in our efforts to build up a solid Catholic manhood for our country, we are laying the foundations for that wholesome family life without which priestly vocations of any kind must ultimately cease to exist."

Vice-President, Fr. Michael Comerford proposed the toast to the guests. In part of his reply Mr. Michael K. O'Connor, a former President of the Union said "We freely admit that were it not for the religious orders, higher education

Fr. Joe Nolan with
Taoiseach Seán Lemass

would have been, and indeed would remain, outside the attainment of the majority of our people. In supplying this great need, Rockwell has played its part right nobly. Successive generations of teachers, clerical and lay, have walked worthily of the vocation in which they have been called. They have deserved well of their country and of us and today I dare to tell them so, in your name, with respect and gratitude. Thank you Rockwell."

The Rockwell centenary celebrations continued on Sunday 26th July with a garden party. Preparations for this event had begun long before Easter. A list of names and addresses of all known past pupils was compiled from every possible source. Four thousand letters were sent enclosing invitations to the garden party and information forms and notices were issued in the daily and provincial newspapers. As a result of this

Archbishop Lefebre, Cardinal Browne,
Fr. Finucane

survey the College obtained the up-to-date record of some three thousand living past students and in each case details of their present address, years at Rockwell, married or single and in many cases, profession.

About three thousand guests attended the garden party. The weather was superb and the Galtees looked supremely beautiful. A dazzling variety of flowers throughout the grounds had burst into bloom dead on time. The trimmed lawns and lightly swaying trees swept gracefully down to the terraces and the lakeside. Refreshment marquees were strategically placed to avoid over crowding. In the middle of the tarmac the Band of the Southern Command played medleys of classical and popular music. Cardinal Browne and Archbishop Lefebre slowly circled around the grounds in an open car attended by past students Lieut-Col Liam Bergin and Comdt. Gerard Glendon. Six past students from the Military College in their uniform adorned the scene.

Throughout the afternoon crowds passed continuously round the lake, visiting the new oratory at St. Joseph's, the Rock and the cemetery. Some guests drifted down to the lake-side near the boat house and just sat enjoying the sun and water. It was an occasion when many half-forgotten faces were recalled, class-room memories were exchanged and old friendships were renewed. From six o'clock on, the visitors melted away leaving many memories. The garden party had rung down the curtain on a wonderful week which had begun with what one newspaper referred to as "a day of pomp and pageantry" and closed in an affectionate family re-union.

Cardinal Browne and Archbishop Lefebre at the garden party

Past student army cadets
B. McCaul, K. White, J. Ahearne, T. Hickey, P. O'Shea, S. Lyons.

Enjoying the garden party

The lay teaching staff of 1964 with Fr. Nolan
Liam Ó Duibhir, Seán O'Donnell, Liam O'Dwyer, Jack Young, Fr. Nolan, John L. Buckley,
Alf O'Sullivan, Jerry Hayes, Thomas Tobin (Absent from the group Martin Farragher)

The Centenary Week was an unqualified success. Its success was due to a great team effort over a long period. The team consisted of the Fathers, Brothers and prefects of the Community, the Sisters and the lay staff. Of the latter special mention was due to Mr. Thomas Tobin, honorary secretary of the centenary committee, whose special gift for large-scale organisation found full scope in the three crowded functions and evoked many tributes of praise. Mr. Hugh Bennett and Mr. Jim Maguire, manager and assistant manager of the Catering School, with their staff of pupil chefs and waiters were responsible for the success of the two formal luncheons and the garden party. The College foreman, Johnnie Moore and his team of workers played a big part in having the grounds in good shape. The army, gárdaí and press were extremely helpful.

THE SCHOOL YEAR

The school year of 1964 proceeded as usual because the centenary celebrations were at a time of summer holidays and therefore did not interfere with the school calendar. There was no change in the number of Fathers since the previous year, being twenty six. The nine Brothers of the previous year continued as did the eleven prefects, two of whom were destined to fill major roles in the College, Fr. Jack Meade as president and Fr. Brendan Hally as Headmaster. The eleven lay teachers were joined in September 1964 by Ms. Margaret Lynch and Mr. Seamus Leahy. Rockwell mourned the death of student Gerard Murtagh who died just a month after completing his Intermediate Certificate in which he had obtained honours in all subjects.

There were 546 students in the Rockwell secondary school in 1964. Of these 523 were boarders with 23 day pupils. 72 of the boarders were scholastics in St.

Joseph's. The fact that Fifth and Sixth years had more students than the junior years reflects a continuing trend whereby many students came to Rockwell having completed their Intermediate studies in other schools.

Students were offered a wide curriculum with a subject choice much wider than many other schools offered at the time. Leaving Certificate students were offered a choice of eighteen subjects. Three of these, Irish, English and Mathematics, were of course mandatory for Irish-born students. Most students took seven subjects for their Leaving Certificate and it is interesting to note how they chose the four non-mandatory subjects. They were influenced of course by their own aptitude, by the interest they had developed in subjects in junior classes and how they had performed in the Intermediate Certificate, by their career expectations and by parental wishes. And at a time when Career Guidance was not yet a formal part of the education system in Irish schools, it can be assumed that the Dean of Studies, Fr. Joe Nolan, had a major influence in subject choice.

The Leaving Certificate results of the previous year provide an insight to how students chose the non mandatory subjects. Of the 89 students who sat the exam that year 73 of them chose Latin at either honours or ordinary level. This can hardly have been due to a love of the classics as only 3 took Greek. French was the choice of 24 with 5 opting for Spanish and one for German. Chemistry was the most popular science subject, attracting 35 while 18 took Physics with 4 of the latter taking Applied Maths. Botany was the choice of 23 while 14 chose Agricultural Science. Of all subjects, Geography was next in popularity to Latin attracting 50 while only 8 opted for History. Commerce was the choice of 39 while 19 chose Drawing. Two university entrance scholarships were obtained by Rockwell students on the results of their Leaving Certificate. Music students took the examinations of the Royal Irish Academy of Music rather than those of the Department of Education. 32 students had taken piano in ranges from Grade 8 to Preliminary. 11 had taken violin examinations ranging from Grade 6 to Preliminary. One took Grade 3 at cello, one took senior at clarinet and three took junior trumpet.

The Intermediate Certificate that year was taken by 82 students. Irish, English, Mathematics and the combined subject of History/Geography were taken by all. Latin was again a popular choice while only 3 took Greek. Commerce, Science, Agricultural Science and Drawing were also popular. European languages were not popular, with only 12 taking French and 9 taking Spanish. The subject choice of the three top performing students was: Irish, English, Mathematics, Latin, Greek, History/Geography and Science. Three Department of Education scholarships were obtained by Rockwell students on the results of their Intermediate Certificate.

Apart from the academic subjects there was no shortage of cultural and educational pursuits available to students outside of the classroom. English debating was strong, especially in senior years while Cumann Díospóireachta na Gaeilge under the direction of Fr. Mullins was vibrant. The Art Club continued to flourish with many paintings on display. The Stamp Club had a collection of stamps of all ages, of all shapes and sizes, of every colour and of a multiplicity of subjects. The Chess Club had many home and away matches before taking part in the Munster Championship. *A Man For All Seasons* was produced by Fr. Campbell and had a cast chosen exclusively from Fifth Year, Third Year and Preparatory.

The Legion of Mary contributed to the spiritual welfare of the students under the direction of Fr. Leonard. In 1964 it had 45 active members with an attendance during the year of 84%. The activities included spiritual reading, preparing for the liturgy in the College Chapel and visiting the sick in St. Patrick's Hospital, Cashel. The praesidium also sponsored concerts given by College students in St. Luke's Hospital, Clonmel and St. Patrick's Hospital. Fr. Jim Barrett was director of the Pioneer Total Abstinence Association which had a large membership and a council of eight.

St. Joseph's, Lake House in 1964 had seventeen new arrivals to the scholasticate in September bringing the total number to seventy five. Fr. Hurley continued as Director assisted by Fr. Leonard. The scholastics were visited by Fr. Connors of the General Council of the Holy Ghost Congregation who gave a talk on the state of the Holy Ghost missions throughout the world. On 1st October Fr. Fitzpatrick who was home on holidays from Africa spoke about the missions. On the following evening Fr. Mullins gave a very interesting talk, illustrated with slides, on St. Thérese of Lisieux, Patroness of the missions. The highlight of the year in St. Joseph's was the blessing of the new oratory on 10th October. The musical tastes of the scholastics were catered for in several music sessions when they listened to the works of Beethoven and Verdi and in a most enjoyable vein to the Irish ballads of the Clancy Brothers who were then the rage. A visit from Fran O'Toole and the College Band was also enjoyed. St. Joseph's was well represented in the College cultural and sporting activities.

The House Games provided an outlet for all ages, all standards and all sporting interests. In the senior Gaelic leagues Billy Coleman's team was prominent while the Wolfhounds and the Wipeouts dominated the senior rugby leagues. Willie Duggan was impressive in the under 14 rugby leagues playing at out-half. The college senior tennis tournament was won by John Hickey while Louis Doyle won the junior. Dermot Cooney's team won the senior basketball league. John Forristal won the senior table-tennis league and Anthony Keane won the junior. Nearly forty students descended on the riding schools of Mr. Garrett Dooley and Miss Ursula Ryan every half-day and under the watchful eye of Fr. Jim Barrett enjoyed more than two hours on horseback.

In 1964 for the first time the annual Union Dinner was held not in a Dublin hotel but in Rockwell on the evening of Saturday 4th April. The function was attended by the president of the Union, Surgeon James Maher, the Minister for Education, Dr. Hillery, the President of Rockwell, the Provincial, the Superiors of Kimmage and Kilshane and a large gathering of past students. It was an occasion for the exchange of memories by all present.

Prize Day in the month of May was the annual awards ceremony when stock was taken of academic progress and achievement rewarded. In May 1964 the prizes were presented by guest of honour Surgeon James Maher, President of the Rockwell Union. Students who had obtained the highest in the Notes system throughout the year received their prizes, known as Galaxy Prizes, and they were also rewarded with a day trip away from the College which was the envy of many students. Distinctions in the public examinations were noted and medals and certificates were awarded for the various educational achievements within the school. At Prize Day in 1964 the William J. Mallen Scholarship was announced. This was an endowment presented to Rockwell by Kevin Mallen in honour of his brother William J. Mallen, a Rockwell student from 1910 to 1915. He was one of six Mallen boys to come to Rockwell from Grangecon, Co. Wicklow and was tragically killed at Ypres in 1917. Following his years in Rockwell Kevin Mallen went to the United States where he had a distinguished career in business and served as an intelligence officer in the U.S. army during World War 2.

Fr. Frank Nolan died during the centenary celebrations in 1964. He was born in 1887 in Derrylahan Co. Laois. From Blackrock College, where he studied from 1903 to 1908, he was sent as a prefect to Rockwell. He stayed for four years during the presidency of Fr. T. A. Pembroke. Ordained in 1919, he was appointed to the American mission. He returned to Rockwell in 1946 and was a diligent teacher up to the time of his death. He was a brother of Fr. Thomas J. Nolan who was also a member of the Rockwell community.[2]

Few years in the history of Rockwell College have been as eventful as that of 1964.

Notes

[1]   RCA 1977
[2]   ISR 418

– 13 –

SUSTAINING ACADEMIC
STANDARDS
1962-1968

The high academic standards of previous years were sustained during the short presidency of Fr. Comerford and the second presidency of Fr. Finucane and were accompanied by a remarkable growth in the Hotel and Catering School.

Fr. Finucane's first term as President ended in September 1961 and he was succeeded by Fr. Comerford who had spent most of his priesthood in Rockwell. He had been a junior scholastic in Rockwell and was appointed Director of St. Joseph's in 1934. He was Bursar from 1940 to 1943 and Vice-President since 1949. Fr. Finucane was to return as President in 1962 and continue in that position until 1968.

PERSONNEL
During Fr. Finucane's second presidency Fr. Comerford continued as Vice-President while Frs. O'Brien and Chamberlain remained as Bursars. Fr. Lehane as Dean of Discipline now had the assistance of Fr. Noel Redmond who was welcomed back to Rockwell, where he had been a prefect, as Dean of the Junior

Visit of past student Cardinal Browne in 1963
Fr. C. Meagher, Fr. A. Chamberlain, Fr. J. Nolan, Fr. J. Mellett (a former contemporary of the Cardinal in Rockwell), the Cardinal, Fr. J. Finucane, Fr. M. Comerford, Fr. Ó hEideán O.P., Fr. Walsh O.P., Fr. J. Hurley.

School. Fr. Nolan continued as Dean of Studies and Fr. Hurley as Director of St. Joseph's. Three new Fathers joined the Rockwell community in 1967, Fr. John C. O'Connor coming from Kimmage, Fr. Desmond Reid who had spent two years in East Africa and Fr Patrick McGlynn who had spent some years teaching in Trinidad prior to his ordination. The same year Fr. Pádraig Leonard departed for the missions in Brazil. Fr. Campbell also left for a French College in Senegal. Fr. Gerard McConnell left for St. Mary's Nairobi and Fr. James Hurley left to do post-graduate work in Catechetics in Brussells. Fr. Bernard Murphy and Fr. Harry Mullen came to Rockwell in 1968 from Biafra, Fr. Murphy to act as Dean as Discipline for a year before returning to Biafra and Fr. Mullen to become Director of Junior Scholastics in place of Fr. Hurley. In 1968 Br. Declan departed for the missions in Sierra Leone.

In December 1967 Rockwell said goodbye to the Sisters of St. Joseph of Chambery who had been in the College since 1954. They were remembered by students for the many areas in which they worked, especially in nursing, laundry and refectory. They were succeeded by the Sisters of St. John of God whose associations with Rockwell went back many years and the Sisters who served up to 1968 were Srs Emerita, Elizabeth, Maire, Mary Augustus, Goretti, Alphonsus, Margaret Mary, Mary Regina and Mary Gerardine.

This period was notable for an increase in lay teachers. In 1966 newcomers were Messrs Patrick Purcell, Seamus King, Gerard O'Beirne, Anthony O'Halpin, Pádraig Breathnach and Laurence O'Dwyer. They were followed in 1967 by Messrs Edmond O'Reilly, Brendan Garvan, Joseph Frawley and Lucy O'Beirne. Mr. Joseph Touhy came the following year. The increase in lay teachers coincided with a decline in the number of prefects from 11 in 1965 to 6 in 1968. These prefects contributed much to teaching, to the supervision of studies and dormitories and to the organisation of sport and recreation. There was an increase in students in these years from 519 in 1965 to 549 in 1968.

For the first time in the history of Rockwell in 1965 a member of the Community celebrated the Diamond Jubilee of his ordination. Fr. Edward O'Shea was born at Ballyragget, Co. Kilkenny in 1876 and was ordained in Paris in October 1905. Having taught at St. Mary's, Rathmines, College of St. Alexander, Quebec and Castlehead, Lancashire, he came to Rockwell in 1930 where he had been teaching French until soon before his jubilee.

Fr. Lehane with Sister Madeline and
Sister Alphonsus in 1968

Preparatory Group 1963
In front: *B. Conroy, A. Shepherd, S. Hillgrove, F. Murphy, F. Haydar, A. Gulbinowicz, J. Burke.*
Seated: *E. Molloy, M. White, Rev. J. Boyle, Rev Sr. Mary, W. Culverhouse, M. Moroney, D. Ryan.*
1st row: *C. Mullen, D. Tanham, T. Hickey, B. Stack, C. Shanley, I. Rostant, N. Gardiner, C. Patience.*
2nd row: *J. Lee, J. McCarthy, A. Howard, M. Ryan, R. Thohig, C. Lewis, J. Mulgrew.*
3rd row: *M. Meade, S. McNamara, M.C. O'Connor, G. Minogue, P. Fitzgerald, G. Blewitt,*
P. Kiersey, M. Spillane.
4th row: *D. Kiersey, E. Lee, D. Shepherd, A. Santiago, P. King, C. Feeney, K. Howard.*

Pioneer Committee 1965
Seated: *B. O'Callaghan, P. Tansey, Fr. Noel Redmond, T. Mitchel, J. Beatty.*
Standing: *B. Glacken, J. O'Mahony, N. McDonnell, L. Doyle.*

In April 1965 the President of the College, Fr. Finucane was conferred by the National University with the degree of L.L.D. *Honoris Causa*. He was introduced by a past student, Professor John J. O'Meara, Professor of Latin at U.C.D. who extolled the achievements of Rockwell. He mentioned that Fr. Finucane had left Rockwell as a student in 1923 to return as President in 1955. He referred to Fr. Finucane's personal modesty which was equalled only by his skill in and dedication to the inspiring of young men. In his reply Fr. Finucane said that the honour conferred on him was an honour conferred on Rockwell College.

HIGH STANDARDS

As Dean of Studies, Fr. Nolan could feel satisfied with the academic progress of his students both past and present. Thirteen past students had graduated from U.C.D. in 1964 and seven from U.C.C. Sixteen were studying medicine at U.C.D. in 1965, twelve were studying Engineering, five Dentistry, seven Veterinary, four Agricultural Science, one Forestry, four Architecture, twenty four Arts, six Commerce, fourteen Science, seven Law, one Pharmacy and eight Public Administration. It seems a fair measure of the academic achievement of Rockwell that in 1965 one hundred and nine of its past students were pursuing graduate courses at U.C.D. In the same year there were thirty Rockwell past students studying at U.C.C and twenty one at U.C.G. The 1966 Intermediate Certificate results yielded six Rockwell university scholarships for Joseph Bergin, John O'Mahony, John Fitzgerald, John Logan, Eamonn Lawlor and Anthony Rossiter.

Prize Day 1965
Fr. Griffin, Fr. Nolan, Mr. George Colley (Minister for Education), Fr. Finucane,
Fr. Comerford, Dr. John Breen (President of Rockwell Union), Fr. Barrett.

Student Council 1968
Seated: *E. Molloy,*
Fr. B. Murphy,
T. O'Sullivan.
Standing: *A. Rossiter,*
E. Lawlor.

1916 ANNIVERSARY

On Friday, 29th May 1966, the national holiday for schools to mark the fiftieth anniversary of the 1916 Rising, Rockwell made a fitting commemoration. After Solemn High Mass, a general assembly of Community, lay teachers and pupils was convened in the Theatre Hall and the Proclamation of the Republic was read in Irish by Fr. Walker and in English by Mr. Jerry Hayes, representing the lay staff. Senator John Nash (Rockwell Leaving Cert. 1923) then unveiled a framed copy of the Proclamation with the portraits of the signatories and in a short address spoke of the part played by Rockwell students in the establishment of the State and its subsequent administration. The National Anthem was then sung, bringing to a close an impressive and dignified tribute to our patriot dead.

In keeping with the 1916 commemoration the Rockwell Union in 1966 made a presentation to Rockwell in memory of past student Thomas MacDonagh. It came in the form of a superbly executed volume of a group of MacDonagh's poems. In making the presentation, the President of the Union, Dr. John Breen, conveyed the regrets of Mr. Justice Donagh MacDonagh and his sister Mrs. Liam Redmond, at their inability to be present at the tribute to their father. Mrs. Redmond kindly sent photostat copies of the last letter written by Thomas at midnight, 2nd May 1916, a few hours before his execution. Finally Dr. Breen announced the foundation by the Rockwell Union of what was to be known as the Tomás MacDonagh Award for Literary Excellence- a gold medal to be presented annually for special merits in prose or poetry composition in one or more languages and open to pupils of all years. The same year the Rockwell Union made a major financial contribution towards the Science Block.

STUDENT ACTIVITIES

The 1916 theme was a matter of discussion by the English Debating Society in 1966. Four past students from UCD visiting the College proposed the motion that "The Rebellion of 1916 was a mistake" Representing Rockwell and

Irish Debating Society 1962
Seated: *K. O'Carroll, Fr. Mullins, J. Collins.*
Standing: *K. Cahill, M. Hickey, L. Ryan.*

opposing the motion were Edward Raymond, Gregory Murphy, Liam Daly and Tony Rossiter. The motion was defeated. In the Muinter na Tíre Public Speaking Competition of 1966 the motion for discussion was "That the ideals of the men of 1916 are the ideals of Young Ireland to-day". Rockwell won the Munster final of that competition and was just pipped in the All Ireland final, the speakers throughout this competition being Edward Raymond, Gregory Murphy, Tony Rossiter, John B. O'Mahony, Martin Roffey Liam Daly, Reggie Walker and Joseph Manning. Fr. Walker presided at a number of debates during the year between Fifth and Sixth Year students and accompanied the team to Thurles for the annual debate with the Ursuline Convent. In the 1967 debating season Fr. Walker had the assistance of Mr. Frawley.

Rockwell students who played chess sometimes found that their brains were as active during recreation hours as they were during class time, although some teachers might not agree. Br. Senan was mentor of the Chess Club during those years and in 1965 he entered four teams in the Munster Junior Chess competition while at the same time coaching a juvenile team. The most interesting feature of that season occurred during the second term when the treasurer of the Munster Chess Club played twenty three Rockwell students in a simultaneous match. Students not engaged in chess who preferred to exercise their literary creativity found expression in the *Rockwellian*, that occasional

The College Orchestra 1964 with Br. Ambrose

student magazine which now and then failed to receive a *nihil obstat* from Fr. Nolan. In 1967 its editor Tony Rossiter stated that his task was to provide "for intellectuals as well as the *Beano*-reading Philistines."

Music and Drama continued to flourish. In 1962 Fr. Campbell produced *Lilac Time* with music directed by Mr. O'Callaghan and design by Br. Ambrose. A four-part choir was available throughout the year for all services in the College Chapel. In 1964 the orchestra, under the direction of Br. Ambrose, with strings, brass and wood wind, obtained 86% in the Department of Education examination. The students organised their own College Band which was in great demand with its repertoire of popular music and the latest "hits". A leading member of the band was Fran O'Toole. Following his years in Rockwell Fran joined the Miami Showband and was one of three members of that band murdered by the U.V.F. on 31st July 1975 as the band returned to Dublin from a performance in Banbridge, Co. Down. Miss Margaret Lynch joined the staff in 1964 as piano teacher and during her long tenure students were prepared for the examinations of the Leinster School of Music rather than as heretofore the Royal Irish Academy of Music. Fr. Reid specialised in choral music.

English Debate Committee 1964
*D. J. O'Mahony,
B. Lynch, J. Dunne,
P. Glacken,
M. Duggan.*

Students continued to participate in the F.C.A. In 1963 three of the previous year's members were selected for cadetships in the Military College, they being Joseph Aherne, Stephen Lyons and Thomas Hickey. Rockwell sent a mortar team each year to a competition in Kilworth The Rockwell Unit of the F.C.A. in 1964 had been decreasing in numbers in the previous two years. There were fifty registered members in 1964 with about forty attending each training session. In an effort to revive interest Captain O'Grady changed the weekly parade from Saturday to Sunday and the monthly parade at the Cahir Camp to be followed by tea in the Galtee Hotel. Field-days were held at the Kilcoran Range and the Kilworth Camp and members attended Spike Island for a fortnight's annual camp during the summer holidays.

English Debating Society 1965
Seated: G. Murphy, J. Dunne, T.A. Murphy, Fr. Nolan, D. McCarthy, L. Byrne, L. Daly.
Standing: J. Gaffney, B. Glacken, E. Raymond, J. Daly, B. Archer, P. Glacken, M. Roffey, N. McDonnell.

English Debating Society 1966
Seated:
E. Raymond,
G. Rosenstock, A. Rossiter, P. Nannery, L. Daly.
Standing:
J. B. O'Mahony,
G. Murphy, R. Walker.

**Clonmel Drama
Festival Winners
1965**
*Brendan Conroy,
Martin Roffey,
Alair Shepherd,
Patrick King.*

**English Debating
Team 1968**
Seated: *E. Lawlor,
A. Rossiter, B. Conroy.*
Standing: *F. O'Dwyer,
F. Murphy, M. Roffey,
M. Cuneen,
D. Kiersey.*

Schola 1968
Front: *A. Vieiera, D. McNamara, R. Thorn, J. Gleeson, B. Egleston, T. Kavanagh.*
Seated: *P. Conaty, N. O'Sullivan, W. Cleary, Fr. Des Reid, F. Fusco, P. McGuire, R. Rosenstock.*
Standing: *J. Healy, J. Cantwell, W. O'Reilly, J. McLoughlin, P. Lennox, G. Purcell.*
Back row: *A. Golden, P. Gorman, M. Barry, J. Colbert, K. Twomey, A. Kennedy, D. Lopes.*

St. Joseph's

Missionaries home on leave continued to visit St. Joseph's and give talks on missionary activities. An event in 1967 which was watched with apprehension in St. Joseph's was the Nigerian Civil War. The Republic of Biafra had been declared in 1967 because of fears that the Nigerian central government was increasingly in the hands of the Hausa tribe. This led the predominantly Ibo Eastern Region to secede under Lt. Col. Odumegwu Ojukwu. On the proclamation of Biafra, civil war ensued. In a bitterly fought campaign federal forces confined the Biafrans to a shrinking area of the interior by 1968 and cut off their supplies of food and assistance. This war had profound repercussions for the Holy Ghost Congregation. Almost three hundred Holy Ghost Fathers, many of them past students of Rockwell, were ministering to the now besieged and starving Ibo people with whom they were determined to remain. Their heroism received world-wide attention, many of them having been captured and imprisoned by federal forces. The war continued until 1970 by which time Biafra had ceased to exist.

The St. Joseph's scholastics were well informed of developments not only in Biafra but also of missionary work throughout the world. They had first-hand information on developments in Biafra from their new Director, Fr. Harry Mullen. In 1965 they had a talk from Fr. John Jordan, Superior of the Holy Ghost Fathers' mission in Brazil. In 1966 St. Joseph's celebrated its centenary and the occasion was marked with an exhibition of missionary pictures and statistics. In 1968 the scholastics said good-bye to Fr. Hurley and presented him with an engraved clock in gratitude for his devoted attention and keen interest in their welfare. Eighteen new scholastics joined St. Joseph's in 1968 which was

Pioneer Council 1962
Seated: B. Kerr, Fr. Joe Nolan, F. McEvoy
Standing: S. Lyons, P. McManus, S. Keating, J. Collins.

The Rockwell Community 1968
Seated: Frs. J. Mullins, S. O'Hanrahan, M. Comerford, F. Griffin, J. Finucane, T. Nolan, M. Neenan,
R. Walker, Br. Eugene.
1st row: Frs: A. Lehane, J. Murphy, F. Marrinan, J.C. O'Connor, C. Meagher, S. Nealon, J. Barrett,
D. O'Brien.
2nd row: Br. Declan, Frs. N. Redmond, D. Reid, M. Lavelle, H. Mullan, Br. Ambrose,
Fr. P. McGlynn.
3rd row: Frs: S. O'Donoghue, B. Murphy, J. Nolan, M. O'Connor, Br. Senan, Fr. A. Chamberlain.

an encouraging number in view of the decline in vocations to all juniorates in recent years. The scholastics in these years engaged very much in the academic and sporting life of the college and they joined in the retreats given by Fr. Patrick Touhy, a former chaplain of University College, Dublin who had been giving retreats in Rockwell for a number of years.

DEVELOPMENTS

In Christmas 1965 the new College Library was opened. One of the two large high-ceilinged class rooms in the Long Hall was set aside for this purpose. Shelving was installed and books were transferred from the various class libraries. Some massive canvasses were hung in the lonely spaces on the high walls and on 30th January 1966 the Library was blessed by the Provincial, Fr. Dinan. Fr. Walker had a major influence in determining its shape. The furnishing and stocking had received great assistance from Tom Manning, furniture manufacturer, of Muinebheag and past student George Mealy, antique dealer and fine art consultant, of Castlecomer. There was a

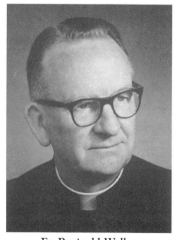

Fr. Reginald Walker

**Junior Debating
Team 1968**
Front: *G. Danaher,
K. Twomey, K.
McKann.*
Back: *K. Kiersey,
E. Grace.*

dramatic increase in the number of students from all years using the Library for project work. The same location of the Library has remained to this day and it has undergone a number of makeovers in the intervening years.

The first cutting of the new main Dublin-Cork road past the College made its appearance at the end of September 1966. It was sad to see the splendid stand of beeches opposite the front gate come crashing down; but such was the price that had to be paid for progress. The new lay-out, however, which remains to this day, made the new approach to the gates even more park-like than before. In 1967 two new buildings were erected. Both were prefabs. The first was a block of four classrooms intended to ease the shortage until such time as planning for future permanent extension had been finalised. It was placed on the terraces outside the Science Rooms. The other was a rather larger complex intended to provide sleeping quarters, washing facilities and classrooms for the Catering School and was placed on the far side of the avenue opposite the Chapel. In 1968 the dormitory known to students for many years as Siberia was completely modernised with new washing facilities including showers and hot water.[1]

ATHLETICS

Athletes brought great honour and distinction to Rockwell throughout the 1960s, due mainly to the influence of Fr. Lavelle. Achievements at the highest level were registered each year. In the All Ireland finals of 1962 in Ballinasloe the intermediate relay team of Anthony Finn, David Hill, Philip Berkley and Joe Cumiskey were winners while Joe Cumiskey came second in the intermediate 220 and Philip Conway came second in the 7lb shot. At the All Ireland finals of 1963 at the Iveagh Grounds, Crumlin John Moroney won the pole vault at 10' 9", Jim Leahy won the intermediate three mile race and the senior relay race was won by Andrew Finn, David Hill, Robert O'Brien and Joe Cumiskey.

Cross country team 1964
Front: *L. Foley, J. Feeney.*
Seated: *J. Moriarty, N. Jones, J. Leahy, J. Lynskey, S. Buckley, T. Delaney, N. Cleary.*
Standing: *G. Hogan, P. Fogarty, H. Sisk, J. Connellan, T. O'Hare, P. O'Dwyer, P. Browne.*

It was a good year in 1964 for Rockwell athletics. Fr. Lavelle had spent endless hours coaching technical events such as the pole vault, shot and discus while Fr. Leonard spent much time training the cross country team. Fr. McConnell trained the junior relay team which came second in the All Ireland. Rockwell won the All Round Cup in the Munster Sports and in the All Ireland tied with Blackrock College for the College of Science Cup. John Moroney, still nursing a broken thumb from the rugby final came second in the All Ireland pole vault, while Brian Lynch came second in the All Ireland javelin. Philip Conway had outstanding performances. Though still an Intermediate, he threw the senior discus 144' 6". As well he won the intermediate shot and brought home the Hugo Flynn trophy. Another intermediate athlete, Jim Leahy won the three miles and 800 yards in the Munster and East Munster Sports, setting new records in each.

Rockwell won the College of Science Cup in 1965 with a total of 28 points, the nearest rival having less than 20. No fewer than six athletes contributed to this total. There had been a build-up in training which resulted in a high quality of fitness and endurance. Just after Easter a team of ten competed in the under 17, under 19 and under 21 Co. Tipperary championships, collecting a total of 16 gold and 8 silver medals. The annual triangular contest between Roscrea, Ballinasloe and Rockwell was held in Rockwell on 12th May. This was always a very friendly and relaxed meeting; there being no individual awards, the only trophy being the Shield presented in honour of the Abbot of Mount St. Joseph's for the school with the highest aggregate points. This Rockwell won with a total of 106 points to Roscrea's 64 and Ballinasloe's 55.

The long road to the 1965 All Ireland began on 23rd May when the East Munster sports were held in Rockwell. Thirty Rockwell athletes qualified for the Munster Championships with a total of 31 firsts and 22 seconds together with the senior, intermediate and junior cups and all three relay batons. In Cork on 29th May competition was keener but Rockwell again excelled, accounting for four of the five records: senior mile Jim Leahy, senior pole vault Percy Hecksher, intermediate pole vault Rodney Hecksher, intermediate relay, Pat Twomey, Dermot O'Donoven, Rodney Hecksher and Ray Cumiskey. Three Rockwell relay teams did well to qualify for the All Ireland championships. Rockwell again won the Munster Colleges Senior Cup which it had held without a break since 1954: also the senior cup and intermediate

Philip Conway Athlete of the Year 1965 with College of Science Cup

relay baton. Philip Conway had a fine double in the senior shot and discus as had Jim Leahy in the 880 and mile and Rodney Hecksher in the intermediate shot and pole vault.

Hopes were high for the All Ireland Sports in Ballinasloe on Whit Monday. Philip Conway, captain of the team, gave Rockwell a good start with a double in shot and discus. Philip had returned two days earlier from the Tailteann Games where he had been just pipped for the Athlete of the Year Award. Rodney Hecksher won the pole vault with his brother Percy second. In the intermediate grade Rodney Hecksher set up a new record in the pole vault. The *Irish Times*, commenting on the event, described Rockwell as "the leading nursery of athletes in Ireland"

Jim Leahy was Rockwell's leading cross-country runner in 1965.

F.C.A. shooting team 1968
Seated: *B. McKenna, N. Gardiner, T. Egan.*
Standing: *J. Kinnerk, S. Carter, M.Casserley, D. O'Gorman.*

In 1966 Roscrea won the tri-angular event. The East Munster was held again in Rockwell. 32 Rockwell athletes qualified for the Munster. In Cork Rockwell won the All Round Cup again. Rodney Hecksher had a fine treble in the senior shot, pole-vault and triple jump. Raymond Cumiskey got first in the 220 and second in the 100. The Rockwell senior relay team broke the record which had stood since 1956. At the All Ireland championships on 4th June in the Iveagh Grounds. Rodney Hecksher won the shot, long jump and pole-vault. Raymond Cumiskey, Dan Finn and Paul Beecher also featured. Willie Duggan, future Irish rugby international, came fourth in the pole vault. On Sports Day. Philip Conway, who was in 6th Year the previous year and was still under age for senior schoolboy competition, gave a spectacular display in the discus which he threw 170 ft. Considering that this was 7ft beyond the then All Ireland record it was a fair indication of the outstanding ability of this athlete.

SENIOR RUGBY

During Fr. Finucane's second presidency Rockwell won the Senior Cup on two occasions, in 1964 and 1967. In 1962 Rockwell reached the final for the fourth year in succession with high hopes of a fourth win. This was not to be, however, when C.B.C. frustrated Rockwell's attempts on the wind-swept plains of Clanwilliam. The team was captained by Jim Molloy and included future international John Moroney. The inter-provincials of 1962 were Joe Cumiskey, Michael Hickey, Roger Cumiskey, Michael Corrigan and Jim Molloy. Fr. Lehane was manager and received good advice from past student and international Tim McGrath and from Ireland's captain Bill Mulcahy, both of whom attended a number of training sessions.

Senior Cup Winners 1964
Front: *R. Butler, B. NcKeon, E. Butler, R. O'Shea.*
Seated: *P. Burkeley, P. O'Donovan, P. O'Donovan, J. Cumiskey, F. Hogan, J. Moroney, E. Teehan.*
Back: *O. Synnott, P. Hecksher, L. Stapleton, L. Hill, D. O'Malley, P. Conway, L. Hodgins.*

In 1963 Fr. Lehane was trainer and Donal Houlihan was captain. For the first time Rockwell was host to a Northern school when Methodist College, Belfast visited in October. Rockwell won by eleven points and became the first Munster school to beat a northern side. Another first was when Rockwell played Ratcliff College, Leicester, in Dublin. Rockwell won by 9-6. The Cup campaign began with a match against Mungret in Thomond Park in which Rockwell had an easy win but lost in the semi-final to C.B.C. by a goal to a try. The inter-provincials of 1963 were David Hill, Joe Cumiskey, John Moroney, Oliver Hickey, and Frank Hogan.

Few events in the course of the school year put such a spring in the step of all Rockwellians as the winning of the rugby Senior Cup. And it was fitting that in its centenary year Rockwell won the Cup for the nineteenth time. The team which represented Rockwell in the early weeks of October as the season got under way was very different from that which beat C.B.C. in the final in Cork on April 19th. In every province they matched themselves against fine teams, one of their better displays being against Methody in Belfast. At the start of the Christmas holidays the team travelled to England where it played Ratcliffe College, Leicester.

The Cup campaign was a marathon. The first match against Crescent in the early days of March was postponed due to bad weather. Played a week later it ended in a draw. A try three minutes from the end, engineered by John Moroney and scored by Eddie Teehan, won Rockwell the right to another chance. The replay in Cashel was played in a gale. Rockwell defended in the first half and managed to keep the score down to 3-0. With the wind in the second half prospects looked good but the only score was a penalty goal from John Moroney. Still no score in extra time. On again to Limerick for the third struggle. Full time came and still no score. Then in extra time after 238 minutes of play came a delightful score. Rockwell heeled from a ruck inside their own half, and Joe Cumiskey cut through the middle, beat four would-be tacklers and crossed midway between the touch line and the posts. The semi-final against Munchins in Clanwilliam in poor weather conditions gave Rockwell a comfortable 16-3 victory.

The final was fixed for Easter Sunday but the weather again intervened. The match finally took place in Musgrave Park on Sunday 19th March after the Easter holidays. The support was splendid and the event was rewarded with a 9-3 win in what was generally agreed was not a classic game. John Moroney had broken his thumb and was incapable of passing the ball. The national

Joe Cumiskey with College of
Science Cup and Munster Schools
Senior Rugby Cup 1964

press hailed him as the best natural footballer that Munster had seen for many a year. Joe Cumiskey, playing on his fourth senior team, played a captain's part. Frank Hogan was an inspiring pack leader. Pat O'Donovan was a reliable vice-captain and proved a core of stability in the front row. These three players together with Philip Conway won their Munster caps

Winning the Cup was always an occasion which led to a degree of exuberance among the students in Rockwell who pined for any escape from the confinement of boarding school life. Such was the case in 1964. On that occasion, when the team returned to the College a number of cheerleaders took advantage of a certain 5th Year student who was noted for his vehicular knowledge and driving skills. He was directed to the farm yard where a tractor was commandeered. The vehicle was then boarded by the flag waving cheerleaders and careered down the back avenue and on reaching the back gate turned in the direction of New Inn. The party arrived in the village in great cheer, much to the displeasure of the local sergeant who mounted his bicycle in pursuit of the offenders as they headed up the main road towards the College. Sensing that the sergeant was gaining ground the driver and cheerleaders abandoned the tractor inside the front gate and hid in the shrubbery, leaving the engine running. A group of more responsible students who were out for a walk spotted the tractor and one of them, who had tractor skills, mounted the vehicle with a view to returning it to the farm yard. As he did, the sergeant arrived and with his baton meted out a robust retribution to the innocent driver.[2]

23. Senior Cup Winning Team 1967
Seated: M. Walsh, J. Blewitt, J. Daly, D. Houlihan, R. Cumiskey, P. Kane, M. Ryan.
Standing: R. Hecksher, G. Hayes, H. Hyland, T. Lawlor, E. Molloy, W. Duggan, P. Edney, J. Monaghan.

Any year when the Senior and Junior Rugby Cups come to Rockwell must be regarded as special occasions in the College calendar. Such was the case in 1967. The Seniors, trained by Fr. Lehane, brought the Cup back for the twentieth time. The series of friendlies prior to Christmas followed the usual pattern with matches against all the Munster schools twice and also against Blackrock, St. Mary's, Terenure and Methodist College Belfast. At the beginning of the Christmas holidays the team set out for England and had games against Ratcliffe College and Loughborough Grammar School.

The first Cup match was against C.B.C. in Cashel which resulted in a good win for Rockwell. And then it was off to Limerick to play Crescent and this match ended in a draw. Rockwell won the replay in Cashel on a wet and windy day. The final was played against P.B.C. in Limerick on St. Patrick's Day. It was a hard tough match but by the sheer concentration of forward power Rockwell wore down the opposition sufficiently to score six points without reply. Team captain David Houlihan had a superb campaign as did Eddie Molloy in his leadership of the forwards. John Blewitt and Andrew Kiely shone throughout while Joe Daly had a splendid game in the final. The seven members of the team who were chosen to play for Munster were Eddie Molloy, David Houlihan, Tom Lawlor, John Blewitt, Tom Hickey, Gerry Hayes and Raymond Cumiskey.

JUNIOR RUGBY
Fr. McConnell trained the J.C.T of 1962 and 1963. The team of 1962 was captained by Liam Stapleton and included Philip Conway but lost in the semi-final to C.B.C. The 1963 team was captained by Philip Conway but again lost in the semi-final, this time to Crescent. Fr. Lavelle took over the training of the J.C.T. in 1964 and continued in this position for a number of years. The 1964 team included veterans such as Landy Hill, Dermot Cooney and David Houlihan but surprisingly lost in the semi-final to Waterpark.

Conor Lewis captained the J.C.T. of 1967 which brought home the Cup for the first time in seven years. The quality of this team can be judged by the fact that in the seventeen matches they played throughout the season they scored an average of fifteen points in each match. Vice-captain, John Coleman, (in later years an All Ireland winning senior Gaelic footballer with Cork) playing at out-half inspired, while John J. Byrne, Tim Ryan, Gerard Richardson, Michael Slattery and Paul Kane were top scorers. The fielding and kicking of Liam O'Sullivan were excellent while Oliver Rowan and Michael Good were two strong props. Four well-taken tries, two converts and a penalty goal were sufficient to defeat C.B.C. in the first round of the Cup. The second round played against Waterpark in heavy rain and a gale-force wind ended in a 3-0 win for Rockwell. Midleton were conquered in the semi-final with nine points to spare and an 11-3 win over Glenstal in the final earned custody of the Cup for Rockwell.

The Junior Cup was won for the second year in succession by Rockwell in 1968. Fr. Lavelle attributed this success to vigorous and determined rucking by the forwards, strong running, accurate handling and crisp passing by the backs

Junior Cup Winning Team 1967
Seated: P. Kane, G. Richardson, J. Coleman, C. Lewis, O. Rohan, L. O'Sullivan, M. Good.
Standing: J. Burke, S. Humpston, D. Condon, G. Deveney, F. Brady, T. Ryan, J.J. Byrne, M. Slattery.

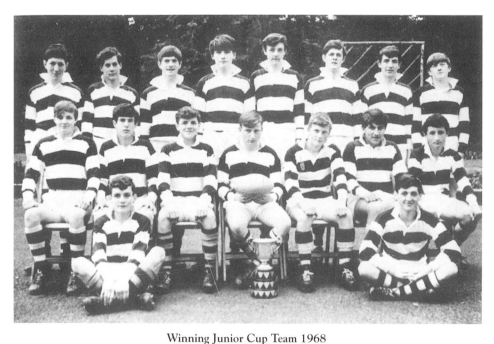

Winning Junior Cup Team 1968
Front: J. Drumm, M. Ryan.
Seated: D. Ormond, M. Ryan, J. Lee, P. Kane, M. Slattery, C. Hayder, P. McIlhinney.
Standing: S. Bradshaw, D. Shepherd, J. Morgan, N. Quinn, F. O'Donovan, M. Morrissey, J. Grennan,
P. McNaughton.

combined with an aggressive defence. These were the elements which Fr. Lavelle felt merited a 12-0 over Munchins in the second replay of the Munster final. Five earlier Cup victories had shaped the team captained by Paul Kane. Michael Ryan at scrum-half had a magnetic pair of hands and a powerful kick with both feet and his ability to pass the ball to Jimmy Lee at out-half who dictated policy to the rest of the backs. Paul McElhinney was an outstanding full-back throughout. David Shepherd and Paul McNaughton were reliable centres while Norman Quinn acquitted himself on the left wing having replaced John Curran and Michael Ryan (3rd Year) who were injured. Michael Slattery had filled the right wing position on the previous year's team and on this occasion by scoring five tries in the Cup campaign he established himself as one of the best wingers in Munster. Charlie Haydar, John Grennan and David Ormond formed a sound front row. In the second row Fergus O'Donovan and Michael Morrissey used their weight to good effect while Paul Kane, John Morgan and John Drumm were reliable in the back-row. Fr. Lavelle was especially pleased at the progress of Paul McNaughton who had never played the game until the previous November. He forecast that Paul would soon make the Rockwell senior team. Little could he have known that Paul would later win his caps as an Irish International and later still would manage the Irish team.

OTHER SPORTS

Fr. Joe Nolan managed the senior Gaelic football teams of the early 1960s which took part in Corn na Mumhan and he acknowledged the regular advice he received from staff member Mr. Jack Young father of the two legendary Cork footballers, Jim and Eamon.

The junior hurlers of 1962 were captained by John Forristal and had a good win over Mount Sion in the first round of the Dean Ryan Cup only to lose to De La Salle, Waterford in the second round. Hurling teams were entered in the senior and junior competitions throughout the sixties and while no trophies were won there were some fine hurlers such as John Forristal, Eddie McManus, Larry Gavin, Noel O'Sullivan, Gerry Keogh, Joe Owens and Dan McHugh. Senior and junior hurling teams were trained by Mr. Leahy and Mr. Doody.

From its earliest days until 1916 Rockwell had a distinguished cricket team. Then it disappeared from college life to re-emerge in 1945 and bring home the Munster Schools Cup in the year of its inauguration. Unfortunately the interest waned after a few years, athletics having made increasing demands on the available playing fields and the game was forgotten. Cricket in Rockwell was born again in 1965. A number of students organised themselves into a cricket team and because they did not have perfect facilities they played all their matches away. Their first outing was to Midleton College where they lost the match but did not lose heart. The next outing was to Waterford where they achieved a morale boosting three wicket win over Bishop Foy School. They returned to Waterford to play Newtown School in the semi-final of the Munster Schools' Cup but had to concede defeat. Those brave cricketers of 1965 included Peter Clerkin, John Shepherd, Gregory Lyder, Dudley Shanley, Fergus

Senior Hurlers 1966
Front: J. Ronayne, S. Kinsella, T. Power.
Seated: S. Corkery, E. Mulkere, P. Twomey. P. Beecher, M. Ahern, A. Meally, P. Browne.
Standing: T. O'Sullivan, J. Devane, M. Murphy, E. O'Toole, L. Collins, G. Keogh, J. Monaghan,
O. Dunne.

O'Donovan and Paul O'Reilly, all of Sixth year, with   Kevin Flynn, Peter Morgan, Niall McDonnell, Ian Rostant and Paul Sheeran of 5th Year and Michael Howard of 3rd Year

The Rockwell Golf Club was gradually taking shape in 1965. The new course looked very well and the boys were so eager to play on it that after a while the course became dangerous with flying balls and swinging clubs. So the Dean of Discipline, Fr. Lehane, decided to put order into Rockwell Golf and he chose a committee. The club was soon full of members. Rules were made and handicaps were established and the first competition was held on 5th December 1964. Annual singles and doubles competitions became very popular over the following years. The Rockwell Golf Course was featured on a junior sports programme on Telefís Éireann in 1968. The same year there were sixty four entrants for the annual singles competition. After some gruelling rounds the four to enter the semi-finals were Austin and Michael Slattery and Raymond and Chris Lynch. Austin Slattery, having beaten his brother went on to become the Rockwell Golf Champion of 1968.

Tennis had become very popular in Rockwell because of the six new first class tennis courts. In 1965 a team was entered in the Munster Senior Schools Cup but lost to Glenstal. A team was entered in succeeding years and in 1967 Rockwell won the Munster Schools Tennis Cup for the first time. Captained by Gabriel Rosenstock, the team included Pat Meenan, John Condon, Joe Murphy, Gregory Kenny (a future member of teaching staff) and Paul McElhinney who was still only in Third Year.

Winners of the Munster Tennis Cup 1967
Pat Meehan, John Condon, Joe Murphy, Gabriel Rosenstock, Gregory Kenny, Paul McIlhinney.

The Rockwell soccer team made good progress in the 1960s and in 1967 entered the Easter Soccer League in Dublin and having been unbeaten in its section beat Catleknock 4-0 but lost to C.U.S. in the semi-final by 4-3.

The Riding School also enjoyed good participation and had some good hunting days with the Clonmel Harriers and Tipperary Foxhounds, thanks to Garret Dooley who supplied the mounts and equipment.

The sporting interests in Rockwell were so wide and so extensive that attending to the facilities was a major responsibility. This task for many years was fulfilled by the grounds-man, Nicholas Tierney, who looked after the pitches, the pavilion, the athletic track and the golf course. He was so efficient that his services were sought by a number of golf courses and leisure centres. It was not by his efficiency, however, that he endeared himself to many Rockwell students. They regarded him as a very knowledgeable man of wide interests who befriended many. They were in awe as he listed the habitats in the College grounds of foxes, squirrels and birds and told of hurling stories of the past. Many students were in contact with him for the remainder of his life.[3]

ROCKWELL UNION
The Union Presidents during Fr. Finucane's second presidency were Frank Mulcahy, James Maher, John Breen and John Nash. The presentation to the College by the Union on the 1916 anniversary has been noted. The Union continued to financially support the College and the Missionary activity of the Holy Ghost

Past Student Bishop Patrick Lennon

Fathers. The annual Retreat was held in Rockwell and past students returned to the College in June every year for Union Day. The annual February dinner was held at the Dolphin Hotel while enjoyable dances were held at Dublin Airport and in Cork.

Union Day 1962
Fr. Comerford with Mr. and Mrs. William O'Neill and Mr. and Mrs. Frank Mulcahy.

Union Dinner 1964
Front row: *Fr. P. Murray (President St. Mary's College, Fr. Francis Griffin (Superior General Emeritus),*
Surgeon James Maher (Rockwell Union President), Dr. Patrick Hillery (Minister for Education),
Fr. V. Dinan (President Blackrock College)
Back row: *Lieut- Col. Bergin, Mr. M. McCormack (President St. Mary's College Union, Mr. F. Purcell*
(President Blackrock College Union), Mr. F. Blair (Secretary Rockwell Union)

HOTEL AND CATERING SCHOOL

A feature of this period from 1965 to 1968 was the remarkable growth of the Rockwell Hotel and Catering School. It had its own independent life and its own staff. In 1967 Fr. Denis O'Brien continued as its director and Mr. Jim Maguire its manager. Its waiting instructors were Peter Collins, Pat Cronin and John Roche while its chef instructors were

Catering School Librarians 1968
B. O'Mahony, M. O'Leary, M.O'Rourke, J. Sheehy.

Franz Knoblauch and Paul Deegan. The domestic economy instructors were Carmel Breen and Denise Hogan. In 1968 three new waiting instructors joined the team, Peter Dowling from Parknasilla Hotel, Michael Meaney from Great Southern Hotel, Killarney and John Muldoon from Shannon. The new chef instructors that year were Jim Bowe who came from Silversprings Hotel, Cork Brendan McGuirk from Travellers' Friend, Ballina and Fred Thoma from the Clare Inn, while the academic staff included Fr. Redmond, Fr. Marrinan, Br. Ambrose, Miss Ennis and Mr. Cristóir Gallachóir. The Hotel and Catering School provided numerous activities for the students and among the most popular were Gaelic Football, Soccer, Rugby and Chess.

The Catering School 1967
Instructors seated: *J. Roche, P. Cronin, F. Knoblauch, J. Maguire, P. Collins, P. Deegan.*

* * *

Fr. Finucane's term as President came to an end in August 1968. During his twelve year presidency he initiated new projects and encouraged many improvements. The physical developments of the College in preparation for the Centenary celebrations of 1964 were a lasting achievement. Fr. Finucane died in 1971.

OBITUARIES

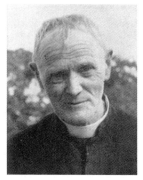

Br. Agathan Fogarty died in February 1966. He was born in Galmoy, Co. Kilkenny in 1876. A pioneer Missionary he had set out for Sierra Leone at the age of twenty six in March 1902 at a time when Missionaries in the "white man's grave" had a life expectancy of only a few years. Brother Agathon defied the norm and survived in Africa for twenty two years. In 1924 he was invalided home and settled down in Rockwell where he had been a postulant in 1898. He shaved off his enormous beard which had been a trademark of early Missionaries in Africa and for the next forty two years he became an indispensable part

Brother Agathon Fogarty

of Rockwell. He rang the bells, dispensed the altar wine, looked after the Brothers' refectory, sold the toothpaste, bootlaces and razor-blades, swept the avenue, served Masses, made and mended Rosary beads and cycled in and out to the bank in Cashel with his outrageously obvious wages bag.[4]

Fr. Michael Neenan died in February 1968. Born in Killimer, Co. Clare in 1891, he had been a student in Rockwell from 1908 to 1912 during which time he had won a Senior Cup medal. After his degree in 1915 he had spent some years prefecting in Trinidad where he returned to teach after his ordination. He came to Rockwell in the early 1940s where his subjects were Spanish and Commerce. During the war he attended lectures at University College Cork for the Higher Diploma in Education and on more than one occasion he cycled all the way from Rockwell to his lectures.[5]

Br. Canice Butler died in 1968. Born in Kyleenascaugh, Co. Kilkenny in 1884, he was a nephew of Br. Auguste Butler who had spent his life in Trinidad and of Br. Regis Butler, one of the great pioneer missionaries who lies buried in Sierra Leone. Br. Canice was attracted to the Holy Ghost Congregation by the example of his uncle. His first appointment, early in the century, was to St. Mary's College, Rathmines. He later moved to Rockwell where he became involved with the farm and became known to students as The Farm Brother. He was noted for his droll sense of humour.[6]

Notes

[1] RCA 1977
[2] Submission by Frank Madden 14/2/2013
[3] Submission by Philip Conway 25/1/2013
[4] ISR 99
[5] ISR 129
[6] ISR 487

– 14 –

NEW STRUCTURES
1969-1974

The building of the Rockwell Agricultural College and a new sports complex and class rooms occurred during the presidency of Fr. Aiden Lehane which lasted from August 1969 to August 1974. These new structures in Rockwell came at a time of major new structures in Irish education. The sudden death of Headmaster, Fr. Joe Nolan, in 1972 was followed by the appointment of Fr. Brendan Hally to succeed him. Fr. Patrick McGlynn became Assistant to the Headmaster.

Fr. Aidan Lehane
President 1968-1974

PERSONNEL

As was always the case in Rockwell, this period was marked with arrivals and departures of Fathers to and from the missions or to and from other Spiritan Colleges. In 1969 Fr. James Hurley returned from his catechetical studies in Brussels to take up his appointment of Dean of Discipline. His stay in this position was short, however, because in the following year he departed again, this time to become President of St. Mary's College, Rathmines. Father Michael O'Connor arrived in Rockwell in 1969 as Dean of Day Students. The same year Fr. Colm Cunningham arrived from Biafra but only remained a year before returning to Biafra. Br. Gerard also came from Biafra in 1969 and provided classes in Drawing and Woodwork. Fr. Tom Meagher came from the missions in East Africa in 1969 and the same year Fr. Brendan Hally, a former prefect, came to Rockwell fresh from his studies in Kimmage. Fr. Desmond Reid assumed the duties of Dean of Discipline (Juniors) in 1969 in succession to Fr. Noel Redmond who took up responsibilities in the Bursar's office. New arrivals in 1970 were Fr. Bernard Frawley from Nigeria

Fr. Colm Cunningham
Home from Biafra in 1969

Br. Gerard Cummins
Home from Biafra in 1969

251

**An Taoiseach Jack Lynch and his
wife with Fr. Lehane. May 1969**

The Librarians 1970
Seated: K. McCann, T. Hastings, G. Wall.
Standing: G. Danaher, J. Healy, J. Callery.

who came to take over as Dean of Discipline of 5th year, Fr. Matthew Knight from Nigeria who was appointed Director of St. Joseph's, Fr. John Buckley from Kimmage who became Bursar and Assistant Director of the Agricultural College and Brothers Finbar, Gregory and Stephen who came from Ardbraccan.

In 1971 Fr. Jack Finucane arrived as Dean of the Hotel School and Fr. Seán Broderick came from Nigeria as Director of St. Joseph's. Fr. Bernard Frawley returned to Africa in 1971. New arrivals to the Rockwell Community in 1972 were Fr. Timothy O'Driscoll, former Provincial and President of Blackrock College, Fr. Patrick Cremins who returned from East Africa, Fr. Patrick Holohan from Nigeria and parish work in the United States, and Fr. Patrick Doody from Kenya. Fr. Naos McCool arrived in 1974. The four sisters of St. John of God in those years were Srs Madeline, Alphonsus, Fabian and Carmelita.

New lay teachers in these years were Gerard O'Beirne, James O'Driscoll, Andrew Bailey, Pádrag O'Mahony, William Gaynor, J. P. Irwin, Criostóir

**Rockwell maintenance
staff in 1971 who
had served for more
than 20 years.**
*Seated: Jack Moloney,
John Pender, John
Carew, Luke Lyons,
Sonny O'Connor,
William Quirke.*
*Standing: Nicholas
Tierney, Johnny Moore,
Fr. Lehane, Fr. O'Brien,
Sonny Dudley,
Br. Senan.*

Community and Staff 1972-73

Seated: *Tom Tobin, Sr. Josephine, Fr. Francis Griffin, John L. Buckley, Fr. Denis O'Brien,*
Fr. Michael Comerford, Fr. Brendan Hally, Liam Ó Duibhir, Jerry Hayes, Margaret Lynch,
Fr. Jim Barrett.
1st row: *Fr. Pat McGlynn, Br. Eugene, Heather Madine, Joseph Irwin, Criostóir Gallagher, Noel*
Moynihan, Seamus King, Maura O'Dwyer, John Pereira, Fr. Patrick Holohan, Fr. Francis Marrinan,
Fr. Noel Redmond.
2nd row: *Pádraig O'Mahony, Fr. Patrick Cremins, Fr. John C. O'Reilly, Fr. Matthew Knight,*
Fr.Timothy O'Driscoll, Fr. Michael O'Connor, Laurence O'Dwyer, Seán O'Donnell, Fr. Bernard
Frawley, Pádraig Purcell, Valerie Quirke.
3rd row: *Br. Finbar, A. O'Rourke, William Gaynor, Fr. Seán Broderick, Fr. Robert Madigan, Joseph Touhy,*
Fr. Christopher Meagher, David Power, Alan Hughes, Fr. Alfred Chamberlain, Fr. Colm Cunningham.
4th row: *Breffni Walker, Fr. Michael Lavelle, Bobby Madine, Seamus Leahy, Adrian Rogers,*
Br. Senan, Nollaig McCarthy, John Kilcrann.
5th row: *Fr. John Buckley, Michael O'Sullivan, Douglas Butler, Brendan Maher.*

Gallagher, Laurence O'Dwyer, Philip Conway, Noel Sweeney, Tom Magner, Adrian Rogers, Thomas Monaghan, Michael O'Sullivan, Douglas Butler, David Power, Robert Madine, Mrs. V. Quirke, Mairéad O'Dwyer, John Pereira, Joan Curtin, David Morris, Caitríona Ní Mhurchadha, Paddy Daly, Tony Smith and Kate O'Leary.

On Friday, 18th December 1971 Rockwell College was *en fete* to celebrate the priestly golden jubilee of Fr. Francis Griffin, Superior General Emeritus of the Holy Ghost Fathers. Fr. Griffin was living in retirement in Rockwell where he was teaching French to senior students. Among the guests at his jubilee celebrations were the Archbishop of Cashel and the Superior General of the Holy Ghost Fathers, Fr. Pere Lécuyer. Br. Eugene Graham celebrated his golden jubilee in October 1972. Born in May 1899 he was appointed to Rockwell in March 1923 and was to spend practically all of those fifty years in the College.

Development

The Rockwell campus underwent unprecedented change in the late 1960s and early 1970s. A development programme for the College was drawn up in 1969. The scheme envisaged an expenditure of over £400,000. This had been made possible by the statuary grants available by the Department of Education and the Department of Agriculture. To meet the balance an appeal was launched to past students and friends of the College with a view to raising £120,000. The appeal fund was quickly filled.

In October 1969 the first students were accepted into the Rockwell Agricultural School. A decision to build this school had been taken in the last months of Fr. Finucane's presidency. In the early months of Fr. Lehane's term, negotiations with the Department of Agriculture were completed. The building was designed by the College architect, Mr. Kelly, and work commenced in early 1969 with Br. Senan as general foreman and Johnny Moore as foreman. The northern wing and the main entrance section of the eastern block were completed in October 1969 to allow the first nineteen students take up residence. The remainder of the eastern block was completed and the building was blessed by former student, Bishop Brosnahan, and was formally opened by the Taoiseach, Jack Lynch, on 8th September 1971. Coinciding with the opening of the Agricultural College, the National Ploughing Championship was held on the Rockwell farm on 22nd and 23rd October 1969. Four months of drought had made ploughing very difficult and one competitor was quoted as saying that they had battled on the toughest-ever ground.[1]

By the end of 1974 the western wing had been added and the Agricultural School then had a capacity for a hundred students. The building was very modern for its time. The sleeping quarters upstairs had wall to wall carpeting in rooms and corridors. The ground floor of the west wing had a reception area, staff rooms and three large class rooms. The north wing ground floor had recreation and changing rooms and in the east wing ground floor was a self-service refectory and modern kitchen. The Agricultural College doubled as a hostel during holidays and was used for seminars and other functions.

On 1st May 1970 Bishop Whelan blessed the site for a new sports centre. Work commenced in 1971 with the same architect and team still at work on the Agricultural College. The completed sports centre consisted of a gymnasium, swimming pool, dressing rooms, a play room, a caretakers' flat, two new class rooms, a furnace and a plant house. The

The Sisters 1973
Sr. Fabian, Sr. Alphonsus, Sr. Carmelita.

Fr. Griffin's Golden Jubilee Celebration 1971
Fr. O'Brien (Provincial), Bishop Achermann, Dr. Daniel Murphy, Fr. Griffin, Archbishop Morris,
Fr. Lecuyer (Superior General), Fr. Lehane.

well-equipped gymnasium is 100ft long, 60ft broad and 21ft high. The swimming pool was then the only one of its type in any school in Ireland or Britain. It is a six-lane 25 metre pool with minimum depth 3ft 4ins and maximum depth 7ft 2ins. The basement combined changing and wash rooms for both the gymnasium and pool. The upper room over the basement is a play room with facilities for billiards and table tennis.

Other structural developments within the College coincided with the building of the Agricultural College and sports complex. Updating of dormitories which had commenced during Fr. Finucane's presidency continued during Fr. Lehane's term. The "Pink" dormitory (Silas Block) was modernised in 1970. The following year St. Joseph's and the Sacred Heart dormitories were refurbished and the updating of St. Patrick's was completed in 1972. Work began in 1968 on what was intended as a new senior refectory. A new cross corridor was built leading towards the Community refectory and then at right angles eastwards to the kitchen, parlours and infirmary. This refectory when complete was used as a junior refectory. (See Chronological Floor Plan) In 1972 work began on a thorough modernisation of the Community corridor with the installation of contemporary facilities.[2]

ADVANCES IN EDUCATION

These developments in Rockwell came at a time of increased involvement by the state in post-primary education. Capital expenditure by the Department of Education in secondary schools had started in 1964-5. *The Investment in Education Report* published in 1966 heralded major change. The chairman of the committee responsible for this report was Professor Patrick Lynch, Associate Professor of Economics in University College, Dublin and chairman since 1954 of Aer Lingus. He had been appointed to this position by the then Minister for Education, Dr. Patrick Hillery, in October 1962 and in the course of his investigation he visited Rockwell for consultation with Fr. Finucane and Fr. Nolan. (Professor Lynch's sister, Margaret, had been a member of the Rockwell teaching staff since 1964)

Senior Orchestra 1970
1st row: G. Barry, P. Pierse, W. Choi, Br. Ambrose, C. Bourke, J. McLoughlin, R. Carter.
2nd row: C. Haydar, B. McNally, K. Gleeson, D. Mulvin, J. Healy, P. Conaty, J. Gleeson, L. Moore.
3rd row: P. Elliott, D. Kiersey, C. O'Carroll, M. O'Brien, E. Hunt, M. Keegan.

One of the outcomes of this report was the opening of the first three state-run comprehensive schools in 1966. The Minister for Education, Donogh O'Malley, declared "free post-primary education" would be made available nationwide from the academic year 1967-8 onwards with free bus transport for pupils living more than three miles from the nearest school. A further dramatic development was the announcement on community schools in October 1970. The concept of the community school was a development of the comprehensive school.[3] In the long term such developments were bound to have repercussions for boarding schools, including Rockwell, which had played a major part in the history of Irish education for more than a century

Highly significant developments in the non-university third-level sector were also taking place at this time with the establishment of the regional colleges, with a technical bias, under the vocational education committees. National institutes of higher education were established in Dublin and Limerick. The emphasis of all these institutions was on technology, applied sciences and business studies. They received most of their academic awards from the National Council for Educational Awards, established in 1972.

Management of secondary schools had to come to terms with these new developments. Teachers in the class room had also to contend with change. New subjects such as metalwork, engineering workshop theory and practice, accounting and business organisation were introduced. Alternative courses were introduced for subjects such as science, history, geography, music and home economics. The post-primary curriculum now offered twenty-six subjects at junior cycle and thirty-three at senior cycle. In 1969 the "honours-pass" nomenclature was dropped and a grading system with six categories from A to F was introduced for Intermediate and Leaving Certificate examinations.

English Debating 1971
Seated: *G. Danaher, F. Higgins, B. Broderick*
Standing: *N.O'Sullivan, B. Cleary, N. O'Dea, B. Gribben, K. McCann.*

Increasingly the importance of career guidance for pupils was recognised. The idea of a "transition year" programme was being promoted by the Minister for Education in 1974. In 1972 posts of responsibility for teaching staff were introduced and it was under this scheme that Rockwell appointed its first Deputy Principal, Liam P. Ó Duibhir. Liam had been a past student of Rockwell and had joined the teaching staff in 1958. He was to hold this position until his retirement twenty two years later.

In the face of all these changes Rockwell College was assessing its own mission and its path to the future. And it was at the annual Prize Day that these assessments were given a public airing. The Catholic ethos of the College with its missionary dimension was always emphasised as a starting point. In 1970 Fr. Nolan spoke of his idea of the task of education in Rockwell which was "to create for some months of every year, a little world, a little republic, where people may be allowed to develop along their own lines, at their own pace, that thy may become their best selves, where, moreover they may be positively assisted to develop". The following year he said that to train to moral virtue was the most formidable duty of the educator today. "Our task" he said "is to instruct, to encourage, to persuade, to inspire to what is right."

Liam Uas. Ó Duibhir
Deputy Principal 1972

Study Prefects 1972
Seated: C. Cosgrave, T. Young, B. Broderick, Fr. Pat McGlynn, J. Donovan, D. Hurley, M. Foley.
Standing: D. O'Neill, E. McAuley, L. Brown, M. Barry, P. Conaty, D. Farrelly, A. Andreucetti.

At Prize Day in 1972, less than two weeks after Fr. Nolan's death, Fr. Lehane reiterated some of the philosophy of education which Fr. Nolan developed and sought to inculcate in his long period as Dean of Studies and during his all too brief period as Headmaster. Fr. Nolan, he said, constantly spoke about religion, saying "We educate to make men with a real love for Christ and the Church, for Ireland and its people. There is about the task of education as there is about Christianity itself, the constant tension between aims and achievement." Fr. Nolan, he said, had aimed at that degree of discipline which allowed boys to develop harmoniously. Where he found self-confidence he did not repress it; and where he did not he tried to create it. He had tried to assert authority with the minimum of authoritarianism. Fr. Nolan, he said, had tried to train our boys to an appreciation of what was fitting, not merely in material things, but in thought and action. It included manner of speaking, politeness, manner of dress and that refinement which revealed itself in the many details of day-to-day living. "We so often confuse roughness with manliness" Fr. Nolan had said, "It is the work of education to show, as Belloc tells us, that the grace of God is in courtesy." Fr. Lehane shared Fr. Nolan's opinion that here in Rockwell we had a tremendous educational advantage in our physical setting where the beauty of our environment should have an elevating effect on us- the lake, the grounds, the Galtees, morning or evening.

The desire for that refinement about which Fr. Lehane and Fr. Nolan spoke could be detected in the appointment of the broadcaster Nollaig McCarthy and the authority on relationships, Angela McNamara to engage with students and in the numerous recitals by leading Irish musicians in the Library. And perhaps it was the thought that women could have a refining influence on an all-male establishment that for the first time in 1969 the wives of teachers and other officials were invited to Prize Day.

Comments of Fr. Lehane on Union Day 1973 that students were then acting as prefects in dormitories suggest that Rockwell had already adjusted to the new reality caused by the dramatic fall in vocations to the priesthood which would lead to the closure of St. Joseph's two years later and to the end of the traditional prefecting system. Since its foundation Rockwell had enjoyed the assistance of clerical students of the Holy Ghost Congregation who acted as prefects in the areas of teaching and supervision. The number of prefects had been on the decrease in recent years and was to cease three years later. (Appendix VIII) On the same occasion Fr. Lehane was probably looking towards the future of Rockwell when he commented that lay teachers were a rewarding addition to the staff and that girls from neighbouring New Inn Convent were attending some senior classes in Rockwell in disciplines that were not available in their own school.

The standing of Rockwell in Irish society had not diminished during Fr. Lehane's tenure judging by the distinguished visitors to the College in those years. President de Valera came on private visits in 1970 and 1971. President Erskine Childers paid an official visit in 1974. Taoiseach Jack Lynch came on a private visit in 1969 and returned in 1972 to officially open the Agricultural College. Taoiseach Liam Cosgrave officiated at the distribution of certificates and diplomas in the Hotel School in 1974 as did Joseph Brennan, Minister for Labour, in 1970 and 1973. Patrick Hillery, Minister for Foreign Affairs paid a private visit in 1970 and returned in 1974 as E.E.C. Commissioner on Prize Day. Minister for Education, Richard Burke was guest at Prize Day in 1973 as was Dr. Patrick Tierney, President of University College, Dublin in 1970 and Professor Patrick Lynch in 1971. Other notable visitors who addressed the Rockwell students in 1970 included T.J. Maher, President of the Irish Farmers Association, Joe Rea, President of Macra na Feirme and Tom Kiernan, legendary Irish rugby player. The following year the students were addressed by Desmond Fennell, academic, journalist and author and by Douglas Hyde the anti-Communist crusader. In 1972, prior to the referendum on Ireland's entry to the European Economic Community, leading advocates on either side of the debate, Raymond Crotty and Gerry Bechener put their case to the students.

Sacristans 1970
Seated: *A. Walkin,*
J. McGoldrick, P. Conaty.
Standing: *J. O'Hare,*
P. Dowling, G. O'Connor.

Day Students 1970
Front: V. O'Reilly, M. O'Loughnan, W. O'Donnell, R. O'Loughnan, T. Shanahan, P. Meagher,
P. O'Loughnan, P. Savage.
Seated: M. O'Donnell, W. Blake, V. Lonergan, T. Mulumby, Fr. M. O'Connor, T. Cleary, T.
Meagher, M. Whelan, T. O'Reilly.
Standing: M. Buckley, W. Halley, B. Irwin, S. Kennedy, M. Fitzgerald, D. Savage, J. English,
L. Bolger, C. O'Reilly, P. Butler, E. O'Neill.

STUDENT POPULATION

Of the 148 Sixth year students in 1970, 40 were from Dublin, 25 from Tipperary, 21 from Cork, 8 from Waterford, 6 from Limerick, 5 from Clare, 4 from Kerry, 4 from Wicklow, 3 each from Kildare, Laoise, Offaly and Galway, 2 each from Carlow, Kilkenny, Westmeath and Sligo and 1 each from Longford and Meath. 13 of the class of 1970 were foreign students. 9 of the 148 6th year students in 1970 were day students. There was little change to this pattern in the Sixth Year class of 1972 with 28 from Dublin, 16 from Tipperary, 15 from Limerick, 11 from Cork, 6 from Kilkenny, 5 from Waterford, 4 from Louth, 3 each from Kerry, Wicklow and Galway, 2 each from Longford, Sligo, Carlow and Kildare and 1 each from Westmeath, Offaly and Meath.

STUDENT ACTIVITIES

Outside of the class-room Rockwell students continued to have many sources of mental stimulation. The new library provided a rich source. Fr. Walker had built a stock of five thousand books. On his death, Mr. Tom Magner was appointed librarian. He acknowledged the help he received in 1972 from the 6th Year librarians Gerard Danaher, John Healy, Declan Bogue and Frank O'Brien.

Teams were entered each year in the Aer Lingus Debating competitions. The team in 1969 was Alair Shepherd, Finbar Murphy, Freddie O'Dwyer, Edmond Grace, Tom Meagher and Kieran McCann, and while it did not win, Alair Shepherd won an individual award. In 1972 the team, consisted of Gerard Danaher, Brendan Broderick and Billy Cleary, a future Rockwell President. An Cumann Díospóireachta under the direction of An tAthair Ó Maoláin with the

English Debating Society 1969
Seated: *A. O'Reilly, F. Murphy, Fr. Joe Nolan, G. Rosenstock, D. O'Neill.*
Standing: *E. Grace, B. Conroy, A. Shepherd, M. Cunneen, F. O'Dwyer, K. McCann.*

assistance of Mac Uí Dhuibhir gave a good performance in the annual Gael Linn competition. In 1972, partly because of the E.E.C. referendum and partly because of the Northern situation, there was a new political awareness among the people of Ireland. This trend was reflected in Rockwell with the launching of *Poblacht Nua,* an organisation which intended to stimulate mature political discussion. It had a nationalist flavour standing for the unification of Ireland and the revival of the Irish Language. Its founding members were Gerard Danaher, Frank O'Brien, Raymond Ryan, Desmond Hurley, John Healy, John Wynne and Michael Barry. Its members were mostly 6th Years and it held regular debates and discussion in Irish and English. It also held collections to support dependents of prisoners in Northern Ireland. It received direction from Mr. Leahy, their English teacher.

Stamp collecting continued to be a popular hobby on Sunday mornings. Br. Ambrose and Fr. J. C. O'Connor encouraged involvement. The Junior Red Cross was revived in 1969 with the aim of fostering service, friendship and health. Almost sixty boys received their membership certificates and badges. In 1969 the Old Rock building was renovated for the Nature Club to give about forty boys a suitable home for pets of their choice. Rockwell grounds are a very natural sanctuary. Boys nursed sick birds. By 1970 the club had evolved into the Ornithology Society following a suggestion by Mr. Gaynor, the Art teacher. The club had numerous outings beyond the College grounds, the most notable being a visit to the Clonmel Falconry, where among remarkable birds, students saw the magnificent Golden Eagle.

Music and drama continued to develop talent. A musical production that differed from any other produced in Rockwell was the production of *Oliver* in 1971. It was performed by the junior school and it differed because it was produced by the students themselves. Billy Cleary of 5th Year produced. John Cantwell on piano was a one-man orchestra and Peter Conaty attended to the costumes. The opening chorus of orphans *Food, glorious Food* had a special resonance for boarding school students. The same team was also responsible for the production of *Pickwick*. In 1972 *King Lear* was performed by the College Dramatic Society. Mr. Irwin directed *The Would-be Gentleman* an English translation of Moliere's comedy in 1973.

The senior choir, conducted by Fr. Reid, entered the Cork international Choral Festival in 1974 and won a trophy. The same year the junior choir, conducted by Mr. Rogers, got great praise from the adjudicator, Eamon Ó Gallchóir, when they took part in the Department of Education Examinations. The Music Society had some excellent concerts during those years, thanks to the Music Association of Ireland, the Arts Council and the Shaw Trust. Some of the country's best known performers came to Rockwell. In 1974 the artists included, Frank Patterson, Geraldine O'Grady, Eily O'Grady, Veronica McSweeney, Peter McBrien and the Hesketh Quartet.

The spiritual development of students was always a priority in Rockwell and in these years The Legion of Mary was promoted. For the Praesidium of "Our Lady of the Woods" the year 1968-69 was successful. About thirty five active members from 6th Year set about the customary works of the Legion in Rockwell. The Legion's most extensive work was once again the dissemination of Catholic literature among the student body. A good selection of Catholic Truth society booklets together with other publications of interest were on sale. At Christmas time trade was brisk in the sale of Catholic Christmas cards. The

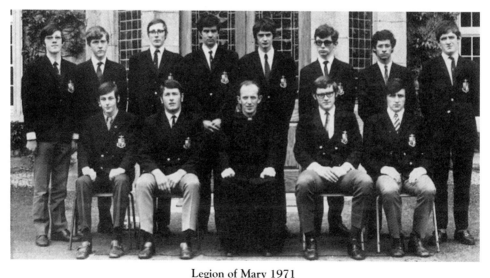

Legion of Mary 1971
Seated: J. Callery, T. McGrath, Fr. Brendan Hally, A. Fewer, N. Gleeson.
Standing: D. Kelly, D. Cuddy, H. O'Neill, F. Power, P. Slattery, F. Higgins, P. Lopes, P. Collins.

weekly visits to the sick in the Cashel hospitals were continued throughout the year. An evening's entertainment was arranged for the old folk several times during the year by the more talented members. Other works undertaken in Rockwell included the training of Mass servers from the Junior House and the distribution of Mass texts and hymn sheets in the Chapel. Fr. Cunningham was spiritual director in 1969 and his accounts of the work of the Legion in Africa were enjoyed

In 1971 spiritual director, Fr. Hally, commented that the greatest difficulty in the efficient running of any apostolic organisation in a boarding school arose from the unavailability of really challenging work in the neighbourhood, a fact that had been evident for several years in Rockwell in connection with the Legion of Mary. In an attempt to redress this problem the membership was reduced to twenty to ensure that each member had a good proportion of work to do each week. Apart from the traditional work of the Legion, students visited two needy traveller families in the neighbourhood and helped to repair their caravan. They also raised money to help a Holy Ghost Father in Sierra Leone fund one of his projects.

Under the auspices of the Legion of Mary, the students of Rockwell in 1971 organised a missionary exhibition on Mission Sunday. A display of posters, statistics and photographs, designed to show the contribution made by the Irish nation to the mission field of the Church, was laid out in the Chapel hall on 18th October. While some may have been interested in the native handcrafts on display, the pathetic scenes of starvation, overpopulation and malnutrition displayed on the various stands were bound to provoke thought.

Students interested in outdoor recreation were spoiled for choice. Enlisting in the F.C.A. was popular because it included activities outside the College and in 1972 there were twenty three new recruits from 5th Year. If horse riding was the choice then it was off to Garret Dooley's stables in New Inn where more than two dozen newcomers in 1969 learned to canter under the supervision of Garret while Fr. Barrett organised proceedings. The more seasoned horsemen enjoyed a few days hunting each season with the South Tipperary Hunt.

St. Joseph's

In 1969 the number of Junior Scholastics was 57. Fr. O'Donoghue departed for Alaska and Fr. J. C. O'Connor took up residence as Assistant Director. After Christmas Fr. Maher filled the post while on leave from East Africa. Br. Gerard came from Biafra and the scholastics enjoyed his classes in woodwork and mechanical drawing. They also enjoyed slide –illustrated talks on the missions from Frs Ray Kennedy and Michael Murphy from Biafra and Frs. Michael Griffin and John Fitzpatrick from Brazil. Under the direction of Fr. Mullan many projects were undertaken, most notably the re-organisation and redecoration of the indoor recreational facilities. Another feature of life in St. Joseph's was the many impromptu concerts.

In 1970 the scholastics welcomed their new Director Fr. Knight and Assistant Director, Fr. Cunningham, both fresh from Africa. During the year they

St. Joseph's 1972
Front: M.Naughton, J. Carre, A. Ryan, H. Connolly, M. Sheehy.
Seated: C. Gough, B. Comerford, M. Kelly, W. Reidy, Fr. Seán Broderick, P. Wallace, T. Jones,
B. Keating, B. Carr.
1st row: A. Nolan, J. Spillane, C. Reddy, D. Maher, M. Gorman, L. Gorman, G. Troy, M. Burke.
2nd row: G. Haugh, J. Basquel, M. Basquel, M. Cahill, S. Sheehan, J. Sheridan, G. O'Rourke,
P. McKenna, C. Daly.

welcomed returned missionaries. Chief among them was Bishop Whelan who spoke about his experiences during the Nigerian Civil War. Other missionaries included Fr. Smithwich and Fr. Patrick Nolan. During the second term scholastics paid their traditional visit to Kilshane to meet the novices and to suffer defeat at their hands in an entertaining soccer match.

Fr. Seán Broderick settled in as Director in 1971. He was no stranger of course to St. Joseph's where he had been a student himself. The retreats and talks on the missions were given in 1971 by Fr. Seán Casey, Director of Vocations and Fr. Keegan. Gerry Nyhan gained an inter-provincial rugby cap in 1971 and this was a first for St. Joseph's in many a year. In 1972 Fr. Raymond Kennedy spoke to the scholastics about Bangla-Desh.

RUGBY
Rockwell won its 21st Senior Rugby Cup in 1970. When the final whistle blew in Thomand Park on 23rd March in a re-played final against Glenstal, spectators, young and old, recognised that this was an exceptional Rockwell team which had had a great Cup campaign. The back row of Paul Kane, Bill Cronin and Val Lonergan were all selected to represent Munster. They combined toughness with alertness and speed. Paul Kane was dynamic and inspirational. Bill Cronin, a virtual novice in September, rapidly proved himself among the best in Munster. Val Lonergan moved irresistibly where the rucking was heaviest.

In the second-row Francis Brady and Michael Morrissey proved an interesting combination. Tall, strong and effective, particularly when roused, they formed a powerful pushing unit. In the front-row, David Ormond, John Grennan and Charlie Haydar were splendid. David, playing a captain's part, showed enthusiasm and effective mobility. Charlie Haydar was a "rock" on which many an opponent perished. John Grennan, experienced and workmanlike, hooked with precision and skill.

The backs did their part. Peter Hanahoe as scrum-half had excellent matches. Always good for a score he was capable of varying his game so that the opponents were always kept on their toes. Aidan Hickey, still under 16, played in every position in the backs during the Cup campaign and displayed a toughness that would have done credit to a much older player. In the centre, Paul McNaughton showed his promising ability. His quick thinking and sense of position saved many tricky moments. He always did something useful with the ball and his ability to move forward as he came into possession was a rare quality. His partner, Michael Ryan had a deceptive style and given the breaks was very effective.

On the wings were Michael Slattery and Pat Lee. Michael had made the score that won the Junior Cup for Rockwell two years earlier and in this final he initiated from his own "25" the move which led to the second splendid score. Pat Lee only joined the team in December and his best match was in the final when his contribution was most needed. At full back seventeen year-old Paul McElhinney was resourceful and competent and put in a capital display in the final. Martin O'Brien and Mark Sullivan were injured for the final but both had made major contributions in earlier matches.

Senior Cup Winning Team 1970
Front: *A. Hickey, M. Slattery (Inset P. Kane)*
Seated: *W. Cronin, P. McNaughton, M. Morrissey, D. Ormond, F. Brady, J. Grennan, V. Lonergan.*
Standing: *P. Hanahoe, P. Lee, M. O'Brien, M. Ryan, P. McIlhinney, C. Hayder.*

Earlier in the season prior to the Cup campaign this team had played the usual challenges including games against Methodist, Rathcliffe College, Leicester and Nottingham High School. The senior team of 1971 had similar matches prior to the Cup campaign but lost the title on an appallingly wet and wintry day in March at Clanwilliam when defeated by C.B.C. in the semi-final.

Fr. Lavelle felt that the junior team of 1970 would not rank among the greatest Rockwell teams as far as football ability was concerned but that very few teams would surpass them in the spirit and courage they displayed. After a scoreless draw in the first round of the Cup against Waterpark they had a 9-0 win in the return game. In the second round they drew with C.B.C. but were well beaten in the replay in Cork.

The Munster Junior Cup returned to Rockwell in 1972 after a lapse of three years. Three of the team, Gerry Clancy, Pádraig Slattery and Liam Fahey had been on the cup team the previous year. Gerry Clancy, the captain and out-half, had also been on the senior team that year and was a rock of strength. Pádraig Slattery at second centre was a fearless tackler. On the right wing Liam Fahey was always a threat to opponents while at full back Michael Quaid was sound in defence. On the right wing Dermot Brown could always be relied on to beat his man for speed while Micahel Gordon was outstanding at first centre. There was a very close contest for scrum-half position between Joe Carroll and Richard Thorn with Richard playing in the first game and Joe in the other two.

The forwards were strong and mobile. Rory Smith, Brendan Egleston and Michael Kelly formed a solid front-row. Two six-footers in the second row, Aidan Molloy and Denis Ormond, used their height to great advantage in the line-

Junior Cup Winning Team 1972
Front: T. Donovan, J. Carroll.
Seated: M. Quaid, B. Egleston, T. O'Sullivan, G. Clancy, L. Fahy, J. Hendry, C. O'Carroll.
Standing: D. Andreucetti, R. Thorn, J. Slattery, M.McInerney, A. Molloy, P.Slattery, M. Kelly, R. Smith, D. Ormond, M. Gordon.

Junior Cup Winning Team 1974
Seated: *W. Norris, G. McAuley, J. Murray, S. Lyons (captain), J. Duggan, T. Broderick, B. Barron.*
Standing: *B. Barron, P. Corcoran, G. Maher, D. Collins, A. Wood, V. Massey, P. Waters, C. Marnell.*

out. The two wing-forwards, Colm O'Carroll and Joe Hendry, were lively and when Colm broke his collar-bone in the first match he was well substituted by Michael McInerney. Eddie O'Sullivan, who had captained the Blackrock junior team the previous year, was at lock and used his strength to advantage. The panel included Dino Andreucetti, John Slattery, Billy Irwin, Tony O'Donovan and Paul Brown who replaced his twin brother Dermot on the wing while the latter was injured.

The Munster Junior Cup was back again in Rockwell in 1974. The potential of the junior team that season was evident from their pre-Cup matches. Competition for places was keen, with the most difficult position to fill being that of hooker. Brian O'Sullivan, Bernard Barron and Walter Norris were all tried at different stages before it was finally taken by Tom Broderick. The front row was completed by Paraic Watters and Gerry McAuley and in the second row were Alister Wood and Vincent Massey. The back-row trio consisted of Gerry Maher, Seamus Lyons and Bernard Barron. John Murray was at out-half and Morgan Pierse at scrum-half. The wings were filled by Bruce Barron and Denis Collins. One of the centre positions fell to John Duggan who took on the place-kicking role. The other centre position altered between Ronnie Fanagan and Canice Marnell while Pat Corcoran at full-back was playing his first season at rugby. Waterpark and Munchins were disposed of before facing Christians in the final. Rockwell were deserving winners in that final and team captain Seamus Lyons was happy to receive the cup.

OTHER SPORTS

In athletics Dermot Brown, a student from 1969 to 1973, established a remarkable record. In 1970 he came first in the 100 metres and third in the triple jump in the junior All Ireland Colleges. In 1971 he came first in the 100 metres and third in the triple jump in the intermediate All Ireland Colleges. In 1972 he came first in the 100 metres and first in the 200 metres, setting a new record in both, in the intermediate All Ireland Colleges. And in 1973 he came first in the 100 metres and 200 metres in the senior All Ireland Colleges. In 1973 he also captured the Irish National 100 metres crown at Santry Stadium.

The Canoe Club had a large membership and in 1970 it travelled to Limerick to compete with the Limerick Canoing Club which was celebrating its centenary. For the first time ever in 1972 the Canoe Club operated throughout the entire season. It had a membership of over thirty and a fleet of fifteen canoes in the boathouse. Eight canoes were built and a twenty-canoe trailer acquired. It took part in the Inter Schools long distance race on the Liffey and in races in Limerick and on the Nore following frequent practice runs on the Suir. Fifty new members joined the club for the 1973-74 season. The first event of the year was the Newbridge College Canoe race in which Mark Clinton and Anthony Walsh were prominent. The club entered the Schools Canoeing Championships on the Liffey in which Mark Clinton and Desmond Molloy came first and second in the under 18 Slalom class. Fr. Reid and Br. Gerard supervised events.

Students keen on water sports had a further facility when the Rockwell swimming pool opened on 25th April 1974. It had the distinction of being the only deck level school pool in Ireland and also the only six-lane school pool. A viewing chamber situated at the deep end was of great help to coach, Mr. Bobby Madine, in correcting faults. Andrew Boyd of 5th Year became the first Rockwell student to win a swimming trophy when in May 1974 he won the Munster Schools Individual Medley Championship.

The new tennis courts were responsible for an increased participation in the sport. In 1969 the senior tennis team had high hopes of regaining the Munster

Golf Committee 1969
Seated: M. *Slattery,*
R. *O'Brien,* A. *Pierse.*
Standing: M.
O'Hanlon, R. *Mulcahy,*
M. *Hanrahan.*

Golfers representing Ireland in 1974
Michael Quaid, Pat McInerney, Des O'Brien and Pat Slattery.

Cup which last adorned the parlours of the College in 1967. After an easy passage to the semi-final the team lost 5-4 to Mungret. The team was: Paul McElhinney, Arthur Pierse, Francis Hayder, Declan Kennedy, Vincent Guerinni and Neil Clancy. The junior team lost to St. Augustine's, Dungarvan in the final.

Rockwell's initial success in the Munster Schools Golf Championship had come in 1968 when the team of Raymond O'Brien, Michael Slattery, Arthur Pierse, Declan Wall and Luke Griffin took the honours only to be beaten in the All Ireland semi-final by the Ulster champions, Bangor Grammar School. The Munster title was successfully defended in 1969 with the team of Raymond O'Brien, Michael Slattery, Arthur Pierse, Michael Cunneen and Brendan Rossiter. Declan Wall won the domestic singles competition and Declan partnered his brother Barry to win the foursomes. The home course continued to improve thanks to the great work of Nicholas Tierney under the direction of Eddie Hackett.

The two most notable achievements in 1971-2 were the affiliation of the club to the Golfing Union of Ireland and the praiseworthy attempt by the golf team to win the Irish section of the Aer Lingus Irish and British Schools Golf Championship. Rockwell won the Munster section in Mallow but lost narrowly to Gormanston College in the final at Royal Dublin. The team was: Kevin O'Keeffe, Pádraig Slattery, Pádraig McInerney and Fergus Caine. Christy Butler succeeded Eddie Hackett as professional advisor to the team.

Rockwell golf reached new heights in the 1973-74 season. Fr. J.C. Ryan was now in charge as the nine holes on the home course were completed. Rockwell won the Munster and All Ireland titles and thus qualified to represent Ireland in the Aer Lingus sponsored international competition at Portmarnock. The

Hunter Trials in 1973
Bryan Ryan, Gerry Lindsay and Willie D'Arcy

team of Michael Quaid, Pat McInerney, Des O'Brien and Pat Slattery came second to a strong English team.

For the mechanically-minded and racing car enthusiasts the Car Club, founded in October 1973 was a new departure. Its purpose was to teach the members about the working of engines. Former student Billy Coleman, then a successful international racing driver, travelled from Millstreet to give a talk to the members on his rallying experiences. The Rockwell Aero Club had been revived in 1967 and in 1969 it had fourteen members. Model aircraft were flown on the recreation fields. John McNally of the Cork aero Club was helpful with advice. A more dramatic event in aerial recreation occurred when Rockwell College invested in a hot air balloon which made its maiden flight on Monday 29th April 1974. It took off from the College grounds with four aboard. It reached a maximum height of 1.500 ft and having flown for eight miles it landed safely at Milltown, Gooldscross. The balloon was to be the centre of an aviation club which the College was establishing for senior boys who were thinking of a career in aviation. The balloon was the brainchild of Fr. Reid.

The greatest student participation in sport was in the house games with leagues organised throughout the year in all sports for all ages. These leagues generated great excitement in rugby, soccer, basketball, tennis and Gaelic. Rugby was the dominant game in Rockwell and every year began with high hopes for the senior and junior teams.

1969 was a good year for Rockwell hurling. It was a year which compensated for many of the defeats of recent years. The seniors brought home the Corn Phádraig and the Keane Cup. The juniors reached the final of the Corn Mhic Ruairí. John Coleman was unanimously elected captain of the senior team. The Keane Cup, in its second year, provided Rockwell with two games In October

Senior Hurling Keane Cup Winning Team 1970
Front: *D. Ryan, M. Horan.*
Seated: *T. Mulumby, J. Devane, W. Devane, P. O'Brien, M. Reynolds, J. Hurley, W. Blake.*
Standing: *Mr. S. Leahy, M. Hanrahan, D. Hurley, R. Murphy, A. Fewer, G. O'Connell,*
P. McNaughton, P. Lee, Fr. B. Frawley.

Rockwell beat Ard Scoil Rís and in the final of the Keane Cup and after Christmas beat Limerick C.B.S. Rockwell travelled to Thurles to to meet Nenagh in the final of the Corn Phádraig. The hero of that game was Liam O'Sullivan who, recuperating from illness, came on as full forward towards the close of the first half. John Coleman was a tower of strength in the half back line. The juniors were out in their first game against Roscrea. They had wins over Doon, St. Colman's and St. Augustines before losing to Nenagh in the final.

Rockwell hurlers retained the Keane Cup in 1970 but lost its hold on the Corn Phádraig. Pat O'Byrne proved to be a very energetic senior captain. His team had a big win over Doon C.B.S. in the Keane Cup, thanks in part to a great goalkeeping display by Willie Blake and a cetrefield performance by Mick Hanrahan. In the final against Limerick C.B.S. Rockwell won by 4-8 to 2-6. In that final prominent displays came from Mick Reynolds, Mick Hanrahan and Willie Blake and the sharp-shooting of Paul McNaughton was effective. It was a great season for Paul featuring on Rugby and Hurling Cup-winning teams. The junior hurlers in 1970 had a few good wins but failed to reach any finals. Hurling in Rockwell was under the capable direction of Fr. Frawley, himself a former Clare senior hurler, and Mr. Leahy of the famous Toberadora hurling family.

Rockwell had been absent from inter-schools Gaelic football competitions for thirteen years but in 1973 it took part in the Tipperary Schools Cup and reached the final but lost to Clonmel High School.

The sporting year in Rockwell concluded with Sports Day, held usually on the first Sunday of June.

ROCKWELL UNION

Rockwell College Union continued its close links with the College under its presidents Kevin Mallen, Fionnán Blair and William Dwyer. On Union Day in 1969 past pupils, their wives and friends attended Mass in the College and afterwards about 175 guests sat down to lunch with catering under the supervision of James McGuire. Union president Kevin Mallen presided. A golf match then took place. The function concluded with afternoon tea followed by Benediction in the College chapel. Other functions held annually included the Mass for deceased members in November, the annual dinner in February and the Retreat in the College on Holy Thursday and Good Friday. During these

Fionnán Blair
Rockwell Union President

years the Union continued to financially support projects within the College and on the Holy Ghost mission fields.

Union Dinner 1971
Mr. Kevin Mallen, Fr. Lehane,
Mr. Ciarán Blair

Past student
Ruairí Brugha T.D.
On Union Day 1973 with
his wife and Fr. Lehane.

HOTEL AND CATERING SCHOOL

Rockwell Hotel and Catering School continued to produce excellent graduates. In 1969 sixteen of the previous year's students had gone to the continent to continue their studies, eight to Munich, four to Geneva and four to Paris. Franz Knoblaugh, chef instructor since 1962 left in 1969 to develop his own establishment, Linden House, in Killarney. Rockwell took part in the C.E.R.T. Cup, an annual competition in Gaelic football for catering colleges. In 1970 Mr. Michael

An Taoiseach Mr. Liam Cosgrave
With Fr. Lehane on Diploma Day 1974

O'Leary, a former student, joined the staff as Assistant Supervisor having completed a period of study in Munich. In 1971 two former pupils, Tom Carroll and John Murray joined the staff as supervisors. In December of the same year Jim McGuire retired as manager, having given ten years of excellent direction to the school. He was succeeded as manager by Pat Cronin. In 1972 The C.E.R.T. Schools Gaelic Football Trophy returned to Rockwell. The 1972 team was managed by Pat Cronin who was a well-known Clare senior hurler.

Hotel School. First Year 1970
1st row: *L, Ryan, Mr. M. O'Leary, Mr. J. Bowe, Mr. H. Leute, Fr. J. Buckley, Mr. J. McGuire, Fr. D. O'Brien, Mr. T. Evans, Mr. B. McGuirk, Mr. P. Cronin, M. Gainey.*
2nd row: *G. Deveny, C. Ó Fionnada, M. Milne, T. Doheney, J. Sweeney, N. Carey, D. Mullane, M. Casey, S. Delaney, L. Dunphy, D. McKenna, L. Ryan.*
3rd row: *T. Hogan, D. Riordan, M. Cussen, J. Maher, L. Cox, P. Parsons, J. Dunne, P. Wallace, P. O'Brien, D. Gorey, J. Rice.*
4th row: *F. Morrissey, L. Carroll, D. McCarthy, L. Cronin, J. Molloy, S. O'Neill, D. Higgins, L. O'Carroll, A. Murphy, G. Buck, P. Duggan.*
5th row: *M. Dunne, W. Farrell, A. Burke, B. McCarthy, M. Finnerty, J. Quaid, M. Walsh, A. Cahill, B. Murphy, S. McEvoy, M. Gleeson.*

First Year Trainee Waiters 1973
Seated: L. Cooke, P. Duggan, Mr. N. Cunningham, Fr. Buckley, Fr. O'Brien, Mr. P. Cronin,
Mr. S. O'Farrell, D. O'Driscoll, J. Flanagan.
1st row: S. Kiely, N. Loughnane, G. O'Connell, D. Dunican, P. Henderson, A. O'Dea, E. Walsh,
P. Gallagher, P. Leonard.
2nd row: M. Doherty, T. O'Sullivan, M. Lee, P. Phelan, S. Dinan.

In 1973 diplomas were presented by the Minister for Labour, Mr. Brennan. He said that in the twelve years that the school had been in existence, 600 pupils had been awarded diplomas. In 1974 diplomas were presented by the Taoiseach, Mr. Liam Cosgrave to 58 students from 16 counties. In 1974 chef instructor Gerry McGourty won a major award at the Salome Culinaire held at the Hotel Olympia, London. Gerry had trained at Rockwell and had been appointed to the staff in 1970.

ROCKWELL AGRICULTURAL COLLEGE
Rockwell Agricultural College was officially opened by Taoiseach Jack Lynch on 8th September 1971. The new school formed part of a federation with the existing secondary school and hotel management school, and the combination of all three made Rockwell, as Fr. Lehane said, "a comprehensive educational campus which is unique in this country". Fr. Denis O'Brien was manager and Fr. John Buckley assistant manager. The staff consisted of Br. Senan, Br. Gerard, Mr. Victor Quinlan, Mr. Timothy Ryan, Miss Annette Bane and Mr. Michael Ryan The first students in October 1969 came from seven counties with different backgrounds and great variation in educational standards. But each student had a specific purpose in mind: some hoping to return to the family farm, others with ambitions of attending university and more with intentions of securing a job.

When the students had received a basic knowledge of the various subjects they then began to relate this to the appropriate activities on the College farm.

Each took part in the ploughing and those who were not familiar with the handling of a tractor were given the necessary instruction. On the livestock side the students gained experience in the use of the milking machine. Various systems of calf feeding and management were studied and participated in on the College farm. This included the management of a large suckling herd. They also became acquainted with the workings of a pig and poultry unit and the problems associated with each, such as feeding, lighting and watering.

In February 1970 the students travelled to the Agricultural Institute station at Grange and later were conducted through Thurles Sugar Factory and through a large mushroom plant. During the year they attended top-class farms in south Tipperary and had various lectures from representatives from the Department of Agriculture. In 1971 nine agricultural colleges took part in a ploughing competition in Rockwell.

In 1972 it was felt that the Rockwell students were getting the ideal training to meet the needs of our entry to the E.E.C. The same year Rockwell won the All Ireland Agricultural Colleges Gaelic Football championship. The team had the advantage of two great inter-county players, Pat Galvin of Kerry at centre field and Kevin Kilmurray of Offaly in attack. In 1973 there were seventy students in attendance. They came mostly from southern counties but there was a sprinkling from areas as far apart as Mayo, Wicklow, Meath and Monaghan. In October 1972 Jude Connellan, a past student of the secondary school, joined the staff. Poultry instructress, Annette Bane retired on her marriage. Patrick Browne, another past student of the secondary school replaced Michael Ryan who left to take up an appointment with the Department of Agriculture. In 1973 Tom Crowe and Lily Kennedy joined the staff. In 1974 the student population reached ninety.

Agricultural College 1970
Seated: Mr. M. Ryan, Br. Gerard, Fr. Lehane, Fr. O'Brien, Mr. M. Quinlivan, Fr. Buckley.
1st row: Mr. T. Ryan, J. McCarthy, J. Doyle, J. Hutchinson, L. Lonergan, J. Fitzgerald, J. Higgins, T. O'Neill, J. Brown, N. Brennan.
2nd row: J. Gorman, J. Looney, D. McSwiney, M. Brown, T. Wall, N. McCarthy, E. Moran, P. Guthrie, S. Troy.

Camp Rockwell 1971
Mr. Sweeney of Camp Rockwell with Audrey D'Alton and Joe Malone of Irish Tourist Board at "Ireland Workshop 71" in Los Angeles.

CAMP ROCKWELL

Camp Rockwell was a summer school directed by Fr. Des Reid which commenced operating in 1971. It seemed appropriate that the many outdoor facilities of the College, especially the golf course, tennis courts, lake and swimming pool, should not lie idle during school vacation and so the new initiative was warmly welcomed. The Camp was widely promoted in Ireland and in the United States with the help of the Irish Tourist Board, and in the summer of 1971 Rockwell College opened its gates to eighty Irish students and forty Americans. The Camp was designed to cater for boys and girls who wished to combine study with relaxation. Classes were provided in European languages and Geography and were combined with trips for Irish students to local locations of interest. For the American students visits were organised to Dublin, Cork, Limerick, Killarney and other destinations of national interest. For all students there was fun and games rounded off by nightly barbecues and sing-songs by the lakeside.

In July 1972 Camp Rockwell was officially opened by the then Parliamentary Secretary to the Minister for Education, Michael O'Kennedy. He said that the number of young visitors who came to Ireland for language courses had increased from 5.600 in 1965 to 30,000 in 1970. In 1972 Camp Rockwell had 32 students from the USA. 9 from Spain and 3 from France with almost 140 Irish students attending the 7 week programme catering for children from 9 to 16 years of age.

OBITUARIES

In 1969 Fr. Stephen O'Hanrahan who had been in Rockwell since 1945 died as did James A. White who had been teaching Music and Latin for many years. In October 1971 Fr. Reginald Walker, who for thirty five years had given unsparingly the fruits of his great mind to generations of past students, died. His history of the first hundred years of Rockwell and his work for the new College Library were among his more recent achievements. He was known throughout the country as a writer, teacher and retreat master. As a boy in Synge Street he was attracted to the Congregation by a talk on the missions given by Bishop Shanahan. He remained a missionary at heart all during his life.

Fr. Seán Nealon passed to his reward in December 1971. He first came to Rockwell as a student from his native Toomevara in 1921. He was ordained in 1935 and served in St. Mary's and Blackrock before departing for the Holy Ghost College, Mauritius. He returned to Rockwell in 1949 where he spent twenty one years teaching French. He was a proficient musician and up to a short period before his death he was organist in the College Chapel. He had a remarkable memory for the activities and whereabouts of past students thus making him invaluable to the Community and the school.

Father Joseph Mullins died in January 1972 in Caerphilly, South Wales while engaged in holiday ministry. Born in 1898 in Dundrum, Dublin, he was ordained at Chevilly, Paris in 1927 and his first appointment was as a teacher in the Holy Ghost College in Mauritius. Fr. Joe, or An tAthair Seosamh Ó Maoláin as he was better known to many, had since he came to Rockwell in 1938 been a champion in the promotion of the Irish language and the Pioneer and Total Abstinence Association. His methods were sometimes unorthodox but always endearing to students and staff.

On May 17th 1972 Rockwell staggered at the sudden death of Headmaster Fr. Joseph Nolan. Born in 1916 in Muinebeag, Co. Carlow, he was ordained in 1944. He served as Bursar at Kimmage until his appointment to Rockwell in 1947 where he first served as Bursar. In 1957 he was appointed Dean of Studies, a post he held until 1971 when he became Headmaster. Possessed as he was of deep reservoirs of physical and intellectual energy, Fr. Nolan's tireless patience, his vast depths of understanding and his incredible memory for detail made him a Rockwell legend. His influence as an educator extended far beyond the walls of Rockwell. In 1971 he became President of the Association of Post Primary Teachers of Ireland. He made many notable contributions to educational theory in his articles and addresses.

Brother Jarlath Hughes died in March 1973. Born in Claremorris, Co. Mayo in 1897 he entered the Holy Ghost Congregation at the age of 29. He was appointed to Bathurst, Gambia in 1934 and returned to Kimmage two years later. He was appointed to Rockwell in 1943, a move which proved to be his last. The death also took place in March 1973 of the former College Librarian, Mr. Thomas Magner. A native of South Africa, he served as a pilot in World War II. Luke Lyons, who had been College chauffeur, died in 1973. He had first come to Rockwell in 1919 and with his brothers Mick and Paddy had been devoted employees.

Fr. James Barrett died in November 1974. He was born in Clonakilty, Co. Cork in 1907. Ordained in 1937, he was first appointed to Rockwell where he served in turn as Dean of Discipline and Dean of Studies. In 1947 he went to Nairobi where he played a leading part in the construction of St. Mary's College, of which he was Headmaster from 1955 to 1960. His next appointment took him to Moshi, Tanzania, where he was Headmaster of Umbwes Secondary

School, near Moshi until 1964. He returned to Rockwell the same year. Fr. Barrett directed the Rockwell riding School until shortly before his death.

*   *   *

Father Lehane had greatly influenced the structure and character of Rockwell during his presidency. When he retired in 1974 his career was only changing rather than ending, as will be seen.

Notes

1   RCA 1977

2   ibid

3   J. Coolahan, *Irish Education: History and Structure*, pp 193 ff.

– 15 –

CHANGING TIMES
1975-1980

Changing times in Ireland were reflected in Rockwell with the closing of St. Joseph's in 1975 and the ending of the prefecting system in 1976. Because of a decline in the number of students studying for the priesthood, the Spiritan Congregation decided to close the scholasticate as such and to place the few students there in the main building. This was the end of an era which started when the Rockwell Juniorate was opened in 1866, two years after the foundation of the College. The closure of St. Joseph's marked a change in the character of Rockwell and came at a time of change in the Catholic Church in Ireland.

Fr. Denis O'Brien
President 1974-1980

Despite these changes, the ideals of Rockwell remained unchanged, as suggested by the College motto *Inter Mutanda Constantia*.

These changes took place during the presidency of Fr. Denis O'Brien who held that office from August 1974 to August 1980. A native of Dublin, he was educated at Rockwell from 1928 to 1933. He studied theology in Rome where he qualified as a Doctor of Divinity and was ordained in 1942. Having lectured in theology in Kimmage for a number of years, he came to Rockwell in 1950 and served as Bursar and director of the Catering School and Agricultural School. During his tenure as President there were many arrivals and departures from the Community and a continuing increase in the number of lay staff.

PERSONNEL
Fr. Hally was Vice-President and Headmaster and he was assisted as Dean of Studies by Fr. McGlynn. Frs. O'Driscoll, Chamberlain and Madigan were Assistant Bursars and Fr. Frawley was Principal of the Agricultural School. In 1977 Fr. Noel Redmond was appointed President of Templeogue College. He had been a prefect in Willow Park and in Rockwell and was ordained in 1963. He returned to Rockwell in 1964 and was successively Dean of Discipline for juniors 1964-1968, assistant Bursar 1968-1969 and Dean of Discipline for seniors from 1969. He was succeeded as Dean of Discipline by Fr. Seán Broderick. Fr. Broderick was ordained in 1965 and went to Nigeria. But the outbreak of war there necessitated his return to Ireland in 1970 when he became Director of St. Joseph's.

Superior General's visit to Rockwell in 1975
Fr. P. McGlynn, Fr. M. O'Connor, Br. Finbar, Br. Pascal, Fr. C. Cunningham, Br. Senan, Fr. B. Frawley, Fr. D. O'Brien, Fr. M. Lavelle, Fr. F. Timmermans (Superior General), Fr. B. Hally, Fr. W. Jenkinson (Provincial), Fr. T. O'Driscoll, Fr. F. Griffin, Fr. F. Marrinan, Fr. M. Comerford, Br. Eugene (partly hidden), Fr. R. Madigan, Fr. A. Chamberlain, Fr. C. Meagher.

Fr. Martin McDonagh joined the Community in September 1976. He studied in Blackrock College, was a prefect in Rockwell and was ordained in his home town, Castleplunkett, Co. Roscommon. Fr. Timothy O'Riordan also joined the Community in 1976. Born in Cork, he was educated at North Monastery. He prefected in Rockwell and was ordained at Clonliffe College in 1951. He ministered in Nigeria from 1952 to 1968. He spent some years in Canada and the United States before his appointment to Rockwell. He died suddenly in 1978.

Two Tipperary-born priests joined the Community in 1977. Fr. Brian O'Connor was a native of Cashel. Educated in the Christian Brothers Cashel and Rockwell, he was ordained at Clonliffe College, Dublin. He spent many years in Sierra Leone before his present appointment. Fr. Tom McCarthy was a native of Tipperary Town and was ordained in 1955. He ministered in Nigeria from 1956 to 1970. Returning to Ireland he became chaplain in the Mater Hospital in Dublin.

Fr. John L. O'Sullivan joined the Community in 1978. A native of Cork, he was a student in Rockwell from 1945 to 1948 and was a prefect in 1951-2. Ordained in 1955 he spent fourteen years in Nigeria and one year in Sierra Leone. On his return to Ireland he held appointments in Kilshane and in St. Michael's College, Ailesbury Road, Dublin. Fr. Brendan Duggan joined the community in 1978. A native of Cappamore, Co. Limerick, he studied in the Christian Brothers' School, Doon before entering the Holy Ghost Congregation. He was a prefect in Rockwell from 1970 to 1972. Following his ordination in 1975 he ministered in Ethiopia until 1978 when health reasons forced his return to Ireland. Fr. Patrick Downes came in 1979. Following his ordination in 1968 he spent ten years on the staff of Willow Park before coming to Rockwell.

Fr. Noel Redmond
Dean of Discipline

Prize Day 1976
*Fr. Griffin and
Fr. O'Brien with
Dr. Donal
McCarthy
(President of
U.C.C. and past
student of Rockwell)*

There were two departures from the Community in 1978. Fr. Alfred Chamberlain left to take up an appointment in Melbourne, Australia. He had come to Rockwell in 1958 as Director of the Junior Scholasticate and later served as assistant Bursar. Before coming to Rockwell he had ministered in Nigeria from 1947 to 1957. Fr. Colm Cunningham left to take up an appointment in Blackrock College. A native of Omagh, Co. Tyrone, he was educated at Omagh and Blackrock College. Following his ordination he ministered in Nigeria until 1970. While in Rockwell he was responsible for guiding the first year students through that delicate transitional period from home to boarding school. The Sisters of St. John of God in those years were Sr. Fabian, Sr. Mechtilde, Sr. Mary Roncali, Sr. Mary Carmelita and Sr. Mary Alphonsus.

The ending of the prefecting system necessitated an increase in lay staff. New lay teachers who joined the Rockwell staff during Fr. O'Brien's Presidency were Anne Noone, John Fitzgibbon, Patrick Daly, David Morris, Gerard Flynn, Greg Kenny, Michael Doyle, Frank McGrath, John Fitzgibbon, Ruth Bracken, Una Dillon, Alan Horne and Ciarán McNamara. Dr. William Ryan continued as house physician and Gerry Pierse as house dentist.

VISITORS IMPRESSED

Fr. Timmermans, the new Superior General of the Holy Ghost Fathers, visited Rockwell in 1975. He cannot but have been impressed by the beauty of the Rockwell environment. Earlier that year the first prize in the post-primary section of the National Gardens competition promoted by Bord Fáilte was won by Rockwell. The official notification of the award contained the following comment: "Rockwell is awarded first place within this section because this year it has in the opinion of the adjudicators, contributed most to an awareness of the adjoining community, insofar as they improved more by superb maintenance

Speech and Debating Society 1980
Seated: *T. Devitt, R. Godson, Fr. Seán O'Donoghue, M. Kelly, J. Reid.*
Standing: *M. Moloney, S. Robinson, D. Keane, M. Collins, R. Bergin.*

than any other action, the entrance area to the College that lies between the main road and the gates. Also the entrance drive with its very beautiful mixture of shrubs and trees has received additional attention, making it a most pleasant example, both in the choice of plant material and in the proportions of height of plants to width of avenue". The success was a personal triumph for Fr. Michael Comerford who directed a team of gardeners with typical dedication and skill and who year after year transformed the Rockwell grounds into a veritable Garden of Eden. Another visitor greatly impressed by the Rockwell environment was the United States Ambassador to Ireland, Thomas Shannon, who visited with his wife in 1978.

STUDENT LIFE
In 1976 between the secondary, hotel and agricultural schools, Rockwell College had a student population of 821. Of the secondary students 168 were from Tipperary and 123 from Dublin with most Irish counties represented. The Secondary School had over fifty foreign students coming from Zambia, England, U.S.A., Canada, Hong Kong, France, Saudi Arabia, Israel, Thailand, West Indies, Kenya, Channel Islands, Nigeria, West Germany and Wales. The largest number from any one country was 13 from the United States.

The quality of life in Rockwell between 1975 and 1980 was a matter which the Headmaster, Fr. Hally, raised annually on prize days. In 1975, when reviewing the work of the previous year, he said that such reviews tend to become littered with clichés about success. While acknowledging success in public examinations, he suggested that success in education surely meant more and that the less quantifiable factors were equally and possibly to some extent

more important and may not
be so easily defined. A College
such as Rockwell, he said,
should be concerned with the
intellectual, the religious, the
social, emotional and physical
development of its pupils.
Were we to over emphasise
any of these, he said, to the
exclusion or downgrading of
any other, we would ultimately
be failing in what must surely
be the role of a school such as
this. In his 1977 review Fr.
Hally said that in recording

Senior English Debating Team 1977
W. Reardon, F. Gleeson, J. Cooke.

progress since the previous year there was not a
problem in doing so in regard to certain aspects
of school life. Examination successes, university
and county council scholarships, the acquisition
of a number of sporting and debating trophies
and such matters were easily recorded. But there
were of course many other dimensions to school
life which, while important, were not subject to
the same clear-cut criteria of measurement. By
what yardstick can one measure progress in the
spiritual and moral formation of a student's
character for example, he asked Yet this was
surely an essential concern of education, he
said. The difficulty of measurement reflected
the difficulty of defining the aims of education.
He continued that some economists, many
parents, and probably even more pupils

Fr. Brendan Hally
Headmaster 1972-1980

subscribed to a quasi-utilitarian philosophy of education, where the measureable,
in terms of job openings and financial reward was everything.

CHARITABLE WORKS

There were aspects of student life in those years, however, which reflected a less
than utilitarian approach to life. In 1975, for instance, there were twenty three
members of the junior Red Cross raising funds for good causes. With the funds
they collected they held a Christmas party for the children in the Dundrum
orphanage. On Shrove Tuesday they held a party for the boys of the Cappoquin
orphanage and in May they organised an outing for the boys of Ferryhouse
Industrial School. And every Monday throughout the year they helped the
students of Scoil Chormaic and Scoil Aonghusa in Cashel when they came to
Rockwell for a swim. They continued with the same activities in 1976.

Fasting for Charity 1975
Vincent Massey, Seamus McCarthy, Pádraig O'Sullivan, Joe Hendry and Des Molloy.

Another well-intentioned student activity which was organised in Rockwell in 1977 was *Renewal and Youth* (R.A.Y.). This organisation had been launched in Dublin in 1972 by Cardinal Conway. It was a movement for young people from fourteen years to twenty one which aimed at tackling problems arising from alcohol. It aimed to help young people know clearly the objective facts about alcohol and to encourage abstinence at least until an informed decision could be made.

R.A.Y. was controlled in Rockwell by a committee of twelve members under the guidance of Fr. Cunningham, R.A.Y.'s spiritual director. It strove to get activities going in the school such as soccer tournaments, swimming galas, chess leagues and it initiated clubs such as the 2nd Year Art Club. R.A.Y. Competitions in all these areas were organised. R.A.Y. Day was celebrated in Rockwell on 20th March 1977 when members from the diocese of Cashel and Emly gathered in the College to celebrate Mass and to view competition entries which were on display. The Mass was celebrated by Archbishop Morris who presented the prizes in the different sections such as poetry, essay and art. He then addressed the gathering and a concert rounded off the proceedings. In 1978 R.A.Y. helped in the organisation of football leagues and initiated a training course for referees.

Since 1969 6th Year students had through various methods been raising funds for the missions. In 1978 they decided to hold a forty eight hours fast, limited to ten members, as a fund-raiser. The fast began on a Wednesday but was complicated by the fact that on the following day Rockwell was involved in a senior cup match and two of the fasters, Louis Fay and Joe O'Connor were cheer leaders. Undaunted by the challenge they performed their sideline duties with traditional gusto on empty stomachs and enjoyed a fine meal when the fast ended on Friday evening. The other fasters were Gearóid McGann, Niall O'Keeffe, David Mongey, Tommy Mulligan, Donal Lyons, Paddy Comber, William Barry and Frank O'Mahony. The £630 collected was donated to Fr. McAlister, a past pupil of Rockwell who was ministering in Sierra Leone and who used the money to help build a church and community centre in his parish.

Student Council 1978
Seated: *M. O'Donovan,
Fr. Broderick, N. Sheedy.*
Standing: *L. Fay, J. Holt,
W. Barry, G. McGann.*

THE S.R.C.

A milestone in student-staff relations was reached in 1977 when the Students'
Representative Council was established. It was born from a meeting of students
with Fr. Hally in November of that year. George Comber, Gearóid McGann
and William Barry discussed the matter with Fr.Hally and later with Fr.
Broderick and it was finally agreed to establish the council. An election was
then held among 6th Years. Twelve candidates presented themselves and the
five successful ones were William Barry, John Holt, Gearóid McGann, Louis
Fay and Niall Sheedy. Weekly meetings between the council and Fr. Broderick
were held. Because of a growing feeling among students that the council was a
6th Year affair, it was decided that a 5th year should be added to the council
and following an election among 5th years Mark O'Donovan was elected. The
aim of the council was to strengthen student-teacher relations and to bring
matters of importance to the notice of the College authorities.

ACHIEVEMENTS AND ACTIVITIES

While academic achievement continued to be high in those years the winning
of three of the Easter Week 1916 scholarships was significant as there were only
seven such scholarships awarded annually in the entire country. In 1976 Kieran
Sheahan obtained the Thomas McDonagh classical scholarship, his teacher of
Latin and Greek being Fr. Lavelle. The following year Jim O'Brien won the
Patrick Pearse scholarship for Irish and Kevin Cotter was awarded the Joseph
Plunkett scholarship for history, their respective teachers being Mac Uí
Dhuibhir and Mr. O'Donnell. These achievements have to be seen in the

Camp Rockwell 1977
Fr. Reid addresses the morning assembly.

context of a speech made by the president of the Rockwell Union, Denis Kelly, at the annual dinner in 1977 when he highlighted the care and attention given to the average and backward student and for which, he claimed, Rockwell was well-known.

Students continued to enjoy numerous out-of-class pursuits. The library provided an outlet for many. The books there were re-classified in 1977 and by 1980 the reference section had four sets of encyclopedias. *The Rock Magazine* was an option for those interested in writing. It re-appeared in 1978 with contributers including Mark O'Donovan, Richard Foley, David Jameson and Stephen Burkart. Mr. Leahy had given helpful direction. The basic principles of photography could be learned in the Camera Club and interesting exhibitions by the Stamp Club were popular. For those interested in travel, the annual school tour was popular. Since the mid 1960s Mr. King had been organising these tours and by 1980 he had taken students to most European major cities. Irish and English debating teams took part each year in the Gael Linn and Muintir na Tíre national competitions. In 1977 the Irish team under the direction of Mac Uí Dhuibhir reached the semi-final of the Gael Linn competition. The following year the English team consisting of Willie Reardon, Maurice McQuillan and Mark Moran did well in the Muintir na Tíre competition. The same year Rockwell entered a debating contest run by Trinity College, Dublin. It was an individual competition and the College was represented by T.J. Meagher and Maurice McQuillan.

MUSIC AND DRAMA

Fr. Reid continued as choral director and in 1975 his choir did a Christmas broadcast on R.T.E. This included hymns from the full choir, junior verse speaking and interviews with some of the overseas members, Canice Marnell from Jerusalem, Pat Curran from Zambia and Paul Gauntley from Toronto. At the Cork International Choral Festival this choir came second. The Gregorian chant choir took part in the Fr. Matthew Feis in Cork in 1977 and 1978 while the junior choir sang at Masses throughout the year. Mr. Ciarán McNamara coached students in many musical instruments and conducted the orchestra. Recitals by professional musicians were regular and in 1978 a recital by the Georgian Brass was especially enjoyed.

Mr. Irwin produced the annual drama. In 1976 he produced *The Importance of Being Earnest*. The production was not without its real drama because on the morning of the second performance the father of James Wright, who had played Miss Prism in the first performance, died. But as the saying goes "the show must go on" and so it did due to the valiant efforts of John O'Sullivan who had originally played Lane but now adopted the role of Miss Prism and played it well. Dave Finan entered the cast only nine hours before the curtains went up to play Lane, the perfect butler. Morgan Pierse played Mr. John Worthing and Francis Gleeson played Algernon Moncrieff. Kevin Cotter captured the jolly old soul of Rev. Dr. Chasuble and Joe Walsh played Merriman the butler. The other ladies' parts were played by Jim O'Brien, Billy Murphy and James O'Sullivan. Mr. Irwin's production in 1977 was *Arsenic and Old Lace* and in 1978 it was *Life With Father* by Clarence Day which was basically a synopsis of the author's childhood memoirs. Good performances were given in that by Maurice McQuillan, Jim O'Malley, James O'Sullivan, and Willie Reardon in the leading roles. In 1979 Mr. Irwin was involved in a novel production. Together with Mr. McNamara and Fr. Reid he produced *Joseph and the Amazing Technicolour Dreamcoat*. And for the first time in Rockwell the cast included twelve girls form the Convent of Mercy, Cahir, who were directed by their teacher Mrs. McGuirk. Ms Kate O'Leary acted as stage director.

RUGBY

Despite great effort Rockwell failed to win the Munster Cup during Fr. O'Brien's presidency. The S.C.T. of 1975 was managed by Fr. Redmond who also looked after the Seconds while Mr. Flynn took charge of the Thirds with Mr. Morris looking after the under 12s. At the beginning of the year Joe Hendry and Pat Curran were elected captain and vice-captain respectively of the senior team. After mid-term break the team almost picked itself. Canice Marnell and Gerry Robinson alternated at first centre with Brian King at loose head prop. Michael Quaid was full back with Michael Wilson and Denis Collins as wingers. Pat Corcoran was at centre and John Murray at out-half. Pat McInerney was scrum-half and Pat Curran tight-head prop. Tom Broderick was hooker while Alister Wood and Denis Ormond were second row. Dino Andreucetti, Seamus Lyons and Joe Hendry were the back-row. The seniors had quite a successful "friendly"

Rugby Inter-provincials 1975-76
T. Broderick, G. Robinson, T. Murray, P. Curran, J. Duggan

season. Of the fifteen matches played they won nine, drew two and lost four. In the first Cup match they beat Waterpark and then had a 15-9 victory over Crescent. They lost in the final to Presentation Brothers by 20-3. Rockwell had four inter-provincials that year in Michael Quaid, Pat Curran, Pat McInerney and Denis Collins. Michael Quaid was selected as full-back on the Irish Schools XV against England, the first Schoolboys rugby international and Pat Curran was on the panel of twenty one. During the year Irish internationals Willie Duggan and Fergus Slattery came to give advice and encouragement. The juniors, trained by Fr. Lavelle lost to Pres in the first round of the Cup.

Pat Curran received two international caps in 1976, one against Scotland and one against Wales, and in 1977 John Duggan was on the team against England and Wales. The four inter-provincials of 1977 were John Duggan, Michael Power, Derek Cowman and Ciarán Ormond. The senior team was beaten in the Cup semi-final by C.B.C. the eventual winners by 11-6. Only four of the previous year's panel were available for selection. John Duggan was the only back while Billy Murphy, Ciaran Ormaond and Michael Power formed the nucleus of a good pack. Billy and John were elected captain and vice-captain respectively. Two new arrivals to the College were decided acquisitions, Derek Cowman at full-back and Andy Hally at centre. Seán Kelly and David Cantwell complemented each other on the wings. David, the more experienced of the two, was fast and elusive whereas Seán was tenacious in the tackle. Seán Booth from the previous year's junior team was skilful at out-half. John Duffy just shaded the scrum-half spot ahead of Andrew Carroll. Compared to former Rockwell teams the forwards were physically small. Mark Higgins and Brendan Barry propped and Ciarán Ormond was an excellent hooker. Michael Power was the star forward ably assisted by Brendan Bagnall. John O'Hanlon at No. 8 was effective while Billy Murphy and Eddie Fitzgerald gave of their best at wing-forward. Willie Duggan visited the team during the year and was generous with

The Junior Cup Team 1977
Front: *B. Flynn, W. Swinburn.*
Seated: *A. McNamara, S. Spollen, B. Watters, J. Lynch, D. Heffernan, M. Holohan, G. Robinson.*
Standing: *M. Griffin, G. Daly, M. Marnell, M. Moran, B. Ryan, D. McMahon, M. O'Connor.*

his time and advice. The junior cup team of 1977 lost to Pres in the Cup semi-final. That team was noted for having the smallest scrum-half in the championship, Walter Swinburn. He was a natural footballer whose tactical and positional sense could exploit the speed of his wingers. His great talent was destined to be channelled later into equine exploits.

Fr. Broderick began his management of the senior team in 1978. The following year Liam Lannen was on the Irish Schoolboys panel against Wales and Scotland. Liam Lannen and John Holt were inter-provincials that year. In 1980 Michael O'Connor was on the Irish team and the inter-provincials were Ian Grogan, Billy Whelan and Michael O'Connor. The junior team of 1980 lost to C.B.C. in the Cup final despite strong displays from future internationals Gary Halpin and Michael Fitzgibbon.

GAELIC FOOTBALL

Rockwell made real progress at Gaelic football between 1975 and 1980 due to the dedication of Mr. Tony Smith. In 1975 he trained teams at under 17, under 15 and under 14. In 1976, for the first time in recent years, Rockwell entered a team in the Munster Colleges senior football championship which beat St. Colman's, Fermoy in the first round but lost in the semi-final to St. Flannan's Ennis. In 1978 the under 15s won the Tipperary Post Primary Schools championship beating St. Joseph's College Cahir in the final with great performances from Tim Buckley, Michael O'Connor, Stanley Barlow, John O'Mahony, Bernard Ryan, Ian Grogan, Paul Booth and Joe Hurley. Mr. Smith had two teams in the under 14 championship that year.

Gaelic Football Cup Winners 1979
Seated: *S. Kelly, J. Hurley, A. Costello, I. Grogan, J. Fitzgerald, G. Irwin, B. O'Dwyer,*
A. McNamara, M. O'Connor (6th Year)
Standing: *P. Slattery, N. Flynn, D. Bolger, F. Hurley, M. Moran, M. O'Connor (5th year),*
B. Deegan, K. O'Hora, S. Barlow, D. Kelly, P. Booth, J. Farrell. Mr. Smith (coach)

Gaelic football reached a new level in Rockwell in 1979 when the seniors won the Munster championship for the first time since 1941 and the under 15s and under 14s became the champions of Tipperary. In the first round of the championship the seniors beat Tipperary C.B.S. by 2-11 to 2-9. They narrowly defeated Douglas Community School in dreadful weather conditions by 2-4 to 2-1.The semi-final was played in Emly against St. Colman's Fermoy and ended in a draw. Rockwell narrowly won the re-play by 2-3 to 0-8. Their opponents in the final were Sacred Heart College, Carrignavar. And after another close encounter in which Rockwell won by 2-5 to 1-5, captain Jack Fitzgerald was presented with the cup. The All Ireland semi-final against St. Fintan's Sutton was played during the Easter holidays but Rockwell failed to live up to their previous form. The team which won the Munster championship in 1979 was: Jack Fitzgerald, Ian Grogan, Mark Moran, Denis Kelly, Michael O'Connor (5th Year), Gabriel Irwin, Michael O'Connor (6th Year), Alan Costello, David Bolger, Barra O'Dwyer, Kevin O'Hora, Adrian McNamara, Stanley Barlow, Gerry Casey, Brendan Deegan, Seamus Kelly, Niall Flynn, John Farrell, Paul Booth, Paul Slattery, Joseph Hurley, Fintan Hurley. The under seventeen team, containing many of the senior team became Tipperary champions with wins over Carrick-on-Suir C.B.S., Tipperary C.B.S. and Clonmel High School. The under fifteen team became county champions with wins over Fethard C.B.S., Tipperary C.B.S. and Clonmel High School.

At Prize Day in 1979 Fr. Hally paid tribute to Mr. Smith and suggested that since coming to Rockwell six years previously, Mr. Smith must have used scores of copy books with his lists of football teams which seemed to appear hourly on the notice boards. There was no doubt, he said, but that the dedication of this man had been the inspiration behind the revival of interest in Gaelic football in Rockwell.

OTHER SPORTS

Mrs Dillon and Mr. Kenny directed matters in the swimming pool while Fr. Reid continued to promote the Canoe Club. Many new members and many new boats on the lake were reported in 1975. A trip to the Nire Valley in the Commeragh Mountains, where there were many rapids and falls, became a regular event. At the Inter Schools canoeing championship on the River Liffey in April 1975 Rockewll came first in the open doubles, the crew being Anthony Walsh and Mark Clinton. Peter Quinn came second in the under eighteen singles class. In 1976 the club started the year with the Ballytiglea to St. Mullins Barrow race but did not appear among the prizewinners. In the Liffey schools race after Easter that year Conor Sandford and John Foley gained fourth place in the under 18 and under 15 slalom classes respectively. In 1978 the Canoe Club had over a hundred members. It took part in the Fermoy Blackwater canoe race and the 3rd annual Suir Descent. After Christmas they were off the the Nire Valley. The treacherous rapids and falls of the White Water river sorted out the skilful from the rest. There were many exciting trips down the Suir at Cahir and Holy Cross.

Mark Kelly
Swims for Irish Schools 1980

Malachy Sheridan
Pole vault champion

Fr. McCool was appointed in charge of the horse riding club in 1976. The riders enjoyed nine meets with the Tipperary Fox Hounds. At the Tipperary Hunter Trials held in Cahir, Rockwell was represented by seniors James Murphy, Bill Doyle and Michael Lynch and juniors Seamus Garvey and Edward Kent. The Fr. Barrett Memorial Cup was competed for at the sports day gymkhana. In 1978 on 21st May the Riding Club held its annual gymkhana in which over fifty riders participated. The Fr. Barrett cup was won by Billy O'Neill.

The Rockwell balloon remained an attraction for the Aviation Club. In 1975 all members had a trip in the balloon at least once. In 1976 flights started in September and weekly meetings were held where those who had partaken in their first flights could discuss the effects it had on them with their fellow members. Seán Morvan was appointed president of the club because he was the holder of a student's pilot licence. All members had at least two flights in the balloon in 1978. In 1979 the Rockwell balloon piloted by Fr. Reid flew over the Alps, coming second in an international competition.

The golf course was slightly redesigned in 1975 to contain five par fours and four difficult par threes. In the same year Rockwell won the Munster section of the Aer Lingus schools competition and lost in the All Ireland final to Belvedere. Fr. J.C. Ryan led his team to win the Munster section in each of the following years. Mr. Morris entered teams in the Munster tennis tournaments at senior, junior and

Athletes at the All Ireland Championships 1975
Seated: *J. Prendergast, D. Andreucetti, B. Barron.*
Standing: *T. Power, D. Collins, D. Ormond.*

under 14 while Mr. Kenny entered basketball teams. Fr. Lavelle with the assistance of Mr. McGrath coached the athletics team with good results in the East Munster, Munster and All Ireland competitions. Good performers in 1975 included Denis Collins, Gerry Barry, Mark Lincheid, Tony Power and Dino Andreucetti. In 1978 Liam Lannen won the shot at the Munster and All Ireland and came second in the discus. Future Olympian, Malachy Sheridan, set a record when winning the junior pole vault at the All Ireland of 1980 while Gary

Table Tennis Team 1980
Seated: *I. Grogan, J. Moriarty, D. Zaidan, P. Fulcher.*
Standing: *G. Lynch, C. Zaidan, V. O'Brien, R. Kennedy, J. Harrison.*

Senior Tennis Team 1980
Seated: *J. Reid, Mr. Greg Kenny (coach), M. O'Brien.*
Standing: *J. Daly, B. Carroll, J. Daly.*

Golf Committee 1975
Seated: *P. Cahill, D. O'Brien, Fr. J.C. Ryan, P. McInerney, J. Lynch.*
Standing: *C. O'Carroll, J. Duggan, M. Quaid, J. McInerney.*

Halpin came second in the junior shot and hammer. Mr. Kenny coached the basketball teams. Mr. Leahy trained the hurling teams and made particular progress with the under 16s.

The curtain came down each year on sporting activity in Rockwell on Parents' Day. Officially known as "At Home Day" it was known to the students as Sports Day. Traditionally it was held on the Sunday before the summer holidays when parents came to see their beloved sons taking part in sporting competitions. It was a day of great activity on the sports fields, the golf course, the gymnasium and swimming pool. Activities included a gymkhana for the horse riders and exhibitions on the main corridor by the stamp club and camera club. The College always looked its best on that day, Fr. Comerford and his team having been at work for a week beforehand.

THE ROCKWELL UNION

The Rockwell College Union celebrated its golden jubilee in 1975. The work which the Union had done for the College and for the missions in the previous fifty years was recalled. The highlight of the celebrations was the gala weekend at Rockwell at the beginning of June when a very large number of past pupils came to pay tribute to their *alma mater*. The weekend activities included a golfing competition, a dinner-dance, a luncheon and a coach tour of the district. The guests at the annual Union dinner of 1975 included Richard Burke, Minister for Education and former President Eamon de Valera who was making one of his last public appearances before his death. In 1977 after a lapse of some years the North Munster branch held their dinner dance in the Parkway Motel in Limerick.

Union Dinner 1975
Eamon de Valera in conversation with Fr. O'Brien and Fionnan Blair, Union President.

Between 1975 and 1980 the annual calendar of events for the Rockwell Union was similar. At the beginning of the new school year in September the ten-years-out returned to Rockwell. The annual general meeting in October was followed by the Halloween Ball in Rockwell. The Southern Region dance in Cork was held in November as was the annual Mass for deceased members in St. Mary's, Rathmines. The annual dinner was held in Dublin in February and the annual retreat in Rockwell was held on Holy Thursday and Good Friday. Union Day was held in Rockwell at the beginning of June when the programme began on a Saturday with the Union Golf Club competition played over the College nine hole course. On Saturday night a dinner dance was held in the main dining room and overnight accommodation was provided in the Agricultural College. On Sunday solemn Mass was celebrated at noon. The annual golf outing was held in July.

Agricultural College

The Rockwell Agricultural School progressed steadily between 1975 and 1980 with changes on the teaching staff and an increase in student numbers. Victor Quinlan, after five and a half years service to the College resigned in 1975 to devote his full time to farming. The same year Dermot O'Mahony from Kilbrittain, Co. Cork took up his appointment as machinery teacher and Jim Fitzgibbon from Castlelyons joined the staff. Willie J. Dwyer, who was new to Rockwell, was a well known Development Officer for Macra na Ferime. Eileen Murphy and Val O'Connor joined in 1977 as did school secretary Breeda O'Donnell.

In October 1975 the new self-service dining room, with its most up to date equipment, was completed and opened. As well as serving the needs of the College the beautifully furnished and finished dining room was used for various functions in the secondary and catering colleges. In 1978 the new machinery workshop was blessed by Bishop Whelan and opened by Mr. Jim Gibbons, Minister for Agriculture. Built with direct labour by the college staff under the

Machinery Workshop Opened 1978
Mr. Ferris M.C.C., Mr. Gibbons, Minister for Agriculture, Mr. Davern T.D., Fr. Knight,
Mr. Byrne M.C.C., Bishop Whelan, Fr. Frawley.

President of I.F.A. Mr. Paddy Lane
With Fr. Frawley and Fr. O'Brien at Prize Day 1979.

supervision of Br.Senan at a cost of £20,000, the new structure consisted of a modern dairy class room, a welding and drilling plant and other up-to-date equipment.

There was a steady growth in the number of students in those years and for the first time it reached a hundred in 1976. Two years later it reached a hundred and eight. Another interesting feature was that 75% of new students in 1977 already had the Leaving Certificate and 42% of the students who graduated that year returned to farming.

President Hillery attended the National Ploughing Championships in Rockwell in 1977 and Paddy Lane, president of the Irish Farmers' Association, was guest of honour at the annual prize day in 1979.

HOTEL AND CATERING SCHOOL

The Hotel and Catering School underwent improvements between 1975 and 1980. A new demonstration kitchen designed to cater for sixteen trainee chefs was built. It included a number of new gas cookers, each containing a built-in work bench and pot rack. Other amenities provided were a practical class room, a games room, a students' television lounge, a study hall and additional sleeping quarters.

Fr. J.C. Ryan continued as Dean of the Catering School in those years. In 1975 diplomas were presented to fifty six graduates of the school by Mr. Michael O'Leary, Minister for Labour. Speaking to a large gathering of distinguished visitors which included many important people in the tourist and hotel industry in Ireland, the Minister praised the school for the contribution it was making to the industry in Ireland. Apart from the diplomas, several special prizes were awarded including scholarships to the Shannon Management School.

The Rockwell Hotel and Catering School entered the annual international catering competitions held in London at Olympia. In January 1977.Seán Davern

First and Second Year Waiters 1977
Seated: *Mr. J. Muldoon (Instructor) Mr. P. Cronin (Manager), Fr. O'Brien (President),*
Mr. M. O'Leary (Instructor), Mr. G. O'Carroll (Instructor)

became the first restaurant trainee from Rockwell on the Irish team and he brought home the silver medal for his orange salad, carved duck and *crepes suzette*. This was the first time that a medal in this competition had been won by an Irish student. Mr. John Muldoon was responsible for Seán's training.

At the annual reunion in 1978 in the Grand Hotel Fermoy among the past pupils present were Eugene McSweeney, head chef at the Berkely Court Hotel Dublin, Tom O'Carroll, Newpark Hotel Kilkenny. Jim Aherne, Strand Hotel Rosslare and Gerry McGourty, Templemore Arms Hotel. The chairman of Bord Fáilte had commented that all the head chef jobs in Ireland had for many years been held by continentals but that had changed due to the excellent training now available in Ireland.

In 1976 Rockwell Hotel and Catering School bid farewell to James Bowe who had given eight years service as chef-instructor. He moved to Dublin and became head chef in the Leopardstown Complex. The school went on a European tour every year and the highlight of the 1977 tour was a visit to Rome and a public audience with Pope Paul VI.

OBITUARIES
Fr. Tom Nolan died in March 1975. Born in Derrylahan, Ballacolla, Abbeyleix in 1886, he pursued his secondary studies in the Blackrock Scholasticate from

1903 to 1908 with his brother Frank. The following two years were taken up with prefect duties in Rockwell. He was professed in Chevilly in 1911 and ordained in Ferndale in 1917. He worked in Louisiana, U.S.A. and was appointed to St. Mary's, Trinidad in 1922. He returned to Rockwell in 1926 where he remained for the rest of his life. He is remembered in Rockwell as an exceptionally great English teacher with the ability to awaken interest in the English literature classics, mainly because of his wide knowledge and his infectious enthusiasm.[1]

Fr. John C. O'Connor died in 1977. Born in Cratloe East, Abbeyfeale in 1916 he entered the Rockwell Juniorate at a slightly later age than the average. Following his ordination he was appointed to Zanzibar in 1947 and he continued his missionary work in East Africa at Mangu High School and in Nairobi as assistant in Our Lady of Visitation parish. He was forced by ill health to return to Ireland in 1964. Despite his ill health he taught for periods in Rockwell and Templeogue and served as chaplain to the Irish Christian Brothers at their novitiate in Baldoyle.[2]

Fr. Francis Marrinan died in 1977 at the age of sixty nine. He was a native of Milltown Malbay, Co. Clare. He studied at Blackrock College and was ordained at Kimmage in 1935. The following year he was appointed to the East African missions. His first appointment was to Bagomoyo in 1936. Later he served in Morogoro at St. Peter Claver's parish, Nairobi and at Nyeri. Suffering from an indisposition which was to afflict him for the rest of his life, he spent some time in hospital before being appointed to Rockwell in 1942 where he taught Mathematics, History and Geography. He was remembered as highly intelligent, uniformly cheerful and a gentle person.[3]

Michael Burke, died in July 1975. Born in Cashel Co. Tipperary in 1950, he was educated at Cashel C.B.S. and Rockwell. He entered Kilshane in 1968 and after his philosophy studies in Kimmage was a prefect in Rockwell from1973 until his death. Three weeks earlier he suffered brain damage in a road accident and never recovered.[4]

Two recent past students of the Rockwell Agricultural School, Noel Kent of Borrisoleigh and Tom Delahunty of Durrow, died in 1975.

Notes
[1] ISR 191
[2] ISR 350
[3] ISR 70A
[4] ISR 416

– 16 –

DISTURBING TRENDS
1981-1986

It was a bleak time for the Irish economy in the early 1980s with high unemployment, mass emigration and political instability. It was inevitable that these circumstances would affect Rockwell where many parents found themselves under financial pressure. The outcome was a fall in student numbers and a decision in 1986 to close the Hotel and Catering School.

When Fr. Patrick Holohan was appointed President of Rockwell in August 1980 he was the first missionary priest to hold that position. Born in Cloneen, Fethard, Co. Tipperary in 1928 he studied at Rockwell from 1942 to 1947. He was ordained in Rome in 1957 and was appointed to

Fr. Patrick Holohan
President 1981-1986

Nigeria the following year where he was supervisor of Holy Ghost schools. He returned to Rockwell in 1971 and was appointed a junior Dean of Discipline. In November 1985 he was specially nominated to receive on behalf of Rockwell the European Cross award. This award had been instituted by General De Gaulle of France and Chancellor Adenauer of Germany and had been awarded to those who had shown exceptional dedication and service in civilian life during World War II. The background to this event involved twelve French students who were accepted in Rockwell as part of the College's contribution towards rebuilding the morale of the European people after the Second World War. Eight of the French students returned to Rockwell in 1985 to present the award to Fr. Holohan.

PERSONNEL

Fr. Brendan Hally, who had been Headmaster since 1972 and Vice-president since 1974 left Rockwell in August 1980 to become Headmaster of Blackrock College. Fr. Desmond Reid also left in August 1980 to take up an appointment in Brisbane, Australia. Fr. Reid had been a prefect in Rockwell from 1959 to 1960 and a member of the Community since 1966 where he was best remembered as the inspiration behind the project known as Camp Rockwell.

Fr. Bernard Frawley became Vice-president and Bursar and Fr. James Hurley became Headmaster in 1980. Fr. Hurley's association with the College went back to 1943 when he came to Rockwell as a student. He had previously been

Prize Day 1981
Dean Lee, Fr. Comerford, Mr. John Lyons (Union President), Archbishop Morris, Fr. Holohan, Fr. Hurley, Liam Uas. Ó Duibhir.

Director of the Rockwell Scholasticate and President of St. Mary's College, Rathmines. Fr. Broderick continued as Dean of Discipline with Fr. John Meade and Fr. Patrick Downes. Fr. Patrick McGlynn continued as Dean of Studies. Fr. John Meade was born in Miltown Malbay, Co. Clare and educated at Blackrock College. Ordained in 1968 he spent ten years in Sierra Leone before coming to Rockwell as a Dean of Discipline. He left in 1984 to take up Missionary work in the United States. Fr. Henry Moloney joined the Community in 1980. A native of Cork, he was ordained in 1967. He had served in St. Mary's College Rathmines from 1968 to 1973 and in Sierra Leone from 1973 to 1979.

The new Principal of the Agricultural School in 1980 was Fr. Michael Moore. A native of Mountrath, Co. Laois, he was educated at Patrician College, Ballyfin and Rockwell. He worked in Nigeria from 1960 to 1969 and then ministered in Kilshane, St. Mary's Rathmines and Jamestown, North Dakota. Fr. James Duggan became the new Dean of the Catering School and Director of Camp Rockwell in 1980. A native of Clonakilty, he was a prefect in Rockwell and following his ordination in 1957 he was involved in mission promotion Fr. James Brett joined the Community in 1983, having served most of his life as a missionary in Trinidad. He celebrated the Golden Jubilee of his ordination in 1986. Fr. Patrick Duggan was appointed Bursar in 1984. A brother of Fr. Brendan, he had served in Nigeria and in the United States and Zambia.

The Sisters of St. John of God in these years were Sr. Mary Fabian Dunne and Sr. Mechtilde Burke. New lay teachers in 1980 were Ms. Nóirin O'Kennedy and Mr. John Mason in 1981, Mr. Declan Crotty, Ms. Ita Cummins and Ms. Anne Moine and in 1983 Mr. Alan Horne. Mr. Tobin continued as Registrar and in charge of the bookshop. The House physician was Dr William Ryan. The College Secretary was Miss Gerardine Kelly and the Bursar's Secretary Miss Teresa Maher.

STUDENT POPULATION AND EDUCATIONAL IDEALS
The student population of Rockwell Secondary School between 1981 and 1985 dropped by nearly a hundred. (Appendix XI). In the same years the population

of the Agricultural School and the Catering School remained steady. Despite the drop in Secondary School numbers, Rockwell continued to attract students from many parts of Ireland and from abroad. In the Leaving Cert class of 1983, for example, twenty two students were from Dublin, nineteen from Tipperary, fourteen were foreign, thirteen from Cork, nine from Waterford and six each from Limerick and Clare. Roscommon had five, Galway four and three each from Wicklow, Longford and Kildare. There were two each from Kilkenny, Carlow and Meath. And there was one student from each of the counties Sligo, Kerry, Donegal, Westmeath, Offaly, Laois, Mayo and Wexford. The number of day students continued to increase.

Speaking at Prize Day in 1981, his first as Headmaster, Fr. Hurley said the priority of educators was to foster mature growth in the faith and in sound and approved doctrine. Our aim, he said, was that enunciated by the Roman document *The Catholic School,* to promote a synthesis of culture and faith and of faith and life. This was not an easy task, he said, because we lived then in an environment in Ireland where consumerism and materialism had created an atmosphere hostile to real religion. "The main danger to religion today is not unbelief but a shallow belief." he said.

At Prize Day in 1984 Fr. Hurley said that each academic year formed part of the life cycle both of student and of school. At the same time it was fashioned by our well-established traditions and by the positive and vigorous contributions made to it by the staff and students alike, he said. He was concerned about the proposed reform of the Irish education system initiated through the establishment by the Minister of Education of the Curriculum and Examinations Board. The Board, he said, should be careful not to shift the core of educational endeavour from the traditional three r's, reading, writing and coping with numbers. In his opinion the finished product of any worthwhile educational system must have a thorough grounding in language and literature. In to-day's world, he felt, there was an ever-growing need for people who were articulate and for whom the old Greek ideal of noble deeds was not something of the dim and distant past.

Prize Day 1982
*Fr. Hurley, T. J. Maher
M.E.P., Enda Marren (Union
President). Fr. Holohan,
Fr. Cooke (Kenya)*

Students' Representative Council 1983
Seated: *A. McCarthy, Fr. Broderick, P. Farrell*,
Standing: *J. Conboy, J. Gold, K. Dennehy.*

The Rockwell Prize Day continued to provide prominent guest speakers. In 1981 it was Archbishop Thomas Morris. In 1985 it was Mr. Paddy Buggy, President of the Gaelic Athletic Association and the following year it was Mr. Kenneth Whitaker, former Governor of the Central Bank. And each year of course the President of the Rockwell Union attended and presented the Union prizes. In 1983 a new prize, the De Valera Prize, was presented. This was a plaque presented to the College at a concert the previous October held to commemorate the centenary of the birth of the former President and his association with Rockwell. The concert was held in the College and was attended by the Taoiseach, Mr. Charles Haughey and among the guest artists was the tenor Frank Patterson.

An Taoiseach Mr. Haughey
Examining the College register with Fr. Holohan and Mr. Seán McCarthy Minister of State and past student.

GOOD WORKS

Rockwell students continued to pursue good works during their hours of recreation. Early in 1981 they joined with students from all over the archdiocese in a youth rally in Holycross. A magnificent mission project was undertaken by the boys of 2nd Year under Fr. McDonagh and Fr. Murphy on Papua New Guinea and it was entered for a Missionary competition for Holy Ghost schools in Ireland. 1981 was the Year of the Disabled and thanks to Fr, McDonagh the students raised £900 for this worthy cause and Fr. Duggan raised £400 from the students for Rockwell's two representatives on the Lourdes Diocesan Pilgrimage. In 1982 a group of seniors and fasters raised a total of £1,100 to send on pilgrimage two senior citizens and two students on the Cashel archdiocesan pilgrimage to Lourdes. The two senior citizens were Johnnie Moore and John Gleeson, both of whom had worked for many years in Rockwell.

For the previous three years the 3rd Year students had been taking part in a religion project organised by the Provincial Animator, Fr. Kane. Rockwell won the trophy for the first time in 1983 for the project "The Refugee Crisis". In June 1983 fifty seven teenagers and eight leaders from the archdiocese set out on a two week overland pilgrimage to Lourdes and Nevers. Three Rockwell students took part and Fr. Brendan Duggan and Mr. Irwin were among the leaders. To raise funds for the project a monster sponsored cycle was held at Hallow'een. More than five hundred teenagers set out for Rockwell from four centres in the archdiocese. Tea was served and a disco followed. £8,000 was raised, £700 of which was raised in Rockwell. R.A.Y. (Renewal and Youth) with Fr. Downes as spiritual director made frequent visits to the Old Folks Home in Cashel each year. In November 1985 a party of students from schools run by

Junior Dormitory Prefects 1983
Seated: *S. Kelly, P. Madigan, Fr. Downes, Fr. McCool, T. Gernez, A. Gallagher.*
Standing: *S. Ryan, D. Higgins, C. Kenny, F, Farrell, P. Dennehy, B. Lansdale.*

the Holy Ghost Congregation departed from Dublin Airport to represent the Congregation at the beatification of Fr. Daniel Brottier C.S.Sp. The party of fourteen was led by Fr. Aidan Lehane and included three Rockwell students and Br. Senan.

STUDENT ACTIONS

It had been decided in 1979 to adopt the Dewey Decimal classification system for the Rockwell Library. The fact that there were over 4,500 books in the library meant that the conversion to the new system was slow. It continued right up to 1986 and librarians who did much of this work included Andrew Rice, Ciarán MacDonagh and Rory Layden with direction from Fr. Moloney and Mr. Daly.

Rockwell students performed well in the Aer Lingus Young Scientists Exhibition held annually at the R.D.S. Dublin. In 1982, under the direction of Fr. Brendan Duggan, John O'Connell entered a project in the intermediate section entitled "The Ecology of Wasteland". It was highly commended. The same year Richard Gallagher and Oisin Hurley entered the junior section with a study of how grass plants grow and again their work was highly commended. In 1985 John O'Connell presented a project on the ecological problems of mallard breeding which won the runner-up award in the senior section, a success which was further recognised by the fact that he was chosen first in his category for Environmental Studies at the International Exhibition organised by Westinghouse and General Motors in Louisiana. Because of his success, the Department of Education asked the school to nominate a representative from Rockwell to join with eight other Irish students in an international congress in Turin. Richard Gallagher was the student chosen and the teacher of both these students was Dr. Butler. In 1986 Rupert Butler was highly commended for his project in the biology/ ecology section of the Aer Lingus Young Scientists Exhibition which researched the area of nest predation and in which he asked himself two basic questions:- a. can the identity of a nest predator be determined by reference to the shell remains that it leaves behind? b. What level of nest predation occurs in Ireland? Rupert's teacher was his father Dr. Douglas Butler.

**French Room Assistants
1985**
Seated:
*J. Kitaka, Ms Ní Mhurchadha,
A. Cronin.*
Standing: *G. Houlihan,
P. Burke.*

Debating Society 1984
Seated: *D. Higgins, P. Madigan, Mr. Morris,*
J. Harte, W. Savage.
Standing: *T. Cronin, F. Moore, J. Fitzgerald, J. O'Connell, N. Hanrahan, G. Moroney.*

In 1983 French teacher Miss Ní Mhurchadha set up Le Coin Français for students of French. This little "corner" of France had over three hundred books of all kinds in French with newspapers and magazines. The club was open on a regular basis and was staffed by four voluntary helpers from 5th Year, in 1985 they being Tony Cronin, Patrick Burke, Greg Houlihan and John Kitaka.

Debating, both in Irish and English, was a regular annual feature. A team, directed by Mac Uí Dhuibhir, was entered each year in the Gael Linn competition and in 1985 the team consisting of John O'Connell, Richard Gallagher, Liam Disney and Gary Moroney did especially well. Debating in English was directed by Mr. Frawley, Mr. Power and Mr. Morris with teams entered in all the national competitions. In 1983 the most competitive of these was the John Dillon National Debating Championship organised jointly by the debating societies of the National University colleges of Dublin, Cork and Galway. Rockwell entered two individual speakers, James Griffin and Denis Hogan and one two-man team of Ian Morley and Michael F. O'Connell. Mr. King was the organiser of the Debater of the Year Competition held annually in May. In 1986 the 5th Year winners were Dylon Dalton and Noel O'Rourke and the 6th Year winners were Mark Heslin and Tim Buckley. Mr. King continued as organiser of the annual school tour which visited places of interest throughout Europe.

The Dramatic Society continued to flourish under the direction of Mr. Irwin and Mr. Gallagher with excellent annual productions. In 1981 *Julius Caesar* was the choice with Patrick Haugh and David Keane playing the parts of Brutus and Cassius and Seán Tobin as Mark Anthony. Other parts were played by Paul McGrath, Joseph Cronin and Brian Moroney. In 1982 the production was *The Strong are Lonely* by Fritz Hochwalder, a play based on the Jesuit State of Paraquay which flourished between 1609 and 1767 with parts played by Patrick Haugh, Michael O'Connell, Paul Gallagher, Gerard Lynam, John Corry, Gerald Tighe, Joseph Mahon, Liam Kelly, John Locke, Malachy Sheridan and James Nolan. *Philadelphia, Here I Come* by Brien Friel was produced in 1985 with parts played by Rory Leyden, Justin Irwin, Michael MacDonagh, Paul O'Donnell, Pierce Kavanagh, Tony Cronin, John Keating, Robert Barrett, Paul Prunty, Brian Fitzgerald, Darren Flynn, Chris Haden, Tim Buckley and Colm Moran. In 1986 T.S. Elliot's *Murder in the Cathedral* was the choice in which Tim Buckley played the lead role with other parts played by Harry O'Meara, Niall Madigan, Roy Hennessy, James Moloney, Michael Keating, Colm Keating, Paul Van Den Bergh, Colm Moran, Pierce Kavanagh, Dylan Dalton Andrew Kennedy, Michael McDonagh, Richard Beirne, Harry Blackmore and Niall McCormack.

The Music Society, under the direction of Fr. Moloney and Miss Lynch, organised regular recitals in the Library by top-class artists. In 1983 the recital by Janet Harbison, harpist, was a highlight. Students were entered each year for the examinations of the Leinster School of Music. The Folk Mass Group was popular in those years under the direction of Mrs. Patsy McGuirk with Miss Angeline Nagle. The aim of the Folk Mass Group was to provide a musical accompaniment to Sunday Mass and on special occasions throughout the year. The musicians in 1985 were Kevin Bolger, Gary Mooney, Tom O'Connor, Aengus Linehan, Antonio Geada, Rory Layden, Harry O'Meara, Harry Blackmore, John McGloughlin and Mark Lawrence.

The economic recession which hit Ireland in the 1980s was reflected in the setting up by the senior students in Rockwell in 1983 of the Young Ireland Group. Its purpose was to promote a "Buy Irish" campaign. The group organised poster competitions and distributed leaflets to shops and spoke to students during class time. They informed parents of their campaign by enclosing a leaflet with end of term school reports. In conjunction with other schools in the district they organised a "Buy Irish" Day in Clonmel at which four thousand leaflets were distributed. Mr. Leahy was involved. More than forty students were members of the group by 1986.

In the early 1980s the use of computers was becoming more widespread and was becoming popular with Rockwell students. Computer Studies gradually became part of the curriculum. Originally it was confined within class hours to junior students not taking Irish. In 1982 a 6th Year student, Joao Geada, was instrumental in forming the Computer Club. Fr. Brian O'Connor was an enthusiastic patron of this club and helped set up Rockwell's first Computer Room. He was assisted by Mr. Purcell. Each evening members crowded the Computer Room. The summer of 1982 was the first occasion on which Leaving Certificate students in Rockwell received certificates for their expertise in computer programming. A colour B.B.C. computer, at that time regarded as a highly sophisticated computer, was presented to the College on Prize Day 1983 by Owen O'Neill on behalf of the Rockwell Union.

The *Rock Magazine* was revived in 1983 by Michael F. O'Connell and Bernard Fanning and some of its light-hearted articles were a source of great amusement. In 1985 Tony Cronin was editor with Paul Prunty and James Moloney, assistant editors and their edition included an interview with the Russian ambassador to Ireland. The three interviewed the American ambassador, Mr. Kane, and the interview was published in the 1986 edition when John O'Neill and Gary Cooney were in charge.

The Stamp Club continued to meet on Sunday mornings and each year attended the *Stampa* Exhibition at the R.D.S. in Dublin with Fr. Knight in charge where it competed for the Windsor Cup. At the Mid-Western Stamp Exhibition in 1983, held at Cruise's Hotel, Brendan Donovan was successful with his depiction of the strides made in space communications over the previous twenty years. Others who took part were Edmond Burke, Kevin Guerin, Gary O'Mahony, Kevin Walsh, Rory Leyden, James Mescell and Tom O'Dwyer. At the same exhibition in 1985 Rockwell took the top prize beating St. Munchin's who had been winners in the previous eight years. Rory Layden and Andrew McGlynn won the individual sections. Also among the prize winners were Ciarán Brophy, Brian Garvey, Michael Whyte, Christopher Walsh, Brendan Donovan, Gareth Cooney, Edmund Burke, Caoimhín Walsh, Gary O'Mahony and Patrick Purtill.

The Arts and Crafts Club under the direction of Fr. Downes engaged in crafts such as basket making and pottery and provided a wealth of material for display on Open Day. The Chess Club, directed by Br. Senan, took part each year in the Tipperary and Munster championship. The team in 1986 was: Martin Quinn, Tom Murphy, Michael Purtill, John Underhill and Denis Keane

Fr. Moloney directed the Orinthology Club and in 1986 together with Mr. Crotty, he helped in a student survey of the Rockwell lake with the aim of further developing an understanding of the lake's ecological balance. Students involved included Louis Keary, Mike Quirke and Martin Kitaka and they soon discovered that the Rockwell lake was a haven for a considerable variety of both animal and plant life

STRUCTURAL DEVELOPMENT

During Fr. Holohan's presidency development and maintenance of the Rockwell infrastructure and environment continued. In the Spring of 1981 a vast programme of tree planting was undertaken. A thousand trees were planted under the supervision of Fr. O'Sullivan, Dr. Butler and Fr. Meagher. The same year three new tennis hard courts were laid beside the gymnasium on the tarmacadam area, thus bringing the number of courts operational to six. Apart from their use during the school year they were a welcome addition to the sporting facilities available to Camp Rockwell students.

In 1982 changes were made in the College Chapel. The altar rails were removed and the priests' choir seats and the sanctuary were restyled and enlarged. The original altar table was brought forward to give it a more central and prominent position. A marble lectern was placed on each side of the main altar. These changes were in keeping with modern developments in the world of liturgy. St. Joseph's was renovated. The building had been used as a dormitory for 3rd Year students since its closure as a juniorate in 1975. In 1982 it was given an internal facelift with rooms papered and fitted with wall-to-wall carpets. Almost one hundred students and six staff members were at that time accommodated in St. Joseph's.

The pavilion, which dated back to 1933-1934, had its interior renovated in 1981. The entire ground floor was covered with quarry tiles and the walls were finished from floor to ceiling with ceramic tiling. The junior section was extended. In 1982 a new telephone system was installed. A new electricity generator was also installed to cater for the entire electrical requirements of the secondary, catering and agricultural schools. Fire prevention facilities were modernised. Two self-service units were installed in the dining halls. A new computer system was introduced. This followed a visit to Dublin and Limerick by Fr. Hurley and a group of science and mathematics teachers. As the number of lay members of the academic staff increased, it was found necessary to provide an adequate staff room. What was formerly the Music Appreciation room on the eastern end of the long hall became the new staff room in 1982.

THE ROCKWELL UNION

The Rockwell College Union continued its activities during Fr. Holohan's presidency when its presidents were Barrie Foley, John G. Lyons, Enda Marren, Owen O'Neill, Paddy O'Dwyer and Bernard Flusk. In 1982 it had a membership of 1,329. Regular events in its calendar included the annual dinner in Dublin in February, the annual Retreat in Rockwell on Holy Thursday and Good Friday, the Cork branch dance in April, the annual general meeting in Dublin in May, the June week-end in Rockwell, the golf outing in July, the ten-year-out return to Rockwell in September, the gala dance in Rockwell at Halloween and the November Mass for deceased members at St. Mary's Rathmines. The Union's donation of a computer system to the College in 1981 and the launching of a special project in 1983 to provide a microcomputer for student training have already been noted. Since 1944 it donated annually gold medals for student of the year and debater of the year and since 1967 for the Thomas McDonagh literary award.

In recent years the Union's assistance to the missionary work of the Holy Ghost Fathers took the form of financial aid for missionary projects. Specific Holy Ghost priests were sponsored each year. It was Fr. Denis Rodgers of Papua New Guinea in 1981 and again in 1982. Fr. Peadar Gallagher of Kenya was selected as recipient in 1983. A burse of £850 was donated to help provide a water supply for his mission complex.

The careers of Rockwell past-students were always followed with interest by the Union and by the College. The ordinations to the priesthood in 1982 of Brendan Carr and William Cleary were noted as was that of Peter Conaty,

**Union Dinner
1984**
*Enda Marren,
Owen O'Neill
(Union President)
and President
Hillery.*

Edmond Grace, Gerard Kirwan and Thomas Mylod in 1983 and of Michael O'Sullivan and Francis Gleeson in 1986. A past student with a different calling was Walter Swinburn who on 3rd June 1981 steered Shergar to an effortless win in the Epsom Derby At the age of nineteen he became only the second teenager to win the Derby in its long history.

THE AGRICULTURAL COLLEGE

The Rockwell Agricultural College in 1981 had a student population of one hundred and eight. It had staff changes from time to time since its foundation. Fr. O'Brien had been its director from 1969 and was succeeded in 1980 by Fr. Frawley. The Principal from 1969 to 1972 was Fr. Buckley and from 1972 to 1980 Fr. Frawley. Fr. Moore became Principal in 1980 with Fr. Fallon as Assistant Principal. By 1985 Fr. Frawley was back as Principal   with Fr. Fallon as Assistant Principal. The other members of staff were: Farm Manager: Mr. Jim Treacy. Dairy Husbandry: Mr. William J. Dwyer, Mr. Patrick Hayes. Crop Husbandry: Mr. William Gleeson, Ms. Eileen Murphy, Mr. Michael Prendergast. Beef: Mr. J.M. O'Dwyer, Mr. John O'Connor. Sheep: Mr. John Crosse, John O'Connor. Pig husbandry: Mr. John J. O'Dwyer, Mr. Denis Carr. Machinery: Mr. Val O'Connor, Br. Gerard, Mr. John Hennessy. Poultry: Mrs. Lily Nolan. Building Construction: Br. Senan. College Secretary: Ms. Breda O'Donnell. Chef: Mr. Peter Grimes.

The new regional administration of ACOT had been established with its headquarters in Kildalton, Piltown, Co.Kilkenny. The transfer of administration from the Department of Agriculture had made no significant difference to the College. It would appear that it was a much more satisfactory system than the previous one with much more personal contact with the regional director of ACOT, Mr. Michael Galvin, and his staff.

Students from the college took part each year in the inter-college farm plan competition and won the Bank of Ireland perpetual trophy in 1981. They also took part in the National Ploughing championships and in the Spring Show stock judging competitions at the R.D.S. In 1983 a great victory came to Rockwell when it won the All Ireland Inter-Colleges hurling championship.

Minister for Agriculture Alan Dukes with Jim Treacy (Farm Manager) and Fr. Frawley

Rockwell beat Mount Bellew and Clonakilty to reach the final at Birr against Mellows College, Athenry which they won by 4-8 to 3-5. The team was coached and trained by Mr. William Gleeson and Mr. William J. Dwyer.

Annual Prize Day in Rockwell Agricultural in those years was attended by the Presidents of the Irish Farmers Association, Mr. Joe Rea and Mr. Donal Cashman

The Rockwell farm, which was essential to the Agricultural College, was in 1981 undergoing changes in keeping with changes in farming trends with a movement towards more winter cereals replacing spring cereals. In 1981 it had sixty acres of winter barley, sixty acres of winter wheat, twenty five acres of winter oats together with ninety acres of spring barley, forty acres of sugar beet, twenty four acres of potatoes, eight acres of vegetables and twelve acres of other root crops. Two thousand eight hundred tonnes of grass silage was conserved each year between 1981 and 1986.

Cattle production was then the two-year beef system with an automatic calf feeding unit. Cattle were wintered on modern slatted accommodation with a capacity for four hundred animals. The dairy herd consisted of two hundred cows. Sheep production at Rockwell was increased substantially in 1981 with the flock consisting of four hundred and eighty breeding ewes and two hundred hoggets. The pig unit had places for two hundred and forty sows with approximately eight thousand fat pigs produced annually. The pig unit was modernised with a new farrowing house and new weaner houses. About seventeen thousand broilers were reared per annum along with over one thousand turkeys. To cater for all the stock on the farm a milling and mixing unit was producing three thousand tonnes of feed per annum. All ploughing and harvesting was done with the farm's own machinery.

HOTEL AND CATERING SCHOOL

The Rockwell Hotel and Catering School celebrated its 24th birthday in 1982. Initiated in 1958 at the request of Bord Fáilte Éireann, it was officially opened in June 1960 by the Minister for Education, Dr. Hillery. In October 1960 the

Prize Winners at Hotel Olympia 1984
Front: *Kevin McCann, George McQuinn, Fr. Holohan, Fr. Duggan, Chris Farrell.*
Back: *James Savage, Pat McSweeney, Chris Bailie.*

Vocational Education Committee of South Tipperary undertook to sponsor the course. In 1963 the Council for Education Recruitment and Training for the hotel industry (CERT) took over from Bord Failte and Rockwell now operated in co-operation with that council. The courses offered were designed to provide a basic training in dining room service or cookery for boys who wished to make careers in the Irish hotel industry as waiters or chefs. Since Rockwell Hotel and Catering School opened, almost 2,000 had graduated up to June 1982.

Fr. Denis O'Brien was Director of the School from 1958 to 1980 except for the year 1967 when Fr. Lehane was Director. Deans of the School in those years were Fr. John Finnucane (1971), Fr. Holohan (1972-1974), Fr. John Buckley (1974-!980). Fr. Jim Duggan became Director in 1980 with Fr. J.C. Ryan as Dean. The Managers of the School were Mr. James Kelly (1958-1961), Mr. Hugh Bennett (1961-1965), Mr. James Maguire (1965-1972) Mr. Patrick Cronin (1972-1986). Waiting and Chef instructors and supervisors in the 1980s were John Muldoon, M. Colbert, M. Hennessy, Brendan McGuirk, Miss P. Dolan, Mr. Hugh O'Donoghue, P. Grimes, M. Orange, J. Casey. Academic staff included Mr. Michael Doyle, Mrs. C. O'Connor and some teachers from time to time from the Secondary school including Mr. Criostóir Gallagher, Mr. Laurence O'Dwyer and Mr. Seán O'Donnell. The Nurse was Sr. M. Mechtilde and the Matron Sr. Mary Fabian Dunne. The school secretary was Ms D. O'Connor and Mrs. McGrath was in charge of laundry.

In 1982 the school had 126 waiters 100 trainee chefs and 26 trainee waiters. The waiters were on a block release system: in college for eight weeks, then in hotel and industry for eight weeks, back in college for a further eight weeks and then to hotel and industry for eight weeks. Sports in the Catering School included athletics, soccer, and house leagues. In 1982 a new club, Carrigeen Cosmos was founded combining staff and students. It was founded by Mr. Smith and Mr. Doyle. The team entered the Tipperary District Shield League.

In the 1980s there was a demand for improved facilities for the Hotel and Catering School and CERT put a lot of pressure on the Rockwell management to build a new one. The proposed cost of a new school was £500,000 so the management judged that there were already adequate State Colleges and Technical Institutes which offered these services, so following much discussion and meetings it was decided to close the Hotel and Catering School in June 1986.[1] Thus ended an institution which had given great service to Rockwell and to the catering and hospitality industry at large.

OBITUARIES

Fr. Michael Lavelle died after a short illness in January 1982. Born in Westport, Co. Mayo in 1925, he was ordained in Fribourg in 1955. He joined the Rockwell Community in 1957. He was teacher of Latin and Greek. The record of his achievement with athletics in the College reached almost folk-epic status. His involvement in this area began in 1958 and he specialised in training for the pole-vault, shot and discus and also the junior rugby cup team. Between 1958 and 1982 Rockwell's success in these fields, especially in athletics was unique, winning the College of Science Cup three times in a row on two occasions. The Munster All Round Cup for athletics rested in

Fr. Michael Lavelle

Rockwell without a break from 1958 to 1968 and four times since 1968.

Mourned at national level both as a coach and as an administrator he was at the forefront in the development of Irish athletics for more than twenty years. His ability, coupled with his vast knowledge of the various disciplines made him one of the greatest coaches in Ireland. While he excelled in throwing and pole-vaulting events his versatility enclosed all the disciplines, sprints, middle distance running, jumps and hurdles. He held the position of National Events Coach from 1971 to 1980.[2]

Fr. Francis Griffin, former Superior General of the Holy Ghost Congregation died on 6th September 1983. He was born in 1893 in Ibrickane, Co. Clare and studied at Rockwell. He was ordained in Fribourg in 1920 and acted as a Dean in Rockwell from 1923 to 1925. He served as a missionary in East Africa from 1926 to 1933. He was General Councillor of the Congregation from 1933 to 1950. From 1950 to 1962 he guided the Congregation as Superior General and during that time the Congregation's membership grew substantially. Missionary activity made great advances and local churches grew rapidly, especially in Africa. New foundations were started in Spain and Canada. He chose Rockwell as his place of retirement and from 1962 until a year short of his death he taught French and was a father-figure and counsel to many. Fr. Griffin's Diamond Jubilee had been celebrated in December 1980. The Jubilee Mass was attended by President Hillery and by the Superior General of the Congregation Fr. Timmermans.[3]

RUGBY

In the period between 1981 and 1986 Rockwell had a number of fine rugby players with Michael Fitzgibbon, Gary Halpin, John Riordan, Brian MacGoey and Jack Clarke winning schoolboy international caps. The Junior Cup was won in 1982 and the Senior Cup returned to Rockwell in 1985.

The senior team of 1981 was managed by Fr. Broderick and had three inter-provincials in Michael O'Connor, Brian O'Donnell and Adrian McNamara. Michael Fitzgibbon was also on that team and he was also on the under 16 Bowen Shield team managed by Fr. Meade. Fr. Broderick also trained the Second Seniors and Mr. Flynn the Third seniors. Fr. Lavelle and Mr. McGrath trained the junior cup team and on that team were Gary Halpin and Malachy Sheridan. Mr. Morris had charge of the under 14s and Fr. Downes was in charge of the under 13s.

The 1982 senior team, managed by Fr. Meade, had Gary Halpin in the front row, with Bryan O'Donnell, Liam Flynn, Ian Slattery and Michael Fitzgibbon getting Munster caps and Michal Fitzgibbon getting an Irish cap. During the year the team had visits from past students Willie Duggan and Johnny Moloney. The Third seniors were trained by Mr. Flynn. Mr. McGrath trained the under 16s. Fr. Dick Lehane and Fr. Duggan were in charge of the under 14s and Fr. Downes managed the under 13s which included Jack Clarke and Gabriel Fulcher. The leagues were organised by Fr. Moloney and Fr. Knight.

The junior team of 1982 brought the cup to Rockwell for the first time since 1974. Fr. Lavelle had shaped this winning team in the months before his death. After Christmas the team was taken over by Mr. McGrath assisted by Mr. Morris. Chris Gibney, Joe Barrett and Liam O'Sullivan formed a formidable front-row that combined character with strength. David Mansfield and Paraic Madigan in the second row proved a veritable powerhouse of industry. Owen Butler on the open-side harried and supported tenaciously. Seamus Kelly at No.8 kept the scrum tight and either J.J. Kelly or Francis Farrell on the "blind" cut off loose breaks effectively. Other forwards who served with distinction were John Walsh and Pat Dennehy.

Schoolboy international Michael Fitzgibbon 1982 with past students Willie Duggan (Triple Crown team 1982 and Bertie O'Hanlon (Triple Crown team 1949)

Junior Cup Winning Team 1982
Front: *N. O'Farrell, P. O'Donoghue, D. Larkin, J. Walsh.*
Seated: *F. Farrell, B. Gillhooley, E. Holland, T. Gregan, J. O'Connor, T. Gernez.*
1st row: *J. Barrett, A. Barlow, C. Gibney, P. Dennehy, J. Kelly, A. Sharkey.*
2nd row: *L. O'Sullivan, O. Butler, P. Madigan, D. Mansfield, S. Kelly.*

The back division was widely regarded as the most talented back-line in Munster capable of intricate passing movements and whipping the ball along the line in record time. Brendan Gilhooly at scrum-half slung out long, crisp passes. Eamonn Holland, the captain, at out-half marshalled his men magnificently and plotted tactics with devastating effect. Peter O'Donoghue feared no one and time and time again stopped opponents' attacks with bone-crushing tackles. Tony Gregan, outside him, carried the ball superbly jinking past centres with relative ease. On the right wing the powerfully built John O'Connor dared anyone to try and pass. On the other wing Neville O'Farrell showed a clean pair of heels to any opposition. At full-back Alan Sharkey, only in his first season of rugby, amazed all who saw him by his safe pair of hands, accurate kicking and determined defence. Alan Barlow, Dixton Larkin and Tristan Gernez on the side-line were ever anxious to pounce on any decline in standards and they too served with distinction throughout the year.

The first cup match was against St. Munchin's in Thomond Park and in horrible weather conditions Rockwell had a narrow win. An easy win over Bandon Grammar followed at Clanwilliam in the semi-final by 24-7. The final against C.B.C. at Thomond Park ended scoreless. The replay after Easter was played in Musgrave Park and again finished scoreless. The second replay a week later at Clanwilliam was again scoreless at full-time. In the last minute of the first half of extra time Rockwell kicked over the bar for the only score of the three finals. It had been a tough but fruitful campaign.

The senior team of 1983 was again trained by Fr. Meade and had visits from Willie Duggan and Hugh McGuire. Gary Halpin was on the Irish schoolboys team and the three inter-provincials were Gary Halpin, John Murphy and John Riordan. They played twenty two matches, won fifteen, drew one and lost six. They were beaten in the semi-final of the Cup by P.B.C. Fr Meade was also in charge of Second seniors and Mr. Horne in charge of third seniors. Fr. Broderick managed the under 16s. Mr. McGrath was in charge of junior cup team which was beaten in Cup semi-final. Fr. Duggan looked after the under 14s A and B which included Gabriel Fulcher on under 14 team.

The 1984 senior team won the Blackrock College Trophy in September. Then followed a trip to Belfast to play Campbell College and wins over St. Clement's, De La Salle and Munster Youths. In the Cup Rockwell had an easy win over Bandon Grammar School but lost to Crescent in the semi-final. Alan Sharkey was a promising full-back. On the wings were John O'Connor and Tony Gregan who had earlier in the season replaced the injured Neville O'Farrell. In the centre were Peter O'Donoghue and Paul McCormack. John Riordan was out-half and was capped for Munster and Ireland. The scrum-half berth was contested by Brian MacGoey and Dixton Larkin. In the front-row were Martin Commane, Barrie O'Connor and Gary Halpin. Barrie O'Connor had warded off the challenge of Joe Barrett and made the hooker position his own. In the second row were Andrew Gallagher, Seán Dookie and Paraic Madigan. The back-row emerged gradually. Both Ronan Kelly and David Williams were new to school rugby but were nursed through the first half of the season by Edmond Walsh in the back row. Others who served with distinction were Joe Barrett and Patrick Bolster. Joe played in every position in the front row and played a total of fifteen games throughout. Patrick was a vital panel member as were Conor Slattery, Anthony O'Reilly and Cathal McDonagh. Fr. Meade spent countless hours whipping that team into shape while Mr. Kenny looked after the fitness. The junior cup team of 1984 was managed by Mr. McGrath with Colm Moran as captain and Jack Clarke as vice-captain. They lost narrowly in the Cup final to P.B.C. despite a great display from Gabriel Fulcher on the wing.

For the first time since 1970 Rockwell regained the Munster Schools' Senior Rugby Cup in 1985 and achieved the victory by 22 points to 4 in the final, a winning margin quite outside the bounds of expectation and perhaps the most decisive ever recorded by the College in its long history. This was Rockwell's twenty second Cup victory. The achievement of this team began in September when it became the first school team to win the Blackrock College Trophy for the second consecutive year.

The path to the Cup decider was smooth. Rockwell accounted for Glenstal by 25 points to 9 and they beat St. Clement's by 18 points to 9. This match marked the scoring debut of out-half Barry Brosnan while Mark Cleary and Dermot Cooney combined to score the second try. Dermot was injured during this game and unfortunately missed the final but Conor Brosnan was a worthy replacement. The victory over Glenstal had come at a high price when full-back Alan Sharkey shattered his kneecap and was out for the rest of the season. Alan, who was one of the mainstays of the team, was a severe loss. Earlier in the season he had been capped for Munster in all the inter-provincials and was also selected for the Irish under 19s team which played the New Zealand schoolboys in Cork.

The final itself unveiled a superb performance, skilfully planned and clinically executed. It was the first time Rockwell had reached the final in eleven years. Mark Boyle had taken over the full-back berth from Alan Sharkey and Jack Clarke took over in the centre. Jack, who had been out of the team for most of the year due to injury, adapted well to this position and his strong running was an asset. Spurred on by a brilliant performance from the pack, Rockwell rarely looked like losing this final. They pushed CBC all over the park in the set scrums and won a fair deal of the line-out possession. A penalty from full-back, Mark Boyle, set Rockwell on course. Five minutes before the change of ends scrum-half Brian MacGoey put Rockwell further ahead with a try which was duly converted by Mark Boyle. On the stroke of half-time Barry Brosnan dropped a splendid goal from over 35 metres and Rockwell surged into a 12-0 lead at the interval.

Christians made it 12-4 in the 49th minute but any hopes of a revival were soon crushed when Brian MacGoey sent flying winger Neville O'Farrell in for the clinching score which Mark Boyle expertly converted, and in injury time Mark scored a try himself. The manager/coach of this winning team was Fr.Broderick assisted by Mr. Kenny. Pat Curran and Willie Duggan had spent time with this team during the year. Five of that team were capped for Munster, they being Martin Commane, Alan Sharkey, Brian MacGoey, Kevin Bolger and

Senior Cup Winning Team 1985
Seated: *Mark Cleary, Colm Moran, Mark Boyle, Conor Slattery, Robert O'Connell, Pat Dennehy, Martin Commane.*
1st row: *Fr. Broderick, Michael Ryan, Kevin Bolger, Jack Clarke, Chris Gibney, John O'Donoghue, Alan Sharkey, Mr. Greg Kenny*
2nd row: *Dixton Larkin, Keith Higgins, Barry Brosnan, Seamus Maher, Michael O'Brien, Dermot Cooney, Conor Brosnan, Neville O'Farrell, Brian MacGoey.*

captain Conor Slattery. Dixton Larkin, who had been injured for much of the season, had put in a courageous performance in the final. Fr. Broderick also looked after the Second and Third seniors and the under 16s. Fr. Duggan was in charge of the under 14s and Fr. Downes of the under 13s.

The junior Cup team of 1985, trained by Fr. Moloney and spurred on by pack leader Gabriel Fulcher and captain Paul Fitzgerald, lost to Pres in the first round of the Cup. The rugby league referees in 1985 were Fr. Downes, Fr. Duggan, Fr. Holohan and Fr. Knight.

The seniors failed to retain the cup in 1986 despite having eight of the previous year's team. The team of 1986 included two future Irish internationals, Gabriel Fulcher and Jack Clarke. Five of the team were inter-provincials, they being Keith Higgins, Jack Clarke, Mark Boyle, Barry Brosnan and Brian MacGoey and three of them Brian MacGoey, Jack Clarke and Keith Higgins were Irish Schoolboys' Internationals. Fr. Broderick coached the senior team in 1986 while Pat Curran and Mr. Kenny assisted with the training. Fr. Broderick also coached the Second and Third Seniors. The under 16s included Gabriel Fulcher in their line-out but failed to progress in the Bowen Shield. This team was trained by Mr. Smith who was making his debut as a rugby trainer. The junior cup team of 1986, trained by Fr. Moloney, was unlucky to lose to St. Munchin's in the semi-final. Fr. Downes made progress with the under 13s.

GAELIC GAMES

The Rockwell Gaelic Football teams between 1981 and 1986 continued to be managed by Mr. Smith with Fr. Brendan Duggan helping with the younger players. The senior team was in the A division of the Munster championship from 1981 to 1983 but returned to the B division in 1984 because of failure to progress in the previous years. The under 17s were seeking their third County Tipperary title in a row in 1981 but lost in the final by a point to Cashel C.B.S. The under 16s took part in the Frewen Cup and the under 15s in the Tipperary championship. They lost to Tipperary Vocational School in the Tipperary Cup. Rockwell had two under 14 teams in the championship each year and had an annual match with St. Brendan's College, Killarney.

When the seniors returned to the B division in 1984 they lost to Bandon Grammar School in the final. The same year the under 17 team won the Tipperary Schools competition. There were twelve teams in this competition and Rockwell beat Fethard in the first round with good displays from Colm Moran, Conor Brosnan, Alan Sharkey, Tony Gregan and Brian MacGoey. In the second round St. Joseph's Cahir were the opposition but Rockwell had an easy win by 3-10 to 0-2 with good performances from Chris Gibney, Seamus Maher, Liam Disney, Mark Boyle, Conor Brosnan, Mark Breen and Ray O'Meara. Rockwell then beat Tipperary C.B.S. and Fethard to qualify for the final against Carrick-on-Suir C.B.S., played in Clonmel. Rockwell were winners by 2-6 to 1-5. Ray O'Meara was a reliable goal-keeper. The full-back line of Conor Geaney, Conor Slattery and David Corcoran was sound. Alan Sharkey and John O'Donoghue were exceptional wing-backs and team captain Conor

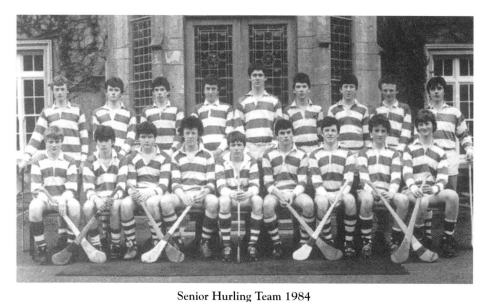

Senior Hurling Team 1984

Seated: *I. Ryan, T. Hudson, S. Finnerty , S. Farrelly, S. Ryan, S. Maher, J. Fitzgerald, P. Walshe, R. Kelly.*
Standing: *P. O'Donnell, L. Disney, R. Walsh, S. Curran, M. Boyle, N. Hanrahan, J. Cottrell,*
J. Keating, B. MacGoey.

Brosnan completed a most formidable half-back line. Tony Gregan and Seamus Maher were industrious mid-fielders. Mark Bolye was a good centre-forward and Maurice Hennessy and Chris Gibney completed a line of great potential. Noel Fitzpatrick proved an able deputy for star full-forward Tristan Gernez who missed the final through injury. Corner-forwards Brian MacGoey and Colm Moran completed a final winning team. In reserve that day were Liam Disney, Mark Breen, Michael Fitzgerald, Michael O'Connor, Maurice Farrelly and James Cottrell. In 1986 the under 14s were the winners of the Munster championship, beating St. Brendan's, Killarney in the final. The leading players on that occasion were Dara Foley, Pat Maguire, Kevin Farrell. Mark Davern, Fergal Gildea, Colm Hayes and David Redmond.

Hurling was revived in Rockwell in 1984 after a lapse of five years with senior and under 17 teams, managed by Mr. Gallagher, entered in the Tipperary championships. 1984 being the centenary of the Gaelic Athletic Association, a special hurling blitz was organised in Rockwell for County Tipperary post primary schools. Forty teams took part and the players were addressed by the President of the Association, Paddy Buggy. The centenary was also marked in Rockwell that year with a thoroughly researched article by Mr. Gallagher in the *Rockwell Annual* on the history of Gaelic games in Rockwell. Prior to the All Ireland Hurling Final of 1984, which was played in Thurles, the Artane Boys' Band stayed overnight in Rockwell.

The senior hurlers of 1985 had wins over Ballingarry and St. Mary's, Newport but lost to Tipperary C.B.S. in the semi-final. The leading players were John O'Dwyer, Mark Breen, Ian Ryan, Willie Tarrant, John Wyse, Seamus

Maher and John Waters. In 1986 the under 17 hurlers, trained by Mr. Gallagher lost narrowly to Newport in the first round of the Canon Fitzgerald Cup in which the team was: Dave Kavanagh, Barry Fitzpatrick, John Corcoran, Tom Murphy, Justin Irwin, Paschal Walsh, Paul O'Donnell, Donal Moloney, Willie Tarrent, Paul Guilfoyle, Anthony Dalton, Seán Moloney, Kieran Walsh, Don Crean, Noel O'Rourke. In earlier challenge matches against Galtee Rovers and St. Mary's, Clonmel, Billy O'Dwyer and Paul Hanrahan were prominent. The under 15 hurlers took part in the Munster B competition.

ATHLETICS

Rockwell athletes won many awards between 1981 and 1986. In 1981 Fr. Lavelle, with the help of Mr. McGrath and Fr. McDonagh, steered the athletes to success in the East Munster, Munster and All-Ireland sports in which Malachy Sheridan was dominant in the pole-vault and Gary Halpin in the shot. The sudden death of Fr. Lavelle in early 1982 was a shock to all athletes but Malachy Sheridan and Gary Halpin gave some consolation that year by again dominating the pole vault and hammer competitions. Gary Halpin represented Ireland in the Western Europen Junior Athletic Competition held in Lisbon, 31st July 1983. A hammer throw of 57.86 metres secured him first place and the only gold medal in the male section. In 1984 Gary Halpin and Jack Clarke established new records in hammer and javelin at the East Munster sports.

Rockwell athletes, under the guidance of Fr. McDonagh, Mr. McGrath and Fr. Moloney were highly successful in 1985 and 1986. In 1985 Michael Howley was dominant in the junior 200m, Rory Warner in the junior hammer and Ivan Barlow in the junior triple jump. In the intermediate grade Colm Moran was leader in the 100m hurdles, shot and discus, Jack Clarke in the javelin, and Darren Flynn was in the hammer and discus. In the senior grade Darren Flynn was first in the hammer and Neville O'Farrell was second in the 100m hurdles

All Ireland Champions 1983
Darren Flynn (junior hammer), Gary Halpin (senior hammer) and David Mansfield (intermediate hammer)

in the All Ireland. In May 1985 Rockwell was host to the first Holy Ghost inter-schools "Superstars" competition. Blackrock College, St. Michael's and Templeogue College travelled from Dublin and a very full day of sporting activity was enjoyed by the four teams. Each team had to select seven out of eight activities which included gym tests, basketball, tennis, cross-country, swimming, sprinting, canoeing and soccer. Rockwell was the winner and the team was: Pat Dennehy, Anthony Rao, Maurice Sheehan and Mussa Rassac.

In 1986 Colm Moran captained the senior athletic team and had a great personal success, coming second in the All Ireland in the shot and 110m hurdles, first in the Munster in the 110m hurdles and shot and second in the discus. Mark MacCloskey was first in the javelin at the Munster and All Ireland intermediate. Other prominent senior athletes included Conor Geaney, Paraic Cliffe, Jack Clarke, Justin Irwin and James Nolan who came first in the pole vault at East Musnter and Munster. In the intermediate section Michael Howley, Alan Glynn, Andrew McGlynn were prominent as was Gabriel Fulcher at the shot and hammer.

OTHER SPORTS

The Horse Riding Club continued to thrive under the guidance of Fr. McCool and the expertise of Mr. Garret Dooley. Early each year members concentrated on the elements of riding, jumping and hacking under the keen eye of Mr. Garrett Dooley. In 1981 the senior members, Noel Delahunty, Kevin O'Donnell and Patrick Lynch assisted by juniors Paul Lenihan, Syl Ryan and Raymond

Horse Riding Club 1981
Front: C. Brophy, J. Lynch, S. Ryan, K. Kelly, J. McInerney, I. Ryan, J. Casey.
Seated: P. Lynch, N. Delahunty, Fr. Naos McCool, K. O'Donnell, C. Moloney, S. Cagney.
1st row: M. Haughton, R. Kelly, J. O'Connor, C. O'Donovan, W. Moore, E. Leung, P. Lenihan,
M. O'Connor.
2nd row: R. Gibbons, R. O'Meara, M. O'Loughlin, A. Cronin, D. Kelleher, G. Smith, A. Hughes.

Swimming Team 1985
Seated: *A. Rao, R. Gallagher. D. McDonnell, Mrs. U. Dillon, S. Keegan, J. Clarke, Y. Fadlu-Deen*
1st row: *J. Gutierrez, G. Moroney, P. O'Donnell, K. Bolger, R. Kelly, C. Brophy, J. Doyle, A. Gomez.*
2nd row: *C. De Costa, E. Spollen, S. Azpiliceuta, R. Warner, A. Geada, R. Llorens, G. Clarke, A. Calvo.*

O'Meara began the building of the cross-country course in preparation for the Inter-schools hunter trials which Rockwell hosted in early March. The course consisted of twenty four obstacles. Forty three teams took part in the team event representing twenty seven schools from Rathnew in Wexford to Limerick. The Rockwell team of John Delahunty, Noel Delahunty and Cyril O'Donovan won the Cup. In March 1982 Rockwell entered three teams in the inter schools hunter trials at Foxboro, Co Wicklow, the riders being Kevin O'Donnell, Alexander Deon, Andrew Hughes, Paul Linehan, Gerard Smyth, Syl Ryan. Kevin O'Donnell rode his father's horse to victory in the Tipperary Hunt point-to-point, the first time a Rockwell student had won this trophy. The same year Kevin won the Fr. Barrett Memorial Trophy which was won in 1983 by Syl Ryan.

In March 1985 Rockwell participated in the sixth inter-schools hunter trials which was hosted in New Ross by St. Mary's Secondary School and in May a team competed in the inter-schools show jumping competition at Greenhills, Co. Kildare at which Paul O'Donnell, Ian Ryan, David Lynch, Harry Blackmore, Aengus McGlynn, Brian Roe, Greg Nolan and Thomas Murphy were prominent riders. At the hunter trials in New Ross in 1986 Rockwell had two teams consisting of Peter Lanigan, Thomas Murphy, James Lyons, Paul O'Donnell, David Lynch and Harry Blackmore. In the inter schools show jumping at Greenhills, Co. Kildare in 1986 Paul O'Donnell, Harry Blackmore, Ian Ryan and Dermot Owens competed. The final curtain for the Horse Riding Club each year was the performance at Parents' Day.

Senior Basketball team 1983
Seated: J. Riordan, S. Dookie, F. Martinez, E. Walsh, E. Somers.
Standing: J. McGee, J. Corry, P. Bolster, J. Asenuga, J. Gold, G. Walsh, R. Olleros.

The Canoe Club lamented the departure of Fr. Reid who had been its inspiring mentor. Fr. Seán O'Donoghue took charge of the club in 1980. In 1981 Mr. Kenny took over and proved to be an industrious and energetic coach with the high standards of the club retained. He took the canoeists on a kayak surfing trip to Tramore which was a new experience for some and was to become an annual event. The sixth annual Suir competition followed and then it was off to Limerick for the race on the Shannon. In the River Bandon race Antoin O'Looney won the McCarthy cup. The Leander Cup was retained by Rockwell in May following the Lifffey Descent. The three fastest canoeists were Morgan Madden, Brian Linehan and Thomas Carroll. Pat Hennessy and John Thompson had damaged their canoes at Lucan. Morgan Madden took first place in the under 18 class while Brian Linehan took first in the under 16 class.

The Canoe Club had a membership of nearly one hundred and twenty in 1982 and as usual beginners spent time in the College swimming pool learning the necessary basic skills. The Leander Cup winning team consisted of John Thompson, Brian Linehan, Aengus Linehan, Pat Hennessy, Michael Hurley, Adrian Madden, Killian Smith, Vincent O'Connor, Thomas Carroll, Joe Kiely and Rory Linehan. In 1983 the leading canoeists in the Liffey Descent were Aengus Linehan, Michael O'Connell and John Thompson. Aengus Linehan and Vincent Bourke were prominent in 1984 and when Rockwell won the Leander Cup for the eight consecutive year in 1985 Vincent Bourke was captain and Brian Donnelly became the new under 18 All Ireland champion. Other prominent members in 1985 were Mark Heslin, William Dwan, Rory Linehan, John Barrett, Tom Lee and Frank Purcell. The leading canoeists in 1986 included Frank Purcell, Grenville Savage, Tom Lee, Trevor Doolan, Ross Thompson, Andrew Kearney, John Barrett, Vincent Bourke, Mark Heslin and Kenneth Kelly.

Canoe Team 1981
Front: *B. MacGoey, A. Linehan, F, Buckley, A. Madden.*
Seated: *S. Kelly, A. O'Looney, B. Linehan, J. Thompson, M Madden, T. Carroll.*
Standing: *Fr. Seán O'Donoghue, T. Crowley, P. McGeogh, W. O'Sullivan, J. Corry, P. Hennessy,*
V. O'Connor, H. Maxwell, M. Hurley.

The table tennis team of 1981 consisting of Desmond Zaidan, Charles Zaidan, Ronan Reid and Brian Shaw retained the Tipperary senior championship and took part in the Cork schools championship. The swimming team directed by Mrs. Dillon competed in the annual gala with Blackrock College for the Shanahan Cup. The golf team, directed by Fr. J.C. Ryan won the Munster championship in 1982 with the team of Brian Shaw, Paul McInerney, Ian Slattery, Kevin Whelan and Declan McInerney and the team which won the Kinane Shield in 1986 at Thurles was Shane Fitzsimons, Keith Coveney, Kevin Kelleher, Ken Lavan, William Coleman, Tim Buckley, Gearóid Clarke, Barry Brosnan and Conor Brosnan.

Notes
[1]   Submission of Fr. James Hurley to DEA in January 2006.
[2]   ISR 46
[3]   ISR 527.

– 17 –

AT A CROSSROADS
1986-1992

In 1986 Rockwell found itself at a crossroads when the very future of the College raised its head for the third time in its history. The Provincial Administration decided to change the administration of Rockwell and opted to put one person at the helm who would combine the roles of President and Principal. Fr. James Hurley was appointed to this position. The *raison d'etre* for this centralisation of functions was to try and render more effective the steps that needed to be taken in planning either the phasing out of the school or its continuity.[1]

Fr. James Hurley
President 1986-1992

Fr. Colm Cunningham became vice-president having returned from Willow Park and having previously been in Rockwell from 1968 to 1979. Fr. Patrick Duggan continued as Bursar. Fr. Patrick McGlynn, who had been Dean of Studies since 1972, went to St. Michael's College and was replaced by Fr. Naos McCool. Liam Uasal Ó Duibhir continued as Deputy Principal. Sister Fabian and Sister Mechtilde who served until 1987 were the last two Sisters of St. John of God to serve in Rockwell.

Fr. Hurley took over the presidency at a difficult time for Rockwell. The Hotel and Catering School had just closed down and the student population of the secondary school had been in decline each year since 1981 and was to continue in decline up to 1990. (Appendix XI) This decline can be attributed in part to the economic depression of the 1980s in Ireland which forced the President and his Council to raise the fees to ensure the viability and future of the school.[2] It can also be attributed to the decline in popularity of boarding schools which was experienced all over Ireland at this time. Children in rural areas had previously little option to boarding but now they had free travel to second level schools in towns throughout the country. The decline in numbers led to the redeployment in 1989 and 1990 of twelve Rockwell teachers who exceeded the quota of teachers to pupils stipulated by the Department of Education.

In His Prize Day address of 1987 Father Hurley observed that the school was then at a crossroads and that some people were asking "whither Rockwell?. "In

Prize Day 1987
Fr. Comerford, Liam Ó Duibhir, Archbishop Clifford, Domhnall Blair (Union President), Dean Lee, Fr. Hurley.

this era of cutbacks and rationalisation we will only survive" he said "if people feel there is a real need for our type of school and secondly that the school offers a genuine programme of formation to meet these needs." Schools are for pupils, he said, and if these are no longer in large supply then one has to seek for reasons why and move in alternative directions.

Continuing, Fr. Hurley observed "Private high fee boarding schools may seem a luxury in our present socio-economic and political climate. The accusation of being elitist and of perpetuating a type of education that in turn keeps the privileged in a position of power and influence has been levelled against Rockwell as against other similar schools. It is difficult to counter these arguments unless the school can show that it is doing its utmost to bring Gospel values of justice and peace into prominence, not only in our own relationships within the school but above all in our awareness of the plight of our less-privileged members of society." Fr. Hurley then announced that it was the intention of the Holy Ghost Congregation to keep this educational establishment open for as long as parents saw it as a viable and productive alternative.

There appeared, he said, to be a need for a post-Leaving Certificate specialist course. Subject to Department of Education approval it was hoped to meet this need in the following September. Rockwell would initiate a special and distinct post Leaving Certificate class aimed at enabling students to get the points rating required for third level. It was hoped, he said, to market this programme and it was also envisaged that it would be co-educational. There would be specialisation in seven Leaving Certificate subjects at higher levels. Religion and Irish would be part of the on-going instruction but the core subjects in the post Leaving Certificate class, to be known as Seventh Year, would be English, Maths, Biology, Chemistry, Physics, History, Business Organisation and Economics.

In 1988 a Provincial Chapter was held in Rockwell and a recommendation was made that the future of Rockwell should be examined by an objective and scientific process. Fr. Hurley sought professional advice and he requested a member of the Education faculty at University College, Cork to initiate the process of evaluation. Dr. O'Sullivan drafted a questionnaire which he requested be sent to the parents of all current students, to a random sampling of past students and to parents of students who did not finish their studies at Rockwell for one reason or another. When Dr. O'Sullivan completed the survey, he submitted his report to the Provincial Administration. It proved to be very favourable with a strong recommendation for the continuity of the school. Accordingly, a decision was taken to continue. The report indicated a high level of all round satisfaction from parents, past pupils and others who had replied to the questionnaire. It showed that Rockwell was a school where pupils felt there was a high level of care and concern for their well-being, where they were allowed develop harmoniously and where the Catholic ethos was fostered and developed and where young men were helped to form their character and grow to be mature persons with the basic skills of goodness, uprightness, honesty and truth.

The question of accepting girls as students was discussed at a staff meeting in 1982 and there was a positive attitude among the staff for going co-educational. However the authorities decided to keep this on hold as they did not wish to create an imbalance for the teacher/pupil quotas in neighbouring schools. When the new schools for Cashel and Cahir were approved by the Department of Education it was felt that the time was ripe for Rockwell to go co-educational.[3]

The announcement that from September 1988 Rockwell would be co-educational in the day section of the school raised some eyebrows. It was unlikely to have been welcomed by the management of girls' schools in the neighbouring towns of Cashel, Cahir and Clonmel who may have feared their numbers would decline. Parents were likely to have had mixed views with some preferring the segregated system while others may have welcomed the convenience of having their sons and daughters in the same school. And of course the old arguments for and against the value of co-education were aired while some hardened rugby followers forecasted the ruination of the game in Rockwell.

NEW DEPARTURES

In September 1988 four girls made history when they enrolled as 7th Year students of Rockwell. Those brave girls were Carlyn Hawe, Marita McGrath, Patricia Moroney and Valerie Strappe. Writing in the *Rockwell Annual* of that

The first Girl Students 1988
Valerie Strappe, Fr. Hurley, Carlyn Hawe and Patricia Moroney.

year Carlyn Hawe described her ordeal. As she sat in the car outside on the first morning she began to have second thoughts when a stampede of boys pounded by. And as she entered from the rain into the main hall, with a hundred staring faces lining the wall on either side she found it difficult to walk straight as she tried to remember where the Girls' Common Room was so that she could go and hide. When she found her three colleagues the tension eased and as the days passed by, the four of them together began to enjoy the attention and the kindness of the Rockwell staff, especially, according to Carlyn, that of Liam Uasal Ó Duibhir and Iníon Ní Mhurchadha. They also enjoyed certain privileges such as skipping the queue at mealtimes and getting immediate counter-top attention in the Dab Shop. Rockwell needed to make adjustments too, she felt, as when in her first report home she was named as Master Carlyn Hawe. Real equality for girls, she felt, would not have come until she could congratulate the first female Rockwellian on getting her name down on Mr. Tony Smith's list on the senior notice board to "be out for SCT rugby training at 4.15 p.m. sharp."

While only four girls arrived in Rockwell in 1988 the number grew each year. It reached thirty three in 1989 and by the end of Fr. Hurley's presidency in 1992 it had reached eighty three and in future years was to reach nearly twice that number. Responsibility for the girls in the fist two years was entrusted to Mrs. Una Dillon and Mrs. Noirin Woodlock and in 1991 and 1992 to Miss Wini Ryan with the title of House Mistress for Girls. The girls integrated remarkably well both in academic and leisure activities and many members of the teaching staff felt that the girls had exercised a refining influence over the boys. The arrival of girls in Rockwell was generally regarded as a success story.

The 7th Year programme initiated in 1988, and coinciding with the arrival of the girls, had twenty four students in its first year, including the four girls and four of Rockwell's 6th Years of the previous years who were repeating their Leaving Certificate. The remaining sixteen students, boys and girls, were all

Seventh Year 1988
Seated: *Niall Cantwell, Kieran Hartigan, Carlyn Hawe, Patricia Moroney, Liam Uas. Ó Duibhir,*
Valerie Strappe, Marita McGrath, Edward Grimson, Robert Galvin.
Standing: *Stephen Connolly, Mel Mannion, Patrick O'Sullivan, Fergal Owens, Seán Doyle,*
Dylan Dalton, Michael Kent, Milo Gleeson, Seamus McDwyer, Paul Tallis.

day-boarders from all regions of County Tipperary. The number in 7th Year had
reached forty by 1992. The increase can be explained firstly because a high
number of students achieved the points they required and secondly because at
that time Rockwell was the only school in Tipperary offering such a programme.

Another development during Fr. Hurley's presidency was the increase in the
number of day pupils. Since its foundation in 1864 the number of day pupils
had been confined to students from the immediate neighbourhood and the sons
of staff members and often numbering less than ten. The fact that Rockwell was
in the middle of sparsely populated countryside at a time of limited travel
facilities was partly a reason for this. From the early 1970s the number of day
pupils began to increase but boarders remained in an overwhelming majority.
In 1986 the number of day pupils reached its highest ever at seventy two which
was 17% of the total student population. Within the next five years there was
a dramatic annual increase and in 1991 for the first time in the history of
Rockwell there were more day pupils than boarders. (Table 17.1) A downside
of the increase of Day pupils was an increase in absenteeism for Saturday class
with the result that it was abandoned in 1992 and a new programme of week-
end activities devised for boarders.

TABLE 17.1: NUMBER OF DAY PUPILS AND GIRLS IN ROCKWELL 1986-1991

Year	Total population	Day Pupils	Girls
1986	412	72	-
1987	397	85	-
1988	366	109	4
1989	353	155	33
1990	399	202	53
1991	463	259	81

Source: RCA 1986-1991.

Girl Students 1989
Seated: A. Casey, J. Gomez-Pablos, D. Gildea, P. Power, S. Foley, Mrs. N. Woodlock, E. Finn,
L. Carrigan, A. Coleman, S. O'Reilly, C. Malone.
1st row: R. O'Meara, G. O'Connor, A. O'Donnell, O. English, Marie Ryan, C. Glynn,
L. Montojo, Y. Kennedy, L. Timoney, C. Corbett, D. Maher.
2nd row: P. Glynn, Marguerite Ryan, S. Flood, E. McGrath, E. Mulcahy, D. Fitzgibbon, T. Ryan,
E. O'Reilly, A. English, M. Disney.

The increase in the number of day pupils was due in part to major changes in post primary education structures in the neighbouring towns of Cashel and Cahir. In 1984 a Community School involving the amalgamation of the three existing post primary schools in the town was planned for Cashel. Because of the severe financial restraints of the 1980s, the Department of Education kept deferring the plan and Cashel Community School did not open until 1994. Similar plans were afoot for the amalgamation of the three post primary schools in Cahir and Coláiste Dún Iascaigh finally opened in 1997. As both towns awaited their new schools there was an air of uncertainty among parents which made Rockwell seem a stable option.

Concern Debating Team 1988
Seated:
Ronan Quirke,
Mr. Frawley,
Damien Tomkins.
Standing:
Aidan O'Connell,
Mark Buckley.

Rockwell offered other attractions. In the late 1980s Rockwell was the only school in County Tipperary offering a supervised night study for its students. This was attractive to some parents who may have worried that their children did not pay sufficient attention to study. It was also attractive in situations where both parents were working. The sporting facilities at Rockwell were also an attraction as was the College's reputation as a centre of learning for more than a century.

ANNUAL PRIZE DAY

During Fr. Hurley's presidency the tradition of a distinguished guest presenting awards on Prize Day continued. In 1987 it was the newly consecrated Archbishop Dermot Clifford who was abiding by the accustomed close ties between the archdiocese and Rockwell maintained by his predecessors. In the following three years the guest was a distinguished past student. In 1988 it was Dr. Seán McCarthy, Minister for Science and Technology followed in 1999 by the President of Ireland Dr. Patrick Hillery and in 1990 by the Attorney General, John L. Murray. Mrs. Mary O'Rourke, Minister for Education, was guest in 1991 and in 1992 it was the Apostolic Nuncio to Ireland, Archbishop Emmanuele Gerada. The presence of these guests was a measure of Rockwell's standing in society.

Prize Day was an occasion when unique achievements in College life were noted. In 1987 a 6th Year student, Peter Power, became the first ever young Irishman to receive the Dermot Harris Memorial Scholarship. This newly instituted scholarship, tenable for four years at the University of Scranton, Pennsylvania, U.S.A. provided complete support to promising young Irish men and women. Dermot Harris was a brother of the renowned actor Richard Harris

Music Awards 1989
Seated: *A. Mackey, Ms Margaret Lynch, F. Hurley*
Standing: *C. O'Sullivan, K. MacDonagh, D. Lee, T. Conway, J. Purcell.*

and had completed his Leaving Certificate in Rockwell in 1945. It was also in 1987 that ten young Irish men and women went to the United States, they being the first to be chosen by the Irish-American Partnership under a unique new scholarship scheme to learn new skills and to bring them back to help development in Ireland. One of the students awarded a scholarship was 6th Year student Robert Disney from Springmount, Clonmel who studied physics at St. Joseph's University, Philadelphia.

Prize Day 1988
Gay Mangan (Union President) Dr. Seán McCarthy (Minister of State for Science, Fr. Hurley.

At Prize Day 1988 the family of the late Denis Jones of Askeaton, Co. Limerick, presented a trophy to the College. The trophy and replica, known as the Denis Jones Cup were to be awarded each year to the Rockwell student who achieved the highest result in the Leaving Certificate. Denis Jones, a Rockwell student of the 1920s died in 1987. He was a Fine Gael T.D. for Limerick and a former Leas Ceann Comhairle of Dáil Éireann.

At Prize Day 1991 Fr. Hurley welcoming Mrs O'Rourke said that since she became minister much had been achieved in the domain of education such as the steering through of the new junior curriculum, the computerisation of exam results and individual print-out results, the rationalisation of entry for third level through the centralisation of CAO and CAS, the establishment of two new universities in Limerick and Dublin, the establishment of a parents' council and the opening up of the debate towards the introduction of an Education Act.

STUDENT ACTIVITIES AND ACHIEVEMENTS

At Prize Day 1988 Fr. Hurley congratulated the boys and girls on the manner in which they had allowed the co-educational experience to develop in a normal and wholesome manner. Boys and girls took part in most of the usual activities alongside of each other. They took part in the efforts to help the missions each year in a new method devised in 1989 by Fr Downes and Fr. McDonagh whereby flag days were organised in the surrounding towns of Cashel, Cahir, Clonmel and Thurles and raising more than a £1,000 each year.

Boys and girls were noted among the Galaxy winners. This was the annual reward for students who had performed well throughout the year in the notes system. Around the middle of May those rewarded departed by bus for a day's outing to a surprise destination under the supervision of Fr. McCool and An tUasal Ó Duibhir. Students who had performed well in other areas were also

Flag Day for the Missions 1992
Seated: *P. Sebuliba, V. McHugh, J. Phelan, M. Hanrahan, Fr. P. Downes, D. Walsh, A. Kearney,*
D. Walsh, A. Gildea.
Standing: *D. Hennessy, J. Morrison, O. Ryan, R. Deane, O. Frawley, M. Dineen, R. Enright,*
M. Dwan, T. Horgan, K. Rockingham.

rewarded. In 1988, for instance two final year students, Michael Quinn and Jonathan Boylan were given awards by Memory Ireland for their computer programme on school records and reports. They had devised this programme in the Computer Club under the direction of Fr. Brian O'Connor. In 1990 Nora Heffernan gained second prize in the Government sponsored European essay competition for which she received a week in Berlin and a financial reward. In 1991 Clodagh Beresford of 5th Year acquired the Lamda Bronze and Silver medals with honours for public speaking. The same year Kevin Ryan and James Phelan entered their project on iodine deficiency in the intermediate section of the Aer Lingus Young Scientist competition for which they were rewarded.

The Rockwell Debating Society was directed in turn by Mr. Frawley, Mr. Morris, Mr. Power and Mr. King. Teams were entered for debates organised by the Philosophical Society of University College Cork and other organisations such as Concern and the Soroptomists. The highlight was the end of year debate organised by Mr. King at which the James Joy senior debating gold medal was awarded. The winner in 1990 was the future well-known journalist, Pat Leahy. A guest adjudicator was invited each year and in 1992 this function was performed by past student Mr. Gerard Danaher S.C.

In 1987 Rockwell decided to enter new territory in its extra curricular activity by joining the contemporary craze, i.e. the quiz scene. Under the tutelage of Mr. Power a four-man team was selected. Gary O'Mahony, Peter Power, Niall Madigan, Brian Kennedy and substitute Ray Moroney took part in a competition open to all secondary schools in South Tipperary and won the prize of £250. The quiz craze continued each year.

Mr. Leahy continued his promotion of the Young Ireland group. In 1987 Ronan O'Connor was voted Young Ireland Student of the Year in recognition of the work he had done in setting up new branches in South Tipperary. The Rockwell branch held action days in local towns when leaflets were distributed encouraging people to buy Irish goods. Poster competitions were arranged and table quizzes were organised to raise funds for charity.

Drama and music continued as popular ingredients of student life. Mr Irwin and Mr. Gallagher produced Bernard Farrell's black comedy *I do not like thee Dr. Fell* in 1987 with parts played by Damien Tomkins, Aidan King, Jason Rock, Justin Doyle, Michael Purtill, Richard Beirne and Justin Irwin. The following year Philip King's comic farce *See How they Run* was the choice and it was the last production of the duo who had done so much for the promotion of drama in Rockwell. For the remainder of Fr.

Pat Leahy, Debater of the year 1990 with his father Mr. Seamus Leahy

Hurley's presidency plays were produced by Mr. Oliver Nolan. *The Importance of Being Earnest* was his choice in 1989 and *Charley's Aunt* by Brandon Thomas in 1990 with parts played by John O'Keeffe, Aidan Mackey, Martin Moloney, Michael Kennedy, Darragh Howard, Jonathan Davis, Eimear O'Reilly and Saoirse Fahey. Brian Friel's *Translations* was performed in 1991 when the actors were Damien Copas, Frank Broderick, Orla Kelleher, John O'Keeffe, Michael Kennedy, Aaron Glynn, Billy Murphy, Ruth Underhill, Mary-Beth Jennings and Martin Moloney. *A Man for All Seasons* by Robert Bolt was the choice in

Concern Debating Team 1992
Gregory Doran, Clodagh Beresford, Fiona Fahey, Robert MacGoey.

Young Irelanders 1987
Arthur Minion,
Harry Blackmore
(with de Valera trophy),
Ronan O'Connor,
Mr. Seamus Leahy
(coordinator)

1992 with parts played by Mary-Beth Jennings, Aaron Glynn, Aisling Gildea, Damien Copas, Gary Colbert, Gregory Doran, James Bolger, Shane McKeon, Michael Kennedy, Tom Horgan, Frank Broderick, Caroline Keane and Brendan Clery. Providing delightful renditions of Handel and Bach at the interval were flautists Dervla O'Sullivan, David Fahey and John Maher and pianist Fionn Hurley.

Fr. Moloney and Miss Lynch directed the Musical Society with recitals each year by eminent musicians including pianists Anthony Byrne, Philip Byrne and Brian McNamara. Fr. Moloney directed three choirs, one of which took part in the Sunday liturgy.

Students interested in continental languages enjoyed lingering in *Le Coin Français* that quiet corner which was a mini-library where students from 2nd Year up could come and browse through books and magazines and listen to tapes and read newspapers under the supervision of Miss Keating and Miss Ni Lannagáin. The Stamp Club under the direction of Fr. Knight was popular with boarders on Sunday mornings. Students with notions of journalism could hone their skills on the *Rock Magazine* which made an occasional appearance. In 1987 it was published by Karl Llewellyn, Justin Doyle, Darren Hudson and Ray Moroney and in 1989 by Gavin Burke as editor assisted by Paula Glynn and Mark Davern.

Soroptomists Debate 1991
Janet Frawley, Jill Walsh.

The annual school tour at Easter under the direction of Mr. King continued to be popular. In 1987 it headed for Moscow and Leningrad, flying from Shannon airport on Aeroflot. It visited a European city in each of the following years and was popular with teachers because it was always during holiday-time with no class-time missed.

CANOE CLUB

The Leander Cup had come to Rockwell in the nine previous years and was to be won again in each year of Fr. Hurley's presidency. Each season commenced with a series of regattas leading up to the Liffey Descent in May. Ross Thompson and John Barrett were joint captains in 1987 when under the direction of Mr. Kenny the Leander Cup was won for the tenth successive time. Together with the joint captains other prominent members that year were Glenville Savage, Kenneth Kelly and Brian Enright. The following year Kenneth Kelly was captain and Andrew Kearney vice-captain and other prominent members were Michael Morrissey, Barry Ivan, John Lehane, Eamon O'Sullivan, Ross Thompson, Bernard Brady and J.J. O'Hara. Following Mr. Kenny's departure from Rockwell Mr. McGrath took charge and when the Leander was won for the twelfth time in 1989 Michael Morrissey was captain and Barry Ivan vice-captain and for the first time three ladies, Alma English, Olive English and Amy O'Donnell, were on the Rockwell winning team. Gerry Rockingham was captain in 1990 and with him in the winners' enclosure were Michael Morrissey, Thomas Neilson, Gus Kearney, Alma English and Amy O'Donnell. In 1991 Gus Kearney was captain and Thomas Neilson vice-captain and they were winners in the Liffey Descent with Gerry Rockingham, Amy O'Donnell, Tarion O'Carroll, Alan O'Dwyer, David Fahey, John Quinlan, Vincent McHugh, James Hally and Cian O'Donoghue. When the Leander Trophy was won for the fifteenth successive year in 1992 James Hally was captain and Cian O'Donoghue vice-captain and they were among the winners at the Liffey Descent with Tarion O'Carroll, David Fahey, Amy O'Donnell, Gerry Rockingham, Tom O'Connor, Tom Neilson, Vincent McHugh, John Quinlan and Michael O'Dwyer.

SENIOR RUGBY

Fr. Broderick coached the S.C.T. in these years. He had the assistance of Mr. Smith and Mr. Dillon and the advice at times of past students Pat Curran, Brian MacGoey, Gary Halpin and Johnny Riordan. The usual pre-Cup matches were played annually.

Gabriel Fulcher captained the 1987 team which lost in the first round to St. Clement's and Gabriel was an inter-provincial that year with Paul Fitzgerald and James Nolan. The following year Tom P. Nolan captained the side, which included inter-provincials John Lane and J.J. O'Hara and which lost to Crescent in the first round of the Cup. In 1989 Seán Moloney was captain of the side which beat St. Enda's in the first round but lost to Crescent in the semi-final. Jeremy Browne was honoured with an Irish jersey that year and he and Frank Fitzgerald were inter-provincials.

Colm Hayes captained the team in 1990 which included internationals Frank Fitzgerald and Denis O'Dowd, both of whom were accompanied on the Munster team by Frank Hogan. The team reached the Cup final for the first time in six years having defeated St. Clement's and St. Munchin's but losing in the final to Crescent. Rockwell was back in the final in 1991 when Mark Smyth was captain and an inter-provincial. Easy wins were recorded against St. Ita's (Newcastlewest), Newtown,

Irish Schoolboy Internationals 1990 Frank Fitzgerald and Denis O'Dowd

St. Enda's and St. Clement's but losing narrowly in the final to PBC.

Denis Finn was captain and an inter-provincial in 1992. Because of falling numbers Rockwell competed in the B competition for the Mungret Cup. The usual pre-Cup fixtures included a trip to Methodist College, Belfast before Christmas. Early Mungret Cup victories were recorded over Waterpark and Midleton followed by a win over Ard Scoil Rís in a hard-fought semi-final. The final was against St. Enda's, and thanks to tries by James Finn and Danny O'Sullivan, Rockwell led at the interval by 10-6. A drop-goal by Dermot O'Brien in the second half and a try by James Morrison converted by Dermot assured victory. In the front-row were Anthony O'Donoghue, Jason O'Dea and John Dineen and in the second row Rafael Sanchez and Wayne O'Dwyer. Michael English and Denis Malone were in the back-row with Denis Finn at Number 8. Scrum half was Colin Murphy with Dermot O'Brien at out-half. The centre positions were filled by Paul Morrissey and Eamon Foley. On the wings were James Morrison and Danny O'Sullivan. James Finn was full back and on the bench were David Walsh, Vincent Peters, Frank Ryan, Shane Foley, Aiden McHugh, Simon Hayes, Declan O'Hanlon and John Murphy.

JUNIOR RUGBY

Fr. Moloney coached the J.C.T. in these years, playing nearly twenty matches in each season but with victories in Cup campaigns hard to come by. First round Cup defeats to Crescent in 1987 and to P.B.C. in 1988 were followed by defeat to St. Munchin's in the 1989 semi-final. The semi-final was reached again in 1990 with victories over Mallow, St. Nessan's and St. Munchin's before defeat to a much bigger P.B.C. side. Rockwell lost in the early stages of the Cup in 1991 and 1992. In those years Fr. Broderick coached the under 16s with Mr McGrath in charge of the under 14s and Fr. Downes the under 13s. Fr. Duggan, Mr. Dillon, Mr. Moran and Mr. Doyle were also involved with teams.

GAELIC GAMES

Mr. Doyle was coach to the senior and under 17 football teams. The senior team, captained by John Hennessy, drew with Douglas in the quarter-final of the Munster championship of 1987 but lost the replay. The under 17s that year lost to Fethard. The seniors of 1988, captained by Eddie Golden, reached the semi-final of the Munster B championship with victories over St. Clement's and St. Patrick's (Shannon) but lost in the semi-final to Skibereen. The under 17s of 1988, captained by Seán Moloney, had great success when they won the Corn Mhic Gabhann. They beat Nenagh C.B.S., Carrick-on-Suir C.B.S. and St. Joseph's Borrisoleigh before beating Tipperary C.B.S. in the final by 2-3 to 1-5. On the winning panel were: Pat McGuire, Mark Cronin, Jeremy Browne, Eoin Lonergan, Donal O'Connell, Damien Tompkins, Ross Thompson, David Geoghan, Colm Hayes, Kevin O'Connell, Frank Fitggerald, John Purcell, Ronan Maher, Declan Moloney, Darragh Foley, Eddie Golden, Brian Donovan, Seán Moloney, Tom.Ryan, Ray Moroney, Seán Fitzpatrick. Denis O'Dowd, Ronan Maher, Pat O'Donoghue. Pat Ryan.

The seniors of 1989 were captained by Seán Moloney and lost in the quarter final to Patrician College, Mallow. Pat McGuire captained the under 17s of 1989 which lost in the semi-final to Cashel C.B.S. Pat McGuire was captain of the seniors in 1990 which lost to St. Flannan's while Robert Hunt captained the under 17s which lost in the final to Clonmel High School. Gavan McGuirk captained the seniors of 1991 which drew twice with St. Augustine's, Dungarvan and lost by a point in extra time in the second replay. The under 17s of 1991, captained by Martin Fagan, lost by a point to Nenagh in the first round.

A feature of Gaelic Football in those years was the annual county Tipperary under 14 blitz held in Rockwell and attracting more that twenty teams. Another

Corn Mhic Gabhainn Champions 1988
Seated: *D. Foley, E. Golden, B. Donovan, S. Moloney, T. J. Ryan, R. Moroney, S. Fitzpatrick.*
Middle: *Mr. M. Doyle, R. Thompson, R. Geoghegan, C. Hayes, K. O'Connell, F. Fitzgerald, J. Purcell, R. Maher, D. Moloney.*
Back: *P. McGuire, M. Cronin, J. Browne, E. Lonergan, D. O'Connell, D. Tomkins.*

feature was the annual fixture between Rockwell and St. Brendan's College, Killarney.

Mr. Gallagher, with assistance from Mr. Leahy was coach to the under 17 hurling team which had a big win over Templemore Vocational School in the first round of the Canon Fitzgerald Cup in 1987. The team was captained by Brian Kennedy and other leading players included Pat McGuire, Seán Moloney, Barry Fitzpatrick, Tom Murphy, Barry Joyce and goalkeeper Dave Kavanagh. Rockwell lost in the second round to Killenaule Vocational School. Seán Moloney captained the under 16s in the Croke Cup that year which lost narrowly to St. Joseph's Borrisoleigh. Following Mr. Gallagher's retirement Fr. Duggan took charge of the under 17s and Mr. O'Mahony of the under 15s. Meanwhile Mr. Phil Lowry of the Tipperary County Board provided coaching in hurling to 1st years.

OTHER SPORTING AND OUTDOOR ACTIVITIES

During Fr. Hurley's presidency Fr. Downes was Games Master and he organised a wide range of sporting activities, with house leagues in each term in all field sports being very popular. Fr. McDonagh was in charge of athletics with the assistance of Fr. Moloney and Mr. McGrath. The intermediate relay team of Michael Howley, Ivan Barlow, Alan Glynn and Stephen Connolly came first in the Munster and All Ireland championship of 1987. Donagh Sheridan had good performances in those years at the pole-vault as had Gabriel Fulcher and Kevin Warner at the hammer. The Finn brothers, Denis and James, were prominent sprinters. Rockwell took part in triangular sports each year with Roscrea and Clongowes Wood.

Mr. Crotty, with the assistance of Mr. Fitzgibbon and Mr. Mason, started the Adventure Sports Group in 1987 to promote mountaineering and orienteering.

Senior Athletic Team 1986
Seated: C. Geaney, K. Hanahoe, J. Clarke, C. Moran, J. Nolan, I. Kiernan.
Standing: P. Cliffe, D. Flynn, G. Fulcher, T. Madigan, J. Irwin, E. McMahon, A. McGlynn.

Mr. Kenny organised mountain climbs on the Galtees while orienteering events were organised in the Glen of Aherlow, in Ballyhooley, Co. Cork, in Rehill Wood near Cahir and in Glengarra Wood near Mitchelstown. Mr. Fitzgibbon organised these events after the departure of Mr. Crotty and Mr. Kenny. Badminton was organised by Mr. Fogarty, Mr. Golden and Miss Ryan while basketball teams were trained in turn by Mr. Doyle, Mr. Townsend, Mr. Dillon and Miss Ryan. Hockey became the principal sport for girls and by 1992 Miss Ryan had a team for

Donagh Sheridan sets a new record in pole vault, 1989

each of the five years and that year entered a girls' team in the County Gymnastics Competition. Mr. O'Donoghue and Mr. Golden managed soccer teams which competed against local clubs. *Tae kwon do*, the modern martial art was introduced to Rockwell by Mr. Foley in 1992.

Fr. Downes succeeded Fr. J.C. Ryan as manager of the golf team which in 1998 won the Munster section of the Aer Lingus Schools competition, the team members being Keith Coveney, Kevin Kelliher, John Lavan, Gavin McGuirk and John Fitzsimon. The following year the team members were John Fitzsimon, Michael McCarthy, Ken Hall, Edward Morrision, Gavin McGuirk and Shane O'Donoghue who later became an internationally known golf commentator. Con O'Driscoll, Emmet Leahy, Alan O'Rourke and Thomas O'Donnell represented Rockwell in 1992. Tennis was organised by Mr. Kenny and later by Miss Ryan and tournaments were organised with Cistercian College Roscrea,

Horse Riding Team 1987
K. Llewellyn,
Fr. N. McCool,
T. E. Murphy,
W. Murphy.

Basketball 1989
Seated: V. Kennedy, O. English, S. Foley, A. English, E. McGrath.
Standing: A. O'Donnell, L. Montojo, P. Power, E. Finn, M. Disney.

Basketball 1991
Seated: T. Hanley, H. Howley, F. Fahey, A. O'Donnell, R. Bell, A. English.
Standing: T. Kinane, T. Fitzgerald, E. Barron, E, McGrath, Mr. Dillon.

Glenstal, Blackrock College and St. Michael's. The Munster Under 19A Cup returned to Rockwell in 1991 for the first time since 1967 when the winning players were Brian Hobbart, James Bolger, Denis Heffernan and Colm O'Mahony.

Mrs Dillon organised the annual swimming gala against Blackrock College for the Shanahan Cup and courses in water safety which in 1990 and 1991 were organised by Mr. Conor Dillon. Fr. McCool continued to look after the Horse Riding Club where beginners were introduced to the elements of riding, hacking, jumping and care of both animals and tack under the keen eye of Mr. Garret Dooley. A team was entered for the inter-schools hunter trials each year in which prominent riders included Thomas Murphy, Karl Llewellyn, William Murphy, Callaghan Cotter, Ronan Rooney, Alan O'Hanlon, Declan Lee, Michael Byrne and Jody Keating. The Fr. Barrett Memorial Cup was keenly contested each year and for the first time in 1991 it was won by a lady, Anthea Browne.

RETIREMENTS
Five members of the lay teaching staff retired during Fr. Hurley's presidency. Criostóir Gallagher retired in 1988 having been on the staff since 1968 as teacher of Irish and English while also teaching in the Hotel and Catering School. Criostóir was a past student of Rockwell and a man of great musical and dramatic talent for which he was noted throughout Tipperary. He put this talent to use in Rockwell when he assisted Mr. Irwin in many dramatic productions. He was passionate about the game of hurling and managed several Rockwell hurling teams and researched the history of hurling in the College.

Willie Gaynor took early retirement in 1991. An Art teacher, he was himself an artist of exceptional ability. He was extremely popular with students and staff and his unhurried style and unflappability was the envy of his colleagues. He had a wide knowledge of animal and bird lore and his discussions on such topics were both enlightening and entertaining. His gentle nature had a wide appeal.

Joe Frawley had been in Rockwell since 1966 and at various times he had taught Latin, English, History and Irish and to all his classes he brought the fruits of wide and discerning reading. He was generous with his time after hours, and despite a career that was dogged by ill-health, he coached for many years debating teams with marked success.

ROCKWELL UNION
The Union presidents during Fr. Hurley's presidency were Bernard Flusk, Domhnall Blair, Gay Mangan, Andy Butler, Matt P.O'Mahony, Jim Peters and Risteard Ó Colmáin. Domhnall Blair is the third member of his family to hold the position, his father and uncle having previously held it.

In 1986 Bernard Flusk reminded members of the importance of the Membership Information Project. He said that they then had on computer the names and addresses of nearly three thousand past students. He said the Membership Information Project was viewed as a two-way process. It was hoped

Union Dinner 1986
Fr. Holohan, Bernard P. Flusk (Union President) and John Rogers (Attorney General and past student)

to reach an even larger number of past students and inform them of Union activities and objectives. At the same time it was hoped that they would c o r r e s p o n d - ingly support the Union and thereby support Rockwell College in its vital educational mission. Despite this ambition, there were only three hundred and fifty paid up members in 1987. A copy of the Union newsletter was sent in 1988 to all past students on the Union list. By 1992 the Union had organisers in North West, West, Mid-West, Northern Ireland and Britain.

Financial contributions were made to the College and to the missionary projects of past students Fr. John C. O'Mahony in Kenya, Fr. Peter Queally in Sierra Leone and Fr. Brendan Carr in Angola. All five Holy Ghost Unions joined forces in a fund-raising drive for the missions.

In May 1987 a new constitution was adopted. It superseded the constitution which had served the Union since 1948. Past students who were forty years out in 1990 were rather startled at the celebration in Rockwell when one of their members, George G. Moloney from Cavan, arrived by helicopter and landed in front of the College Chapel. The annual Retreat, dinners and golf outings were held as usual. In 1990 a dinner was held in London for the first time and in 1992 a dinner was held in Washington.

ROCKWELL AGRICULTURAL COLLEGE

The personnel with responsibility in the Agricultural College during Fr. Hurley's

Union Dinner 1988
Fr. Hurley, Domhnall Blair (Union President), John L. Murray (Attorney General and past student)

The Class of '61
John L. Murray
(Attorney General),
Andy Butler (Union
President),
Senator Maurice Manning.

presidency were: Principal: Fr. Bernard Frawley. Chaplain: Fr. John Fallon. Crop Production: William Gleeson, Michael Prendergast. Dairying: Pat Hayes, William Dwyer. Horticulture: Eileen Murphy. Building Construction: Br. Senan Smith. Farm Manager: Jim Tracey. Livestock: John O'Dwyer, John O'Connor, John J. O'Dwyer, John Crosse. Machinery: Val O'Connor, John Hennessy, Br. Gerard Cummins. Poultry: Mrs. E. Nolan. Secretary: Miss Breda O'Donnell.

The 1980s introduced a new era as the Agricultural Colleges around the country passed from the control of the Department of Agriculture and became part of a new body A.C.O.T. An Comhairle Oiliúna Talamhaíochta, Council of Development in Agriculture. The new body was dedicated to training and education and had to look at the total scene of people entering farming.

At the beginning of each school year in September the Agricultural College accommodated two courses for adult farmers who wished to do a management

Macra na Feirme Efficiency Team 1988
Front: *J. Hayes, P.J. Ryan, D. Maher, M. Corbett, H. Delaney.*
Back: *Mr. William Dwyer, H. Bourke, M. Foran, K. O'Connell, R. Barry, J. Heffernan, Fr. Frawley.*

course so that they would be eligible for the stamp duty exemption at that time in operation by the government to enable the transfer of land to young people. In total the college accommodated 240 in these two courses. Prior to this five weeks in June/July had been given over to courses to fulfil the college part of the Certificate in Farming. It was not difficult to fill the 110 places in the residential one-year course. In 1997 the number of girls increased to nine. The transfer of land to women was no longer frowned upon. In the late 1980s the overwhelming number of students who went through Rockwell found immediate employment.

During term the College was used as a venue for conferences and seminars both by Teagasc and the Irish Farmers' Association. The I.F.A. seminar of 1990 was attended by Alan Gillis, President of the Association. Students were active in Macra na Feirme and attended the annual National Ploughing Championship and Spring Show.

Rockwell continued to dominate in sport, especially in Hurling and Gaelic football. In 1990 the hurlers won the All Ireland for the third time with victories over Gurteen and Multhfarnham and in the final over Mellows College, Athenry played at Cusack Park, Ennis. The hurlers won the All Ireland again in 1992 when the winning players were: Pat Reynolds, Tom O'Riordan, Anthony O'Gorman, John Murphy, Paul Phelan, Larry Quinn, Mark Leonard, Donal O'Brien, James Sheehan, Joe Murphy, Pádraig Bourke, Owen Dalton, Tom Cantwell, Aidan Meade, Ken Cummins.

OBITUARIES

John L. Buckley died on March 18th 1986. He had been on the teaching staff of Rockwell for forty five years. A past student of North Monastery, Cork and a graduate of U.C.D., John joined the staff of Rockwell in 1928. As a teacher of Science and Applied Mathematics, he was deeply respected by his students and colleagues. He was a founder member of the Tipperary branch of the A.S.T.I. and one of its earliest chairmen. He gave valuable service to the town of Cashel as a member of its Urban District Council. John Buckley was forthright in expressing his views on many subjects, especially politics, history and education. He greeted the advent of a broadly based post-primary curriculum with great enthusiasm. He was a man of consummate integrity and deep Catholic faith.

Gerry Hayes died in 1987. He had been teaching in Rockwell for forty two years and was a familiar figure to generations of boys and countless members of the Holy Ghost Congregation. His interest in history was legendary and his favourite subjects on which

Mr. John L. Buckley who retired in June 1973

he spoke with much authority and conviction were the English Reformation, the French Revolution and the fall of Parnell. His taste in literature was that of the old Catholic scholar and his views on life itself, as on literature, were the products of a profoundly Catholic background. He had a particular liking for Belloc and Chesterton with their Catholic view of history.

John McGrath, a member of the maintenance staff for thirty five years, died in June 1988. He was a droll character who never failed to see the bright side of life. His outstanding characteristic was his concern for others. Mrs Peggy Joyce, who worked in the linen room for many years, died in 1988. She was regular in her work and always cheerful when meeting people.

Dr. Daniel Murphy C.S.Sp. died in 1988. Born in Knocknagoshel in 1890, he came to Rockwell in 1903. He later earned an M.A. in classics from the National University and a doctorate in philosophy and theology from University of Fribourg in Switzerland. He returned to Rockwell as Dean of Studies in 1924 and held this position for ten years. In 1934 he became Provincial of the Irish Province of the Holy Ghost Congregation, a position he held until 1948 when he went to East Africa as Superior of the missionary priests of the Congregation serving in that area. In 1950 he was appointed Procurator General of the Congregation to the Holy Sea in Rome. He remained in this position until 1962 when he went back to Fribourg as Director of the International Scholasticate. In 1968 he retired to Kilshane and in 1984 to Rockwell.[4]

Ciarán Blair died on 28th November 1988. He became a Rockwell student in 1932 and was a life-long generous supporter of the Rockwell Union of which he was president in 1970. He was looked on as father-figure in the engineering profession and was held in great respect and affection by his colleagues. He had a genuine love for Rockwell and a deep concern for its well-being.

John J. Nash died in a road accident in Gran Canaria in 1988. He was President of the Rockwell Union in 1966-68. Elected to Seanad Éireann in 1961 he served with distinction for twelve years. He was a life-long member of the Incorporated Law Society and President of it in 1961. He had legal practices in Thurles and Templemore.

Michael Ryan died in November 1990. He farmed next-door to Rockwell He was only 47. He was a member of the famous Ryan sporting family with Rockwell associations in the early 1900s. He was an outstanding athlete in his youth excelling at the 400m and was offered a scholarship to Villanova University but turned it down in favour of his commitment to his business.

Fr. Tom Maher C.S.Sp. a native of Knockraffon died in 1991. Born in Lagganstown, New Inn, he had been a student in Rockwell from 1918 to 1921 and on joining the Holy Ghost Congregation he was ordained in 1930. He was assigned to Kenya where he was to spend the next fifty one years. He was among those who welcomed Edel Quinn to Kenya, giving her his full support in her work as an envoy of the Legion of Mary. He was to be at her death bed years later to say the last prayers for her. In 1982 he retired to Rockwell but was always ready to help in local parish work and as confessor.[5]

Fr. Michael J. O'Connor died in 1992. Born in Dingle, Co. Kerry in 1915 he received his secondary education in Rockwell and was among the first group to do their novitiate in Kilshane, being professed in 1935. Following his ordination in 1943 he served for some time on the island of Zanzibar before working in St. Mary's School in Nairobi as teacher and in charge of the liturgy. He served in four different missions in Kenya before returning to Rockwell in 1965. In Rockwell he taught Irish, he being a native Irish speaker, and took charge of the liturgy.[6]

Brother Eugene Graham C.S.Sp. died in 1992. Born in Belfast in 1899 he entered the Congregation in 1920 and was professed in 1922. His first and only appointment in 1923 was to Rockwell where he was to serve for the rest of his long life. As an experienced electrician, he took charge of the electricity generator which provided power and light to the College in the days before Rockwell was linked to the national grid. He showed films to the students, looked after the wages for the staff and took care of the distribution of the post for staff and students.[7]

Notes

[1]   Submission of Fr. James Hurley to DEA, January 2006
[2]   ibid
[3]   ibid
[4]   ISR 204
[5]   ISR 391
[6]   ISR 443
[7]   ISR 396

– 18 –

A NEW BEGINNING
1993- 1999

New legislation for Irish schools and a review by the Congregation of the Holy Spirit of the role of its schools in the future of education were among features of the 1990s which marked another dawn in the progress of Rockwell College.

Fr. Colm Cunningham was President from 1992 to 1994 when he was succeeded by Fr Seán Casey. Fr. Cunningham had been on the missions in Nigeria before becoming a member of the Community from 1968 to 1979 and again from 1986. He was chosen to be assistant to the Provincial at the 1994 Provincial Chapter. Fr. Casey had for a long time previously been engaged in giving retreats to schools throughout Ireland. The outgoing President, Fr.

Fr Colm Cunningham
President 1992-1994

James Hurley, was appointed General Secretary of the Holy Ghost Congregation and was based in Rome, but was to return to Rockwell later.

A TIME OF CHANGE
These two presidencies came at a time of dramatic change in Irish society. This change was reflected in the education system with a move towards democratisation and a greater recognition of the rights of parents. During this period the curricula at primary and post-primary levels were revised to take account of the growth of knowledge and new developments in teaching and learning as well as the opportunities provided by information and communication technologies. At second level the proportion of an age group taking the Leaving Certificate increased from less that 20 per cent in the mid-1960s to more than 80 per cent in the mid 1990s.[1]

Fr. Seán Casey
President 1994-1999

While these changes were taking place, the Irish Province of the Congregation of the Holy Spirit was considering the role of its schools in the future of Irish education. The Provincial Chapter of 1988 decided that the

Prize Day 1993
*Fergus Ahearne (Union President) with Fr.Michael Comerford, Fr. Christopher Meagher and
Fr. Seán O'Donoghue.*

Provincial Council would ensure that there would be ongoing evaluation of the
type of education provided in Spiritan schools, in accordance with the criteria
of the Spiritan mission of evangelisation outlined in the Spiritan Rule of Life.
The Chapter also established a broad based commission to look at present and
future needs of Spiritan schools.[2]

The 1994 Provincial Chapter affirmed the efforts of the schools to implement
the recommendations of the previous Chapter but it also challenged them to
explore the possibility of admitting or helping disadvantaged students, to ensure
that new management structures would guarantee continuity of the Spritan
ethos and the rights of local Spiritan communities and the Congregation, to
provide a good pastoral programme in each school, and to educate the whole
school community in the Spiritan education ethos so that it would be a lived
reality.[3]

The Education Act 1998 was a major development in the history of Irish
education with legislation on such issues as the ownership and management of
schools and the inspection of schools by the Department of Education and
Science. The Education (Welfare) Act, 2000 established the National
Educational Welfare Board. These two Acts did much to clarify the changed
role and responsibilities of school trustees. Within the Congregation of the Holy
Spirit there had been widespread consultation and debate following the 1994
Chapter on the way forward for their schools and this culminated in the
establishment in 1999 of the Des Places Educational Association (DEA), a
company limited by guarantee, to act as patron of the Spiritan schools in
accordance with the Education Act 1998. It was named after Claude Poullart
Des Places, founder of the Congregation of the Holy Spirit. This Spiritan
response to the Education Act was the first by any Irish religious congregation.

On his appointment as President, Fr Seán Casey carried out a review of the Rockwell farm and had an external scientific assessment done which proved to be both timely and beneficial. This prepared the way for the Provincial Administration to take over complete control of the operation of the farm under its existing management.

On his retirement as President in 1999 a further change was made in the Rockwell administrative structure. The President would no longer be the religious superior of the Community, the new superior being Fr. Paddy Reedy.[4]

PERSONNEL

Fr. Seán Broderick continued as Vice-President and as Head Master until 1997. Fr. Patrick Duggan who had been Bursar since 1984 was succeeded in 1996 by Fr. William Kingston. Fr. Naos McCool continued as Dean of Studies until 1996 and Fr. Pat Downes as Games Master until 1999 when he was succeeded by Fr. John McEvoy. Lay deans replaced Community members.

There were many changes in the position of deans of discipline in the 1990s. The senior deans in 1992 and 1993 were Coleman Kelliher, Colin Moran and Fr. Brendan Duggan. In 1994 and 1995 the senior deans were Gerard Dunne, Paul Kilraine and Michael Lynch while Michael Coughlan was senior dean on his own in 1996 and 1997. He was succeeded in 1998 by Denis Gibbons and in 1999 by James Keating when Fr. John McEvoy became dean of the boarding school.

**Rockwell College
Teaching Staff 1996**
Front: *M. Doyle, M. Coughlan,
P. Kilraine, M. Hally.*
1st row: *P. Sullivan, W. Ryan,
F. O'Rourke, M. Lynch,
M. Niland-Ryan, M.McHugh,
G. Buckley.*
2nd row: *J. Fitzgibbon,
N. Woodlock, I. Tungler, D. Power,
Fr. B. O'Connor, D. O'Donoghue.*
3rd row: *S. Leahy, S. O'Donnell,
A. Smith, D. Hally, P. O'Mahony,
D. Butler, L. Fennell.*
4th row: *M. Daly, Fr. N. McCool,
L. Ó Duibhir, L. O'Dwyer,
Fr. P. Downes.*
5th row: *Fr. S. Broderick,
F. McGrath, Fr. S. Casey,
P. Daly, S. King.*

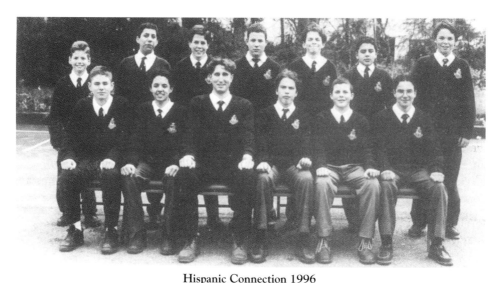

Hispanic Connection 1996
Seated: R. Alvarez, B. Torres, T. Dezcallar, A. Castellanos, G. Altamirano, J. Aguilar.
Standing: L. Alvarez, P. Fernandez, P. Asua, J.P. Niembro, J.I. Urquiza, A. Aguilar, J. Montojo.

Junior deans of discipline in 1992 and 1993 were Breffni Carroll and Edmond Golden and in 1994 Breffni Carroll and Donagh O'Donnell and the following year David O'Donoghue and Donagh O'Donnell. Paul Kilraine and David O'Donoghue were junior deans in 1996 and in 1997 Paul Kilraine was accompanied by Michael Doyle. Declan Murphy and Michael Doyle followed in 1998 and 1999. Ms Winni Ryan was dean of girls in 1992 and 1993 and in 1994 she was succeeded by Mrs. Kathleen Smyth who held that position to the present day.

Two notable changes during the presidency of Fr. Casey were the retirement of Liam Uasal Ó Duibhir in 1996 and the appointment of Mr. Pat O'Sullivan in 1997 as the first lay Principal in the history of Rockwell College. An t-Uasal Ó Duibhir had been a student at Rockwell and as a member of the Leaving Cert class of 1951 he was awarded one of the three South Tipperary University Scholarships. He was a member of the teaching staff since 1958 and was appointed Deputy Principal in 1972 when posts of responsibility were first introduced. He was highly regarded by his students, school management and colleagues. His subject was Gaeilge and he did much to promote the language among students. He was succeeded by Dr. Seán O'Donnell who had been teaching History and Gaeilge at Rockwell since 1963. Mr. Pat O'Sullivan had previously been Principal of a Christian Brothers' School and in his first Principal's Report at Prize Day in 1998 he noted how the task of running Rockwell as a boarding school moved well beyond the requirements of the normal 9 to 4 school and depended equally on both the academic and ancillary staff. Over the next fifteen years he was to introduce major development to Rockwell. Previous to his appointment the term "Principal" had never been used in Rockwell. From 1864 the holder of this position was known as Dean of Studies and from 1972 as Head Master.

Mrs Noreen Woodlock retired in 1998 having taught Maths and French for eighteen years. Mr. Paddy Hall also retired in 1998 having been on the maintenance staff since 1963. Mr. Thomas Tobin retired in 1999.

OBITUARIES

Fr. John Cathal Ryan C.S.Sp. affectionately known as J. C., died in 1994. Born in Tipperary Town in 1911, he studied at Blackrock College before joining the Congregation. Ordained in 1938 he was appointed the following year to Nigeria. He worked in the missions of Amigbo and Emekuku until 1967 when he was forced to leave because of the Biafran War. He continued his pastoral work in San Jose and in Jacksonville, Florida and later in Bluebell parish, Dublin before his appointment to Rockwell in 1973. He was a dean in the Hotel and Catering School and director of golf in the Secondary School. He lived life to the full and enjoyed his golf and horse racing. He was a popular member of the Community who endeared himself to all.[5]

Fr. Michael Comerford C.S.Sp. former President of Rockwell and long-time Vice-President, died in 1997. Born in Urlingford, Co. Kilkenny in 1903, he was a junior Scholastic in Rockwell from 1917 to 1921 He went to Kimmage for his novitiate and was a prefect in Blackrock College. Ordained in 1933, his first and only appointment was to Rockwell where he was Director of St. Joseph's (1934-1940), Bursar (1940-1943), Vice-President (1949-1961), President (1961-1962) and again Vice-President (1962-1974). He continued teaching Mathematics until 1981. He was noted for tending to the shrubs and flowers which adorned the front avenue and front of house and was a renowned authority on matters horticultural. He was also an authority on the physical development of Rockwell and its environment from 1864 to the time of his death.[6]

Brother Pascal C.S.Sp. died on Easter Sunday 1997. Born Hugh Mawhinney on the Falls Road Belfast in 1924, he left school at fifteen and spent five years as an apprentice electrician before qualifying as and electrical engineer. He joined the British Navy and served on an aircraft carrier in the Pacific during the war and endured many close calls following attacks from Japanese aircraft. He retired from the Navy in 1950 and joined the Holy Ghost Congregation and was professed as Brother Pascal. He served in Kilshane and Kimmage before being appointed to Nigeria in 1961. Following the Biafran War he was appointed to Sierra Leone where he served until his appointment to Rockwell in 1977. He suffered very poor health for many years in Rockwell which he endured with patience and humility.[7]

Fr. Robert J. Madigan C.S.Sp. died in January 1998. Born in Cobh in 1914, he was educated at Rockwell junior Scholasticate and was ordained in 1942. His first appointment was to Sierra Leone where he served until 1950. Following his return to Ireland he was appointed assistant novice master at Kilshane for a short period before his return to Sierra Leone for a further two years. Due to ill health he returned to Ireland and served as Director of Junior Postulant Brothers at Kimmage until 1955. Following the opening of Ardbaccan in Co. Meath in 1956 he served as novice master, bursar and superior. He was appointed to Rockwell in 1971 where he served as assistant to the Bursar.

Miss Brigid Sharkey, who had been nurse in Rockwell for a number of years, died in 1998. She had nursed in England for many years before coming to Rockwell. On her retirement in 1997 she went to live with her brother in Roscommon where she died.

DEVELOPMENT

In 1993 there were major developments to the Crehan wing. The top floor, which was previously a dormitory, became a study hall for First Years. The Concert Hall on the middle floor was converted into a number of classrooms and the senior refectory became a venue for plays and concerts and for such public occasions as Prize Day.

Heat preservation and fire protection were adopted as projects in the following years with new double glazed windows and insulation being installed throughout the College. At either end of the main hall a fire-protection wall with exit was installed which shortened the hall slightly but was in keeping with its character. On the exit from the main hall to the Crehan Wing a porch was built with electronic doors in a further effort to conserve heat. A protective shield was installed over the stained glass windows in the senior refectory and at the stair case on the main hall. Heat-preservation methods were also carried out in St. Joseph's. The architect for all these projects in the College and St. Joseph's was past student Jim Peters (class of 1945) who had been President of the Union in 1991-92.

During the summer of 1997 major works were carried out on the lake. Silt had accumulated over the previous two hundred years. It needed deepening to reduce the algae and the construction of new islands to absorb the silt and the seeding and planting of these to improve its general appearance. The contractors for this project were Hanlys of Longford. This and all the development in Rockwell since 1984 had been spear-headed by the Bursar, Fr. Paddy Duggan.

A major change to the Lake House, St. Joseph's, occurred in 1999 when the Provincial Administration decided to convert the building into a retirement residence for the Province of the Spiritan Congregation. The building was redesigned by architect Jim Peters, helped by the Bursar Fr. William Kingston with twenty six *en suite* rooms provided. It was opened in August 2000 by the Provincial Fr. Martin Keane and with Fr. Michael Moore named Director. As well as being a house of retirement it soon became a very popular guest house for Spiritan members of the Province who wished to have a few days of quiet repose. In addition to the renovations inside and outside the building, a new roadway was constructed to link up with the Cashel/New Inn road, so that access and regress to the road from the Lake House did not necessarily have to pass through the College grounds.[8]

Prize Day 1998
Dr. Seán O'Donnell (Deputy Principal), Mr. Brendan Sutton (Rockwell Union), President Hillery,
Fr. Seán Casey (President), Mr. Pat O'Sullivan (Principal)

Detective Garda Jerry McCabe Award
Fr. Seán Casey, Deputy Commissioner, P.J. Moran, Mrs. Ann McCabe, Fergal Ryan, Fergus Ahern,
Chief Supt. Michael Lynch.

PRIZE DAYS

Rockwell continued to be honoured on its annual prize days with the attendance of distinguished guests. In 1993 Mrs. Monica Shannon, Principal of Scoil Chormaic in Cashel was guest and the following year it was the renowned sociologist Fr. Harry Bohan. The Nigerian ambassador to Ireland was guest in 1995 and in 1996 it was Sister Eileen Fahey of the *Aiseirí* Centre in Cahir. Brian Crowley M.E.P. was guest in 1997 and in 1998 it was Pat Cox M.E.P. The

President of Ireland, Patrick Hillery, making one of his many visits to his *alma mater*, was guest of honour in 1999. The President of the Rockwell College Union was always in attendance to present gold medals to the Student of the Year, to the winner of the Thomas MacDonagh literary award and to the winner of the James Joy senior debating award.

It was at Prize Day in 1997 that the Jerry McCabe Civic Award was instituted. It was to honour the memory of Detective Gerry McCabe, a past student of Rockwell, who had been assassinated in the course of his duty in June 1996. His widow and other family members were present for the occasion.

Student Life

The annual student population stood between 450 and 500 in these years, approximately 150 of whom were boarders. The number of girls continued to increase. It was 83 in 1992 and for the first time it reached 100 in 1999. Because of the increased number of day students the Saturday class schedule had been suspended and replaced by a series of Saturday morning activities for boarders. Another effect of the increase of day students was mentioned by Fr. Broderick at Prize day in 1994 when he referred to the greater involvement of parents. This was probably due, he said to the fact that day students were part of the school from 9am to 9pm and like the full time boarders developed that sense of community which had been and was so important to the school. When the school was completely boarding, he said, parents were involved to a much lesser degree. A notable development was the involvement of parents in the end of year Mass and dinner for final year students.

Foreign Languages Room Prefects 1993
Seated: *P. Drew, Ms I. Tungler, B. Morrissey.*
Standing: *F. Kinsella, K. O'Reilly, E, McGrath, D. Butler.*

Prefects 1998-99
Seated: *G. Browne, P. Keogh, J. Hurley, J.Lundi, C. O'Leary, J. Lane, C. Foley.*
1st. row: *Mrs. K. Smyth, B. Crowley, A.M. Murphy, C. Flynn, J. Grace, T. Gallaghy, B. Murphy, Mr. J. Keating.*
2nd row: *A. Daly, C. Moran, C. Flanagan, J. Dalton, S. Brosnan, K. Brennan, M. Van Dulken.*

DEBATING

As ever in Rockwell, debating was an important after-class activity. 5th and 6th Years had their own teams which clashed on occasion and were involved in the annual Debater of the Year in the month of May organised by Mr. King with a guest adjudicator. On two occasions in these years the guest was a prominent past student. In 1993 it was the R.T.E. broadcaster Eamon Lawlor and in 1998 it was Seamus Mulligan President of Elan Pharmaceutical Technologies. The winners of the Union Gold medal and the Fr. Walker plaque in those years were Robert MacGoey, Cian Toomey, Patrick MacGoey, Aonghus Fitzgibbon, P.J. Flynn, Angela Quinlan and John Prendergast.

Rockwell debaters took part in debates throughout the years organised by Concern, the Soroptomists, The Mental Health Association of Ireland and the U.C.C. Philosophical Society. In 1998 the Garda Siocbána in Cashel invited the schools in the district to take part in a debate on the whole area of drug culture. Many of the debaters also took part in the many table quizzes organised by Mr. Power.

MUSIC AND DRAMA

Music and drama continued to flourish in those years. Mr. Oliver Nolan produced plays in 1993 and 1994. In the 1993 production of *Juno and the Paycock* the leading players were Alan Cavanagh, Kate Rockingham, Michael Ahearne, Arlene Murphy, Jude Bolger, Aisling Gildea, David Butler Louise Carey, Breffni O'Sullivan Tom Horgan, Dominic Bonny and Frank Carmody. In the 1994 production of *Our Town* by Thornton Wilder, parts were played by Jude Bolger, John Brennan, Kevin Geraghty, Kate Rockingham, Olivia Frawley, Aonghus

Fitzgibbon, Sarah Galvin, Cathal Ferris, Patricia McInerney, Jonathan Carey, Michael Ahearne, Emer O'Sullivan, Tom Kearney, Alan Kavanagh, Ellen Foley, Kevin Ryan, Kevin Ray and Daniel Hennessy.

West Side Story was produced by Mr. Kilraine with Mr Donagh O'Donnell in 1995 when the members of the cast were Oliver Wall, Tom Kearney, Mark Barry, John Fogarty, Patrick Phelan, Jonathan Carey, Maura Long, Marcella Ryan, Ruth Cooney, John Brennan. Maria Gleeson, Patricia McInerney, Caoimhe Cantwell, Gordon Spain, Colin Enright, Patrick O'Sullivan, Gareth Ahearn, Michael Lyons, Alice O'Connor, Susan O'Reilly, Aisling Ryan and Georgina Touhy

The choice of Mr. Kilraine in 1996 was *Oliver* and for the first time it was staged outside of the College in the Brú Ború Theatre in Cashel. The members of the cast were Ray Blewitt, Daniel Aytour, Maria Gleeson, Eoin O'Keeffe, Roy Horgan, Louise Horgan, Valerie O'Reilly, Darren Murphy, Mark Barry, Niamh O'Donoghue, Marcella Ryan, Ciarán Young, Arlene Gibbs, Jack Mulcahy, Gordon Spain, Caitriona O'Reilly, Georgina Touhy, Ian Brennan, Jonathan Maher, Michael Rockingham, Hugh Fitzpatrick, Peter Boylan, Aoife Holohan, Patrick Dolan, John Silke, Patricia Ryan, Gerry Purcell, Paul Horgan, Michael O'Connor, Alec Spain, Ian Walsh, Yvonne Hannigan, Karol Cusack, Karl Sutcliffe, Peter Fallon, Liam Marmion, Senan Gardiner, James Moloney, Paul Clarke, Paul Ahearne and Hugh Daly.

Mr. Kilraine produced *Grease* in 1997 when the players were Willie O'Donnell, Fiona Coughlan, Niamh O'Donoghue, Vincent Canavan, Patricia

Christmas Choir 1995
Seated: *A. Drew, J. Lynch, S. McDonald, J. Carey, N. Mangan, D. Walsh, J. Waddock, G. Purcell, V. O'Shea.*
1st row: *I. Brennan, J. Ward, D. Kieran, S. Canavan, T. Kearney, C. Enright, M. Lyons, J. Bolger, K. Rockingham, G. Sidman.*
2nd row: *P. Ryan, D. Julian, R. Horgan, C. Ryan, B. Kennedy, D. O'Brien, L. Ryan, D. Aytour, P. Horgan, H. Fitzpatrick.*

Music Awards 1995
Seated: Ms M. Lynch, P. Ryan, J. Martin, M. Quinn.
Standing: E. O'Keeffe, S. Gardiner, A. Shealy, P.J. Flynn.

Ryan, Alana Durack, Rickard Creedon, Patrique Kelly, Fiachra Fitzgibbon, Gerard Casey, Yvonne Hannigan, Fergal Ryan, Conor Martin, Gareth McGlinchey, Damien O'Connor, Arlene Gibbs, David O'Brien, Edward O'Connor, Christopher Agom, Roy Horgan, Elaine Cleary, Dawn Manning, Aoife Holohan, Katie Ryan and Avril Mulcahy.

Choral music, with particular emphasis on liturgical choirs, continued as a prominent feature of student life under the direction of Fr. Moloney and later Fr. Raftery following his appointment to Rockwell in 1997. Recitals by visiting artists continued to impress students with some of the most memorable including the visit by the Douglas Gunn Ensemble in 1993 and of the internationally renowned pianist, Veronica McSweeney in 1995.

CULTURAL EXCHANGE
As for many years there was a continuous international dimension to student life in Rockwell. Students from Spain, Mexico and Germany were the dominant nationalities among foreign students who exercised a global influence over the natives. College management further encouraged this development by promoting inter-school exchanges. In 1994, for instance, an exchange was arranged with *Realschule, Rotenburg,* a German second level academy which sent a group of students and teachers to Rockwell for a fortnight followed by a return visit by Rockwell students under the care of Ms. Tungler and Mr. Mason. A similar exchange was arranged in 1998 with *L'Institute de Assumption,* a Catholic second level school situated in the centre of Brussels. This exchange was organised by Fr. John McEvoy and Mrs. O'Rourke. The annual Easter

international tour organised by Mr. King was further evidence of the international dimension. And *Le Coin Francais*, that space within Rockwell originally established by Iníon Ní Muurchadha for the promotion of French, was now supervised by Ms Keating and Ms Tungler and was rightly renamed the Modern Language Room because of the increased interest in other modern languages.

GOOD WORKS

A new development in the good works performed by Rockwell students from 1993 was the opportunity provided for them to help with children with special needs and young people with learning difficulties in Scoil Chormaic, Cashel. This exercise became part of the Religion programme for 5th Year students in the College. It took the form of students involved visiting Scoil Chormaic three times a week over a period of five weeks, each visit lasting for half an hour. Parallel to this, the Rockwell swimming pool was put at the disposal of the Scoil Chormaic students for a couple of visits a week when they were assisted in enjoying the facilities of the pool. It proved to be a rewarding and continuous exercise. The Rockwell branch of the St. Vincent de Paul Society raised funds for Scoil Chormaic.

Fr. Downes continued to direct the annual Flag Day for the missions when 5th Year students collected funds in the neighbouring towns of Cashel, Cahir, Clonmel and Thurles. Sums amounting to nearly £1,500 were raised on each occasion. Fr. Stirling gained great notoriety in the district for the project he spear-headed when Rockwell joined forces and resources with her sister college, Blackrock College in collecting money for the charities Goal and Aid Link. Funds collected were divided equally between the two organisations to be used to help needy people in the Third World. More than fifty students helped collect in the local towns. St. Patrick's Day emblems were sold for £1 each. Nearly £2,000 was collected annually.

Goal-Aid Link 1997
Seated: *Fr. E. Stirling,
A. Buttimer, B. Halley,
L. Heffernan.*
Standing: *G. O'Driscoll,
D. Julian, T. O'Neill.*

RUGBY

Despite the fact that in the 1990s Rockwell produced two future Irish internationals, Denis Leamy and John Fogarty, the Munster senior Cup did not come to the College in that decade. Instead for the second and final year Rockwell competed in the Mungret Cup and won it again in 1993 when the team was captained by Dermot O'Brien with wins over Ard Scoil Rís, Waterpark, Crescent and Glenstal. Other members of the winning panel were Daniel O'Sullivan, Bosco Ryan, James Morrison, Gary Colbert, Geoffrey Coman, Colin Murphy, Dwyer Ryan, Denis Malone, Brian Murphy, John J. Waddock, Alan O'Rourke, Patrick Kelly, Thomas Walsh, Michael Hanrahan, Thomas Connolly and Eugene Fortune.

Denis Leamy
Schoolboy Rugby International 1999

The S.C.T. of 1994 lost to Munchins but had three inter-provincials in Colin Murphy, Brian Murphy and James Morrison. Munchins were the victors again in 1995 and the inter-provincials were John Morrison, Patrick Hickey-Dwyer, Fergal Buttimer and John Fogarty. The 1996 team was beaten by P.B.C. and the inter-provincials were Fergal Butttimer, Evan Lonergan and John Fogarty who was also honoured with an Irish Schoolboys International cap. The 1997 team

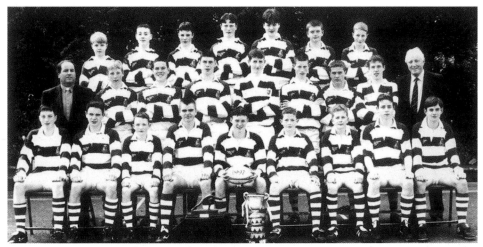

Junior Cup Winning Team 1997
Seated: *V. O'Keeffe, P. Carey, G. Purcell, K; Sutcliffe, J. Silke, P. Morrissey, P. Ahearne, T. Ryan, A. Earley.*
1st row: *Fr. J. McEvoy, P. Mullane, T. Fennessy, D. Leamy, P. Ryan, L. Marmion, J. O'Brien, A. O'Donnell, Mr. E. Tierney.*
2nd row: *J.P. Julian, P. Horgan, J. Hurley, E. Tierney, L. Ryan, O. Cleary, M. O'Connor.*

won the inaugural Munster/Connaght League but lost to St. Munchins in the Cup. The inter-pros of 1997 were Eoin Kelly, John Hadnett, Wayne Hyde and Ian Brennan. In 1998 the S.C.T. lost to C.B.C. in the Cup and the inter-provincials were Danny Noonan, Aidan O'Sullivan, John Hadnett, John Dalton, Ronan O'Brien and Colin Morrissey who was later to become a prominent Tipperary senior hurler. In 1999 Mr. Hogan Chapman of New Zealand took charge of the S.C.T. in succession to Mr. Tony Smith who had been in charge throughout the 1990s and was now involved with the Munster team. Rockwell lost to Munchins in the Cup; and the inter- provincials of 1999 were John Dalton, Nabil McNaughton and Denis Leamy who was an Irish Schoolboys International player that year and representing his country for the first of many times to come.

The J. C.T. won the Cup once in the 1990s and that was in 1997 when Fr. McEvoy and Mr. Ned Tierney were in charge with John Silke as captain of a team powered by Denis Leamy at Number 8. Victories were recorded over Munchins, P.B.C and Ard Scoil Rís. The winning panel was: Vincent O'Shea, Peter Carey, Karl Sutcliffe, John Silke, Pat Morrissey, Paul Ahearne, Tim Ryan, Alan Earley, Emmet Flynn, Pat Mullane, Owen Cleary, Tom Fennessy, Denis Leamy, Philip Ryan, Liam Marmion, Jarleth O'Brien, Liam Ryan Alec Spain, John Paul Julian, Paul Horgan, Gerry Purcell, John Hurley, Patrick Ryan, Edward Tierney, Daniel Aytour, Michael Quinn, Diarmuid Terry, Alan O'Donnell, Michael O'Connor and Michael Kearney.

OTHER SPORTS

Rockwell never failed to provide individual surprises "outside of the box" in the sporting arena as in 1998 when William Loughnane took part in a number of boxing tournaments and was crowned under14 Munster boxing champion.

The Canoe Club was noted for its annual performance in the Leander Cup. It won it for the sixteenth time in succession in 1993 and was to win it again annually for the remainder of the decade. Mr. McGrath continued to direct operations each year. The students who were part of this continuing achievement in those years included David Fahey, Michael O'Dwyer, James Halley, Vincent Pierce, Vincent Mc Hugh, John Quinlan, Alec O'Riordan, Cathal Ferris, Philip Feitz, John Quinlan,

David Bennett
Schoolboy Basketball International 1999

James O'Dwyer. Brendan McHugh, Eimear Burke, Arlene Gibbs, Páraic Lonergan, Seán Lonergan, John Nolan, Richard O'Donnell, Alistair Forsyth, Liam Lee, Aoife Holohan, Eve Nolan, Louise Heywood, Dirk Hau, Rory Sheehan, Michael O'Riordan, Eamon Hayes, Kevin Murphy, Dominic Rodgers, John Madden, Colm Lonergan, Orla McGrath and Muireann Nolan.

In Gaelic Games the Annual County Schools under 14 football blitz continued to be held in Rockwell each year and in 1996 it was won by the home team. Up to 1995 Mr. Doyle entered teams in the Munster senior championship on occasions and regularly in the MacGahhainn County Schools competition . Prominent players in

Under 14 Tennis Internationals 1999
Emma Heffernan, Clodagh McMorrow

the early 1990s included John Heaney, Tom Galvin, Colm Heaney and John Kennedy. From 1996 to 1999 Gaelic football teams were managed in turn by Mr. Donagh O'Donnell, Mr. Coughlin and Mr. Gibbins. Hurling teams were managed by Mr. O'Mahony at under 16 and under 15 levels and entered in the County championships in 1993 and 1994. From then until 1999 Mr. Donagh O'Donnell took charge.

Inter-Schools Show-Jumping Team 1995
Joe Hartigan, Elen Phelan, Michelle Hanrahan, Ian Brennan

Large numbers of girls were involved in hockey which was organised by Ms Winnie Ryan. By 1993 junior and senior teams were entered in the Tipperary leagues and championship and a team was organised for each year in the school. Teams were later entered in the Munster championship in which Rockwell made a good impression. Ms Ryan also entered gymnastic teams in competitions. Basketball for boys and girls was organised at all levels by Mr. Fennell and teams were entered successfully in national championships. In 1999 the under 14 team won an All Ireland blitz and David Bennett became an under 16 Basketball schoolboy international.

Athletic teams were entered each year for the East Munster and Munster sports and good performances were recorded as in 1993 at the Munster sports when Daniel O'Sullivan came first in the 100 m and James Long first in the shot. Cross Country remained popular with boys and girls. Boys and Girls tennis teams were entered in the Munster championships each year. Clodagh McMorrow of 2nd Year was a member of the Munster tennis team which won the inter-provincial championship in Nenagh in August 1997. In April 1998 Clodagh was selected on the Irish under 14 team to play Wales. Clodagh was selected on the Irish team again in 1999 and this time Emma Heffernan of Rockwell was also selected on the Irish team. Emma had been a finalist the previous year in the under 12 competition at Fitxwilliam

Horse Riding at Mr. Garret Dooley's stables continued to be organised by Fr. McCool with teams entered for the Irish schools hunter trials and the Fr. Barrett Memorial Cup being keenly contested each year. Brian Curran Cournane and Edward Tierney were especially prominent in this field. Swimming galas and life-saving classes for boys and girls were organised by Mr. Martin Daly and later by Mr. Michael Kelly and an annual home-and-away gala with Kilkenny College was especially popular. Fr. Downes looked after the golfers in the early 1990s when prominent golfers included Emmet Leahy, Con O'Driscoll, Geoffrey Coman, Fergal Buttimer and John Morrison. In the later part of the decade Mr. Doyle was in charge and prominent golfers included Fintan McGuirk, Conor O'Leary, Brian Curran Cournane, Ciaran Moran, James Moloney, William O'Connor, Martin Gildea, Denis McGrath, John Devereaux, and William Prendergast.

The organisation of sport in Rockwell was a time-consuming affair with making fixtures and organising venues and transport. It was a duty that was fulfilled annually and to the appreciation of all until 1997 by Fr. Downes.

AGRICULTURAL COLLEGE

The number of people applying to do agricultural courses increased throughout the 1990s and Rockwell, as one of the eleven Irish agricultural colleges, was full to capacity. There were no major changes in management personnel with Fr. Bernard Frawley continuing as Principal and the same lecturers dealing with dairy, grassland, tillage, environmental matters, sheep, veterinary, beef, buildings and machinery. Different projects were carried out each year and in 1996, for instance, it concentrated on farm safety. In 1993 the

Camp Rockwell Staff 1999
1st row: *Liz O'Riordan, Siobhán O'Toole, Nicola Carew, Pádraig Lonergan, David Morris,*
Fr. William Kingston, Marie Quinlan, Paul Tuohy, Anna Craddock, Br. Gerard Cummins,
Máirin Farrell, Gayle Noonan.
2nd row: *Jennifer Beary, Margaret-Ann O'Donoghue, Catriona O'Dwyer, Colm Fitzpatrick,*
Alice O'Connor, Damien Byrne, Sandra Hedigan, Alistair Forsyth, Shane Flynn, Brendan O'Connor,
Adrian Flynn, Hogan Chapman.
3rd row: *Georgina Duggan, Jim Kennedy, Karen Molan, Ronán Morris, Patrique Kelly, Edmund Golden,*
Anne-Marie O'Connor, Karena Hayes, Shane Stapleton, Raymond Bourke, Colm Heaney.
Back row: *Liz Cullen, Eadaoin O'Mahony, Kate Lonergan, Emma Tuohy, Julia Hayes,*
Frances Mulcahy, Laura Ryan, Andree Walkin, Marie Donovan, Paula Morris, Emma Ryan.

Student of the Year was Lilian Gash from Co. Cork, one of three girls in the college.

Rockwell was a major force among the agricultural colleges on the sporting field. In 1994 a rare distinction was the winning of both the All Ireland football and hurling championship. The footballers, captained by Aidan Ahearne, beat Warrenstown College in the final. The team was: Pat Hernan (Wexford), Damian O'Sullivan (Cork), Vincent Fahy (Cork), Ken Walsh (Kilkenny). Brendan Hogan (Tipperary), Brendan Joyce (Kilkenny), Rody Aherne (Tipperary), Ger Hanrahan (Cork),Aidan Ahearne (Waterford), Paul Connery (Waterford), Donnacha Tobin (Waterford), Enda Seale (Wexford),Oliver Looney (Cork), Martin Ryan (Tipperary), Paul McCarthy (Cork).

In the hurling Rockwell defeated Mountbellew College, Galway. The hurlers were: Paul Connery (Waterford), John Rafter (Laois), Pat Hernan (Wexford), Vincent Fahy (Cork), Rody Aherne (Tipperary), Ken Walsh (Kilkenny), Brendan Hogan (Tipperary), Aidan Ahearne (Waterford), James Murphy (Cork), Danny Ryan (Tipperary), Brendan Joyce (Kilkenny), Martin Ryan (Tipperary), Donal Doyle (Wexford),Joe Smyth (Tipperary), Enda Seale

(Wexford), Oliver Looney (Cork), Paul McCarthy (Cork), Willie Keating (Tipperary).

ROCKWELL UNION

The Union presidents in these years were Risteard Ó Colmáin. Fergus Ahearne, Hilary Healy, Joe Cumiskey, Gerard Quinn, Ken Maguire and Seán Cronin. The Union continued its generosity to the College and to the missions. In July 1993 a garden party was held which raised £3,460 for Fr. Brian Starkin, a past student and future Provincial of the Congregation, who was working with displaced people in Sierra Leone. The same year the Union contributed £!,000 towards the restoration of the College organ. A financial contribution to missionary projects of the Holy Ghost Fathers was made every year.

In 1998 Kevin Mallen, one of five brothers from Grangecon, Co. Wicklow who studied in Rockwell between 1914 and 1926, made a large financial contribution to upgrade computer facilities. The same year the Ciarán Blair Award was launched. It was a silver plate and medal for the sciences awarded to honour Ciarán who had been a student of the 1930s and who had died in 1988. It was presented by his son Domhnall who had been President of the Union in 1987-88.

The Union made a major contribution to career guidance and mock interviews by sending as many as thirty past students to the College each year to deliver their expertise.

Bishop William Lee, class of 1959, consecrated Bishop of Waterford and Lismore.

Careers Advisers 1994
Bernard Flusk, Brian Kavanagh, Fr. Cunningham, Michael G. Ryan, John Duffy.

Bishop Lee with Some Classmates of 1959
Front: *Fr. Christy Meagher, Nicholas Cotter, Joe Jones, John O'Dwyer, Bishop Lee, Gay Mangan, Frank Caplice, James Meehan, Pierce Hickey*
Back: *Fr. Matt Knight, Frank Hickey, Kevin Prendergast, Pat Leydon, John Prendergast, Owen Ryan, Seán Cooney, Paddy Hickey, John Clancy, Fr. Colm Cunningham.*

SPIRITAN GATHERING
Members of the Congregation of the Holy Spirit present at the celebration of the centenary of
St. Patrick's Chapel Rockwell, June 1999.

Standing front left: Frs. Bernard Frawley, Frank Barry, Seán O'Connell, Paddy Cleary, Jim Stapleton,
Patrick Holland, Vincent O'Grady.
Standing front right: Frs. Christy Meagher, Richard Gavin, Tom McCarthy, Norman Fitzgerald,
Jim Shanley, Willie Kingston, Bryan O'Connor, Tom Cleary.
Seated: Frs. J. C. O'Mahony, Tim O'Driscoll, Hugh Boyle, Br. Gerard Cummins,
Frs. Colum Cunningham, Martin Keane, Tom Roche, Brendan O'Brien, Frank Comerford,
Ned Tiernan, John O'Neill, Oliver Dowling, John Buckley.
1st row: Frs. Pat Downes, Seán Casey, Willie Walsh, Br. Finbar Kelly, Br. Coleman,
Frs. Seán Broderick, Vincent Browne, Dick O'Dwyer, Joe Sheehan, Alo Dempsey. James McNulty.
2nd row: Frs: Denis O'Brien, Denis Kennedy, Finbar Horgan, John Flavin, Michael Kilkenny,
Breffney Walker, Patrick M. Ryan, Jim Duggan, Noel Redmond, Joe Beere, Edward Stirling.
3rd row: Frs. Paddy Dundon, Henry Moloney, Patrick Reedy, Patrick Devine, Edward O'Farrell,
Noel O'Meara, Patrick J. Ryan, Valentine O'Brien, Jack Meade, Seán O'Shaughnessy.
4th row: Frs. Vincent McDevitt, Peter Casey, Pat McNamara, Peter Conaty, John Fitzpatrick,
Br. Augustin O'Keeffe, Fr. Des Kenny.
5th row: Frs. John Kingston, John McEvoy, Paddy Carroll, Peter Raftery, Matthew Knight,
Michael Hickey, Peter Queally, Pat Palmer, Martin McDonagh.

Notes

[1] Áine Hyland, *Education*, The Encyclopedia of Ireland
[2] Congregation of the Holy Spirit Irish Province: Provincial Guideline Document on Primary/Secondary Education in Ireland 2006
[3] ibid
[4] Submission of Fr. James Hurley to the DEA, January 2006.
[5] ISR 17
[6] ISR 257
[7] ISR 196
[8] Submission of Fr. James Hurley to the DEA 15/1/2006.

– 19 –

GOING FORWARD
2000-2006

A new plan for Rockwell College was devised in accordance with the Education Act of 1998 and in the early years of the new millennium a facelift was delivered to a number of the College landmarks.

Speaking at Prize Day 2003 Mr. O'Sullivan stated that the entire teaching staff had begun to engage in the production of a whole school plan for the future of the College. "This involves an examination of our current and future needs" he said. Continuing, he said "We are obliged under the requirements of the new Education Act to produce such a plan. The work will take several years and must then be made available to the different partners in education, the Department of Education and Science, the trustees, the staff, the students themselves and of course the parents. An important part of the work will be to examine the current state of our infrastructure, our plant, our classrooms, our dormitories, our science laboratories and so on. We will then have to move on and find the capital to develop the resources we need for the future. Clearly important decisions lie ahead. We must not be afraid to move forward and to engage all those who will need to be involved. We cannot bask in the shade of former glories".

In 2006 a joint fund-raising appeal by the President, Fr. William Cleary, and the Principal, Mr. Pat O'Sullivan, was launched in support of a new development plan for Rockwell which was to be carried out in three phases. The first phase concerned work which had already been completed.

Fr. Seán Broderick
President 1999-2004

Fr. William Cleary
President 2004-2007

From April to August 2005 the former Agricultural College was refurbished and was opened as Shanahan Hall on 8th September 2005 by the Provincial, Fr. Pat Palmer. It was managed under the newly appointed Director, Mr. Frank Fitzgerald (Class of 1990). Named in honour of the distinguished past pupil and former College Dean, Bishop Joseph Shanahan C.S.Sp., this new accommodation provided excellent facilities as a Hall of Residence for 116 "Seven Day" boarding students. The cost of this refurbishment was €248,900. The electrical work in this refurbishment amounted to €50.000 and was paid for entirely by the Rockwell College Union.

Joe Moran
Union President 1999-2000

The Libermann Hall, named after the founder of the Congregation, opened in October 2005. It occupied the area of the College, formerly the Priests' Corridor and directly above the former Big Study and was designated as an accommodation facility. With marvellous views of Rockwell lake and the Galtee Mountains, this Hall offered twin-bedded accommodation with common room, study and kitchenette facilities for 34 "Five Day" boarding students. The cost of this facility was €28,000.

The College Finance offices were relocated to the main College building providing fully equipped and spacious offices necessary for an expanding service to College management and staff at a cost of €15,000. The new surgery and sick bay provided a much valued facility at the heart of the College to attend to the physical well-being of students and staff. The cost of this facility was €55,000.

Phase Two of the Development Plan began towards the end of 2005 with the construction of a floodlit, multi-purpose all-weather pitch measuring 100 meters by 60. Its surface is to International Hockey Federation specification and its

Amnesty International 2002
1st row: *Mukhtar Shegaya, Claire Cremmins, John O'Kelly, Michael O'Connor, Daryll Curran.*
2nd row: *Mr. Pat Egan, Robert Ryan, Laura O'Connell, Niamh Conneally, Jeff Quirke.*
3rd row: *Jack Pearson, Laura Prenderville, Alison Duffy, William Purcell, David Darmody,*
Cathy O'Donoghue.

location is on the former soccer pitch which was relocated to the front of Shanahan Hall. The cost of this pitch was €540,000. An all weather training area measuring 60 meters by 35 and located between the tarmac and the pavilion was completed at a cost of €130,000. The tennis courts were re-surfaced and upgraded at a cost of €90,000. These new developments greatly enhanced the sporting facilities of the College and were complete in June 2006.

For some years the senior refectory had doubled as a School Hall. This changed when work began in July 2006 in relocating the Big Study on the Chapel corridor to two independent studies on the top floor of the school. The Big Study was the chosen location for the new School Hall. It was known as the Crosbie Hall, because of the generous donation of €180,000 towards its cost by past student Harry Crosbie. It was to be the venue for musicals, plays and concerts (with a permanent stage in place), as well as parent-teacher meetings, general meetings and lectures. Centrally located, this new meeting area beside the College Chapel and library, became the focal point for the Rockwell cultural programme.

Art in Rockwell College is seen as "a visual language" and is greatly valued in the current high-tech, highly visual modern era. The space and lighting of an art studio is critical to the educational value of art as a modern subject. As such the new Art and Craft Studio was well positioned on the top floor overlooking the lake, with excellent lighting and an inspiring vista of the Rockwell campus. The cost of this Studio was €120,000.

Teaching and learning facilities were extended on the top and middle floors. The top floor of the main College building was transformed into a modern environment for teaching and learning accessible by lift for disabled access and general staff use. It consisted of two spacious study areas, one for 3rd Year and another for Transition and 5th year students, five new classrooms and a modern Transition Year resource room and four offices for deans. The cost of the top floor facilities was €800,000. The middle floor was renovated to include a new staffroom with kitchenette and cloakroom and a board room for meetings of the new Board of Management and other meetings at a cost of €65,000.

PERSONNEL

Fr. Seán Broderick was President from 1999 to 2004, having ministered in Nigeria until his appointment to Rockwell in 1971 where he had served as Director of St. Joseph's, Dean of Discipline and Vice-President. In 2004 he commenced a new ministry in the United States. A major development in 2002 had been the closure of the Agricultural College. Fr. Bernard Frawley, who had been its Director since 1983, was appointed Community and Farm Bursar.

Fr. William Cleary was President from 2004 to 2007. He had been a student in Rockwell from 1966 to 1972. He studied at U.C.D. where he obtained an M.A. in psychology and at Maynooth where he obtained a B.D. in theology. Following his ordination in 1982 he was appointed to the Gambia in West Africa where he worked until 1993. He worked as Vocations Director for the Irish Spiritan Province becoming Manager of St. Michael's College in 1998.

Chapel Choir 2003
Seated: *Jeffrey Quirke, Alejandro Gomez Mont, Ciaran Dolan, Alberto Bullejos, Fr. Peter Raftery, Guillermo Garcia, Patrick Naughton, Seán Joyce, Fernando Gallego.*
2nd row: *Kevin Buckley, Gerry Tin Sin, Jack Pearson, Denis Motchalov, Yuk Man Pak, Anthony Yiu, Javier Nabal, Alejandro Figueras.*
3rd row: *Alex King, Wilson Chan, Brendan Mulcahy, Michael O'Connor, Andy Cheung, Eduardo del Villar, Juan Salcedo.*
4th row: *Patrick Farrelly, Liam Mainstone, Vincent Chan, Peter Shallow, Alec Frazer, Xavier Navarette, Rodolfo Sondoval.*

During these two presidencies there were many personnel changes, most of them due to retirements of long-serving members of the teaching staff. Mr. Seamus Leahy (English) and Mr. Laurence O'Dwyer (Business Studies) retired in 2000 and the following year Mr. Seamus King (English) retired and Fr. Naos McCool (Dean of Studies), who had served in Rockwell for twenty eight years, was assigned to Duquesne University, Pittsburg, Philadelphia, United States. In 2003 Dr. Seán O'Donnell retired as Deputy Principal and was succeeded by Mr. Michael Doyle. Mr. Pádraig O'Mahony (Irish) and Mr. David Power (English) retired in 2004 and Miss Margaret Lynch (Music) and Mr. Paddy Daly (Physics) in 2005. Dr. Douglas Butler (Biology) retired in 2006. All of these retired teachers had served Rockwell since the 1960s or early 1970s and had in their own way made a long and significant contribution to the academic life of the College and had made an impression on the mind of many a student. They were replaced by a younger staff

PRIZE DAY
Prize Day in Rockwell continued to attract guests of honour who were influential in Irish life. People of influence in the field of education were represented in 2000 by the visit of past student Dr. Maurice Manning, Chancellor of the National University of Ireland, in 2004 by Professor Kieran Byrne, Director of Waterford Institute of Technology and in 2006 by Ms. Mary Hanafin, Minister of Education and Science. Mr. Ruairi Quinn, who was guest

in 2001, was then leader of the Irish Labour Party with a noted interest in educational matters and was to become a future Minister of Education and Science. The guest in 2002 was past pupil Mr. Harry Crosbie, one of Ireland's most successful businessmen who was always a close friend of his *alma mater* and whose practical advice was treasured by students. John O'Shea, director of Goal, was represented by his daughter at Prize Day in 2003 in acknowledgement of the work which Rockwell students continued to perform for the Third World.

Prize Day was always an occasion for the Principal to annually review educational developments in the College. In 2002 Mr. O'Sullivan mentioned that he had always stated that the single most important factor in the success in any school was the quality of the relationship between the pupil and teacher. In a year of industrial action, which had throughout the country seen a challenge to that relationship, he was pleased to say that in this College, the quality of the relationship had endured. The year had been characterised by the same sense of goodwill and generosity of spirit on the part of the teaching staff which had always prevailed.

Referring to curriculum development Mr. O'Sullivan reported that 6th Year students took the Leaving Certificate Vocational Programme for the first time in 2000 and the same year also marked the introduction of a most successful Transition Year programme in which students had learned a whole range of new skills in communication, public speaking, in music and drama and in acquiring lifesaving skills through work experience. Further progress in curriculum

College Staff 2004
Seated: *Cliona Geary, Pádraig O'Mahony, Margaret Lynch, Eileen McCormack, Fr. Seán Broderick, David Power, Anne Mulcahy, Pat O'Sullivan, Frank Fitzgerald.*
2nd row: *Neasa O'Halloran, Lena Hally, John Mason, Patrick Daly, Maureen McHugh, Margaret Niland-Ryan, June O'Brien, Alvara Duggan, John McBride, Joan Kennedy.*
3rd row: *Frank McGrath, Eleanor Kilroy, Wini Ryan Patrique Kelly, Orla O'Dwyer, Martin Daly, Caroline Kelly, Gemma Walsh, Pat Egan, Breda Marnane.*
4th row: *Michael Rennie, Gerard Hough, Seán Ryan, Fr. Patrick Downes, John Fitzgibbon, Michael Doyle, Audrey O'Byrne, Douglas Butler.*

development was highlighted in 2006 with Religious Education and Physical Education becoming Leaving Certificate subjects. Home Economics was then being taught in all years and Music was available as an exam subject.

Mr. O'Sullivan noted that in 2005 Rockwell had welcomed many pupils whom it was known in advance had certain learning difficulties. He noted that the support and resources services in the College had been enhanced which provided learning support to more than twenty five pupils that year. This was, he said, evidence of the inclusive nature of the College enrolment policy.

For the first time in more than twenty years the student enrolment had moved beyond the five hundred mark in 2002. This came at a time of falling demographics in secondary schools and Mr. O'Sullivan suggested it represented a huge vote of confidence by both parents and students in the work being done in Rockwell. More than 90% of the previous year's Leaving Certificate students had progressed to third level education in Ireland, England, Scotland, Germany Spain, Mexico, Russia and the U.S.A. The international nature of the Rockwell student body was not always recognised by the Irish media who may look only to Irish universities to measure academic success, according to Mr. O'Sullivan. He referred to the achievement of one Rockwell student in 2002 who achieved not just 7 A's but 7 A1's which was a unique distinction..

Debating continued as a popular outlet for students outside of the classroom. Ms Audrey O'Byrne acted as co-ordinator of the Debating Society with teams in 5th and 6th Years and the highlight of the year being the Student of the Year

Board of Management and Finance Committee 2006
Seated: Mr. John Mason, (Teachers' rep.), Ms Olwyn Kingston (Parents' rep), Dr. Seán O'Donnell
(Chairperson), Sr. Regina Powell (Trustees' rep) Fr. Matthew Knight (Trustees' rep.)
Standing: Ms. Joan Kennedy (Finance Manager), Mr. John Fitzgibbon (Teachers' rep.) Mr. William
Irwin (Finance Committee) Mr. Pat O'Sullivan (Principal), Ms. Clodagh Beresford (Trustees' rep.),
Mr. Martin Healy (Parents' rep)

debate in May. The guest adjudicators for that debate in 2001 were two past students Pat Leahy, political editor of the *Sunday Business Post*, and Shane O'Donoghue of R.T.E Sport. Teams competed each year in debates promoted by Concern, the Munster Schools competition and the University College, Cork Philosophical Society. Rockwell was represented at these competitions by Tiernan Fitzgibbon, Aidan Byrne, Kieran McCarthy, Sarah Long, David Cashman and Emma Coffey.

Fr. Raftery's choirs occupied nearly a hundred students each year with performances at liturgical services at Sunday Mass, Mass for deceased members, Christmas Carol recital, annual school concert, Prize Day recital and in competition at the Cork International Choral Festival, the Arklow Music Festival, the Wesley College inter-schools competition and the Dublin Feis Ceoil where in 2005 Rockwell won the prize for mixed-voice choirs. The choir was accompanied in 2005 and 2006 by pianist and music student of the year Yuk Man Pak.

Fr. Joe D'Ambrosia continued to inspire chess players with teams entered each year in the National Secondary Schools finals in Dublin, in the Checkmate finals in Limerick sponsored by the E.S.B. Competitions against Blackrock College, Glenstal and Middleton College were regular.

In keeping with the ethos of Rockwell College, students continued their involvement in charitable works. Fr. Stirling directed the Goal/Aidlink campaign in which students raised large sums of money each year for the Third World. Students were also involved in collecting money for Fr. Peter Qeeley's Missionary fund and in fundraising for the Christina Noble Foundation. Fifth Year students continued their link with Scoil Chormaic and Scoil Aonghusa.

ROCKWELL UNION
Between 2001 and 2006 the Rockwell Union under Presidents Brendan Sutton, Brian Goff, Patrick Curran, Billy Murphy and John Duffy continued to raise funds for Spiritan missionary projects. In 2003 the President Brian Goff attended the Spiritan celebrations in Rome marking the 300th anniversary of the founding of the Holy Ghost Congregation. From 2003 the Union became involved in fundraising for the Rockwell Development Fund and as has been seen, their contribution in that regard was significant. The Union also continued its important and greatly appreciated role as career advisers to students.

OBITUARIES
Fr. Christopher Meagher C.S.Sp. died on his 87th birthday on Christmas Day 2000. He was born in Clonmel in1912. He studied at Rockwell and then entered the Holy Ghost novitiate at Kimmage. He studied at U. C.D. and prefected in Trinidad and did his theological studies at the University of Fribourg in Switzerland. He was ordained in 1941. He had brief appointments in Blackrock College and the Kilshane novitiate before coming to Rockwell in 1949 where he was to spend virtually the rest of his long life. For a number of years he was

Director of St. Joseph's. Those were the years of exceptional growth in the numbers opting for the religious life and he presided over a full house during his period there as Director. His talent for foreign languages was exceptional and he excelled as a teacher of Latin in the classroom. He also found time to publish Latin and Spanish text books.

Brother Finbarr Kelly C.S.Sp. died unexpectedly in March 2000 at the early age of 62. He had served as stores manager. In a place like Rockwell where over 1,000 meals a day were prepared, served and eaten, his role was pivotal and essential. Donal Kelly was born in Dunmanway, Co.Cork in 1937. In his late twenties he realised he had a vocation to the religious life and he entered the Holy Ghost Congregation, making his profession in 1968 after his novitiate at Ardbraccon Co. Meath. His choice of name in the religious life was obviously inspired by his love for his native place.

Fr. James Brett C.S.Sp. died in June 2000 at the age of 92. His departure left a gap in the Community, despite the fact that he had spent nearly half a century in Trinidad in the apostolate of education. Although his latter years in Rockwell were mainly spent in retirement, his gentle and undemanding presence was missed by all. He was born in 1908 at Kilmoyler, not far from Rockwell and did his secondary studies in Rockwell. He was ordained in 1936 and received his appointment to the teaching staff of St. Mary's College, Port-of-Spain, Trididad and there he was to work for forty years.

Fr. Tom Cleary C.S.Sp. died in December 2001. A native of Kilfeakle, Co. Tipperary, he was born in 1924 and studied at Rockwell. He entered the novitiate at Kilshane and was ordained in 1952. He left for the missions in Nigeria in 1953 and spent the next fourteen years in the parish of Nnewi. Due to ill-health he had to leave Nigeria in 1967 and following a short time in Ireland he departed for the United States where he worked in parishes in New York and Florida. He retired from the United States in 1993 and joined the Rockwell Community where he became involved in a new form of ministry, organising prayer groups that were linked with the Marian movement of Priests.

A former President of Rockwell, Fr. Denis O'Brien C.S.Sp. died in March 2002. He was born in Donabate, Co. Dublin in 1914 and was a student in Rockwell from 1928 to 1933. Following his studies in Rockwell he entered the novitiate in Kilshane and was ordained in 1942 having earlier obtained a Doctorate of Divinity from the Gregorian University in Rome. He took up a teaching post in the Congregation's House of Studies in Kimmage lecturing to seminarians who were preparing for the priesthood in the Congregation.

In 1950 he was appointed to Rockwell where he was to spend the next thirty years serving as a teacher, a Dean of Discipline, Bursar and President from 1974 to 1980. The Rockwell Catering School and the Rockwell Agricultural College were both his brainchild and he watched over their beginnings and their growth. In 1980 he became Bursar of the Spiritan Community in Ardbraccan, Co. Meath and later Provincial Bursar. In later years as a member of the Willow Park Community he served as assistant Chaplain in the St. John of God Hospital in Stillorgan.

Fr. Patrick Cremins C.S.Sp.died on St. Patrick's Day 2003. He had been part of the Rockwell scene for over a quarter of a century. Born in Dublin in 1915 he attended Blackrock College and entered the Holy Ghost Novitiate in 1933 and was ordained in 1944. His first appointment was to the mission in Kenya where he spent the next twenty two years. He served in Mangu, Holy Family Parish, Nairobi and St. Mary's School, Nairobi. He spent the years 1955-1958 in Rome where he obtained a Licenciate in Canon Law. When he returned to Ireland he spent a short terms teaching in Templeogue College and Ballymun Comprehensive School before coming to Rockwell in 1972 where he spent the next 28 years. He taught Latin and Italian and when he retired from teaching he looked after the Sacristy and Community Library. As the dress code among members of he Community became more relaxed, he remained faithful to the very end in wearing the traditional habit of the Congregation- probably the last member of the Community to do so.

When the name of Stephen McHugh was called out on Prize Day, May 2003, to receive the De Valera Trophy for courage, the entire assembly of students, teachers, parents and guests rose to its feet in a spontaneous gesture of affection, admiration and respect. Although it was known that Stephen was seriously ill, nevertheless his death less than two months later was a cause of deep sorrow to all his friends in Rockwell College. Sympathy was extended to his mother Maureen, a member of the College teaching staff, his father Bernard and his sister Marie.

Mr. Tom Tobin, who died in September 2003, was known and respected by generations of Rockwell students. Born in Buttevant, Co. Cork in 1910 when Rockwell was less than fifty years in existence, he lived to see the school celebrate its centenary in 1964 and continued to fulfil a vital role in the everyday life of the school until 1997.

On completion of his secondary studies at Blackrock College in 1928 he entered the Congregation of the Holy Ghost as a religious Brother when he took the name of Benedict. After five years teaching in St. Mary's College, Port of Spain, Trinidad, he was appointed to St. Mary's College, Rathmines and in 1942 he was assigned to Rockwell College. In addition to teaching classes in Commerce, Technical Drawing, Accounting and Business Studies, his manifold talents ensured that he was constantly in demand in a wide variety of departments throughout the school. He produced a memorable series of Gilbert and Sullivan operas in the late 1940s and 1950s.

Although he decided to leave the Congregation in the early 1950s, his work in the school continued uninterrupted. He played a pivotal role in the lead-up to and the actual celebration of the College's centenary in 1964. His encyclopaedic memory and his attention to detail meant that important occasions in the school year such as Prize Day and Sports Day were largely dependent on his organisation. Despite his duties as College "Registrar" he had time to write school textbooks and run the College Book Shop.

Fr. Bryan O'Connor C.S.Sp. died in March 2004. Born in Cashel in 1922 he completed his secondary studies at Rockwell after which he joined the

Congregation. He obtained an honours degree in Science at U.C.D. and was ordained in 1949. He was then posted to Sierra Leone where he spent the next twenty five years in both pastoral and educational work. His teaching was done in St. Edward's College, Freetown and in Christ the King College, Bo.

Fr. Bryan left Sierra Leone in 1975 and after a year of parish work in England, began what might be termed the second half of his teaching career, this time in his *alma mater*, Rockwell. He taught Physics and was to the fore in developing the vital area of Computer Studies in the school. He was the pioneer in this area and was responsible for building up the first Computer Room in the College. He also established an extensive video library in the College and went to endless trouble in making video recordings of various cultural and sporting events in the school. He also saw to it that tape recorders, required by teachers in teaching the revised new courses in French and German, were kept in good working order.

Fr. Bryan celebrated the Golden Jubilee of his ordination in Rockwell in the summer of 1999 when a large number of family and friends were in attendance to express their affection and respect.

Ms Lucy O'Beirne died in 2005. A teacher of French for a few years in the 1970s she was well remembered by students for the high standards she set for them.

Fr. Alfred Chamberlain C.S.Sp., who was a member of the Rockwell Community from 1958 to 1979, died in 2006. He was born in Calcutta, India in 1916 and completed his secondary studies at Blackrock College. He entered the novitiate at Kilshane and following his studies at U.C.D. he prefected at Blackrock College. Following his ordination in 1943 he was appointed Dean of the Boarding School at Blackrock College. He then went to Nigeria where he spent over a decade working in education; teaching at the College of the Immaculate Conception in Enugu, Principal of St. Anthony's Teacher Training College in Agula and finally Rector of the Spiritan Junior Seminary in Ihiala.

On returning to Ireland he was appointed Director of St. Joseph's House, Rockwell. He later became an assistant Bursar of Rockwell. In 1979 he left Rockwell for Australia where he provided much appreciated pastoral help in Spiritan parishes in Melbourne and Ringwood, Victoria. In 1983 he returned to Ireland, this time to St. Michael's where he remained until his death.

The tragic death of Sheola Keaney in July 2006 was a source of great grief and profound sadness to many individuals and groups, chief among them her classmates and friends in Rockwell College. Sheola was a student in Rockwell from 1999 to 2004 and she fully participated in the life of the school. Her vibrant presence in the classroom, her broad smile, her unmistakable yet attractive lisp endeared her to her fellow students and teachers. The shocking circumstances of her death struck a raw nerve with all who knew her.

RUGBY
The S.C.T won the Cup in 2001, the first time since 1985 and the only time between 2000 and 2006 despite producing some fine individual players in those

years including eight Schoolboy internationals. The 2000 team under coaches Mr. Hogan Chapman and Mr. Tony Smith lost in the final to C.B.C with inter-provincials Denis Leamy, Diarmuid O'Riordan, Karl Sutcliffe and James Clifford while Denis Leamy and Diramuid O'Riordan were honoured with international jersies. Mr.Alan Rutherford was coach for the next three years with Mr. Smith and coached the Cup winning team of 2001 captained by Eoin Macken with wins over Glenstal, C.B.C. and St. Munchins in the final. The winning panel was: Morgan Lyons, Frank Quinlan, Cormac McNaughton, Brendan Mackey, Michael Costello, Mark Melbourne, Brendan O'Connor,

Schoolboy Internationals 2000
Diarmuid O'Riordan and Denis Leamy.

Conor O'Gorman, Jim Mackessy, Gerry Hurley, Brendan Crowley, Rory Brosnan, James Clifford, Eoin Mackey, captain. Denis Fogarty, Michael Barry, Daragh Lyons, Shane Nolan, Kieran Lyons, Steven Mee, Michael Golden, Donnacha Duggan, John O'Donnell, Stuart Mangan, Ray O'Neill and John Ryan. The inter-provincials of 2001 were Daragh Lyons, Denis Fogarty, Brendan Mackey, Brendan O'Connor and James Mackey while Denis Fogarty and James Clifford were honoured with international caps.

Denis Fogarty captained the team of 2002 which lost in the semi-final to St. Munchins, the defeated finalists of the previous year. The inter-provincials of 2002 were Denis Fogarty, Cian McNaughton, James Mackessy and Mark Melbourne while Denis Fogarty was honoured for the second year in a row with an international cap. Cian McNaughton and James Mackessy were also honoured with the green jersey. Kevin Leamy captained the team of 2003 which lost to Ard Scoil Rís in the quarter final. Cian McNaughton and Neville Melbourne were inter-provincials that year while Cian McNaughton was honoured with an international cap for the second year in a row.

Mr. Frank Fitzgerald, himself a schoolboy international in 1990, took charge of coaching the S.C.T. in 2004 with Mr. Smith for the next three years. Eoin Culliton captained the team of 2004 while also performing as goalkeeper on the Laois minor football team which won the All Ireland. The S.C.T. lost to P.B.C. in the semi-final of 2004 while the inter-provincials were Peter Shallow and Tom Barry. Peter Shallow was Rockwell's representative on the Irish schoolboys' team of 2004.

The team of 2005, captained by Courtney Canning lost to a much stronger Munchins team while Courtney was accompanied at inter-provincial level by Stephen O'Dwyer, Killian Roche, Marcus O'Driscoll and Patrick Thompson.

The team of 2006 captained by Rory O'Connor again lost to Munchins. Rory was honoured with an international cap while he was accompanied at inter-provincial level by Eoghan Grace, Ian Duffy, Stephen O'Dwyer and Marcus O'Driscoll.

The Junior Cup team between 2000 and 2002 was coached by Mr. Ned Tierney with the assistance from time to time of Mr. Frank McGrath, Mr. John McNamara, Mr. Simon Maher and Mr. Ray Bourke. The team reached the final in 2001 but lost to a much stronger PBC team. Mr. Martin Daly took over coaching in 2003 assisted that year and in 2004 by Mr. Dermot Brislane and in 2005 by Ms Patrique Kelly. Mr. Trevor Breen and Mr Gerorg McInnes were coaches in 2006 when the "back door" system was first introduced for the Junior Cup. The under 17s, 14s and 13s meanwhile were coached in turn by Fr. Brendan Hally, Mr. James Keating, Mr.Niall McGonagle, Mr. Seán Ryan, Mr. John Power and Mr. John Hartnett.

Ladies rugby was fast becoming popular in schools throughout Munster and when it was announced in 2003 that Rockwell would enter a team, more than fifty girls turned up for training in September. The fact that staff member, Ms Patrique Kelly, was a member of the Irish Ladies team was a bonus for Rockwell as she coached the girls into shape. Two Rockwell girls, Gráinne O'Sullivan and Marina Quinlan were selected for the Munster under 19 team that year. In the next two years Rockwell ladies teams took part in the tag rugby blitz at Shannon Rugby Club and at Musgrave Park, winning the trophy twice at Shannon.

6. Senior Cup Winning Team 2001
Seated: *Gerry Hurley, Brendan Crowley, Rory Brosnan, James Clifford, Eoin Macken, Mr. Pat O'Sullivan, Denis Fogarty, Michael Barry, Daragh Lyons.*
2nd row: *Mr. Tony Smith, Morgan Lyons, Frank Quinlan, Cormac McNaughton, Brendan Mackey, Michael Costello, Mark Melbourne, Brendan O'Connor, Conor O'Gorman, Jim Mackessy, Mr. Alan Rutherford.*
3rd row: *Shane Nolan, Kieran Lyons, Stephen Mee, Michael Golden, Donnacha Duggan, John O'Donnell, Stuart Mangan, Ray O'Neill, John Ryan.*

Girls Rugby 2005-6
Seated: *Jane O'Connor, Molly Walsh, Nicola Henry, Rosie Lynch, Aideen O'Brien, Nicola Kingston, Niamh Londrgan.*
2nd row: *Chelsey O'Doherty, Ursula O'Sullivan, Daisy Welsh, Lydia Kelly, Elayne Mulcahy, Sarah Crowe, Ms. Patrique Kelly (coach)*
3rd row: *Niamh Kenneally, Lean McMorrow, Siobhán Kelly, Aisling Kenneally, Emma Wilson, Tara Dirilgen.*

HOCKEY

Hockey continued as the most popular sport for girls in Rockwell with a high degree of participation at all ages. In 2000 the under 16 team won the North Munster League for the first time, thereby becoming the first team to win a hockey tournament in the history of the College. The members of the winning team, coached by Ms Ryan, were: Clodagh-Marie O'Connor (captain), Margaret Kennedy, Marianne Kennedy, Emma Heffernan, Fiona Cummins, Natalie O'Donoghue, Clodagh McMorrow, Clare Mainstone, Maeve O'Sullivan, Niamh Lyons, Susan McGivern, Aoife Lyons, Sheree Moroney, Rachel Ryan, Niamh Daly, Elizabeth English, Louise Heywood, Siobhán Fahey, Niamh Durack, Sheila Ryan, Muireann Nolan, Nicole Thornton. The title was retained the following year.

Rockwell won the Intermediate League in 2003 beating Loreto Clonmel in the final. Coached by Ms. Ryan the winning panel was: Marina Quinlan (captain), Niamh Lyons, Aoife Lyons, Susan McGivern, Emma Coffey, Siobhán McMorrow, Rachel Cummins, Noreen O'Callaghan, Roslyn Rochard, Gráinne O'Sullivan, Audrey McGrath, Emma Jane Morrissey, Lorna Pierse, Philippa Leahy, Mary O'Connell, Lauranne O'Reilly, Gillian Barry, Sarah Maher, Elaine Devereaux, Amy Ryan, Doireann McMorrow, Jessica Long.

Teams were entered at all levels in the following years with coaches Ms Alvara Duggan, Ms Emma Gleeson and Ms Patrique Kelly and were especially successful at senior and under 16 grades.

OTHER SPORTS

Fr. Hally, as Games Master, was responsible for the organisation of all sport in this period. Participation in Athletics in Rockwell had declined in recent years but signs of a revival were evident in 2003 when the relay team of Peter Shallow, Cian McNaughton, John Curran and Des Morrissey qualified for the All Ireland as did William McCarthy in the intermediate pole-vault. The following year Peter Shallow won the National Indoor 60 metre hurdle championship and Finbar Horgan won the National Indoor 800 metre event, these events held at Nenagh.

Under 14 G.A.A. football teams continued to take part in the annual Rockwell blitz and in 2002 the team, managed by Mr. Keating, won the annual quadrangular competition in Newbridge College. A hurling team, managed by Mr. Kenny, took part in the Lord Mayor's Cup in Cork in 2005 and 2006.

The Canoe Team, directed by Mr. McGrath won the Leander Cup for the 23rd consecutive time in 2000, the members of the team being: Louise Heywood, Dirk Hau, Rory Sheehan, Michael O'Riordan, Eamon Hayes, Kevin Murphy, Dominic Rodgers, John Madden, Colm Lonergan, Orla McGrath, Muireann Nolan. In 2003 at the Liffey Descent three 6th Year students, Dominic Rogers, Kevin Murphy and Michael O'Leary came first, second and third respectively in their class. In 2005 Paul Russell was selected to represent Ireland in the junior mens' section in the World Cup.

The under 15 Boys' basketball team of 2000 won a competition in Denmark in which teams from nine European countries had taken part. Ms Alavaro

Leander Cup Winners 2000
Seated: *Kevin Murphy, Dominic Rodgers, John Madden, Colm Lonergan, Orla McGrath, Muireann Nolan.*
Standing: *Mr. Frank McGrath, Louise Heywood, Dirk Hau, Rory Sheehan, Michael O'Riordan,*
Eamon Hayes.

Senior Girls Basketball 2002
Front: *Noreen O'Callaghan, Marina Quinlan, Erin Gleeson.*
Back: *Gráinne O'Sullivan, Laura Prenderville, Susan McGivern, Jeanienne McCarthy.*

Duggan managed the teams of 2003 when three members, J.D. Flynn, Herman Heuvinck and Kojo Boama were under 19 inter-provincials. Ms Neasa O'Halloran managed basketball teams in the next few years with Mr. John Kilbride and Mr. Simon Kenny.

The equestrian team with Mr. Brislane as Chef d'Equipe reached 7th place out of 72 teams in the National Hunter Trial of 2002 with Jessica Long honoured at international level. The team members were: Aaron Leonard, Mark Flunn, Niamh Lonergan, Jessica Long, Conor English, Michael R. Kelly, Gerard Gleeson, Claire Cremmins, Robert Keogh, Seán Ronan. In 2004 Rockwell won the National Show Jumping championship in Port Laoise with Mark Flynn winning a bronze medal in the European Pony championships and Ruth McGarry obtaining first place in the All-Ireland Pony Club championships. The National Show Jumping championship was won again in Eniscorthy in 2006 when the team consisted of Tom Lalor, Anna Geraghty, Peter O'Donnell and Ruth McGarry.

A rare achievement in tennis was recorded in 2002 when Rockwell won the Munster Girls' under 19 championship for the first time. The team was led by Clodagh McMorrow with her sister Doireann and ably supported by Emma Heffernan and Clodagh-Marie O'Connor. Previously Clodagh McMorrow had won the National Under 18's Championship held at Fitzwilliam and reached the semi-final of the National Senior championship and she won the Riverview Indoor Championship. Clodagh was nominated as one of Tipperary Sportspersons of the Year for 2002 and was awarded a civic reception in her native Tipperary Town. The under 16 team of Gillian Barry, Lorna Pierse, Siobhán McMorrow and Bronagh McMorrow performed well in competition in 2002. Rockwell won the Munster under 14 Boys'Shield in 2004 when the team members were Patrick Butler, Peter Acheson, Alex McAlpin and Aidan Burke. There was a notable Squash achievement in 2002 when Stephen O'Dwyer was ranked fourth in Ireland at under 15 level and represented Ireland in international competition.

Swimming galas were organised each year by Mr. Martin Daly and Ms Ryan. In 2004 Hugo Morrissey and Andrew Yates were selected to represent Munster at the National Swimming championships. In 2005 for the first time Rockwell won the Munster Relay Shield for Senior Boys, the team being Eoghan Anderson, Kyle Kophamel, Hugo Morrissey and Michael Coyne. Medal winners at

Munster Senior Tennis Cup Winners 2002
Front: *Doireann McMorrow, Clodagh McMorrow*
Back: *Emma Heffernan, Clodagh-Marie O'Connor.*

the Munster championships in 2006 were Hugo Morrissey, Michael Coyne, Gavin Yates, Alan Anderson and Michael Coyne.

Munster Swimming Relay Champions 2004
Hugo Morrissey, Eoghan Anderson, Kyl Kophamel, Michael Coyne.

Girls Golf Team 2002
Front: *Lorna Pierse, Jacqui Ryan.*
Back: *Mary O'Connell, Mr. M. Doyle.*

Soccer Players 2001
Seated: *Ken Feely, Matthew McCabe, Ronan Ryan, Patrick Nugent, Mr. Gerard Hough,*
Laurence Phelan, Karol Keane, Danny Flynn, Ray O'Sullivan.
2nd row: *Colm Lonergan, Eoin Hartigan, Ryan Hennessy, Patrick Prendergast, Francis Strumble,*
Tadhg Carroll, Edward Manning, David Moloney, Tom Devane.
3rd row: *Gerard Collins, Michael Delaney, Jorge de Beascoa, Marcos Van Dulken, Liam Hyland, Rory*
Sheehan, Tom Kelly, William English.

Interest in soccer increased when Mr. Hough took charge in 2001. The highlight of this period was the winning of the North Munster Senior Cup in 2004 with the winning panel of David Roche, Donal Collins, Shane O'Sullivan, Neville Melbourne, Brian Hogg, Aaron Nolan, Damien Ryan, Eamon Peters, Ben Lynch, Michael Strickland, Eoin Culliton, Alan Rockett, Des Morrissey, Daniel Schmidt, Shane Collins, Kevin Quinlan, Aidan Scannell, Paul Halley (captain), Conor McEvoy, Tom Barry, Jamie Kelly. Ladies soccer was introduced in 2006 when games were played against Cashel, Thurles, Borrisokane and Pallaskenry.

Students interested in playing golf were catered for by Mr. Doyle who entered teams each year in the Munster Schools championship with the hope of qualifying for the British and Irish Schools competition. Of local interest was the annual competition against Cahir Community College referred to as the Ryder Cup. When Rockwell won this competition in 2002 the players were Patrick Ruddy, Stuart Mangan, Fintan McGuirk and John Fahey. The following year the team consisted of Christopher Kendrick, Patrick Ruddy, John Devereaux, Tiarnan O'Sullivan and Arthur Pierse.

– 20 –

TOWARDS THE SESQUICENTENARY
2007-2014

As Rockwell College approached its sesquicentenary it completed phase three of its development programme while at the same time adapting to more new changes required by the 1998 Education Act and to the challenges of rapid technological advances.

It was possible to complete phase three of the development programme because over €2 million had been raised by parents and supporters and because of grants by the Department of Education and Science. A Past Pupils' fundraising committee, chaired by Andy Butler, was especially generous.

During 2007 the new all-weather pitch was officially opened and it immediately became the centrepiece of the Physical Education programme and a facility enjoyed by many sports. A new and highly furnished staff room was completed and when a grant was sanctioned by the Department of Education and Science work commenced on the development of two new science laboratories and a music room. These were located on the bottom floor of the Crehan Wing.

New Lecture Theatre

384

The revamped library

A new lift was installed in 2008 connecting all floors in the main building at a cost of €100,000. In 2010 a new reception area was completed as was a new lecture theatre and a new I.T. facility, the latter two being located in the area recently vacated by the old science laboratories off the main hall. A grant from the Department of Education and Science was secured. There was an upgrading of the communications, broadband and inter-com links throughout the entire plant and an alternative biomass energy system was installed which took account of carbon costs and environmental obligations. If past students were bewildered by all these changes they may have even been more confused when trying to access the College now that the new M8 motorway on the Dublin-Cork route deprived the passer-by of a sight of the imposing front entrance gates with a mere glimpse of the tower in the distance a poor substitute.

The Education Act of 1998 had, among other matters, specified the setting up of boards of management and inspection of schools by the Department of Education and Science. Accordingly, boards of management were established in all Spiritan schools acting as agents for the DEA. The Rockwell College Board of Management was established in September 2006. Like all boards of management it consisted of four nominees of the trustees, two nominated by teachers and two by parents. The Principal acted as secretary to the Board. The term of office of this first Board expired in 2012 when it was succeeded by the second Board.

In October 2006 the Department of Education and Science informed the College that during the following weeks a team of inspectors would be conducting a Whole School Evaluation on every aspect of the College management, curriculum teaching and student welfare. Following this inspection a report, which was a 50,000 word document, was issued in March 2007 with an introduction outlining the history and character of the school. It assessed the quality of school management, the quality of school planning, the quality of curriculum provision, the quality of learning and teaching in subjects and the quality of support for students. In all cases the findings were highly positive. This report was available to the public on the internet and was a great advertisement for Rockwell. Inspections of individual subjects followed which were again highly positive.

Maintenance Staff 2012
Seated: *John Byrne, John Keating, Monica Moore, Tommy Keating, James C. Mangan, Eimear O'Neill.*
Standing: *John Shanahan, Myles Ryan, Paddy Currivan, Catherine Moore, Justin Cleary, Billy Lawlor, Danny Ryan.*

Fundraising for Good Causes 2010
Orla Heffernan, Ms Caroline Kelly, Eoin O'Donoghue, Andrew Desmond, Kieran Lyons, Kevin Bartley, Robbie Lyons, Ella Guionneau, Odhran McCarthy, Ms June O'Brien.

Catering Directors 2012
*Mr. Hugh O'Donoghue (Catering Manager), Mr. Garrett Sheehan (Chef), Dr. Seán O'Donnell
(Chairperson Board of Management), Mr. Barry Sheehan (Union President),
Ms Audrey O'Byrne (Principal), Mr. Gearóid O Sullivan (Head Chef), Mr. John O'Donoghue (Chef)*

In response to the great advances in technology since the new millennium, Rockwell College, like other educational institutions, responded by adopting a policy on the acceptable usage of the computer network and internet. It recognised that the main purpose of the College computer and network resources was to support the pedagogic and day-to-day operation of the school. These resources include hardware, software, user accounts, local and wide area network facilities as well as services accessed via the internet. They are powerful resources enabling technologies for accessing and delivering information and knowledge.

These resources and the dramatic advances in facilities such as U-Tube, Facebook, Twitter, the iPad, Tablets and Smartphones, demanded that the policy on their use within the College be reviewed on a regular basis. Students were asked to sign an acceptance form agreeing to use the internet and other resources in a responsible way and to obey all rules within the policy. They were warned that violation of this policy could result in disciplinary action, including possible suspension or expulsion and that Rockwell College reserved the right to report any illegal activities to the appropriate authorities. Parents and guardians were also asked to sign this acceptance form.

The years leading to Rockwell's one hundred and fiftieth celebrations were also the years when the so-called Celtic Tiger was coming to an end and Ireland was plummeting into another deep economic recession. This put a severe strain on all concerned parties. Some parents had to cope with unemployment and negative equity while the Department of Education and Science had to trim its budgets by increasing teacher-pupil ratio and enforcing severe operational restrictions. Rockwell College was faced with major challenges at a time of great change in its personnel.

PERSONNEL

Fr. William Cleary retired as President in 2007 and returned to the missions in Zimbabwe. He was succeeded as President by Fr. John Meade who also took over from Fr. Reedy as Superior of the Community. Fr. Meade was a native of Miltown Malbay and having studied at Blackrock College was ordained in 1968. He spent ten years in Sierra Leone before his appointment as Dean of Discipline in Rockwell in 1980 and his later return to the missions. This was also a time of notable retirements. Fr. Pat Downes retired in 2007 having served in Willow Park for eleven years before coming to Rockwell in 1979 where in addition to his classroom work he served as Junior Dean (1880-1986) and Games Master (1986-1998)

Fr. John Meade
President 2007-2011

Fr. Joseph D'Ambrosia returned to Africa in the summer of 2010 to continue the missionary work which he had begun there in the late 1970s. Since coming to Rockwell in 1999 he endeared himself especially to foreign students as their teacher of English. He also involved himself with the promotion of chess and all the while he acted as sacristan in the College Chapel.

Fr. Peter Raftery also retired in 2010. He had come to Rockwell in 1997 as a teacher of French and Music. His passion was choral music and he formed choirs which performed at liturgical services and at inter-schools competitions. He acted as editor of the *Rockwell Annual* and excelled in recording the daily life of the College.

Catering Staff 2012
Seated: *Debbie Ramsey, Ann Marie O'Donoghue, Tetyana Lapco, Yvonne Reddy, Joan O'Reilly.*
Standing: *Garret Sheehan, Lillija Andliraskaja, Ita Holmes, Galina Morozona, Elena Gluata,*
Mary Ramsey, Donna Harding, John O'Donoghue.

There were notable retirements among the lay teaching staff. Ms. Margaret Niland-Ryan retired in 2008 having served since 1991 as teacher of Accounting, Economics, Maths and Business Organisation. Mr. Tony Smith, who retired in 2012, had been teacher of Maths and Economics since 1973 and a prominent mentor of rugby and Gaelic Football teams. Mr. John Mason also retired in 2012. He had been teacher of French and German from 1980 until his redeployment in 1989. Returning in 1991 he continued his involvement with the annual school tours.

Fr. Peter Raftery at the Chapel organ 2009

The Principal, Mr. Pat O'Sullivan, took early retirement in 2012. Since his appointment as the first lay Principal of Rockwell in 1997, he had steered the College over the next fifteen years through a period of great development of its infrastructure, notably the new classrooms and science block, the new halls of residence, the new all-weather pitches and the enhanced security systems. And during his term of office the student population was retained at a very high level; in 2007, for instance, there were seventy international students from Spain, Mexico, China, Japan, Russian, Germany, Luxembourg, the United Kingdom, the United States and other countries.

Mr. Pat O'Sullivan
Principal 1997-2012

It was an occasion of historic significance for Rockwell in 2012 when Ms. Audrey O'Byrne was appointed the first lady Principal. Ms. O'Byrne had been a member of the teaching staff since 1999 when her chief subject was English. She devoted much of her time to the promotion of debating and under her direction the College achieved notable success in this area, winning the schools competition run by University College Cork Philosophical Society on two occasions and being runner-up in

Ms. Audrey O'Byrne
Principal

Mr. Michael Doyle
Deputy Principal

the All Ireland competition organised by University College Dublin in 2010. Her appointment as Principal was greeted by her teaching colleagues with enthusiasm and optimism.

STUDENT ACTIVITY

Students continued to involve themselves in various organisations which help the under-privileged. The Hope Foundation, a charity which works for the street children of Calcutta, involved Rockwell students in raising large sums of money to help these children and in journeying to India with assistance. Fundraising for other charities such as Trócaire, Temple Street Childrens Hospital, Operation Smile, a charity to help children with facial deformities and the Niall Mellon Township Trust also involved students, especially Transition Year students under the direction of Mr. Pat Egan

Choral music was conducted by Fr. Raftery until he was succeeded in 2010 by Mr. John White. The development of the new theatre afforded an opportunity for stage productions leading to a series of popular musicals. In 2007 it was *Once on this Island* with Ms Lena Hally as musical director and production by Ms Gemma Cummins assisted by Ms Eleanor Gilroy and Mr. Brendan Ferris with the leading parts played by Eimear Collins, Gavin Ryan, Brendan Cullinane, Charlie Purcell and Neil Farrell. The same team directed *Jesus Christ Superstar* in 2008 when the leading players were Tom Sharpe, Jane O'Connor, David Farah, Mark Loveday. Ronan Maher, Darragh McEniry, Darragh Bourke, Sarah Long and Sal Molumby and Emma Wilson.

Seven Brides for Seven Brothers in 2010 was directed by Ms O'Dwyer with production by Ms Cummins and Ms O'Byrne. Leading parts were played by Ursula O'Sullivan, Jane O'Connor, Emma Wilson, Eva Cummins, Elayne Mulcahy, Eimear Barron, Elaine Long, Dermot Maher, Colm Summers, Nicholas Ryan, Michael Butler, Jack Sutcliffe, Jack Jeffries, Ause Abdelhaq, Richard Moran, Laurens van Bussell, Joanne Irwin, Paraic Ryan, Kate Ryan. David Smyth. *All Shook Up* in 2010 was directed by Ms O'Dwyer, production

Senior Chess Team 2007-8
Wilson Pak, Ivan Gliancev, Fr.J. D'Ambrosia, Nikanor Khalin, Guillermo Carrasco.

College Choir 2007-8
Seated: *Johanna Butler, Finbar English, Maximilian Pucklitzsch, Fr. Peter Raftery, Mark Loveday,*
Pepe Moreno, Zack O'Connell,
2nd row: *Ciara Cremmins, Ursula O'Sullivan, Ross Kerrigan, Lydia Kelly, Marcel Beaucamp,*
Zoe Finnegan, Elayne Mulcahy, Adrian Walshe, Carlo Cuellar.
3rd row: *Nicky Purcell, Eva Cummins, Siobhán Kelly, Jack Sutcliffe, Micheál Butler, Dermot Maher,*
Aideen O'Brien, Michael Fitzgerald.

Debating Team retains Munster Trophy 2010
Jack Jeffries, Ms. Audrey O'Byrne, Jack Moloney, Joey Doverman

College Staff 2011-2012
1st row: *John Mason, Kathleen Smyth, Pat O'Sullivan, Audrey O'Byrne, Michael Doyle, Brendan Ferris Michael Doyle jn.*
2nd row: *Pat Bennis, Pat Egan, Jeanette Hickey, Joan Kennedy, Tom Hogan Frank McGrath.*
3rd. row: *Brede Corcoran, Eileen McCormack, Tom Ryan, Nicola McGrath, Maureen McHugh, Gemma Walsh Cummins.*
4th row: *Frank O'Sullivan, Nicola Fahey, Tony Smith, Lisa Cosgrove, Fr. Brendan Hally, Mary Hyland.*
5th row: *Cathal Maher, Caroline Kelly, Seán Ryan, Kate Heaney, Elaine O'Sullivan, Fiona McGillicuddy.*
6th row: *Aoife Mulcahy, Simon Kenny, Wini Ryan, Patrique Kelly, Alvara Duggan, June O'Brien.*
7th row: *William Ryan, John White, Frank Fitzgerald, Martin Daly, John Fitzgibbon, Anna Dunne.*

Ms Cummins Ms O'Byrne. Leading parts played by Mandy O'Dwyer, Natalie Haller, Jessie Barlow, David Farah, Odhrán McCarthy, Sophie Sharpe, Alison O'Connor, David Smyth, Ciara Cremins, Jack Looby.

West Side Story in 2011 had Ms Lena Hally as musical director with Ms Audrey O'Byrne and Ms Gemma Cummins as producers. Taking part were Colm Summers, Cian Farrell, Adam Horgan, Ata Dirilgen, Michael Boland, Charles Croome-Carroll, Michael Fitzgerald, Ódhrán McCarthy, Connor Joy, Emma Ryan, Charlotte Ashmore, Ashley Maher, Rachel Breen, Mary Anne Browne, Rachel Doyle, Kate Benson, Ause Abdelhaq, Neville Flynn, Micahel Purcell, Cormac O'Donnell, Jack Morrissey, Conor Godsil, Harvey Blackmore, Chloe Maher, Jane O'Donovan, Alison O'Connor, Sophie Sharpe, Elaine Long, Jenna Belghafria, Maeve Quinlan, Elizabeth Doherty, Kate Harney, James Houlihan, Cormaxc English, Michael Morrissey and Jack Looby.

Back to the 80s was produced by Mr. Tom Ryan in 2012 and taking part were Andrew Smyth, Cormac Looby, Simon Sharpe, Peirce Maher, Mimi Lane, Chloe Maher, Eilidh Rogers, Robyn Barlow, Charles Croome-Carroll, Cian

Overseas Student of the Year 2010
*Mr. Michael Doyle (Deputy Principal, Mr. Paul Marren (Union President), Jay Theis,
Mr. Pat O'Sullivan (Principal)*

Flavin, Joey Doverman, Eireamhóin McCarthy, Oisin Fiuza, Laura Moloney, Jean O'Donnell, Emily Nolan, Jane O'Donovan, Ause Abdelelhaq, Toby Kane, Michaela Kavanagh, Michaela Waissel, Áine Heffernan and Oonagh Hynes.

Camp Rockwell, which had been founded by Fr. Des Reid, was still thriving in 2013. Following Fr. Reid's departure it continued for many years under the management of the College Bursar with Marie Quinlan and David Morris as Directors. The Camp was outsourced for the years 2008 to 2011 and was taken back under the management of Rockwell College in 2012 when the Directors were Ms Joan Kennedy and Mr. Pat O'Sullivan. The Camp was fully booked for 2013 with Ms Joan Kennedy as Director.

RUGBY
The SCT recorded losses in the Cup to PBC in 2007 and to Castletroy in 2008 when the captains were Ian Duffy and Conor Sweeney respectively. The inter-provincials in 2007 were Ian Duffy, Derry O'Neill, William Devane and Kevin Buckley and in 2008 Paddy Butler, Shane Luby, Brendan Cullinane and Brian Smith. James Ryan was an international in 2007 and Paddy Butler in 2008. The teams were coached in those two years by Martin Daly, Tom Mulcahy, Tony Trehy, Dermot Brislane, Ken O'Connell and Paudie Butler.

What proved to be a record sequence of success for the SCT began in 2008 when Rockwell was to contest the Cup final for five seasons in-a-row. Paddy

Butler was captain in 2009 and the coaches were Mark Butler, Fergus Timmons and Tom Mulcahy when for the first time the "back door" system was in operation for the senior Cup. Rockwell lost to Castletroy in the first round but beat Glenstal and then St. Munchins but lost to CBC in the final by 33-19. The internationals in 2009 were Paddy Butler and Shane Buckley and the inter-provincials with Paddy Butler and Shane Buckley were Brian Smith, Brendan Cullinane and Gavin Ryan.

Rockwell reached the final for the second year in a row in 2010 when Shane Buckley was captain but lost to P.B.C by 22-10. On the way to the final victories were secured over St. Munchins, Ard Scoil Rís and Castletroy. The internationals in 2010 were Shane Buckley and J.J. Hanrahan and together with these two inter-provincials was Cian O'Donnell. The coaches were Mark Butler, Tom Mulcahy, Kevin Leamy, Frank Fitzgerald and Tony Smith and the physiotherapist was Frances Mulcahy.

For the first time since 2001 and for the third successive year in the final, Rockwell won the Cup in 2011. One hundred and twenty training sessions were held and fifty players contested for fifteen places. Cian O'Donnell was captain and on the way to the final victories were recorded over Bandon, St. Munchins, Ard Scoil Rís, CBC and against PBC in the final at Musgrave Park. The panel was: Aidan Barron, Aidan O'Sullivan, Billy Duggan, Richard Moran, Eddie

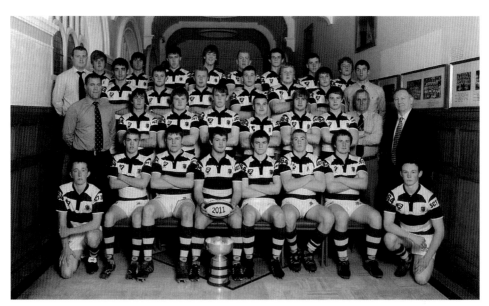

Munster Senior Rugby Cup Winners 2011
1st row: *Aidan Barron, Billy Duggan, Eddie Phelan, Cian O'Donnell, Sonny Dwyer, Aidan O'Sullivan, Richard Moran, Luke McGrane*
2nd row: *Mr. Frank Fitzgerald, Ronan Maher, Cathal Ryan, Conor Holland, Dara Mulcahy, Donough MacGillicuddy, Shaun Horgan, Mr. Tony Smith, Mr. Pat O'Sullivan.*
3rd row: *Alwx Rio-Lynch, Brian Haugh, Rob Jermyn, Cillian Kiely, David Kennedy, David Johnston, Mr. Kevin Leamy.*
4th row: *Mr. Mark Butler, M.J. Murphy, Harry McNulty, Brendan Crosse, Seán McCarthy, Luke Cahill, Neville Flynn, Aidan Butler, Aaron Sweeney.*

Munster Senior Rugby Cup Winners 2012
Seated: *Mr. Frank Fitzgerald, Steve McMahon, Mr. Kevin Leamy, Cillian Kiely, Mr. Pat O'Sullivan, Seán McCarthy, Mr. Mark Butler, Sonny Dwyer, Mr. Tom Mulcahy, Shaun O'Donoghue, Mr. Tony Smith.*
2nd row: *Darragh Mulcahy, Aaron Sweeney, Jack McCormack, Cathal Ryan, James Maxwell, Neville Flynn, Seán McNulty, James Feehan, Willie O'Dwyer, Ronan Maher, Aidan Moynihan, Rob Jermyn.*
3rd row: *David Johnston, Alex Rio-Lynch, Darragh Foley, Dylan McGragh, Aidan Butler, Robert Lyons, Aidan Barron.*

Phelan, Luke McGrane, Cian O'Donnell (captain), Sonny Dwyer, Shaun Horgan, Ronan Maher, Cathal Ryan, Conor Holland, Dara Mulcahy, Donough MacGillicuddy, Neville Flynn, Alex Rio-Lynch, Aidan Butler, Brian Haugh, Harry McNulty, Aaron Sweeney, Rob Jermyn, Brendan Crosse, Cillian Kiely, Seán McCarthy, David Kennedy, Luke Cahill, David Johnston. The management team was: Tom Mulcahy, Frank Fitzgerlad, Ross O'Callaghan, Mark Butler and Kevin Leamy and the physiotherapist was Frances Mulcahy.

The S.C.T. was in the final for the fourth year in succession in 2012 and captained by Seán McCarthy, the Cup was successfully retained. The campaign opened with a narrow win over Glenstal at Clanwilliam followed by an unexpected easy victory over Castletroy. In a repeat of the previous year's semi-final, Rockwell travelled to Musgrave Park to take on C.B.C. A try and two penalties secured a Rockwell victory and left the Corkmen scoreless. The final against Munchins was at Thomond Park. Trailing by 5 to nil at half time, Rockwell had a stiff task ahead. With a solid scrum and accurate line-outs in the second half Rockwell were soon ahead by 6-5 and survived a late onslaught by Munchins. The winning panel was: David Johnston, Alex Rio-Lynch, Darragh Foley, Dylan McGagh, Aidan Butler, Robert Lyons, Aidan Barron , Darragh Mulcahy, Aaron Sweeney, Jack McCormack, Cathal Ryan, James Maxwell, Neville Flynn, Seán McNulty, James Feehan, Willie O'Dwyer, Ronan Maher, Aidan Moynihan, Rob Jermyn, Steve McMahon, Cillian Kiely, Seán McCarthy, Sonny Dwyer and Shaun O'Donoghue. The management team was similar to the previous year.

Rockwell was in search of three-in-a-row when the S.C.T. set out on their 2013 campaign and they got off to a solid start with a 15-5 victory over Crescent. In the quarter final at Clanwilliam Rockwell proved far too strong for Castletroy winning by 25-7 and keeping alive their hopes of a three-in-a-row success. As a contest it was over by half time at which stage Rockwell was leading 18-0, all the points having come from centre Rory Parata. In the semi-final against the previous year's finalists, St. Munchin's, Steve McMahon was the toast of Rockwell after his try three minutes into stoppage time gained a dramatic 13-6 victory and earned his side a place in the final for the fifth successive year with the prospect of Sonny Dwyer and Neville Flynn picking up their third medal. The opponents in the final were Crescent whom Rockwell had easily disposed of earlier in the season. In the final, however, Crescent sprang a major surprise to overcome Rockwell by 27-5. It was a great disappointment. The panel which reached the final was: Steve McMahon, D. O'Mahony, S. O'Donoghue, Rory Parata, W. Coffey, A. Moynihan, Ben Riley, D. O'Connell, Seán McNulty, J. Maxwell, N. Flynn Adam Horgan, S. O'Connor, Jimmy Feehan, S. Dwyer, Aidan Butler, E. Mulcahy, A. McMahon, R. Horgan, T. Anglim.

The J.C.T. had not won the Cup since 1997 and between 2007 and 2012 it remained elusive. Glenstal beat them in 2008 and 2009 and Castletroy in 2010 and 2011. In 2012 they lost to Castletroy and Ard Scoil Rís. Their fortunes improved in 2013 with a 13-10 win over St. Munchins followed by a 13-13 draw with CBC. In the replay, however, they lost narrowly by 22-21. The J.C.T. teams were trained in those years by Brendan Ferris and Patrique Kelly. Girls' rugby took off for the first time in 2007 and again in 2009 with Patrique Kelly in charge on both occasions. In those years Mollie O'Donnell, Rosie Lynch, Lean McMorrow and Kelly Dwyer were picked to represent Munster.

Other Sports
There was a low level of participation in athletics in these years although teams were entered in the East Munster each year. The canoeists made their annual trips to the Suir and Nore and enjoyed kayak surfing at Tramore and Lahinch. Cricket had a revival in 2007 and 2008 with the new all-weather pitch being used for practice sessions. Rockwell had great success at show jumping winning the national schools championship for the second time in 2009 and Joseph O'Brien and Nicola Harvey being selected on the Irish team in 2008. Mr. Brislaine took charge of equestrian sport and the team competed in the British Schools championship at Hickstead.

David Hannigan and Joseph O'Brien represent Rockwell at Hickstead 2008

Equestrian Team 2007
Front: *David Bergin, Greg Henry, Joseph O'Brien, David Hannigan, Patrick Bolger.*
Back: *Mr. D. Brislane, Michael Davoren, Anna Geraghty, Niamh Barry, Ruth McGarry,*
Peter O'Donnell, Niall Flynn, Eddie Phelan.

Rockwell golfers, under the direction of Mr. Doyle, distinguished themselves in those years. In 2007, for the first time in eighteen years the senior team won the North Munster championship at Rathbane, the members of the team being Brian McEvoy, Ross O'Dwyer and Patrick Butler while Sarah Crowe was selected for the Munster Schools inter-provincial team. In 2008 the senior team won the Munster section of the Irish strokeplay championship and finished second in the All Ireland final, the leading golfers being David Ruddy, Neil Farrell and Patrick Butler. Sarah Crowe was again on the Munster team and on the basis of her performance she was chosen for specialised coaching at St. Andrews. Jill Pierse, playing off a handicap of eight, was also prominent.

Basketball continued as a popular sport for girls and boys. The senior girls team in 2008 reached the All Ireland final at the National Basketball Arena but lost in the final to St. Mary's, Charlestown. Ms Neasa O'Halloran was coach and the team was: Molly Walsh, Zoe Finnegan, Ellen O'Shea, Tara Dirilgen, Eimear Collins, Rosie Lynch, Laura Enright, Zoe O'Connor, Sarah Long, Julie Irwin (captain) Jennifer Quinlan, Mollie O'Donnell. Ms Whelan and Mr Kenny were in charge of the other basketball teams.

The hockey players enjoyed the new all-weather pitch. The senior Cup and the senior League were won in 2009 with wins over Villiers and St. Anglea's Cork but because of this they were upgraded to the B class where competition was more difficult. Teams were managed by Ms Alvara Duggan, Fiona Noonan and Patrique Kelly. The seniors lost narrowly in the 2011 final of the Munster Cup.

The under 14 Gaelic football team, which was managed each year by Mr. Keating, took part in the annual Newbridge blitz and the annual Rockwell blitz.

Senior Hockey Cup and League Winners 2012
Seated: *Emma Ryan, Alison O'Connor, Betty Barlow, Siobhán Hennessy, Sarah O'Sullivan,*
Áine O'Dwyer, Sorcha Sweeney.
Standing: *Elaine Long, Jane Hannigan, Ally Barlow, Sinéad Kennedy, Kate Binchy, Jackie O'Gorman,*
Mr. John Ryan, Aisling McCarthy, Amy Sweeney, Aoife Purcell, Betty Barlow, Rachel Doyle,
Cliona Doyle, Edel Cummins.

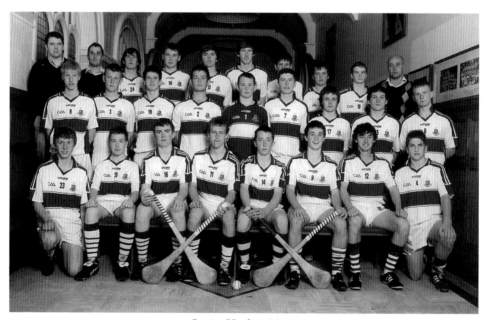

Senior Hurlers 2010
1st row: *Liam Fahey, Cillian Walsh, Joe O'Neill, Eamon Morrissey, Aidan Barron , Liam Murchan,*
Gregory Henry, William Coffey.
2nd row: *Conor Hayes, James Costello, Robert O'Donnell, Colin Meagher, Killian Farrell,*
Tommy Sweeney, Conor Moloughney, T. J. Ryan, Elliot Mulcahy.
3rd row: *Mr. Seán Ryan, Mr. Brendan Ferris, Ronan Maher, Kevin Maher, Colman Kennedy,*
Philip Quirke, John Feehan, Shane Skelly, Jonathan Yates, Mr. Simon Kenny.

All Ireland Minor Football Champions 2011
Rockwell members of that Tipperary team: T.J. Ryan, Greg Henry, Jimmy Feehan, Philip Quirke,
Niall McKenna, Colman Kennedy.

**Munster Tennis Shield
Winners 2007**
*Louise Quinlan, Jill Pierse,
Lean McMorrow,
Elena Moreno.*

Mr. Kenny took charge of the under 17 hurling team which took part each year in the Fitzgerald Cup which was the competition for Tipperary schools.

Soccer teams for boys and girls were managed by Mr Hough and a unique distinction was achieved in 2008 when Peter Acheson was picked on the under 18 Irish team for games against Northern Ireland, Wales and England. Eoin Farrell was honoured at under 15 level the same year while Tom O'Hanlon was chosen on the Irish Clubs team and Alex McAlpin on the Munster team.

Rockwell swimmers, boys and girls, took part in the Munster Schools championship each year. In 2007 the relay team of Andrew Balfour, Jamie Willgrass, Michael Coyne and Alan Anderson were winners and they came third in the All Ireland in Belfast. The same quartet was again winner in 2008 in both the medley and freestyle relays. In 2007 Andrew Yates won the butterfly event in the national championships.

The under 19 tennis players won the Munster Shield in 2008 and 2009 when the players were Lean McMorrow, Louise Quinlan, Jill Pierse, Elena Moreno and Zoe O'Connor. The under 14 boys' team of Geronimo Farres, Jack Marshall, Aidan Butler and Denis O'Connell won the Munster Shield in 2007.

ROCKWELL COLLEGE UNION

The Union Presidents in those years were Robert Gallagher, Jim Holmes, Joe Barrett and Liam Flynn and as usual they made very generous donations towards the Spiritan mission, towards the upkeep of the College and towards other good causes. Among notable donations were a €40,000 gift towards the building of the new science laboratories, the purchase of a new College minibus, €3,000 towards the Spiritan House in Zimbabwe, €1,500 towards the Hope Foundation and €1,000 towards the Stuart Mangan Fund.

OBITUARIES

Mr. Joseph Irwin, a member of the teaching staff, died in January 2007. He had retired in 1990. Joe came to Rockwell in 1968 having previously taught in Glenstal, Ennis and Cashel. At U.C.D. he was a member of the Dramatic society, the beginning of a lifelong interest in all aspects of the theatre. In Rockwell he taught Englsih, History and Geography at all levels, but both staff and students will always associate him with the annual school play. For twenty years he devoted most of the first term to converting inexperienced youths into actors capable of creating parts in productions of a high standard. Students lucky enough to have undergone the transformation were greatly enriched by the experience and grateful for a love and understanding of the theatre.

Fr. Patrick Holohan C.S.Sp. President of Rockwell 1981-1986, died in June 2007. A native of Ballinard, near Fethard, he was born in 1928 and received his secondary education at Rockwell. Having studied in Kimmage and in Rome he was ordained in 1956. His first appointment was in Nigeria where he was involved principally in pastoral and educational work. He became Education Secretary for the Archdiocese of Onitsha and also served on the staff of the Cathedral Parish. Like nearly three hundred other Spiritans, Fr. Paddy had to leave Nigeria on the outbreak of the Biafran War. He spent a time in the United States before arriving in Rockwell in 1972 where he filled the role of Dean in the Boarding School before becoming President. In 1986 he was transferred to St. Michael's College in Dublin where he worked until 1995. He was then assigned to the Spiritan Regional House in New York where he served until the time of his death.

Fr. Tom McCarthy C.S.Sp. died in June 2007. He was born in Tipperary Town in 1929. After his secondary education with the Christian Brothers in his native Tipperary, he entered the Holy Ghost novitiate at Kilshane in 1947. He spent two years prefecting in Blackrock College and was ordained to the priesthood in 1955. His first appointment was to Nigeria where he worked in the Diocese of Onitsha until 1968 and like Fr. Holohan he was forced to leave Nigeria on the outbreak of the Biafran war. He served in the Archdiocese of Dublin and in Willow Park School before coming to Rockwell in 1977. In Rockwell he worked as a chaplain to the Hotel and Catering School.

Fr. John Buckley C.S.Sp. died in June 2007. He was born in Upperchurch, Co. Tipperary in 1928 and received his secondary education in Rockwell. He entered the novitiate in Kilshane in 1949 and during his studies for the priesthood he spent two years as prefect in Rockwell. He was ordained in 1957 and his first assignment was as a Bursar in Kimmage while at the same time he was deeply involved in fundraising for the education of missionary priests and brothers. In 1969 he was appointed to Rockwell where his task was to help with fundraising for the College. The success of the fundraising programme at that time can be seen in the huge building programme that took place in the 1970s. He then moved as Director of the Agricultural College and later as Director of the Hotel and Catering College. In 1978 he became involved in pastoral work in the United States, in the parish of St. James in Jamestown, Dakota. He returned to Ireland in 1986 and was again appointed to Rockwell. Failing health, however required a move to Kimmage Manor where he was able to avail of the exceptional nursing and care facilities in Marian House. His brother, Fr. Edward, was also a member of the Congregation and served for many years in Nigeria.

Mr. Pat Purcell, a member of the teaching staff who had retired in 1990, died in December 2007. A graduate of U.C.C., he joined the Rockwell staff in 1965. Earlier he had taught in Dublin and in Mitchelstown. Best known as a Maths teacher, he also taught Science, Mechanical Drawing, and Irish and English, and even before Computer Studies had become a curriculum subject he was actively promoting interest in computers. His success in sharing his enthusiasm for the new science resulted in some of his students gaining awards in national competitions.

Fr. Jack Fallon C.S.Sp. died in September 2008. a native of Clara, Co. Offaly, he was born in 1926. In his youth he aspired to becoming a missionary priest, but family circumstances dictated that he was in his early forties before he could realise his dream. He entered the novitiate at Kilshane and during his studies for the priesthood he was a member of a group of seminarians who were at least half his own age. However, he never let that become an obstacle. He was ordained in 1976 at the age of 50. His first appointment was to Sierra Leone in West Africa. To his disappointment, he found that his age made the adaptation to a completely new climate and culture too difficult. After a short period he returned to Ireland. He spent some time on the staff of St. Mary's College, Rathmines before his appointment to Rockwell. His time in Rockwell was divided between working in the Secondary School and the Agricultural School. When his term in Rockwell ended he spent time with a group of confreres in the promotion of the Province's magazine *Mission Outlook*. He later spent some time on the staff of Marian House, Kimmage taking care of the pastoral and spiritual needs of his elderly and infirm confreres.

Fr. Edward Stirling C.S.Sp died on Christmas Day 2008. Born in Dublin in

1933 he entered the Holy Ghost novitiate at Kilshane in 1952 and was ordained in 1961.He was appointed to the Diocese of Umuahia in Nigeria but was prevented by ill-health from travelling to Africa. Instead He joined the teaching staff of Willow Park School in 1963. In 1968 he responded to an appeal from the Archbishop of Anchorage in Alaska for priests for his vast diocese. He spent ten years there before returning to Willow Park.

His desire to serve on overseas mission became a reality when he was assigned to Kenya where he ministered for a number of years in the Archdiocese of Mombasa. He then went to the United States where he ministered in the Archdiocese of San Francisco. One particular aspect of his pastoral ministry was his concern for the elderly and the housebound. This was recognised by the civic authorities who presented him with an award for this work. His time in Rockwell too was marked by his care for those in retirement homes in Cashel and Cahir.

On returning to Ireland he was appointed to Rockwell where he served the Community and the school in different ways. For a number of years he spearheaded the Goal-Aidlink campaign which produced St. Patrick's Day badges. The proceeds were used to help development projects in the Third World. He also served as College archivist. He loved to cycle and to fish. He had a great interest in traditional Irish music and was a regular visitor to *Brú Ború* in Cashel as well as serving for a time as President of the local branch of *Comhaltas Ceolteoirí Éireann*.

Miss Margaret Lynch died in February 2009. She had been teaching music in Rockwell since 1964. Margaret was the younger sister of Paddy Lynch who became the distinguished economist Professor Patrick Lynch whose wise counsel and wide-ranging expertise were sought by many Government Departments over the years, particularly the Department of Education. Margaret was immensely proud of Paddy and her sitting room in Carrigeen contained many photographs of him pictured with some of the leading statesmen, Irish and international, of the day. In Rockwell Margaret prepared students each year for the examinations of the Leinster School of Music and many of them were awarded the much coveted Gold Medal.

Fr. Patrick Duggan C.S.Sp. Died in June 2009. He had been familiar with three aspects of life in Rockwell as student, prefect and priest. Born in Cappamore, Co. Limerick in 1930, he studied for his Leaving Certificate in Rockwell in 1948. He entered the novitiate and returned to Rockwell in 1952 for a two-year period as prefect. Returning to Kimmage he was ordained in 1957. He was appointed to Nigeria in the Diocese of Owerri. The Biafran War in the late 1960s saw the uprooting of a considerable number of missionaries, Paddy included, who were obliged to leave the country.

Fr. Paddy took a temporary assignment in the Diocese of Trenton in the United States. The call to Africa proved to be a strong one and Fr. Paddy returned there, this time to Zambia in 1972 where he ministered in schools, parishes and prison chaplaincy. In 1981 he went to Philadelphia where he ministered in a hospital in that city until 1984. He returned to Rockwell in that year and served the Community and school faithfully in the demanding role of Bursar for twelve years. For some of those years he was joined in the Community by his brother Fr. Brendan who taught in the school during that time. In 1997 he was asked to go to the Spiritan Community of Ardbarccan as Bursar and later to St. Michael's College in Dublin. In Rockwell in 2007 he celebrated the Golden Jubilee of his ordination.

Fr. Maurice Curtin C.S.Sp. died in September 2009 at the age of 96. Rockwell students of the 1940s and early 1950s will have memories of him having been their Dean of Studies during that time. Born in Tournafulla, Co. Limerick in 1913, he was educated at Blackrock College after which he joined the Holy Ghost Congregation in Kimmage Manor. Following his graduation from U.C.D. in 1934 he spent the following year as a prefect in Rockwell. He studied theology at Fribourg in Switzerland and was ordained in 1939. Two years later he was awarded a doctorate in theology.

His first appointment was to Rockwell where he worked as teacher and Dean of Studies until 1953. He loved Rockwell and later in life he often spoke of the years he spent there as having been the happiest years of his life. He often referred to the College environs as being "the most beautiful in the whole Congregation". From 1953 to 1957 he was Dean of Studies at St. Mary's, Rathmines. From 1957 to 1966 he taught philosophy and catechatics in Kimmage before being appointed to the Department of Philosophy at UCD where he taught metaphysics and moral philosophy. Then at the age of 67 he went to West Africa, teaching philosophy, initially at the Benedictine seminary in Ewu, Nigeria and later at St. Paul's seminary in Monrovia, Liberia. Before returning back to Ireland he taught for one year at the Mill Hill, London. He played an active part in the affairs of the Community in Kimmage for many years where he was always unfailingly courteous and welcoming.

Brother Senan Smith C.S.Sp. died in November 2009. He was born in Ennis, Co. Clare in 1926. Before entering the Holy Ghost Congregation, he worked in the building and construction industry for a number of years. In 1956 he entered the Brothers' Novitiate at Ardbaraccan, Co. Meath and was responsible for the development of the living accommodation of the Brothers there. He was assigned to Rockwell in 1962 and his contribution to the College over the next 47 years was enormous. He played a major role in the building of the Chapel at St. Joseph's, the Agricultural College (now Shanahan Hall), the junior dining hall, the swimming pool and the gymnasium.

The year 2009 was especially poignant with the untimely death of two students and two immediate past students.

Stuart Mangan died in August 2009 after a brave fight to cope with catastrophic injuries received as a result of an accident while playing rugby in London. Stuart was a member of the Leaving Certificate class of 2002 and had been a member of the SCT panel which won the Cup that year.

Tomás Kennedy, while still a student in Rockwell, died tragically in September 2009. He was a popular student from Dingle who had begun to follow in the footsteps of his father, the well known Dingle fisherman Tom Kennedy.

Andrew Walsh died in a road accident in October 2009. Andrew was a member of the Leaving Certificate class of 2009 and during his years in Rockwell he enjoyed all aspects of school life. He was a keen sportsman and played Gaelic Football, rugby and soccer and in his final year won the Soccer Player of the Year Trophy.

Noel Julian, of the Leaving Certificate class of 2005, died tragically in November 2009. During his years in Rockwell Noel displayed a keen intellect with a particular interest in the environment.

Mr. Críostóir Gallagher died in January 2011. Críostóir had been a highly respected member of the teaching staff from 1968 to 1988 and a student at Rockwell from 1945 to 1950. He taught Irish and English and was deeply involved in the promotion of drama with Mr. Irwin. He also trained the College hurling teams, an experience he greatly enjoyed. He was a man of great talent and his early retirement, because of failing health, was a source of disappointment to all.

Fr. Aidan Lehane C.S.Sp. died in August 2011. He had been President of Rockwell College from 1968 to 1974. Rockwell College had undergone major changes during his presidency. Born in Dublin in 1926 he studied at Blackrock, Kilshane and Kimmage before being awarded the S.T.L for his study of theology in Rome. He was later awarded a Ph.D in Education from Toronto University. Following his ordination in 1955 his first appointment was to Rockwell as Dean of Discipline. Following his presidency of Rockwell, he served as President of Blackrock College from 1977 to 1983 and held the same role in St. Michael's College from 1983 to 1992. He served as Chaplain in St. Mary's, 1993-94, and Manager of St. Michael's until 1998. He then moved to Templeogue College where he undertook pastoral work and acted as Chairperson of the Board of Management.

Fr. Seán O'Donoghue C.S.Sp. died on 10th March 2012. Born in 1925 in Bandon, Co. Cork, he studied at St. Finian's College, Mullingar and entered the Holy Ghost novitiate in 1945. He served as a prefect in Rockwell for two years and following his ordination in 1955 he was appointed to Nigeria where he taught at All Hallows Seminary in Onitsha. Ill health forced him to return to Ireland and he was appointed to Rockwell in 1959 where he taught until 1968 when he was appointed to do missionary work in Alaska. He returned to Rockwell in 1979 where he taught English, Religion and Business Studies and acted as Bursar with responsibility for students' accounts. He suffered greatly from ill health which forced his retirement to Kimmage.

Fr. John L. O'Sullivan C.S.Sp.died on 30th March 2012. Born in Ballydehob, Co. Cork in 1924, he studied at Rockwell and following his Leaving Cert he entered the Holy Ghost novitiate at Kilshane and returned to Rockwell as a prefect in 1951. Following his ordination he was appointed to Nigeria in 1956 where he spent the next thirteen years in the Diocese of Umahia. Obliged to leave the country because of the Biafran War he served for two years in Sierra Leone before returning to Ireland. On his return he taught at St. Michael's College, Bandon Vocational School, the Cork Regional Technical College and the Rockwell Catering School. From 1991 he ministered in SS. Peter and Paul's in Cork City before retiring to Kimmage.

Fr. Jack Nugent C.S.Sp.died on 4th September 2012. Born in Clonmel in 1926, he studied at Rockwell and following his novitiate he served as prefect in Blackrock College and Rockwell. Following his ordination in 1953 he was appointed to Sierra Leone where he spent over fifty years in ministry. He served as pastor at Pendembu and vicar general of the diocese. When civil war broke out in the early 1990s he helped refugees and in 1994 he had the sad task of assisting in the burial of his fellow Spiritan and past student of Rockwell, Fr. Felim McAlister, who had been killed in an ambush. He returned to Ireland in 2007 and was happy to be appointed to Rockwell.

Fr. John Cahill C.S.Sp. died on 14th September 2012. He was born in Cork in 1922 and following his education at the North Monastry he entered the Holy Ghost novitiate at Kilshane in 1941. He spent two years as prefect in Rockwell and following his ordination in 1950 he was appointed to the Owerri District in Nigeria where he worked for the next fifteen years, teaching in Stella Maris College, Port Harcourt and St. Mary's Teacher Training College in Azaebulu. Returning to Ireland because of the Biafran civil war, he taught at St. Mary's College. He then served in parish ministry in Athy and Carrick Beg before joining the Rockwell Community.

Fr. Tim O'Driscoll C.S.Sp., one of the most respected members of the Rockwell Community, died on 10th October 2012 at the age of 102. Fr. Tim was born on Valentia Island and was educated at Blackrock College where he gained a reputation as a fine rugby player, gaining schoolboy inter-provincial honours with Leinster. Ordained in 1938, among those present at his first Mass was Bishop Joseph Shanahan. He served as Dean of Discipline and Bursar at Rockwell and

Fr. Tim O'Driscoll

later as Provincial Bursar and Superior at Kimmage. He was chosen as Irish Provincial in 1956 and during his term he witnessed the expansion of the Province into new missions in Brazil and Canada.

In 1965 he was appointed President of Blackrock College and on completion of his six-year term he returned to Rockwell where he taught Business Studies and Religious Education. In his retirement he loved to walk the farm to see how the crops and animals were doing. He loved to work in the gardens where he experimented with the planting of vines and oak trees. He was a man of great vision whose advice was sought by many.

Fr. William (Liam) Murphy C.S.Sp. died on 8th March 2013. Born in Tarbert, Co. Kerry in 1927, he entered the novitiate at Kilshane in 1945 following his secondary education at Rockwell. He was back as a prefect in

Rockwell in 1949 and 1950 and following his study of theology at Kimmage, he was ordained in 1953. On his appointment to Nigeria he combined pastoral work and teaching in Owerri and Kabba and taught Liturgy and Moral Theology at the Owerri Senior Diocesan Seminary from 1959 until the outbreak of the Biafran War which forced his return to Ireland.

He ministered and studied in New York from 1968 to 1972 and taught at Templeogue College and Rockwell until 1985 when he was appointed Provincial Secretary. He returned to the USA in 1988 where he ministered in St. Luke's Parish, Fort Worth, Florida while also studying in counselling and psychology. He returned to Rockwell in 1991 where he took on an extensive ministry in counselling and retreats.

Fr. Peter Raftery C.S.Sp. died on 19th March 2013. Ordained in 1978 he served in St. Mary's College, Rathmines for seventeen years teaching French and music, editing the College Annual and acting as photographer of all College events. He served in Rockwell from 1997 to 2009 performing the same duties. As in St. Mary's, his choral work in Rockwell was meticulous with his choirs taking part in competitions at national level. He was greatly missed by students and staff when he departed to take up an appointment at St. Eunan's Cathedral in Derry. Following two years there he was appointed to the Templeogue Commuity and to the role of Provincial Archivist.

Epilogue

The Rockwell crest encapsulates what Rockwell College is and what it has been about since 1864. The crest is rich in colour and symbolism and near to heraldic correctness. The dove with the seven descending rays represents the Holy Spirit. The four quarters on the crest have separate symbolisms. The castle standing on a rock rising from the water is related to the arms of Cashel and is suggested by the tower on the rock at the Rockwell lakeside and symbolises constancy. The three fleurs-de-lis symbolise Our Lady and also the

original French connection of Rockwell, with the red background representing the Holy Spirit. The three books represent scholarship while the fourth quarter is the crest of Munster. The motto *Inter Mutanda Constantia* means amidst things of necessity changing, there is constancy.[1]

As Rockwell College approached its hundred and fiftieth anniversary, it could reflect with satisfaction on its life and achievements. It had been founded as a junior seminary and from the beginning it educated countless young men who served as members of the Spiritan Congregation in mission fields throughout the world and many others who served in other religious orders and as diocesan clergy in Ireland and abroad. Fourteen of its students were ordained as bishops and one a cardinal. A number served as Provincials of the Spiritan

Congregation in Ireland and one became Superior General of the world-wide Spiritan Congregation. It was only in the 1970s and 1980s when new cultural values prevailed in Ireland that this trend of educating future priests diminished.

While serving as a junior seminary Rockwell College also became one of the best known second level boarding schools in Ireland. In post-famine Ireland when second-level education for Catholics was less than widespread, Rockwell originally provided a French schooling system and later adapted to the often criticised Intermediate system. Later still it embraced the secondary education system of the new Irish State and all the changes to that system which have been introduced over the years. For a while its Hotel and Agricultural Colleges catered for needs in the Irish economy at a time when such facilities were in short supply elsewhere.

Rockwell College educated students from every county in Ireland and from many foreign countries. Apart from those who chose the religious life, some of these students later graduated to the highest positions in Irish and international society in business, public service and the professions. Among the most notable to pass through its halls were the 1916 leader Thomas MacDonagh, the two Presidents of Ireland, Eamon de Valera and Patrick Hillery, the writers Liam O'Flaherty and Pádraig Ó Conaire, and the architect Kevin Roche. Past students of Rockwell have shown a remarkable loyalty to their *alma mater* and over the years have been generous in their support of every development in the College and in the Spiritan mission fields. Their interest has always been a source of sustenance to College authorities.

As its motto suggests, Rockwell College has in the past one hundred and fifty years adapted to changes in society, at times dramatic, while at the same time adhering to the principles of its founder and patron the Irish Spiritan Congregation.

Notes

[1] RCA 1941 p. 8.

APPENDICES

APPENDIX I: PRESIDENTS OF ROCKWELL COLLEGE

1864-1880	Fr. Pierre Huvétys
1880-1889	Fr. Prosper Goepfert
1889-1893	Fr. Amet Limbour
1893-1894	Fr. James Cotter
1894-1895	Fr. John Stephens
1895-1905	Fr. Nicholas Brennan
1905-1912	Fr. Thomas A. Pembroke
1912-1916	Fr. Hugh M. G. Evans
1916-1925	Fr. John Byrne
1925-1934	Dr. Edward Crehan
1934-1939	Fr. John McCarthy
1939-1949	Fr. Vincent J. Dinan
1949-1955	Fr. Andrew Egan
1955-1961	Fr. James M. Finucane
1961-1962	Fr. Michael F. Comerford
1962-1968	Fr. James M. Finucane
1968-1974	Fr. Aidan Lehane
1974-1980	Fr. Denis O'Brien
1981-1986	Fr. Patrick Holohan
1986- 1992	Fr. James Hurley
1992- 1994	Fr. Colm Cunningham
1994-1999	Fr. Seán Casey
1999-2004	Fr Seán Broderick
2004-2007	Fr. William Cleary
2007-2011	Fr. John Meade

APPENDIX II: FATHERS AND BROTHERS OF ROCKWELL COMMUNITY

Fr. Peter Huvéths	1864-1880	Br. Hippolyte Matasse	1864-1916
Br. Alban Cran	1864-1865	Br. John Aloysius McGrath	1864-1867
Br. Vincent de Paul McNally	1864-1868	Br. John Joseph O'Donoghue,	1864-1872
Fr. Bartholomew Stoffel	1865-1867	Fr. Prosper Mary Goepfert	1867-1889
Fr. Jacques Richet	1867-1872	Br. Edward Flynn	1867-1868
Br. James Elzear	1868-1874	Br. Tobias Fitzpatrick	1868-1872
Fr. Denis O'Farrell	1868-1869	Br. Silas Laffan*	1868-1922
Fr. Bernard Joseph Graff	1869-1878	Br. John Jerome Hayes	1869-1873
Fr. Anthony Clauss	1871-1872	Br. Roger Manning	1871-1876
Br. Celsus McCabe	1871-1889	Br. Aidan Ryan*	1871-1908
Fr. Edward Mooney	1872-1874	Br. Roland Mahony	1872-1873
Br. Raul Condon*	1873-1910	Br. Mary Ignatious O'Dea*	1873-1897
Fr. Jean Artaud	1874	Fr. James Cotter*	1874-1922
Br. Colmcille Heffernan	1875-1879	Fr. John Francis Berkessel	1876-1884
Fr. John O'Keeffe*	1876-1877	Br. Senan Mulligan	1877-1890
Fr. John T. Murphy	1878-1886	Br. Kieran Egan*	1879-1905
Br. Achille Banbury*	1881-1893	Br. Nicephorus Barrett*	1881-1925
Br. Dalmas Colgan*	1881-1927	Br. Dunstan Dunne*	1881-1893
Fr. Patrick McDermott	1881-1882	Fr. Thomas Fogarty	1882-1887

Fr. Edward Conyngham	1882	Br. Anthony Nolan	1882-1887
Br. Palermo Cunningham	1882-1888	Br. Congal Gleeson	1883-1884
Fr. Lawrence Healy	1883-1891	Fr. Martin Kenneally	1883-1884
Fr. John George Off	1883-1889	Br. Paulinus Colgan	1884-1889
Br. Tobias Hogan*	1884-1918	Br. Omer O'Connell	1884-1890
Br. David Doran,	1885-1893	Br. Aloysius Feely	1885-1888
Fr. Peter McBride	1886-1887	Fr. Achille Lemire	1887-1888
Fr. Martin Kelly	1887-1891	Fr. Louis Leiniger	1887-1892
Fr. Amet Limbour	1888-1894	Br. Patrick Coman	1890-1891
Fr. Edward Crehan 1890-1900	1925-1934	Br. Nicholas Quinlan*	1890-1905
Fr. Louis Demaissan	1890-1891	Fr. Peter Leimann	1890-1895
Br. Contran Meehan*	1890-1895	Fr. Daniel Murphy	1891-1896
Fr. Cornelius O'Rourke	1891-1894	Br. Gregory Power	1891-1911
Br. Albert Coady* 1892-1893	1909-1942	Fr. William Maher	1892-1893
Fr. Christian Schmidt*	1882-1938	Fr. John Stephens	1892-1898
Fr. Louis Fortemps	1893-1894	Br. Valerian Bielman	1894-1899
Fr. Michael O'Shea	1894-1907	Fr. Richard Dooley	1895-1898
Fr. Nicholas Brennan	1896-1905	Fr. Martin Moloney	1896-1898
Br. Adelme Walshe 1896-1900	1905-1906	Fr. Michael Colgan	1897-1941
Br. Francis De Sales O'Connell	1897-1904	Fr. Jean Desnier	1898-1900
Fr. Hugh Evans 1898-1903	1912-1920	Fr. Paul Meistermann	1898-1900
Fr. John Muller	1898-1938	Br. Patrick McCarthy*	1898-1932
Br. Brendan Coffey*	1899-1925	Br. Elimien Gaschy 1899-1901	1903-1933
Br. Virgilius Ryan*1899-1906	1913-1920	Fr. John Byrne* 1900-1925	1937-1953
Fr. John McGrath	1900-1925	Fr. Joseph Shanahan	1900-1902
Br. Edgar Stafford	1900-1920	Fr. Michael Walsh	1900-1909
Fr. Henri Blanchot 1901-1905	1913-1916	Br. Agricole Kennedy	1901-1905
Fr. Joseph Baldwin	1902-1904	Br. John Baptist Hourigan*	1903-1924
Fr. James McGurk	1903-1904	Fr. Thomas O'Brien	1903-1904
Fr. Daniel Egan*	1904-1922	Br. Mary Bernard Schikarski	1904-1910
Fr. Patrick Brennan* 1905-1917	1921-1931	Fr. Bernard Carey	1905-1906
Fr. Thomas Naughton	1905-1911	Br. Edmond McSweeney*	1905-1918
Br. Epiphane O'Leary	1905-1912	Fr. Thomas Pembroke	1905-1912
Fr. Edward Cleary	1906-1920	Fr. James O'Neill	1906-1926
Br. Muterne Compte	1907-1912	Br. Ailbe Merrigan	1907-1917
Br. Kieran O'Neill*	1907-1950	Fr. Eugene Berbech	1908-1912
Br. Alphonsus Biggermann	1909-1913	Fr. Peter Meagher	1909-1910
Br. Martenan Reutter	1909-1910	Fr. Martin O'Mahony*1910-13	1932-1944
Fr. Philip O'Shea	1910-1912	Br. Eusabius Aherne*1913-14	1930-1948
Br. Protasio Gomes	1913-1914	Br. Gerald Heffernan	1913-1918
Fr. Charles Meyer	1913-1922	Fr. Michael Meagher	1914-1919
Fr. John English	1915-1919	Br. Canice Butler*	1916-1929
Fr. John Kingston*	1916-1939	Fr. Daniel Leen 1916-34	1936-1967
Fr. Patrick Walshe* 1916-21	1933-1946	Fr. Bartholomew Wilson	1917-1918
Fr. Patrick McAllister* 1918-24	1936-1947	Br. Malachy Fleming*	1920-1959
Fr. John McCarthy	1920-1939	Br. Aiden Cahill	1921-1937
Fr. Timothy Cunningham*	1922-1955	Br. Kevin Walker	1922-1933
Br. Eugene Graham*	1923-1992	Fr. Griffin Francis*1923-25	1962-1983
Fr. David O'Brien	1923-1932	Br. AgathonFogarty*	1924-1966
Fr. David Heelan	1955-1963	Fr. Daniel Murphy*1924-34	1984-1988
Br. Sabbas Devlin	1925-1934	Br. Finbarr O'Sullivan	1925-1931
Br. John Berchmans Casserly	1927-1928	Fr. Andrew Egan 1928-34	1949-1955
Fr. James Nolan	1927-1933	Fr. Thomas Nolan*	1927-1975

Fr. William O'Donnell	1927-1928	Br. Austin Tobin*	1927-1940
Br. Gomblem Hartmuth	1928-1930	Br. Gerald Joseph McCoy	1930-1931
Fr. Edward O'Shea*	1930-1967	Fr. Herbert Farrell	1931-1932
Fr. Thaddeus O'Connor	1931-1960	Br. Dominic O'Reardon	1931-1940
Fr. Michael Neenan*	1933-1968	Fr. Michael Comerford*	1934-1997
Fr. Cornelius Daly	1934-1939	Fr. Michael Sexton	1934-1939
Fr. James White	1934-1937	Fr. James Burke*	1935-1958
Fr. Thomas Gough*	1935-1936	Fr. Thomas Kinsella	1935-1940
Fr. Reginald Walker*	1936-1971	Fr. John Cahill 1937-38	1951-1952
Fr. James Barrett* 1938-1947	1963-1975	Fr. Joseph Mullins*	1938-1972
Fr. Vincent Dinan	1939-1949	Fr. James Kromer	1939-1949
Fr. Timothy O'Driscoll*1939-47	1971-2012	Fr. Maurice Curtin	1940-1954
Fr. Edward Holmes	1940-1951	Fr. Patrick Nolan	1940-1949
Br. Benignus Flood	1942-1944	Fr. Michael Frawley	1942-1944
Br. Jar;ath Hughes*	1944-1973	Fr. Francis Marrinan*	1944-1977
Br. Xavier Morrissey	1944-1945	Fr. John O'Donoghue	1944-1949
Fr. Patrick Curtin	1945-1946	Fr. Patrick Doyle	1945-1946
Fr. Robert Farrelly	1945-1946	Fr. John Flavin	1945-1947
Fr. Charles O'Donoghue	1945-1946	Fr. Stephen O'Hanrahan*	1945-1969
Br. Columba Sheehy 1945-48	1962-1964	Fr. Timothy Crowley	1946-1947
Fr. Michael Higgins*	1946-1955	Br. Joseph Jennings	1946-1949
Fr. Anthony Meany* 1946-47	1953-1957	Fr. Frank Nolan*	1946-1964
Fr. Patrick Noonan	1947-1948	Fr. Joseph Likely	1948-1949
Fr. Joseph Nolan*	1948-1972	Fr. Terence O'Brien	1948-1950
Fr. James Cronin	1949-1970	Fr. Christopher Meagher*	1949-2000
Fr. James Harrison	1949-1951	Fr. James Murray	1949-1963
Br. Ambrose O'Boyce	1949-1971	Fr. Andrew O'Carroll	1949-1951
Fr. Redmond Walsh	1949-1958	Fr. William Butler	1950-1951
Fr. John McAsey	1950-1953	Fr. Seán Nealon*	1950-1971
Fr. Demis O'Brien	1950-1981	Br. Boneventure Scott	1950-1953
Br. Fintan Walsh	1950-1951	Fr. Thomas O'Byrne	1951-1952
Fr. Michael O'Quigley	1951-1958	Fr. Michael Grogan	1952-1965
Fr. Patrick Murray	1953-1958	Fr. James Finnucane*	1955-1970
Fr. Patrick McMahon	1955-1956	Fr. Aidan Lehane	1956-1974
Fr. Alfred Chamberlain	1957-1979	Fr. Michael Lavelle*	1957-1982
Fr. Patrick Campbell	1958-1966	Fr. Patrick Leonard	1958-1966
Fr. James Hurley 1959-69,1980-92, 2000-		Fr. Seán O'Donoghue 1959-68	1979-2000
Br. Joseph Brennan	1960-1964	Fr. Gerard McConnell	1961-1967
Br. Declan Cashin	1962-1968	Br. Senan Smith*	1962-2009
Fr. John C. O'Connor	1963-1970	Fr. Noel Redmond	1964-1977
Fr. Michael Harkins	1966-1967	Fr. Patrick McGlynn	1966-1985
Fr. Michael O'Connor*	1966-1992	Fr. Desmond Reid	1966-1980
Fr. Henry Mullin	1967-1968	Fr. Bernard Murphy	1967-1968
Fr. Joseph Murphy	1967-1968	Br. Gerard Cummins	1968-
Fr. Colm Cunningham 1968-69,70-79, 86-		Fr. Brendan Hally 1968-1980	2002-
Fr. John Buckley	1969-1977	Fr. Bernard Frawley	1969-1970 1972-
Br. Finbar Kelly*	1969-2000	Fr. Matthew Knight	1969-
Fr. John A. Finnucane	1970-1971	Fr. Patrick Cremins*	1971-2003
Fr. Seán Broderick	1971-2004	Fr. Patrick Doody	1971-1972
Fr. Robert Madigan*	1971-1998	Fr. Patrick Holohan*	1971-1986
Fr. John L. O'Reilly	1972-1973	Fr. John C. Ryan*	1973- 1994
Br. Pascal Mawhinney*	1974-1997	Fr. Liam Murphy *	1974- 2013
Fr. Naos McCool	1974-2001	Fr. Martin McDonagh	1976-1998

Fr. Brian O'Connor*	1976-2004	Fr. Thomas McCarthy*	1977-2007
Fr. Timothy O'Riordan*	1977-1978	Fr. Brendan Duggan	1978-1994
Fr. John L. O'Sullivan*	1978-1981	Fr. Patrick Downes	1979-
Fr. James Duggan	1980-1985	Fr. John Meade 1980-1984	2000-
Fr. Henry Moloney	1980-1994	Fr. Michael Moore	1980
Fr. John Fallon	1981-1982	Fr. Richard Lehane	1981-1985
Fr. Desmond O'Farrell	1981-1982	Fr. Thomas Maher*	1981-1991
Fr. Maurice Kiely	1983-1984	Fr. James Brett*	1983-2000
Fr. Patrick Duggan*.	1984-1997	Fr. Edward Nealon	1987-1988
Fr. Allan Collins	1987-1989	Fr. Edward Stirling	1991-2008
Fr. Thomas Cleary*	1993-2001	Fr. Seán Casey	1994-1999
Fr. Lloyd Rebeyro	1995-1996	Fr. William Kingston	1995-
Fr. Joseph D'Ambrosio	1997-2010	Fr. John McEvoy	1996-98
Fr. Peter Queally	1997-	Fr. Patrick Reedy	1997-2005
Fr. Peter Raftery	1997-2009	Fr. Michael Moore	2000-2005
Fr. Seán O'Connell	2000-	Fr. Finbarr Horrigan	2000
Fr. Noel Murphy	2000-	Fr. John Cahill*	2002-2003
Fr. William Cleary	2004-2007	Fr. Patrick Moore	2004-2005
Fr. Jack Nugent	2006-2011	Fr. Timothy Connolly	2006-
Fr. Thomas Cunningham	2007-	Fr. Gerard Griffin	2009-

* Interred in Rockwell Cemetery.
Source: Archives of The Congregation of the Holy Spirit

APPENDIX III: DIRECTORS OF ST. JOSEPH'S

1867-1880	Fr. Prosper Goepfert
1881-1883	Fr. Patrick Mc.Dermott
1884-1887	Fr. Thomas Fogarty
1887-1888	Fr. Achilles Lemire
1888-1889	Fr. Paul Meistermann
1890- 1891	Fr. Louis Demaison
1891- 1892	Fr. Louis Leiniger
1893- 1894	Fr. John Stephens
1900- 1903	Fr. Hugh Evans
1904-1907	Fr. Daniel Egan
1910-1917	Fr. Edmund Cleary
1917- 1918	Fr. John English
1918-1921	Fr. Patrick Walsh
1921- 1934	Fr. John J. McCarthy
1934- 1942	Fr. Michael Comerford
1942- 1949	Fr. Patrick J. Nolan
1949-1959	Fr Christopher Meagher
1958-1960	Fr Alfred Chamberlain
1960-1968	Fr. James Hurley
1968- 1970	Fr. Harry Mullan
1970-1971	Fr. Matthew Knight
1971-1975	Fr. Seán Broderick

APPENDIX IV: BOARD OF MANAGEMENT

2006-2012

Dr. Seán O'Donnell	Chairperson
Ms Clodagh Beresford	Trustees nominees
Sr. Regina Powell	
Fr. Matthew Knight CSSp.	
Mr. John Mason	Staff nominees
Mr. John Fitzgibbon	
Ms. Olwen Kingston	Parent nominees
Mr. Martin Healy	
Ms. Catherine Phelan	
Mr. John O'Dwyer	
Ms. Joan Walsh	

2012-

Sr. Ena Quinlan
Ms. Sheila Murray
Fr. Brendan Hally CSSp
Mr. William Irwin
Ms. June O'Brien
Mr. Tom Ryan
Mr. John O'Dwyer
Ms. Marie Russell

APPENDIX V: DEANS OF STUDIES, HEADMASTERS AND PRINCIPALS*

Fr. Jacques Richert	1867-1868
Fr. Bernard Joseph Graf	1869-1878
Fr. John T. Murphy	1879-1887
Fr. Laurence Healy	1887-1890
Dr. Edward A. Crehan	1890-1900
Fr. John Byrne	1900-1907.
Fr. Peter Thomas Naughton	1908-1911
Dr. James O'Neill	1911-1916
Fr. John Kingston	1916-1918
Fr. John McGrath	1918-1924.
Dr. Daniel Murphy	1924-1934
Fr. Cornelius Daly	1934-1939
Fr. James Barrett	1940-1942
Fr. Maurice Curtin	1942-1954
Fr. Patrick J. Murray	1954-1957
Fr. Joe Nolan	1957-1972.
Fr. Brendan Hally	1972-1980
Fr. James Hurley	1980-1992
Fr. Seán Broderick	1992-1997
Mr. Pat O'Sullivan	1997-2012
Ms. Audrey O'Byrne	2012-

* The term Dean of Studies denoted the principal teacher until 1972. From then the term Headmaster was used until 1997 when the term Principal was in use. From 1972 the term Dean of Studies was used to describe the assistant to the Headmaster and this position was held by Fr. Patrick McGlynn from 1972 to 1985 and by Fr. Naos McCool from 1985 to 2003.

APPENDIX VI: DEPUTY PRINCIPALS

1972-1996	Liam Uasal Ó Duibhir
1996-2003	Dr. Seán O'Donnell
2003-	Mr. Michael Doyle

APPENDIX VII: EDITORS OF ROCKWELL ANNUAL

1926-1932	Fr. Daniel Murphy
1933-1934	Fr. Andrew Egan
1935-1936	Fr. Cornelius Daly
1937-1966	Fr. Reginald Walker
1967-1968	Fr. Aidan Lehane
1969-1970	Fr. Noel Redmond
1971-1986	Fr. Patrick McGlynn
1987-2004	Fr. Naos McCool
2005-2009	Fr. Peter Raftery
2010-	Mr. Frank McGrath

APPENDIX VIII: ROCKWELL PREFECTS*

1864-1875: Michael Clarke, John O'Dwyer, Jules Botrel, Prosper Duval, Edward Gallagher, John Quinn, Edward Schmitz, John Corry.

1876-1886: William Quinn, John Norris, Joseph Muller, Robert Tobin, Thomas Pembroke, Hugh Evans, Christian Schmidt.

1887-1897: Prosper Bisch, Frederick Rausch, Thomas Molloy, Patrick Coffey, John Byrne, John Stafford, Patrick Walsh, James J. McGurk, Thomas MacDonagh, Joseph Cronenberger, Joseph Shanahan.

1898-1908: Edward Cleary, Daniel Egan, John Kingston, Michael Kelly, John O'Brien, Joseph Baldwin, Thomas Kelly John Heelan, Leonard Graf, James Dowling, James Murphy, Martin O'Mahony, John Heelan, Thaddeus O'Connor, John Leen, Michael Martin Francis Howell 1901, Edmond Cleary, Edward Lean, Timothy Cunningham, Richard Hartnett, Frank`Howell, John Heelan, James Ryan, Henry Gogarty, David J. Lloyd. Cornelius Liddane

1909-1919: Frank Nolan, James Mellett, Kerry Keane, Thomas J. Nolan, Denis Joy, Charles Heerey, John C. McCarthy, William O'Donnell, Daniel Liston.

1920-1922: Messrs Brassil, Meehan, Wallis, Kennedy, Mansfield, Murren, Finn, Egan, White, Maguire, O'Sullivan, Nagle, Andrew Egan, David Heelan, Messrs McCarthy, Finnegan, Mansfield, Liston, Maguire, Neville, McGree, Foley, Danagher, Neville, Mullane, Mackey, Hanrahan, Reidy, William Law.

1923: William Brolly, Michael Murren, Michael Mackey, Michael Flanagan, Martin Reidy.

1924: Colman McMahon, Daniel Shields, Austin Fennessy, Michael Harkins, Michael Flanagan, Martin Reidy.

1925: Michael Flanagan, John Cahill, Colman McMahon, Tom Macken, Robert Farrelly, Tom Kennelly. Austin Fennessy.

1926: Michael Flanagan, Colman McMahon, Austin Fennessy, Tom Macken, Robert Farrelly, Tom Kennedy, John Cahill, Henry O'Sullivan

1927: Robert Farrelly, Tom Kennedy, John Cahill, Michael Doody, B. Keane, Niall McCormack, Thomas McEnnis, Tom McKenna, Edward Fitzgerald

1930: Francis Marrinan, Stephen Cloonan

1931: D Madden, Jim Millar J Andrews, John Jordan, D. Morgan, John Thompson, David Law, Michael Higgins, John Flavin, Francis Marrinan, P. Quinn. William Guinan

1935: J. O'Neill, Edward Holmes, Maurice Curtin, J. Nordelle, P. Kennedy, J. Mulcahy, Denis O'Keeffe, J. Doyle, P. Gilsenan, W. McGuinness. Henry J. Byrne.

1936: J. Mulcahy, P. Brett, John P. Morrissey, A. O'Connell, D. O'Callaghan, J. O'Brien, G. Fitzgerald, William O'Connor, Patrick Murray, John C. Ryan, T, Walsh., Richard Joyce, Patrick J. Murray

1937: D.J. Morrissey, A.F. O'Connell, Paddy Holly, Joe Lynch, Walter Kennedy, William O'Connor, M.G. O'Connor, John O'Donoghue, M. J. O'Connell, James Meade.

1939: Joseph P. Nolan, D.C. Crowley, W.X. Deasy, W.F. Dennehy, J.P. Harrison, Patrick Kinnerk, Declan McGoldrick, Patrick Meaney, Paddy Noonan, Con Woulfe.

1940: M. O'Connell, John Enright, Joseph Nolan, Richard Caplice, Edward Darcy, Richard Woulfe, Richard Lehane, D. Egan, Joseph Tobin, J. Ryan.

1942: Frank Comerford, Patrick Smyth, Mr. O'Byrne, Mr. Lyons, John L. O'Reilly, Oliver Barrett, Mr. Corry, Mr. Divane, Mr. Roche, Mr. Corrigan, Michael McCarthy

1945: Edward Buckley, Desmond. Connaughton, Edward Downey, Patrick Liddane, Frank Martin, Charles McCarthy, Michael McCarthy, Frank McCabe, Seosaimh O'Malley, Pat Sheridan, Pat Walsh, Redmond Walsh.

1946: Desmond Connaughton, Pat Sheridan, Tom McDonnell, Seosaimh O'Malley, J. Dooley, Charles McCarthy, Michael McCarthy, Redmond Walsh, Eamon McSweeney, J. Fahy, John Cahill, Tom Cleary, John O'Mahony.

1947: Desmond Connoughton, John O'Mahony, John Cahill, Owen Carton, Denis Rodgers, P. O'Connor, Eamon McSweeney, T. Buckley, D. Gully, Paddy Holland, T. Clery, P. Crosbie, P. Hogan.

1948: D. Rodgers, T. Buckley, A. Lindsay, W. Costello, L. Layden, P. Holland, B. Murphy, J. O'Mahony, Timothy O'Riordan, P. Scahill, J. Aherne, M. Courtney, P. Crosbie, M. Keegan.

1949: M. Courtney, M. Flynn, M. Keegan, J.O'Mahony, C. Foley, P.Scahill, A. Lindsay, D. Cahill, P.Keegan, M. Smithwick, B. Murphy, T. Rock, L. Laydein, J. Mulqueen.

1950: W. Nugent, T. Rock, G. Boran, J. Nugent, Michael Flynn, C. Foley, J. Mulqueen, W. Murphy, J. Delaney, M. Sheedy, Michael S. Smithwick, D. O'Connor, John Spriggs.

1951: J. Delaney, John Spriggs, C. Ó Nualláin, W. O'Brien, Seán O'Donoghue, F. Boran, P. Henry, S. Owens, J. Corcoran, M. Eivers, W. Graham, P. Newman, J. O'Keeffe, A. Kelly, James Duggan.

1952: J. Corcoran, Seán O'Donoghue, P. Henry, S. Owens, A. White, M. Eivers, T. Maguire, P. Newman, J. O'Keeffe, James Duggan, D. Kiely, P. Leonard, J. O'Doherty, John L. O'Sullivan, Philip Shannahan, J. O'Connell.

1953: P. Leonard, James Duggan, C. Corrigan, D. Kiely, J. O'Connell, S. O'Shaughnessy, J. Dunne, P. Duggan, B. McCormack, P. Ryan, G. McConnell, N. Gavin, John Buckley, M. Cunniffe, J. O'Reilly, H. Curneen.

1954: J. Dunne, Patrick Duggan, G. McConnell, John Buckley, John O'Reilly, T. O'Connor, M. Grogan, S. Murray, M. Buckley, J. Byrne, P. Gunning, O O'Donnell, P. Fleming, A. Finucane, M. Doyle, F. O'Connor.

1955: A. Finucane, P. Fleming, M. Doyle, J. Byrne, P. Gunning, B. Carey, P. Mullen, H. Mullin, J. Kelly, R. Deadman, H. Boyle, C. Lynch, N. Delaney, P. Nolan, H. Fagan.

1956: H. O'Boyle, J. Geary, P. O'Loughlin, H. Mullin, R. Maher, C. Murray, J. Kelly, A. Fallon, N. Maguire, N. Dalaney, M. O'Hara, T. Barron, P. Nolan, H. Fagan, B. Hayes

1957: J. Geary, N. Maguire, C. O'Byrne, B. O'Flynn, T. Barron, D. Kavanagh, T. Cromien, W. Ellison, G. O'Grady, A. Fallon, J. Dolan, C. Brennan. M. O'Hara, Matthew Knight, A. O'Brien.

1958: B. O'Flynn, Noel Redmond, C. Brennan, T. Cromien, Matthew Knight, Edward Scott, W. Ellison, C. O'Byrne, J. Flynn, J.Dolan, G. O'Grady, Anthony Duffy, J. McDonagh.

1959: J. McDonagh, J. Kiely, P. Taylor, E. Scott, D. Kennedy, C. Burke, J. Flynn. P. Ryan, J. Hogan, R. Curran, John Finucane.

1960: M. Waldron, J. Kiely, John Finucane, D. Reid, J. O'Mahony, F. Burke, S. Harpur, D. O'Farrell, M. Breslin, R. Curran, K. Dempsey.

1961: M. Waldron, J. O'Mahony, M. Breslin, K. Dempsey, P. Guckian, S. Malone, F. Burke, S. Walsh, C. Kennedy, P. Reidy.

1962: F. Burke, S. Walsh, M. Malone, P. Guckian, P. Reidy, S. Lovett, J. Malone, D. Coffey, M. Casey, P. Daly.

1963: M. Casey, P. McGeever, J. O'Doherty, J. Dunne, R. Grimshaw, Brendan Hally, A. Burke, J. Feeney, J. Doyle, B. Eburne, John Meade.

1964: J. Dunne, J. O'Doherty, P. McGeever, A. Burke, Brendan Hally, B. Allen, J. Fagan, John Meade, D. Moloney, V. McDevitt, P. Doody.

1965: P. Doody, V. McDevitt, D. Moloney, W. McNamara, F. Carty, M. Hickey, D. O'Casey, W. Gardiner, C. Walsh, V. Hardiman, P. Nugent.

1966: W. Gardiner, M. Hickey, D. Casey, C. Walsh, V. Hardiman, M. Cahill, J. Considine, P. Ridge, J. Fitzgerald.

1967: J. Considine, C. Sweeney, J. Byrnes, J. Fitzgerald, J. Farrelly, S. Doyle, P. Byrne.

1968: C.N. Sweeney, P. Byrne, S. Doyle, K. Gavin, P. Roe. B. Rickard.

1969: C. P. Sweeney, V. Costello, B.Rickard, M.Whelan. J. Doyle, Naos McCool, B.O'Sullivan.

1970: V. Costello, J. Brady, Naos McCool, P. Doherty, Martin.McDonagh, B. O'Sullivan, L. Flanagan

1971: M. McDonagh, P. Doherty, C. Ó Laochdha, P.McNamara, P.Burke, S. McNally.

1972: Brendan Duggan, S. McNally, E. Flynn, C Ó Laochdha, A. Hughes, P.J. Burke, J. Kilcrann.

1973: Breffni Walker, J. Kilcrann, A. O'Boyle, E. Flynn, N. Moynihan, A. Hughes, B. Maher.

1974: N. Moynihan, A, O'Boyle, Michael Burke, B. Maher, P. Murphy.

1975: M. Burke, M. Foran, O. Kavanagh, W. Dunne, C. Kane.

1976: T. Chadwick, J. Jackson.

---

* Prior to 1924 prefects served within the timeframe mentioned for periods varying usually from one to five years.

APPENDIX IX: LAY TEACHING STAFF

Mr. Reidy 1864-1865
Mr. Etterlen 1864-1868
William Griffin 1894-1895
Daniel Shanahan 1897-1898
Thomas Morrissey 1898-1899
Jack Barrett 1903-1904
Eamon de Valera 1903-1905
Daniel Cahill 1909-1910
Michael J. Ryan 1909-1920
Patrick V. O'Flaherty 1909-1910
Denis Harte 1915-1921
Seán Gallagher 1919-1926
Michael Nagle 1920-1927
James O'Shea 1922-23
Patrick J. O' Hanlon 1926-1927
E.J. Hally 1927-1931
M.L. Powell 1927-1929
1928-1973 John L. Buckley
Timothy Shannon 1931-1932
Martin Farragher 1934-1970
Patrick Walsh 1934-1940
John Horgan 1934-1935
Thomas Geary 1934-1935
James A. White 1935-1964
Patrick J. O'Connor 1939-1956
Xavier Gibson 1942-1954
Patrick Walsh 1947-1948
Liam Ó Duibhir 1958-1996
Hans Schreinert 1959-1960
Brendan Kelly 1960-1961
Michael O'Callaghan 1961-1962
Liam O'Dwyer 1961-1972
Thomas Kyne 1962-1963
Seán O'Donnell 1963-2003
Seamus Leahy 1964-2000
Joseph Touhy 1967-1975
Pádraig Breathnach 1965-1966
Patrick Purcell 1965-1990
P.J. Irwin 1968-1990
Brendan Garvan 1967-1968
Pádraig O'Mahony 1968-2004
Thomas Magner 1969-1972
Laurence O'Dwyer 1970-2000
Douglas Butler 1972-2006
Adrian Rogers 1972-1973
David Power 1972-2004
Máiréad O'Dwyer 1972-1974
John Pereira 1972-1973
Caitríona Ní Mhurchadha 1973-1989
Joan Curtin 1973-1975
Michael Doyle 1976-

Mr. Courtney 1864-1865
Thomas Griffin 1880-1882
Michael Walsh 1894-1895
Michael Smithwick 1898-1899
James Cremer 1903-1904
Tom O'Donnell 1903-1904
Denis J. O'Connor 1908-1909
Francis O'Callaghan 1909-1910
Michael Cremin 1909-1954
Seamus O'Neill 1915-1920
Michael O'Brien 1916-1917
John McGinty 1919-1920
John Twomey 1920-1923
John Mansfield 1922-1923
Michael Conway 1927-1928
Michael Hally 1927-1928
Michael Power 1928-1932
Edward J. Hally 1931-1932
Thomas Coppinger 1931-1932
Michael Kiernan 1931-1932
Jerry Hayes 1934-1976
Thomas McHugh 1934-1935
Patrick Clune 1934-1935
James Cahill 1934-1935
Thomas Tobin 1942-1987
James G. Croghan 1942-1943
Patrick Ryan 1954-1958
John Enright 1959-1960
Conrad Schmitte 1960-1961
Paul Tansey 1961-1962
Pádraig Conroy 1961-1962
Jack Young 1961-1964
Alfred O'Sullivan 1963-1967
Owen O'Neill 1962-1965
Margaret Lynch 1964-2006
Seamus King 1965-2001
Anthony O'Halpin 1965-1966
Joseph Frawley 1966-1991
Cristóir Gallagher 1968-1988
Edward O'Reilly 1967-1968
William Gaynor 1969-1991
Andrew Bailey 1970-1971
Gerard O'Byrne 1966-1975
Lucy O'Byrne 1972-1975
Thomas Monaghan 1972-1973
Michael O'Sullivan 1972-2001
Valerie Quirke 1972-1974
David T. Morris 1973-1989
Kate O'Leary 1973-1978
Patrick Daly 1973-2006
Tony Smith 1973-2012

John Fitzgibbon 1974-
Anne Noone 1974-1976
Greg Kenny 1975-1989
Frank McGrath 1977-
Ruth Bracken 1979-1980
Declan Crotty 1981-1989
Edward Neenan 1983-1984
Colin Townsend 1988-1989
Conor Dillon 1990-1991
Ina Tungler 1990-2006
Maureen McHugh 1991-
Colin Moran 1991-1992
Gabriel Buckley 1992-
Gerard Dunne 1993-1994
Michael Lynch 1993-1994
Donagh O'Donnell 1993-1994
David O'Donoghue 1994-1995
Denis Gibbons 1997-1999
Pat O'Sullivan 1997-2012
James Keating 1998-
Seán Ryan 1998-
Patrick Egan 2001-
Dermot Brislane 2001-2013
Regina Flynn 2001-2002
Anne-Marie O'Dwyer 2001-2002
Joan Ryan 2000-
Martin Daly 1992-1996, 2001-
Nora Kennedy 2002-2003
June O'Brien 2001-
Christopher Roberts 2002-2003
Eleanor Kilroy 2002-
Brian Comerford 2002-2003
Patrique Kelly 2002-
Sarah Drohan 2002-
John Hartnett 2002-2005
Simon Kenny 2004-
Nicola Fahey 2005-
Anna Dunne 2005-
Fiona Noonan 2006-
Elaine O'Sullivan 2007-2013
Kate Heaney 2011-
Claire Whelan 2009-2011
Máirín Gallagher 2010-2011
Lisa Cosgrove 2012-2013

Gerard Flynn 1974-1989
Alan Horne 1977-1980
Frank McNamara 1978-1979
John Mason 1980-1988, 1991-2012
Nóirín Woodlock 1980-1998
Anne Moine 1981-1982
Fionula NíLanagáin 1989-1991
Winnie Ryan 1990-
Margaret Keating 1990-
Edmond Golden 1990-1991
Margaret Niland-Ryan 1991-2009
Siobhán Ní Gabhann 1991-1999
Liam Fennell 1992-2001
Faoill O'Rourke 1993-
Breffni Carroll 1993-1994
Paul Kilrane 1994-1997
Michael Coughlin 1996-1998
Declan Murphy 1997-2000
Niall McGonagle 1996-
Audrey O'Byrne 1999-
Thomas Ryan 2000-
Anne Minehan 2000-2001
Pat McEvoy 2001-2002
Alvara Duggan 2000-
John McNamara 2001-2002
Gerard Hough 2000-
Donal Breen 2002-2003
Gemma Cummins 2001-
Caroline Kelly 2001-
Debbie Lynch 2002-2003
Orla O'Dwyer 2001-2013
Maura Fallon 2002-2003
Lena Hally 2002-2003, 2006-2011
Neasa O'Halloran 2003-2011
Fiona Roche 2005-
Emma Gleeson 2004-2005
Brendan Ferris 2006-
Tony Trehy 2005-2006
John White 2010-2012
Bríd Whelan 2010-2011
Aoife Mulcahy 2011-
Cathal Maher 2012-
Andrew Flynn 2012-2013

Appendix X: Non-Teaching Lay Staff

2013
Director of Residence: Frank Fitzgerald
Dean of Girl Students: Kathleen Smyth
College Finance Manager & Director of Camp Rockwell: Joan Kennedy
College Secretary: Eileen McCormack
Administration Secretary: Jeanette Hickey
Students' Accounts: Breda Marnane
Receptionist: Nicola McGrath
Physician: Dr. William Ryan (Junior)
Nursing Staff: Mary Lonergan, Mary Hyland, Nuala Kavanagh.
Catering Manager: Hugh O'Donoghue
Chefs: Gearóid O'Sullivan (Head Chef), Garrett Sheehan, John O'Donoghue
Catering Staff: Ann Corcoran, Mary Lonergan, Ann Marie O'Donoghue, Donna
    Harding, Mary Riordan, Elena Gluata, Galina Morozona, Yvonne Reddy, Yvonne
    Hoare, Ita Holmes, Debbie Ramsey, Mary Ramsey, Joan O'Reilly, Nicola Ryan,
    Tetyana Lapco, Mary Ryan, Lillija Andliraskaja
Facilities Manager: Tommy Keating
Maintenance Staff: John Byrne, Pat Currivan, John Keating, James C. Mangan,
    Oliver Keating, Myles Ryan, Eoin Ryan, John Shanahan, David Shiels, William
    Lawlor.
Farm Manager: Jim Treacy
Farm Secretary: Josie Treacy

Some Previous Non-Teaching Lay Staff
Physicians: Dr. McCormack (1860s) Dr. Moloney (1870s & 1880s), Dr. Cusack (1900-
    1920), Dr. Dowling (1920s), Dr. Arthur Foley (1934-1940), Dr. Hennessy (1941-
    1944), Dr. James O'Connor (1945-1961), Dr. William Ryan (1962-1999)
Oculist: Dr. Mary O'Connor (1942-1956)
Dentist: Jerry Pierse (1963-1981)
Nursing Staff: Ms. Armstrong (1914-1917), Ms. Marrinan (1918-1925), Ms Foley
    (1925-1940), Ms. O'Shea (1950s), Ms. Lyons (1960s), Joan O'Dwyer (1980s), Brigid
    Sharkey (1989-1995), Anne Mulcahy (1994-2005), Mary Duane (1994-1998),
    Breda Ryan (1996-2000), Joan Moloney (1999-2002), Barbara Rutherford (2001),
    Mary O'Reilly (2003)
College Secretary: Anne O'Donnell (1973-1975), Helen King (1975), Mary Walsh
    (1976-1979), Gerardine Kelly (1980-1997) Siobhán Long (1993)
Bursar's Secretary: Teresa Maher (1980-2000)
Students' Accounts: Cliona Geary (2002-2004)
Receptionist: Ester O'Dwyer (1990-1992), Joan Turner (1993-1998), Deborah Ramsey
    (1993-1998), Breda Marnane (1999-2004)
Elocution Instructress: 1964 Miss Lenihan 1960s. I. Cummins 1980s
Communications: Nollaig McCarthy (1973-1981)
Orchestra: Ciaran McNamara (1973-1978)
Ballroom and Irish Dancing: Ms. Penny (1960-1967), Ms O'Carroll (1968-1972), Ms.
    Proctor (1972-1981)
Gymnastics, Physical Education, Swimming: John Frazer (1935-1960), John O'Driscoll
    (1970), Philip Conway (1971-1972), Robert Madine (1973-1975), Edward Byrne

(1975-1977), Una Dillon (1978-1992), Martin Daly (1993-1996), Michael Kelly (1997-2012)

Golf Coach:1967-1974 Eddie Hackett. 1974-1978 Christy Butler

Tennis Coach: Michael Hickey (1970-1988), Tadhg Lambe (1989-1993)

Housekeeping and Catering: Peggy Joyce, Mary O'Flaherty, Joan Hoare, Angela Turner, Ann Corcoran, Bridget Byrne, Donna Harding, Mary Boles, Mary Claffey, Mary Heaney, Mary O'Shea, Maureen Spellman, Monica Moore.

Farm and Maintenance: Albert Doyle, Denis Carr, Paddy Hall, Patrick Hayes, Michael Prendergast, Patrick Currivan, Seán Horan, Patrick Griffin, Stephen Byrne, Michael Halpin, John Hennessy, Frank Kelly, Frank O'Meara, John Healy, John Walsh, Joe Moloney, Johnny Moore, John Gleeson, Joe Golden, John McGrath, Michael Connor, Tim Enright, Joe Moloney, Luke Lyons, Michael Lyons, Paddy Lyons, Patsy Carey, John O'Brien, Patsy Heaney, Tom Meehan, Nicholas Tierney, John Seerey, Martin Hewitt, John McGrath, John Ryan, Jack Moloney, John Pender, John Carew, Sonny O'Connor, William Quirke, Sonny Dudley

Staff recorded in 1901 Census: Thomas Meehan, David Lonergan, Patrick Doherty, Joseph Convey, Patrick Carew, John Molloy, Patrick Lowery, Thomas Dunne, Terence Murphy, Michael Cunningham, Pierce Buckley, Joseph Moloney, Michael Grace, Patrick Heney, William Duhy, Patrick Cunningham, James Farrell, Patrick Beary.

APPENDIX XI STUDENTS IN JANUARY1869.

Junior Scholastics

James Hickey, John Hogan, Nicholas Lundy, Laurence St. Laurence, John Thornton, Thomas O'Connor. (6)

Scottish Seminarians

Stephen McGlinchy, James Harris, Daniel Donnelly, Laurence Finin, Thomas Tighe, John Graham, Joseph Lynch, Archy McLaughlin, Peter Donnelly, James Conaghan, John McDonald, Laurence McGlinchy, William Golden, Colin McDonald. (14)

Boarders

William Mullins, Richard Mullins, John Connors, Paul Fahy, Andrew Hennessey, Robert Wood, Thomas Carew, Francis Curren, Robert Carew, Edmund Connelly, James Dwyer, James Conroy, James Byrne, John Power, William Corcoran, Michael O'Shea, David O'Gorman, John O'Gorman, Michael Ryan, John O'Dwyer, Edmund Gubbins, Patrick Phelan, John Culhane, William Mahony, Edmund McCarthy, Robert Donovan, John Francis McCarthy, William Moran, John Carroll, Cornelius Dwyer, John Butler, George Butler, Fitzmaurice Butler, John Ryan, James Ryan, William Mullally, Austin Meagher, Robert Gubbins, John Quinlan, Thomas Hayden. (40)

Day Boys

Patrick Ryan, Cornelius O'Sullivan, John Cleary. Michael Cleary, John Nolan, Cornelius Doherty, Thomas Downey, Michael Moloney, William Nolan, Daniel O'Sullivan, Edmund Hyland, James Coughlin, James Loughnane, Charles O'Farrell, William Lonergan, Denis McGrath, William Purcell, Michael Purcell, William English, Daniel Heffernan, Andrew Heffernan, Patrick Duggan, Michael Hanley. (23)

Source: JNL 19/1/1869.

APPENDIX XII. STUDENTS RECORDED IN 1911 CENSUS AND THEIR PLACE OF BIRTH

Barry, Gerard	Cork	Barry, John	Cork
Blackburn, Philip	Tipperary	Blake, Thomas	Clare
Bolton, Patrick	Tipperary	Boyce, William	Cork
Brassil, William	Kerry	Brennan, Patrick	Kilkenny
Britton, Henry	Tipperary	Cahill, Edmund	Tipperary
Calleary, John	Tipperary	Canty, John	Limerick
Chadwick, William	Tipperary	Cleary, Michael	Tipperary
Coen, Patrick	Mayo	Coghlan, Patrick	Cork
Collins, Arthur	Dublin	Collins, Thomas	Dublin
Crowley, Patrick	Limerick	Coyle, Michael	Meath
Costelloe, Michael	Clare	Daly, Owen	Limerick
Curran, John	Galway	Daly, Stanly	Westmeath
Daly, Richard	Kerry	Dowling, Thomas	Galway
Darmody, John	Limerick	Duane, Thomas	Queen's
Downey, David	Tipperary	Duggan, Patrick	Wexford
Duffy, Albert	Tipperary	Fahy, John	Mayo
Dwyer, Michael	Galway	Fitzgerald, Frank	Mayo
Fennelly, William	Tipperary	Fitzgerald, Patrick	Kerry
Fitzgerald, John	Tipperary	Fitzgerald, William	Queen's Co.
Fitzgerald, Thomas	Kildare	Fyans, Thomas	Roscommon
Fitzpatrick, John	Mayo	Grary, Augustin	Tipperary
Godfrey, Michael	Clare	Griffin, Francis	Clare
Gray, Gerald	Tipperary	Grogan, Thomas	King's
Griffin, Martin	Tipperary	Guerin, Michael	Kerry
Guerin, Gerome	Clare	Hanlon, Arthur	Dublin
Hand, John	Kerry	Hannon, James	Limerick
Hanly, James	Kerry	Hannon, Timothy	Clare
Hannon, Joseph	Tipperary	Hayden, Leo	Dublin
Hayden, Denis	Limerick	Healy, Thomas	Tipperary
Hayes, William	Dublin	Heelan, David	Limerick
Healy, Thomas	Wexford	Hewitt, Patrick	Tipperary
Heffernan, Michael	Waterford	Hickey, Thomas	Tipperary
Hickey, David	Tipperary	Holohan, Thomas	King's Co.
Holloway, Michael	Tipperary	Horgan, Joseph	Kerry
Holohan, William	Tipperary	Hurley, James	Clare
Hourigan, William	King's Co.	Hyland, Michael	Tipperary
Hurley, William	Clare	Jeffers, John	Cork
Irwin, Robert	Cork	Kavanagh, John	Wexford
Jones, Louis	King's Co.	Keane, Maurice	Limerick
Keane, Denis	Galway	Keane, Michael	Galway
Keane, Michael	Limerick	Kelly, Thomas	Tipperary
Keane, Thomas	Galway	Kennedy, William	Tipperary
Kennedy, Crusick	Dublin	Kenny, Terence	India
Kenny, Patrick	India	Kinsella, Edward	Carlow
Kinane, Thomas	Tipperary	Lee, Michael	Tipperary
Lambe, John	Tipperary	Leonard, Daniel	Cork
Leen, Patrick	Limerick	Lesley, Timothy	Limerick
Leonard, Paul	England	Longford, Michael	Kerry
Long, John	Cork	Maher John	Tipperary
Lynch, James	Clare	Mallon, William	Wicklow

Mahony, Michael	Tipperary	Mangan, George	Kerry
Malone, Edward	Kildare	Mariana, George	Burmah
MacAleer, John	Tyrone	McCarthy, Denis	Kerry
McCarthy, William	Kerry	McCarthy, John	Clare
McCormack, John	Sth. America	McClare, Thomas	Westmeath
McDonald, James	Scotland	McDonagh, Redmond	Clare
McDonnell, John	King's	McDonnell, James	Tipperary
McGing, Patrick	Mayo	McGillicuddy, Thomas	Kerry
McGlade, Charles	Derry	McGlade, Bernard	Derry
Meade, Thomas	Galway	McGlade, Patrick	Derry
Mevelehan, Edward	Westmeath	Mevelehan, Christy	Westmeath
Moloney, John	Clare	Moloney, Michael	Clare
Monaghan, John	England	Moore, Michael	Kilkenny
Morrissey, William	Queen's	Murphy, James	Wexford
Murphy, Leo	Dublin	Murphy, Patrick	Cork
Neenan, Michael	Clare	Nolan, Martin	Kerry
O'Brien, Daniel	Clare	O'Brien, David	Tipperary
O'Brien, Donald	Mayo	O'Brien, Edward	Tipperary
O'Brien, Joseph	Clare	O'Brien, William	Limerick
O'Callaghan, John	Limerick	O'Callaghan, Thomas	Limerick
O'Connor, Michael	Kerry	O'Connor, Patrick	Limerick
O'Donnell, James	Tipperary	O'Donnell, John	Tipperary
O'Donnell, John	Tipperary	O'Donnell, Martin	Clare
O'Dwyer, James	Tipperary	O'Dwyer, Philip	Tipperary
O'Flaherty, Morgan	Kerry	O'Flaherty William	Galway
O'Grady, Laurence	King's Co.	O'Hara, Patrick	Wexford
O'Loughlin, Paul	Tipperary	O'Mahony, Brian	Kerry
O'Mahony, Charles	Kerry	O'Rourke, Joseph	Wicklow
O'Rourke, Maurice	Wicklow	O'Rourke, Timothy	Limerick
O'Shea, Daniel	Kerry	O'Sullivan, Daniel	Kerry
O'Sullivan, Eugene	Kerry	O'Sullivan, James	Kerry
O'Sullivan, Lawrence	Kerry	O'Sullivan, Michael	Kerry
O'Sullivan, Michael	Kerry	O'Sullivan, Philip	Kerry
O'Sullivan, Thomas	Kerry	O'Toole, Joseph	Wicklow
Powell, Edward	Limerick	Powell, John	King's Co.
Power, Faney	Tipperary	Power, James	Wexford
Quigley, James	Wexford	Quigley, John	Wexford
Quinlan, Michael	Tipperary	Quirk, William	Tipperary
Reddy, Patrick	King's Co.	Ring, George	Kerry
Roche, John	Kildare	Roche, Philip	Kildare
Ronan, James	Tipperary	Ryan, Edward	Tipperary
Ryan, James	Tipperary	Ryan, Martin	Tipperary
Ryan, Thomas	Carlow	Ryan, Michael	Tipperary
Ryan, Thomas	Dublin	Ryan, Thomas	Tipperary
Russell, John	Australia	Sadlier, Thomas	Tipperary
Scully, Patrick	Cork	Shannon, William	Clare
Slattery, Richard	Tipperary	Slattery, William	Tipperary
Stokes, Edward	Tipperary	Tierney, Francis	Tipperary
Tobin, James	Cork	Tobin, Michael	Tipperary
Tobin, Patrick	Tipperary	Waldron, Thomas	Galway
Wall, John	Tipperary	Wall, Maurice	Tipperary
Wallace, Michael	Limerick	Walsh, Joseph	Tipperary

APPENDIX XIII: STUDENT POPULATION OF ROCKWELL COLLEGE 1944-2013

	1944	1945	1946	1947	1948	1949	1950	1951
6th Year	92	91	77	77	95	95	98	91
5th Year	92	84	84	88	92	100	92	85
4th Year	109	127	137	138	150	139	114	120
3rd Year	69	101	98	100	97	84	76	73
2nd Year	38	53	66	69	63	66	51	47
Total	400	456	462	472	497	484	431	416

	1952	1953	1954	1955	1956	1957	1958	1959
6th Year	101	90	85	91	60	91	82	98
5th Year	78	85	87	54	85	80	96	82
4th Year	120	121	105	66	68	76	74	104
3rd Year	64	67	74	79	93	84	100	90
2nd Year	38	40	32	140	91	89	79	84
1st Year						46	44	34
Total	401	404	383	430	456	466	475	492

	1960	1961	1962	1963	1964	1965	1966
6th Year	74	108	110	115	120	127	113
5th Year	108	109	111	107	125	116	104
4th Year	109	107	103	130	80	76	91
3rd Year	87	104	114	93	85	99	100
2nd Year	85	107	95	72	105	109	104
1st Year	34	16	32	31	23	18	--
Total	497	551	565	548	538	545	512

	1966	1967	1968	1969	1970	1971	1972
6th Year	113	115	132	132	148	125	140
5th Year	104	121	116	127	107	123	127
4th Year	91	93	92	73	102	111	96
3rd Year	100	94	92	106	101	90	124
2nd Year	104	93	119	102	107	119	107
1st Year	--	22	--	25	22	14	10
Total	512	538	551	565	587	582	604

	1973	1974	1975	1976	1977	1978	1979
6th Year	155	135	134	152	123	138	122
5th Year	121	125	144	113	133	115	135
4th Year	123	117	104	122	121	119	119
3rd Year	113	103	121	121	113	113	118
2nd Year	114	119	120	110	116	112	92
Total	626	599	623	618	606	597	586

	1980	1981	1982	1983	1984	1985	1986
6th Year	132	125	116	121	111	114	117
5th Year	141	134	127	121	112	122	97
4th Year	123	95	97	86	85	67	77
3rd Year	97	108	88	82	67	81	67
2nd Year	95	78	74	74	75	58	54

Total	588	540	502	484	450	442	412

	1987	1988	1989	1990	1991	1992	1993
7th Year		24	30	40	34	39	33
6th Year	97	92	75	80	89	92	80
5th Year	116	80	91	94	102	85	110
4th Year	70	61	66	59	50	98	88
3rd Year	56	62	53	47	102	89	104
2nd Year	58	47	38	79	86	100	84
Total	397	366	353	399	463	503	499

	1994	1995	1996	1997	1998	1999	2000
7th Year	42	50	54	25	30	19	23
6th Year	97	95	96	101	85	98	90
5th Year	104	101	102	97	112	98	94
4th Year	103	86	61	88	70	66	91
3rd Year	89	65	81	68	71	78	74
2nd Year	60	76	63	66	71	79	78
Total	495	473	457	445	439	438	450

	2001	2002	2003	2004	2005	2006	2007
7th Year	21	28	19	30	32	19	16
6th Year	81	89	106	112	84	78	91
5th Year	76	116	121	106	91	116	101
Transition	23	21	12	17	40	50	47
3rd Year	72	90	84	90	86	76	71
2nd Year	87	80	88	92	84	81	92
1st Year	71	84	83	88	71	85	64
Total	431	508	513	535	488	505	482

	2008	2009	2010	2011	2012	2013
7th Year	8	8				
6th Year	77	78	108*	106*	120*	89*
5th Year	132	128	92	128	90	104
Transition	52	52	57	58	60	72
3rd Year	70	72	93	71	98	88
2nd Year	99	95	84	96	91	78
1st Year	72	72	92	89	83	62
Total	510	505	527	548	542	493

* 7th and 6th Years.

Source: RCA passim.

Appendix XIV Final Year Students 1935-2013

1935

Brennan, James A.
Bresnahan, Seán
Bunworth, Richard
Burke, Denis
Burrell, Eric
Byrne, John J.
Cahalane, John
Cahalane, Denis J.
Campion, John
Caplice, Richard A.
Cleary, John
Coghlan, James
Condon, Philip G.
Corry, Patrick
Crowley, William A.
Crowley, Michael B.
Curtin, John
Daly, Matthew
Daly, John
Danaher, Patrick
Dore, James C.
Duffy, Thomas
Egan, James
Enright, John
Feehan, Seán M.

Felle, Robert.
Foley, Walter
Gleeson, Christopher J.
Guilfoyle, Daniel
Hanly, Patrick
Hayes, Henry F.
Headen, William P.
Healy, Thomas
Holly, Cornelius C.
Keating, William
Keena, Kieran
Kelly, Richard
Kennelly, Timothy
Kissane, Richard
Leahy, William J.
Lennon, Edward
Liddy, Martin
Lynch, Thomaas
Mangan, Colman H.
Meagher, James J.
Moynihan, Timothy J.
Murphy, Thomas
Mc.Auliffe, Denis
Mc.Carthy, James C.
McCarthy, Denis

McCarthy John
McCarthy, John P.
McDyer, Andrew
McElligot, James
McGovern, John
McGrane, Michael
McGuinness, Anthony P.
McSweeney, Eugene
Nolan, Joseph
Noonan, William,
Nunan, James A.
O'Flaherty, Timothy
O'Grady, Seán
O'Grady, Thomas
O'Keeffe, James
O'Neill, Owen R.
O'Sullivan, Patrick J.
Rooney, Christopher T.
Ryan, Denis
Ryan, Patrick
Rynne, John
Toner, Peter
Walsh, Michael
Whelan, Stephen
Woulfe, Cornelius C.

1936

Blair, Ciarán
Breen, Thomas
Carey, Patrick F.
Casey, John P.
Connolly, Edward
Coughlan, Patrick J.
Cronin, Daniel N.
Cronin, Timothy
Crowley, Cornelius
Crowley, Patrick
Curran, Patrick
Daly, John
Danaher, Patrick
Darmody, Joseph
Delaney, John J.
Delaney, Kevin
Dennehy, Thomas
Diamond, John
Doyle, John J.
Duggan, James
Dunne, Philip
Dwan, Michael
Egan, Thomas J.
Egan, James
Fitzgerald, James
Fogarty, Patrick

Healy, Thomas D.
Hennessy, William
Hickey, Edward
Holohan, John C.
Holohan, Patrick
Jolly, John A.
Jordan, Thomas
Keane, Michael
Keane, Patrick
Kissane, Maurice
Lavery, John
Lehane, Richard
Liddy, Michael
Maguire, Patrick
Meagher, Martin
Moffat, Eamon
Mulcahy, Francis
Mulcahy, Martin
Murphy, John P.
Murphy, Richard
Murray, Patrick
McEvoy, Laurence B.
McNamara, John L
McNamara, Matthew
Noonan, Patrick J.
Noonan, William

O'Driscoll, Desmond
O'Gorman, Michael
O'Leary, Denis
O'Leary, Martin
O'Neill, Eoin
O'Neill, Fergus
O'Neill, James J.
O'Sullivan, Cornelius E.
O'Sullivan, Declan F.
O'Sullivan, Timothy
Prout, John
Reidy, John
Ring, Christopher
Rosney, Peter J.
Ryan, Neil A.
Ryan, Patrick
Ryan, Peter P.
Russell, David
Savage, John C.
Scott, timothy
Sheehy, John
Sheridan, Farrell
Toomey, Noel,
Treacy, Arthur
Troy, Michael
Van de Velde, Rene

Going, James
Griffin, Patrick
Headon, Thomas

O'Connell, John P.
O'Connor, Denis
O'Connor, John

Walsh, Redmond
White, James

1937

Aherne, John
Archdeacon, John
Barrett, David O.
Burke, John
Burke, John J.
Cantwell, John
Casey, John
Cleare, Gerard
Comerford, Francis
Crosse, William
Crowley, Dermot
Crowley, Seamus
Daly, John
Darmody, James
Delaney, John J.
Domoney, Liam
Dwan, Michael
Fitzpatrick, Patrick
Fogarty, Patrick
Gilman, John
Gohery, Lawrence

Going, James
Griffin, Patrick
Gunne, Lawrence
Hackett, Patrick
Henebery, Robert
Hennessy, William
Holohan, Patrick
Jordan, Thomas
Kirby, James
Kissane, Thomas
Liddane, Patrick
Lynch, Joseph
Lynch, Patrick
Madden, Liam
Maguire, Patrick
Malone, John
McCarthy, Denis
McGrane, Christopher
Moloney, Walter
Morrissey, Patrick
Mulcahy, Martin

Murphy, Michael
Murphy, Peter
Noonan, Denis
Nugent, Thomas
O'Brien, James
O'Byrne, Thomas
O'Connell, Seán
O'Connor, Michael
O'Donovan, Michael
O'Driscoll, Michael
O'Keeffe, John
O'Sullivan, James
O'Sullivan, Timothy
Reilly, Michael
Reynolds, Thomas
Rosney, Timothy
Ryan, Patrick
Sheehy, John
Sheridan, Farrell
Smith, William
Teihan, Edward

1939

Collins, Michael
Corry, Senan
Crowley, Seamus
Culloo, Michael
Darcy, Kevin
Diamond, Patrick
Doyle, John
Dillon, Jim
Doyle, James
Fahy, John Francis
Flaherty, Cornelius
Faraher, John
Finn, Seán
Hanrahan, John
Holohan Bernard
Layden, Michael
Lafford, Liam
Leahy, Patrick J.

Leen, Denis
Lee, Eamon
Lowe, Colm
Martin, John
Mascarenchas, Felix
Moriarty, Liam
Murphy, Jerry
Murnane, John
McCarthy, Michael
McGrath, Terence
Nugent, Thomas
O'Brien, John
O'Connell, Joseph
O'Connor, Denis
O'Connor, Patrick
O'Driscoll, Denis
O'Driscoll, James Francis
O'Driscoll, Timothy

O'Dwyer, Seamus
O'Farrell, Thomas
O'Keeffe, John Joseph
O'Mahony, Conor
O'Mahony, Eamon
O'Mahony, Jeremiah
O'Neill, Oliver Plunkett
O'Shea, Timothy
O'Sullivan, Thomas
Russell, Patrick
Ryan, Eamon
Ryan, John
Ryan, Michael
Wall, Donagh
Walsh, John Francis
Walsh, Patrick

1940

Barry, Eamonn
Blackwell, Patrick
Carroll, Gerald
Connaughton, Lawrence
Conron, Joseph
Corbett, James

Hughes, Gerald
Joyce, Thomas
Kane, Vincent
Kelly, Denis
Killeen, Patrick
Lawlor, Arthhur

O'Connor, Patrick
O'Donnell, Thomas
O'Donoghue, Michael
O'Keeffe, Dermot
O'Loughlin, Andrew
O'Shea, Timothy

Crowe, William
Crowley, Edward
Culloo, Michael
Danaher, Colm
Doyle, Finian
Doyle, James
Dunican, William
Fergus, William
Hartnett, Denis
Hartnett, William
Hickey, Philip
Hoare, Paddy

Leahy, Patrick
Loughnane, Michael
McCarthy, Timothy
McCluskey, Peter
McCullough, Michael
McDonnell, Harry
McDonnell, Richard
Moran, Thomas
Morris, Peter
Murphy, Timothy
O'Connell, Hugh
O'Connor, John

O'Sullivan, Donal
O'Sullivan, Thomas
Roche, Aiden
Roche, Kevin
Roycroft, William
Ryan, Michael
Sheridan, Patrick
Sweeney, John
Sweeney, Joseph
Tanney, Donal
White, Michael

1943

Ahearne G.
Breen, D.
Buckley, T.
Burke, J.
Burke, R.
Chadwick, J.
Cleary, T.
Colbert, C.
Cummins, F.
Conlon, F.
Corcery, M.
Creamer, P.
Davern E.
Derivan, P.
Dinan, P.
Egan, D.
Enright, T.
Fitzgerald, G.
Fitzgerald, J.
Fitzgerald, N.
Foyle, C.
Gogarty, H.
Gully, D.
Harney, G.
Healy, D.
Heenan, M.
Holland, P.

Hussey, M.
Hussey, T.
Joyce, D.
Keating, S.
Keogh, M.
Layden, G.
Leahy, R.
Ledaire, L.
Lynch, H.
Maher, P.
Mannion, S.
McCarthy, D.
McCarthy, F.
McCarthy, G.
McGrath, D.
McGuinness, E.
Minihan, G.
Moloney, M.
Morgan, J.
Murphy, J.
Murphy, P.
Murphy, S.
Murtagh, E.
Neenan, M.
Nolan, T.
Nugent, W.
O'Brien, M.

O'Brien, T.
O'Connell, M.
O'Connor, T.
O'Dea, N.
O'Dwyer, J.
O'Dwyer, M.
O'Hanlon, B.
O'Mahony, G.
O'Mahony, J.
O'Mahony, P.
O'Reilly, L.
O'Shea, J.
O'Sullivan, D.
Ryan, C.
Ryan, J.
Ryan, P.
Scahill, P.
Shine, J.
Sweeney, P.
Walshe, D.
Walshe, P.
Walshe, P.J.
Warren, P.
White, J.
Wilkinson, C.

1945

Beddy, D.
Blackwell, P.
Boran, F.
Burke, P.
Cahill, D.
Calnan, F.
Carmody, W.
Conlon, B.
Conway, P.
Conway, R.
Corish, P.
Crean, J.

Gaynor, W.
Gleeson, J.
Glynn, J.
Griffin, M.
Harrington, J.
Harris, D.
Heelan, F.
Heffernan, J.
Hoare, B.
Horrigan, F.
Keane, J.
Keating, B.

O'Byrne, S.
O'Carroll, J.
O'Dea, S.
O'Donovan, T.
O'Dowd, J.
O'Farrell, F.
O'Mahony, J.
O'Regan, T.
O'Sullivan, D.
O'Sullivan, J.
O'Sullivan, T.
Peters, J.

Curran, P.
Cusack, L.
Daly, J.
Delaney, M.
Devlin, P.
Donovan, R.
Doyle, A.
Dunne, J.
Fahey, M.
Farrell, T.
Finucane, T.
Fitzpatrick, J.
Flavin, J.
Forde, P.
Kennedy, Jn.
Kennedy, Jas.
Keyes, J.
Lynch, J.
Lynch, L.

Mackey, K.
Maher, D.
Maher, M.
Martin, C.
McBrinn, J.
McGrath, J.
McGrath, P.
McInerney, B.
McNeela, M.
Miley, J.
Moroney, T.
Moynihan, J.
Mulvihill, P.
Murphy, M.
Murphy, T.K.
Murphy, W.
Murray, P.
Murtagh, P.
Nolan, W.
Nunan, D.

Power, M.
Riordan, E.
Roche, P.
Ryan, C.
Ryan, J.
Ryan, P.
Ryan, W.
Shanahan, R.
Sheedy, M.
Sheedy, V.
Shelley, P.
Sweeney, M.
Sweeney, T.
Tobin, J.
Walsh, S.
Ward, T.
Whelan, J.

1946

Armstrong, Ivor
Arrigan, Patrick
Baynton, Patrick
Berkery, John
Bermingham, Donal
Bondoe, Denis
Brosnan, James
Burke, James
Burke, Louis
Cahill, Ronald
Canney, Michael
Collins, John Denis
Collins, Timothy
Collins, William
Conway, Seán
Cotter, Nicholas
Dee, Thomas
Deegan, Brendan
Duggan, Patrick
Egan, John
Egan, Michael
Egan, Thomas Joseph
English, John
Enright, Jeremiah
Enright, Thomas
Fahey, Patrick
Feehan, Michael
Gallway, Patrick
Gavin, Noel
Grau-Bassas, Alejandro
Hanna, Herbert
Harrington, John
Herlihy, Donal

Hickey, Paul
Hogan, James
Hulgraine, Michael
Hurley, James
Hussey, Brendan
Hyland, Louis
Irwin, John
Keane, Noel
Keane, Timothy
Keating, Vincent
Kelly, Anthony
Kelly, James
Kelly, Jeremiah
Kelly, Patrick
Kennedy, William
Kiernan, Charles
Layden, Brendan
Layden, Vincent
Leavy, Michael
Lefevre, Francois
Loftus, Joseph
Lynch, Brendan
Lynch, John
Lyon, Brendan
McAuliffe, Michael
McCarthy, Patrick
McConnell, Gerald
McCormack, Bernard
McInerney, John
Moloney, Raymond
Montes, Manuel
Murphy, James
Murphy, Joseph

Murphy, Michael
O'Brien, Alphonsus
O'Brien, Henry
O'Brien, Timothy A.
O'Connor, Brendan
O'Dinneen, Lee
O'Donnell, Michael
O'Halloran, Patrick
O'Mahony, Brian
O'Mahony, William
O'Neill, Daniel
O'Reilly, Liam
O'Sullivan, John
Rafferty, Nicholas
Rafferty, Seán
Richardson, Seán
Reidy, John
Ryan, Edmund
Ryan, Laurence
Scully, Patrick
Shanahan, Francis
Sheedy, Francis
Sheedy, John
Smyth, James
Smyth, Michael
Sweeney, Frank
Switzer, John
Thompson, Kieran
Tierney, Maurice
Walsh, John
Walsh, Kevin

1947

Allen, Geoffrey	Higgins, John	Nunan, Joseph
Barry, Thomas	Hogan, Denis	O'Connor, James
Blackledge, Denis	Holohan, Patrick	O'Dwyer, Eugene
Broderick, Patrick	Keating, Michael	O'Farrell, Brendan
Broderick, Thomas	Kelly, Seán	O'Loughlin, Kevin
Brosnan, James	Kennedy, Patrick	O'Regan, Michael
Buckley, Jeremiah	Kingston, Samuel	O'Shaughnessy, Seán
Buckley, Joseph	Kissane, Patrick	O'Shea, Donal
Burke, Alexander	Larkin, Austin	O'Sullivan, Edward
Clarke, Joseph	Larkin, Hugh	O'Sullivan, Joseph
Corrigan, William	Layden, Brendan	Owens, Hugh
Creed, Patrick	Maloney, Thomas G.	Phelan, John
Dillon, Edward	Martin, Rory	Power, James
Duffy, Sylvester	Masterson, Peter	Prendergast, Francis
English, Patrick D.	Mason, Michael	Quirke, David
Enright, Jeremiah	McConnell, Gerard	Ryan, Edmund
Farrell, James	McGough, William	Ryan, George
Farrell, Leo	McSweeney, David	Ryan, James
Florido, Gaspar	Moloney, John	Ryan, Liam
Foley, Dermot	Morrissey, James	Ryan, Michael
Forster, Francis	Murphy, Daniel	Ryan, Michael Enda
Fleming, Joseph	Murphy, Finbar	Shanahan, Patrick
Flynn, Thomas	Murray, Seán	Wall, Thomas
Gallaher, Thomas	Murray, Timothy	Whyte, Michael
Groarke, Ignatius	Nash, Seán	Williams, Seán
Hartnett, Desmond	Nunan, Bernard	

1949

Agnoli, Enzo	Hallinan, Gerald	McMahon, Peter
Barry, Kevin	Hannon, Edward	McManus, John
Bernard, John	Harrington, Edmund	Meaney, Michael
Bredin, John	Hayes, Patrick	Moloney, Marcus
Buckley, John	Hennessy, Paschal	Moran, Patrick
Buckley, Michael	Hodkinson, Henry	Murphy, Patrick
Burke, Thomas	Horgan, Patrick	Murphy, Richard
Connaughton, James	Irwin, John	Newman, John
Crean, Thomas	Keane, Noel	O'Brien, Patrick
Cronin, Patrick	Keane, Timothy	O'Connor, John
Cuniffe, Michael	Kearney, Francis	O'Mahony, James
Devlin, Leo	Keegan, Maurice	O'Mahony, Thomas
Duffy, Dermot	Kelly, Patrick	O'Mahony, William
Durkin, William	Kelly, Patrick	O'Riordan, Kenneth
Dwane, Seamus	Kennedy, Desmond	O'Shea, Owen
English, John	Kennedy, Patrick	O'Sullivan, Seán
Feehan, Michael	Kenny, Gerald	Powell, Derek
Fennelly, Joseph	Kent, Donald	Reilly, Thomas
Finlan, Michael	Kilkenny, Desmond	Roche, Anthony
Finnucane, James	Landers, Daniel	Sampson, Thomas
Fitzgerald, Thomas	Larkin, William	Sexton, Michael
Flood, Eoin	Lawless, Fergus	Sexton, Timothy
Flynn, Noel	Layden, Edmund	Siung, Manfred
Fogarty, Patrick	Lynch, Cornelius	Stack, William
Funchion, Pierce	Lynch, Michael	Sweeney, Robert
Gallagher, John	Mackey, Noel	Thompson, Thomas
Gaule, Gerald	McAuliffe, Michael	Traynor, Michael
Gavin, Noel	McCarthy, Brendan	Tynan, Aidan
Geary, John	McConville, William	Verschoyle, Frederick

Glasgow, Rian
Grogan, Matthew
Griffin, Denis

McGrath, James
McKenna, Peter
McMahon, Michael

Walsh, Francis
Walsh, Patrick

1950

Beary, Timothy
Bernard, Denis
Bourke, Donal
Brosnan, Cornelius
Brosnan, Michael
Buckley, James
Burke, Thomas
Burke, Thomas
Cahill, Thomas
Cantwell, Charles
Casey, Patrick
Cogans, Denis
Colbert, William
Condon, John
Conway, Vincent
Creedon, Jeremiah
Cronin, Edmund
D'Arcy, Christopher
D'Arcy, Seán M
D'Arcy, Seán N
Davern, Patrick
Devlin, Leo
Dodd, Kieran
Doran, Patrick
Dwyer, Martin
Dwyer, William
English, Michael
Fitzpatrick, Anthony
Flusk, Bernard
Gallagher, Christopher
Gallagher, Joseph
Gallagher, S. Finbarr

Gannon, Martin
Gunning, Patrick
Healy, Daniel
Healy, Oliver
Heenan, Joseph
Holland, Timothy
Keane, Noel
Kelly, Brendan
Kelly, Seán
Landers, Maurice
Langan, Christopher
Larkin, James
Layden, Gabriel
Layden, Patrick
Lowney, John
Lynch, Lionel
Lynch, Patrick
Maloney, George Vincent
Manning, John
McCarton, Eugene
McCarton, Joseph
McCarthy, John
McCarthy, Timothy
McCrea, Anthony
McGrath, Brendan
McKiernan, Cataldus
McMurray, Robert
McSweeney, James
Meaney, Michael
Miller, Alexander
Moran, John
Mullens, Patrick

Murphy, Edward
Murphy Noel
Neerman, Paul
Newman, John
Nolan, Seán
O'Brien, Andrew
O'Connor, Brendan
O'Connor, Brian
O'Donnell, Owen
O'Farrell, Patrick
O'Gorman. Patrick
O'Hara, Patrick
O'Keeffe, Finbarr
O'Kelly, Brendan
O'Leary, Simon
O'Neill, Patrick
O'Regan, Colum
O'Riordan, Kenneth
O'Sullivan, Bernard
O'Sullivan, John
Quill, Patrick
Rafferty, John
Redmond, Thomas
Rogers, Thomas
Schmeltz, Stefan
Shanahan, Richard
Shine, Michael
Stack, Paschal
Sweeney, Hugh
Tynan, Aidan
Wall, Richard
Zaidan, Raymond

1951.

Arrigan, John
Bamin, Edward
Bartley, Philip
Bennett, James
Bird, Terence
Breen, Arthur
Breen, Owen
Brew, Patrick
Browne, Laurence
Buckley, Michael
Butler, David
Cahill, Patrick
Carron, Desmond
Cody, James
Cogans, Denis
Connolly, Dermot
Cosgrove, John
Cotter, Richard
Cusack, Patrick

Geary, Dermot
Hannon, William
Hayes, John
Hernandez, Jose
Hickey, John
Horgan, Seamus
Jacob, Liam
Jones, Philip
Keenan, Noel
Kelly, Michael
Lynch, Patrick
Maloney, Thomas
McCarthy, Cathal
McCarthy, Denis
McCarthy, Edward
McCarthy, John
McCarthy, Joseph
McDonald, Patrick
McDonnell, Brendan

Murphy, Cornelius
Murphy, Michael
Murphy, Patrick
Murray, Patrick
Nolan, Nicholas
Nolan, Patrick
Nolan, Peter
O'Brien, Leo
O'Connell, Vincent
O'Connor, Desmond
O'Dea, Joseph
O'Driscoll, Michael
O'Dwyer, William
O'Farrell, Thomas
O'Hara, Michael
O'Reilly, Seamus
O'Sullivan, Dermot
O'Sullivan, Michael
Quinn, James

Dalton, John
Davern, Patrick
Deehan, Thomas
Drea, Henry
Dwyer, William
Fagan, Hubert
Farrell, John
Fitzgibbon, Joseph
Forster, Frederick
Flanagan, Brian
Frawley, Martin
Gallagher, Joseph

McElligott, John
McEvoy, Malachy
McGrath, Philip
McGrenra, Marcus
McKenna, Seamus
McLoughlin, Edward
McMahon, Desmond
McSweeney, Brian
Millar, Alexander
Mocklar, Patrick
Moloney, Basil
Moriarty, John

Reidy, Donal
Ruttledge, Robert
Ryan, Philip
Ryan, William
Sheehan, Joseph
Stokes, Michael
Twomey, William
Woods, Paul
Woulfe, Patrick
Xavier, Francis

1952

Allman, Timothy
Andrefouet, Tanneguy
Bamin, Edward
Barron, Thomas
Bowman, Michael
Campbell, Albert
Casey, Patrick
Casey, Timothy
Cashman, Michael
Cawley, John
Cleary, Patrick
Coffey, Ailbe
Collins, John
Considine, Patrick
Cotter. Richard
Creagh, Thomas
Crofton, Derek
Deady, Brendan
Dempsey, Gerard
Dolan, Joseph
Drea, Thomas
Dunne, John
Dwyer, Brendan
English, Christopher
Farrell, Seamus
Fitzgerald, Edmond
Gallagher, Seamus
Gilligan, Michael
Hannon, Daniel
Harris, Michael
Hayes, Philip
Healy, Patrick
Hennessy, Paschal
Hogan, John

Horan, William
Horgan, Eamon
Horgan, Patrick
Hughes, Peter
Hynes, James
Keohane, Michael
Kiely, George
Kingston, William
Lenehan, John
Lynch, Donal
Lynch, Francis
Lynch, Patrick
Lyons, Clement
Manning, Michael
McCarthy, John
McEntee, Eamon
McGrath, Timothy
McInerney, John
McLoughlin, Dermot
McManus, Brendan
McSweeney, Brian
Meehan, Joseph
Moore, Patrick
Molloy, Patrick
Moran, Francis
Moran, James Francis
Moroney, Brendan
Morris, Francis
Mulcair, Michael
Murphy, Brendan
Murphy, Joseph
Murray, Senan
Neville, Richard
O'Byrne, Colm

O'Connor, Noel
O'Connor, Vincent
O'Donnell, James
O'Donoghue, Joseph
O'Donovan, Cornelius
O'Dwyer, Denis
O'Gorman, Thomas
O'Keeffe, Cornelius
O'Keeffe, Patrick
O'Reilly, William
Reid, Owen
Reidy, Brian
Ryan, David
Ryan Edmond
Ryan, John
Ryan, Liam
Ryan, Patrick
Shanley, James
Sheahan, Gerald
Sheehan, John
Sheehy, john
Sheerin, Francis
Smith Seán
Smythe, Michael
Stack, John
Swan, Patrick
Tackaberry, Jeremiah
Taylor, Gerard
Thompson, Brendan
Tobin, Thomas
Treacy, Dermot
Walsh, Michael
Walshe, Thomas

1953

Allen, Vincent
Allmen, Denis
Boland, Flannan
Brown, William
Buckley, Edward
Burke, Seán
Burke, Thomas

Hurley, Patrick
Kaufmann, Hans
Kavanagh, Dermot
Kelly, Xavier
Keogh, Daniel
Kiely, James
Kinnane, John

Ó Caoimh, Pádraig
Ó Caoimh, Tomás
O'Connor, Noel
O'Daly, Arthur
O'Dea, Patrick
O'Donovan, David
O'Gorman, Thomas

Cardozo, John
Casey, Donal
Collins, Patrick
Cooke, Patrick
Cotter, Patrick
Cronin, Seán
Donlan, Aengus
Donnelly, Louis
Duggan, Michael
Duggan, Peter
Dunne, Seán
Du Crest, Maxime
Egan, Gerald
Evers, Paul
Foley, Seamus
Givens, Seán
Hale, Daniel
Hanley, Bernard
Harrington, Daniel
Hayes, Seán
Heron, Michael
Holway, James
Hughes, Peter

Lynch, Austin
Lynch, Florence
Maher, Seamus
Maher, William
Marren, Enda
McDermott, Patrick
McEvoy, Gerald
McKiernan, Eucharius
McMahon, Gerald
McManus, Kevin
Meade, Benedict
Meagher, Emmet
Moloney, Joseph
Moore, Michael
Moore, Patrick
Mullins, George
Mullins, Michael
Murphy, Barry
Murphy, Cyril
Nolan, Daniel
O'Boyle, Martin
O'Brien, Brendan
O'Callaghan, Noel

O'Grady, Gerald
Olisa, Geoffrey
O'Kelly, Gerald
O'Neill, John G.
O'Neill, John J.
O'Reilly, Gabriel
O'Shaughnessy, Kevin
O'Sullivan, Bernard
O'Sullivan, James
O'Sullivan, Michael
Prendergast, Kevin
Prendergast, Patrick
Reidy, Jeremiah
Savage, Richard
Sexton, George
Sheedy, John
Sheehan, Patrick
Siung, Michael
Smith, Patrick
Sodiende, Oyedola
Stokes, Stephen
Twomey, Jeremiah
Walker, Charles

1954

Allen, Ailbe
Behan, John
Bree, Seán
Briody, Hugh
Broderick, Seán
Byrne, Valentine
Casey, Luke
Coffey, Thomas
Coghlan, Daniel
Corbett, Michael
Conlon, Patrick
Cotter, Robert
Curtin, Maurice
Delaney, Daniel
Devlin, James
Dunne, Colm
Ferris, Gerard
Fitzpatrick, John
Fogarty, James
Frawley, Michael
Gallagher, Donal B.
Gallagher, Thomas F.
Glio, Giorgio
Gleeson, Anthony
Hanly, Noel
Harrington, Daniel
Harte, John
Jones, Patrick
Joy, Laurence
Joye, Patrick

Keyes, Patrick F.
Kirwan, Patrick
Lovett, Anselm
Lynch, Owen
Lynch, Robert
Lynch, Terence
Madigan, Patrick
Maher, Stephen
McCarthy, Seán
McDonald, Anthony
McGillycuddy, Thomas
McGrath, Michael
Meade, Gerard
Molloy, Edward
Molloy, Patrick
Moran, Patrick J.
Mulcahy, Donal
Murphy, Leo
Mullins, Denis
Neary, Patrick
Neville, Maurice A.
Nolan, Brendan
O'Brien, George B.
O'Brien, Joseph
O'Brien, Patrick
O'Callaghan, Thomas
O'Connell, Leo
O'Connor, Hugh
O'Flaherty, Thomas
O'Gorman, Maurice

O'Gorman, Thomas
O'Hart, Henry B.
O'Leary, Michael O.
O'Leary, Thomas C.
O'Mahony, James
O'Regan, Liam
O'Reilly, Ciarán
O'Sullivan, Michael
Phelan, Donal
Riordan, Richard
Ryan, Thomas A.
Scott, Edward
Scully, Patrick
Sewell, John
Sexton, George
Sheehan, Michael
Smith, Cornelius
Smith, Joseph
Smith, Seamus
Stokes, Stephen
Stritch, Paul
Tobin, Augustine
Treacy, Niall
Twomey, Jeremiah
Wong Hen, Arthur

1955

Aherne, John	Frewen, Thomas	Nesdale, Joseph
Allen, Michael	Hanley, John	Nunan, Matthew
Barron, Martin	Hanlon, William	O'Brien, Conall
Bidwell, Joseph	Higgins, Paul	O'Brien, Conor
Bresnan, Vincent	Hurley, Patrick	O'Brien, Fergus
Briody, Hugh	Hurley, Timothy	O'Connell, Daniel
Brosnan, Michael	Jacob, Joseph	O'Daly, Kevin
Browne, Cornelius	Keenan, John	O'Driscoll, John
Burke, Francis	Kehoe, Walter	O'Dwyer, Edmond
Byrne, Valentine	Kenny, Andrew	O'Dwyer, Michael
Casey, Benjamin	Keyes, Fergus	O'Flaherty, John
Clancy, Thomas	Kirwan, Patrick	O'Hart, Brendan
Coffey, Thomas	Kobba, Mansaley	O'Mahony, Joseph
Conroy, Seán	Kowa, Joseph	Ormond, Michael
Cooke, Thomas	Layden, Dermot	O'Sullivan, Donal
Daramy, Evans	Liston, Edward J.	O'Sullivan, Timothy
Deegan, Aiden	Liston, Edward T.	Palmer, Geoffrey
Devlin, James	Lynch, Daniel	Reidy, Vincent
Donovan, Peter	Mallen, Anthony	Rice, Dermot
Doran, Eamonn	McCabe, Joseph	Ryan, Edward
Dorr, Damien	McLoughlin, Michael	Ryan, Noel
Driscoll, Kevin	McMahon, Cornelius	Ryan, Patrick
Dunne, Colm	McSweeney, Michael	Ryan, Patrick F.
Dwan, Conor	Mellamphy, Ninian	Ryan, Patrick S.
Farragher, Pierce	Moloney, Vincent	Ryan, Thomas
Feore, John	Moran, William	Sheehan, Michael
Feore, James	Morkan, Thomas	Smyth, Frederick
Ferris, Gerard	Murphy, Jeremiah	Stanton, Joseph
Fleming, Anthony	Murphy, William	Stapleton, William
Flood, Eamonn	Nash, Jeremiah	Treacy, Kevin

1956

Allman, Dermot	Flood, Eamon	Mulligan, Declan, J.
Begley, Diarmuid	Frazer, Joseph	Mullins, Maurice
Boateng, Laurence	Gillan, Thomas	Murphy, Seán
Burke, Francis	Glendon, Seamus	O'Brien, Edward
Byrne, Francis	Henihan, Patrick D.	O'Donnell, Roger, J.
Byrne, Michael	Hickey, Patrick F.	O'Driscoll, John
Campbell, Brendan	Hurley, James	O'Farrell, John
Clifford, Michael	Kenny, Andrew	O'Leary, James
Collins, John	King, Joseph	O'Mahony, Stephen
Collins, Patrick	Lee, John	O'Shaughnessy, Vincent
Cusack, Senan	McCarthy, John	Quane, Patrick J.
Comerford, Michael	McCormack, Liam G.	Riordan, Desmond
Conway, Thomas L.	McElwain, John	Ryan, Conor
Daly, Noel	McKiernan, Finian	Ryan, Edward
Daly, Vincent	Magourty, Brendan	Ryan, Francis
Daly, William	Malone, Cecil	Ryan, Patrick F.
Donovan, Michael	Maloney, Stephen	Tooher, Terence
Fitzgerald, John G.	Meighan, Patrick R.	Walsh, Liam
Flannery, Edward	Milne, Robert	Whelan, Patrick
		Wyer, Edward

1957

Allen, Kieran	Egar, William	Meade, Conor
Barry, Derek	Elichondo, Jean	Meade, Thomas

Beere, Joseph
Behan, Hugh
Bissette, Paul
Blain, Anthony
Bodley, Desmond
Brassel. Patrick
Brennan, Gerald
Byrne, Michael
Byrne, Patrick
Cantwell, Alfred
Caplice, Michael
Casey, Michael
Casserly, Basil
Cavanagh, Cathal
Coakley, John
Concannon, Malachy
Cooke, Ciaran
Cosgrave, Stuart
Costelloe, John
Cregan, James
Crowley, Michael
Crowe, John
Daly, William
De Chambaud, Antoine
De Lacy, Desmond
Dillon, Kevin
Downey, Gerald
Edwards, Thomas

Fenoughty, Patrick
Foley, Maurice
Galvin, Patrick
Genet, Alain
Gillen, Kevin
Gilsennan, Noel
Hamill, David
Harte, Michael
Heffernan, James
Heffernan, Joseph
Hoade, Anthony
Joel, John
Keating, Bernard
Kelly, Brendan
Keogh, Edward
Keown, Ciaran
Khama, Leapeetswe
Kingston, Noel
Lewis, Liam
Linehan, Peter
Lonergan, Eamonn
Lonergan, Edmond
Lovett, John
Mahon, Barry
Malone, John
Maloughney, Diarmuid
Martin, Peter
McLoughlin, Michael

Mooney, Michael
Morris, Patrick
Murphy, Patrick
Murray, Paul
Nash, Henry
Neville, Grattan
O'Brien, John
O'Brien, Thomas
O'Callaghan, Bernard
O'Connor, Thomas
O'Donoghue, Michael
O'Regan, John
O'Rourke, John
O'Sullivan, Donal
O'Sullivan, Eamonn
O'Sullivan, Jeremiah
Reidy, Francis
Ryan, Conor
Sawh, Paul
Sheehan, David
Sheehy, Patrick
Synnott, John
Toohy, James
Treasy, Brian
Tuffy, Eamonn
Walton, Thomas
Wrixon, Henry
Yaghmour, Michel
Yzebe, Antoine

1958

Allen, Thomas
Barry, Aidan
Bohsali, Nassir
Bowe, Edward
Boylan, Andrew *
Brennan, Austin
Brennan, Pierce
Browne, Thomas
Burke, James
Cahill, John
Cahill, William
Carroll, Patrick
Casserly, Basil
Comerford, John
Condon, John
Conroy, Michael
Cooke, Patrick
Costelloe, Thomas
Croke, John
Cronin, John
Crowe, William
Crowley, Michael
Dillon, Kevin
Donaghy, Paul
Doyle, James
Egan, Thomas
Fagan, Fintan
Farragher, Seán

Ferris, Cornelius
Flynn, Patrick
Foley, Jerome
Galvin, Gerard
Galvin, Michael
Gardiner, James
Garvey, Joseph
Geaney, David
Grant, Michael
Hanley, Theo
Hazel, Finbar
Healey, Philip
Healy, Patrick
Heeley, Robert
Heelan, Michael
Hoade, Anthony
Holmes, John
Jones, Daniel
Kirby, Michael
Khama, Leapetswe
Lalor, Fergus
Lee, William
Lim, Henry
Maguire, Thomas
Mallen, Vincent
Martin, Thomas
McCarthy, Anthony

McCarthy, John
McElligott, Richard
McGovern, Paul
McGrath, Matthew
McLaughlin, Vincent
McNamara, Matthew
Moran, Paul
Moriarty, Kevin
O'Brien, Gerard
O'Brien, Turlough
O'Donnell, Edmond
O'Donnell, Michael
O'Donoghue, Martin
O'Dowd, Brendan
O'Dwyer, Patrick
O'Farrell, Michael
O'Leary, Francis
O'Leary, Ian
O'Reilly, Austin
O'Rourke, Dermot
Park, Jeremiah
Peters, Patrick
Prendergast, Kevin
Reidy, Francis
Sequeira, Raphael
Tangney, Seán
Wall, James

1959

Ahearn, Liam
Anyanwu, Innocent
Behan, Seamus
Bermudez, Louis
Brennan, Matthew
Brophy, Liam
Buckley, Joseph
Buggle, Joseph
Byrne, Joseph
Butler, Michael
Callanan, Timothy
Caplice, Francis
Carty, Bernard
Carty, Denis
Clancy, John
Coleman, Brendan
Condon, James
Conway, Ultan
Cooke, Thomas
Cooney, Seán
Corcoran, Anthony
Correa, Raynor
Corry, Declan
Cotter, Nicholas
Coughlan, Arthur
Cronin, John
Dennehy, Michael
Delaney, John
Doyle, Brian
D'Souza, John
Duffy, Francis
Duggan, Martin
Elliot, Neal
Enwezor, Joseph

Flemming, John
Flynn, Seamus
Gardiner, James
Gillen, Seán
Gillespie, Liam
Goncalves, Kenneth
Guiney, Cornelius
Hannon, James
Harris, John
Hickey, Francis
Hickey, Patrick
Hickey, Pierce
Hogan, Seán
Hughes, Frederick
Jones, Joseph
Kelliher, Donal
Kennedy, Dermot
Kennedy, Donal
Kerins, Tadhg
Kirby, Michael
Kirby, Thomas
Lacey, Liam
Leamy, Michael
Lee, William
Lim, David
Madigan, Anthony
Mangan, Colm
Mangan, Gabriel
Mangan, Henry
McAlister, Philip
McGrath, Patrick
McGrenra, Paschal
McNamara, Michael
Meehan, James

Modile, Abedowale
Moloney, Daniel
Mullins, Maurice
Murphy, Denis
Murphy, Patrick
Naughton, Raymond
Neary, Jeremiah
Nolan, Bernard
O'Brien, Gerard
O'Brien, Maurice
O'Doherty, David
O'Donoghue, Olaf
O'Donovan, Charles
O'Dwyer, John
O'Farrell, Roderick
O'Flynn, Thomas
O'Gorman, Liam
O'Grady, William
O'Leary, Michael
O'Loughlin, Francis
O'Mahony, James
O'Mahony, James E.
O'Neill, Michael
Pedro, Adebayo
Prendergast, John
Prendergast Kevin
Ryan, Martin
Ryan, Owen
Ryan, Patrick
Ryan, Percy
Sheehy, Edward
Tobin, Stephen

1960

Aherne, Francis
Browne, Vincent
Brogan, Gerard
Byrne, Maurice
Carey, Michael
Carmody, Peter
Chan, Michael
Collins, Joseph
Connaughton, Noel
Costelloe, James
Cotter, John
Crowley, Jeremiah
Dalton, John
Daly, John
Daly, Patrick
Davey, Gerard
Davey, Louis
Deevey, Anthony
Demby, Samuel
Doody, Parrick
Drew, Noel

Franquira, Juan
Gallagher, Michael
Gardiner, William
Goncalves, Kenneth
Guiney, Cornelius
Harte, Joseph
Hayes, Joseph
Henihan, Martin
Hickey, Michael
Hollder, Hayden
Keating, Seán
Kelly, Donal
Khama, Sekgoma
Lannen, Patrick
Leyden, Patrick
McKeon, Seán
McNamara, Michael
Mercer, John
Moody, Hugh
Morrissey, John
Murray, John

O'Connor, Patrick
O'Connor, Patrick
O'Donnell, John
O'Donovan, Donal
O'Driscoll, Denis
O'Dwyer, Vincent
O'Leary, Tadhg
O'Mahony, Edward
O'Shaughnessy, Justin
O'Shea, Denis
O'Shea, Donal
O'Sullivan, Denis
O'Sullivan, Donal
Power, John
Purcell, Gerald
Ryan, Patrick
Ryan, Pierce
Shanahan, Carl
Shanahan, Denis
Timlin, David
Wall, Patrick

Enright, Michael
Finucane, Joseph
Fitzpatrick, Francis
Fox, John

Neal, Michael
Nyhol, Richard
O'Brien, John
O'Brien, Richard

Wallace, Justin
Walshe, Thomas
Walshe, Patrick

1961

Acton, Francis
Anderson, Conor
Baldwin, Thomas
Berkeley, Alfred
Bermudez, Louis
Blair, Domhnall
Breen, Oliver
Broderick, Oliver
Buckley, Conor
Buckley, Denis
Butler, Andrew
Cantwell, Oliver
Comerford, Ciaran
Conroy, Aloysius
D'Arcy, Brendan
Daly, Patrick
Doyle, Francis
Duffy, Kenneth
De'Souza, Agnelo
Dwyer, Gerard
Egan, Finbarr
Egar, Anthony
Farragher, Francis
Farrelly, Patrick
Flanagan, Lawrenc
Flanagan, Richard
Fleming, Philip
Foley, John
Forrest, Seán
Frayne, John
Freeney, Christopher
Gallagher, Francis
Gavin, Thomas
Geary, Patrick
Gonzales, Graham
Hackett, Michael
Hannafin, Michael

Harrington, James
Harris, Derek
Haughton, Finbarr
Hayes, Brendan
Healy, Donal
Healy, James
Heaphy, John
Higgins, Malachy
Hogan, Patrick
Holland, Francis
Holmes, William
Houlihan, Tadhg
Hurley, Barry
Keane, Martin
Landy, John
Lannen, Raymond
Leamy, Paul
Lennon, Peter
Lewis, Kevin
Liddy, Christopher
Lynch, Donal
Lyras, Emile
Maher, Anthony
Maloughney, Fergus
Mangan, Alan
Manning, Maurice
McLean, Charles
McKeon, Gerard
McLoughlin, John
McSweeney, Anthony
Mercer, Michael
Milne, Robert
Mitchell, Robert
Morgan, Michael
Moroney, Jeremiah
Moynihan, Barry
Mulcahy, Donal

Murphy, Gary
Murphy, Terence
Murray, John L. *
O'Connor, Kevin
O'Connor, Terence
O'Donnell, Donal
O'Donnell, John
O'Donnell, Joseph
O'Donoghue, Desmond
O'Donoghue, Michael
O'Donovan, Thomas
O'Hourihan, Peadar
O'Keeffe, Brian
O'Mahony, Matthias
O'Neill, Terence
Onwu, Simon
O'Riordan, Seán
O'Rourke, Seán
O'Shea, Donal
O'Sullivan, Gerard
O'Sullivan, Seán
Power, Carroll
Ronayne, James
Rossat, Dominic
Ryan, Michael G.
Ryan, Michael J.
Sheehan, Joseph
Sheerin, James
Shine, Michael
Shorthall, John
Stapleton, Fintan
Synnott, Thomas
Tierney, Seán
Vaughan Buckley, Denis
White, Eoin

1962

Aherne, Joseph
Aherne, Noel
Barrett, Noel
Becton, Pierce
Blair, Ciaran
Brennan, Desmond
Brennan, Neil
Browne, Patrick
Buckley, Neil
Byrd, Stephen
Cahill, Kevin
Cahill, Sylvester

Gleeson, Joseph
Goncalves, Brent
Gough, Joseph
Gray, Desmond
Hale, Brendan
Hanna, Francis
Hayes, Brendan
Hawkins, John
Healy, Conor
Hegarty, John
Hickey, Michael
Hickey, Thomas

McGeough, Patrick
McGrath, Paul
McManus, Patrick
McSweeney, Cyril
Molloy, James
Mooney, Leo
Mullalley, Timothy
Nugent, James
O'Brien, John
O'Brien, John A.
O'Byrne, Dermot

Callinan, William
Carmody, Maurice
Chute, Frederick
Cleary, Kieran
Cole, Michael
Concannon, Robert
Conroy, Jarlath
Corcoran, Colum
Corrigan, Michael
Costello, Peter
Costigan, Martin
Cumiskey, Roger
Darmody, John
De Cevins, Louis
Dowling, Thomas
Doyle, Seán
Dudley, Hugh
Duggan, Thomas
Farragher, Noel
Fitzgerald, James
Fleming, Garrett
Gallivan, Daniel
Gannon, Patrick
Gaschinard, Michel
Gomez, Michael

Hourigan, Patrick
Hughes, John
Hurley, Michael
Johannes, Joseph
Kelly, Aidan
Kennedy, John
Kenny, Francis
Kerr, Bernard
Lancaster, Keith
Landy, Maurice
Langton, David
Lannen, Killian
Lowry, Vincent
Lyons, Michael
Lyons, Stephen
Lyras, Emile
Lynch, Dominick
Mackey, Gerard
Mangan, Joseph
Mannion, Oliver
McCabe, Jeremiah
McCann, Brian
McCarthy, John
McCormick, Mark
McEvoy, Francis

O'Carroll, Kevin
O'Connor, Hugh
O'Connor, Pádraig
O'Donnell, Joseph
O'Dowd, Brendan
O'Malley, John
O'Reilly, Bernard
Pantin, Michael
Parsons, Edward
Power, William
Rodgers, Patrick
Ryan, Liam
Sharpe, Raymond
Sheehan, Michael
Smyth, Adrian
Solomon, Aneurin
Suarez, José
Sutton, Ivan
Taylor, Edmond
Taylor, Patrick
Thomas, James
Walsh, David
Whelan, Seán
White, Kevin

1963

Aherne, Niall
Aherne, Terence
Barry, Anthony
Barry, Conor
Behan, Harold
Brennan, Donal
Browne, Michael
Burke, Michael
Carey, Brendan
Carey, John
Carroll, Brian
Carty, Nial
Casey, John
Casey, Thomas
Cashman, Cornelius
Clancy, Daniel
Clancy, Eamon
Clancy, Patrick
Cleary, John
Cleary, Kieran
Collins, John
Condon, Michael
Conlon, Michael
Cumiskey, Joseph
Curran, Albert
Curran, Patrick
Curtin, Cyril
Cussen, Edward
Daly, Cornelius
Daniels, Albert
Delahunty, John

Farragher, Noel
Finn, Anthony
Flanagan, Seamus
Fogarty, Patrick
Gaschinard, Michel
Glynn, John
Haddad, Gabriel
Hannon, Vincent
Hawkins, John
Hayes, Patrick
Healy, Daniel
Hegarty, Peter
Hennessy, Donal
Hickey, Oliver
Hill, David
Hogan, Francis
Houlihan, Donal
Hume, Enda
Keane, Michael
Keating, Seamus
Keeley, Paul
Kelly, Edward
Kelly, Michael
Kennelly, Joseph
Kenny, Thomas
Keoghan, Leo
King, Karl
Kinsella, Austin
Lalor, Stephen
Leyden, Michael
Lloyd, Finbarr

McMahon, Bernard
McManus, Edward
Meany, John
Moloney, Norbert
Moroney, John
Morrissey, Edward
Mullally, Timothy
Mullen, Raymond
Murphy, Thomas
Murtagh, Michael
Neale, John
Nolan, Terence
O'Brien, Robert
O'Brien, Thomas
O'Carroll, Donnan
O'Connor, Joseph
O'Connor, Liam
O'Connor, Martin
O'Donnell, Eugene
O'Donnell, Seamus
O'Donoghue, Desmond
O'Dwyer, Stephen
O'Laughlin, Augustine
O'Shaughnessy, Michael
O'Shea, Patrick
Power, James
Quinn, Anthony
Quinlan, Matthew
Quinlan, Matthew
Ryan, Thomas
Soloman, Aneurin

Dempsey, Brendan
De Meillac, John
Dolan, Michael
Doyle, Eugene
DuCoudray, Frederick
Enright, Timothy
Farrelly, John

Macdowall, Roderick
Mackey, Gerard
Madden, John
McCarthy, Joseph
McCarthy, Liam
McCaul, Bernard
McLoughlin, Anthony

Stapleton, Thomas
Tam, Stephen
Tampin, Ian
Tangney, Michael
Thavenot, Gordon
Thunder, Michael
White, Kevin
White, John

1964

Archer, Brian
Barry, Michael
Brennan, Thomas
Browne, Seán
Buckley, Cathal
Buckley, Seamus
Burkley, Philip
Butler, Eoin
Butler, Michael
Carroll, Brian
Carroll, Liam
Cashman, Thomas
Cleary, Noel
Collins, Malachy
Condon, Kieran
Conway, Seán
Costello, Vincent
Coughlin, James
Cuddy, William
Cumiskey, Joseph
Crosbie, Harry
Deevy, Edward
Delaney, Thomas
Devane, Thomas
De Villeneuve, Jean
English, Patrick
Enright, Timothy
Fallon, John
Fallon, Michael
Fewer, Lawrence
Ffrench, Nicholas
Fitzgerald, Eamon
Fitzgerald, Peter
Fraher, Kevin
Frayne, Edward
Gavin, Lawrence
Goon, Denis
Grace, Brian
Hayden, James

Heffernan, Patrick
Hegarty, Michael
Hickey, John
Hodgins, Liam
Hogan, Francis
Hogan, Thomas
Houlihan, Michael
Hourihane, John
Hume, Enda
Hyde, Francis
Ibrech, Robert
Jones, Noel
Kelliher, Raymond
Kelly, Michael
Kennedy, John
Kennedy, Seán
Kiely, Daniel
Kiely, Denis
Lalor, James
Lancaster, Anthony
Lannen, Shane
Lynch, Brian
Lynsky, John
Madden, Francis
Maguire, Hugo
Martin, Nyron
McCambridge, John
McCann, Alan
McCarthy, Patrick
McCluskey, Thomas
McCormick, Denis
McDermott, Patrick
McDonnell, Frederick
McKeown, Joseph
Moran, Patrick
Moroney, John
Moriarty, John
Mullins, Noel
Natton, Kenneth

Naeuboonien, Nacw
Nolan, David
Nowlan, William
O'Brien, Austin
O'Brien, Brian
O'Carroll, Brendan
O'Connor, Francis
O'Connor, James
O'Doherty, Patrick
O'Donovan, Patrick
O'Donovan, Patrick
O'Keeffe, Denis
O'Mahony, Denis
O'Malley, Derry
O'Neill, Edward
O'Rourke, Pacelli
O'Shea, Robert
O'Toole, Francis
Parson, James
Renehan, Thomas
Riordan, Michael
Ryan, John
Rocke, Thomas
Shine, Thomas
Sisk, Hugh
Stapleton, Liam
Sutton, Brendan
Tam Pui Gun, Patrick
Tard, Patrick
Taylor, Anthony
Teehan, Edwin
Thomas, John
Toohey, Michael
Walton, Kevin
Wailes, Francis
Ward, James
Whelan, Donal
White, Michael
Wrixon, John

1965

Aherne, Edward
Barry, Paul
Beatty, John
Brett, John J.
Butler, Richard
Byrd, Bernard
Byrne, Paul

Harkin, Brian
Haughton, Francis
Healy, John
Hecksher, Percy
Henehan, Pat
Hill, Landy
Hoare, David

O'Connor, Michael
O'Doherty, Patrick
O'Donnell, Brian
O'Donovan, Fergus
O'Dwyer, Patrick
O'Gorman, Michael
O'Kane, Eoin

Canavan, Pat
Cantwell, Peter
Carmody, Paschal
Clancy, Brian
Cleary, Bernard
Clerkin, Peter
Coleman, William
Condon, Alexis
Condon, Brian
Connellan, Jude
Conway, Philip
Cooney, Declan
Cooney, Dermot
Cremin, Patrick
Crowley, Conor
Daly, Aidan
Deveney, Donal
Dhanasunthorn, Y
Dunne, Joseph
Dunne, Patrick
Egan, Brendan
Farrell, Paschal
Farrell, Paul
Finnan, Arthur
Fleming, Canice
Fogarty, Patrick
Forrest, Frank
Forrestal, John
Gaffney, James
Glacken, Paul
Goon, Denis
Gough, Richard
Gray, Vincent
Hale, Maurice
Hanahoe, Michael

Hogan, Patrick
Hogan, Seán
Holmes, Thomas
Jones, Michael
Kehelly, Oliver
Kelly, Michael
Kennedy, John
Kennedy, Patrick
Kiely, Timothy
King, Mark
Kissane, John
Leonard, Richard
Lively, Gerard
Lyder, Gregory
Lynch, John P.
Madden, Francis
Maguire, James
Maguire, Kenneth
Mangan, Terence
McCann, Alan
McCarthy, James
McCluskey, Thomas
McCormack, Pat
McGlynn, Michael
McHugh, David
Murphy, Noel
Naughton, Peter
Neale, Manfred
Nolan, James
O'Byrne, Roger
O'Callaghan, Brian
O'Carroll, John
O'Connell, Seán
O'Connor, Brendan
O'Connor, Brian

O'Leary, Coleman
O'Neill, David
O'Neill, Hugh
O'Neill, Seamus
O'Reilly, Paul
O'Reilly, Philip
OShaughnessy, Dave
O'Sullivan, Noel
O'Sullivan, Philip
Owens, Joseph
Parsons, James
Power, Edmond
Quinn, Gerard
Rostant, Alan
Rowell, Sydney
Ryan, Patrick
Scanlan, Raymond
Scanlan, Robert
Seery, Michael
Shanley, Dudley
Sheeran, Paul
Shepherd, John
Sheridan, James
Spillane, Michael
Starkin, Brian
Synnott, Oliver
Tansey, Pierre
Tippins, Dermot
Volgo, John
Wallace, Brian
Ward, Joseph
Woolley, Joseph
Wright, Robert

1966

Aherne, Michael
Archer, Bruce
Beecher, Paul
Bergin, Joseph
Betes, Miguel
Bird, Michael
Byrne, Leo
Cantwell, coleman
Caplice, Michael
Carey, Patrick
Casey, Brendan
Casserley, Michael
Choe, Anthony
Clancy, Eoin
Clancy, Maurice
Cleary, Kevin
Comerford, Anthony
Connolly, Adrian
Corbett, Patrick
Corkery, John
Courbier, Bertrand

Finucane, Anthony
Fitzgerald, John
Flynn, Gerard
Garvey, Anthony
Gavin, Patrick
Glacken, Brendan
Glendon, Liam
Heffernan, Frank
Hegarty, John
Hennessy, Robert
Hodgins, Seán
Hogan, Noel
Holly, Maurice
Hourihane, John
Hoskins, Harry
Hughes, Patrick
Hume, John
Jordan, James
Keane, Anthony
Kearney, Eamon
Kelly, Vincent

Morrissey, Michael
Mulcahy, Michael
Mulkere, Enda
Murphy, Anthony
Murphy, Chris
Murphy, Gregory
Murphy, Michael
Nolan, James
Nowlan, Peter
O'Brien, Michael
O'Carroll, Aodhán
O'Carroll, Ciaran
O'Donoghue, Kieran
O'Donovan, Derry
O'Haire, Thomas
O'Hare, Eric
O'Hanlon, John
O'Keeffe, David
O'Keeffe, John
O'Mahony, John
O'Neill, Kevin

Cuddy, Chris
Culhane, Robert
Cullen, John
Culverhouse, William
Curran, Michael
Daly, James
Daly, John
Daly, Liam
D'Arcy, Thomas
Desmond, William
Devane, James
Donoghue, Vincent
Doyle, George
Doyle, Lewis
Dunne, Oliver
Dunne, Robert
Edney, David

Kinnerk, Conor
Leahy, James
Ledwith, Eamon
Lennox, David
Lynch, John
Martin, Anthony
McCarthy, Donal
McDonnell, Niall
McInerney, Eamon
McKeon, Brendan
McKeon, Cyril
McLoughlin, Joseph
McManus, James
McNulty, John
Meally, Alphonsus
Menton, Raymond
Morgan, Peter

Paul, Farrelli
Quinn, Gerard
Quirke, David
Rajinvat, Ong
Raymond, Edward
Rickard, William
Rostant, Ian
Savage, Barry
Sullivan, Timothy
Thompson, Jeffrey
Tracey, Michael
Twomey, Patrick
Whelan, Morgan
Whelan, Thomas
Young, Thomas

1967

Armitage, Eric C.
Ashe, David P.
Barry, John J.
Blewitt, John J.
Brocklebank, Gerard L.
Brosnan, John
Browne, Patrick J.
Carmody, Finbarr
Carter, Seán G.
Choi, Antonio
Cleary, Gerard
Collins, William J.
Condon, John F.
Cooke, Nicholas P.
Corrigan, Brian
Courbier, Bertrand
Courtney, Edward T.
Culhane, Robert T.
Cumiskey, Brian J.
Cumiskey, Raymond
Cunneen, Tiernan J.
Curry, Joseph P.
Daly, Joseph P.
Desmond, William H.
Donoghue, Brendan P.
Duggan, Kieran, P.
Duggan, William
Dunlea, Richard A.
Dunne, Thomas J.
Edney, Paul M.
Elliott, John J.
Fawsitt, Dirmuid S.
Fewer, Michael
Finn, Daniel J.
Fitzgerald, Michael
Fitzgerald, Simon
Flynn, Edward A.
Foley, J. Fergus
Gough, John

Grace, Michael
Griffin, Noel J.
Hanahoe, Terence J.
Hanratty, Paul J.
Headen, John F.
Hecksher, Rodney A.
Hickey, Michael P.
Hogan, Francis
Hogan, Gerard
Hogan, Thomas M.
Hooper, Patrick B.
Houlihan, David G.
Hume, John
Hurley, Michael J.
Keeley, Stephen H.
Kentgens, Joseph
Kett, Senan
Kinsella, Seán
Lacy, John F.
Lambe, Oscar A.
Lavelle, Brian P.
Lawlor, Thomas J.
Leonard, John
Lynch, John F.
Madden, James G.
Manning, Joseph T.
Martin, Edward J.
Mc.Donnell, Raymond J.
McMahon, Desmond
Mealy, Francis M.
Meenan, Patrick J.
Monahan, John
Moore, Anthony P.
Morrissey, John J.
Mulcahy, Patrick D.
Mullane, Donald J.
Mullins, Kevin J.
Murphy, John T.
Nannery, Peter G.

Neale, Paul R.
Oates, Guillaume C.
O'Carroll, Thomas A.
O'Connor, Michael F.
O'Donovan, Diarmuid F.
O'Donovan, Michael A.
O'Dwyer, John M.
O'Hanlon, Thomas J.
O'Keeffe, Thomas
O'Neill, Brian F.
O'Neill, Kevin F.
O'Reilly, Michael J.
O'Shea, Thomas W.
O'Sullivan, Daniel G.
O'Sullivan, Thomas Patrick
O'Sullivan, Thomas Peter
O'Toole, Eamonn
Power, Thomas
Quinlan, William P.
Regan. Patrick N.
Relihan, Jeremiah
Rogers, Michael T.
Rosenstock, Gabriel S.
Ryan, James B.
Ryan, Michael A.
Seery, Thomas P.
Stuart, Timothy L.
Tam, Thomas V.
Teehan, Thomas F.
Tobin, Eamonn P.
Walker, Reginald J.
Walsh, Michael A.
Ward, John
Whelan, Oliver
White, Timothy
Young, Peter J.

1968

Basquel, Thomas
Brassil, Daniel J.
Breaden, Thomas J.
Burke, Michael M.
Burke-Moran, Michael
Byrne, Barry L
Caplice, Seán
Carter, Seán
Casey, John J.
Casserly, Martin A.
Cleary, Gerard
Cleary, Michael G.
Clifford, Michael F.
Coady, James E.
Collins, Donal A.
Collins, Michael W.
Comer, Jeoffrey
Conroy, Brendan J.
Conroy, Michael T.
Conroy, Patrick M.
Corcoran, Colman M.
Cotter, Thomas M.
Craul, Martin E.
Cummins, Stephen
Curran, John G.
Curran, Peter Anthony
D'Arcy, Patrick H.
Doherty, Patrick J.
Duffy, Diarmuid J.
Egan, Thomas J.
Feeney, Colm W.
Finn, Martin H.
Fitzgerald, Jude
Fitzgerald, Piers D.
Flanagan, James C.
Fleetwood, John F.
Foley, William M.
Gardiner, Michael Noel
Gilmartin, John M.
Gleeson, John A.
Griffin, Luke P.
Hanratty, Paul
Hayes, Gerard M.
Hegarty, Denis M.

Graham, Gerard A.
Hegarty, William Finbarr
Hickey, Michael
Honan, Martin Adrian
Hooper, Patrick B.
Howard, Clifford Arthur
Howard, Michael G.
Hume, Hubert D.
Hurley, Peter J.
Hyde, Bernard W.
Hyland, Hugh
Kane, Peter J.
Kenny, Gregory T.
Kentgens-Bos, Joseph
Keyes, Michael John
Kiely, Andrew G.
Kiersey, Patrick D.
Kiersey, Paul A.
King, Patrick B.
Kinnerk, John M.
Laffan, Patrick P.
Lambe, Vincent M.
Lambert, Thomas P.
Lawlor, Eamonn J.
Leavy, Ciaran J.
Ledwith, Michael J.
Lewis, Cornelius P.
Logan, John G.
Long, Thomas Declan
Lynch, Christopher G.
Maher, Timothy M.
Martyn, Peter M.
McCarthy, Gerald J.
McGuire, Michael P.
McKenna, Brendan P.
McNamara, John P.
Milne, Vincent, M.
Molloy, Edward J.
Morgan, Raymond
Mulcahy, Patrick D.
Mulcahy, Roderick F.
Mullaney, Charles A.
Murphy, John T.
Murphy, Joseph S.

Murphy, Thomas G.
Nicke, Robert
O'Connell, Leonard
O'Connor, Thomas F.
O'Connor, Thomas Vincent
O'Dea, John
O'Doherty, Hubert
O'Donnell, Edward
O'Donovan, Ciaran G.
O'Donovan, Donal F.
O'Driscoll, Cornelius A.
O'Dwyer, John V.
O'Dwyer, Michael G.
O'Gorman, David
O'Hanlon, Michael P.
Ohie, Thomas J.
O'Keeffe, Dermot N.
O'Sullivan, Anthony G.
O'Sullivan, Thomas
O'Toole, Eamonn
Oxley, Joseph P.
Parsons, John G.
Patience, Colin A.
Pender, Kenneth P.
Quinn, Thomas P.
Roffey, Martin, M.
Rogers, John F.
Rossiter, William Anthony
Rostant, Derek F.
Ryan, Diarmuid S.
Ryan, Joseph V.
Ryan, Timothy D.
Santiago, Ephrem M.
Shepherd, Alair P.
Slattery, Austin M.
Spillett, Eric D.
Stack, William Brendan
Stringer, Richard A.
Tansey, Jerome P.
Taylor, John J.
Thoma. Francis P.
Walsh, R. Colman
Weber, Eugene K.
White, Matthew E.

1969

Blewitt, James M.
Bolger, Thomas Peter
Brady, Michael Francis
Brady, Richard R.
Brennan, Martin J.
Brown, Grant A.
Browne, Michael J.
Buckley, John Emmanuel
Buckley, John T.
Buckley, Martin G.

Hart, David P.
Haydar, Francis J.
Hayes, Gerard M.
Hegarty, James D.
Hickey, Thomas
Howard, D.J. Keith
Hume, D. Matthias
Humpston, James A.
Jones, Peter M.
Keane, Joseph R.

Neale, Richard D.
O'Brien, Cornelius M.
O'Brien, Raymond J.
O'Byrne, Patrick J.
O'Connor, Aloysius
O'Connor, Michael F.
O'Connor, Roderick P.
O'Dea, Kevin P.
O'Doherty, Hubert
O'Donnell, Roderick M.

Byrne, John Cosmos
Byrne, John Joseph
Carmody, Noel G.
Carroll, Seán P.
Choi, William
Clery, Thomas
Clifford, William J.
Clyne, Thomas A.
Coleman, John A.
Condon, David C.
Conroy, Brendan J.
Corcoran, Colman
Costelloe, John M.
Cotter, John P.
Cotter, Michael G.
Crowley, Patrick J.
Cunneen, Micahel P.
Dillon, Michael K.
Doheny, Michael A.
Donohoe, Peter A.
Echingham, Arthur J.
Fahey, Richard
Farrelly, Terence T.
Fealy, Patrick J.
Fitzgerald, Piers
Fleetwood, John F.
Fox, John J.
Furlong, Timothy
Good, Michael P.
Haddad, Elias G.
Hanahoe, Peter P.
Hanna, B. Conleth
Hardiman, K. Gerard
Harding, Liam J.

Kelly, John J.
Kelly, Patrick J.
Kennedy, J. Declan
Keogh, William M.
Kiersey, J. David
Lebert, Dominique
Leo, John M.
Lewis, John E.
Lonergan, Valentine M.
Long, R. finbarr
Lyons, Jarlath E.
Maher, Brian P.
Maher, Timothy M.
Mangan, Leo F.
Manibal, Daniel A.
Martin, Patrick John
McCabe, Michael I.
MacCarthy, Edward A.
McCarthy, Gerard M.
McCarthy, Jeremiah F.
McCarthy, John J.
MacCarthy, Seamus
McDermott, Thomas
McGuire, Michael P.
MacLochlainn, Colm
Morgan, Edward V.
Mulcahy, John V.
Mulcahy, Paul E.
Mulcahy, Roderick F.
Mulligan, Ultan O.
Murphy, D. Finbarr
Murphy, Eamonn A.
Murphy, Richard J.
Murray, Eamon M.

O'Driscoll, Bernard P.
O'Dwyer, Frederick M.
O'Dwyer, Michael G.
O'Hanlon, Michael P.
O'Neill, Declan F.
O'Reilly, Aidan P.
O'Shea, Michael J. G.
O'Sullivan, Thomas V.
O'Sullivan, William J.
Parkes, Michael R.
Pender, Kenneth P.
Peters, David M.
Pierse, Arthur D.
Quinn, Michael W.
Reddy, Brian O.
Rohan, Oliver L.
Rosenstock, O. Gregory
Rowell, Bernard C.
Russell, John
Ryan, U. Eoin
Shanahan, Michael J.
Sheehan, Don
Shepherd, Alair
Shepherd, David L.
Stakelum, Seán P.
Stringer, Richard A.
Sutton, Patrick Gerard
Taylor, Paul J.
Thompson, David
Wall, Declan A.
Walsh, Fergus Edward
Walsh, R. Colman
Willaims, Declan P.
Woodford, Terence J.H.

1970

Aherne, Thomas
Bambury, William
Blake, William
Brady, Conor
Brady, Francis
Breen, Patrick
Burke, Aidan
Buckley, Martin
Byrne, John .
Carroll, Kevin
Casey, Timothy
Choi, William
Clery, Thomas
Clifford, William
Clyne, Thomas
Condon, Declan
Coneys, Thomas
Connolly, Fergus
Cotter, Richard
Daly, Bartholomew
Daly, Stephen

Hanahoe, Peter
Hanrahan, Michael
Haydar, Charles
Hayden, John
Hennessy, Patrick
Hickey, Aidan
Holmes, Francis
Horan, Michael
Hughes, Aidan
Hume, Matthias
Jones, Philip
Kane, Paul
Keogh, Michael
Keogh, William
Kelly, John
Kennedy, Patrick
Kenny, John
Kiersey, David
Kiersey, Kenneth
King, Edward
Lanigan, James

O'Brien, Eamonn
O'Brien, Martin
O'Brien, Laurence
O'Byrne, Patrick
O'Carroll, Conor
O'Connell, Gabriel
O'Connor, Donal
O'Dea, Kevin
O'Donovan, Fergus
O'Driscoll, Fachtna
O'Driscoll, Gearóid
O'Flynn, Philip
O'Hara, Robert
Ohle, Brian
O'Neill, Shane
O'Riordan, Kieran
Ormond, David
O'Shea, Gerard
O'Sullivan, Matth
Pierse, Arthur
Purcell, Pierce

De Freyne, Leo
Dempsey, Terence
Devane, James
Devane, William
Doheny, Canice
Donovan, Cornelius
Drumm, John
Dunne, Kieran
Egleston, Kieran
Fanagan, David
Flannery, William
Frawley, Michael
Frayne, Robert
Gleeson, Francis
Grace, Edmond
Gray, Aiden
Greene, Alan
Grennan, John
Griffin, Greville
Guihan, Killian
Hackett, John
Haddad. Elias

Lee, Patrick
Leonard, Thomas
Loftus Patrick
Lonergan, Valentine
Lyons, Jarleth
Martin, John
McCann, Hugh
McDermot, Roger
McElhinney, Paul
McGuire, Paul
McNaughton, Paul
Meagher, Thomas
Meehan, Roderick
Moore, Adrian
Moore, Denis
Morgan, Edward
Morrissey, Michael
Mulcahy, David
Mullins, James
Murphy, Rory
Murray, Eunan
Nolan, Michael

Quigley, Patrick
Reilly, Rory
Reynolds, Michael
Ryan, Eoin
Ryan, James
Ryan, Michael A.
Ryan, Michael S.
Ryan, Noel
Slattery, Michael
Smyth, Anthony
Spillett, Clive
Stavely, Barry
Stuart, Thomas
Sullivan, Mark
Thompson, David
Treacy, Patrick
Twomey, Michael
Wall, David
Ward, Declan
Whelan, Michael
White, Thomas
Younger, Paul L.

1971

Ahern, Stephen
Andreucetti, Cecil R
Barry, Gerard
Bradshaw, Stephen
Bridges, Harold
Burke-Moran, Anthony
Callery, John T.
Carey, Anthony R.
Carter, Russell
Clancy, Neil
Clinton, Joseph
Collins, Paul
Condon, John
Connolly, Peter
Cooney, James
Counihan, Gerard
Cronin, William
Crosse, Seamus
Crowley, Francis
Cuddy, David
D'Arcy, Colm
D'Arcy, John
Devahastin, Fiat
Donohoe, John
Elliott, Paul
Fewer, Anthony
Fitzgerald, Garrett
Fitzgerald, Maurice
Fleming, Brian
Frawley, Flannan
Fusco, Franco
Gleeson, Noel
Grennan, John
Gribbon, Norman

Henry, Paul
Hickey, Denis
Higgins, Francis
Hynes, Patrick
Jodhan, Shaun
Keating, Patrick
Keller, Niall
Kennedy, John
Kennedy, Michael
Kilmartin, Fergus
Lennox, John
Lonergan, James
Lopes, Paul
Lynch, Kyran
Maguire, Paul
Mangan, Martin
Martin Jeffrey
McAnena, Francis
McCann, Kieran
McCrea, Paul
McDunphy, Pádraig
McGrath, Thomas
McLaughlin, John
Meaney, John
Meenan, Ernan
Mendoza, Jose
Moloney, William
Molumby, Thomas
Moore, Adrian
Moran, Lawrence
Murphy, Paul
Nyhan, Gerald
Nowlan, Francis
O'Brien, Daniel

O'Connor, Gerard
O'Dea, Declan
O'Donnell, Martin
O'Dwyer, Seán
Ojukwu, Lotanna
O'Keeffe, James
O'Kelly, Patrick
O'Mahony, Cian
O'Neill, Anthony
O'Neill, Raymond
Onwu, Peter
O'Regan, Timothy
O'Reilly, Tomás
O'Reilly, William
O'Sullivan, Cormac
O'Sullivan, Gerard
O'Sullivan, Noel
Pierse, Patrick
Power, Fintan
Reidy, Robert
Rossiter, Brendan
Savage, Donal
Sisk, William
Slattery, Patrick
Spillane, Patrick
Staveley, John
Stuart, Thomas
Sweeney, Michael
Terry, Christopher
Treacy, John J
Treacy, John J.R.

Hanley, John
Hastings, Timothy
Hecksher, Jason
Hegarty, Donal
Hegarty, Timothy
Hennessy, Colm

O'Brien, John
O'Connell, Vincent

1972

Angelinos, Stratos
Barron, Eamonn
Barry, Michael D.
Barry, Michael P.
Barry-Walsh, Eugen
Bogue, Declan
Booth, Richard
Bourke, Cyril
Bridges, Edmund
Broderick, Brendan
Browne, Alphonsus
Burke, Aiden
Butler, John
Carey, Terence
Carr, Brendan
Carroll, Michael
Cass, Michael
Cleary, William
Colbert, John
Comerford, Brendan
Conaty, Peter
Corcoran, Matthew
Corcoran, Noel
Counihan, David
Cronin, Patrick
Crowley, Brian
Danaher, Gerard
Davis, Robert
Dennehy, Cornelius
Dineen, Francis
Dixon, Thomas
Doherty, Patrick
Donovan, James
Dowling, Paul
Doyle, Gilmar
Doyle, Kieran
Doyle, Patrick
Droussiotis, George
Elliot, Peter
English, Denis
English, James

Fewer, Vincent
Fitzgerald, Declan
Fogarty, Ronald
Gillman, Richard
Gleeson, John
Gleeson, Michael
Godley, Richard
Golden, Anthony
Gonsalves, Gerard
Gorman, William
Gough, Cornelius
Grennan, Daniel
Griffin, Anthony
Hayes, John
Healy, John
Heffernan, John
Higgins, Liam
Higgins, Gregory
Higgins, Patrick
Holly, Cornelius
Hurley, Desmond
Hurley, John
Jones, Thomas
Kavanagh, Terence
Keegan, Michael
Kelly, Derek
Kelly, Nicholas
Kennedy, Noel
Kingston, Daniel
Krzywinski, Eugene
Lehane, Michael
Lopes, Duane
McAuley, Michael
McGoldrick, John
McGovern, Garry
McInerney, John
McKenna, James
McMahon, Brendan
McNamara, Desmond
Maher, John
Maher, Thomas

Molloy, John
Moran, Donal
Mullins, Brian
Murray, Oliver
Nalty, Peter
Nolan, Anthony
O'Brien, Francis
O'Callaghan, Gearo
O'Connor, Brian
O'Donnell, Martin
O'Flynn, John
O'Keeffe, Kevin
O'Neill, Hugh
O'Reilly, John
O'Shea, James
O'Sullivan, Eugene
O'Sullivan, John
O'Sullivan, Michael
Porter, David
Power, Declan
Power. Denis
Prendergast, Patrick
Purcell, Gerard
Redmond, Eoghan
Reidy, William
Reynolds, John
Ryan, Raymond
Sexton, Simon
Sheehan, Michael
Sheeran, Joseph
Sheikh, Daniel
Sossi, Robert
Spillane, James
Timmons, Mel
Townsend, Robert
Tynan, Pierce
Wallace, Patrick
Wynne, John
Young, Thomas

1973

Andreucetti, Anthon
Barry, Peter
Begley, Arthur
Bohmeke, Jan
Bowers, Paul
Boyle, Adrian
Boyle, Eugene

Fyfe, Robert
Gleeson, Kieran
Gordon, Michael
Gorman, Michael
Guy, Peter
Hedigan, Peter
Hendry, Michael

Maher, Daniel G.
Maher, Daniel V.
Manning, Thomas
Molloy, John
Moran, Declan
Murphy, Patrick
O'Brien, Oliver

O'Driscoll, Tim
O'Dwyer, Desmond
O'Hara, John
O'Keeffe, Brendan
O'Loughlin, Patrick
O'Neill, Diarmuid
O'Neill, Eoghan

Brady, John
Brown, Dermot
Brown, Liam
Brown, Paul
Brown, Timothy
Buckley, Michael
Burke, Michael
Burke, William
Cahill, Michael A.
Cahill, Michael T.
Caine, Fergus
Carroll, Joseph
Clancy, Gerard
Clancy, Thomas
Cotter, Maurice
Cotter, Timothy
Cronin, John
Crowley, Patrick
Cunningham, Aust
D'Arcy, William
Dempsey, Ivan
Devane, Patrick
Egleston, Brendan
Elliot, Jeremy
Fahy, Patrick
Fahey, Thomas
Fahy, William
Farrelly, Donal
Farrelly, Donal F.
Feeney, Francis
Fitzgerald, Colman
Fitzgerald, Michael
Foley, Matthew
Foley, Robin
Frayne, Robert

Higgins, Daniel
Higgins, Michael F.
Higgins, Michael G.
Hope Ross, Michael
Howard, Donal
Hyland, David
Ivers, James
Jones, James
Kavanagh, Patrick
Kearns, Tom
Keating, Brendan
Kelly, Maurice
Kelly, Michael
Kelly, Thomas
Kennedy, Edward
Kennedy, Noel
Kenny, Paul
Keogh, William
Kerins, Brendan
Kiely, Jeremiah
Killeen, Maurice
Knoblauch, Peter
Lee Heung, Richard
Lordan, Jerome
Lynch, William
Mackenzie, Monty
McAuley, Edmund
McCready, Kieran
McDonagh, Hugh
McGuire, Hugh
McHugh, David
McMahon, Brendan
McInerney, Michael
McKeever, Brian
McNally, Brendan

O'Brien, Ronald
O'Brien, William
O'Connor, John
O'Connor, Peter
O'Connor, Rory
O'Donnell, Walter
O'Driscoll, Michael
O'Driscoll, Tim
O'Dwyer, Desmond
O'Hara, John
O'Keeffe, Brendan
O'Loughlin, Patrick
O'Neill, Diarmuid
O'Neill, Eoghan
Onwu, Feani
O'Reilly, Conor
O'Sullivan, Vincent
McMahon, Brendan
McInerney, Michael
McKeever, Brian
McNally, Brendan
Maher, Daniel G.
Maher, Daniel V.
Manning, Thomas
Molloy, John
Moran, Declan
Murphy, Patrick
O'Brien, Oliver
O'Brien, Ronald
O'Brien, William
O'Connor, John
O'Connor, Peter
O'Connor, Rory
O'Donnell, Walter
O'Driscoll, Michael

Onwu, Feani
O'Reilly, Conor
O'Sullivan, Vincent
Quinlan, Thomas
Quinn, Frank
Reddy, Colm
Riordan, James
Ross, Richarad
Ryan, Brian
Ryan, Leo
Ryan, John
Ryan, Michael
Savage, Peter
Shanahan, Edward
Shanahan, Michael
Shanahan, Thomas
Sheahan, William
Sheridan, Francis
Sinadinos, Alesande
Slattery, Denis
Slattery, John
Slattery, William
Stapleton, Paul
Stapleton, Robert
Sweeney, Michael
Tam, Edward
Taylor, Eamon
Thorn, Richard
Todd, Kevin
Tomkins, Brendan
Troy, Martin
Wall, Gerard
Walsh, Brendan J.
Walsh, Brendan P.

1974

Ahern, Daniel
Ashe, Brendan
Barker, Desmond
Barrett, John
Barron, Kevin
Basquel, John
Basquel, Martin
Begley, Michael
Behan, Richard
Brady, Philip
Bolger, William
Browne, Joseph
Byrne, Fergus
Caffrey, Thomas
Carre, James
Carroll, Joseph
Cashin, Gerard
Cass, James
Coady, Donald
Coghlan, Gerald
Connolly, James
Corbett, Michael
Cotter, Francis

Gayer, Austin
Geoghan, Patrick
Ginnell, Philip
Griffin, Michael
Harnett, James
Hastings, John
Haugh, Gerard
Headen, David
Higgins, Daniel
Higgins, James
Holly, Denis
Holmes, Michael
Hoskin, Richard
Hourihan, Patrick
Humphries, Robert
Irwin, William
Kelliher, James
Kelly, Michael
Kennedy, Donal
Kennedy, James
Kenny, Paul
Kerins, Brendan
Lahart, Nicholas

McInerney, Patrick
McKenna, Peter
McMahon, James
McNaughton, John
Meagher, Patrick
Meehan, Patrick
Molloy, Aidan
Moloney, Gerard
Moriarty, Bartholo
Mulvin, David
Murphy, Richard
Mylod, Thomas
O'Brien, Desmond
O'Brien, Noel
O'Brien, Richard
O'Carroll, Colum
O'Connor, David
O'Connor, Maurice
O'Connor, Michael
O'Connor,Michael J
O'Connor, Patrick
O'Connor, Thomas
O'Doherty, Thomas

Rocca, Angelo
Rowan, Patrick
Ryan, Aidan
Ryan, Pat
Sheahan, Thomas
Shepherd, Myron
Sheridan, Francis
Sheridan, John
Sinadinos, Anastase
Slattery, Pádraig
Smith, Brian
Smithwick, Mark
Solan, Brendan
Spillane, Brendan
Stuart, Edward
Sweeney, John
Taylor, Martin
Thorn, Richard
Todd, Kevin
Tozer, Joseph
Tyrrell, Reginald
Volgo, Edmund

Cotter, Liam
Cronin, William
Cunningham, Charl
Curran, James
Daly, Martin
Devane, Michael
Doyle, John
Duffy, Patrick
Farrelly, Francis
Fennelly, James
Fenton, Malcolm
Fitzgerald, Patrick

Layden, Peter
Leonard, Diarmuid
Lindsay, Garry
Lincheid, Christoph
Lyons, Morgan
McBride, Joseph
McCarthy, Charles
McCarthy, Eamonn
McCarthy, Michael
McCarthy, Patrick
McGonagle, Patrick
McInerney, Brian

O'Donovan, Anthon
O'Dwyer, Seán
O'Halloran, Patrick
O'Keeffe, Kieran
O'Loughnan, Micha
O'Neill, Eamonn
Onwu, Edward
O'Sullivan, Edward
O'Sullivan, Gerard
O'Sullivan, Liam
Parsons, Kevin
Pierse, John

Walkin, Ambrose
Wallace, John
Wallace, Kevin
Walsh, John
Ward, Barry
Wendel, Erwin
Whelan, Griffith
Young, Seamus

1975

Andreucette, Dino
Basquel, John
Basquel, Joseph
Basquel, Martin
Begley, John
Bolger, William
Buckley, Thomas
Butler, Paul
Byrne, Martin
Byrne, Peter
Cahill, Paul
Cantwell, Francis
Carroll, Andrew
Clinton, Mark
Collins, Stephen
Connolly, Hugh
Coogan, Brendan
Cooney, Patrick
Corbett, Fergus
Corcoran, Patrick
Creedon, Shane
Cronin, William
Daly, Caimin
D'Arcy, Fergus
Dempsey, Maurice
Donohue, Brendan
Donohue, Noel
English, William
Farrell, Paul
Fennelly, James
Fennelly, John
Fitzgerald, Thomas
Fine, Michael
Gallagher, Patrick
Gleeson, Thomas

Griffin, Michael
Guy, Patrick
Hannon, Joseph
Harris, Kevin
Hedigan, Philip
Hendry, Joseph
Higgins, Peter
Hogan, Mark
Hyland, Paul
Kearns, Joseph
Keating, Sarsfield
Kelly, Brian
Kelly, Denis
Kelly, Pádraig
Kennedy, Patrick
Kerins, John
King, Brian
Little, Brendan
Long, Patrick
Lynch, John
Lynch, Terence
Lynch, William
Lyons, Seamus
Madden, James
Maher, Vincent
Marshall, John
Massey, Vincent
Mawe, Patrick
McBride, Joseph
McCarthy, Eamonn
McCarthy, Seamus
McDonnell, Patrick
McGann, Brian
McInerney, Cyril
McInerney, Patrick

McKeogh, David
Meaney, Tomás
Molloy, Brian
Molloy, Desmond
Moloney, Raymond
Moran, Brian
Moran, Michael
Mulholland, James
Murphy, Thomas
Mylod, Thomas
O'Brien, Desmond
O'Brien, John
O'Carroll, Colm
O'Doherty, James
O'Donnell, Seán
O'Donnell, Thomas
O'Neill, Michael
Onwu, Edward
O'Reilly, Vincent
Ormond, Denis
O'Rourke, Gerard
O'Shea, Patrick
O'Sullivan, Donal
O'Sullivan, James
O'Sullivan, Pádraig
Oxley, Peter
Peppard, Thomas
Power, Anthony
Quaid, Michael
Quinn, Tiernan
Reilly, David
Rocca, Angelo
Ryan, Edmund
Ryan, Matthew
Ryan, Michael

Sheehan, Kiernan
Shepherd, Myron
Smith, Paul
Stapleton, John
Sutton, Francis
Sweeney, John
Tyrrell, William
Walsh, Anthony
Walsh, David
Waterfouse, James
Wilson, Michael
Wood, Alister

1976

Ashe, Fergus
Barron, Bernard
Barron, Bruce
Barry, Michael
Barry-Walsh, D.
Bolger, Henry
Boucher, Richard

Finan, David
Fine, David
Flanagan, Michael
Fleming, Anthony
Flynn, Brian
Forrest, John
Gannon, Paul

Maher, George
Maher, Ken
Maher, Gerard
Maher, John
Maher, Michael
Manning, Michael
Marnell, Canice

O'Sullivan, Barry
O'Sullivan, Gerard
O'Sullivan, Hans
O'Sullivan, James
O'Sullivan, Karl
O'Sullivan, M.P.
Pierse, Morgan

Bourke, Diarmuid
Breen, Anthony
Broderick, Patrick
Broderick, Thomas
Buckley, Patrick
Burdon, Andrew
Burkart, Norman
Burns, Anthony
Butler, Declan
Butterly, Nicholas
Byrnes, Christopher
Chan, Daniel
Cleary, Michael
Coffey, Liam
Coffey, Michael
Collins, Denis
Collins, Michael
Condon, Michael
Connellan, Pádraig
Cooney, David
Corcoran, Kieran
Courtney, Conor
Creagh, Michael
Cribben, Raymond
Crowley, Eoghan
Curran, Patrick
Dalton, Thomas
De Larminat,Michel
Donovan, Michael
Doyle, William
Ellis, Declan
Fagan, Anthony
Fanaghan, Ronald

Gavin, Michael
Gibson, Senan
Gillen, Seán
Gleeson, Timothy
Goff, Brian
Hamilton, Paul
Healy, Michael
Healy-Rae, John
Hennessy, James
Hennigan, Michael
Holmes, James
Howard, Barry
Howard, Fintan
Irwin, Edmond
Kelly, Alexander
Kelly, Eugene
Kelly, James
Keogh, Patrick
Kerwick, Michael
Kilgarriff, Michael
Kingston, Barry
Lahart, Liam
Lambe, Paul
Leddin, Gerard
Lincheid, Mark
Lynch, Anthony
Lynch, Barry
Lynch, Brendan
Lynch, Gerard
Lynch, Philip
Lynch, Raymond
Mackey, Noel
Mackey, Paul

Matthews, Robert
Maydew, Brendan
McCaffrey. D.M.
McCormack, Paul
McGrainne, Cormac
McInerney, Thomas
McMahon, Gerald
McMenamin, Fergu
Moloney, Simon
Morrissey, Joseph
Morrissey, Patrick
Morvan, Seán
Moss, Brian
Mullane, Patrick
Mullins, Gerard
Murphy, James
Murphy, Timothy
Murray, John
Murray, Seán
Norris, Walter
O'Brien, Michael
O'Connor, Jeremiah
O'Connor, John
O'Connor, Kevin
O'Connor, Rory
O'Connor, Thomas
O'Donnell, Michael
O'Dwyer, Dermot
O'Farrell, Kenneth
O'Flaherty, Dara
O'Loughnan, N.F.
O'Meara, John
O'Neill, John

Power, John
Power, Robert
Prendergast, J.P.
Prunty, Michael
Quinn, Peter
Redmond, Patrick
Roberts, Peter
Robinson, Gerard
Russell, Seamus
Ryan, William
Scully, Eamon
Shanahan, Timothy
Sheedy, Finian
Slattery, Kevin
Slattery, Mahon
Smyth, Hugh
Tipping, Roger
Walsh, Brian
Walsh, Richard
Watters, Paraic
Whitney, Alan
Wilson, Eric

1977

Bagnall, Brendan
Barron, Bruce
Bird, Michael
Booth, John
Boucher, Peter
Burkart, Edward
Burke, William
Caffrey, Michael
Cantwell, David
Cashin, Patrick
Chadwick, David
Coffey, Liam
Connolly, Kieran
Cooney, David
Cooke, Dermot
Cooke, John
Cotter, Kevin
Cowman, Derek
Delaney, Noel *
Duggan, John
Fitzgerald, Edward
Fitzpatrick, Andrew
French, Andrew
French, Paul

Grace. Patrick
Hahessy, Tomás
Hale, Patrick
Hally, Andrew
Healy, Michael
Higgins, John P.
Higgins, Mark
Hogan, Seán
Holland, Michael
Holohan, Mark
Hourihan, Roderick
Howard, Fintan
Humphries, Andrew
Jameson, Raymond
Johnson, Joseph
Kavanagh, Francis
Keegan, Joseph
Keenan, Donal
Kelly, Seán
Kennedy, Barry
Kiely, Anthony
Lynch, Barry
Lynch, Michael
Lyons, Gerald

Marren, David *
McCarthy, Patrick
McConville, Harold
McDonnell Brendan
McKeogh, Henry
McMahon, Michael
McQuillan, Neil
Meagher, John
Moloney, Paul
Morrin, Michael
Morris, Patrick
Moylan, Phelim
Mulcahy, Thomas
Mulligan, Seamus
Murphy, Michael A.
Murphy, Michael K.
Murray, Seán
O'Brien, James
O'Farrell, William
O'Flaherty, Niall
O'Loughnan, John
O'Malley, Harold
Ormonde, Ciaran
O'Shea, Laurence

Power, Lawrence
Power, Michael
Quaid, Alan
Quaid, John
Raddawi, Mouanna
Raftery, Dominic
Raymond, David
Reilly, John
Roberts, Peter
Roche, Anthony
Roche, John
Ryan, Daniel
Ryan, Donal
Ryan, Philip
Shanahan, Timothy
Sheehan, Thomas
Shorten, Donald
Siegfried, John
Simpson, John
Sweeney, Declan
Tipping, Edward
Wall, William
Walsh, Joe
Whelan, Aidan

Gallagher, Eamon
Gallagher, Michael
Gillen, Rory
Gleeson, Francis

Madden, Philip
Madigan, Kieran
Maher, Canice
Maher, Declan

O'Sullivan, John
O'Toole, Paul
Pillai, Hari
Power, Anthony

Whooley, Conor
Wright, James J.

1978

Barrett, Patrick
Barron, Declan
Barry, Brendan
Barry, William
Blackmore, Charles
Breen, John
Brannigan, Michael
Brennan, Geoffrey
Brosnan, Michael
Broderick, Anthony
Buckley, Joseph
Burdon, Paul
Burke, James
Burke, Thomas
Burke, William
Carroll, Andrew
Carroll, Martin
Casey, Dermot
Cass, John
Comber, George
Comber, Patrick
Connelly, Eamon
Cooke, Patrick
Courtney, David
Crosse, Michael
Currivan, George
Cully, Gerard
Deegan, Aidan
Devereaux, Patrick
Doherty, Niall
Doige, Karl
Donovan, Laurence
Donovan, Noel
Duffy, John

English, Mark
English, Paul
Farrell, John B.
Farrell, John V.
Fay, Louis
Flanagan, Fintan
Geoghan, John
Goulding, Aidan
Hannon, Gerard
Heffernan, Daniel
Higgins, Brendan
Hoctor, Jeremy
Hoctor, Patrick
Hope-Ross, Ian
Irwin, Philip
Joy, James
Kelly, Michael
Kenny, Paul
Kerins, David
Kiernan, John
Killoran, Gregory
Kingston, Alan
Klimmek, Markus
Lannen, William
Lee, Lawrence
Leech, John
Lonergan, David
Lordan, Patrick
Lynch, Patrick
Lyons, Donal
Maher, Noel
Marren, Paul
McCan, Pierse
McGann, Gearóid

McGinley, James
McGovern, Breffni
McMahon, Paul
McQuillan, Maurice
Meade, Gerard
Mongey, David
Morris, David
Mulligan, Thomas
Murphy, Anthony
Murphy, Denis
Murphy, Philip
Murphy, William
Naik, David
Nardone, Raffaele
Nolan, Tom
O'Brien, Vincent
O'Connell, Philip
O'Connell, Robert
O'Connor, Desmon
O'Connor, James
O'Connor, Joseph
O'Connor, Kevin
O'Dea, Noel
O'Donnell, Edmond
O'Dwyer, John
O'Dwyer, Thomas
O'Hora, Liam
O'Keeffe, Niall
O'Mahony, Francis
O'Meara, Raymond
O'Neill, William
O'Reilly, Shane
O'Reilly, Eugene
O'Shea, Maurice

O'Shea, Stephen
O'Shaughnessy, C.
O'Shaughnessy, D.
O'Sullivan, Edmund
O'Sullivan, James
O'Sullivan, Jonatho
O'Sullivan, Michael
Phillips, Michael
Poon, Frank
Porter, Stanley
Power, Aidan
Quinn, Donal
Reardon, William
Roche, Patrick
Ryan, Allan
Ryan, James
Sandford, Conor
Shanahan, Paul
Sheedy, Niall
Sheehy, Richard
Shelly, John
Slattery, Edmond
Smyth, Vincent
Stevenson, Peter
Tohme, Charles
Walsh, Joseph
Walsh, Stephen
White, Conleth

1979

Bergin, Colin
Bolger, Paul
Brannigan, Michael
Brosnan, Michael
Burkart, Stephen
Butler, Paul
Cavanagh, Conor
Conroy, Niall
Cooney, Peter
Corrigan, Andrew
Costello, Alan
Craul, Joseph
Curneen, Hugh
Daly, Brian
Daly, Gary
Deane, Peter
Deegan, Brendan

Flynn, Niall
Flynn, Patrick
Flusk, Mark
Gallagher, Robert
Gallagher, William
Gleeson, Michael
Griffin, Matthew
Hayes, Thomas
Headon, William
Hickey, Fergal
Holohan, Michael
Holt, John
Hoynes, Patrick
Hurley, Daniel
Hurley, Fintan
Jameson, David
Johnson, Patrick

Kingston, Kieran
Kingston, Robert
Klimmek, Knut
Lawlor, Seamus
Lannen, William
Leavy, Donal
Leung, Leo
Lynch, Jerome
Madigan, William
Maher, Thomas
Maigrot, Bernard
Marnell, Mark
Marren, Padraic
McCarthy, Karl
McDonnell, Patrick
McEnroe, Dermot
McMahon, John

O'Brien, Michael
O'Connell, William
O'Connor, Edward
O'Connor, Patrick
O'Donnell, John
O'Donoghue,Finbar
O'Donovan, Mark
O'Donovan, Simon
O'Loughlin,Roderic
O'Malley, Anthony
O'Reilly, Eugene
O'Rourke, Gerard
O'Shea, Timothy
Phelan, Michael
Renehan, Jeremiah
Ryan, Brian
Ryan, Joseph

Dodd, Denis
Downey, Michael
Doyle, Brian
Doyle, Peter
Doran, Ciaran
Doran, Declan
Farrell, John V.
Fitzgerald, John
Fitzgerald, Seamus
Flood, Ronert
Flynn, Barry

Jones, Edward
Jones, Niall
Jones, Seamus
Kampff, Paul
Kavanagh, Terence
Keane, Patrick
Kelly, Denis
Kelly, Richard
Kelly, Seamus
Kennedy, Paul
Keogh, Basil

McNally, Vincent
Meagher, James
Moloney, Paul
Molony, Martin
Moran, Mark
Mulligan, Ronan
Mullins, Seamus
Murray, Gerald
Naik, Eic
Naik, SooWoon
Nugent, Gerard

Scallan, Philip
Scarry, Aidan
Shanahan, Francis
Sheehan, Brian
Sit, Oliver
Sweeney, Francis
Tohme, Alain
Waters, David
Webster, Brian
Willoughby, Francis

1980

Allen, Peter
Barlow, Stanley
Bergin, Laurence
Bolger, David
Buckley, John
Buckley, Raymond
Buckley, Timothy
Bugler, Henry
Burkart, Gregory
Burke, Cyril
Butler, Michael
Byrne, John
Carr, Kevin
Carroll, Breffni
Collins, Michael
Comber, William
Cooney, Kieran
Cowley, Martin
Cronnelly, Eamon
Crowley, Jeremiah
Curley, Paul
Daly, Alan
Daly, James
Daly, John
Deane, David
Devitt, Thomas
Doherty, Ian
Fearon, Patrick
Fennelly, Paul
Finnegan, John
Finneran, John
Fitzpatrick, James
Flannery, Frank
Flynn, Thomas
Foley, Richard

Garland, Darach
Gibbons, John
Gillin, John
Godsil, Leonard
Godson, Rory
Grogan, Ian
Halpin, John
Harrison, John
Hawe, John
Hazel, Richard
Holland, Michael
Hughes, Michael
Hurley, Vincent
Hynes, Julian
Irwin, Gabriel
Kelly, Myles
Kelly, Paul
Kelly, Seamus
Kennedy, Ronan
Kennedy, Sydney
Kenny, George
Kiernan, Michael
Lalor, William
Layden, Michael
Leonard, Daniel
Loughnane, Edward
Lynam, Ciaran
Lynch, Gregory
Marnane, Con
McAlinden, Mark
McCan, David
McDonagh, Donogh
McDonagh, Michael
McGrath, Alphonsu
McGrory, Liam

McManus, Patrick
Moloney, Martin
Moore, Patrick
Moriarty, John
Morrissey, James
Mulroy, Seán
Murphy, Brian
Murphy, Declan
Murphy, William
Nallen, John
O'Brien, Vincent
O'Connor, Brian
O'Connor, David
O'Connor, Declan
O'Connor, Jerome
O'Donnell, Raphael
O'Donovan, Chris
O'Dwyer, Philip
O'Flaherty, Cristóir
O'Hora, Kevin
O'Malley, James
O'Neill, Brendan
O'Neill, John
O'Rourke, Francis
O'Sullivan, Dermot
O'Sullivan, Trevor
Pentony, Seamus
Prunty, Gabriel
Rattigan, Paul
Reardon, Patrick
Reid, John
Reidy, Donal
Roberts, Brian
Robinson, Seamus
Roche, James

Ryan, Bernaard
Ryan, Michael
Ryan, Seán
Sheehan, Barry
Sheehan, Don
Sheridan, Ciaran
Slattery, Paul
Smyth, Noel
Spollen, Oliver
Stevenson, Patrick
Stokes, John
Tewelde, Samson
Walsh, Martin
Waters, David
Whelan, William

1981

Baez, Kenneth
Barry, Kevin
Bergin, Michael
Bernard, Jeremiah
Booth, Paul
Bowe, Danny
Breen, Mark
Bresnan, Adrian

Forkan, John
Fulcher, Peter
Gallagher, David
Garland, Daragh
Gillin, Richard
Habelrih, Elias
Halpin, Mark
Halpin, Peter

McGee, Michael
McGrath, Paul
McKevitt, Paul
McNamara, Adrian
McNamara, John
Molumby, Michael
Morris, Dermot
Morrissey, Brendan

Sherlock, Andrew
Slattery, Patrick
Spollen, John
Stafford, Aidan
Sweeney, Finian
Tewelde, Benjamin
Tobin, Seán
Trant, Ian

Broderick, John
Broderick, Peter
Buckley, Seán
Butler, Kieran
Butler, Michael
Byron, Kerrill
Carolan, Matthew
Cassidy, Pearase
Cleveland-Peck, Ch
Coghlan, Peter
Collins, Maurice
Costello, Valentine
Cronin, Joseph
Crowley, John
Curran, Michael
Dalton, Francis
Delahunty, Noel
Devlin, John
Dillon, Rory
Doige, Christian
Donovan, Cyril
Doorley, Teremce
Doyle, Damian
Duffy, Mark
Flynn, Donal
Flynn, William
Foley, David
Foley, Maurice

Hannon, Maurice
Hannon, Thomas
Healy, Daniel
Hewitt, Desmond
Hindle, Frank
Hogan, Stephane,
Holohan, Seán
Hughes, Anthony
Hurley, Joseph
Irwin, John
Kavanagh, Peter
Keane, David
Kelly, Mark
Kennedy, Denis
Kennedy, Michael
Layden, David
Linnane, Frank
Lonergan, Thomas
Madden, Morgan
Madigan, Paul
Maher, Thomas
Marnell, Michael
McCarthy, Alan
McCarthy, Seán
McCormack, John
McDonagh, Diarmu
McDonagh, Stephen
McGee, Edwin

Murphy, Colin
Murphy, Thomas
O'Brien, Michael
O'Connor, Michael
O'Connor, Paul
O'Donnell, Hugh
O'Donnell, Gerard
O'Donnell, James
O'Donovan, Steven
O'Hara, Dermot
O'Hora, Pádraig
O'Keeffe, Edmund
O'Keeffe, John
O'Mahony, John
O'Meara, Michael
O'Neill, John
O'Neill, Padraic
O'Sullivan, Chris
O'Sullivan, Eugene
O'Sullivan, Frank
Peppard, Anthony
Ramalho, Pedro
Reidy, Allen
Rice, Richard
Ryan, Patrick J.
Ryan, Patrick O.
Ryan, Paul
Sheehan, William

Troy, Aidan
Twohill, John
Walsh, Martin

1982

Bernard, John
Blackwell, Donal
Boyd, Gary
Boyd, Kieran
Brosnan, Paul
Browne, Liam
Browne, Paul
Burns, Ian
Cabo, Ricardo
Campion, Patrick
Carroll, Thomas
Chan, Tommy
Clarke, John
Clifford, Peter
Condon, Vincent
Cronnelly, James
Cullen, Dermot
Curry, Joseph
Dalton, Dermot
Desmond, Pascal
Dooley, Adrian
Dowling, Paul
Egan, Carl
Farabaugh, Michael
Fitzgerald, John
Fitzgibbon, Michael
Flynn, Liam
Foley, Hugh
Gallagher, Paul

Gildea, Cathal
Grealy, John
Halpin, Patrick
Haugh, Patrick
Healy, Gerard
Healy, Nicholas
Hennessy, Patrick
Hughes, Thomas
Kavanagh, Brian
Kavanagh, John
Kearney, Michael
Kelly, Aidan
Kelly, Seán
Knoblaugh, Josef
Lawrence, Kevin
Linehan, Brian
Linehan, Steven
Loughnane, Martin
Lynam, Gerard
Lynch, Brian
MacDonagh, Seán
Martinez, Carlos
McAleese, Thomas
McGee, Brian
McGee, Prionsias
McGeogh, Patrick
McInerney, Paul
McKenzie, Desmon
McKeon, Vincent

McKevitt, David
McNaughton, Mich
Mahon, Joseph
Mitchell, John
Moroney, Brian
Murphy, Aidan
Murray, Paul
Neale, Paul
Neenan, David
Norris, James
O'Brien, Ronan
O'Callaghan, Rory
O'Connell, Derry
O'Connor, Vincent
O'Doherty, Conor
O'Donnell, Bryan
O'Donnell, Kevin
O'Dwyer, James
O'Hora, Donal
O'Hora, Gerard
O'Keeffe, Andrew
O'Neill, Brian
O'Reilly, Terence
Osborne, John
O'Shaughnessy Nev
O'Sullivan, Seán
Phelan, Finbarr
Phelan, James
Ramalho, Nuno

Regan, Joseph
Reidy, Graham
Reilly, Seán
Renehan, David
Roe, Michael
Ryan, Noel
Ryan, Paul
Sheehan, John
Sherlock, Liam
Slattery, Brian
Slattery, Ian
Sloane, Diarmuid
Smyth, Joseph
Somers, Benedict
Talbot, Frank
Tighe, Gerard
Toohey, William
Twohill, Conor
Whelan, Kevin

1983

Acheson, Brian
Alexander, Nial
Barlow, Raphael
Barrett, Brian
Barry, Andrew
Bernard, Denis
Bolger, Peter
Bourke, David
Brennan, Reginald
Burke, Diarmuid
Byrne, Dermot
Byrne, Gerard
Callanan, Conor
Capetto, Amedeo
Chan, Benedickt
Chan, Tommy
Cleveland-Peck, Mi
Cooney, Brian
Corry, John
Courtney, Alan
Coyle, Patrick
Curtin, Donal
Dennehy, Kevin
Deon, Alexander
Dillon, John
Drohan, Davitt
Duffy, David
Duffy, Paul
Egan, Patrick

Fallon, Coman
Fanning, Bernard
Farrell, Páraig
Feely, Thomas
Flynn, David
Fulcher, Timothy
Geada, Joao
Grene, Morgan
Griffin, James
Haden, Simon
Hannon, Joseph
Harty, James
Hearn, William
Hester, Kevin
Hogan, Denis
Holland, Eamon
Holohan, David
Howard, Brendan
Hurley, Michael
Hynes, Justin
Jameson, Stephen
Kearney, Paul
Keegan, Aaron
Kelly, Liam
Loughlin, Anthony
Madigan, Thomas
Maguire, Patrick
Mahon, Seán
Manning, Conor

Marnane, Edmond
Martin, Brian
Martinez, Fernando
McCarthy, Anthony
McCarthy, Eoin
McCormack, Daniel
McGonagle, Robert
McNamara, Conor
Mongey, Cyril
Moore, Patrick
Moore, William
Morley, Iain
Mulenga, Mwenya
Mullins, Michael
Murphy, Brian
Murphy, John
Murphy, Michael
Murtagh, Garrett
Neiland, Jason
NG, Paul
Nolan, James
O'Brien, Jack
O'Brien, Patrick
O'Connell, M. F.
O'Connell, M.K.
O'Connor, Brian
O'Connor, Kevin
O'Connor, Mark
O'Connor, Michael

O'Connor, Richard
O'Dea, Karl
O'Donnell, Brian
O'Donoghue, John
O'Donovan, David
O'Farrell, Edward
O'Kelly, Liam
O'Leary, Kieran
O'Looney, Antoin
O'Neill, David
O'Neill, James
Prendergast, John
Quillinan, Matthew
Reardon, Louis
Reid, Ronan
Rice, John
Riordan, John
Ryan, David
Ryan, Peter
Ryan, Timothy
Shanahan, Patrick
Shaw, Brian
Sheehan, Patrick
Sheridan, Malachy
Stack, Robert
Thompson, John
Tighe, Anthony
Walsh, Gearóid
Walsh, John

1984

Asenuga, Joseph
Badri, Yusef
Barlow, Alan
Barrett, Joseph
Bolster, Patrick
Brosnan, Michael
Butler, Owen
Carberry, Ronan
Chan, Benedict
Chan, Gino
Conboy, John
Connery, Shane
Crowley, Gerald
Daly, Liam
Dennehy, Seán
Dennis, Mark
Dookie, Seán
Dowd, Aidan
Dunican, Thomas
Farrell, Francis
Feely, Michael
Finan, John
Flynn, Pierce
Fulcher, Kieran
Gallagher, Andrew
Garvey, Hugh
Gernez, Tristan

Halpin, Garrett
Harte, John
Haughton, Mark
Hayes, Desmond
Hennigan, Seán
Hickey, David
Higgins, Donal
Howard, Thomas
Hudson, Timothy
Keelaghan, Nial
Kelly, Seamus
Kennedy, Gerard
Kennedy, William
Kenny, Clement
Kiely, Joseph
Kirby, James
Lawrence, Thomas
Layden, Brendan
Leahy, Kevin
Leonard, Aidan
Leung, Eric
Locke, John
Logan, Brian
Lynch, John
MacDonagh, Cathal
Madigan, Páraic
Maguire, Peter

McArdle, James
McAuliffe, Don
McCormack, Gerard
McCormick, Paul
McDonagh, Thomas
McDonnell, Rory
McGee, John
McHugh, Kevin
McInerney, Declan
McInerney, James
McNamara, Conor
Medir, Javier
Mekitarian, Lorcan
Moran, Seán
Morris, Michael
Morrissey, Michael
Murphy, Paul
Neiland, Richard
O'Brien, Allister
O'Brien, Anthony
O'Brien, Garrett
O'Connor, John
O'Connor, Michael
O'Dwyer, Anthony
O'Gorman, John
O'Gorman, Seán
Olleros, Ramon

Pearce, Damien
Peltz, Ingo
Purcell, Joseph
Quinn, Cathal
Riordan, John
Ryan, Richard
Ryan, Sylvester
Schaeuffele, Mamo
Sheahan, Keith
Somers, Emmet
Sweeney, Kevin
Walshe, Edmond
Whelan, Patrick
Williams, David

Gibbons, Ruairi
Girvan, David
Gregan, Anthony

Mansfield, David
Maxwell, Shane
McAlpin, Timothy

O'Meara, Raymond
O'Reilly, Anthony
O'Sullivan, Liam

1985

Barrett, Michael
Beyene, Abel
Bolger, Kevin
Borrell, Andres
Brannigan, Paul
Brennan, Frank
Bruce, Craig
Cantwell, Adrian
Carey, Noel
Casey, John
Chan, Marvin
Coen, David
Commane, Martin
Cooney, Dermot
Corcoran, David
Cottrell, James
Cronin, Timothy
Curran, Seamus
Daly, Donal
Deegan, Seán
Dennehy, Brian
Dennehy, Patrick
Dineen, Michael
Disney, William
Dowdall, Adrian

Drennan, Philip
Dunne, Joseph
Fadlu-Deen, Yazid
Farrell, Simon
Farrelly, Seamus
Finnerty, Seán
Fitzgerald, Brian
Fitzgerald, John
Fitzpatrick, Noel
Fitzsimons, Dermot
Gallagher, Richard
Gavin, James
Geada, Antonio
Gibbons, Declan
Gibney, Christopher
Goulding, Alan
Grace, Donal
Grealy, Anthony
Haden, Christopher
Hanrahan, Neil
Hayes, William
Hennessy, Maurice
Hurley, Oisín
Keating, John
Kelly, Ronan

Kennedy, Carl
Larkin, Dixton
Linehan, Aengus
Loftus, John
Long, Nicholas
MacDonagh, Ciaran
MacHugh, Owen
Maher, Seamus
Marnane, Seamus
McCormack, Micha
McDonnell, David
McDonnell, Donagh
McGloughlin, Mark
McGlynn, Angus
McGrath, Ciaran
McMahon, Michael
Moore, Fintan
Moroney, Gary
Murphy, David
O'Brien, Michael
O'Connell, John
O'Connell, Robert
O'Connor, Thomas
O'Donoghue, John
O'Donoghue, Peter

O'Farrell, Neville
O'Gorman, Patrick
O'Gorman, Peter
O'Kirwan, William
Rao, Anthony
Rassac, Musa
Reilly, David
Rice, Andrew
Rose, Richard
Russell, Thomas
Ryan, Kevin
Savage, William
Sexton, Shane
Sharkey, Alan
Sheahan, Davitt
Sheehan, Maurice
Sim, Ronald
Slattery, Cornelius
Slevin, David
Spillane, John
Spollen, Maris
Walsh, Raymond
Walshe, Edmond
Waters, John
Whelan, Rory

1986

Barrett, James
Barrett, Robert
Bolger, Raymond
Bourke, Vincent
Boyle, Mark
Breen, Mark
Brennan, Shane
Brophy, Ciaran
Brosnan, Barry
Brosnan, Conor
Buckley, Timothy
Chan, Benny
Chan, Matthew
Christianakis, Leon
Clarke, Jack
Cleary, Mark
Cliffe, Páraic
Coleman, William
Connery, James
Connolly, Paul
Cotter, Christopher
Cronin, Anthony
Cunningham, Franci
Daly, Brendan
Daly, Donal
Datsomor, Divine

Donovan, David
Doyle, Peter
Duggan, Declan
Farrell, Colm
Fitzgerald, Michael
Fitzsimons, Shane
Garvey, Brian
Geaney, Conor
Gibney, Vivien
Gillin, Patrick
Grace, Stephen
Griffin, Colin
Guilfoyle, Paul
Hanahoe, Karl
Haughton, Carl
Hayes, John
Heskin, Mark
Higgins, Keith
Hogan, Paul
Kavanagh, Pierce
Kearney, Pat
Keegan, Simon
Kelly, Raymond
Kiely, Daniel
Kiernan, Ian
Kitaka, John

Linehan, Rory
Lynam, Eoin
Lynch, David
MacGoey, Brian
Madden, Adrian
Madigan, Timothy
Maher, Conor
Malone, David
Mangan, John
McElhatton, Brenda
Moloney, James
Moran, Colm
Mullally, Robert
Murphy, Michael
Nolan, Edward
O'Donnell, Aidan
O'Donnell, Paul
O'Dwyer, John
O'Dwyer, Thomas
O'Neill, Donal
O'Reilly, John
Paassen, John
Prunty, Paul
Quinn, John
Quinn, Martin
Quinn, Gerard

Sheahan, Donald
Spollen, Bosco
Tang, Stanley
Tarrant, William
Tynan, James
Underhill, John
Walsh, Christopher
Walsh, Paschal
Walsh, Paul
Walsh, Peter
Whyte, Michael
Williams, Kevin
Wong, Casey
Wong, Felix
Wyse, John

Delahunty, Barry
Delaney, Darragh
Doherty, David
Donnelly, Brian

Lavan, Kenneth
Layden, Rory
Lee, Koon-Yum
Lewis, Ian

Romeo, Juan
Ryan, Leo
Ryan, Ian
Ryan, Micahel

1987

Beirne, Richard
Bermingham, James
Blackmore, Harry
Bolger, Ciaran
Brannigan, Martin
Burke, Patrick
Butler, Rupert
Carmody, John
Cliffe, Páraic
Coleman, Brian
Clarke, Gearóid
Cooney, Gray
Cooney, Kevin
Corcoran, John
Costello, David
Crean, Daniel
Cronin, Seán
Dalton, Anthony
Datsomor, Alex
Davern, Don
Disney, Robert
Doolan, Trevor
Edwards, Kevin
Finn, Kevin
Fitzgerald, Declan
Fitzgerald, Paul
Flynn, Darren
Fulcher, Gabriel
Gonzalez, Juan
Gonzalez, Ricardo
Gordon, Patrick

Griffin, Barry
Guerin, Kevin
Haughton, Carl
Heaphy, John
Hennessy, Paul
Heslin, Michael
Houlihan, Gregory
Irwin, Justin
Kawar, Tarif
Keary, Louis
Keating, Colm
Keating, Michael
Kennedy, Andrew
Kennedy, Brian
Kent, Michael
Kiely, Donal
Lawrence, Mark
Lee, Thomas
Llamas, Javier
Lynam, Adrian
Lysaght, Seamus
MacCloskey, Mark
MacDonagh, Brendan
MacDonagh, Michael
Martin, Ronan
Martinez, Alfredo
McCormack, Niall
McElhatton, Brian
McGlynn, Andrew
Morales, Jose
Moreno, Luis Mig

Mulvihill, Stephen
Moloney, Donal
Murphy, Barry
Murray, Brian
Naburi, David
Nsubuga, Martin
Nolan, James
O'Connor, Ronan
O'Connor, Patrick
O'Donnell, Liam
O'Donnell, Ruairi
O'Dowd, Cathal
O'Dwyer, William
O'Keeffe, Patrick
O'Mahony, Gary
O'Meara, Henry
O'Neill, John
O'Rourke, Noel
Power, Peter
Prieto, Guillermo
Prieto, Juan
Purcell, Francis
Purtill, Robert
Quirke, Michael
Rooney, Ronan
Ryan, Adrian
Savage, Grenville
Van Den Bergh, Paul
Valdez, Francisco
Walsh, Kieran
Wogan, Philip

1988

Barlow, Ivan
Barrett, John
Bermingham, James
Bevan, David
Boylan, Jonathan
Brady, Bernard
Butler, John
Campbell, Cian
Cantwell, Niall
Carey, Shaun
Carr, Jason
Cleary, Michael
Connolly, Stephen
Costello, Morgan
Cotter, Callaghan
Coveney, Keith
Dalton, Dylan
Davern, Don
Doyle, Justin

Gleeson, Milo
Glynn, Alan
Glynn, Francis
Golden, Edmond
Grimson, Edward
Halpin, Derek
Hannan, Martin
Hartigan, Kieran
Hawe, Carlyn
Healy, Thomas
Hennessy, John
Hogan, Anthony
Howley, Michael
Keane, Denis
Kelliher, Kevin
Kennedy, Brian
Kent, Michael
King, Aidan
Lane, John

McCarthy, Hugh
McCarthy, Hugh
McCarthy, John
McCarthy, Michael
McCorry, Keith
McDwyer, Seamus
McGrath, Marita
McGrath, Timothy
McCorry, Keith
McLellan, William
Moroney, Patricia
Moroney, Raymond
Murphy, Thomas E.
Murphy, Thomas P.
Murray, Anthony
Murray, Ronan
Nagle, Rory
Neville, Thomas
O'Connell, Donal

O'Sullivan, Patrick
Owens, Fergal
Purcell, Thomas
Purtill, Patrick
Purtill, Thomas
Quinn, Michael
Rock, Jason
Roe, Brian
Rowan, Brian
Ryan, Thomas
Ryan, Thomas J.
Sheahan, Philip
Sheehan, Gerard
Silke, William
Sperath, Neill
Spearman, John
Strappe, Valerie
Tallis, Paul
Tarrant, Peter

Doyle, Seán
Eivers, Frank
Enright, Brian
Fahey, Edmond
Fitzgerald, Anthony
Fitzgerald, Michael
Fitzpatrick, James
Fitzpatrick, John
Fitzsimon, John
Flaherty, Desmond
Galvin, Robert

Lavan, John
Lawrence, Mark
Lehane, John
Long, Andrew
MacGoey, John
Madigan, Niall
Maher, Brian
Mannion, Mel
Marnane, John
McCarthy, Aidan
McCarthy, Brian

O'Connell, Fintan
O'Donnell, Thomas
O'Donoghue, Patric
O'Donovan, Brian
O'Dwyer, Anthony
O'Dwyer, Patrick
O'Gorman, Thomas
O'Hara, James
O'Looney, Clement
O'Neill, Gerry
O'Sullivan, Eamon

Thompson, Ross
Tomkins, Damien
Van den Bergh, Ste
Wall, Shane
Warner, Rory

1989

Ambat, Andrew
Asmar, Leon
Bell, Desmond
Brennan, Conor
Browne, Kristian
Buckley, Mark
Byrne, Michael
Carrigan, Lucy
Casey, Anne
Casey, Joseph
Cheung, Ming
Cleary, Michael
Clinton, Simon
Coleman, Aisling
Coleman, John
Corbett, Claire
D'Costa, Cecil
De La Hoz, Enrique
Earley, Paul
Edwards, Brian
Finn, Eleanor
Fitzgibbon, Deborah
Fitzpatrick, Barry
Fitzpatrick, Seán
Fleming, Conor
Foley, Darragh
Foley, Sinéad
Fitzsimon, John
Garcia San Miguel, Julian
Gildea, Derbhail
Gil De Barroeta, Anna
Glynn, Carla

Gorman, David
Hall, Kenneth
Hayes, Colin
Higgins, Paul
Horan, Enda
Joyce, Kevin
Kavanagh, Michael
Kearney, Andrew
Keating, Joseph
Kelly, Kenneth
Kirby, Timothy
Lane, Patrick
Lynch, Colin
Lynch, Gerard
Madden, Conor
Maher, Ronan
Maher, Thomas
McCarthy, Aidan
McCarthy, John
McCarthy, Michael
McCarthy, Niall
McCorry, Clement
McGloughlin, John
McGrath, Fergal
McHugh, James
Moloney, John
Moran, Thomas
Morris, David
Morrissey, John
Murphy, Kevin
Neville, Richard
Nolan, Gregory

O'Connell, Kevin
O'Connell, Richard
O'Donnell, Eoin
O'Donoghue, Shane
O'Flaherty, Eoin
O'Meara, P.J.
O'Reilly, Sylvia
O'Shea, James
Power, Patricia
Purcell, John
Purcell, Thomas
Purtill, Michael
Quirke, Ronan
Riva, Juan
Ryan, Teresa
Ryan, Thomas
Ryan, Marie
Saeed, Richard
Shanahan, Thomas
Sheedy, John
Sheehan, Gerard
Sheridan, Donagh
Smyth, Douglas
Spearmon, John
Ssebunnya, Jerome
Timony, Louise
Tynan, Brian
Vesey, Paul
Wall, Francis
Walsh, Eoin
Whelan, Fintan

1990

Aberham, Matthew
Brennan, Conor
Browne, Jeremy
Burke, Gavin
Byrne, Leslie
Canavan, Pádraig
Cashman, Isaac
Chawke, Fergus
Cleary, Evelyn
Cliffe, Deirdre

Graham, Bernard
Griffin, Michael
Griffin, Nicholas
Hannafin, John
Hassett, Ross
Hayes, Colm
Heffernan, Nora
Hennessy, David
Hickey, Graham
Hickey, James

McGrath, Brian
McKeon, John Paul
McLoughlin, Barry
Moloney, Declan
Moloney, Galen
Moloney, Sheevan
Mooney, Catherine,
Moran, Thomas
Morgan, Robert
Morrisson, Edward

Connery, Mark
Costello, John
Cotter, Deirdre
Cronin, Mark
Dalton, Donal
Dalton, Patrick J.
Dalton, Patrick
Dalton, William
Davern, Mark
Davis, Jonathan
Disney, Marian
Dooley, Suzanne
Duffy, Seán Óg
Duke, Avik
Esquardo, Tristan
Fahey, Saoirse
Fitzgerald, Frank
Fitzgibbon, Deborah
Fitzpatrick, Paul
Fitzpatrick, William
Flanagan, David
Fogarty, Michael
Geraghty, George
Gildea, Fergal
Gleeson, Conor
Glynn, Paula

Higgins, Clive
Hobbert, Mark
Howard, Darragh
Ivin, Barry
Joyce, Barry
Juantegui, Jose
Kelly, Angela
Kennedy, Alan
Kennedy, Yvonne
Kiely, Kevin
Lacey, Darren
Leahy, Eimear
Leahy, Pádraig
Lonergan, Eoin
Lyons, Gavan
Lysaght, Michael
MacDonagh, Kevin
MacNamara, Colette
Malone, Ciara
Maher, Derbhile
Mahon, Gregory
Martin, Conan
Marnane, John
McDonagh, Lorraine
McDonnell, Aaron
McGloughlin, Paul

Morrissey, Michael
Mulcahy, Elaine
O'Connell, Aidan
O'Connor, Gillian
O'Connor, Lawrence
O'Connor, Ronan
O'Donnell, Eibhlin
O'Donnell, Kevin
O'Donoghue, Michael
O'Dowd, Conor
O'Dowd, Denis
O'Dwyer, Siobhán
O'Farrell, Thomas
O'Gara, Seamus
O'Gorman, David
O'Hanlon, Alan
O'Keeffe, Murray
O'Leary, Noel
O'Leary, Raymond
O'Neill, Darac
O'Reilly, Eimear
Ryan, Marguerite
Ryan, Valerie
Scanlon, Joseph
Van Der Wel
Walsh, Thomas

1991

Ahern, Carita
Betoret Catala, David
Bolger, Ian
Brennan, Anthony
Brosnan, Gregory
Browne, Gormlaith
Campion, Patrick
Carmody, William
Carrasco, Francisco
Carrington, Michael
Cleary, Kevin
Conway, Thomas
Dalton, Liam
English, Philip
English, Philip
Espinosa, Alvaro
Fagan, Martin
Feely, Patrick
Fitzgerald, Neil
Fitzpatrick, Darran
Flood, Susan
Flynn, Joseph
Fogarty, Damian
Foley, David
Frawley, Janet
Fuller, Breffni
Gallagher, Seamus
Glynn, Paula
Golden, David
Grace, Emily-Jean
Graham, Peter

Hourihan, Sinéad
Howe, John
Hunt, Philip
Hunt, Robert
Jackman, Jonathan
Julian, Ann-Marie
Kaikati, George
Keary, Olivia
Kelleher, Orla
Kelly, David
Kelly, Patrick
Kenneally, John
Kennedy, Valerie
Kiernan, David
King, Ruadhan
Kierans, Ian
Lavin, David
Lee, Declan
Lim, C. Boon
Lysaght, Michael
Mackey, Aidan
Maher, Michelle
McAuley, Colum
McCarthy, Timothy
McDonnell, Aaron
McGuire, Patrick
McGuirk, Gavin
McInerney, Ian
Merry, Colin
Moloney, Ian
Moloney, Martin

O'Brien, Fergal
O'Callaghan, Denis
Ó Cobhthaigh, Fearghal
O'Connell, Martin
O'Connor, Michael
O'Donnell, Patrick
O'Dowd, Joseph
O'Driscoll, Grace
O'Dwyer, Marina
O'Dwyer, Tríona
O'Dwyer, Patrick
O'Farrell, Mark
O'Gorman, Margot
O'Keeffe, John
O'Leary, Raymond
O'Meara, Rosemary
O'Sullivan, Conor
Owens, Jeremy
Owens, Joseph
Powell, Oisín
Purcell, James
Purcell, Thomas
Rockingham, Gerald
Ronan, John
Ruxton, austen
Ryan, Michael
Sexton, Victor
Smith, Seán
Smyth, Evelyn
Smyth, Mark
Toomey, Brendan

Hally, Ann-Marie
Hanlon, Conor
Heffernan, Denis
Hennessy, Claire
Hennessy, Michael
Higgins, Peter
Hogan, Frank
Horgan, Eamon

Moran, Caroline
Mulcahy, Geoffrey
Murphy, Jonathan
Murphy, Lisa
Murphy, Michael
Murphy, Niall
Murphy, William
Nolan, Daragh

Wallace, James
Walsh, Celia
Walsh, Donal
Walsh, Jill
Walshe, Myles
Warner, Kevin

1992

Addie, Christopher
Barron, Emily
Barry, John
Bell, Raelleen
Beresford, Clodagh
Bolger, James
Bourke, Michaael
Bradley, Olan
Broderick, Frank
Browne, Anthea
Browne, Emmet
Browne, Oonagh
Butler, Barry
Butler, Michael
Butler, Paul
Carey, Timothy
Carthy, Paul
Chawke, Gearóid
Cooney, Kevin
Cotter, Aaron
Copas, Damien
Coyle, John
Daly, Seán
Deane, Johathan
Delaney, Anthony
De Souza, Ian
Devane, Anthony
Devery, Aonghus
Dineen, John
Doran, Gregory
Dwan, Michael
English, Alma
Fahey, Fiona
Fahey, Linda
Finn, Denis
Finn, James
Fitzgerald, Ciaran
Fitzgerald, Teresa
Fitzgibbon, Mark
Fleming, Fergal
Foley, Alan
Foley, Eamonn
Foley, Shane

Fuller, Kirsten
Gardiner, Seán
Gillen, Ronan
Gleeson, Richard
Glynn, Keith
Gubbins, Gary
Hanley, Davina
Hanrahan, Enda
Harte, Andrew
Hayes, Simon
Horan, Conor
Howley, Helen
Hurley, Fionn
Jennings, Mary Beth
Keane, Andrew
Keane, Caroline
Keary, Kilian
Kelly, Aaron
Kelly, Kieran
Kennedy, Michael
Kinane, Caitríona
Kirwan, Ross
Luby, Anne-Marie
Lynam, Seán
Maher, John
McCarthy, Maria
McCoy, Wayne
McDonald, Mark
McHugh, Aidan
McGrath, Niall
McMorrow, Dermot
Moran, Denis
Morrissey, Paul
Moylan, Cormac
Mulcahy, John
Murphy, Jonathan
Nagle, Helen
Neilsen, Thomas
O'Brien, Thomas
O'Connor, Paul
O'Donnell, Amy
O'Donnell, Arthur
O'Donnell, Kevin

O'Donnell, Thomas
O'Donoghue, Anthony
O'Donoghue, Thomas
O'Donovan, Timothy
O'Dwyer, Aidan
O'Dwyer, Brian
O'Dwyer, James
O'Dwyer, Neasa
O'Dwyer, Paul
O'Dwyer, Seán
O'Dwyer, Wayne
O'Hanlon, Declan
O'Mahony, Colm
O'Reilly, Stanley
O'Riordan, Aoifa
Ortiz-Ayela, Nicolas
O'Shaughnessy, P.Ryan
Owens, Patrick
Prendergast, Gina
Prendergast, John
Purcell, Thomas
Rockingham, Gerald
Ryan, Ciaran
Ryan, Frank
Ryan, Karise
Sanches-Gavilan, Rafael
Smyth, Evelyn
Steinle-O'Carroll, Tarion
Sweetman, Richard
Swift, Gary
Thompson, Thomas
Tierney, James
Tracy, Colm
White, Roy
Woodlock, David

1993

Ahern, Salome
Aherne, Liane
Archibold, Robert

Hannigan, James
Heaney, John
Hobbert, Brian

O'Dea, Jason
O'Donnell, Amy
O'Donnell, Eoin

Balfe, Cillian
Blackwell, Brendan
Boylan, Patrick
Browne, Emmet
Carey, Anna-Louise
Carmody, Francis
Claffey, Barry
Clancy, John
Colbert, Gary
Cole-NcColgan, Justin
Coman, Geoffrey
Condon, Niamh
Corbett, Brian
Costello, Bernard
Crowley, Peter
Daly, Seán
Denby, Aidan
Drew, Patrick
Dumigan, Ryan
Dunne, Ivan
English, Michael
English, Olive
Enright, Jason
Enright, Roy
Feehan, Paula
Fitzgerald, Patrick
Fortune, Eoin
Gildea, Aisling
Griffin, Nigel
Hadnett, Michele

Hogan, Tanya
Horgan, Thomas
Kearney, Augustine
Keavney, David
Kingston, Dermot
Kirwan, Stuart
Leahy, Emmet
Leahy, Shane
Lonergan, Jeanne
Lonergan, William
Lucy, Morgan
Lynch, Anthony
Malone, Denis
MacGoey, Robert
McGrath, Elaine
McHugh, Aidan
Meagher, Patrick
Moloney, Helen
Moloney, Kevin
Moynihan, Gerry
Murphy, Arlene
Murray, Paul
Nealon, Fergal
Nugent, John
Ó Briain, Donough
O'Brien, Dermot
O'Brien, Joseph
O'Connor, Ruairi
O'Connor, Tom
O'Connor, Tomás

O'Donoghue, Cian
O'Driscoll, Conn
O'Dwyer, Alan
O'Dwyer, John
O'Flaherty, Nigel
O'Loughlin, Clodagh
O'Malley, Diarmuid
O'Reilly, Edmond
O'Reilly, Kevin
O'Rourke, Alan
O'Shea, Derek
O'Sullivan, Daniel
Owens, Kathleen
Phelan, Liam
Power, Ruadhan
Quinlan, Marie
Reidy, Brian
Ronan, Maurice
Ryan, Barry
Ryan, Dwyer
Ryan, Philip
Ryan, Ronan
Simo, Jose
Skehan, Thomas
Traynor, John
Waddock, John
Wallace, Adam
Walsh, Aidan
Walsh, David
Woodlock, Mark

1994

Ahearne, Michael
Bourke, Annette
Bourke, Stephen
Browne, Alan
Butler, Ciaran
Butler, David
Carey, Brian
Carey, Louise
Carrigan, William
Casey, Patrick
Cavanagh, Alan
Coffey, Ted
Conway, Paul
Connolly, Thomas
Cooney, Eimear
Commins, Diarmuid
Coyle, Killian
Cunnane, Una
Dalton, Eamonn
Devery, Eoghan
Disney, Jean
Doyle, Ronan
Dunne, Michelle
Durack, Seamus
Dwyer, Shane
Fahey, Conor
Fahey, David

Frawley, Olivia
Garcio, Amancio
Gardiner, Paul
Glynn, Aaron
Glynn, Conor
Golden, Alan
Halley, James
Halley, Oliver
Halpin, Seamus
Hanrahan, Michael
Hennessy, Martina
Higgins, Susan
Horgan, Cora
Julian, Gavin
Julian, Thomas
Keary, Brian
Kelleher, Seamus
Kelly, Patrick
Kennedy, James
Kennedy, John J.
Kennedy, Monica
Kennedy, Richard
Kiely, Ruth
Kirwan, Carroll
Leahy, Susan
Lonergan, Eileen
Maher, Jack

Moloney, Brian
Morris, Brian
Murphy, Brian
Murphy, Colin
Murphy, Gregory
Naewboonnien, Nundhivad
Nugent, Nora
O'Brien, Dan
O'Brien, Darren
Ó Cléirigh, Shane
O'Connor, Denis
O'Connor, Dolores
O'Connor, Lynda
O'Connor, Nicholas
O'Donnell, Eugene
O'Dwyer, James
O'Flaherty, Colm
O'Flaherty, Nigel
O'Gorman Ann-Marie
O'Gorman, Annemarie
O'Gorman, Eoin
Okoronkwo, Hope
O'Reilly, Audrey
O'Reilly, Conall
O'Sullivan, Emer
Peters, Vincent
Phelan, James

Ryan, Siobhán
Ryan, Susan
Samarokoon, Jason
Sebuliba, Peter
Sheehy, Marcella
Spillane, Alaine
Stokes, William
Tierney, Philip
Toomey, Cian
Walsh, Nicole
Walsh, Thomas
Wyse, Frank

Farrell, Leah
Fitzgerald, John
Flynn, Rory
Flynn, Seamus
Fogarty, Bridget
Fogarty, Niamh
Foley, Ellen
Fortune, Eugene

Mason, Alan
McCormack, Margaret
McDonagh, David
McGrath, Jennifer
McHugh, Vincent
McInerney, Patricia
McInerney. Vincent
Meehan, Lucy

Purcell, Emer
Quinlan, John
Quirke, Anthony
Rea, Triona
Reidy, Brian
Ryan, Kevin
Ryan, Kieran
Ryan, Oisin

1995

Ahern, Maurice
Archer, Graham
Barry, Kevin
Bates, Carmel
Bolger, Jude
Borras, Jordi
Brennan, John
Broad, Julianne
Browne, Colin
Burke, Eimear
Butler, Elaine
Campion, Martin
Canavan, Shane
Cantwell, Caoimhe
Carey, Jonathan
Carey, William
Carr, Seán
Carrigan, Conor
Casey, Ann-Marie
Casey, Donal
Coffey, Derek
Condon, Ronan
Cooney, Niall
Costello, Fergus
Delahunty, Aidan
Delahunty, Kevin
Delane, Desmond
Delap, Anthony
Devereux, George
Dolan, Paul
Drew, Alan
Dwyer, Paul
Dwyer, Shane
Earley, Seán
Egan, Patrick
Enright, Colin
Everard, Arvin
Farrell, Aoife

Fitzsimons, Patrick
Flynn, Kieran
Fuller, George
Galvin, Sarah
Gardiner, Paul
Geraghty, Anthony
Geraghty, Kevin
Gibson, Mark
Goodbody, Darnan
Hanrahan, Oliver
Heaney, Colm
Hegarty, Richard
Hennessy, Thomas
Hickey-Dwyer, Patric
Higgins, Susan
Hogg, Caroline
Kearney, Thomas
Keating, Albert
Keating, Cameron
Kelleher, Deborah
Kelly, Jerry
Kennedy, Monica
Kieran, Daniel
Kinsella, Frederick
Lane, Timothy
Landy, John Oliver
Lonergan, John
Lynch, Justin
Lyons, Michael
MacGoey, Patrick
Magnier, Geraldine
Mangan, Niall
Martinez, Rafa
McDonald, Gavin
McDonald, Seán
McGrath, Jenifer
McHugh, Fiona
McInerney, Patricia

McLoughlin, Adrian
Mills, Gary
Moloney, Marie
Morrison, James
Morrissey, Brian
Murray, Michael
O'Brien, Canice
O'Brien, James
O'Brien, Nigel
O'Connor, Alice
O'Connor, Cornelius
O'Donoghue Declan
O'Donovan, Annabell
O'Dwyer, Colum
O'Dwyer, Michael
O'Dwyer, Philip
O'Gorman, Mairéad
O'Gorman, Virginia
O'Gorman, William
O'Grady, Seán
O'Mahony, Kenneth
O'Mahony, Sheila
O'Reilly, Conal
O'Reilly, Jacquie
O'Reilly, Susan
Peters, Elaine
Pesquera, Gerardo
Phelan, Patrick
Phelan, Vincent
Pilkington, Simon
Powell, Cian
Purcell, Michael
Reddy, Sive
Roche, Andrea
Roche, Paul
Rockinngham, Kate
Russell, Jane
Ryan, Conleth

Ryan, Emma
Ryan, Kaye
Ryan, Martina
Ryan, Noel
Shanley, Owen
Shee, Jane
Sheehy, Martina
Shine, Catherine
Stapleton, Michael
Staunton, Mark
Sweeney, Paddy
Thompson, Olive
Tierney, David
Timony, Seán
Treacy, Jonathan
Ustiani, Marco
Vega, Diego
Waddock, James
Wall, Oliver
Walsh, David
Walsh, Patricia

1996

Ahearn, Garret
Ahearn, Patrick
Anchell, Thomas
Barry, Mark
Beary, Elizabeth
Beary, Patrick
Brett, Michael
Browne, David
Burke, Niall

Fitzgibbon, Aonghus
Flynn, Thomas
Fogarty, John
Foley, Ciarán
Foley, Louise
Galvin, William T.
Gibbs, Adrian
Goss, David
Griffin-Harney, Mand

Lenane, Joseph
Leonard, Timmy
Littleton, James
Lloyd, Donnacha
Lonergan, Evan
Long, Maura
Manning, Thomas
Martin, Darragh
Martin, Jennifer

O'Malley, Deirdre
O'Riordan, Alec
Ormond, Jilian
O'Sullivan, Seán
Power, Derek
Quigley, Aidan
Reidy, Fiona
Ronan, Frances
Ryan, Emmett

Buttimer, Fergal
Callaghan, Margaret
Callanan, Cathal
Carthy, David
Casey, Alex
Casey, David
Cashin, Aodhgan
Coffey, Brendan
Collins, Lorraine
Crowley, John Paul
Cummins, Mark
Cunniffe, Noel
Cunningham, Fiachra
Curran, Gareth
Curtin, Michael
Dalton, Brian
Dalton, Jacinta
Dempsey, Colm
Disney, Jean
Dolan, Brian
Durack, Conor
Dwyer, William P.
English, Barbara
Everard, Zane
Falvey, Niamh
Feitz, Philip
Fitzgerald, Alan
Fitzgerald, Barry
Fitzgerald, William

Grogan, Denis
Hadnett, Lorraine
Halley, Robert
Hanrahan, Michelle
Harnett, Michael
Hartigan, Joseph
Hassett, Tom
Hayes, Cathal
Hickey, John
Hickey, Pierce
Hogan, Claire
Horgan, Edward
Horgan, Marie Loui
Howley, Thomas
Hudner, Richard
Hyland, Pádraig
Katumbo, Kennedy
Keary, Vivienne
Kelleher, Avril
Kelleher, James
Kelly, Shane
Kennedy, Michael
Kennedy, Nora
Kiely, Ronan
Kinsella, Alan
Kinsella, Rhoda
Kitaka, Kizito
Leahy, Adrian
Leahy, Colm

McHugh, Brendan
Moloney, Alan
Moloney, Eamon
Moloney, Maeve
Moran, Shane
Morrison, John
Murphy, David
Murphy, Gemma
Nolan, Gráinne
Norris, Colm
Nugent, Elizabeth
O'Brien, Elizabeth
O'Connor, Jacqueline
O'Connor, Lee
O'Connor, Lisa
O'Connor, Noel
O'Connor, Stephen
O'Donovan, Finbarr
O'Driscoll, Clare
O'Dwyer, Claire
O'Dwyer, John
O'Flaherty, Brendan
O'Flaherty, Ciarán
O'Gorman, Finn
O'Gorman, Rosmarie
O'Gorman, Thomas
O'Gorman, Ursula
O'Keeffe, Bill
O'Keeffe, Josef

Ryan, Geraldine
Ryan, Marcella
Ryan, Maurice
Ryan, Mary Beth
Ryan, Shane
Samarakoon, Jason
Senior, David
Silke, Peter
Smith, Eamonn
Spain, Gordon
Spillane, Eamon
Treacy, Jonathan
Touhy, Georgina
Touhy, Michael
Walsh, Gilian
Walsh, Sinéad

1997

Agom, Christopher
Ahearne, Eileen
Bohner, Marcus
Bourke, Robert
Boyle, Michael
Breen, Trevor
Brennan, Ian
Burke, Donal
Canavan, Vincent
Casey, James
Casey, John Paul
Cashman, Alan
Cosgrove, Andrew
Courtney, Nicholas
Cunningham, Alan
Cusack, Karol
Day, Cathy
Darmody, Barry
Devereux, John
Dillane, Fiona
Dolan, John
Dooley, Patrick
Dower, Fergus
Durack, Alana
Dwyer, Michael
Dwyer, Rowena
English, John

Ennett, John
Fahey, Nichola
Fahy, Richard
Fallon, Peter
Finn, James
Flynn, P.J.
Gibbs, Arlene
Gleeson, Maria
Glynn, Elaine
Halley, Margaret
Halley, Robert
Hannigan, Yvonne
Hayes, Adrian
Hayes, Deirdre
Hayes, Michael
Hennessy, John Paul
Higgins, John
Hogg, Andrew
Holohan, Aoife
Horgan, Louise
Horgan, Roy
Horgan, Sara
Horne, Douglas
Hyde, Wayne
Ivin, Brian
Julian, Patrick
Joyce, Antonia
Keenan, Niamh

Kelleher, Eoin
Kelly, Eoin
Kennedy, Nora
Killeen, Conor
Kinsella, Rhoda
Kitaka, Lukka
Landy, David
Lennon, Cathal
Livonius Constantine
Lonergan, Marita
Lonergan, Suzanne
Maher, Daire
Maher, John
Maher, Jonathan
Mangan, Colin
Martin, Conor
McCormack, Declan
McGann, Donald
McGettigan, Brian
McMahon, Ronan
Meagher, Bill
Moloney, John
Murphy, James
Murray, Paul
O'Brien, Dennis
O'Brien, Ike
O'Brien, Michelle
O'Connor, Philip

O'Donnell, Richard
O'Donnell, William
O'Donoghue, Niamh
O'Dwyer, Noel
O'Gorman, David
O'Halloran, Pádraig
O'Keeffe, Eoin
O'Keeffe, Vincent
O'Sullivan, John
Peters, John Paul
Powell, Darach
Power, Davnett
Quinn, Mary
Reyels, Hannes
Roche, Brian
Roche, William
Ryan, Fergal
Ryan, Patricia
Scully, Michael
Shanahan, Maeve
Shealy, Alan
Shine, Patrick
Tierney, Robert
Toomey, Eoin
Toomey, Tadhg
Townsley, David
Yanguis, Luis
Young, Ciaran.

1998

Aytour, Daniel
Beary, Jenny
Blunnie, Mark
Boden, Peter
Boland, John
Boylan, Peter
Butler, Liam
Buttimer, Andrea
Byrne, James
Carthy, Adrian
Casey, Gerard
Casey, John
Clarke, Kevin
Cleary, Kieran
Conroy, John
Corbett, Joannne
D'Arcy, John
Earley, Brian
Egan, Kevin
English, John
Fahey, James
Ferris, Ciara
Finnucane, Niall
Fitzgerald, Edward
Fitzgibbon, Fiachra
Gardiner, Senan
Gleeson, Richard
Hadnett, John

Halley, Brigid
Hally, Michael
Hannigan, Anne-Marie
Hartley, James
Hayes, John
Hayes, Niamh
Healy, Tom
Heffernan, Anthony
Heffernan, John
Heffernan, Laura
Hennessy, Cathal
Ho, Leon
Hogan, Simon
Horgan, Barry
Julian, Darragh
Kavanagh, Patrick
Kavanagh, Paul
Kelly, Mark
Kelly, Patrique
Kennedy, Aodh
Littleton, Mark
Lonergan, Seán
Lonergan, Thomas
Long, John
Long, Shane
Maher, Niall
Martin, Anthony
Martin, Ross

Martin, Sylvia
McCarthy, Ciaran
McCarthy, Paul
McEntee, Ben
MvGlinchey, Gareth
McSweeney, Adrian
Moran, Shane
Moroney, Heather
Morrissey, Clare
Morrissey, Colin
Mulcahy, Frances
Mulcahy, Jack
Nolan, Brian
Nolan, John
Noonan, Danny
Noonan, Nora
O'Brien, David
O'Brien, Michael
O'Brien, Thomas
O'Connor, Damien
O'Connor, Edward
O'Connor, Patrick
O'Donoghue, Margaret-Ann
O'Dowd, Michael
O'Driscoll, Gareth
O'Dwyer, Jerry
O'Dwyer, Michael
O'Neill, Timothy

O'Reilly, Triona
O'Sullivan, Aidan
O'Sullivan, Gerard
O'Toole, Denis
Phelan, Orla
Quinlan, Angela
Rockingham, Michael
Russell, James
Ryan, Aisling
Ryan, Anthony
Ryan, Jennifer
Ryan, Liam
Ryan, Patricia
Scully, Gerard
Sheahan, Theodore
Stapleton, Shane
Stokes, Nessa
Swords, James
Tierney, Ronan
Waddock, Barry
Walsh, Alan
Walsh, Barry
Walsh, Karl
Weldon, Rory
Woodlock, Paul

1999

Ahearne, Paul
Anchell, Jake
Beresford, Patrick
Brett, Valerie
Brosnan, Seán
Browne, Gary
Browne, Tanya
Burke, Caoimhghin
Burke, Elaine
Byrne, Deirdre
Clarke, Paul
Cleary, Elaine
Cleary, Hazel
Cleary, Stephen
Collins, Ailish
Collins, Jennifer
Commins, Jennifer
Cregan, Michael
Dalton, John
Daly, Hugh
Dolan, Patrick
Dunlea, Claire
English, Jane
Fiesco Flores Rodrigo
Fitzgerald, Anne-Marie
Fitzgerald, Brendan
Fitzpatrick, Hugh

Foley, Cian
Forsyth, Alistair
Grace, John
Griffin, Hilda
Heap, Mark
Heffernan, James
Hogan, Karol
Hogan, Matthew
Horgan, Donna
Horgan, Paul
Howley, Noel
Joyce, Richard
Kearney, Michael
Keary, Jonathan
Keating, Noreen
Keogh, Patrick
Kiersey, Ken
Kirby, Vincent
Landy, Elaine
Lane, Jody
Lee, William
Little, Seán
Lonergan, Kate
Long, Vincent
Lundi, Justin
Magnier, Edward
Mason, Stephen

McGrath, Denis
McNaughton, Nabil
Moran, Ciaran
Morris, Muireann
Morris, Ronan
Morrissey, Patrick
Moylan, David
Mulcahy, Avril
Murphy, Brian
Murphy, Darren
Nolan, Eamon
Noonan, Forbes
O'Brien, Catherine
O'Brien, Maurice
O'Carroll, Seán
O'Connor, Anne-Marie
O'Connor, Brendan
O'Connor, Eleanor
O'Connor, William
O'Donnell, Alan
O'Driscoll, Timothy
O'Dwyer, Paul
O'Haloran, Michael
O'Leary, Conor
O'Mahony, Eadaoin
O'Meara, Ray
O'Shea, Vincent

Purcell, Gerard
Reynolds, Cathal
Ryan, Áine
Ryan, Garrett
Ryan, Katy
Ryan, Laura
Ryan, Patrick
Ryan, Philip
Ryan, Timothy
Scotland, Danielle
Shortall, Barry
Silke, John
Spain, Alec
Sutcliffe, Karl
Terry, Diarmuid
Touhy, Emma
Touhy, Paul
Underhill, Andrew
Walsh, Ian

Flanagan, Colm
Flynn, Emmet
Flynn, Thomas

McCarthy, Conor
McCloskey, Daniel
McGrath, Damien

Phelan, Ellen
Phelan, Rory
Prendergast, John

2000

Adey Odelade, Toyin
Agom, John
Barrett, Brian
Beary, Caroline
Boama Bonsu, Nana
Boyle, Patrick
Brennan, Keith
Buckley, Eamon
Callagy, Timothy
Casey, Joanne
Chui, Edward
Cleary, Hazel
Cleary, Thomas
Collins, Sinéad
Comerford, Peter
Commins, Jason
Courtney, Claire
Cronin, David
Culliton, P.J.
Curran Cournane, Brian
Dowling, Daniel
Doyle, John R.
Doyle, Michael
Drohan, Michael
Earley, Alan
Egan, James
Fennessy, Thomas
Fitzgerald, Sinéad

Flynn, Catriona
Garland, Wayne
Gildea, Martin
Hally, Gearóid
Hanley, Mark
Hau, Dirk
Hayes, Karena
Heereman, Lucas
Jenkins, Ciaran
Kennedy, Claire
King, Paula
Kinsella, Richard
Leahy, Seán
Leamy, Denis
Lee, David
Macken, Eoin
Mackey, Brendan
Mainstone, Ciaran
McDonnell, Elaine
McLoughlin, Paul
Mikhailov, Sergei
Moloney, James
Moloney, Oliver
Molumby, Mark
Moran, Eavan
Moylan, Ross
Mulcahy, Avril
Murphy, Anne-Marie

Murtagh, Grant
Nathan, Emmanuel
Nathan, Fukaino
Nolan, Eve
Nolan, Teresa
Noonan, Joanne
O'Brien, Robert
O'Connor, Eimear
O'Donnell, Shane
O'Dwyer, Mark
O'Flynn, Tadhg
O'Mahony, Cian
O'Neill, Shane
O'Riordan, Diarmuid
O'Sullivan, Laura
Phelan, Alan
Phelan, Lewis
Prendergast, William
Quinlan, Antoinette
Quinlan, Edwina
Quinlan, Ken
Renehan, Avril
Renehan, Edmond
Roche, David
Ryan, Eoin
Ryan, Fergal
Ryan, Sharon
Shine, Enda

Shine, Patrick
Shortt, Kristian
Stapleton, Shane
Sutcliffe, Karl
Tierney, Edward
Tobin, Stephen
Tuohy, Mark
Van Dulken, Gerardo
Van Dulken, Juan
Van Dulken, Marcos
Von Freyend, Gregor
Von Roebel, Wenzel

2001

Anchell, Katy
Anderson, Clive
Barry, Michael
Bennett, Francis
Brennan, Peter
Carroll, Tadhg
Clifford, James
Collins, Gerard
Costelloe, Michael
Coughlan, Michael
Crowley, Brendan
Cummins, Fiona
Cunningham, Shane
Curtin, David
Daly, Adrian
De Beasco, Jorge
Delaney, Michael
Devane, Thomas
Dowling, Jennifer
English, William
Fahey, Laura
Fahy, Adrian

Goodbody, Ben
Graham, Fergus
Griffin, Joseph
Halley, Lisa
Hally, Lena
Hannon, Timothy
Hartigan, Eoin
Hayes, Eamonn
Healy, Marie
Hennessy, Ryan
Hurley, John
Hyland, Liam
Keane, Karol
Kelly, Lynda
Kelly, Thomas
Kennedy, Margaret
Kennedy, Marianne
Lee, Ailish
Linehan, Noel
Lobkowicz, Maximilian
Lonergan, Colm
Lyons, Morgan

Manning, Edward
Martin, Thomas
McCabe, Matthew
McGonigle, Paul
McNaughton, Corma
Moloney, David
Moloney, Michael
Mullally, Sheena
Nolan, Shane
Nugent, Niamh
Nugent, Patrick
O'Brien, Brendan
O'Connor, Brendan
O'Donnell, John
O'Donnell, Shane
O'Donoghue, Brenda
O'Donoghue, Natalie
O'Flaherty, Brian
O'Gorman, Conor
Olagbegi, Dami
Oruche, Adaora
Oruche, Chike

Power, Michelle
Prendergast, Patrick
Rosenberg, Paul
Ryan, Shane
Sheehan, Rory
Slattery, Elizabeth
Slattery, Martin
Strumble, Francis
Udoeyop, Edidong
Von Schierstaadt, Anton
Walsh, Barry

Feeley, Kenneth
Fitzgerald, Sinéad
Flynn, Danny
Foy, Declan

Macken, Eoin
Mackey, Brendan
Madden, John
Mainstone, Clare

O'Sullivan, Laura
O'Sullivan, Raymond
O'Sullivan, Sarah
Phelan, Laurence

2002

Bechinger, Jakob
Bourke, Andrew
Boyle, Siobhán
Britton, Adrian
Brosnan, Rory
Butler, Michael
Casey, Killian
Collins, Deirdre
Collins, Gráinne
Costello, Irma
Coughlan, Kevin
Daly, Evan
Daly, Niamh
Darmody, David
Devereaux, John
Doocey, Michael
Duffy, Alison
Doyle, Edward
Durack, Niamh
Duttemeyer, Raphael
Echterhoff, Philipp
English, Elizabeth
Farrell, Amanda
Fogarty, Denis
Gaffney, James
Gahan, Eimear
Gallagher, Sarah

Gete, Gonzalo
Golden, Michael
Hall, Jonathan
Hallinan, Sarah
Heffernan, Emma
Hewitt, Clark
Heywood, Louise
Horan, John
Howard, Niall
Hurley, Gerard
Joyce, David
Kealy, Niall
Keating, Anne-Marie
Kehoe, Cormac
Kehoe, Karen
Kelleher, Claire
Leamy, Edmund
Le Voir, Mark
Lyons, Daragh
Macken, Oliver
Mackessy, James
Magnier, Lavinia
Malone, Karl
Mangan, Stuart
McGrath, James
McGuiirk, Fintan
McMorrow, Clodagh

Meaney, Eoin
Mee, Steven
Mejekodumni, Tunde
Melbourne, Mark
Moroney, Sheree
Mulcahy, Sheena
Mullally, Damian
Murphy, Brendan
Murphy, Daniel
Murphy, Niamh
Nolan, Muireann
O'Brien, Aileen
O'Connell, Kevin
O'Connor, Clodagh Mar
O'Connor, Diarmuid
O'Connor, Patrick
Odelade, Oluwkatay
O'Donoghue, Natalie
O'Donoghue, Thomas
O'Dwyer, Maria
O'Gorman, Conor
O'Gorman, Evan
O'Keeffe, Siobhán
Olaghere, Olufemi
O'Mahony, Niall
O'Neill, Raymond
Onile-Ere, Adewele

O'Sullivan, Maeve
O'Sullivan, Raymond
Perrozzi, Gabriella
Phelan, Donal
Prendergast, Patrick
Quillinan, Joy
Quinlan, Frank
Ryan, John
Ryan, Jordan
Ryan, Morgan
Ryan, Rachael
Ryan, Ronan
Ryan, Sheila Cummins
Ryan, Sheila Merchant
Scannell, Barry
Shanahan, Nicole
Stapleton, Ross
Sutton, Andrew
Thornton, Nicole
Toomey, Neil
Udensi, Veronica
Vierhout, Alexander
Walsh, Aisling
Walsh, Conor
Walsh, Leo
Ward. Julianne
White, Siobhán

2003

Ahern, Ian
Anglim, Áine
Barrett, Aoife
Barrionuevo, Pedro
Barry, Thomas
Blake, Kevin
Boama, Kojo
Bourke, Rita
Boyle, Cormac
Boyle, Kate
Burke, Hayley
Cashman, David
Colton, Paul
Cooney, Conor
Corbett, Siobhán
Corcoran, Martin
Corrigan, Michael
Cummins, Rachel
Curran, John
Dalton, Michael
Daly, Sarah
Domenech, Eduardo

Farrell, Brian
Feeney, David
Fields, Joseph
Fitzpatrick, Darren
Fox, Caroline
Fox, Paul
Gilmore, David
Gulati, Daksh
Hall, Coliosa
Hayes, Alan
Hayes, Jemma
Hearn, Ronan
Hennessy, Joe
Heywood, Grace
Hogan, Catherine
Hogan, Deirdre
Houlihan, David
Jenkins, Michael
Keary, Adrian
Kendrick, Christopher
Leahy, Brian
Loughnane, William

McGivern, Susan
McGlinchey, Oliver
McGrath, Audrey
McGrath, Johanna
McGrath, Orla
McMorrow, Siobhán
McHugh, Stephen
McManus, Conor
McNaughton, Cian
Montenegro, Alvaro
Morrin, Joseph
Mulcahy, Elaine
Mulcahy, Michael
Murphy, Kevin
Murray, Gerard
Murtagh, Tara
Nolan, Éibhín
O'Brien, John
O'Callaghan, Noreen
O'Connor, John
O'Dwyer, Edward
O'Flynn, Seán

Quinlan, Kevin
Quinlan, Marina
Quinlan, Mark
Quinn, Anthony
Quinton, Ciaran
Redfern, Rebecca
Rochard, Roslyn
Rodgers, Dominic
Ruddy, Patrick
Russell, David
Ryan, Alan
Ryan, Conor
Ryan, James
Ryan, Nuala
Ryan, Shane
Tobin, Thomas
Tuohy, Frank
Vidal, Xavier
Walsh, Eoin
Wenzel, Constantin
Yiu, Anthony

Dawodu, Sameat
Dowling, Sinéad
Duggan, Donnacha
English, Carmel
English, Conor
English, Philip
Fahey, Siobhán

Lyons, Aoife
Lyons, Kieran
Lyons, Niamh
McCarthy, Conor
McCarthy, Jeanienne
McCarthy, Michael
McGann, Paula

O'Gorman, Patrick
O'Halloran, Robert
O'Hanlon, Karl
O'Rahelly, Niall
O'Reilly, Alan
O'Riordan, Michael
O'Sullivan, Gráinne

2004

Aamir, Fahd
Bargary, Amy
Barry, Anthony
Barry, Gillian
Barry, Thomas
Bini, Marina
Blake, Kevin
Boyle, Roisin
Britton, Philip
Burke, Victoria
Byrne, Aidan
Carroll, Gerard
Cheung, Andy
Cleary, Damien
Coates, Robert
Collins, Bill
Collins, Leah
Collins, Shane
Cooney, Zoe
Corr, Peter
Crean, Patrick
Crosse, Ronan
Culliton, Eoin
Daly, Caoimhghin
Devereaux, Elaine
Dolan, Conor
Downey, Ciaran
Doyle, Sarah Jane
Duane, Fiona
Duffy, Aoife
Dunne, Anne

English, John
Fahey, John
Farrelly, Patrick
Fitzpatrick, Jennifer
Flynn, John D.
Foley, Siobhán
Foley, Tuan
Foley, Ultan
Frazer, Alec
Freiberg, Damien
Gembruch, Christoph
Gembruch, Oliver
Greaney, Siobhán
Griffin, Florence
Hall O'Mahony, Conor
Halley, Paul
Hanly, Colm
Hartnett, Gerard
Hayes, Christopher
Hennessy, Marie
Heuvinck, Herman
Hogg, Brian
Hunter, Bill
Igoe, John
Ilochi, Pearl
Iqbal, Usman
Keaney, Sheola
Kennedy, Daniel
Kumar, Divij
Leahy, Pádraig
Leamy, Kevin

Lonergan, Niamh
Long, Gillian
Longworth, Nicholas
Lynch, Benjamin
Lynch, Kevin
Lyons, Niamh
Maber, Brendan
Maher, Sarah
McCarthy, William
McGrath, Áine
McGrath, Joanna
McGrath, Philip
McLoughlin, John
Meade, Shane
Melbourne, Neville
Moloney, Cian
Moloney, Peter
Morris, Deirdre
Morrissey, Desmond
Morrissey, Emma Jane
Mulcahy, Brendan
Mulcahy, Michael
Ní Chonchubhair, Hazel
Nolan, Aaron
O'Connell, Emma
O'Connell, Mary
O'Connor, Brendan
O'Connor, Michael
O'Donnell, Johnny
O'Reilly, Alan
O'Reilly, Laurann

O'Shea, Joan
O'Sullivan, Darren
O'Sullivan, Owen
O'Sullivan, Shane
Peters, Eamonn
Pierse, Lorna
Power, Fiona
Prendergast, Michael
Purcell, William
Quinlan, Marina
Quinton, Ciaran
Quirke, Thomas
Reidy, Stephen
Roche, David
Rockett, Alan
Ronan, Seán
Russell, Neil
Ryan, Amy
Ryan, Michael
Ryan, Rachele
Schmidt, Daniel
Shanahan, Robert
Shealy, Danielle
Thornton, Philip
Von Roebel, Kasimir
Walsh, Eoin
Walshe, John
Weitz, Clemens

2005

Abdel-Haq, Ady
Anderson, Eoghan
Aversberg, Douglas
Badiya, Titlope
Bargary, Amy
Borzenco, Daniil
Bradley, Ross
Brett, Ronan
Buanga, Stefanie
Buckley, Micheál
Canning, Courtney
Casey, James
Coffey, Emma
Coffey, Stephen
Collins, Donal

Gilpin, Tom
Hayes, Patrick
Healy, Bryan
Hennessy, Tommy
Heuvinck, Laura
Heywood, Sarah
Hogan, Cian
Hogan, Jennifer
Hogan, William
Hyland, Fiona
Julian, Noel
Kamogowa, Yuko
Kelly, James
Kelly, Jamie
Kelly, Rhea

Molloy, Frank
Moloney, Luke
Morris, Olwyn
Mulcahy, John
Mullaney, Aaron
Nolan, Ruth
O'Callaghan, Patricia
O'Connell, Laura
O'Donnell, John
O'Donoghue, Catherine
O'Driscoll, Marcus
O'Flynn, Conny
O'Flynn, Niall
O'Neill, Kate
O'Neill, Melissa

Quinlan, Conor
Roche, Killian
Russell, James
Russell, Paul
Ruttle, Edward
Ryan, Damien
Ryan, Shane
Ryan, Tim
Sahay, Shruti
Scannell, Aidan
Scannell, Jerome
Shallow, Peter
Sherlock, Andrew
Showell, Emily
Spillane, Susan

Conneally, Niamh
Corcoran, Daire
Crowley, David
Davis, Michael
Del Villar, Eduardo
Duane, Fiona
Dwyer, Alan
Farrelly, Terence
Fitzgerald, Seán Óg
Fitzgibbon, Tiernan
Flynn, Mark
Foley, David

Kennedy, Aidan
Kenny, Paul
Kiel, Liane
Kophamel, Kyle
Leahy, Philippa
Lonergan, Anita
Long, Jessica
McEvoy, Conor
McMorrow, Doireann
Mee, David
Meehan, Ailish
Melbourne, Brian

O'Rahelly, Ian
O'Regan, Tadhg
O'Reilly, Claire
O'Shea, Peter
O'Sullivan, Bernard
O'Sullivan, Frank
O'Sullivan, Tiarnan
Payne, Caitriona
Perigoe, Luke
Power, Fiona
Prendergast, Mark
Purcell, Dorothy

Thompson, Patrick
Tigges, Sebastian
Vasiliev, Alexy
Von Alvensleben, Max
Von Thielmann, Rupec
Walsh, Noreel
Walsh, Peter
Walsh, Ronan
Walshe, Sarah
White, Peter
Wiseler, Cathy

2006

Acheson, Kate
Barrau, Gonzalo
Boland, Darragh
Buckley, Sarah
Cleere, Grace
Collins, Donal
Collins, Kate
Condon, Eoin
Corcoran, Jonathan
Cremmins, Clare
Cummins, Kieran
Delahunty, Eoin
Delventhal, Niall
Farrell, Ronan
Fox, Ann Marie
Geraghty, James
Gleeson, Gerald
Grace, Eoghan
Hale, Christopher
Hall, Adele
Hannover, Otto
Holden, Hannah
Howley, Eimear

Jeffries, Grace
Jones, Fiona
Kelly, Michael Wm.
Kendrick, Emer
Kolbasin, Sasha
Lalor, Thomas
Lane, Eamon
Leonard, Aaron
Long, Patrick
Longworth, Oliver
Maher, Cathal
McCarthy, Kieran
McCarthy, Timothy
McDonnell, Barry
McEvoy, Conor
McGrath, Seán
McHugh, Marie
McKeown, Conor
McMorrow, Bronagh
Melbourne, Stephen
Meyer, David
Moloney, Catherine
Morrissey, June

Motchalov, Denis
Naughton, Patrick
O'Brien, Patrick
O'Brien, William
O'Connor, Jack
O'Connor, Rory
O'Donnell, Caitriona
O'Donnell, Lorraine
O'Donovan, Cathal
O'Donovan, John Paul
O'Dwyer, Jack
O'Dwyer, Niamh
O'Dwyer, Stephen
O'Halloran, Barry
O'Keeffe, Ian
O'Leary, Tadhg
O'Mahony, Joseph
O'Mara, Niall
O'Neill, Con
O'Regan, Amy
O'Shea, Jakki
O'Sullivan, Ciara
O'Sullivan, Frank

O'Sullivan, Grace
O'Sullivan, Louise
O'Sullivan, Niall
O'Sullivan, Rebecca
Pierse, Arthur
Purcell, Sandra
Quirke, Claire
Quirke, Jeffrey
Rockett, Patrick
Russell, Emma
Ruttle, Geoffrey
Ryan, Jacqui
Shadyzhev, Berd
Teehan, Claire
Thornton, Jeanine
Von Alvensleven, Max
Walsh, Brendan
Walsh, Orla
Walsh, Paul
Zhuchenko, Lev

2007

Adam, Constantin
Barry, David
Barry, Roger
Barron, Eamonn
Boland, Cailin
Buckley, Kevin
Coffey, Donnchadh
Corcoran, Michael
Corry, David
Costello, Arthur
Crosse, Michael
Cummins, Jennifer
Cummins, Rebekah
Curran, Daryll
Devane, William
Duffy, Caoimhe
Duffy, Ian
Duffy, Orlaith
Duggan, Joanna

Friemann, Christian
Garcia, Jose
Gill, James
Hally, Claire
Heywood, Judith
Hickey, David
Higgins, Donncha
Himayat, Faryal
Hogan, Daore
Holohan, Patrick
Jenkins, Evan
Joy, Robert
Joyce, Andrew
Joyce, Seán
Kelly, Michael
Kennedy, Laura
Kramer, Viola
Lawlor, Ciara
Leamy, Maeve

Martin, Eda
Mason, Rodney
Matsuo, Marin
McCarthy, John
McCarthy, Kieran
McDonald, Ciara
McEvoy, Brian
McGarry, Ruth
McGivern, Robert
Moore, Raphael
Morrissey, Hugo
Mullins, Shirley
Murphy, Lauren N.
Murray, Clare
Nagle, James
Nolan, Robert
O'Brien, John
O'Brien, Robert
O'Callaghan, Luke

O'Neill, Derry
Oppermann, Klemens
O'Reilly, Hazel
Ortlepp, Gerold
O'Sullivan, Brian
O'Sullivan, Gerald
O'Sullivan, Kevin
Ould Boye, Abdoullah
Phelan, John
Powell, Elaine
Power, James
Ryan, James
Ryan, Michael
Ryan, Niamh
Schmidt, Malte
Schmitz, Sebastian
Sheehan, Eimear
Von Woellwart, Ernst
Walsh, Bríd

Eisenberg, Leonard
English, Kenneth
Fatrekdinov, Ramil
Feehan, Martin
Fitzpatrick, Alice

Lonergan, Catherine
Magar, Fiona
Maher, Cathal
Maher, Sinéad
Maher, Susan

O'Connell, Eoin
O'Connor, Martin
O'Connor, Patrick
O'Dwyer, Ross
O'Flynn, Ciaran

Walsh, Deirdre
Walsh, Ronan
Willhelm, Katharina
Yates, Gavin
Zipplies, Maximilian

2008

Acheson, Peter
Alvarez, Patrick
Amoros, Sergio
Anderson, Alan
Arigho Stiles, Joseph
Balfour, Andrew
Burrows, Declan
Busch, Johann
Butler, Johannah
Coffey, Aidan
Coffey, Tiarnan
Coyne, Michael
Croke, Ian
Crowe, Sarah
Davydenko, Vladimir
De Lojendio, Luis
Dennehy, David
Derbasova, Daria
Drohan, Eric
Droney, David
Eleker, Shereen
Farrelly, Fiona
Fiedler, Jan
Fitzgerald, Ellen
Fitzpatrick, James
Fitzpatrick, Sarah

Flynn, Niall
Fogarty, Dan
Garrigan, Ben
Greaney, Robert
Gupta, Kushal
Hayes, Philip
Horgan, Julie
Hoyne, David
Irwin, Julie
Katsukawa, Shohei
Kearney, Robert
Keating, Aidan
Keating, Alan
Kelly, Edward
Kelly, Rachel
Kelly, William
Kehoe, James
Kelleher, Hugh
Kennedy, Eoin
Kiely, Joseph
Kingston, Nicola
Kirwan, Del
Lawlor, Conor
Lenhardt, Maximilian
Lonergan, Niamh
Luby, Shane

Magar, Leon
Martin, Leanne
Martin, Michelle
Matas, Fernando
McCarthy, Críomhthann
McEvoy, Paul
Meskele, Habtamu
Moreno, Pepe
Munnich, Stuart
Murphy, Sinéad
Neuschaffer, Georg
Nolan, William
O'Brien, Jerry
O'Connell, Zack
O'Connor, Mark
Oda, Hideo
O'Doherty, Darragh
O'Donnell, Christopher
O'Donnell, Luke
O'Donnell, Peter
O'Donovan, James
O'Kelly, John
O'Leary, Andrew
O'Mahony, Alexander
O'Reilly, Hazel
O'Sullivan, Jack

Phelan, Emmet
Purcell, Daelyn
Quigley, James
Rafferty, Niamh
Rafferty, Rory
Ridley, Alexander
Rogers, Brian
Russell, Jean
Ryan, Niamh
Ryan, Robert
Shealy, Vicki
Silke, Brian
Svirkov, Nikita
Sweeney, Conor
Teehan, Patrick
Theis, Joe
Thompson, Hugh
Thornton, Robert
Wall, Thomas
Walsh, Gilda
Walsh, Ronan
Whelan, Barry
Wilgress, Jamie
Wynne, James

2009

Abaladejo Costello, Aur
Atkinson, Claire
Binchy, Daniel
Boland, Seán
Burke, Aidan
Butler, Patrick
Byrne, Keelin
Collins, Eimear
Corcoran, Donnchadh
Cullinane, Brendan
Deeleman, Ivor
Dirilgen, Tara
Dwyer, Kenneth
English, Finbarr
Farrell, Neil
Flanagan, Tracey
Finnegan, Zoe
Foley, Liam
Gill, Barry
Gill, Niamh

Hannigan, Peter
Haugh, Maeve
Hayes, Thomas
Hennessy, Ciaran
Hennessy, Claire
Higgins, Noel
Hillmann, Friederike
Horgan, Luke
Hyland, John
Irwin, Philip
Keane, Edmond
Kelly, Eoghan
Kennelly, Bridie
Khalin, Nikanor
Killian, Richard
Koch, Patrick
Leahy, Michael
Lonergan, Jack
Long, Sarah
Lynch, Rosemary

Lyons, Jason
Lyons, Maedhbh
McAlpin, Alexander
McCarthy, Brian
McEvoy, Paul
Molumby, Sarah
Nagle, Andrew
Neylon, Lisa
Nolan, James
O'Brien, Paddy
O'Connor, Aoife
O'Connor, Joseph
O'Connor, Seán
O'Connor, William
O'Connor, Zoe
O'Donnell, Colm
O'Donnell, Luke
O'Dwyer, Robert
O'Flynn, Shane
O'Neill, Aoife

O'Sullivan, Barry
Pucklitzsch, Maximilian
Purcell, Charlie
Quinlan, Jennifer
Rakhmatulina, Elina
Roche, Aisling
Ryan, Gavin
Shanahan, Bill
Smith, Brian
Tarasenok, Artjom
Taylor, Edward
Teehan, David
Wai-Shun-Pak, Wilson
Walsh, Andrew
Walsh, Katie
Walsh, Molly
Yates, Andrew
Weitz, Benedikt
Woodlock, Tom
Yau-Sze-Wai, Sharon

2010

Aamir, Zahrish	Finnegan, John	Maher, Laura	O'Donovan, Aoife
Anchell, Simon	Fitzgerald, Louise	Manton, Samuel Gerard	O'Leary, Hugh
Barron, Eimear	Fitzgerald, Owen	Marshall, Liam	O'Rahelly, Bryan
Bartley, Lauren	Foley, Andrew Joseph	McDonnell, Katie	O'Reilly, Keith
Bourke, Darragh	Gehling, Constantin	McEniry, Darragh	Ortlepp, Hagen
Breedy, Robert	Gerrard, Daniel	McEvoy, Barry	O'Sullivan, Aidan
Brett, Orla	GrafBeissel Von Gymnich	McGillycuddy, Donough	O'Sullivan, Conor
Buckley, Shane	Hallinan, Dominique	Meagher, Joseph	O'Sullivan, Ursula
Byrne, Feargal	Hanrahan, J.J.	Moloney, Brian	Pierse, Andrew
Chow, Simon	Healy, Isabel	Morrissey, Charlotte	Pierse, Jill
Clancy, Flann	Heuston, Gavin	Morrissey, William	Prendergast, Conor
Cleary, Elizabeth	Heywood, Honor	Mulcahy, Elayne	Prendergast, Michael
Coffey, Myles	Horgan, Shaun	Mullane, Ross	Purcell, Julie
Collins, Barry	Howley, Erika	Mullins, Ivan	Purcell, Nicholas
Cooney, J.J.	Hughes, Yvonne	Mullins, Michael	Quinlan, Louise
Cummins, Eva	Hyland, Christopher	Murray, Conall	Rafferty, Tim
Cummins, Liam	Kavanaagh, Conor	Murtagh, Ryan	Roche, Niamh
Cummins, Mark	Kehoe, Ellen	Mutaaga, Isabel	Ryan, Seán
De Bhulbh, Laoise	Kelly, Lydia	Nolan, Robert	Schletihoff, Lukas
Dilleen, James	Kenneally, Aishling	O'Brien, Aideen	Schmidt, Hendrik
Donoghue, Laura	Kenneally, Niamh	O'Brien, Joseph	Schoenebeck, Johannes
Doyle, Jonathan	Khan, Arham Ikram	O'Connell, Colm	Stone, Aisling
Doyle, Tom	Konn, Leonard	O'Connell, Jack	Thompson, Niall
Drew, Haydn	Kopp, Lorenz	O'Connor, Annemarie	Tobin, Laura
Dwyer, Aime	Lonergan, Andrew	O'Connor, Conor	Trucksaess, Maximillian
Dwyer, Edward	Magee, David	O'Connor, Jane	Van Bussel, Laurens
Dwyer, Kelly	Maguire, Stephen	O'Doherty, Liam	Walsh, David
Farrell, Eoin	Maguire, Stephena	O'Donoghue, Charlie	

2011

Arce Bayibam Jose	Hally, Aisling	Manton, Samuel G.	O'Donnell, Rory
Barron, Michael	Hannigan, David	Martin, Alvarez Luis	O'Neill, Keith
Bergin, David	Haugh, Brian	McCarthy, Seán	O'Sullivan, Aidan G.
Birgel, Jan Lukas	Haurie, Alejandro	McDonald, Katie	O'Sullivan, Cian
Bourke, Darragh	Hickey, Áine	McDonald, Roisin	O'Sullivan, Matt
Breedy, Robert	Holland, Conor	McEniry, Darragh	Phelan, Edward
Buckley, Emma	Horgan, Shaun	McGillycuddy, Donough	Pierse, Charles
Buckley, Laura	Hospital, Luis Serra	McKenna, Eoin	Possenti, Carlos
Butler, Michael	Hynes, Matthew	McNulty, Harry	Purcell, Alex
Cahill, Luke	Irwin, Danielle	Meagher, Joseph P.	Rehman, Hafsa
Carroll, Robert	Irwin, Joanne	Meaney, Alexander D	Riley, Jack Edward
Conneely, Lee	Jeffries, Jack	Mitryashkin, Stepan	Roberts, Jamie
Corbett, Karen	Jiang, Mingxu	Moloney, Aidan	Ryan, Kate
Cremins, Ciara	Joyce, Pádraig	Moloney, Jack	Ryan, Nicholas
Crosse, Brendan	Kelly, Siobhán	Moran, Richard J.	Ryan, Paraic
Dolan, Fiona	Kenneally, Niamh	Morrissey, Eamonn	Ryan, Stephen
Doverman, Katherine	Kennedy, David J.	Morrissey, William P	Schlupp, Merle Marie
Doyle, Cliona	Kerrigan, Ross	Mulcahy, Luke	Sheehy, Eoghan J.
Duggan, Billy	Khan, Arham Ikram	Murphy, Michael J.	Skehan, Katie
Dunne, Lee	Khan, Rohaan	O'Connell, Jack	Smyth, David
Dwan, Louis	Kingston, Paul	O'Connor, Annemarie	Sutcliffe, Jack
	Konn, Valentin	O'Doherty, Chelsey	Theis, Jay
Feeney, Owen	Maher, Colleen	O'Doherty, Conor	Wade-Ryan, Toni
Gehling, Alexander	Maher, Dermot	O'Donnell, Cian	Wai Chyan, Wong,
Ricky			
Gustav, Ritz Carl	Maher, Kealan	O'Donnell, Eoghan	Wallace, Andrew
Guttes, Lukas	Maher, Shauna	O'Donnell, Mollie	Welsh, Daisy

2012

Barlow, Jessie	Greed Aideen	Looby, Jack	O'Leary, Aoife
Barron, Aidan	Greenslade, George	Lyons, Robert	O'Mahoney, Susi
Barry, Sarah	Guionneau, Ella	Lyons, Kieran	O'Regan, Adam
Belghafria, Jenna	Hannigan, Jane	Magnier, Zoe Chantelle	Oseguera Riohas, Joaquin
Binchy, Kate	Harney, Kate	Maher, Kevin	Quinn, Meghan
Bolger, Pádraig,	Hayes, Conor	Maher, Ronan Matthew	Quirke, Philip John
Bourke, Staphanie	Healy, Gregory	Manton, Faye	Rehman, Hafsa
Brennan, Simon	Healy, Michael	Marshall, Jack Conor	Rio-Lynch, Alexander
Campion, Conor	Heffernan, Orlagh	Martines, Cristina Llabres	Rogers, Kenneth
Carroll, Robert	Hennessy, Siobhán	McCarthy, Odhran	Ruth, Dervla
Casey, Fiona	Henry, Gregory	McCarthy, Seán	Ryan, Cathal
Cleary, Dillon	Hough, Julian	McCormack, Jack	Ryan, Emma
Collins, Robert	Hughes, Maria	McGagh, Dylan	Ryan Louise
Corbett, Karen	Jermyn, Robert	McGrane, Luke Edward	Ryan, T.J.
Costello, Jamie	Johnston, David Keith	McKenna, Niall	Scannell, David
Delany, Gavin	Kendrick, Callum	McNulty, Ella	Sharpe, Sophie
Desmond, Andrew	Kenneally, Deborah	Meagher, Colin Gerard	Smyth, David
Donohue, Owen	Kennedy, Colman	Meagher, Paul	Smyth, John
Donworth, Tim	Kennedy, Richard	Moloney, Aidan	Sumida, Kyosuke
Doyle, Cliona	Kennedy, Sinéad	Mulcahy, Darragh,	Summers, Colm Robertson
Drew, Kenny	Khan, Ibrahim	Murchan, Liam	Sutcliffe, Adam Patrick
Dwyer, Sonny James	Khan, Maham	O'Connell, Michael	Sweeney, Aaron Philip
Dziengel, Anton	Khan, Rohaan	O'Connor, Alison	Sweeney, Saidhbh
Farrell, Killian	Kiely, Cillian	O'Donnell, Robert	Sweeney, Sorcha
Feehan, Ann	Lannigan-Ryan, Daniel	O'Donoghue, Erin	Sweeney, Thomas R.
Fitzgerald, Kate	Leahy, Oisín	O'Donoghue Eve	Tolmachev, Anton
Fitzgerald, Michael J.	Loening, Jacob	O'Donoghue, Shaun	Walsh, Johnny
Fiuza, Constantino	Long, Andrew	O'Donovan, Deirdre	Yates, Jonathan
Foley, Darragh	Long, Emily	O'Dwyer, Amanda	
Graf Beissel, Adrian	Long, Elaine Andrea	O'Dwyer, William	

2013

Abdekhaqom Ause	Eppert, Cody	Livianos, Vicente	Parata, Rory Otaki
Acheson, Courtney	Falvey, Conor	Maher, Ashley	Pattison, Jade
Aragoneses, David	Farrell, Cian	Martin, Alvarez	Peters, Bridget
Barlow, Ally	Fitzgerald, Kate	Maxwell, James	Purcell, Aoife
Barrett, Ted	Fitzpatrick, Gwen	McCowen, Kevin	Purcell, Michael
Barry, Sarah	Flynn, Neville	McMahon, Steven	Quinlan, Brian
Bergin, Keith	Hanrahan, Matthew	McNulty, Seán	Quinlan, Dvid John
Boehlke, Timo	Harrington, Aisling	Moloughney, Conora	Quinn, Selena
Boland, Haxel	Harrington, Nicola	Morrissey, Michael	Rafferty, Elizabeth
Boland, Mairead	Haurie, Alejandro	Morrissey, Tristan	Riley, David
Boland, Rian	Hayes, Claire	Mulcahy, Elliot	Ryan, Aida
Butler, Aidan	Healy Rae, Jackie	O'Brien, David	Ryan, Emma
Cossio, Jose Rodrigo	Heffernan, Kate	O'Connell, Denis	Sharpe, Simon
Croome Carroll, Charles	Hennessy, James	O'Connor, John James	Skelly, Shane
Cummins, Edel	Holohan, James Patrick	O'Donnell, Cian James	Smith, Saoirse
Doheny, Clara	Horgan, Adam	O'Donnell, Lily	Smyth, John
Donovan, Caolin	Hughes, Paul	O'Donoghue, Shaun	Sylver, Jordan
Doyle, Rachel	Irwin, Nicky	O'Donovan, Jane	Trunov, Daniel
Drohan, Seán	Kaminski, Lukas	O'Dwyer, Aine Marie	Wallace, Mark
Dwyer, Sonny James	Keating, Luke William	O'Keeffe, Thomas	Walshe, Adrian
English, Mary Ellena	Kenneally, Patrick	O'Neill, Joseph	
Enright, Sally	Leahy, Caitriona	O'Sullivan, Sarah	

Appendix XV Prize Winning Students

	Student of the Year	James Joy Senior Debating Gold Medal	Thomas MacDonagh Literary Award
1944	William O'Brien,	William Kingston	
1945	John A. Tobin	Terence O'Regan	
1946	Edward J. Hayes	Edward J. Hayes	
1947	Patrick Holohan	Hugh Larkin	
1948	James Brosnan	Laurence Ryan	
1949	Francis Walsh	John Geary	
1950	Finbarr Gallagher	Finbarr Gallagher	
1951	Denis Cogan	Alec Miller	
1952	Timothy McGrath	John Hogan	
1953	Not Awarded	Paul Evers	
1954	Joseph Moran	Thomas O'Flaherty	
1955	Edmond O'Dwyer	Patrick Kirwan	
1956	Edward O'Brien	Diarmuid Begley	
1957	Cahal Cavanagh	Maurice Foley	
1958	Matthew McNamara	Liam Brophy	
1959	Michael Butler	Joseph Jones	
1960	William Gardiner	Jeremiah Crowley	
1961	Matthew O'Mahony	Not Awarded	
1962	Bernard Kerr	Neil Buckley	
1963	John Collins	John Collins	
1964	Joseph Cumiskey	Pacelli O'Rourke	
1965	Paul Glacken	Not Awarded	
1966	John O'Mahony	Not Awarded	
1967	Tom Teehan	Anthony Rossiter	Gabriel Rosenstock
1968	Anthony Kiely	Eamon Lawlor	Anthony Rossiter
1969	Timothy Furlong	Kevin O'Dea	Not Awarded
1970	Michael Slattery	Terence Dempsey	Leo de Freyne
1971	Thomas McGrath	Noel O'Sullivan	Peter Onwe
1972	Hugh Maguire	Gerard Danaher	John Healy
1973	Paul Kenny	Robin Foley	Arthur Begley
1974	Patrick McGonigle	Diarmuid Leonard	Diarmuid Leonard
1975	Desmond Molloy	Gerard McMahon	Patrick Mawe
1976	John Murray	Gerard McMahon	Michael Healy
1977	John Booth/Wm Murphy	Francis Gleeson	Conor Whooley
1978	Maurice McQuillan	Seamus McGinley	Maurice McQuillan
1979	Mark Moran	Mark Moran	Stephen Burkart
1980	David Bolger	John Reid	Tom Flynn
1981	Liam Flynn	Maurice Collins	Maurice Collins
1982	Ian Slattery	P.J. Hough	Ian Slattery
1983	Anthony McCarthy	Iain Morley	Iain Morley
1984	Pauric Madigan	Francis Farrell	John Riordan
1985	Seamus Maher	Neil Hanrahan	Richard Gallagher
1986	Conor Brosnan/Rory Leydan	Mark Heslin	Mark Heslin
1987	Harry Blackmore	Brian Coleman	Gary O'Mahony

1988	John Hennessy	Dylan Dalton	John MacGoey
1989	Kevin O'Connell	Aidan O'Connell	Ronan Quirke
1990	Patrick Maguire	Patrick leahy	Gavin Burke
1991	Thomas Purcell	Michelle Maher	Thomas Purcell
1992	Fionn Hurley	Dermot McMorrow	Helen Howley
1993	Thomas Horgan	Robert MacGoey	Oran O'Donohue
1994	James Kennedy	Cian Toomey	Leah Farrell
1995	Eimear Burke	Patrick MacGoey	Shane Dwyer
1996	J. P. Crowley	Aonghus Fitzgibbon	Josef O'Keeffe
1997	Robert Bourke	P. J. Flynn	P. J. Flynn
1998	Angela Quinlan	Angela Quinlan	Brigid Halley
1999	John Dalton	John Prendergast	John Prendergast
2000	Brendan Crowley	Mark Hanly	James Moloney
2001	Brenda O'Donoghue	Michael Griffin	Sarah Jane Hallinan
2002	Maeve O'Sullivan,	Diarmuid O'Connor	Sheila Ryan
2003	Tom Barry	Emma Coffey	Gráinne O'Sullivan
2004	Emma Jane Morrissey	Tiarnan Fitzgibbon	Peter Moloney
2005	Cathy O'Donoghue	Seán Óg Fitzgerald	Tiernan Fitzgibbon
2006	Owen Delahunty	Claire Quirke	Kieran McCarthy
2007	Ruth McGarry	Robert Joy	Declan Burrowes
2008	Tom Wall	Patrick Alvarez	Niamh Raftery
2009	Aiden Burke	Sarah Long	Daniel Binchy
2010	John Finnegan	Eva Cummins	Lydia Kelly
2011	Jack Jeffries	Jack Jeffries	David Smyth
2012	Killian Farrell	Jack Looby	Susan Binchy
2013	Ally Barlow	Cody Eppert	Cian Farrell

APPENDIX XVI. ROCKWELL COLLEGE UNION PRESIDENTS

1925	Mgr Innocent Ryan	1926	Mgr Innocent Ryan	1927	Mgr Innocent Ryan
1928	Timothy Cleary	1929	Timothy Cleary	1930	Patrick J. Duffy
1931	Patrick J. Duffy	1932	Edwd McLoughlin	1933	John P. McAvin
1934	Andrew Butler	1935	James A. Nugent	1936	James A. Nugent
1937	Malachi Martin	1938	Edward C. Powell	1939	John Gleeson
1940	William Chadwick	1941	William Chadwick	1942	James J. Comerford
1943	James J Comerford	1944	Robert V. Walker	1945	Martin Gleeson
1946	Martin Gleeson	1947	T. J. Horgan	1948	Michael O'Connor
1949	Michael O'Connor	1950	P.J. Roche	1951	P.J. Roche
1952	Thomas Collins	1953	Martin Byrne	1954	Stanislaus O'Brien
1955	Edward Morkan	1956	James G. Maher	1957	James G. Maher
1958	Jack Condon	1959	Jack Condon	1960	William J. O'Neill
1961	William J. O'Neill	1962	Frank Mulcahy	1963	James G. Maher
1964	John Breen	1965	John Breen	1966	John J. Nash
1967	John J. Nash	1968	T. K. Mallon	1969	T. K. Mallon
1970	Ciarán P. Blair	1971	Ciarán P. Blair	1972	W. F. Dwyer
1973	W.F. Dwyer	1974	W.F. Dwyer	1975	Fionnán Blair
1976	James Joy	1977	Denis Kelly	1978	Seán Kennedy
1979	John McElwain	1980	Barry Foley	1981	John J. Lyons
1982	Enda Marron	1983	Owen O'Neill	1984	Paddy O'Dwyer
1985	Bernard Flusk	1986	Bernard Flusk	1987	Domhnall Blair
1988	Gay Mangan	1989	Andy Butler	1990	Matt O'Mahony
1991	Jim Peters	1992	Risteárd Ó Colmáin	1993	Fergus Ahearn
1994	Hilary Healy	1995	Joseph Cumiskey	1996	Gerard Quinn
1997	Kenneth Maguire	1998	Seán Cronin	1999	Joe Moran
2000	Brendan Sutton	2001	Brendan Sutton	2002	Brian W. Goff
2003	Patrick Curran	2004	Billy Murphy	2005	John Duffy
2006	Robert Gallagher	2007	Jim Holmes	2008	Joe Barrett
2009	Liam Flynn	2010	Mark Smyth	2011	Paul Marren
2012	Barry Sheehan	2013	Hugh Garvey		

APPENDIX XVII SPORTING AWARDS

RUGBY

Rockwell Irish rugby internationals:

1897-1904	Jack Ryan	1962	Frank Byrne
1897-1904	Mike Ryan	1968-1969	John Moroney
1911	Michael R. Heffernan	1965-1967	Pat McGrath
1913-1922	Paddy Stokes	1975-1984	Willie Duggan
1920	Decco Browne	1978-1981	Paul McNaughton
1933-1938	Joseph J. O'Connor	1990-1995	Gary Halpin
1947-1950	Bertie O'Hanlon	1991-1992	Jack Clarke
1952	Michael Dargan	1992	Michael Fitzgibbon
1955	David McSweeney	1994-1998	Gabriel Fulcher
1956-1961	Tim McGrath	2004-2011	Denis Leamy
1958-1963	Mick English	2010	John Fogarty

Rockwell British and Irish Lions:
1959 Mick English   1977 Willie Duggan
Rockwell Womens International:
2000-2008 Patrique Kelly

Rockwell Irish Schoolboy Internationals:

1975	Michael Quaid	2000	Diarmuid O'Riordan
1976	Patrick Curran	2001	James Clifford
1977	John Duggan	2001	Denis Fogarty
1980	Michael O'Connor	2001	Jim Mackessy
1982	Michael Fitzgibbon	2001	Cian McNaughton
1983	Gary Halpin	2004	Peter Shallow
1984	John Riordan	2007	James Ryan
1986	Brian MacGoey	2008	Paddy Butler
1986	Jack Clarke	2009	Shane Buckley
1990	Fraank Fitzgerald	2009	J.J. Hanrahan
1990	Denis O'Dowd	2010	Seán McCarthy
1996	John Fogarty	2012	David Johnston
1998	Denis Leamy	2013	Seán McNulty

Munster Colleges Senior Cup: 1910 (P. Salmon) 1911 (P. Kenny) 1912 (L. O'Grady), 1914 (D. Heelin) 1915 (J. Hennerbry), 1917 (P. Breen), 1928 (T. Brockert) 1929, 1930 (W. Kennedy), 1937 (P. Ryan), 1940 (M. O'Donoghue), 1942 (M. Dunne), 1950 (M. Brosnan), 1953 (D. Hale), 1955 (T. Coffey), 1959 (M. Butler), 1960 (P. Leyden), 1961 (T. Holohan), 1964 (J. Cumiskey), 1967 (D. Houlihan), 1970 (D. Ormond), 1985 (C. Slattery), 2001 (E. Macken), 2011 (C. O'Donnell), 2012 (S. McCarthy)

Munster Colleges Junior Cup: 1934, 1935, 1936, 1937, 1942, 1943, 1947, 1948, 1949, 1955, 1956, 1958, 1959, 1967, 1968, 1972, 1974, 1982, 1997.

ATHLETICS
College of Science Cup: 1929, 1930, 1931, 1958, 1959, 1964, 1965.
Munster Colleges Senior Cup: 1954, 1955, 1956, 1957, 1958, 1959, 1960, 1961, 1962, 1963, 1964, 1965, 1966.

BASKETBALL
1999: David Bennett was a schoolboy international.

CANOING
Leander Cup: Every year from 1975 to 2003 when the schools' committee, which organised the competition, was dissolved.

CRICKET
Munster Schools Senior Cup 1945

EQUESTRIAN
National Schools Show Jumping Championship 2007, 2009
Epsom Derby Winners: 1981, 1986, 1995: Walter Swinbourne, 2012: Joseph O'Brien.

GAELIC FOOTBALL
Munster Colleges Senior Cup 1917, 1919, 1941, 1979.

GOLF
Munster Colleges Championship 1968, 1969, 1972, 1973, 1974, 1975, 1998, 2008.
All Ireland Colleges Championship 1974
Walker Cup:1963 David Sheehan. 1983: Arthur Pierse.

HURLING

Harty Cup 1918, 1923, 1924, 1930, 1931.
All Ireland Colleges Hurling Cup: 1923, 1924.
Munster Colleges Senior Hurling Cup: 1940, 1941, 1943, 1946.
 Keane Cup 1969, 1970.
Dean Ryan Cup: (under 16), 1928, 1929.

OLYMPIANS

1972 Munich Philip Conway. 1992 Albertville Malachy Sheridan

ROWING

Metropolitan Challenge Cup: 1940, 1941, 1942, 1943, 1944, 1945.

SWIMMING

1974: Munster Schools Individual Medley Championship
2004: Munster Schools Relay Championship
2007: Munster Schools Relay Champpionship

SOCCER

2008: Peter Acheson was a schoolboy international.

TENNIS

Munster Schools Senior Cup: 1967, 1991, 2002.
1998: Clodagh McMorrow schoolgirl international.
1999: Clodagh McMorrow and Emma Heffernan schoolgirl internationals.

SELECT BIBLIOGRAPHY

Official Publications
Griffith's Primary Valuations.
Intermediate Education (Ireland) Act 1878
Census of the Population 1901
The Irish Universities Act 1908
Census of the Population 1911
Intermediate Education (Amendment) Act 1924
Department of Education Rules and Programmes for Secondary Schools 1924-25
Investment in Education: Report of the Survey Team 1966
Higher Education Authority Act 1971
Education Act 1998
Education (Welfare) Act 2000

Journals
Rockwell College Annual
Tipperary Historical Journal.

Newspapers
Cashel Gazette
Cashel Sentinel
Tipperary Free Press
Cork Examiner
Clonmel Chronicle
Clonmel Nationalist
Freeman's Journal
Irish Independent

Books and articles
Aan de Wiel, J., *The Catholic Church in Ireland 1914-1918: War and Politics* (Dublin 2003)
Augusteigin, J.. The Operations of South Tipperary IRA 1916-1921 (Tipperary Historical Journal 1996
Boyce, D.G., *Nineteenth Century Ireland: The Search for Stability* (Dublin, 1990)
Colmcille, An tAthair, The Third Tipperary Brigade from Truce to Civil War (Tipperary Historical Journal, 1990, 1991, 1992.
Coolahan, J., *Irish Education: History and Structure* (Dublin 1981)
Comerford, R.V.. *The Fenians in Contex: Irish Politics and Society 1848-1882* (Dublin 1985)
Corbett, W. & Nolan, W., (eds.) *Thurles the Cathedral Town* (Dublin, 1989)
Cruise O'Brien, M., *The Same Age as the State* (Dublin, 2003)
De Breffny, B., *Ireland: A Cultural Encyclopaedia* (London, 1982
De Búrca. M., *The G.A.A.: A History* (Dublin, 1980)
Farragher, S. P., *Blackrock College 1860-1995* (Dublin 1995)
   Irish Spiritans Remembered (Dublin n.d.)
   Père Leman: Educator and Missionary 1826-1880 (Dublin 1998)
   The French College: Blackrock 1860-1896 (Dublin 2011)
Dev and his Alma Mater: Eamon de Valera's Lifelong association with Blackrock College 1898-1975(Dublin& London 1984)
Hayes, W. & Kavanagh A., *The Tipperary Gentry* (Dublin 2003)
Lee, J., *The Modernisation of Irish Society 1948-1918* (Dublin, 1973
Lyons, F.S.L., *Ireland Since the Famine* (London, 1971)
Maher, W. A., *A History of St. Mary's College Rathmines, Dublin 1890-1990* (Dublin 1994)

Marnane, D.G., *Land and Violence: A History of West Tipperary from 1660* (Tipperary 1985)
    The Famine in South Tipperary (Tipperary Historical Journal 2000)
Moody, T.W., *Davitt and the Irish Revolution 1846- 82* (Oxford, 1981)
Nolan, W. Patterns of Living in Tipperary 1750-1850 in *Tipperary: History and Society* (Dublin 1985)
O'Donnell, S., *Clonmel 1840-1900: Anatomy of an Irish Town* (Dublin, 1999)
    Clonmel 1900-1932: A History (Clonmel 2009)
Nolan, W.& McGrath, T.G, (eds.) *Tipperary: History and Society* (Dublin 1985)
O'Shea, J., *Priest, politics and society in post-famine Ireland: A Study of County Tipperary 1850-1891* (Dublin 1983)
Ryan, P. J., *Kimmage Manor: 100 Years of Service to Mission* (Dublin 2011)
Skehan, W. G., *Cashel & Emly Heritage* (Tipperary 1993)
Tierney, M., *Croke of Cashel: The Life of Archbishop Thomas William Croke, 1823-1902,* (Dublin 1876)

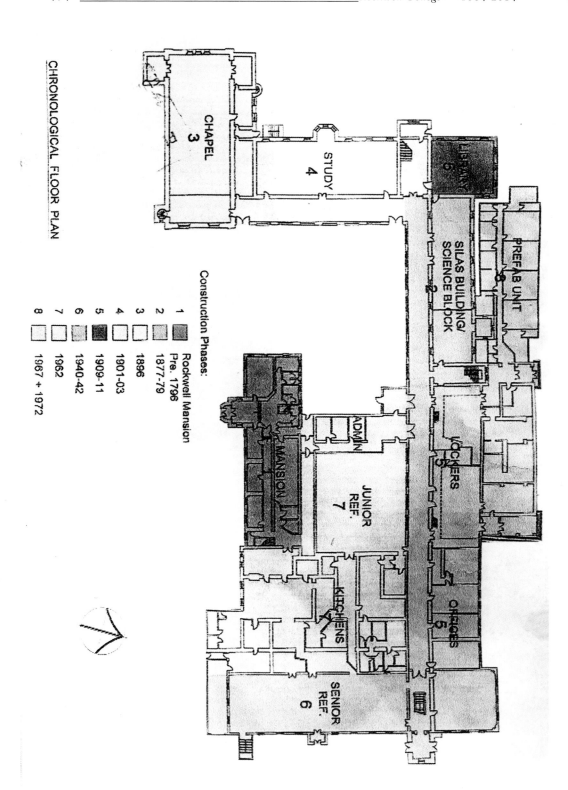

CHRONOLOGICAL FLOOR PLAN

Construction Phases:

1		Rockwell Mansion
		Pre. 1796
2		1877-79
3		1896
4		1901-03
5		1909-11
6		1940-42
7		1962
8		1967 + 1972

CHAPEL 3

STUDY 4

LIBRARY 8

SILAS BUILDING/ SCIENCE BLOCK 2

PREFAB UNIT

MANSION 1

ADMIN

JUNIOR REF. 7

LOCKERS 5

KITCHENS

SENIOR REF. 6

OFFICES 5